Economic Policy in Sri Lanka

For Gamani,

Scholar, Mentor and Friend

Economic Policy in Sri Lanka
Issues and Debates

A Festschrift in Honour of Gamani Corea

Editor
Saman Kelegama

Sage Publications
New Delhi/Thousand Oaks/London

First published in 2004 by

Sage Publications India Pvt Ltd
B-42, Panchsheel Enclave
New Delhi 110 017

<table>
<tr><td>

Sage Publications Inc
2455 Teller Road
Thousand Oaks, California 91320

</td><td>

</td><td>

Sage Publications Ltd
1 Oliver's Yard
55 City Road, London EC1Y 1SP

</td></tr>
</table>

Published by Tejeshwar Singh for Sage Publications India Pvt Ltd, typeset in 10/12 Goudy Old Style by Prism Graphix, New Delhi and printed at Chaman Enterprises, New Delhi.

Library of Congress Cataloging-in-Publication Data

Economic policy in Sri Lanka: issues and debates/editor, Saman Kelegama.
     p. cm.
    "A festschrift in honour of Gamani Corea."
    Includes bibliographical references and index.
    1. Sri Lanka—Economic policy. I. Kelegama, Saman. II. Corea, Gamani, 1925–
HC424.E218   330.95493—dc22   2004   2004014911

ISBN: 0-7619-3278-X (Hb)   81-7829-410-9 (India-Hb)

Sage Production Team: Ankush Saikia, Vineeta Rai, Rajib Chatterjee and Santosh Rawat

CONTENTS

List of Tables and Figures

Figures

List of Abbreviations

ADB	Asian Development Bank
AGBEP	Area Based Growth and Equity Programme
AMDP	Accelerated Mahaweli Development Programme
AMP	Assistant Medical Practitioner
ARC	Administrative Reform Committee
BCCI	Bank of Credit and Commerce International
BOI	Board of Investment
BOP	Balance of Payments
BTT	Barter Terms of Trade
CAA	Consumer Affairs Authority
CAP	Change Agent Programme
CBOs	Community Based Organizations
CCP	Ceylon Communist Party
CCPI	Colombo Consumers' Price Index
CD	Central Dispensaries
CF	Common Fund
CIMA	Chartered Institute of Management Accountants
CIM	Chartered Institute of Marketing
CNC	Ceylon National Congress
CPC	Congress Policy Committee
CPI	Consumer Price Index
CWE	Co-operative Wholesale Establishment
DDT	Dichlorodiphenyltrichloroethane
DFCC	Development Finance Corporation of Ceylon
DIR	Department of Inland Revenue
DIT	Department of Internal Trade
DSt	Divisional Secretariat
EEF	Extended Fund Facility
ERD	External Resources Department
ESAF	Enhanced Structural Adjustment Facility
ESOP	Employee Share Ownership Plan
FAO	Food and Agricultural Organization
FDI	Foreign Direct Investment
FEECS	Foreign Exchange Entitlement Certificate Scheme
FPD	Fiscal Policy Department
FTC	Fair Trading Commission
GDCF	Gross Domestic Capital Formation
GDP	Gross Domestic Product
GMOA	Government Medical Officers' Association

GNP	Gross National Product
GoBU	Government owned Business Undertakings
GPS	Guaranteed Price Scheme
GST	Goods and Services Tax
HDI	Human Development Index
HFA	Health for All
HIDCs	Highly Indebted Poor Countries
HPAEs	High Performing Asian Economies
IBRD	International Bank for Reconstruction and Development
ICA	International Commodity Agreements
IFIs	International Financial Institutions
IGA	Income Generating Activities
ILFTA	Indo-Sri Lanka Free Trade Agreement
ILO	International Labour Organization
IMF	International Monetary Fund
IPC	Integrated Programme of Commodities
IR	Investment Ratio
IRDP	Integrated Rural Development Programme
ISIC	International Standard Industrial Classification
IT	Information Technology
ITT	Income Terms of Trade
JEDB	Janatha Estate Development Board
JICA	Japan International Co-operation Agency
JSP	Jana Saviya Programme
JVP	Janatha Vimukhti Peramuna
LSSP	Lanka Sama Samaja Party
LTTE	Liberation Tigers of Tamil Eelam
MEs	Micro-Enterprises
MEP	Mahajana Eksath Peramuna
MFA	Multi Fibre Arrangement
MH	Maternity Homes
MNCs	Multinational Corporations
MO	Medical Officer
MP	Member of Parliament
MT	Metric Tonnes
NDB	National Development Bank
NGOs	Non-Governmental Organizations
NICs	Newly Industrialized Countries
NIEO	New International Economic Order
NIPO	National Intellectual Property Office
NPC	National Planning Council
NSL	National Security Levy
OECD	Organization for Economic Cooperation and Development
OPEC	Organization of the Petroleum Exporting Countries
PA	People's Alliance
PAYE	Pay As You Earn

PC	Provincial Council
PDMO	Public Debt Management Office
PIPU	Public Interest Program Unit
PRGF	Poverty Reduction and Growth Facility
PRS	Poverty Reduction Strategy
PS	Pradeshiya Sabha
PSDG	Provincial Specific Development Grant
PSIP	Public Sector Investment Programme
PTF	Presidential Task Force
PUC	Public Utilities Commission
QRs	Quantitative Restrictions
R&D	Research and Development
REAP	Regional Economic Advancement Programme
REER	Real Effective Exchange Rate
RER	Real Exchange Rate
RMP	Registered Medical Practitioner
RRISL	Rubber Research Institute of Sri Lanka
SAPTA	South Asian Preferential Trade Arrangement
SDHC	Sub-Divisional Health Centre
SDRs	Special Drawing Rights
SEC	Securities and Exchange Commission
SLBFE	Sri Lankan Bureau of Foreign Employment
SLFP	Sri Lanka Freedom Party
SLSPC	Sri Lanka State Plantations Corporation
SMEs	Small and Medium Enterprises
SMF	Social Mobilization Foundation
SOEs	State-owned Enterprises
S&T	Science and Technology
STPD	Science and Technology Personnel Development
TFP	Total Factor Productivity
TFR	Total Fertility Rate
TULF	Tamil United Liberation Front
UN	United Nations
UNCTAD	United Nations Conference on Trade and Development
UNDP	United Nations Development Programme
UNF	United National Front
UNP	United National Party
USOs	Universal Service Obligations
VAT	Value Added Tax
VERs	Voluntary Export Restraints
VLSSP	Viplavakari Lanka Sama Samaja Party
WHO	World Health Organization
WIDER	World Institute for Development Economics Research
WPI	Wholesale Price Index

ACKNOWLEDGEMENTS

I am most grateful to the contributors to this volume for their discerning papers and for patiently complying with the tight editorial timetable. I acknowledge with gratitude the encouragement provided by Nimal Sanderatne, Nihal Kappagoda, Sisira Jayasuriya, Prema-chandra Athukorala, Laksiri Jayasuriya and Godfrey Gunatilleke. The editorial support I received from D.D.M. Waidyasekera, Dushni Weerakoon, Ruvani Fernando and Sonali Peiris is greatly appreciated. The secretarial support on the manuscript by Asuntha Paul and miscellaneous work by Malini Fernando and Nirmala Meegama went a long way in finalizing the manuscript on time. I am most grateful to them. The views expressed in this volume are the authors' own and do not necessarily represent the views of the organizations they belong to.

18 December 2003   **Saman Kelegama**
                                                                        Editor

INTRODUCTION

ECONOMIC POLICY IN SRI LANKA: ISSUES AND DEBATES

ˋ Saman Kelegama

This volume of essays titled *Economic Policy in Sri Lanka: Issues and Debates* is dedicated to Gamani Corea—one of the foremost Sri Lankan economists, both nationally and as internationally. There are a number of recent compendiums of essays on post-independence economic policy and programmes in Sri Lanka (Lakshman, 1997; Indraratna, 1998; People's Bank, 1999; Lakshman and Tisdell, 2000, etc.). However, this volume that brings together contributions by well-known Sri Lankan economists, social scientists and other scholars is unique in the comprehensiveness of its subject coverage. The 22 chapters contained in the volume discuss the evolution of policy over the years, the ideology governing the evolution, the debates on policy, and the key economic issues in contemporary Sri Lanka to which Gamani Corea made his own substantial contribution at one time or another.

COREA AND THE ECONOMIC POLICY DEBATE

The milestones of Gamani Corea's career are easy to summarize. After graduating from the Oxbridge Universities in the UK, Corea joined the Central Bank of Ceylon in 1950 in the first batch of young recruits (Chapter 18). In 1952, he was seconded to the newly formed Planning Secretariat and soon became its Director. He played a key role in the preparation of the first Six-Year Plan of the Government. Thereafter, he was appointed the Secretary of the Planning Council formed in 1956 (by the then Prime Minister S.W.R.D. Bandaranaike) and was instrumental in preparing the first Ten-Year Plan of Ceylon: 1959–68 (Chapter 3).

In 1960, Corea returned to the Central Bank, and worked there till 1965. It was during this time, in 1963, that Corea first met Raul Prebisch, the renowned Latin American economist, at a meeting in Geneva. Prebisch subsequently invited Corea to New York to join the team involved in the preparation of the World Conference on Development, which later became known as UNCTAD-I. Prebisch became the first Secretary General of United Nations Conference on Trade and Development (UNCTAD) and Corea made a mark in the UNCTAD fora as an articulate spokesman and a skillful negotiator for Sri Lanka and the Third World countries.

In 1965, his career took a new turn when the new Prime Minister of Sri Lanka (Dudley Senanayake) appointed him as the Permanent Secretary of the newly created Ministry of Planning and Economic Affairs. In this position, which was under the direct purview of the Prime Minister, Corea virtually became the sole architect of economic policies of the nation during 1965–70. This was also a period when his role as a spokesman of the Third World became more pronounced. In 1972 he became the Chairman of the United Nations (UN) Committee for Development Planning.

In 1970, with the change of Government, Corea went back to the Central Bank as the Deputy Governor, but decided to resign from the Bank shortly afterwards to undertake various UN assignments, notably chairing the conference setting up the UN Environment Programme. In 1973, he became the Sri Lankan Ambassador to the European community in Belgium, a position that set the stage for him to build up an effective network within UNCTAD circles.

In a nutshell, Corea played a key role in shaping Sri Lankan policy during 1950–72: from 1950–59 he was involved in national planning, during 1960–64 and 1971–72 he was primarily a central banker and during 1965–70 he played a key role as the supreme policy maker of the country.

From 1950 to the mid-1970s, Corea made a number of scholarly contributions to academic journals. He was in fact one of the first contributors to the *Ceylon Economist*—the first post-independent economic journal of Sri Lanka. Later, he made contributions to the *Marga Quarterly Journal* during the early 1970s. Corea's doctoral dissertation which he completed under the supervision of Lady Ursula Hicks at Oxford (1953) was published by the Marga Institute in 1975. The book titled *Instability of an Export Economy* clearly demonstrates his early thinking regarding developing trends in world market and the need for caution by developing countries in aggressively promoting exports (Corea, 1975).

In 1974, Corea was elected to the prestigious post of the Secretary General of UNCTAD, a position he held for 11 years till 1984. To quote the Minister of Foreign Affairs of Sri Lanka:

> Within weeks of his assuming office, it became clear that he was going to wield significant influence on the development of international economic affairs. His public presentations and speeches were fluent, clear, and elegantly phrased. They drew the admiration of the entire global economic community. They certainly made all the Asian delegations, indeed all Third World delegations extremely proud because in Gamani Corea they had found a man who walked tall, stood his ground and was more than a match for his interlocutors from the developed countries. (Kadirgamar, 2002: 8)

Under Corea's leadership, UNCTAD became a hive of intellectual activity. A stream of studies on a wide range of subjects touching almost every conceivable aspect of international trade and commerce—banking, insurance, shipping, the transfer of technology, restrictive business practices, commodities and so on were issued from the

UNCTAD Secretariat. The codes of restrictive business practices, multi-modal transport, linear conferences, the charter on rights and duties of states, the cancellation of debt by poor countries, the concept of 'generalized system of preferences' were all achievements of UNCTAD via a dialogue with developed countries. Corea was instrumental in introducing the Integrated Programme for Commodities—commonly known as the 'Corea Plan'—which 'was among the finest of his achievements' (Dell, 1988: xii).

Recognizing the fact that developing countries wielded little influence individually and found it difficult to protect their interests, Gamani Corea did more than most in promoting efforts to strengthen the bargaining power and negotiating capacity of developing countries as a group. It was one of Gamani Corea's many strengths as Secretary General of UNCTAD that he never became cynical or embittered about the North-South deadlock that he faced continually, and always retained confidence in the power of persuasion and in the ultimate victory of reason over unreason. These efforts did not stop when he ceased to be Secretary General of UNCTAD. In the 1990s, the report of the Non-Aligned Movement's Expert Group on Third World debt, which he chaired, was important in influencing the decision to establish the Highly Indebted Poor Countries (HIDC) initiative.

In 1986, Corea was offered a Visiting Fellowship at Corpus Christi College, Cambridge, to work on a book on UNCTAD, which finally came out in 1992 (Corea, 1992). In the 1990s, he made important contributions to the analysis of the emerging global economic system from the perspective of developing countries, and worked assiduously to assist developing countries define a common platform. He also put his energies into consolidating the position of the South on these matters by working with the South Commission, the South Centre, the Non-Aligned Movement and indirectly with the Group of 77. In recognition of his lead role in developing country concerns, he was appointed as the Chairman of the South Centre in 2002 after the death (1999) of Julius Nyrere—the former President of Tanzania (Luis Fernando Jaramillo of Colombia took over the remainder of the term of Nyrere).

In Sri Lanka, in the post-1984 period, he became the first President of the Sri Lanka Economic Association and held this position for six years (1985-91). He became a regular contributor to local journals such as the *Sri Lanka Economic Journal* and *Economic Review* (People's Bank). Corea was a much sought after speaker in public gatherings and was frequently in the limelight articulating his long-held views—effortlessly holding the attention of an audience with his remarkable memory, clarity of thought, imaginative ideas and dry wit.

Some of Corea's views on various subjects are worth highlighting. With regard to industrialization, he always argued for some degree of protectionism, stating that it was not only the infant industry argument that one should look at but also the fact that most developing countries were 'infant economies' (Corea, 1987: 72–73). Corea did not believe in the textbook case for the invisible hand of the market, nor did he advocate full-scale state intervention in an economy. Corea often used the parallel of the colonial economy of Sri Lanka where there was no intervention and markets were free to operate, but where industrialization hardly took place (Corea, 1993: 34).

Corea did not believe in the so-called 'level playing field', stating that under such a field 'the stronger team will keep winning year after year' (Corea, 2003: 170). He always believed in an international regulation mechanism under which the initial disadvantaged conditions of the developing countries in developmental efforts were explicitly taken into account. He referred frequently to globalization and liberalization as a 'fast express train' that everyone had been requested to get into to be carried to new heights, and if they did not get in, they would be left behind and marginalized. He viewed the current policy prescriptions to developing countries as a 'do-it-yourself kit', a self-help apparatus, with emphasis almost exclusively on domestic policy, soft peddling and underplaying the external economic environment (Corea, 1993).

Corea's policy prescriptions are of course not free from criticism. On the domestic policy front, critics argue that Corea was too concerned with the decline in terms of trade and thus pessimistic about exports taking off. It is alleged that the policy transition in Sri Lanka towards export-oriented industrialization was in fact delayed by nearly 10 years. In 1965, when partial liberalization of the economy took place under Corea's leadership, Sri Lanka had an opportune moment to adopt an export-led growth strategy, but the opening was not fully exploited due to prevalent views on export pessimism. He was pessimistic about market prospects for traditional exports and opportunities for diversifying exports into more product lines. Import liberalization seems to have been perceived largely as an aid to import substitution by way of ensuring the availability of imported machinery and inputs for domestic industry and agriculture, and export promotion was implemented only partially (Cuthbertson and Athukorala, 1991: 340). It is perhaps due to this reason that a recovery programme was put into operation in the late 1960s (Kelegama, 1999).

Gamani Corea was instrumental in setting up the multiple exchange-rate system in the late 1960s, the first time the exchange rate was deliberately used as a policy tool for export promotion in Sri Lanka. What emerged was a compromised policy of import substitution and export promotion clearly seen from the half-hearted dual exchange rate policy which the International Monetary Fund (IMF) described as 'the wrong step in the right direction' (Corea, 1985: 12). Of course, there was at that time no adequate literature on the East Asian model to emulate their strategy. Critiques point out that instead of the recovery programme that Sri Lanka pursued in the late 1960s, had it pursued an aggressive export-promotion policy similar to those the East Asian countries were following during that period, Sri Lanka would have achieved a higher growth rate and laid the foundation for a comprehensive export-led strategy.

It should be noted that in Sri Lanka the transition to import-substitution industrialization from the classic 'export economy' was delayed by 10 to 12 years compared to a number of developing countries (Lakshman, 1997). This obviously had a knock-on effect on the transition to the export-oriented industrialization stage. Moreover, the reservations in regard to export diversification were based on the fact that it would take time to achieve results from such a strategy—illustrating the influence of electoral politics in determining crucial economic policies in Sri Lanka. When the political economy factor is taken into account, the pessimism towards export diversification can be seen more clearly and one can be more sympathetic towards Corea (Bruton et al., 1992: 345).

On the planning side, Snodgrass (1966) has shown that the Six-Year Plan was 'purely a pro forma exercise and probably had no influence on policy'. The Ten-Year Plan that came out in 1959 was more or less disowned by the Government that came to power in 1960. In Chapter 3, some of the anomalies of this Plan are highlighted. In fact, Chapter 11 shows how the Plan completely ignored the relevance of science and technology for the future development of Sri Lanka. It must be noted however that planning never got institutionalized in Sri Lanka as it did in India (Chapter 3), thus most of these criticisms are not totally justified from a political economy perspective.

On international policy, the Integrated Programme of Commodities (IPC) and the Common Fund (CF) have also been subject to criticism. It has been argued that the failure of the IPC was partly due to disagreement with regard to what it was meant to achieve, with producers more interested in the level than the variability of prices, and partly due to discontent about the division of the spoils when an agreement did manage to raise prices (Gilbert, 1996).

The CF was finally established after Corea's term in UNCTAD in 1989, but it never became operational given that by the late 1980s market economy policies had begun to spread globally, and in such an environment, there was no enthusiasm to support a CF by the international community.[1] According to Corea, the main weakness of the CF was not the finances but the linking of its operation to, and total dependence on, International Commodity Agreements (ICAs). Corea compares the situation of a CF without ICAs as akin to 'a bank without clients and one that could do little to create its own clientele' (Corea, 1992). Dell (1988: xiii) states that 'although it has more recently become fashionable to deride the CF and to urge that the solutions to the commodity problem must be sought in other directions, the fact remains that no other solutions have been proposed or are available'.

In his initial years in UNCTAD, Corea's ideas on commodity market stabilization, increase in financial flows from rich to poor countries, increase of access to goods from developing countries to developed country markets by trade preferences and a host of others as well, had some impact due to the dominance of Keynesian economics in global economic management. However, with the conservatism Reagan and Thatcher dominating the world scene in the early 1980s there came the gradual falling apart of these ideas, and with the collapse of the Soviet bloc in the late 1980s, there was complete marginalization of the UNCTAD.

In his magnum opus *Taming Commodity Markets: The Integrated Programme and the Common Fund at UNCTAD* (1992), Corea acknowledged that the new international climate did not favour commodity price stabilization. But he made a strong case for it by arguing that despite industrialization and diversification of exports, most developing countries remained crucially dependent on commodities for a substantial part of their foreign exchange earnings. Thus, the instability and downward trend in commodity prices continued to be the underlying reason for underdevelopment.

He writes: 'It is not acceptable that in the world where there is increasing concentration and cartellization over widening range of productive activities, the commodity sectors of developing countries, virtually alone, should remain vulnerable to the adverse forces in the name of free markets and allocative efficiency' (Corea, 1992). Corea considered supply management to be an essential strategy in commodity price stabilization and saw lessons in the experience of the Organization of the Petroleum Exporting Countries (OPEC), despite the wide differences in commodities. However, Corea emphasizes that supply management by producer countries cannot be undertaken entirely by developing countries alone, as a number of commodities are produced and exported by developed countries as well. A central theme in Corea's thinking is that developing and developed countries should cooperate in ensuring the stabilization and strengthening of commodity prices, as this is in the long run interest of global economic management.

Despite various criticisms, Corea has remained a highly respected figure in economic policy circles. His work has been the epitome of political economy, both at the national and international level. The breadth and depth of his knowledge on development issues and his concern to find practical measures and appropriate national and international policies to try to resolve the many problems confronting developing countries have been widely recognized. This is reflected in the number of important positions he has held in the international arena. His eloquence made him a formidable negotiator in all the posts he held. In recognition of Corea's contribution to Sri Lanka he was awarded the highest national title of 'Deshamanya' in the year 1987. Corea is a recipient of a number of international honours too. Corea's bibliographical data is listed at the end of this volume, which summarizes his achievements both nationally and internationally.

An Overview of the Chapters

The national planning and partial liberalization exercise of the Sri Lankan economy that was initiated by Corea generated a policy debate within the country. It was this debate that laid the foundation for a more radical liberalization in 1977 that continues till today. The chapters of this volume shed light on this debate and highlight other contemporary economic issues of Sri Lanka. The 22 chapters in the volume are divided into six parts, namely; (I) Development Strategy and Ideology, (II) Macroeconomic Policy, (III) Agriculture, Industry and Technology Development, (IV) Employment and Labour, (V) Institutional and Governance Issues, and (VI) Social Welfare. The key themes of these chapters are summarized as follows.

Part I—Development Strategy and Ideology—begins with a chapter by Prema-chandra Athukorala on the terms of trade debate, which has been at the centre of the policy ideology that shaped Sri Lanka's post-independence development strategy (Chapter 1). Athukorala analyses the behaviour of the terms of trade in Sri Lanka in the post-independence era with emphasis on the implications of the structural shift in exports from primary products to manufactured goods. He traces Corea's thinking on this issue, starting with the prominence of import substitution development strategy in the 1950s and 1960s, the efforts to tame commodity markets during his tenure as Secretary General of the UNCTAD, and to his continued pessimism regarding export-led industrialization following the market oriented reforms of 1977. Athukorala perceives the Sri Lankan experience as having provided an excellent testing ground for the validity of Corea's allegiance to the new export pessimism and the recent terms of trade debate. The debate was centred on two hypotheses: first, the Prebisch-Singer thesis with four major explanations for the long run deterioration in terms of trade between primary products and manufactures; and second, the 'fallacy of composition' involved in adoption of export promotion policies by developing countries.

Athukorala attempts to test the validity of these hypotheses using time-profile analysis of the terms of trade behaviour of Sri Lanka from 1948 to 2000. Due to the limitations of solely focusing on Barter Terms of Trade (BTT), he makes a case for using Income Terms of Trade (ITT) together with BTT in the study. The trend rate estimates for ITT reinforce the inferences for BTT, suggesting that the Sri Lankan experience with manufacturing export expansion clearly rebuts the new terms of trade pessimism and, as such, diversification into manufacturing from structurally weak conventional commodities has enabled the country to escape from unequal exchange relations in world trade.

In Chapter 2, Dushni Weerakoon examines the influence of development ideology in Sri Lanka's macroeconomic policy reform process. Sri Lanka's economic policies since independence have, not surprisingly, tended to follow contemporary ideological commitments shaping the design of appropriate policies for economic development. Following a survey of the development thinking of industrialization based on import substitution in the 1950s and 1960s, the resurgence of neo-classical economics with its focus on markets, prices and incentives in the 1970s and 1980s at the global level, she goes on to discuss the Sri Lankan experience with its three distinct phases of economic development and the neo-liberal development agenda that was adopted to respond to the critical economic shocks of 1973 and 1979. Weerakoon points out that this also marked the beginning of economic policy convergence between the primary political forces in Sri Lanka. The emerging 'consensus' on economic policy was a reflection of the broader acceptance of the 'Washington Consensus' that was expected to generate a degree of policy certainty for developing countries. However, the experience by not being positive has left developing countries exposed to the vagaries of the 'development' debate as in the past.

The general ideas derived from the stabilization and structural adjustment programmes of the 1980s that were epitomized under the 'Washington Consensus' were quick to give way to fundamental divisions about the pace and sequence of reforms. Weerakoon points out that the East Asian financial crises brought to the forefront recommendations that also ran counter to the 'Washington Consensus.' For policy-makers in developing countries, the changes that were expected were becoming progressively more complex and often, politically difficult to implement. The search for new answers recognized the need for a broader set of reforms—referred to collectively as 'second generation' reforms—focused around the need to develop institutional capacity for reforms. Weerakoon discusses the key concerns generated by this reform idea. She concludes that the current emphasis on 'institutions', 'transparency' and 'governance' is just as likely to yield to a new set of prescriptions—progressively raising the bar and stretching the capacity of developing countries such as Sri Lanka to tackle infinitely more complex issues.

An overview of the lessons of national planning in Sri Lanka is presented by Godfrey Gunatilleke in Chapter 3. It is noted that from the outset, national planning in Sri Lanka never acquired the institutional clarity and continuity it enjoyed in most other developing countries. The position of national planning within the system, the methodology and application of planning to the development problems of the country and the commitment that planning gained from political rulers altered with almost every change in government. As such, the critical issues relating to the impact of national planning in Sri Lanka needs to be seen in this ideological context in which the fortunes of national planning fluctuated according to the party in power. Particular emphasis is placed on how national planning focused on and dealt with the critical development problems of Sri Lanka in different phases.

The author firstly considers the state of three fundamentals of development at the time of independence—the economy, social and human capital, and the political system that had key problems and as such needed to be addressed. He carries out an in-depth study of: (a) Planning under the United National Party (UNP): 1947–56, (b) The New Ten-Year Phase in Planning: 1956–65, (c) Macroeconomic Management and Sectoral Planning: 1956–70, (d) The Alterations to Planning in the 1970s, and (e) The Scenario after Liberalization. Special reference is given to the two phases of national planning under the leadership of Gamani Corea. The concluding section of the chapter presents some of the author's reflections on the nature of planning in a market economy and the future of planning in Sri Lanka. Gunatilleke argues that Sri Lanka needs to envision its future development and planning path in terms of the three main value systems in today's global debate on development. What is saddest he points out, is that when Sri Lanka began its journey in planning, it had elements of all three value systems, but still managed to lose its way.

In Chapter 4, Lal Jayawardena reviews some aspects of the Sri Lankan economic reform experience in comparison with East Asia. According to Jayawardena, Sri Lanka's principal economic achievement was the high quality of life attained on a modest per capita income, and its most spectacular failure the inability to translate this social sector achievement into rapid economic growth. Jayawardena uses different indicator values to reinforce his views. He introduces four developments which led to Sri Lanka's low growth performance: (a) election pledges to make Sinhala the sole official language, (b) introduction of 'standardization of marks' to help children from rural areas enter universities at the expense of their urban counterparts, (c) government investment in large high-cost projects for electoral gains, and (d) the combination of a high literacy rate and an oversupply of graduates coupled with low growth.

Jayawardena goes on to discuss the three main attempts made at reforms and their outcomes: first, the conversion of the food subsidy to investment in 1977; second, the 1989 Enhanced Structural Adjustment Facility (ESAF) programme designed by the

IMF; and third, the 2001 IMF conditionality to maintain a managed float of the exchange rate. A critique of reform issues follows where Jayawardena raises questions which are discussed in the context of Sri Lanka, and incorporates the views of Stiglitz and Soros, both of whom analyse the issues in relation to Africa and East Asia: (a) why do countries undertake major reform measures? (b) what is the relationship between political and economic reform? (c) what is the threshold level of economic development that must be reached before reform can be effective? and (d) when should a country liberalize its capital account? Jayawardena concludes by examining the future perspectives for reform and points out that there is currently a real opportunity for a deal between Sri Lanka and the donor community provided they commit themselves to the conditionalities imposed.

In Chapter 5, J.B. Kelegama analyses the role of the public sector in the Sri Lankan economy with a critical look at the premise that 'the invisible hand' of market forces should accord supremacy with no state interference. The limitations of this 'one size fits all' formula are discussed in detail and the argument further strengthened with highlights from the Report of the South Commission which included Gamani Corea.

Kelegama consolidates this view by incorporating extracts from the work of Stiglitz and Sen. He argues that without public investment in infrastructure, there will be little private investment, and then goes on to review Sri Lanka's pre-1977 emphasis on operating a mixed economy with co-existing public and private sectors and the subsequent decline in the relative importance of the public sector with the adoption of free market policies. The author points out to the presence of a large public sector in developed countries, although developing countries are advised to maintain a small public sector. This is shown by analysing government spending figures, levels of taxation and the many forms of state intervention present in the developed world.

Kelegama goes on to examine the view that the high growth rates experienced by the East Asian countries were in a major part due to the active role played by the state, despite IMF pressure to shrink the public sector in these countries. The high level of public investment stimulated greater domestic private investment, which in turn raised the level of Foreign Direct Investment (FDI) to East Asia. In comparison, Kelegama emphasizes that the current level of public investment in Sri Lanka is too low and considers the importance of increasing this in order to promote economic growth. Many economic, political and social factors are presented to highlight the need for an active public sector and the author concludes that both the public and private sectors are engines for growth and must co-exist in a growing economy, as one alone is inadequate.

Part II—Macroeconomic Policy—begins with a chapter by D.D.M. Waidyasekera on fiscal policy issues and debates in Sri Lanka (Chapter 6). Sri Lanka's fiscal and tax system is at a critical juncture, resulting in much debate on current policy issues and the future direction of policy. The author analyses the effectiveness and efficacy of the prevalent fiscal and taxation system and discusses the declining trend in government revenue in relation to gross domestic product (GDP) over time, the reasons for the decline, and the paucity of direct taxes like income tax in relation to the increasing importance of consumption taxes such as value added tax (VAT), import taxes and excise duties.

Other important issues examined in the chapter include the relationship of taxation to savings, capital formation and investment, the elasticity and buoyancy of the fiscal system and to what extent consumption taxes can be utilized to further increase revenue. The VAT system which has evoked considerable controversy is discussed at length, bringing to light some of its structural and implementational deficiencies. Waidyasekera expresses doubt as to the effectiveness and cost of the fiscal incentive system in the development process. Further, while there is no question of the presence of large-scale tax evasion and black money in the economy, the measures periodically taken to remedy this situation have so far proved ineffective. In this context, the author critiques the effectiveness of the regular amnesties granted, including the latest across-the-board amnesty of 2003. The final sections discuss the topical issue of fiscal devolution. It stresses that in devising any form of political devolution, careful attention must be paid to the economic and fiscal aspects of devolution right from the inception.

Chapter 7 by Nihal Kappagoda presents a detailed analysis of the current situation of public debt in Sri Lanka and related institutional issues. According to Kappagoda, public debt and its management has become an important policy issue for Sri Lanka at present as compared to the 1980s due to factors that have altered the international financial environment. The changes and new requirements for debt management have led governments of developing and transition countries to review their institutional arrangements for public sector borrowing and its management. The author goes on to discuss nine vital requirements for effective management of public debt and four principal debt management objectives appropriate for any country which should be met. Kappagoda charts the organizational structure of a Public Debt Management Office (PDMO) and points out the functions of each office.

The final section on future action discusses the way out of the present public debt situation from an institutional and policy point of view. As regards the government decision to establish a PDMO office to deal with all aspects of debt management, Kappagoda identifies the need for an appropriate institutional structure to build on existing capacities and a review of laws dealing with public sector borrowing. Consideration is given to adopting annual borrowing plans, introducing effective budget-management measures, and a borrowing policy that covers both quantitative and qualitative issues. Monitoring should also be carried out on accumulation of arrears on debt service payments and loan implementation on government borrowing. In the long run, all these activities performed by the departments of the Ministry of Finance and the Central Bank should be brought under the umbrella of the PDMO.

In Chapter 8, Sisira Jayasuriya looks at some of the main issues related to exchange rate policy and the surrounding debates in recent years, a period during which the exchange rate regime as well as the broader policy environment has changed in quite fundamental ways, with the shift to a floating exchange rate regime marking the culmination of a series of measures towards a market responsive policy regime.

Jayasuriya examines the behaviour of both nominal and real exchange rates since the early 1980s, and discusses the underlying factors driving phases of appreciation and depreciation in the context of structural factors causing macroeconomic imbalances which generate real exchange rate appreciations and misalignments. The empirical evidence suggests that regular small adjustments to the nominal exchange rate can help maintain the level of the real exchange rate only in the short run because underlying misalignments of the real exchange rate necessitate periodic large currency depreciations. These impose significant real economic costs by entrenching inflationary expectations, lowering export and income growth, and increasing costs of investment and trade. Jayasuriya argues that the Central Bank's attempts to counter the macroeconomic impacts of fiscal imbalances with monetary policy have probably aggravated growth instability and distributional inequity.

Part III—Agriculture, Industry and Technology Development—begins with a chapter by Nimal Sanderatne on selected issues of agricultural development. The author introduces the main events influencing agricultural policy commencing with the emphasis on institutional change and government support for paddy farming in 1956 to attain self-sufficiency in food in the post-independence era. He examines the controversial tenancy reforms of 1958, the import substitution programme of the 1960s, the implementation of ceilings on land ownership and the subsequent nationalization of estates in the 1970s, as well as the Accelerated Mahaweli Development Programme of the late 1970s and early 1980s.

The author goes on to discuss the controversies surrounding these policies. He examines in depth six of these controversies which were at the political, technical and academic levels: (*a*) Cost and Benefit of Colonization, (*b*) Protective Tenure, (*c*) Paddy Lands Act of 1958, (*d*) Land Reforms, (*e*) Privatization of Estates, and (*f*) Protection, Subsidies and Environment. Sanderatne's concluding reflections provide some useful insights. Despite the important bearing that many of the policies had on agrarian structure, controversies on agricultural development issues were limited. The author examines reasons for the agricultural-fundamentalist views of the post-independence politicians in terms of colonization, land resettlement, legislature and the prevailing economic conditions. While political and public debate on agricultural policy was limited, there was controversy at the academic level. It is also interesting to note that current controversies in agriculture are due to policy recommendations by international institutions.

In Chapter 10, Sarath Rajapatirana critically examines the new revisionist case for an active industrial policy with a focus on the private sector. The author defines both types of policies and sets out reasons why the debate has special significance in the Sri Lankan context. Rajapatirana goes on to examine the main elements of the case for industrial policy, which is based on four prime propositions concerned with the infant industry argument. Each element is analysed in depth to see which ones support the case for industrial policy. As economists used the East Asian Tigers as a role model for Sri Lanka's growth performance, the author evaluates the case put forward for an industrial policy based on the East Asian countries' experiences, especially following the crises faced by those countries during the period 1997–2000.

Rajapatirana uses data on Sri Lanka's manufacturing export performance to consider whether one would be better informed by looking at actual experience rather than conjectures as to what would have happened if one type of policy was followed rather than the other. The author suggests that a neutral policy towards industry be implemented as an alternative to industrial policy, as it is more likely to maximize national income than industrial policy. According to the author, the stellar performance in East Asia can be ascribed to getting the fundamentals right and not to industrial policy per se. Rajapatirana concludes by pointing out that specific interventions through appropriate institutional arrangements should be formulated, and discusses the conditions that must be met to ensure successful selective intervention.

In Chapter 11, Chandana Perera and Sarath Dasanayaka provide a study on key issues of technology development. The authors state that technology, innovation and research and development (R&D) are recognized as important factors in the economic growth and development of a country. However, the history of technology development in Sri Lanka is not marked by much success. The study is divided into two major periods: (a) pre-independence period in which the state deliberately ignored technology issues which were not within the domain of plantation agriculture, and (b) post-independence period in which a significant reason for failure was the lack of high level political commitment and support for R&D activities. After the economic reforms of 1977, the government took considerable efforts to develop Sri Lanka as a newly industrialized country based on science and technology (S&T). Despite all this, due to many reasons, the effort towards S&T development has not been very successful.

Perera and Dasanayaka carry out an in-depth analysis on R&D expenditure, highlighting that Sri Lanka's expenditure is well below the recommended value for developing countries. They examine the future directions of R&D and trace the main drawbacks that exist, including the position of universities and R&D institutions in technology development. They observe that the lack of commercialization of R&D is a major problem in all the institutions. The authors suggest that Sri Lanka should develop the acquisition, adaptive, operative and innovative capabilities in line with the country's factor and resource endowments. When acquiring technology, they argue that all its components should be obtained in order to gain maximum benefit and to enhance national technology capabilities.

Part IV—Employment and Labour—begins with a chapter by Ravindra A. Yatawara on labour productivity growth and employment generation (Chapter 12). According to Yatawara, the dual goals of productivity growth and employment generation are tantamount to the development process. Productivity growth reflects greater efficiency, enhances competitiveness of a nation and leads to higher living standards, while employment creation is a powerful tool to eliminate poverty and stem social unrest. There is an implicit debate over the preference of goals due to the traditional belief of a trade-off existing between the two. Yatawara argues that such a debate is not useful and detracts from effective policy formulations to facilitate economic take-off. He utilizes disaggregated industry-level data to examine the relationship between productivity, employment growth and wages. Two interesting observations from the results are highlighted. Real wage growth and thus increases in living standards are determined by productivity growth. Policies to improve productivity are vital for Sri Lanka's development and can be consistent with employment creation. Yatawara points out that a multi-pronged approach is needed to stimulate both productivity growth and job creation, and discusses a range of policies that will promote both goals.

An often cited (and contentious) obstacle to achieving both these goals is the excessive level of labour regulations in Sri Lanka. Evidence suggests more labour market flexibility is desirable, but the move to it must involve higher wages as job security is reduced, and a credible system of worker adjustment assistance. The other main issues include the accumulation of local and foreign capital, technological innovation, work force development, improving labour-management relations and encouraging entrepreneurship.

In Chapter 13, W.D. Lakshman analyses issues related to youth unemployment in Sri Lanka. The topic is a worldwide phenomenon, and Sri Lanka offers an interesting case study of youth unemployment in a developing country as its experience in this area brings out both unique features as well as common elements, both of which Lakshman considers. The author sets out the background for the study of youth unemployment by examining the extent of overall unemployment in the country as well as its change over time using empirical data. He then identifies the nature and extent of youth unemployment in Sri Lanka during the past two decades—its composition, links between educational attainment levels and unemployment, etc.

The core of this chapter is an exploration of the major causal factors behind high rates of youth unemployment and the observed structural characteristics of this problem. The exploration is interdisciplinary and goes into economic, social and political spheres. Some comments are also made here on the strengths and weaknesses of general and employment-orientated policies under the programme of liberalization carried out in Sri Lanka since 1977.

The essay concludes by providing several policy insights. Lakshman discusses the most widely adopted policy framework for raising growth and employment as well as measures particularly adopted by Sri Lanka. He reviews the reliance placed on FDI and the need for outward-oriented economic strategy along with systems of manpower planning, selective state intervention and appropriate institutional arrangements.

In Chapter 14, Raja B.M. Korale examines migration and brain drain in Sri Lanka. The author attempts to make an assessment of the dimensions of brain drain and its impact on Sri Lanka, and to review existing policies and analyse appropriate interventions to deal with its possible adverse effects. Korale examines the migration dimensions in which emigration has exceeded immigration—the available data roughly indicate the number of persons who migrated annually for employment and residence abroad, and by the level of illegal migration. The study traces migration patterns to selected countries based on empirical host-country data. Host countries analysed in depth included Australia, Canada, New Zealand, the United States, Norway and others. The concept of the brain drain is discussed as the adverse effects of migration include the loss of skilled and experienced employees.

Korale selects a few occupations such as engineering, accountancy and medicine in order to examine growth in the stock of human capital with the additions of output from education and training institutions while emigration and other losses are taking place. International migration was assumed to be a temporary phenomenon, but in the Sri Lankan case, Korale points out many factors that contribute to maintaining the high migration outflows. He goes on to identify the impact of migration on Sri Lanka in terms of demographics and the effects on the labour force, employment and households. The remainder of the chapter discusses other topics related to international migration including migrant remittances, prospects for migration, clandestine and out-migration and the protection of migrant workers abroad. He concludes by observing that Sri Lanka will have to accept brain drain as a medium-term phenomenon, and as such analyses seven possible strategies that have been formulated to meet the effects of skilled migration.

In Part V of this collection—Institutional and Governance Issues—David Dunham deals with the debate on the nexus of economic liberalization and institutional reform in Chapter 15. This chapter looks at the alternative views in the discussion on institutions and institutional change in relation to economic policy reforms in contemporary Sri Lanka. The first, described as a 'getting policies right' approach, emphasizes the mainstream position where the driving force is a need for greater efficiency in the economic reforms process. He argues that many of the specific policy measures that have been proposed run squarely counter to the strategic thinking of the political leadership, and consequently, institutional reform has been an uphill struggle.

On the other hand is the 'politics first' approach in which reform is seen as part of the broader programme of particular governments, stressing political leadership, path dependence and macro-institutional change. In this case, since policy is structured largely on political patronage, almost any policy may be viewed and implemented to serve the leadership's purposes. The main difference between the two approaches is that in the first model rent-seeking will be eliminated through the institutional reform process and a coalition against reform will vote the politicians out of office. In the second model, initial conditions, political culture and macro-political institutions emerge as qualifying factors and the reform process will be slow.

Dunham goes on to examine Sri Lanka's history of reform and institutional change. He traces and analyses the policies of successive governments, starting with the Jayawardena government of 1977–89, to the Premadasa years of 1989–93, Kumaratunga during 1994–2001 and finally the Wickremesinghe Government of 2002 and beyond. He describes the major changes in political ideology and in political culture and institutions that have shaped the country's development trajectory over the past 25 years. He points out that effective institutional change needs perceived legitimacy. What is happening must be known, understood and seen as wrong. It remains part of the tragedy of Sri Lanka that discussions of policy and analysis of context remain far apart.

In Chapter 16, A.D.V. de S. Indraratna discusses the Consumer Affairs Authority (CAA) Act in the overall context of competition policy in Sri Lanka. Under perfect competition, not only are resources allocated efficiently but also consumer welfare is maximized. Since in practice this ideal situation does not exist and markets are imperfect in varying degrees, a competition policy backed by legislation is necessary to promote competition.

Indraratna examines in detail the objectives of the Fair Trading Commission (FTC) and considers its main function of conducting investigations on its own motions or on a request made to it by other bodies. Indraratna identifies several weaknesses of the FTC Act including questions regarding its definition, anti-competitive practices, discrimination and transparency and procedural fairness. In order to remedy the limitations of the FTC, the CCA Act was passed in 2003. This Act too was a mixture of competition and consumer protection legislature, but with greater weightage given to the latter than in the FTC Act. It is in several ways an improvement on the preceding legislation. The author provides a critique of the CCA Act in terms of its inadequacy as competition legislation and on its other weaknesses. He points out the need for amendments to the Act to provide an interface between it and the Public Utilities Commission (PUC) Act. After the strengths and weaknesses have been assessed, the Act must be streamlined and complemented by monopolies and mergers legislation in order to have an effective competition policy.

Policy issues relating to privatization and regulation are addressed in Chapter 17 by Malathy Knight-John. This chapter provides some useful insights on the dynamics of reform and of institutions in the Sri Lankan context. Knight-John traces the evolution of policies and institutional changes with regard to privatization and regulation since the opening up of the Sri Lankan economy. Before privatization, policy formulation and the institutional structures created by the different governments in power were in many cases designed to satisfy the political needs of the time and this manifested in the form of rent-seeking, crony capitalism and weak regulation. Privatization was formally announced as a state policy in 1987 and coincided with the second wave of liberalization. Its primary objectives were to ease the fiscal burden and improve the efficiency of enterprises through the infusion of private sector norms. The author discusses in depth the reform proposals and changes made, starting with the Premadasa years in the late 1980s to the People's Alliance (PA) Government of the 1990s and finally to the new United National Front (UNF) Government post-2001.

Knight-John goes on to analyse some of the 'big picture' questions and controversies on privatization and regulation as they relate to policy, process and outcome issues faced by reformers, in an attempt to gain a better understanding of the dynamics of institutional change in Sri Lanka's political economy milieu. The author examines fundamental issues such as why successive policy regimes chose privatization as a development strategy, the actual results of privatization and issues related to regulation. Some of the challenges remaining in this area that have not received adequate attention include the need to develop a generic competition law. Also, with respect to the current wave of regulation, the new legislation is inconsistent in several instances with the devolution of power to local government bodies under the Constitution. Knight-John also returns to the recurring theme of her chapter—the dynamics of institutions and institutional change in Sri Lanka.

One of the main lessons emerging from this discussion that is integral to the success of future reform efforts is that any reform is essentially a political exercise, and, as such, it is vital that the reform process have national ownership. According to Knight-John, it is this notion that leads us to the core of the reform problem—the nature of the state in Sri Lanka and the need for political will when implementing institutional change.

Chapter 18 by H.N.S. Karunatilake examines reforms in the banking sector. Proposals were made starting from the late 1940s to establish a central bank to look at policies critically and tender objective advice to the government. Controversy surrounded the issue as the public and politicians had different convictions. Many critics were influenced by the orthodox thinking and practice of central banking in Europe and as such did not consider the medium and long-term impact on the country of a central bank. Despite opposition, the Central Bank commenced operations in 1950.

In it's first Annual Report issued in 1951, the views expressed by the Central Bank on subsidies, inflation and budget deficits have been the position maintained by the Bank ever since its inception, and there has been no variation in its stand since then on these issues. Karunatilake considers the Central Bank's approach to monetary and fiscal management and government policy. The Bank cautioned the government that the consequences of lax fiscal policy would affect monetary management. However, different governments with differing ideologies often resulted in the Central Bank not being completely in harmony with government policies, but conflict was generally avoided. The post-1977 liberalization reforms and policies were welcomed by the Central Bank.

From an institutional standpoint, the Development Finance Corporation of Ceylon (DFCC) was established in the mid-1950s to finance private sector investment. The early 1960s were of special significance as the nationalization of the Bank of Ceylon and the establishment of the People's Bank laid a firm foundation for the development and expansion of domestic banking, a process aided by the reforms of 1977. The government also found that the DFCC was not up to the task of financing new projects on a broad front and as such, the decision was taken to set up the National Development Bank (NDB) as a new institution with the object of financing long-term projects in the private sector.

The failure of several finance companies between 1983 and 1990 threatened the stability of some domestic banks and led the Central Bank to usher in a new era in the regulation and supervision of banking and financial institutions. The 1990s saw the appointment of a Banking Commission which had broad terms of reference. According to the author, recently, due to many weaknesses including its politicization, poor management and an inability to think in national terms, the Central Bank had undergone restructuring. The chapter provides an in-depth analysis of the reasons behind the streamlining and the changes undertaken.

Part VI of this volume on Social Welfare has Laksiri Jayasuriya in Chapter 19 providing an in-depth analysis of the colonial roots of the Sri Lankan welfare state, a relatively neglected aspect of post-independence policy history of the country. It is found that the Sri Lankan welfare state, a coordinated institutional system that emerged in the 1960s and 1970s, was largely a legacy of Sri Lanka's British colonial past, extending from the 19th century to the ending of colonial rule in 1948. Adopting a distinctly historical focus, the author endeavours to highlight, without discounting domestic social and cultural influences, the impact of British colonial policy on the development of Sri Lanka's social policy. The chapter identifies three main phases of social policy development. The early phase extending from 1833 to 1931 denotes the early colonial state in Sri Lanka, and is marked by the development of a colonial export economy and the modernization of Sri Lankan society. The second phase from 1931 to 1948 represents the late colonial state; this features a period of partial self-rule, which also serves as a development prelude to the emergence of the welfare state. The third, most recent phase covers the first two decades of independence (1948–70), and stands out as a transitional phase in which the late colonial state moved into the post-colonial era.

Jayasuriya provides a detailed examination of all three phases of social policy development and discusses the constitutional reforms associated with each phase. In contextualizing the evolution of social policy leading to the welfare state, the author shows that British liberalism imposed on Sri Lanka helped shape the political economy on the basis of three elements: free trade, evangelicalism and philosophical radicalism. In effect, the social and political institutions of Sri Lanka, including the welfare state of the 1960s, lie firmly anchored to the social and political ideology of British colonialism.

Jayasuriya also discusses, among many other points, the transformation of the Sri Lanka polity from welfare to warfare in the post-colonial era. In concluding, the author identifies three distinctive features of the British colonial legacy—the influence of a liberal ideology, the processes of democratization and the relative autonomy of the late colonial state. However, Jayasuriya points out that there still remain many challenging and unanswered questions in understanding the evolution of social policy in Sri Lanka.

Chapter 20 by Amala de Silva presents an overview of reforms in the health sector in Sri Lanka. The chapter examines the evolution of the health system in Sri Lanka, focusing on provision and financing. It notes that Sri Lanka has been a success story in the health arena achieving excellent health indicators while expending a low share of the gross domestic product (GDP) on health care. Two policies are considered to have led to this success: free health care and the provision of services close to the client. According to the author, both demographic and epidemiological transitions are now posing a challenge to the health system and this has been further intensified by the impact of economic transition and the rise in aspirations that have resulted from social transition. The lack of a national health policy, despite attempts by Health Task Forces in 1992 and 1996, have led to ad hoc developments in the health sector and to growing imbalances with regard to provision and financing.

De Silva in particular focuses on three debates that have persisted over time and are now crucial at the begining of the 21st century. The first is whether referral or 'voting with the feet', as occurs presently, is the best way of providing public services. The second relates to the government's role in financing health care, while the third focuses on market imperfections within the private sector and its impact on provision, pricing and efficiency. The chapter argues that there is a vital need to consider whether the existing policies in the health care sector are outmoded given the current challenges. The main conclusion however, is that there exists an urgent need for a comprehensive national health policy, incorporating health financing explicitly, and focusing on the coordination of public and private sector activity in Sri Lanka.

In Chapter 21, Harsha Aturupane provides a study of conceptual foundations and achievements of public investment on education. Aturupane identifies the many economic and social benefits of efficient and equitable investment in education. Consideration is given to the economic and social arguments that justify public investment in education as opposed to private investment. The Sri Lankan public education system, as is normal in most countries, is divided into three main cycles: primary, secondary and tertiary schooling. The central characteristic of the education policy framework is the commitment of the state to provide universal access to basic education. The chapter highlights empirical testing of the composition of public education expenditure and of recurrent and capital education budgets. The results provide some useful observations for analysis and policy planning.

Aturupane presents the main sources of financing of government educational expenditure as domestic revenue, foreign aid loans and foreign grants. He points out the educational attainments of Sri Lanka, including quantitative attainments as well as indicators of internal efficiency, which are well above those of neighbouring South Asian countries, and close to rates in countries at considerably higher economic levels. The author finds through econometric testing the impact of education investment on poverty and economic welfare. Empirical data shows that poverty declines steeply as education levels rise. Economic welfare is also closely related to education, and the analysis of household expenditure of poor families indicates that consumption increases sharply as the education level of the household head rises, among both male and female headed households. Other findings also suggest that there may be considerable scope for raising private investment in education through the creation of a favourable environment for private sector investment.

The final chapter (Chapter 22) by Buddhadasa Hewavitharana examines the achievements and policy challenges in the sphere of poverty alleviation. The chapter encompasses past as well as current policy debates on poverty alleviation issues in relation to impediments and obstacles, welfare and income transfers, reformulation and reorientation of programmes and the dynamics of growth, equity and poverty. The debate considers two critical phases of economic policy-making in Sri Lanka: the first in 1977 which centred on structural adjustments to activate market forces, and the second from 1989 onwards which emphasized the private sector as the engine of growth, and as such attempted to link the poor to the growth process. Policies and strategies suited for the first round are examined for their relevance to the second. The impediments and obstacles to alleviating poverty are analysed using a thematic diagram which depicts the complex linkages between the poor and the environment that controls their economic and social well-being.

The poor are casualties of four forms of marginalization: economic, political, social and spatial, and the aim of all targeted and specific alleviation programmes have been to reach out and lift them out of poverty through micro-level interventions. Hewavitharana points out that some macro/national policies/programmes run contrary to or at cross purposes with micro-level interventions. Thus for achieving sustainable poverty alleviation there needs to be consistency between macro-policy frameworks, institutional change and action at the micro-level. The author also goes on to argue that bad governance associated with the politicization of the public service, coupled with a bureaucratic culture that is not service orientated, works directly to disempower the poor. As such, it is necessary to build up a countervailing power of the poor that could catalyse a process of building up a non-party political culture for poverty eradication.

In the final section, Hewavitharana examines pro-poor structural change for pro-poor growth. The chapter presents issues raised by evaluators/analysts and highlights the innovative concepts of pro-poor growth and pro-poor structural change. The author also raises the question of how to manage growth-equity-poverty dynamics in a private sector led process of economic growth.

NOTE

1. The First Act of the CF which was linked to price stabilization agreements never got operational; however, a diluted version of the CF (Act 2) where commodity development activities—R&D and market promotion activities—were emphasized became operational.

REFERENCES

Bruton, H. et al. (1992), *Sri Lanka & Malaysia: The Political Economy of Poverty, Equity, & Growth*, Oxford University Press for the World Bank.

Corea, G. (1975), *Instability of an Export Economy*, Colombo: Marga Publication.

——— (1985), 'Adjustment and Growth', in Sri Lanka Association of Economists (eds), *Structural Adjustment and Growth*, Colombo: SLAE.

——— (1987), 'The Prospects for our Poor', *Sri Lanka Economic Journal*, 2(1).

——— (1992), *Taming Commodity Markets: The Integrated Programme and Common Fund in UNCTAD*, Manchester: Manchester University Press.

——— (1993), 'Development in Asia: Prospects and Issues for the Nineties', *Sri Lanka Economic Journal*, 8(2).

——— (2003), 'The Legacy of Dr. Raul Prebisch', *South Asia Economic Journal*, 4(1).

Cuthbertson, A.G. and P. Athukorala (1991), 'Sri Lanka', in D. Papageorgiou, M. Michaely and A.M. Choksi (eds), *Liberalizing Foreign Trade*, Vol. 5, Oxford: Blackwell.

Dell, S. (1988), 'Preface', in S. Dell (ed.), *Policies for Development: Essays in Honour of Gamani Corea*, London: Macmillan.

Gilbert, C.L. (1996), 'International Commodity Agreements: An Obituary Notice', *World Development*, 24(1).

Indraratna, A.D.V. de S. (1998), *Fifty Years of Sri Lanka's Independence: A Socio-Economic Review*, Colombo: Sri Lanka Institute of Social and Economic Studies.

Kadirgamar, Lakshman (2002), 'Gamani Returns to the Third World', in *The Sunday Times*, 20 October 2002, Colombo.

Kelegama, S. (1999), 'Economic Development in Sri Lanka during the 50 Years of Independence: What Went Wrong?', in *People's Bank* (1999).

Lakshman, W.D. (1997), *Dilemmas of Development: Fifty Years of Economic Change in Sri Lanka*, Colombo: Sri Lanka Association of Economists.

Lakshman, W.D. and C.A. Tisdell (2000), *Sri Lanka's Development since Independence: Socio-Economic Perspectives and Analysis*, New York: Nova Science Publishers.

People's Bank (1999), *Milestones to Independence*, A Publication of the People's Bank to Commemorate the Golden Jubilee of National Independence, Colombo.

Snodgrass, D.R. (1966), *Ceylon: An Export Economy in Transition*, Homewood: Richard D. Irwin Inc.

Part I

DEVELOPMENT STRATEGY AND IDEOLOGY

Part I

1

Growth of Manufactured Exports and Terms of Trade: Pessimism Confounded

Prema-chandra Athukorala

Introduction

This chapter examines the behaviour of the terms of trade of Sri Lanka during the post-independence era, with emphasis on the implications of the structural shift in the export composition into manufactures over the past two decades under market-oriented reforms. The theoretical underpinning for the analysis is provided by the 'new' terms of trade pessimism, the views that export diversification from primary products to manufactures may not necessarily bring about terms of trade gains for commodity-dependent developing countries. The empirical analysis of this chapter focuses on trends in both BTT and ITT.[1] Previous studies on this subject have focused solely on BTT. This practice however tends to miss an important part of the story because, compared to primary products, manufactures have a greater capacity to strengthen the external payments position of a country through volume expansion for a given level of BTT.

The implications of terms of trade deterioration for the development efforts of commodity-dependent developing countries has been a dominant theme throughout Gamani Corea's long and highly influential career. In the mid-1950s, when Corea entered development policy-making in Sri Lanka, the Prebisch-Singer thesis of the declining terms of trade of primary commodities (Prebisch, 1950; Singer, 1950) and the advocacy of import-substitution industrialization as an escape from the resultant unequal distribution of gains from trade had begun to dominate development thinking. As part of his doctoral research at Oxford, Corea had closely followed the new debate in relation to future growth prospects for Sri Lanka's classical export economy (Corea, 1952). His conviction of this ideology was further buttressed by the precipitous fall in Sri Lanka's terms of trade following the ending of the tea boom in 1956, undermining the very foundations of the export economy inherited from the colonial era (Corea, 1965). Thus, cushioning the growth dynamism of the economy against terms of trade deterioration turned out to be the prime concern of the development strategy of the first Ten-Year Plan (1959–68) designed by the Planning Secretariat under his leadership. The Plan spoke of 'turning the country's existing export sector into the equivalent of a capital goods sector by the domestic production of consumer import substitutes' so that growth of both industry and agriculture would be accelerated without being impeded by the external payments crisis. When Corea commenced his second term as the head of the planning organization in Sri Lanka in 1965, there were no signs of abating the terms of trade collapse and the nascent import-substituting manufacturing industries were in deep trouble because of shortages of imported intermediate goods. In this context, he engineered a major shift in the focus of national development policy in favour of domestic food production (Corea, 1973).[2] This gave rise to the 'Food' Drive (renamed 'Cultivation War' following the change in political leadership in 1970), which remained the main pillar of the government's economic policy for the next 10 years.

During his tenure as Secretary General of the UNCTAD (1974–88), Corea fought hard to tame commodity markets (Corea, 1980, 1992). As the result of a deliberate initiative by the Secretariat of the UNCTAD under his leadership, reforming the international trading system for commodities became the key issue of the North-South dialogue on establishing a New International Economic Order (NIEO). The IPC (Corea Plan) proposed by the UNCTAD as one of the main planks of the NIEO sought to establish a series of commodity agreements covering a wide range of products of interest to developing countries and to create an entirely new institution (CF) for financing of these agreements. In its original form, the Corea Plan had two key objectives: indexing commodity prices to the prices of manufactured products (essentially meaning arresting decline in BTT faced by primary producers), and moderating short-term fluctuations in commodity prices. The former objective was lost in the battle to win acceptance of the programme by consumer countries, and the final programme explicitly emphasized reducing price fluctuations as the operational norm of the commodity agreements. However, Corea considered the implementation of the IPC in this watered down form as an essential first step in accomplishing the objective of arresting adverse trends in terms of trade faced by primary exporting countries through price indexation. On this he wrote:

> [While] indexation is a valid goal it cannot be implemented merely through the adoption of resolutions. Until the instruments for regulating markets exist there is no way of implementing the objective of indexation. Once there is a commodity agreement, of course, it would be possible to include in its price provisions something akin to an indexation process. (Corea, 1980: 14)[3]

Corea's emphasis on import-substitution development strategy in the 1950s and 1960s was much in line with the prevalent style of economic thinking when the post-war period of development planning began. But he has always been prepared to change his views when facts change. For instance, by the late 1960s he had already begun to discuss openly the limitations of the inward-oriented growth strategy of Sri Lanka during the first two decades and the need for an outward-looking policy shift (Corea,

1971a, 1971b). Corea emphasized that Sri Lanka's lacklustre economic record could not be explained in terms of unfavourable world market conditions alone as many other countries facing the same market conditions had done much better, and argued for a new policy framework based on a reappraisal of 'the relative attractiveness of production for the domestic market and the production for exports' (1971b: 27). During his tenure at UNCTAD, he considered international commodity control only as a means of facilitating national developmental efforts of primary-dependent developing countries to restructure their lop-sided colonial economies, not as an end in itself. Perhaps based on the lessons learned from Sri Lanka, he emphasized export-led industrialization as an important element of such national efforts (Corea, 1992: Chapter 11; 1993). However, Corea has continued to maintain the view that widespread adoption of an export-led industrialization strategy by developing countries is unlikely to bring about the desired results, unless this policy shift is combined with an effort to harness 'the potential for greater exchange among developing countries themselves—South-South trade—as a means of ... (averting) possible saturation of markets if exports are aimed at only the industrialized countries' (1986a: 14). Though not explicitly stated, this view is much in the logical line of the fallacy of composition argument—one of the two pillars of the new terms of trade pessimism (see below).

This chapter takes Corea's allegiance to the new export pessimism as an invitation to undertake an empirical analysis of the terms of trade implications of the expansion of manufactured exports from Sri Lanka. Market-oriented policy reforms initiated in 1977 and sustained over the past two decades have dramatically transformed Sri Lanka's colonial export structure, something which had a profound impact on Corea's economic thinking. The combined share of primary exports in total merchandise exports (in gross terms) declined from over 85 per cent in the late 1970s to about 16 per cent in 2002 (Table 1.1). Sri Lanka is now classified among a handful of developing countries that have achieved a clear policy shift from import-substitution to export-oriented industrialization (Athukorala and Rajapatirana, 2000). While the composition of manufactured exports is still dominated by textiles and garments, there has been a significant increase in the relative importance of other manufacturing products over the years. The share of natural rubber (the second largest of the traditional 'trio') in total exports has declined sharply (reaching less than 1 per cent in 2002) as a result of the rapid growth of rubber-based manufactured products. The Sri Lankan experience over the past two decades thus provides an excellent opportunity for testing the validity of the new terms of trade debate.

The remainder of this chapter is structured into three sections. The first section provides an overview of the debate on the terms of trade implications of export diversification into manufacturing in a traditional primary-exporting country in order to set the stage for the ensuing analysis. In the second section, trends and patterns of the terms of BTT and ITT in Sri Lanka during the post-independence era are examined, with particular emphasis on the experience during the two-and-a-half decades following the liberalization reforms initiated in 1977. The final section presents some concluding remarks.

Table 1.1

Export Structure of Sri Lanka, 1965–2002

(percentage composition at current prices, two-year averages)

	1965/66	1976/77	1979/80	1984/85	1989/90	1994/95	1999/2000	2001/02
Primary exports	99.1	85.7	72.5	63.1	47.4	29.5	16.1	16.5
Tea	59.8	50.3	36.3	37.6	25	12.5	13.0	14.2
Rubber	17.2	16.4	15.5	8	4.7	1.7	0.6	0.5
Coconut products	13.1	8.7	8.7	6.5	4.4	1.9	2.5	1.7
Other primary products[a]	9	10.3	12	11	13.3	13.3	4.7	5.0
Manufacturing	0.9	4.6	12.3	26.9	47.9	66.0	75.6	75.7
Food and beverages	0.6	2	2.1	3.8	4.3	3.7	2.3	2.6
Textile and garment	—	1.8	8.4	21.1	33.1	42.9	53.4	52.2
Rubber products	—	—	0.2	0.4	1.6	3.3	3.5	3.7
Ceramics	—	0.4	0.6	0.5	0.8	1.1	0.9	0.9
Leather and footwear	—	0.1	0.2	0.2	0.6	3.1	3.7	2.5
Diamond and jewellery	—	—	0.3	0.4	4.3	4.6	3.6	4.1
Machinery and equipment	0.2	0.2	0.2	0.2	1.7	3.7	4.4	5.4
Other manufacturing[b]	—	—	0.3	0.3	1.5	3.6	3.7	4.3
Petroleum products[c]	0	9.7	15.2	10	4.7	2.0	1.7	1.5
Total[d] (US$ million)	393	645	1,023	1,401	1,735	3,507	5,066	4,758

Source: Compiled using data from Central Bank, *Annual Report* (various years).
Notes: [a] Minor agricultural products and minerals.
[b] Mostly toys, sports goods and plastic products.
[c] Shipping and aviation fuel supplied by the state-owned Sri Lanka Petroleum Corporation.
[d] Including re-exports (which amounted to less than 1 per cent in all years).
— Zero or negligible.

THE NEW TERMS OF TRADE DEBATE[4]

The majority opinion in policy circles in developing countries and within the international policy community is that primary-exporting developing countries can achieve terms of trade gains through diversification into manufactured exports. This view is often rationalized on the basis of the Prebisch-Singer thesis that postulates a structural tendency for the barter (or commodity) terms of trade, or BTT, of primary commodities in world trade to deteriorate relative to manufactures (Prebisch, 1950; Singer, 1950). Whether this postulate necessarily implies that a shift away from primary commodities to manufactures will bring about terms of trade gains for developing countries has, however, become the subject of an interesting debate in the recent trade and development literature. The point of contention in the 'new' terms of trade debate is whether there are 'commodity-like' characteristics in manufacturing processes in developing countries which place these countries in 'double jeopardy' in their attempts to escape from unequal exchanges in world trade (Thirlwall, 2003: 443).

The debate is centred on two main hypotheses. The first, which is dubbed 'the Singer hypothesis', is an adaptation of the old Prebisch-Singer thesis. Prebisch (1950) and Singer (1950) present four major explanations of the long run deterioration in the BTT between primary products and manufactures. These are: (a) lower price and lower income elasticity of demand for primary products than for manufactured goods, (b) technical progress that economises on the use of primary raw material in the manufacturing process, (c) technological superiority of developed countries and the control exercised by multinational corporations (MNCs) based in these countries on the use of sophisticated manufacturing technology, and (d) monopolistic market structures in developed countries combined with competitive conditions in both commodity and labour markets in developing countries. Of these, the first two factors are essentially 'commodity specific' and hence, so argues Singer (1987), imply that a shift from primary commodities to manufactures would lead to terms of trade gains. By contrast, the remaining two factors are 'country specific' and are presumably relevant in determining the BTT of both primary commodities as well as manufactures exported by developing countries. If the negative influences of country-specific factors outweigh the positive influences of commodity-specific factors, a shift away from primary commodities may not dispose of the problem of terms of trade deterioration.

The second, and perhaps the most prominent, hypothesis is the 'fallacy of composition' involved in the widespread adoption of export-promotion policies by many developing countries (Cline, 1984; Faini et al., 1992; Wood, 1994). Put simply, this hypothesis stipulates that the entry of many countries into the market in labour-intensive manufactures will intensify competition, tending to drive down the world price of these products relative to capital- and skill-intensive products exported by developed countries. Both these hypotheses are not immune to counter arguments, however. For instance, the Singer hypothesis relates only to the terms of trade of manufactured exports from developing countries compared to that of developed countries, and not to the net terms of trade outcome of export diversification into manufactures in a given primary-producing country. The latter depends not only on relative prices of manufacturing trade but also on the price patterns of manufactured goods relative to that of traditional primary products (which gradually lose their relative importance as an outcome of the diversification process). The fallacy of composition argument ignores the fact that opportunity for changing the product mix is generally greater, both across countries at a given point in time and over time within a given country, in manufacturing compared to primary production, even within the confines of labour-intensive manufactures. Since different developing countries are characterized by different initial condition and policy postures, these countries embracing export-led industrialization would presumably mean different countries producing goods with different attributes at different points in time, even in the hypothetical case of many countries embarking on policy reforms in this direction at the same time (Ranis, 1985). Moreover, comparative advantage in international production is not static but evolving. As early starters in the manufactured-exports arena (the newly industrialized countries or NICs) gain maturity and wages in these countries increase, they will move up the production ladder leaving room for newcomers (Balassa, 1989). Given these characteristics on the production side, one can reasonably assume that terms of trade movements are at least partly endogenous to the export growth process, with export success generating terms of trade improvement over time.

Given these considerations, the terms of trade outcome of export diversification into manufactures away from primary commodities is very much an empirical issue. The available empirical studies on this issue have predominantly focused on the terms of trade for aggregate manufactured exports from developing countries (e.g., Sarkar and Singer, 1991; Athukorala, 1993; Rowthorn, 1997; Lucke, 1993; Minford et al., 1995).[5] The results of these studies are at best mixed, and meaningful generalization is not possible because of differences in terms of mythology, country coverage and data quality (Athukorala, 1998: Chapter 11).

Even if taken at face value, the results from aggregate analyses are of limited value for policy analysis in individual developing countries. As discussed, whatever overall trends there may have been between aggregate exports of developing and developed countries, individual countries may experience favourable or unfavourable trends in BTT, depending on their particular basket of export products and compositional shifts in the commodity mix (the 'ladder effect'). Moreover, even if manufactured exports from a given developing country experience price disadvantage vis-à-vis its manufactured imports, the overall BTT can still improve, provided price trends of the former are relatively more favourable compared to that of traditional primary products. Therefore, a more meaningful approach to the issue at hand is to undertake time-profile analysis of terms of trade behaviour of individual developing countries that have undergone significant changes in their export structures through diversification into manufactures. Interestingly, the few available time-series analyses of individual country experiences have generally come up with results which run counter to the new terms of trade pessimism (Mayer, 2003).

Finally, a common limitation of the existing literature (both on the old and new terms of trade debates) is the sole focus on BTT. This is, however, not an adequate measure of the balance of payments implications of export performance, particularly in relation to trade in manufactured goods, since it does not take into account changes in the volume of trade that may be associated with a given change in BTT. For instance, countries often deliberately attempt to depreciate their real exchange rate (and hence lower the BTT) in order to raise export earnings (Bleaney, 1993). Under such policy choice, the adverse effects of real exchange-rate depreciation (or BTT deterioration) on the level of real income may be offset by volume movements. Another reason why export prices may be falling (and the BTT deteriorating) but favourable volume movements compensating for the adverse effect, is an increase in productivity in the export sector, which releases resources for other purposes, including more exports (Thirlwall, 2003: 667) In these cases, it is the combined effect of relative price and volume movements which is of direct relevance in analysing growth implications of export diversification in the typical developing economy whose growth process is typically constrained by balance of payments.

The above considerations make a strong case for the use of ITT together with BTT in examining terms of trade implications of manufacturing export expansion from developing countries. The ITT brings together BTT and export volume (see note 1) to yield a useful indicator of change in import purchasing power of exports. If, as a result of a decrease in BTT, the volume of exports increases sharply, then the net effect in terms of total import purchasing power is desirable. The income terms of trade capture this beneficial effect.[6]

EVIDENCE

This section examines Sri Lanka's terms of trade experience in two stages. First, an overview of terms of trade behaviour during the period 1948–2000 is provided with an emphasis on changes during the post-reform years. Second, a disaggregated analysis of the terms of trade developments during the latter period is undertaken with a view to identifying the role of manufactured exports in determining the observed trends.

The empirical analysis is based on annual export price (unit value) and volume indices compiled by the Central Bank of Sri Lanka.[7] The Central Bank has revised its trade indices with effect from 1978 by adding separate indices for total manufactures and two sub-categories therein—textiles and garments, and other manufactures. This two-way disaggregation of manufactured exports is important for the purpose at hand because it permits us to allow for possible bias resulting from the possible price-raising impact of voluntary export restraints (VERs) imposed on clothing exports under the Multi Fibre Arrangement (MFA). In the presence of binding quantitative restrictions, exporters from even a small country like Sri Lanka will be able to influence the price of their exports. In constructing the BTT and ITT series used here, the price of petroleum has been purged from the import price index (the denominator). This adjustment is needed in order to separate market-detrained trends in the two terms of trade series from the impact of periodic adjustments of petroleum prices by OPEC from the early 1970s.

BTT and ITT series for total merchandise exports are shown in Figure 1.1. Estimated trend rates of the series for the total time period and the pre- and post-reform period (1948–77 and 1978–2002) are given in panel (A) of Table 1.2.

In the first half of the1950s, Sri Lanka experienced exceptionally favourable terms of trade movements thanks to the rubber price hike during the period of the Korean War (1950–51) and the subsequent world tea boom (1954–55). The ensuing two-and-a-half decades were however characterized by a precipitous fall in both BTT and ITT, with only a few hikes. Sri Lanka's two major exports, tea and rubber, were among the commodities which experienced sharpest falls in price in world markets during this period (MacBean and Nguyen, 1987). The adverse impact of the resultant deterioration in BTT on the Sri Lankan economy was compounded by supply problems faced by the export industries. Reflecting the combined effects of the anti-export bias inherent in the import-substitution policy regime, the fear of nationalization that pervaded the plantation sector from the late 1950s and the dismal performance of state-owned

Figure 1.1

Sri Lanka: Barter Terms of Trade (BTT) and Income Terms of
Trade (ITT), 1948–2000 (1990 = 100)

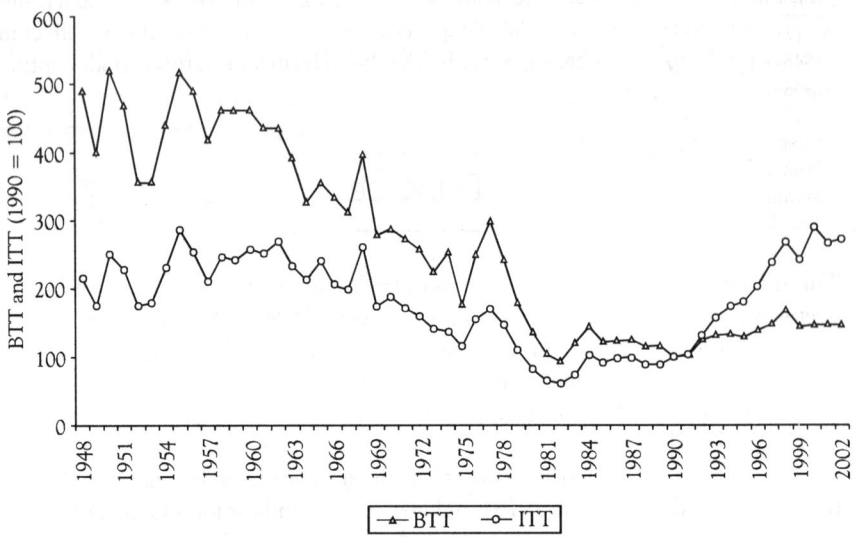

Source: Appendix Table A-1.

plantation companies following nationalization in the early 1970s, there was no significant volume growth to counterbalance adverse price trends (Athukorala and Jayasuriya,
1994: 51–55; Athukorala, 1998: Chapter 9). Consequently, BTT and ITT exhibited
remarkably similar trends.

A gradual stabilization and then an improvement in BTT is clearly observable
following the policy reforms initiated in 1977. BTT recorded an annual compound rate
of 1.8 per cent during 1978–2002, compared to 2.6 per cent deterioration during the
pre-reform period from 1948 to 1977.[8] In a clear departure from the historic patterns of
close co-movements in BTT and ITT, the latter has increased at a much faster rate
during the post-reform years. The compound growth rate of ITT during this period
(7.9 per cent) was almost three times that of the BTT (1.8). This comparison suggests
that market-oriented policy reforms can generate a superior ITT outcome by improving supply elasticity of exports.[9] From the point of view of development, measured by
per capita income, ITT is of course the more relevant concept to consider than BTT.

The disaggregated data for the post-reform period clearly point to the role played by
manufactured export expansion in determining the overall trends in BTT and ITT
noted above (Figures 1.2 and 1.3 and panel [B] in Table1.2). To comment first on the
results for BTT (panel [B] in Table 1.2), for total manufactures as well as the two
manufacturing sub-categories, the trend coefficient is statistically significant at a 5 per
cent level or better with the positive sign. Growth rates for textiles and clothing, and

Table 1.2

ANNUAL COMPOUND GROWTH RATES OF NET BARTER TERMS OF TRADE (BTT)
AND INCOME TERMS OF TRADE (ITT)[a] (%)

Export Category/Time Period	BTT	ITT
(A) Total exports[b]		
1948–2002	−2.82 (3.78)*	+1.48 (0.43)
1948–77	−2.60 (4.66)**	−1.69 (2.13)**
1978–2002	+1.77 (2.30)**	+7.90 (7.70)**
(B) Exports by commodity group: 1978–2002		
Primary products	−0.17 (0.13)	+1.61 (1.13)
Manufactured goods[c]	+4.08 (4.85)**	+12.22 (2.71)*
Textile and clothing	+3.82 (3.49)**	+12.42 (3.40)**
Other manufacturing[c]	+4.26 (3.49)**	+15.31 (10.39)**

Source: Estimates based on data reported in the Appendix.

Notes: [a] Growth rates have been estimated by fitting a log linear trend equation in error-correction formulation:

$$\Delta x_t = \alpha + \beta T - \theta x_{t-1} + \mu$$

where, x is the logarithmic value of the given data series (BTT or ITT), T time trend, t time subscript, and u_t a disturbance. The compound growth rate is given by $-(\beta/\theta)$, which is the long-run solution to the estimated equation. (For details on this formulation of the trend equation, and its desirability over the conventional [log linear] formulation in its application to terms of trade analysis, see Bleaney and Greenaway, 1993; Athukorala, 2000.) The t-ratios of growth coefficients are given in brackets, with the level of statistical significance (one-tailed t-test) is denoted as: ** = 5% and *** = 1%.

[b] The Chow test statistics for the structural shift in the growth trends in BTT and ITT during 1978–2000 compared to 1948–77 are, F (3,48): 7.19 and F (3,48): 7.23 respectively. Both are statistically significant at the 1-per cent level.

[c] Excluding petroleum products.

other manufactures, are 3.8 per cent and 4.6 per cent respectively, leading to a trend rate of 4.1 per cent for total manufactures. Despite a near zero growth in BTT for primary products, the favourable terms of trade implications of the expansion of manufactured exports were powerful enough to generate an annual average increment of 1.7 per cent in BTT for total exports. Clearly, the favourable terms of trade movement for total manufacturing is not simply a passing phenomenon brought about by special market conditions enjoyed by textile and clothing exports under the MFA. As already noted, BTT of 'other manufactures' has increased at a faster rate (4.3 per cent) compared to that of textiles and clothing (3.8 per cent).

The trend rate estimates for ITT basically reinforce the above inferences (Figure 1.3). For the period 1978–2002, the statistically significant (all at 1-per cent level) trend rates for ITT in textiles and clothing, and other manufactured goods and total manufactures are 12.4 per cent and 15.3 per cent respectively, which are much higher than their BTT counterparts. The upshot is that the positive relative price trends of these exports have been reinforced by much more powerful volume trends to yield an impressive increase in import purchasing power of export earnings of the country. Despite stagnation of ITT of agricultural exports, ITT of total exports increased at a compound

Figure 1.2

BARTER TERMS OF TRADE (BTT) FOR TOTAL, PRIMARY AND MANUFACTURED EXPORTS,
1978–2002 (1990 = 100)

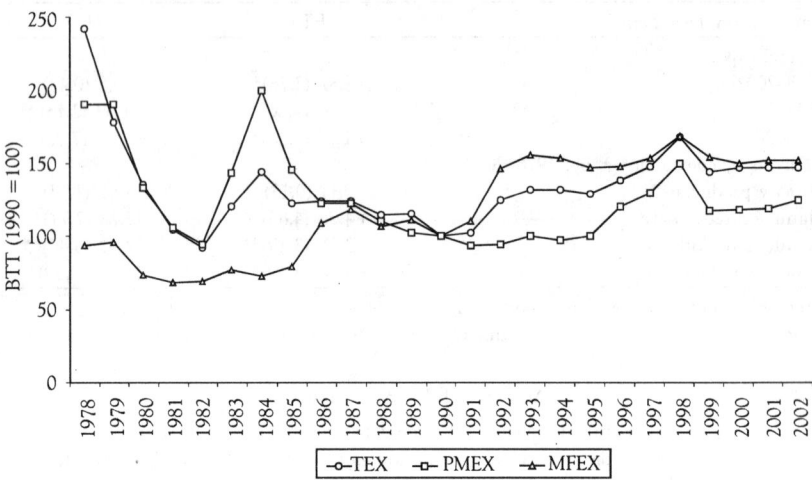

Source: Appendix Table A-2.
Legend: TEX: Total exports (excluding petroleum products).
PMEX: Primary exports.
MFEX: Manufactured exports (excluding petroleum products).

Figure 1.3

INCOME TERMS OF TRADE (ITT) FOR TOTAL, PRIMARY AND MANUFACTURED EXPORTS,
1978–2002 (1990 = 100)

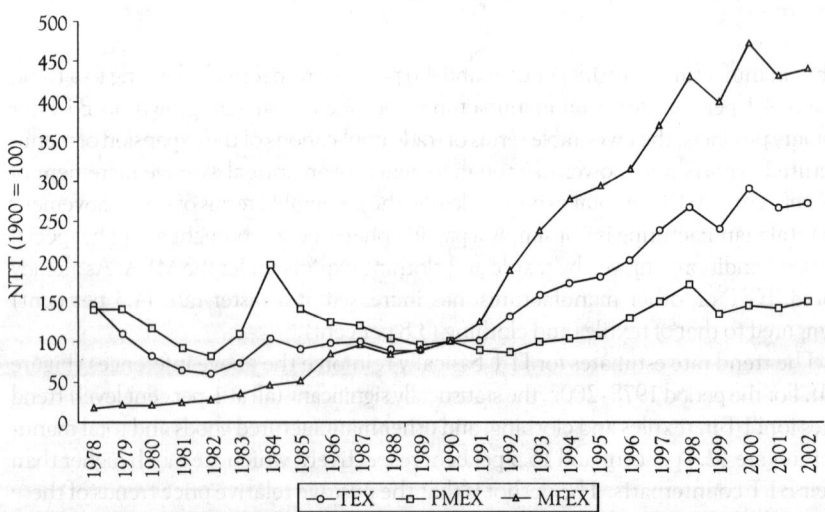

Source: Appendix Table A-3.
Legend: TEX: Total exports (excluding petroleum products).
PMEX: Primary exports.
MFEX: Manufactured Exports (excluding petroleum products).

rate of 7.9 per cent during this period, thanks to impressive gains in ITT of trade for manufactures.

CONCLUDING REMARKS

In his presidential address to the inaugural meeting of the Sri Lanka Economic Association in 1985, Gamani Corea revisited his popular subject, the role of the terms of trade behaviour in shaping the economic fortune of Sri Lanka, and made the following remarks:

> When I looked at some of the indicators to our economic performance there was one that struck me with particular force. That was the truly extraordinary deterioration we have seen in our terms of trade .... I was startled to see in the statistics presented by the Central Bank that the index of our terms of trade—the ratio of export to import prices—which registered a figure of 187 in the year of independence in 1948, today stands at 50! Even this reflected an improvement in the last two years because two years ago the index was 38! This is surely an extraordinary phenomenon particularly for a country so heavily reliant on foreign trade, so open to world economy, so dependent on the impulses generated from outside for its growth and development .... Had our terms of trade remained what they were at the time of independence the resources at our disposal would have been so much greater, the options open to us so much wider, that we would have been in a better position to speed up the transformation of the economy. (1986b: 4) [10]

I believe that Corea would be delighted to learn from this chapter that the mild upturn in BTT which he observed in the above remarks was in fact the beginning of a notable turnaround in the terms of trade during the ensuing years. The empirical evidence harnessed in this chapter clearly suggests that diversification into manufactures from structurally-weak conventional primary commodities under the market-oriented policy reforms intitiated in 1977 has enabled the country to escape from unequal exchange relations in world trade. In a clear departure from the historic primary commodity dependence, during the post-reform era, both the net barter terms of trade and income terms of trade (import purchasing power of export earnings) have significantly improved, thanks to the rapid growth in manufactured exports. The positive trends of the ITT are even stronger, which means that the positive relative price trends have been reinforced by positive volume trends. Thus, the Sri Lankan experience with manufactured export expansion clearly rebuts the new terms of trade pessimism about the gains from diversification into manufactured exports in a traditional primary-exporting country.

It is of course not possible to generalize from a single country case. However, the findings of this chapter do serve to cast doubt on the robustness of results coming from statistical analysis of price trends in aggregate manufactured exports from developing countries. Thus, further systematic empirical studies covering individual developing countries which have achieved a decisive diversification into manufactured exports from their historical primary commodity dependence are needed before valid general-izations on the issue at hand can be made. The results also bring home the point that the reliance on BTT as the sole focus of analysis is likely to miss an important part of the story relating to the terms of trade implications of manufactured exports expansion.

Notes

1. BTT = $[P_x/P_m] \times 100$ (the ratio of export to import price), and ITT = $[Q_x P_x]/ P_m$ = BTT $\times Q_x$ (import purchasing power of export earning), where P_x and P_m are price indices of exports and imports, and Q_x is an index of export volume (quantity).

2. At the time food accounted for over 20 per cent of the country's import bill. Most, though not all, of these food items were, from a technical point of view, capable of being produced locally (Corea, 1973).

3. Corea's great vision for taming commodity markets turned out to be 'a veritable saga' (Corea: 1992: viii). Under the IPC, only one new commodity agreement (for natural rubber) was negotiated and six other existing agreements were renegotiated, as against the original aim of having 16 agreements to cover over 90 per cent of total commodity trade of interest to developing countries. The CF was finally established in 1989 but it never became operational. By late 2000 all these had either lapsed or collapsed. For Corea's own reflections on the fate of IPC, see Corea (1992). Gilbert (1996) provides an insightful alternative view. According to Gilbert, the failure of the IPC was partly the result of a continuing disagreement with regard to what the international commodity agreements were meant to achieve, with producers more interested in the level than the variability of prices, and partly due to discontent about the division of the spoils when an agreement did manage to raise prices (1996: 2).

4. This section draws heavily on Athukorala, 2002.

5. For a comprehensive survey of this literature, see Mayer, 2003.

6. Another concept of terms of trade which is relevant for the issue at hand is the single factor terms of trade, SFTT = BTT $\times Z_x$, where, Z_x is an export productivity index. SFTT is important because it shows how much a unit of resources can buy. Thus, if BTT falls but the domestic economy becomes more productive in that it now uses less resources for each unit of export, then there is no reason to believe that the trading conditions have deteriorated for the domestic economy. The SFTT takes this into account. The productivity data required for the implementation of this measure are not available for Sri Lanka. Spraos (1983) provides a useful synthesis of various terms of trade indicators.

7. For Sri Lanka, as is the case with many developing countries, the only available trade price measures are the unit value indices. It is well known that a unit value index captures not only 'true' price movements but also quality improvement in composite commodities and compositional shift within a given commodity category for which the index is constructed. Consequently, it is not possible to provide any evidence about whether the 'fallacy of composition' effect might exist in its pure form (which would require a true price index adjusted for quality improvement). Using unit values it is, however, possible to examine (as done here) whether adverse price implications of the fallacy of composition is more than offset by the ladder effect. This is a useful result from a policy point of view.

8. It is not realistic to anticipate a repetition of the terms of trade experiences of the early 1950s, when a boom in world market price of a single commodity could change the entire export picture. The most favourable long term outcome of export diversification into manufactures would be one of BTT stability. In the medium term, some mild increase in BTT (as we have observed here) can be expected as a result of the gradual shift in export composition high value items (the ladder effect).

9. The structural shift in both BTT and ITT during the post-reform period over the pre-reform era is statistically significant in terms of the Chow test. See note b to Table 1.2.
10. The figures quoted here are BTT indices computed with 1978 as the base year.

REFERENCES

Athukorala, Prema-chandra (1993), 'Manufactured Exports from Developing Countries and Their Terms of Trade: A Re-examination of Sarkar-Singer Results', *World Development*, 21(10): 1607–13.

_____ **(1998),** *Trade Policy Issues in Asian Development*, London: Routledge.

Athukorala, Prema-chandra and Sisira Jayasuriya (1994), *Macroeconomic Policies, Crises, and Growth in Sri Lanka, 1969–90*, Washington D.C.: World Bank.

Athukorala, P. and S. Rajapatirana (2000), *Liberalisation and Industrial Transformation: Sri Lanka in International Perspective*, Oxford University Press: Oxford and New Delhi.

Balassa, Bela (1989), 'Outward Orientation', Chapter 31, in Holis Chenery and T.N. Srinivasan (eds), *Handbook of Development Economics*, Amsterdam: North-Holland, 1646–89.

Bleaney, Michael F. (1993), 'Manufactured Exports of Developing Countries and Their Terms of Trade Since 1965: A Comment', *World Development*, 21(11): 1615–16.

Bleaney, Michael F. and David Greenaway (1993), 'Long-run Trends in the Relative Price of Primary Commodities and in the Terms of Trade of Developing Countries', *Oxford Economic Papers*, 45(3): 349–63.

Cline, William R. (1984), *Exports of Manufactures from Developing Countries: Performance and Prospects for Market Access*, Washington D.C.: Brookings Institute.

Corea, Gamani (1952), *The Economic Structure of Ceylon in Relation to Fiscal Policy*, Doctoral Dissertation, Oxford University (published in 1972 as *The Instability of an Export Economy*, Colombo: Marga Institute).

_____ **(1965),** 'Ceylon', in Cranley Onslow (ed.), *Asian Economic Development*, London: Wieden feld and Nicholson, 29–65.

_____ **(1971a),** 'Aid and the Economy', *Marga Quarterly Journal*, 1(1): 19–54

_____ **(1971b),** 'Ceylon in this Sixties', *Marga Quarterly Journal*, 1(2): 1–30

_____ **(1973),** 'Economic Planning, the Green Revolution and the "Food Drive" in Ceylon', in Wilfred L. David (ed.), *Public Finance, Planning and Economic Development: Essays in Honour of Ursula Hicks*, London: Macmillan, 273–303.

_____ **(1980),** *Need for Change: Towards the New International Economic Order*, Oxford: Pergamon Press.

_____ **(1986a),** 'Adjustment and Growth', in *Structural Adjustment and Growth* (papers presented at the 1985 Annual Sessions), Sri Lanka Association of Economists (SLAE), Colombo: University of Colombo, Department of Economics, 11–18.

_____ **(1986b),** 'Inaugural Address', *Sri Lanka Economic Journal*, 1(1): 1–11.

_____ **(1992),** *Taming Commodity Markets: The Integrated Programme and the Common Fund in UNCTAD*, Manchester: Manchester University Press.

Faini, Ricardo, Fernado Clavijo and Abdel Senhandji-Semlali (1992), 'The Fallacy of Composition Argument: Does Demand Matter for LDC Manufactured Exports?', *European Economic Review*, 36(4): 865–82.

Gilbert, Christopher L. (1996), 'International Commodity Agreements: An Obituary Notice', *World Development*, 24(1): 1–19.

Lucke, Matthias (1993), 'Developing Countries' Terms of Trade in Manufactures, 1967–87: A Note', *Journal of Developing Studies*, 29(3): 588–95.

MacBean, Alasdair I. and D.T. Nguyen (1987), *Commodity Policies: Problems and Prospects*, London: Croom Helm.

Mayer, Jorg (2003), 'The Fallacy of Composition: A Review of the Literature', Discussion Paper No. 166, UNCTAD/OSG/DP/2003/1, United Nations Conference on Trade and Development (UNCTAD), Geneva.

Minford, Patrick, J. Riley and E. Nowell (1995), 'The Elixir of Growth: Trade, Non-Traded Goods and Development', Discussion Paper No. 1165, Centre for Economic Policy Research (CEPR), London.

Prebisch, Raul (1950), The Economic Development of Latin America and Its Principal Problems, New York: UN Commission for Latin America.

Ranis, Gustav (1985), 'Can East Asian Model of Development be Generalized? A Comment', World Development, 13(4): 543–45.

Rowthorn, Robert (1997), 'Replicating the Experience of the Newly Industrializing Economies', Centre for Business Studies Working Paper 57, Economic and Social Research Council, London.

Sarkar, Prabirjit and Hans W. Singer (1991), 'Manufactured Exports of Developing Countries and Their Terms of Trade Since 1965', World Development, 19(4): 333–40.

Singer, Hans W. (1950), 'The Distribution of Gains between Investing and Borrowing Countries', American Economic Review, 40(2): 473–85.

————— (1987), 'Terms of Trade', in John Eatwell, Murray Milgate and Peter Newman (eds), The New Palgrave: A Dictionary of Economics, London: Macmillan, 626–28.

Spraos, John (1983), Inequalising Trade? A Study of Traditional North/South Specialisation in the Context of Terms of Trade Concepts, Oxford: Clarendon Press.

Thirlwall, Anthony P. (2003), Growth and Development (8th Edition), London: Palgrave Macmillan.

Wood, Adrian (1994), North-South Trade, Employment and Inequality: Changing Fortunes in a Skill-Driven World, Oxford: Clarendon Press.

SELECT READINGS

Athukorala, Prema-chandra (2000), 'Manufactured Exports and Terms of Trade of Developing Countries: Evidence from Sri Lanka', Journal of Development Studies, 36(5): 89–104.

Corea, Gamani (1993), 'World and Asian Development Perspectives in the 1990s', in K. Dharmasena et al. (eds), Essays in Honour of A.D.V. de S. Indraratna, Kelaniya: Vidyalankara University Press, 35–53.

Singher, Hans W. (1991), 'Terms of Trade: New Wines and New Bottles?', Development Policy Review, 9(3): 339–51.

Appendix

Table 1.1A

INDICES OF EXPORT PRICE (UNIT VALUES), EXPORT VOLUME, NET BARTER
TERMS OF TRADE (BTT) AND COMMODITY T OF TRADE (ITT) (1990 = 100)

Year	Export Price (XP)	Import Price (MP)	Import Price Net of Petroleum (MP*)	Export Volume (XQ)	BTT ([XP/MP*] × 100)	ITT ([XP × XQ]/ MP*)
1948	3.9	0.8	0.8	43.8	489.3	214.3
1949	4.4	1.1	1.1	43.8	397.6	174.1
1950	5.7	1.1	1.1	48.1	519.9	250.1
1951	7.0	1.5	1.5	48.7	467.1	227.5
1952	5.3	1.5	1.5	49.3	355.9	175.5
1953	5.3	1.5	1.5	50.5	355.9	179.7
1954	5.7	1.3	1.3	52.4	440.4	230.8
1955	6.2	1.2	1.2	55.4	516.5	286.1
1956	5.9	1.2	1.2	51.8	489.3	253.5
1957	5.4	1.3	1.3	50.5	415.9	210.0
1958	5.5	1.2	1.2	53.6	462.1	247.7
1959	5.5	1.2	1.2	52.4	462.1	242.1
1960	5.5	1.2	1.2	56.0	462.1	258.8
1961	5.2	1.2	1.2	57.8	434.9	251.4
1962	5.2	1.2	1.2	62.1	434.9	270.1
1963	5.1	1.3	1.3	59.7	391.4	233.7
1964	5.2	1.6	1.6	65.2	326.2	212.7
1965	5.3	1.5	1.5	67.6	355.9	240.6
1966	5.0	1.5	1.5	61.5	333.6	205.2
1967	4.7	1.5	1.5	63.9	311.4	199.0
1968	7.5	1.9	1.9	65.8	397.1	261.3
1969	5.5	2.0	2.0	62.7	277.3	173.9
1970	5.7	2.2	2.0	65.2	288.0	187.8
1971	5.6	2.3	2.1	63.3	271.7	172.0
1972	5.5	2.4	2.2	62.1	257.1	159.7
1973	6.5	3.2	2.9	62.7	224.6	140.8
1974	10.3	5.7	4.1	54.2	252.5	136.9
1975	9.6	6.6	5.5	65.2	175.3	114.3
1976	11.2	5.9	4.5	62.1	248.9	154.6
1977	18.2	7.3	6.1	57.2	298.0	170.4
1978	33.0	13.5	13.7	60.9	241.7	147.2
1979	36.0	20.5	20.2	61.5	178.0	109.5
1980	41.6	29.3	30.7	60.3	135.5	81.7
1981	42.6	38.0	40.9	62.1	104.2	64.7
1982	41.7	39.5	45.1	65.2	92.5	60.3
1983	53.2	41.4	44.2	61.5	120.2	73.9
1984	68.1	43.3	47.2	72.0	144.4	103.9
1985	60.4	46.8	49.4	74.5	122.2	91.0
1986	53.6	43.3	43.4	79.5	123.6	98.3
1987	62.1	49.0	50.1	80.7	123.9	100.0
1988	76.2	67.0	66.5	77.4	114.6	88.7
1989	91.7	80.2	79.4	77.1	115.5	89.1
1990	100.0	100.0	100.0	100.0	100.0	100.0
1991	105.0	103.9	102.9	101.1	102.0	103.1
1992	131.8	108.8	105.4	105.1	125.0	131.4
1993	144.7	114.6	110.0	120.2	131.6	158.2
1994	151.7	121.0	114.8	131.5	132.1	173.7

(Contd. on next page)

Year	Export Price (XP)	Import Price (MP)	Import Price Net of Petroleum (MP*)	Export Volume (XQ)	BTT ([XP/MP*] × 100)	ITT ([XP × XQ]/ MP*)
1995	174.2	140.2	135.1	140.9	129.0	181.7
1996	194.9	153.2	140.9	146.4	138.4	202.6
1997	213.0	156.8	144.1	161.9	147.8	239.4
1998	244.7	158.8	145.6	159.5	168.1	268.1
1999	244.1	179.7	169.5	167.6	144.0	241.3
2000	266.7	196.3	181.7	198.2	146.8	290.9
2001	297.4	218.9	202.6	182.0	146.7	267.1
2002	304.8	224.4	207.4	185.8	147.0	273.0

Sources: XP and MP: Central Bank of Sri Lanka, *Annual Report* (various issues).

MP*: Derived by purging petroleum price from MP for the period after 1970. For this purpose, the Central Bank Petroleum price (unit value) index which starts in 1978 was extended back to 1970 using petroleum import unit values derived from import data from the United Nations Comtrade database. The latter is also the source of data on petroleum import share in total imports (in all years) used for purging the petroleum price index from MP.

Table 1.2A

BARTER TERMS OF TRADE (BTT) FOR TOTAL EXPORTS AND SUB-CATEGORIES

Year	Total Exports	Primary Products	Total Manufactures	Textiles and Clothing	Other Manufactures
1978	241.7	189.9	93.4	85.6	110.0
1979	178.0	190.1	95.5	88.1	111.4
1980	135.5	133.5	73.7	70.0	87.6
1981	104.2	105.6	68.2	66.3	75.3
1982	92.5	94.7	69.4	66.8	75.9
1983	120.2	143.5	77.0	74.8	84.8
1984	144.4	199.5	72.7	70.8	80.1
1985	122.2	145.9	79.3	76.9	87.2
1986	123.6	122.5	108.7	108.9	108.2
1987	123.9	122.7	117.9	115.3	125.7
1988	114.6	110.0	106.4	96.7	129.8
1989	115.5	102.7	111.1	100.4	133.6
1990	100.0	100.0	100.0	100.0	100.0
1991	102.0	93.5	110.4	110.8	109.6
1992	125.0	94.4	146.6	141.0	160.5
1993	131.6	100.0	155.6	148.3	172.4
1994	132.1	97.2	153.5	127.3	206.3
1995	129.0	100.4	147.0	123.5	193.0
1996	138.4	120.1	148.0	125.7	192.2
1997	147.8	130.0	153.8	140.9	179.4
1998	168.1	149.5	168.9	160.4	187.5
1999	144.0	117.4	154.5	138.4	190.0
2000	146.8	117.9	149.5	146.2	157.2
2001	146.7	118.7	151.7	148.5	158.7
2002	147.0	124.5	152.3	146.0	165.7

Source: Compiled from data obtained from the Central Bank of Sri Lanka, *Annual Report* (various issues).

Notes: 1. The import price index used in constructing all BTT series is the total import price index net of petroleum (Table A-1).

2. Based on average (value share weighted) of export unit value indices for agricultural products and minerals.

3. Based on average (value share weighted) of textiles and clothing, and other manufactures.

Table 1.3A

INCOME TERMS OF TRADE (ITT) FOR TOTAL EXPORTS AND SUB-CATEGORIES

Year	Total Exports	Primary Products	Total Manufactures	Textiles and Clothing	Other Manufactures
1978	147.2	99.8	12.5	10.2	17.2
1979	109.5	100.2	15.2	13.5	19.0
1980	81.7	107.9	18.7	19.5	15.5
1981	64.7	101.9	27.1	28.8	21.1
1982	60.3	95.8	32.4	31.9	33.4
1983	73.9	119.6	37.0	39.5	28.2
1984	103.9	214.8	50.7	54.6	36.1
1985	91.0	149.9	52.7	56.1	41.5
1986	98.3	113.5	76.2	80.2	66.0
1987	100.0	115.5	91.2	98.3	69.9
1988	88.7	102.8	80.8	83.8	73.5
1989	89.1	94.3	86.5	86.7	86.0
1990	100.0	100.0	100.0	100.0	100.0
1991	103.1	86.6	119.7	124.6	108.1
1992	131.4	82.6	177.4	188.9	148.5
1993	158.2	94.0	222.1	232.8	197.6
1994	173.7	95.0	240.5	243.8	233.8
1995	181.7	99.3	260.7	258.7	264.6
1996	202.6	116.1	270.3	264.0	282.7
1997	239.4	141.8	343.5	349.2	332.2
1998	268.1	156.5	385.5	407.5	337.2
1999	241.3	127.2	363.8	377.8	333.1
2000	290.9	136.9	442.3	467.3	383.6
2001	267.1	134.0	404.1	419.9	369.0
2002	273.0	140.9	412.1	418.5	398.3

Source: Compiled from data obtained from the Central Bank of Sri Lanka, *Annual Report* (various issues).

Notes: 1. The import price index used in constructing all ITT series is the total import price index net of petroleum (Table A-1).

2. Based on average (value share weighted) of export unit value and volume indices for agricultural products and minerals.

3. Based on average (value share weighted) unit value and volume indices for textiles and clothing, and other manufactures.

2

THE INFLUENCE OF DEVELOPMENT IDEOLOGY IN MACROECONOMIC POLICY REFORM PROCESS

Dushni Weerakoon

INTRODUCTION

At the time of independence in 1948, Sri Lanka had three primary developmental objectives driving its economic policy: the desire to achieve a reasonable rate of economic growth, greater equity, and greater self-reliance or national control over economic activities. In pursuing these objectives, post-independence governments were understandably influenced by, and adapted from, the dominant strands that were shaping development thinking in the post World War II era. De-colonization in the post World War II era was an important catalyst in focusing attention on emerging nations whose standards of living and institutions were very different from the advanced capitalist economies of Europe and North America. Political independence in low income countries in regions such as Asia, Africa and Latin America necessitated an understanding of the forces of development and the design of appropriate policies for 'economic development'.

Another important impetus was to be found with the post-war formation of the UN and its attendant agencies such as the World Bank and the International Monetary Fund. Development thinking in the 1950s and early 1960s was to be influenced by increasing pessimism about external conditions of development. Maximization of growth through industrialization based on import substitution was to dominate the discourse. During the late 1960s and early 1970s, maximization of growth began to encompass more directly the issues of poverty and inequality. The most pervasive change in development thinking, however, came in the 1970s and early 1980s with the resurgence of neo-classical economics and with it the focus of attention on markets, prices and incentives.

Sri Lanka's development policies and its macroeconomic policy management in turn has ebbed and flowed in response to such ideological policy shifts in economic thinking. Having inherited a fairly 'liberal' open economic policy regime from the British colonial powers, and a strong foreign exchange position, there was little impetus for a major policy change in the immediate post-independence period. A relatively peaceful transition of power also contributed to this sense of policy continuity. However, with the rise of nationalist political ideology and associated developments in the political economy front, there was a marked shift towards inward-looking dirigiste policies in the 1960s and 1970s. The emphasis on import substitution as a viable strategy of economic development was not seriously challenged until 1977 when Sri Lanka once again changed direction with the introduction of a package of economic reforms that was in line with outward-oriented growth strategy policies.

The analysis of the economic progress of Sri Lanka is multifaceted in light of the complex economic and political history of the country. The complexity in isolating economic policy developments is deepened by the fact that for much of its early post-independent history, the country was governed alternatively by two major political parties demonstrating some element of divergence with respect to their approach to development. The UNP has been typically associated with a right-of-centre political ideology and an adherence to a more laissez-faire approach to economic policy than that of the more left-of-centre socialist-oriented Sri Lanka Freedom Party (SLFP). Nevertheless, both parties engaged in state intervention in economic activity, the difference being largely in the intensity of intervention.[1] Economic policy, particularly in the early decades of independence, thus tended to follow swings in the political pendulum, burdening the country with a marked lack of consistency in policy planning. The shift to neo-liberal economic orthodoxy and economic policy convergence between the primary political parties from the 1980s onwards was expected to generate a degree of policy certainty in the development process. The experience, however, has been that the variety and volatility of policy prescriptions has not abated.

This chapter attempts to examine the extent to which prevailing ideology in development thinking influenced the policy response during two critical shocks to the Sri Lankan economy at distinct points in the country's economic evolution. In doing so, it will also examine the extent to which the ascendance of neo-liberal orthodoxy has generated policy convergence for developing countries engaged in the process of economic reforms. The chapter is organized as follows: section 2 will give a brief overview of the evolution of development theory, section 3 will examine the policy response to economic shocks in Sri Lanka, section 4 will assess the reality of policy consensus of the 1980s and 1990s, and section 5 will conclude.

EVOLUTION OF 'DEVELOPMENT' THEORY: A BRIEF OVERVIEW

In the immediate post-World War II years, the primary concern remained the reconstruction and industrialization of Europe. But with de-colonization, modern development theory began to emerge increasingly as a complementary strand geared not only to the analysis of growth, but also to the post-World War II institutions which could induce and accelerate growth. While economic development theorists such as Kuznets, Lewis and Myint attempted to analyse the issue of 'developing countries' as a distinct subject, early economic development theory was nevertheless a mere extension of conventional economic theory, equating 'development' with growth and industrialization. Newly independent countries in Asia, Latin America and Africa were therefore seen mostly as 'underdeveloped' and on the path of a linear historical progress towards development exemplified by the experience of more advanced economies.

Work by economists such as Chenery to define the concept of 'underdevelopment' led to a general acceptance that while countries did not necessarily follow linear stages in development, there was nonetheless evidence to suggest that they exhibited similar patterns of development. Underdeveloped countries therefore could yet leap over a few stages and 'catch up' with more advanced economies. Capital formation was identified as the crucial component to enable countries to accelerate the 'catching-up' process. Such reasoning was the outcome of early development theorists such as Nurske in equating development with output growth. While Lewis stressed the importance of savings in development, other early Keynesian economists such as Kaldor and Robinson took the issue further to stress the importance of income distribution as a critical determinant of savings and growth.

Development strategy in the 1950s and early 1960s increasingly turned to maximization of growth through capital accumulation and industrialization based on import substitution. The early emphasis on savings continued, but with the proviso that savings themselves could be manipulated by government intervention. The notion of turning the 'vicious circle' of low savings and low growth into a 'virtuous circle' of high savings and high growth by government intervention, put forward by theorists such as Singer and Myrdal, was to gain emphasis. Government involvement, whether through planning or effective demand management, was regarded as a vital for economic development.

Alongside these developments, the notion that 'underdevelopment' was merely a stage in the process towards greater industrialization came to be challenged. This school of thought evolved into the 'structuralist' thesis which drew attention to the distinct structural problems of underdeveloped countries such as specific rigidities, low elasticities of supply and demand, etc., which affect economic adjustments to policy. Given that industrialization in underdeveloped countries was to take place alongside already advanced industrialized countries, economists such as Singer and Prebisch argued that such a relationship in turn could give rise to a form of 'dependency'. According to this view, developing countries would be condemned into a 'centre–periphery' relationship, producing raw materials for advanced country manufacturers, and play a dependent role in the global economy. Some degree of protectionism in trade was recommended as a means of ensuring self-sustained development. Import substitution, enabled by protection and government policy, was regarded as an appropriate development strategy for industrialization and growth.

As these policies seemed to fail to yield their promised results, a neo-liberal counter-movement began to emerge and gain more adherents. The dominance of Keynesian demand management policies in developed countries was being challenged by economists such as Friedman, who argued that high rates of inflation cause unemployment to increase. This was to mark the pre-eminence of monetarism (advocating a rule of slow but steady growth in money supply).[2] Economists in the monetarist tradition turned their attention to 'supply side' constraints that reinforced a whole gamut of reforms aimed at privatization and deregulation. Increasing criticism of policy-induced distortions and failures associated with the implementation of public policies led to a critique of administrative controls by economists such as Little, Balassa and Krueger. Government intervention was regarded as hindering rather than improving development, where the emergence of administrative controls suffocated private investment and distorted prices making developing economies extremely inefficient. Export-led growth encompassing economies of scale, learning effects and competitive gains of X-efficiency were touted as the dynamic considerations in favour of outward-orientation.

The collapse of the Bretton Woods system of fixed exchange rates in 1971, the Latin American debt crisis of the 1980s and the increasing involvement of the IMF in stabilization efforts fashioned and encapsulated the shift to more market-oriented policies within a particular policy matrix. The key elements were to achieve balance of payments (BOP) viability in context of low inflation and improved growth performance. The set of measures typically included monetary restraint, interest rate policies, reduction in fiscal deficit, exchange rate action, policies to reduce external debt and introduction of structural reforms.

EXTERNAL SHOCKS AND POLICY RESPONSES

For newly independent developing countries engaged in the twin tasks of economic development and 'nation' building, grappling with shifting trends in development theory has proved to be an arduous task. For Sri Lanka, while its vulnerability to external conditions was manifest throughout its post-independence economic history, the policy response has varied in line with the dominant ideology of the time and prevailing political economy constraints.[3] Two clear examples of shocks to the Sri Lankan economy were visible in 1973 and 1979 when the country was following fundamentally different approaches on the macroeconomic front. The rest of the section will examine the extent to which the policy instruments employed to withstand the shocks were governed by the debates shaping development thinking.

Political independence for Sri Lanka brought to the forefront many issues and problems relating to the country's future economic development, not least of all the overwhelming dependence on a narrow range of primary export commodities.[4] Ever since the end of World War II there were indications of unfavourable structural changes in the demand for primary export commodities. A World Bank mission to Sri Lanka in 1951 in its report reinforced that view with the observation that 'the old momentum in the export sector is unlikely to be maintained' (World Bank, 1952: 2). The observation was made in the midst of a severe deterioration in external conditions for the economy.

The need to diversify Sri Lanka's export base, both for foreign and home markets, was stressed as a vital element to sustain development (Loganathan, 1952). But the government's response was muted, echoing the emerging trend towards planning as an instrument of economic policy to direct capital, rather than turn its attention to diversification of the export base.[5] Not surprisingly, attention was focused increasingly on capital accumulation as a key component to achieve Sri Lanka's developmental objectives as the influence of early development theorists permeated to the policy response of a newly independent economy. Thus, reflecting the optimism of dominant thinking with respect to what could be achieved by emphasizing investment in new physical capital, a draft Six Year Programme of Investment (Planning Secretariat, 1955) was developed for the country on the heels of the World Bank mission in 1951. Heavy emphasis was laid on investment in agriculture and infrastructure with a view to encouraging the private sector to take on a dominant role in economic development.

The government's apathy with regard to the core issue of export diversification can perhaps be explained by the fact that Sri Lanka had experienced a decade-long period of prosperity from 1942. A favourable BOP position and boom conditions on the heels of the Korean war boom of 1950–51 contributed to a sense of complacency. The strong external position prompted the removal of some restrictions on import and foreign exchange inherited from the colonial government during this period, but little effort was made in other areas, even in the face of a deteriorating fiscal position. Thus, economic policy appears not to have been directed at effecting structural changes to deal with the adverse repercussions the economy was likely to experience in terms of long-term growth prospects, but rather to continue with the inherited structure of production, dependent almost entirely on the performance of key primary export commodities. Thus, it has been variously argued that the government failed to make use of the opportunity offered during an initial period of prosperity to place the economy on a firmer foundation (Weerawardena and Wadinambiaratchi, 1954).

Despite a turnaround in external conditions as result of the tea boom that the country experienced during 1954–55, the government appeared incapable of coming to grips with the development needs of the country. Buffeted by a faltering economy—the combined impact of a sharp increase in the world price of rice in 1953 and falling tea and rubber prices in the world market from the mid-1950s—and a general loss of popularity, its investment programme was also largely ignored.[6] The early apathy with respect to lessening the country's vulnerability to volatility in external market conditions left the country open to greater influence emanating from the 'dependency' school of thought. Even in the early 1950s, there had been calls for a policy shift. For example, Sarkar (1951) commenting on the UNP budget argued that 'a country that is struggling hard to develop its own industries cannot but look with great concern at the policy of free imports of goods and export of capital' (ibid.: 53). These ideas took form in a Ten-Year Plan put forward in 1959 indicating a marked shift in industrial policy arguing the case for industrialization primarily based on import substitution. The development of industry and domestic agriculture within the framework of a protected market to meet domestic demand was the priority objective of the Plan. Although the Plan never became a fully operational document, it was to provide policy makers with a blueprint for policy guidelines up to the late 1960s.[7]

On the external front, a rapid depletion of external reserves prompted the abandonment of the relatively liberal import and foreign exchange policies and the introduction of a system of rigid import restrictions in 1961.[8] Nonetheless, the government's early ideological commitment towards industrialization based on import substitution has also been questioned. Athukorala and Jayasuriya (1994) argue that its policies were based on pragmatism and that 'import substitution rhetoric provided a radical façade that was politically useful' (ibid.: 12). The SLFP had organized itself as a 'centrist' political force, and sought to convey the image of itself as a party committed to policies that would bring about changes to the existing status quo and drew on the increasing emphasis on issues of equity in development theory to appeal to a growing nationalist political ideology (de Silva, 1987). Given the predominance of import substitution across the developing world during this period, it is hardly surprising that Sri Lanka was to adopt similar policies in pursuit of its developmental objectives. Not surprisingly, the UNP too had 'nationalized' its image in the intervening period, taking up many of the characteristic socio-economic positions of its main political opponent.[9]

An alternative option to the BOP crisis would have been drastic expenditure cuts, including cuts in consumer subsidies, an option fraught with political risk that the government was obviously not willing to contemplate. With little room to manoeuvre, the foreign exchange position was to be preserved by import controls, a policy that was also being advocated by the Central Bank. It was reasoned that the government had to hold a large volume of foreign reserves to stabilize economic conditions of an economy subject to volatility in export incomes (Rasaputram, 1960). Therefore, it was argued that 'in times of economic expansion (as well as in depression) it is necessary to forego some imports while at the same time encourage and develop import competing industries' (ibid.: 68). Thus, the underlying assumption appears to have been to stem a deteriorating external account through savings of foreign exchange rather than by earning it through diversification into manufactured export growth.

However, on the eve of a major supply shock to the economy in the form of a five-fold increase in international oil prices in 1973, two decades of a progressive policy stance to make the economy less vulnerable to external conditions failed to offer any protection.[10] On the face of it, the emphasis since the early 1960s on encouraging domestic production to reduce the heavy dependence of the economy on foreign trade should have lessened Sri Lanka's vulnerability to adverse movements in the terms of trade. A decline in the direct share of export agriculture in total domestic output and a concurrent increase in the share of output of domestic manufacturing and agriculture was visible from the early 1960s. In addition, it has been noted that the ratio of imports in final consumer expenditures fell from 32 per cent in 1958–60 to 17 per cent in 1970–73 (Athukorala and Jayasuriya, 1994). These trends, however, failed to lessen Sri Lanka's exposure to external shocks. The structural transformations masked a greater dependence on intermediate and investment goods imports as domestic

Table 2.1

Selected Macroeconomic Indicators: 1970–75

		1970	1971	1972	1973	1974	1975
GDP growth	%	4.3	0.2	3.2	3.7	3.2	2.8
Agriculture	%	3.8	−2.4	3.1	−0.8	5.8	−2.4
Manufacturing	%	5.6	3.7	1.8	−2.4	−4.5	4.6
Services		2.8	1.0	4.9	3.1	6.6	4.8
Investment	% of GDP	18.9	17.1	17.3	13.7	15.7	15.6
Savings	% of GDP	16.7	16	16.1	12.5	8.2	8.1
Exports	$ million	338.7	325.4	317.9	366.4	511.2	563.4
Imports	$ million	391.8	373.7	360.6	412.9	701.1	767.3
Export volume	1990 = 100	65.2	63.3	62.1	62.7	54.2	65.2
Import volume	1990 = 100	43.2	38.1	37.6	33.6	23.5	29.2
TOT	1990 = 100	259.9	244.7	231.1	203.9	180.6	144.8
Current A/C on BOP	% of GDP	−2.6	−1.5	−1.3	−0.9	−3.8	−2.9
Govt. expenditure	% of GDP	26.9	27.8	28.3	27.3	24.5	27.0
Govt. revenue	% of GDP	20.0	20.0	21.5	21.9	20.1	19.1
Fiscal balance	% of GDP	−6.9	−7.7	−6.8	−5.4	−4.4	−7.9
Rate of inflation	%	5.9	2.7	6.3	9.7	12.3	6.7
Interest rate[a]	%	6.5	6.5	6.5	6.5	6.5	6.5
Money supply (M2)	% change	9.3	10.3	15.7	4.5	10.0	4.6
Exchange rate	Rs/US$	5.96	5.96	6.70	6.75	6.69	7.71

Source: Central Bank of Sri Lanka, Annual Report, 2002.
Note: [a] Bank rate.

production activities expanded and made the country more dependent on external trade (in the face of a fall in the share of export earnings to GDP). In turn, the sharp decline in non-essential imports[11] left little room to compress total imports in the face of pressure on foreign exchange.

The impact of the crisis was exacerbated by domestic political conditions, coming as it did on the heels of a youth insurrection in 1971 that disrupted agricultural production (given the concentration of unrest in rural areas). The insurrection also conveyed an important message to the government and prompted a series of radical economic and social policy changes that were to reinforce state involvement in the economy. The inherent pessimism with regard to external conditions of development was strengthened in the minds of Sri Lanka's policy-makers. Even while the limitations of import substitution were being recognized in the early 1970s, the reasoning appeared to be that sufficient export expansion would take considerable time to provide a solution to the looming BOP crisis (Corea, 1971a, 1971b). Implementation of import controls was the preferred option in a scenario where external conditions were likely to worsen even more. The Finance Minister was to reiterate such concerns in view of what he termed the 'impending disaster that hangs over the world' in the budget speech of 1974.[12] The government's response was to strengthen ownership in trade and industry—a process that had already gained momentum— with the nationalization of the plantation sector in 1975 (Table 2.1). By 1976, agency houses, banking, insurance, most of the press, and much of wholesaling and retailing were to be under the control of state corporations and cooperatives.

Under pressure from rising inflation, the government's response was the adoption of orthodox fiscal austerity measures with little input from monetary policy. Total expenditure was slashed, but with a more significant role assigned to government in economic affairs, the pressure for fiscal transfers rose in the face of declining revenue for the government.[13] Monetary policy was not considered as a possible tool to restrain inflation with interest rates remaining unchanged. The exchange rate was also not considered as a tool for addressing external balance. In fact, it did not figure in policy discussions, a fact attributed to the overwhelming conviction that direct controls have a more immediate impact on the level of imports. An unwillingness to adjust exchange rates—a resulting scenario that Bhagwati (1987) has referred to as regimes of 'reluctant exchange-rate adjustments'—which implies continuing overvaluation is in itself a reinforcing factor for a strategy of import substitution.[14] The Sri Lankan rupee did depreciate as a result of cross exchange-rate effects between the US dollar and other major currencies in the aftermath of international currency volatility with the breakdown of the Bretton Woods system in 1971. Athukorala and Jayasuriya (1994) have argued that evidence of a high black market rate and need for stringent exchange controls suggest that the rupee was grossly overvalued throughout this period. Pervasive export pessimism only served to relegate any discussion on currency devaluation to the sidelines. And in the absence of recourse to foreign finance, import restrictions for import substitution reasons were reinforced by the need to achieve a current account equilibrium. Import controls were enforced more or less indiscriminately, disregarding the priorities of import substitution and affecting the availability of imported inputs and finished goods. The near 30 per cent compression in import volume in 1974 had a severe knock-on effect in dragging down manufacturing output.

As the economy faced a crisis on the external front in the early 1970s, there were emerging policy discussions to re-orient economic strategy towards more outward-looking policies, with the example of the high performing East Asian economies undoubtedly exerting its own influence towards an attitudinal shift. Attempts by the SLFP as early as 1973 to move towards reduction of import restrictions were thwarted by its more radical coalition partners. The UNP, on the other hand, adopted a policy of economic liberalization in 1973 as part of its political platform for re-election. Its return to power in 1977 saw the adoption of far-reaching reforms in almost all spheres of economic activity. These included many of the standard reforms of a structural adjustment programme, including dismantling currency controls and adopting a single exchange rate, eliminating price controls, lowering import tariffs, easing restrictions to foreign investment and deregulating the financial sector.[15]

Not only was the government assisted in pushing its reforms through by an overwhelming majority in Parliament, but the external conditions were surprisingly robust in the wake of a mini-boom in international tea prices during 1976–77. There was a sharp and immediate resurgence in growth, fuelled by a massive public investment programme that was in turn to induce significant macroeconomic instability by the early 1980s (Table 2.2). In the midst of a demand shock (induced by government policy), the country was also subject to a sharp deterioration in the terms of trade following the second oil price hike of 1979. Sri Lanka's policy response, unlike in the

Table 2.2

SELECTED MACROECONOMIC INDICATORS: 1977–82

		1977	1978	1979	1980	1981	1982
GDP growth	%	10.4	5.4	2.0	3.1	6.9	2.6
Agriculture	%	−0.6	7.8	4.6	0.8	5.2	4.8
Manufacturing	%	4.8	7.6	7.8	8.0	6.4	7.0
Services							
Investment	% of GDP	14.4	20.0	25.8	33.8	27.8	30.8
Savings	% of GDP	18.1	15.3	13.8	11.2	11.7	12.1
Exports	$ million	767.1	845.1	981.4	1064.7	1065.5	1013.7
Imports	$ million	726.2	1025.4	1449.4	2051.2	1876.9	1994.1
Export volume	1990 = 100	57.2	60.9	61.5	60.3	62.1	65.2
Import volume	1990 = 100	40.9	56.1	69.0	74.5	81.3	81.3
TOT	1990 = 100	249.2	244.7	175.4	142.1	111.9	105.5
Current A/C on BOP	% of GDP						
Govt. expenditure	% of GDP	24.2	41.5	36.6	42.7	33.0	33.8
Govt. revenue	% of GDP	18.4	27.4	22.8	19.6	17.4	16.3
Fiscal balance	% of GDP	−5.8	−14.1	−13.8	−23.1	−15.6	−17.4
Rate of inflation	%	1.2	12.1	10.8	26.1	18.0	10.8
Interest rate[a]	%	10.0	10.0	10.0	12.0	14.0	14.0
Money supply (M2)	% change	37.9	24.9	38.3	31.9	23.1	24.8
Exchange rate	Rs/US$	15.56	15.51	15.45	18.00	20.55	21.32

Source: Central Bank of Sri Lanka, *Annual Report*, 2002.
Note: [a] Bank rate.

earlier decades of pessimism of external conditions for development, remained highly optimistic. The deterioration in the current account was regarded largely as a typical 'J-curve' response—based on the assumption of an increased inflow of imports not matched equally by a rise in exports in the immediate aftermath of trade liberalization. Access to unprecedented levels of foreign capital—by way of aid, concessional loans and migrant-worker remittances—appear to have boosted the belief that re- source constraints were a thing of the past. Unlike the earlier crisis, such access also meant that there was little pressure on the government to curb its deteriorating exter- nal account by tighter controls on imports (with the volume of imports showing an upward growth unlike in the earlier crisis). The national economic debate had shifted focus from 'encouraging import competing industries' to adjustments in interest rates 'with a view to arresting the prevailing inflationary tendencies' (Central Bank, 1980: 298).

The means by which the government attempted to restore macroeconomic stability was by adopting orthodox fiscal and monetary measures. Tighter discipline was im- posed on government expenditure—a major component of which came from cuts in capital spending—with the public investment programme being confined to on-going projects. However, unlike in the earlier episode, fiscal efforts were complemented by a progressively tighter monetary policy stance to curtail rising inflation. Inflation was no longer considered to be a result of 'structural' conditions, and the idea that large public deficits and loose monetary policies fueled inflation was accepted. Interest rates were raised progressively from 1980 to stem the rapid growth of money supply. While the measures were effective in decelerating the growth in money supply quite sharply in the immediate short term, real money supply growth continued to go up. Heavy government borrowing persisted in exerting pressure on monetary growth. Direct measures in the form of a temporary credit ceiling on commercial banks were imposed by the Central Bank in 1981 with further interest rate hikes.

Exchange rate policy was also used as an explicit tool to address the burgeoning deficit on the current account and was deemed to 'help ease pressure on the BOP'(Central Bank, 1981: 9). Nonetheless, despite the significant nominal devaluation, it was insufficient in counteracting high domestic inflation. Most estimates of real exchange-rate behaviour suggest unequivocally that there was a sharp appreciation of the real exchange rate in the period 1980–84 (Lal, 1985; White and Wignaraja, 1992) with adverse implications for Sri Lanka's international export competitiveness. In effect, the country was subject to the 'Dutch Disease' associated with high capital inflows. Athukorala and Jayasuriya (1994) argue that contrary to the assertion put forward by Lal (1985) that the increase in the price level and real exchange-rate appreciation was consistent with the changes required to absorb the capital inflows, the magnitude of the terms of trade decline was not compensated by sufficient cuts in expenditure. Capital inflows were bolstered by higher commercial borrowing to meet the rising current account deficit during this period. Therefore, the government is argued to have adopted a policy to maintain the level of real expenditure,[16] the outcome of which was a continuous appreciation of the real exchange rate and a weaker performance by the export sector.

Thus, rhetoric on export-led growth was not matched equally by a strong policy response to give the export sector the highest priority. The government certainly strengthened the institutional structure to support export growth and diversification—such as the establishment of the Greater Colombo Economic Commission that was given the responsibility to set up free trade zones and attract FDI, and the establishment of the Export Development Board—but there was no concerted effort to push forward the trade liberalization programme initiated in 1977–78. Rather, there were policy slippages in response to pressure from the emerging instability in the domestic economy.[17] And despite emerging evidence from the experience of the high performing East Asian economies of the application of 'selective intervention' to promote rapid export growth and diversification, Sri Lanka appeared largely content to subscribe to the belief that price incentives generated from trade policies alone would be sufficient to achieve industrialization of the economy (Kelegama, 1992).

While Sri Lanka's experiment with market reforms remained limited and partial in nature in the 1980s (though extensive in comparison with the previous policy regime), there was an emerging policy consensus between the major political parties on economic policy for the first time since independence. Domestic policy convergence was a reflection of a more gradual shift that was taking shape across South Asia (and much of the developing world) that was to coalesce with the arrival of the 'Washington Consensus'. The broad policy measures of orthodox macroeconomics and structural adjustments appeared to offer prescriptions that would enable developing countries to withstand unanticipated shocks so long as 'correct' policies were followed. While Sri Lanka had made the first initial steps in re-orienting its macroeconomic policy management in this direction in the early 1980s—albeit not entirely successfully—it was to continue its programme of attempting to achieve strong macroeconomic 'fundamentals' and structural reforms in the following years.[18]

The pace of reforms undoubtedly slowed down as the country became embroiled in social and ethnic conflict from the mid-1980s. The staggered and slow pace of reforms—particularly in areas of trade policy and privatization—have had its critics (Lal and Rajapatirana, 1989; Athukorala and Rajapatirana, 2000) who argued that delayed implementation stunted the outcome of liberalization reforms. Others have argued that tensions between the stabilization and structural adjustment programmes—in timing, sequencing and problems of transition—played a key role in the hesitant implementation of the liberalization process in Sri Lanka (Dunham and Kelegama, 1997). Conflicting tensions in turn are argued to have imposed domestic social and political pressure on the reform agenda. The situation is not unique to Sri Lanka. It could well be argued that the impression of arriving at a clear convergence on policy that offered unambiguous prescriptions was misleading. In fact, the 1980s and 1990s have been marked by a high degree of volatility of policy prescriptions that left developing countries as exposed to the vagaries of the development debate as in the past.

THE WASHINGTON CONSENSUS: WHAT CONSENSUS?

The latter half of the 1980s and the 1990s saw the rapid integration of trade and financial markets with more countries in developing and transitional economies embracing market driven economic policies, propelled to some extent by the collapse of the Soviet Union and its experiment with central planning. The inexorable pull also exerted its influence on Sri Lanka's policy agenda. The 1980s were to mark the beginning of a gradual convergence in economic policy between the two major political forces in Sri Lanka, the UNP and SLFP, with a commitment to ideals of 'open market' policies. The reform agenda has progressed—albeit with fits and starts—uninterrupted for over two decades. The neo-liberal policy agenda reigns virtually unchallenged at the government and policy-making levels in the country. But while its central thesis has gained greater adherence globally, the evidence is still ambivalent and disputed.

The general ideas derived from the stabilization and structural adjustment programmes of the 1980s coalesced into a list of 10 policy recommendations coined under the term 'Washington Consensus'[19] in 1989, and had considerable influence in shaping the economic reform programmes of many developing and emerging transitional economies. It appeared to offer a clear agreement about the policy matrix that developing countries were to follow in order to ensure sustainable growth. Nevertheless, the original 10 policy prescriptions reigned unchallenged only for a short time.[20] Notwithstanding emerging evidence of direct state involvement in the industrial policy and export development of the East Asian 'miracle' economies (Amsden, 1989; Wade, 1990), there was also disagreement amongst economists who subscribed to the set of ideas embodied in the 'Consensus'. Fundamental divisions about the pace and sequence of reforms—the desirability of 'shock therapy' approach to policy reforms—have existed since the beginning beneath the façade of a 'Consensus'.

New realities also impinged to create problems that the 'Consensus' did not envisage. The early 1990s was a period of rapid financial integration with unprecedented volumes of private capital flowing to 'emerging' market economies in the developing world. However, Mexico was to suffer a financial crisis in 1994, a consequence of an overdependence on short term foreign capital in the absence of a low rate of domestic savings in the economy. Alternatively, the high performing East Asian economies were held up as exemplary illustrations of countries with enviable levels of domestic savings and foreign capital, and sound macroeconomic 'fundamentals'. Three years later, the lessons of the 1997–98 financial crises in East Asia served to highlight the complexities of macroeconomic management in the face of capital inflows. The crises brought to the forefront recommendations—about controls on foreign capital and 'appropriate' exchange rate regimes—that also ran counter to the 'Washington Consensus'.

Criticism of the orthodox macroeconomic policies of the 'Washington Consensus' was also to gather momentum in the wake of the financial crises and its handling by international financial institutions, particularly by the IMF. Stiglitz (2002) for example, has argued that the imposition of fiscal austerity measures in the midst of a downturn aggravated the crisis. While the long-term benefits of trade liberalization, privatization and a low inflationary environment were not being disputed, a key argument made was the need to phase in 'Washington Consensus' policies rather than impose them with strict and largely artificial deadlines. The need to establish a sound regulatory framework prior to a push for privatization or financial sector reforms, for example, began to be recognized as an irrefutable factor. Such concerns emerged from the new 'lessons' of the financial crises in East Asia pointing to distortions arising out of 'crony capitalism'. A poor regulatory environment and weak institutions were held partly responsible for the financial meltdown. For policy-makers in developing countries, the changes that were expected were becoming progressively more complex, and often, politically difficult to implement.

The call to eliminate distortions and inefficiency in markets provided the motivation for the 'first generation' of reforms. But increasingly, while stabilization and structural adjustment were considered to have had a measure of success in jump-starting economies, their inability to ensure sustainability of renewed growth and address core concerns of reducing the poverty gap—within and between nations—were being questioned. While poverty alleviation remained a core concern, the nuance was more on the increase in inequality and its consequences.[21] With the emphasis on reducing the disparity between the rich and poor countries, the search for new answers recognized the need for a broader set of reforms—referred to collectively as 'second generation' reforms—focused around the need to develop institutional capacity for reforms.

Questions on the structure of right institutions, improvement of the administrative, legal and regulatory functions of the state, and incentives and actions required for private sector development were key concerns. Nonetheless, international financial institutions such as the IMF and the World Bank have been at pains to argue that the 'first' and 'second' generation reforms were not sequential, but where earlier attention on monetary policy and growth and stability were seen as preconditions for attacking the question of poverty through a broader set of reforms aimed at sustainable and equitable growth.[22]

For the international financial institutions, the reform policies themselves had to be seen as something broader than the 'structural adjustment' policies of the past. In 1999, the IMF and the World Bank created a new lending programme called the Poverty Reduction and Growth Facility (PRGF), which replaced the existing Enhanced Structural Adjustment Facility (ESAF), as an answer to their critics. Its aim was broadly to explore alternative approaches to the reform programmes and to commit to poverty reduction as an explicit goal of lending and macroeconomic policies.

The mixed results achieved during the decades of neo-liberal policies have also been echoed in the debate on Sri Lanka's experience with the reform programme. While the economy did indicate an improved outcome in terms of GDP growth, most data suggest that poverty may not have changed much over the period (World Bank, 2002). In fact, perceptions of inequity in access to the benefits of market driven policies is argued to have been a contributory factor in heightening social and political tensions in Sri Lanka in the latter part of the 1980s (Dunham and Jayasuriya, 2001). In response, the government adopted a considerably more populist and expansionary policy stance in what has been termed the 'second wave' of liberalization that included an ambitious poverty alleviation programme (the Janasaviya programme). The government's efforts were supported by an IMF/World Bank Structural Adjustment Facility with renewed emphasis on macroeconomic stability and further structural reforms, but retaining the core elements of the poverty alleviation programme. Thus, Sri Lanka's experience appears broadly in line with emerging evidence that prescribed orthodox macroeconomic policies have limits in terms of how far they can take countries on the path toward equitable growth. Despite the mixed results achieved so far, Sri Lanka has signed on to the core issues of 'second generation reforms' as articulated in its poverty reduction strategy paper that includes an increased role for the private sector in education and health care, and substantive components of labour and land law reforms.[23] The structural reforms are complemented by orthodox medium term fiscal and monetary frameworks.

The core concern will be whether the emphasis on stronger and more effective institutions to complement macroeconomic policy changes is adequate to ensure sustained and equitable growth in the long run. Implementing 'second generation' reforms are likely to prove more difficult for governments. Strengthening the institutional capacity relevant for the establishment of effective regulation, rule of law or provision of health and education to the poor require complex administrative resources not readily available in developing countries. The impact of such reforms is less immediate and less visible, making them politically less attractive. Moreover, adjustment costs are more likely to be concentrated in specific groups that can, in turn, encourage focused resistance (Naim, 1999). A firm agenda to guide such reforms is also not clearly in evidence, leaving countries to improvise in transferring experience gained from limited case studies across countries.

CONCLUSION

It has been variously argued that Sri Lanka mismanaged its economic policies in the 1960s and 1970s by turning its back on the world trading system at a time of rapid and sustained growth in the global economy, particularly in international trade. By turning to market-oriented policies and promoting export-led growth, the country was expected to benefit from emerging convergence in policy advice and experience across the developing world. However, the reality was often far less clear-cut. As Sri Lanka began its experiment with liberalization in the 1980s, conflicting evidence on the role of selective intervention, pacing, timing and sequencing of reforms were to emerge alongside the established view of a 'Washington Consensus'.

The realization that sound macroeconomic fundamentals are not a goal in themselves but a precondition for sustained growth has been accompanied by a broader and noticeably more complex reform agenda. As developing countries such as Sri Lanka sign on to these 'second generation' reforms—alongside an as yet incomplete attempt at 'first generation' reforms—their capacity to tackle infinitely more complex issues is likely to stretch governments to hitherto unchallenged levels. The emphasis on 'minimum' government has yielded to 'strong' government, supported by sound regulatory and enforcement capabilities. It would almost appear that 'development theory' has come full circle to reinforce the early emphasis on the need for institutions which could induce and accelerate growth, the difference being perhaps the precondition requiring strong macroeconomic 'fundamentals'.

There is certainly a need for institutional reforms. However, countries that are embarking on such reforms will need to be pragmatic in their approach, balancing the pacing of reforms while ensuring social and political stability. The lesson of the 1990s has been that achieving sound macroeconomic 'fundamentals' are not an end in themselves, but rather a precondition to a broader reform programme to achieve sustained and equitable growth. How individual countries set about achieving those objectives will differ, and should differ, according to particular cultural and historical experiences. As amply demonstrated by Sri Lanka's experience of social and ethnic conflagrations, perceptions of rising inequality can act as a catalyst in engineering conflicts that ultimately undermine efforts at structural reforms. The current emphasis on 'institutions', 'transparency' and 'governance' is just as likely to yield to a new set of prescriptions. For developing countries such as Sri Lanka, the challenges of keeping abreast of changing international opinion on the 'development debate' are likely to mount in the current era of 'second generation reforms'.

NOTES

1. This has prompted some to suggest that both the UNP and the SLFP governments worked essentially within the framework of a 'mixed' capitalist system to achieve the twin objectives of economic growth and social equality, with the vital difference being the degree of priority each attached to the two elements (Lakshman, 1986).

2. Building on monetarism, economists such as Lucas argue that monetary and fiscal policy can only affect the 'real' portion of the economy when their use is unexpected. Anticipated government action is concluded to have no impact on the economy.

3. For a detailed discussion, see Lakshman (1997) and Kelegama (1998).

4. The undiversified nature of the economy may be gauged by the fact that in 1950 more than 50 per cent of its GDP was accounted for by the agricultural sector—tea, rubber and coconut production alone accounting for 37 per cent (Balakrishnan, 1977). Manufacturing output in contrast (excluding the processing of export crops), accounted for only 4 per cent of GDP in 1950 (Snodgrass, 1966).

5. A Six-Year Plan was enumerated by the Finance Minister as early as 1948, although it failed to materialize as a published document.

6. The decline in popularity of the government was exacerbated by a general perception of remoteness of the Colombo-based leadership on the part of its rural supporters (Jupp, 1977) and growing electoral disillusionment channelled into defeat for the government in 1956.

7. In support of a greater role for the state in economic activities a wide variety of economic enterprises, both foreign and local, were nationalized, including the import and distribution of petroleum products with the creation of the Ceylon Petroleum Corporation in 1961. Government control over the banking system was also strengthened. The People's Bank was established primarily as a means of providing commercial loans to the rural sector, while the largest commercial bank operating in the country, the Bank of Ceylon, was brought under government control. In addition, foreign banks were prohibited from opening new branches in the country.

8. As part of the policy aimed at stabilizing BOP, quantitative restrictions were imposed on imports, initially to cover only manufactured consumer goods, but later extended to intermediate and capital goods as well.

9. For instance its leadership began to preach a policy of 'democratic socialist objectives' from the late 1950s (Bandaranayaka, 1958; Jupp, 1977).

10. While a brief return to power of the UNP (1960–65) witnessed a partial attempt at import liberalization and reform of the exchange rate regime, the entrenched belief in import substitution was not seriously challenged.

11. Estimated to have declined from 20 per cent of total imports in the late 1950s to less than 5 per cent by the early 1970s (Athukorala and Jayasuriya, 1994).

12. Quoted in Athukorala and Jayasuriya (1994).

13. Sri Lanka's options in responding to the policy shock were to some extent curtailed by limited access to external financing. The government's policies and heavy state involvement in economic activity did not encourage the involvement of international financial institutions. Nonetheless, there was some increase in aid flows, including funds from the IMF.

14. Governments may use the exchange rate as a tool to keep down the price of imported industrial inputs through a deliberate policy of maintaining an overvalued real rate of exchange.

15. These policy reforms have been well documented. See Lal and Rajapatirana (1989), Cuthbertson and Athukorala (1991).

16. Expenditure levels were maintained until 1981 when some cuts were made, but such efforts were reversed once again in 1982.

17. For example, the government imposed a 10 per cent cess on all imports dutiable at over 50 per cent in 1980 while the Ministry of Finance introduced substantial selective duty increases on certain items already at high duty rates in 1982.

18. Although in the next two decades it made progress in terms of achieving a reasonable rate of GDP growth, macroeconomic stability was to remain elusive in view of fiscal pressures (resulting largely from high defence expenditures).
19. These were fiscal discipline, restructuring of public expenditure, tax reforms, financial liberalization, competitive exchange rate, trade liberalization, elimination of barriers to FDI, divestiture of public enterprises, deregulation and secure property rights (see Williamson, 1990).
20. It was also acknowledged in the early 1990s that not all 10 recommendations enjoyed the same degree of consensus. Consensus was deemed to have been achieved in five, with three (trade, financial liberalization and deregulation) still controversial, while the remaining two (restructuring budgets and FDI) were considered to be controversial (see Williamson, 1993).
21. Inequality in developing countries itself may tend to reduce growth when saving and investment become the preserve of a small rich elite.
22. See Camdessus (1999), Wolfensohn (1999).
23. See GOSL (2003).

REFERENCES

Amsden, A. (1989), *Asia's Next Giant: South Korea and Late Industrialization*, London: Oxford University Press.

Athukorala, P. and S. Jayasuriya (1994), *Macroeconomic Policies, Crises, and Growth in Sri Lanka, 1969–90*, Washington D.C.: World Bank.

Athukorala, P. and S. Rajapatirana (2000), *Liberalization and Industrial Transformation: Sri Lanka in International Perspective*, New Delhi: Oxford University Press.

Balakrishnan, N. (1977), 'Industrial Policy and Development Since Independence', in K.M. de Silva (ed.), *Sri Lanka: A Survey*, Colombo: C. Hurst and Co.

Bandaranayaka, M.N. (1958), 'Visionary Planning', *The Ceylon Economist*, 4(2).

Bhagwati, J. (1987), 'Outward-orientation: Trade Issues', in V. Corbo, M. Goldstein and M. Khan (eds), *Growth Oriented Adjustment Programmes*, IMF and World Bank, Washington D.C.

Camdessus, M. (1999), 'Second Generation Reforms: Reflections and New Challenges', Opening Remarks at a Conference on Second Generation Reforms, 8–9 November, IMF, Washington D.C.

Central Bank of Ceylon (1980), *Review of the Economy*.

———— (1981), *Annual Report*.

Corea, G. (1971a), 'Ceylon in the Sixties', *Marga Quarterly Journal*, 1(2).

———— (1971b), 'Aid and the Economy', *Marga Quarterly Journal*, 1(1).

Cuthbertson, S. and P. Athukorala (1991), 'Sri Lanka: Country Study', in M. Michaely, D. Papageorgiou and A.M. Choksi (eds), *Liberalizing Foreign Trade: Lessons of Experience from Developing Countries*, London: Basil Blackwell.

de Silva, K.M. (1987), 'Historical Background', in W. Rasaputram (ed.), *Facets of Development in Independent Sri Lanka*, Colombo: Ministry of Finance.

Dunham, D. and S. Jayasuriya (2001), 'Liberalization and Political Decay: Sri Lanka's Journey from Welfare State to a Brutalized Society', *Pravada*, 7(7).

Dunham, D. and S. Kelegama (1997), 'Does Leadership Matter in the Economic Reform Process?: Liberalization and Governance in Sri Lanka, 1989–93', *World Development*, 25(2).

GOSL (2003), *Regaining Sri Lanka: Vision and Strategy for Accelerated Development*, Colombo.

Jupp, J. (1977), *Sri Lanka: Third World Democracy*, Colombo: KVG De Silva and Sons.

Kelegama, S. (1992), *Liberalization and Industrialization: The Sri Lankan Experience of the 1980s*, Industrialization Series No. 2, Colombo: Institute of Policy Studies.

_____ (1998), 'Economic Development in Sri Lanka during the 50 Years of Independence: What Went Wrong?', Occasional Paper No. 53, Research and Information System for the Non-Aligned and Other Developing Countries, New Delhi.

Lakshman, W.D. (1986), 'State Policy in Sri Lanka and Its Economic Impact, 1970-85: Selected Themes with Special Reference to Distributive Implications of Policy', *Upanathi*, 1(1).

_____ (1997), 'Introduction', in W.D. Lakshman (ed.), *Dilemmas of Development: Fifty Years of Economic Change in Sri Lanka*, Colombo: Sri Lanka Association of Economists.

Lal, D. (1985), 'The Real Exchange Rate, Capital Inflows and Inflation in Sri Lanka, 1970-82', *Welfwirtschaftliches Archiv*, 121(4).

Lal, D. and S. Rajapatirana (1989), *Impediments to Trade Liberalization in Sri Lanka*, London: Trade Policy Research Centre.

Loganathan, C. (1952), 'Some Problems of the Ceylon Economy', *The Ceylon Economist*, 2(2).

Naim, M. (1999), 'Fads and Fashion in Economic Reforms: Washington Consensus or Washington Confusion?', working draft of a paper prepared for a Conference on Second Generation Reforms, 8-9 November, 1999, IMF, Washington D.C.

Planning Secretariat (1955), *Six Year Programme of Investment, 1954-59/60*, Colombo.

Rasaputram, W. (1960), 'Economic Expansion and Balance of Trade in Ceylon', *The Ceylon Economist*, 5(1).

Sarkar, N.K. (1951), 'The Budget Debate' *The Ceylon Economist*, 2(1).

Snodgrass, D. (1966), *Ceylon: An Export Economy in Transition*, Illinois: Homewood.

Stiglitz, J. (2002), *Globalization and Its Discontents*, London: Penguin.

Wade, R. (1990), *Governing the Market: Economic Theory and the Role of Government in East Asian Industrialization*, New Jersey: Princeton University Press.

Weerawardena, I.D.S. and G.H. Wadinambiaratchi (1954), 'Notes and Comments', *The Ceylon Economist*, 3(1).

White, H. and G. Wignaraja (1992), 'Exchange Rates, Trade Liberalization and Aid: The Sri Lankan Experience', *World Development*, 20(10).

Williamson, J. (1990), *Latin American Adjustment: How Much Has Happened?*, Washington D.C.: Institute for International Economics.

_____ (1993), 'Democracy and the Washington Consensus', *World Development*, 21(8).

Wolfensohn, J.D. (1999), Keynote Address at a Conference on Second Generation Reforms, 8-9 November, IMF, Washington D.C.

World Bank (1952), *The Economic Development of Ceylon*, Baltimore: John Hopkins University Press.

_____ (2002), 'Sri Lanka Poverty Assessment', Report No. 22535, Washington D.C.

3

THE LESSONS OF NATIONAL PLANNING

Godfrey Gunatilleke

There is nothing new in the world except the history you do not know
—Harry Truman

INTRODUCTION

Planning in its quintessential sense is present in almost all activities where human beings organize their effort to achieve a desired outcome in the future. In each of these activities there are certain elements which are fundamental to planning in general—a clearly identified goal, the time span within which it is to be attained, the assessment of resources required to achieve the desired outcome, the mobilization of resources selecting the best options from the various alternatives that are available and organizing the various activities within these parameters. As we move from the small to the large, the micro to the macro, the elements of planning vary in complexity and the degree of knowledge and skill, depending on the activity in question.[1]

The debate on national planning is normally related to the question as to whether there is much purpose in planning for a unit which we describe as the national economy. Some of the issues regarding the raison d'etre of national planning arise from the ideological assumptions underlying the debate. What is the *economic system* we have in mind—socialist or capitalist? What is the *type of planning* we have in mind—short term, long term, indicative, directive? In an attempt to remove ideological distortions we might proceed to distinguish between the 'market economy' and the 'planned economy'. At that point the debate begs the question. The very definitions suggest that a market economy is what it is because it is not planned. But then, do we not have to do a great deal of planning to ensure that the market operates freely, efficiently and, above all, equitably? Is not 'the level playing field' and equality of opportunity all about a particular type of planning?

The story of national planning in Sri Lanka takes us through many of the perplexities of this unresolved debate with its shifting definitions. At the very outset it has to be noted that national planning in Sri Lanka never acquired the institutional clarity and the continuity it has enjoyed in most other developing countries. The position of national planning within the system, the methodology and application of planning to the development problems of the country and the commitment that planning gained from the political rulers changed with almost every change of government. In striking contrast, the National Planning Commision of India which was established in 1950 became a permanent institution with a mandate to produce national five-year plans, which it continued to do regularly with only a few lags and delays that were caused by war and internal crises.

The Sri Lankan planning activity in a formal, structured sense began with a Cabinet Planning Committee and a small secretariat in the early 1950s which produced the 'Six-Year Programme of Investment' in 1955. After a change of government in 1956, the planning activity was organized under a National Planning Council. In 1960, the Council ceased to function and a National Department of Planning took over. With the next change of government in 1965, planning was elevated in status and came under a separate Ministry of Planning and Economic Affairs. In 1970 national planning retained its ministerial status, but the portfolio was divided and the function of progress control and monitoring of plan implementation was given to a new Ministry of Plan Implementation.

The economic reforms of 1978 mark another decisive turning point for planning in Sri Lanka. The type of national planning that had been hitherto attempted fell into disfavour with the new set of policy-makers. The National Department of Planning continued under the Ministry of Finance, but its activities were limited to the control of the government capital budget and the preparation of the six-year programme of public investment. Thereafter, there were further changes. There has been a noteworthy change of nomenclature. The term 'policy planning' was used and the term 'national planning' itself avoided, re-emphasizing the new orientation given to planning activity within the market economy. In the most recent reallocation, the word planning itself was dropped from the ministerial nomenclature and the Ministry which contained the National Department of Planning was named the Ministry of Policy Development and Implementation.

Most of these changes had to do with the political ideology of the party in power. The SLFP-led governments, which were socialist in their orientation and relied heavily on the expansion of the public sector, tended to give a central place to national planning and the production of a national plan. The UNP governments with their private-sector orientation were less enthusiastic about national planning of the SLFP type. Many of the critical issues relating to the impact of national planning in Sri Lanka need to be seen in this ideological context in which the fortunes of national planning fluctuated according to changes in government.

The narrative and analysis that follow do not attempt to examine or evaluate the methodologies and techniques of planning as they were used and developed in Sri Lanka. The scope and focus of this chapter are limited to issues which are best described as issues of political economy—the need for planning as perceived by governments and the political leadership, and the practice of planning by professional planners in response to these needs. The chapter focuses on the changing role of planning under successive governments and attempts to unravel the underlying causes that often led to disappointing outcomes. The discussion that follows is organized in three sections. The second section deals briefly with the ideology and concepts of planning as they evolved before independence and set the stage for national planning. The third section briefly examines how national planning focused and dealt with the critical development problems of Sri Lanka in different phases. It provides a brief narration of the main planning exercises in Sri Lanka, with special reference to the two phases of national planning under the leadership of Gamani Corea. The fourth section presents some reflections on the nature of planning in a market economy and the future of planning in Sri Lanka.

CONCEPTS AND IDEOLOGY OF PLANNING IN THE PRE-INDEPENDENCE ERA

The issues that have a bearing on national planning can be traced back to the political discourse in the years preceding independence. They are contained in the manifestos and agendas of the main political organizations that were active during this period, including the Ceylon National Congress (CNC), the Marxist parties and the Tamil parties.

While the Marxist approach to a planned economy had a strong influence on the politics of planning in Sri Lanka, what is of greater relevance is the approach of the political group which was in a majority and which was organized under the CNC. It is the leadership of this group which took over the reins of government when Sri Lanka became independent and remained the dominant force in Sri Lankan politics, whether it be under the UNP or the SLFP.

Some of the earliest references to national planning in an explicit sense occur in the statements produced by the CNC on the eve of Sri Lanka's independence. The first of these is entitled 'A Policy and Programme for the Ceylon National Congress' produced in 1935. The document contains the rudiments of the development programme that came to be implemented by the government that assumed office after independence. It gives high priority to health and education; it outlines a strategy of import substitution in agriculture; it proposes the establishment of a vigorous system of local government in which local communities will assume responsibility for health, education, sanitation, agriculture and irrigation, etc.

In the later documents , the Congress Policy Committee (CPC) begins to define in more elaborate terms its ideology of development. The first document produced in 1939 reflects the strong presence of two intellectual traditions—the Buddhist and the socialist. For the authors of the Congress document, the Buddhist value system was in consonance with a non-acquisitive, anti-capitalist social order. The two later documents of the CPC have several significant revisions and omissions. The strong socialist, anti-capitalist ideology of the first draft is altogether absent in the later two drafts. The pervasive tone of the document is pragmatic and its agenda points in the direction of social democracy.

In all the aforementioned documents that have been cited, there is no explicit reference to the process of national planning that is needed to formulate or implement the development programme. The notion that the development programme has to be implemented over a period of time and needs a coordinated national effort is implicit in the documents. The first document with its socialist orientation comes closest to the concept of planning. The later documents avoid any mention of planning, until we come to a document entitled 'A Congress Memorandum on the Problems Facing Ceylon'.[2] It begins with a brief analysis of the high vulnerability and instability of the Sri Lankan economy on account of its dependence on three export products whose terms of trade had sharply deteriorated. This was the first time that an economic analysis of this nature appeared in a Congress document. The food import-substitution strategy it proposed was presented as the means of reducing the instability of the external sector. The document recognized the need for national planning and outlined the measures that needed to be taken. The proposals both in regard to development strategy and institutional framework of planning anticipated some of the directions that were taken by the government after 1956.

The two documents that followed this memorandum which are given the title of 'Manifesto' are apparently the drafts that were used for the official version of the Congress Manifesto of 1947. While both omitted the explicit reference to planning found in the earlier document, they introduced a new conceptual frame which included some fundamental freedoms and a programme of action to achieve those freedoms. The concept of freedom in the two documents encompassed all its three dimensions—political, economic and social—and some of these concepts that were current found their way into the political discourse in Sri Lanka.[3] While the two documents dropped any explicit references to planning, there was an implicit recognition of the need for comprehensive or complete planning based on full information and scientific study, as well as planning in selected sectors such as agriculture.

The UNP was the virtual successor to the CNC, and a minority in the Congress was pushing for a strategy of a planned socialistic type in which the state was the principal actor, but in the bargaining for power within the party, this pro-planning socialistic minority lost out to the larger more moderate and conservative leaders. One can speculate that these would have included the leader who broke away and formed the SLFP a few years after independence. On the whole, it would appear that the leadership of the CNC was politically committed to some degree of planning for the future of the country they were going to govern.

From this ambiguity regarding planning that we find among the political leaders at the time of independence, it is clear that the issue of national planning itself would be subordinated to the more critical political issue of the choice of political and economic systems. On this count, the situation in Sri Lanka was very different from that of India at the time of independence. In India, the commitment to planning and a mixed economy with a socialist bias was unequivocal. Even so, there were some important elements in the discourse regarding development that took place in Sri Lanka on the eve of independence that provided an ideological framework and long-term direction. The leadership had identified the main goals and elements of the development strategy with a fair degree of clarity. These included:

- Import substitution in agriculture, with a focus on self-sufficiency in rice.
- Development of available human resources through expansion of health and education.
- Alleviation of poverty and satisfaction of the basic needs of the population— food, housing, water and sanitation.

The planning activity that was initiated and organized after independence has to be seen against this background. Independence meant different things to different political groups led by opposing schools of thought. The best expression that they were able to give to this vision was a mixed economy with a welfare state, influenced by Buddhist ideals and values. It was an approach that contained many contradictory elements which remained irreconcilable. The challenge was to develop the variant of national planning that was appropriate to the type of mixed economy-cum-welfare state that they envisioned in a manner which was adequate for the critical social, economic and political problems that lay ahead.

THE ALTERNATIONS OF NATIONAL PLANNING AFTER INDEPENDENCE

The Diagnosis of Development Problems

Any planning exercise has to begin with the diagnosis of the problems which it seeks to address. Some of the key problems that Sri Lanka had to address in any national planning exercise—problems that have persisted in varying forms up to the present day—could be broadly summarized as follows:

1. The first problem was that of managing an economy highly dependent on an external sector which was facing sharp short-term fluctuations together with the prospect of a long-term declining trend in the terms of trade. The strategies for major structural adjustments and the diversification of the economy could be regarded as among the highest priorities of a national planning process. What was the response of national planners to this problem?
2. The welfare system, the political imperatives pertaining to it, and the trade-offs between social goals and objectives of growth and productive investment have always been issues of overriding importance in designing and steering a development strategy. To what extent did these enter into the calculations of planners and how were they handled within planning, if at all?

3. In the conditions of uncertainty which beset the BOP and the government budget, the formulation and implementation of programmes of investment had to be closely linked to efficient macroeconomic management. How was investment planning linked to macroeconomic policy formulation?

4. How did the planning process deal with critical problems such as massive unemployment among educated youth or the urgent need for policy initiatives in the field of population control? Was it structured and oriented to anticipate, identify and respond to the major social and demographic transitions that were taking place?

5. The changes of government and the accompanying alternations of policy posed a serious problem to national planners. This problem was linked to the special character of the mixed economy and the ideological disposition of different governments to the relative roles of the public and private sectors. How were these dichotomies reconciled in planning, if at all ?

6. Finally, the youth insurrection and ethnic conflict bring into focus the critical importance of the political foundation of economic growth and development. They raise fundamental issues concerning the manner in which planning is related to the socio-political context in which it operates. How did national planning in Sri Lanka address them?

The foregoing summary has focused on the state of the three fundamentals of development at the time Sri Lanka became independent—the economy, social and human capital, and the political system. The story that unfolds after independence illustrates the tragic consequences that follow the failure to orchestrate all three critical components of development and ensure progress in all three that is simultaneous and mutually reinforcing. In the terms used by the Planning Commission of India, national planning must play 'an integrative role in the development of a holistic approach to the policy formulation in critical areas of human and economic development'. For a variety of reasons, national planning in Sri Lanka was unable to acquire the capacity to play that integrative role. The variables with which professional planners dealt were almost always economic in their focus.

Planning under the UNP: 1947–56

National planning in a formal sense and as a recognized function of government began in 1952 with the establishment of the Planning Secretariat under the Cabinet. But before it started its work, there were several documents that were produced which had some of the ingredients of a national plan. The first such attempt was the document published as the Six-Year Plan for the period 1947–53. The Six-Year Plan was no more than the combination of the two budget speeches of the then Minister of Finance J.R. Jayawardene for the years 1947–48 and 1948–49.[4] The budget speeches gave in broad outline the objectives of the government for the development of the country for the six-year period from 1947 to 1953. The speeches, although they were commendable as presentations of budgets, did not satisfy some of the basic requirements of a national plan.

Nevertheless, the Six-Year Plan identified several broad areas of action. First, there were the wet-zone cropes—tea, rubber and coconut. The wet zone is seen as 'fully exploited' and the resources available capable of generating their own momentum. Second, the programme placed emphasis on import substitution in both agriculture and industry. In agriculture, the programme included the development of the dry zone for food production, particularly self-sufficiency in rice. In industry, the Six-Year Plan underscored the need to develop the capacity 'to supply as far as possible the goods that are imported'. Import substitution was conceived as the panacea to all economic maladies.

Although the UNP was ideologically opposed to a dominant role for the state in the productive sectors of the economy, the Six-Year Plan envisaged a major role for the state in both agriculture and industry. The government defined its commitment to a mixed economy in which the state would undertake large public expenditures and play a significant role. A central feature of the Plan was the place given to state welfare in government outlays. Free mass education, food subsidies and free public-health services made up the most important components of the welfare package. Third, the development of economic infrastructure, power, transportation, and posts and communications were also given an important place in the government's capital outlay.

Thus, the Six-Year Plan contained most of the development components of a national plan although each part was not analysed in depth and integrated into an internally consistent whole as in a national plan that is professionally designed. There was, however, an attempt to bring the development programme and the public expenditures of the budget within a broad national accounting framework. For such an exercise, the statistical base that was relied upon appears to have been wholly inadequate. The macroeconomic aggregates that were consequently derived for the purpose of the budget turned out to be grossly inaccurate.[5] The Plan does not give any firm estimate of the rate of economic growth that was expected, but talks of a higher standard of health and comfort and an increasing measure of social security and employment. On the whole the rate of growth would have been barely sufficient to keep pace with population growth.

The diagnosis of the problems of Sri Lanka's economy which were implicit in the Six-Year Plan were not unmindful of such problems. What was at fault was the failure to assess the full gravity and fast growing intensity of these problems. There is hardly any mention of the rapid growth of population and how it was transforming the development scene. The economic forecast on which the Six-Year Plan was based was highly optimistic—a weakness which we find in almost all planning exercises up to 1978. The instability of world markets which were an endemic problem for small open economies such as Sri Lanka were never internalized as a persistent and severe constraint in the planning process.

At the start of planning, we find this feature in the first exercise itself.[6] The availability of domestic and external resources and a relatively favourable BOP was taken for granted in the Six-Year Plan. In his general comments in introducing the budget, the Minister of Finance expressed a general concern about rising public expenditure on social welfare but did not perceive the real dimensions of the dangers ahead. Any minor disequilibria were to be settled through borrowings from the IMF. Finally, the proportions of public-sector and private-sector investment were estimated and set in such a way as to give the state the principal role in investment. Private investment was expected to make its contribution without any special encouragement and promotion from the state. There was no clearly defined, systematic drive to stimulate and direct private enterprise to new investment fields.

This first exercise in 'planning' also foreshadowed some of the problems regarding the status of the professional planning activity that was to plague the planning process throughout. What is important to note is that at this initial stage as the government set about planning, the activity was generated in the Ministry of Finance and integrated with the budgetary exercise. This approach had far-reaching effects on national planning and the changing roles it assumed over the years. One set of effects was positive; planning in such an approach would be linked firmly with the exercise of managing available resources and implementing the programmes and policies required. The Six-Year Plan satisfied these criteria. It was kept within a short-term horizon which was clearly perceived. The negative outcome of such an approach lay in the mindset it generated. It made policy-makers and administrators approach planning as a simple extension of budgeting and administration.[7] Such an approach implied that planning did not need to be established as a separate activity for which new expertize and specialized skills had to be mobilized and applied. Planning could be managed by politicians and skilled administrators. Throughout its brief history, this mindset played an important part in the destiny of national planning in Sri Lanka.

Finally, this first plan had a political dimension significantly different from the exercises that followed. The Six-Year Plan was a political exercise in that it communicated a strong political commitment to the plan goals and gave a vision of the future Sri Lanka. This political dimension of the planning exercise had both opportunities and dangers. In its positive form, the political dimension encouraged the political and social thought that should underpin the planning process and develop the human involvement that made it more than a merely technical process. On the negative side, these also fed some of the emotions that fueled the ethnic conflict that resulted in a two-decade long war between the Tamil separatists and the Sri Lankan Armed Forces. Jayawardene imbued his statements with Buddhist values which 'stressed the development of the mind rather than the mere acquisition of worldly riches'. In this vision, economic growth was tempered by spiritual values, expressed more clearly in the International Bank for Reconstruction and Development (IBRD) report that was produced a few years later. When modern specialties and professional disciplines were each going in their own direction with methods and analytical tools which were value neutral and positivistic, it is impossible to imagine what planners who were new to their task in the early 1950s could have made of these many diverse elements in Jayawardene's Six-Year Plan, or how they could have helped to give planning its integrative role in the cultural matrix in which it had to operate.[8]

The document which explicitly dealt with Sri Lanka's economic and social development and deserves fuller treatment is the report produced by the IBRD mission which visited Sri Lanka in 1951. It pointed out that the problem was not one of correcting maladjustments that had already become severe, but 'forestalling a clearly seen threat of such maladjustments in the future', thereby sharply focusing on the main challenge of planning—that of shaping and giving direction to the future. The mission gave a comprehensive analysis of the economy, its current problems and future prospects. Drawing on the latest statistical information available, it provided a more reliable framework of national accounting than the Six-Year Plan. It assessed the domestic and external resources that would be available and proceeded to formulate a comprehensive development programme. On the whole, the IBRD mission endorsed the policies that were being pursued and the development programme that was being implemented. They urged the government to continue the sound fiscal macroeconomic policies that they had pursued, but in doing so strongly recommended the phased removal of the food subsidy within two to three years with appropriate adjustments in wage rates and government salaries, and the tax burden of export industries. This last recommendation was the only recommendation of a strategic nature affecting the government budget and the economy.

On the role of the private sector, the mission recommended policies to 'encourage further investment of private capital, both Ceylonese and non-Ceylonese', and more specifically it proposed the establishment of a development financing institution in the form of the Ceylon Development Corporation. The Corporation was to be created with the joint participation of government, commercial banks and the investing public. The mission had givien overriding importance to financial stability. It was not in favour of expansionary financing of development as they considered it 'especially hazardous for Ceylon because of its dependence on foreign trade'. It was very cautious about the planned utilization of the accumulated reserves for investment and development. Within these constraints the mission came up with a development strategy that yielded growth rates which were quite low.

The mission visited Sri Lanka in 1951, during the term of office of the first government formed after independence, when the political party in power was the UNP. The mission report had the effect of reassuring the government that it was on the right course. This may have led the government to a state of complacency over the problems that were gathering momentum. This was unfortunate as the evaluation made by the mission should have provided the opportunity for a searching reappraisal of the development challenges facing Sri Lanka.

Rapid population growth and the social advancements that were being made were to create needs in the medium and long term which required a significantly faster rate of economic growth and structural change if they were to be satisfied. The trends in the international market were soon to render the assumptions regarding external resources unrealistic. By the mid-1950s, the entry of new political parties and the growing divisions and tensions between the Sinhala and Tamil communities would be undermining the foundations of political stability that were essential for development. Sri Lanka was, however, entering the decade of the 1950s without a sober appreciation of the emerging realities and the magnitude of the challenges that she was facing. The policies that were proposed assumed a continuation of the socio-economic status quo with hardly any significant growth of per capita income. The staid perspective of fiscal prudence with low per capita income growth altogether missed the demographic socio-economic and political scenario that was fast emerging.

Meanwhile, new political forces were emerging which saw the short-term problems of Sri Lankan society as not the economic problems but rather cultural and ethnic imbalances. Correcting these imbalances was seen as a precondition of social and economic change. The mounting resentment against the small English-educated privileged minority and English as the language of administration, the position of the Sinhala Buddhist majority, the rehabilitation of Sinhala Buddhist culture as the dominant shaping force and a reactive Tamil regionalism were issues which pushed themselves to the forefront. It was in this setting that the Planning Secretariat was established and the work of professional planners began.

The Planning Secretariat that was established in 1952 was based on the recommendations of the IBRD mission—although it did not recommend a planning secretariat as such—for the formation of an Economic Committee of the Cabinet composed of the ministers in charge of the main development portfolios and the minister of Finance. This Committee was to be serviced by a small secretariat of senior professionals. The substantive work of preparing projects and programmes was to be initiated by the ministries concerned. These were to be received and evaluated by the Secretariat and submitted to the Committee for decision-making. This Secretariat was later expanded. It was formally headed by a senior civil servant, but the substantive head for the professional work was Gamani Corea himself who was seconded for service from the Central Bank.

The task of planning was conceptualized primarily as one of coordination at the highest decision-making level. This concept did not provide for a large professional body. Planning in the view of the IBRD dealt with the activities that were already initiated at the sectoral level; it had to be closely integrated with decision-making at the Cabinet level. Finally, the substance of planning consisted of the preparatory professional work that had to be done to ensure that there was effective coordination and informed decision-making at the national level.

The Six-Year Programme of Investment was a compilation of the projects under-taken and proposed by the government to be implemented in a phased manner over the next six years. It did not contemplate any significant changes of policy or new directions for investment. It analysed the rationale of existing policies and programmes and explained the nature of the problems and constraints faced in financing the budget. The detail and thoroughness with which the Six-Year Programme was pre-pared imposed new discipline on the preparation of the capital budget. Although the work on the Six-Year Programme provided no scope for the more substantive tasks of planning, the first and last chapter are analytical essays which introduce the reader to some basic concepts of economic development and planning. The first chapter contains an outline of the economic problem elucidated in clear and simple terms that are intelligible to the administrator and politician alike. It is a virtue that the author, Gamani Corea, demonstrated at all times in his professional writing. The problem is set in terms of population, the minimum rate of growth of the economy to keep pace with population growth, and the investment and output needed. The last chapter deals with more complex issues relating to the process of development and is more technical in content, covering a wide range of topics such as terms of trade, the determinants of output, capital formation, techniques of production, etc. The discussion is largely at the level of general principles and its purpose is to provide the theoretical background to economic planning.

Interestingly enough, the author underscores the limits within which he works; drawing attention to the term 'economic development' he says, 'the process of development however is complex and involves far-reaching changes in the entire pattern of life and work'. This insight however has not been pursued in the work of national planning that followed. There was no effort to elicit this complexity and adapt and develop the methodologies of planning to address and manage the human complexity of the development process. The author provides some clues when he proposes a methodology of planning that approaches its task from the consumption and distribution end. In such a model one captures the improvements in the standard of living of households at different levels of income and 'the far-reaching changes' at a fuller and more comprehensive level. Unfortunately, there was no effort to develop this model further.

The New Ten-Year Phase in Planning: 1956–65

A new left-oriented government was voted to power in the Sri Lankan general elections of 1956. The political front which opposed the UNP and defeated it consisted of a coalition of parties led by the SLFP. The SLFP could be regarded as a party of the centre, with economic policies favouring a mixed economy in which the state assumed a dominant role. The new government included smaller parties which were Marxist in their approach and wanted the country to move more decisively in the direction of a socialist system. This coalition was, however, short-lived. Policy differences aggravated by personality conflicts led to the withdrawal of the Marxist group from the government in 1958.

The period immediately following the change in government marked a major change of direction in national planning in Sri Lanka. The government made it clear that it was firmly committed to the formulation of a comprehensive national plan which was to be the main instrument for directing the development of the country. A National Planning Council (NPC) was established by an Act of Parliament, with the Prime Minister as Chairman, the Minister of Finance as Deputy Chairman, and eminent professionals drawn from various fields, both in the public as well as private sectors, as additional members. Its role was exclusively advisory. It was serviced by a Planning Secretariat manned by economists and other professionals which included those who were responsible for the preparation of the Six-Year Programme of Investment. The head of the Planning Secretariat under the UNP government, Gamani Corea, continued as such under the SLFP.

The NPC was conceived essentially as an agency for the formulation of a national plan. Preparation of the plan took three years. According to the mandate given to the Council it was required to undertake its work as a scientific, professional body, examining the problems of the economy in depth and planning for structural changes in the economy in a manner which would be of lasting value to whichever government was in power. Planning was thus defined primarily as an intellectual and technical task. The objective was to give a continuity to the planning process and enable it to deal with the essential problems in a manner which would provide an indispensable technical resource for all governments. This, which was its main strength, also contributed to its weakness.

The Ten-Year Plan has to be recognized as the high watermark of national planning in Sri Lanka. Given the state of the economy, the Ten-Year Plan fulfilled all the technical and professional requirements of a sound economic-development plan. The Plan was acclaimed internationally for its high professional quality. It was in many ways a pioneering exercise for small developing economies and was recognized as such. The path-breaking part of the Ten-Year Plan was its diagnosis of the development problem and its effort to move planning beyond the concepts of stabilization and slow growth that characterized the approach of the Six-Year Plan and the IBRD report. Through a detailed analysis of demographic trends and the existing system of production, it convincingly demonstrated that the future potential of agriculture in creating new employment was fast reaching its limit and that a strategy of industrialization was inescapable. In designing its strategy, the Ten-Year Plan identified the need to create new employment as the critical starting point. In doing so, it was focusing on the problem which was to have the most far-reaching social and political consequences.

In this manner, the Ten-Year Plan helped to change Sri Lanka's perception of the development problem and to recognize the crucial importance of achieving a high rate of economic growth with a rapidly increasing role for industrialization. The Plan envisaged an increase in the rate of investment from 12.9 per cent of GDP in 1957 to 21.1 per cent in 1968. The national income over the period was expected to increase at an annual average of 5.9 per cent, and per capita income to increase at 2.9 per cent. The Plan projected significant changes in the sectoral composition of GDP, with the manufacturing industry increasing its share from 7.6 per cent, in 1957 to 13.7 per cent in 1968 (according to the data available to the planning agency). The sectoral programmes that were to contribute to this increase in output were prepared in elaborate detail and phased over the 10-year period. The domestic and external resources for the implementation of the Plan were carefully estimated, and the projections of government finance and BOP were shown to be consistent with the Plan requirements. On the basis of these calculations, the Ten-Year Plan appeared to be an implementable plan.

There was, of course, no opportunity to test the implementability of the Ten-Year Plan. Soon after its publication, the Prime Minister S.W.R.D. Bandaranaike was assassinated, and with his demise the Ten-Year Plan lost its most powerful political protagonist. Immediately thereafter, the country was embroiled in the politics of succession. Parliament was dissolved in 1960, and after a brief tenure in power by the UNP, the SLFP returned to power in July 1960. The NPC was replaced with a National Planning Department under the Prime Minister. The Finance Minister, Felix Dias Bandaranaike, who was the Prime Minister's chief advisor and played a key role in directing the affairs of the government and virtually took over the function of planning, had little sympathy for the Ten-Year Plan. This led to a change of personnel. Although there was no explicit disavowal of the Ten-Year Plan, it was not formally adopted by the SLFP government that assumed office in 1960 and it ceased to play the active role of a national plan in resource allocation and decision-making.

Regardless of the political fate that overtook it, the Ten-Year Plan became a major resource for planners, policy-makers and administrators. By focusing on growth, it altered the main parameters of the future discourse on planning. Almost all the sectoral plans, with the exception of the section on social services, were prepared with great thoroughness, and many of these sectoral plans such as the fisheries plan have stood the test of time. The intensive preparatory work of the Ten-Year Plan left a wealth of information and data for future use, and both administrators and policy-makers continued to refer to the Ten-Year Plan in developing sectoral programmes and policies. For all these reasons, the Ten-Year Plan contributed significantly to the improvement of planning, policy-making and administration.

The Ten-Year Plan provides a good vantage point to reflect on some of the deeper causes that underlay the problems that beset national planning in Sri Lanka. No one would dispute that the main reason for the failure to implement the Ten-Year Plan was a combination of political events that left the Plan without the necessary political leadership and support. The opportunity to demonstrate the feasibility of the Plan was aborted. But when this has been said, we still need to answer the question whether the Plan would not have had sufficient intrinsic strength and worth to resist uninformed efforts to discard it? As we may find in the best of plans, there were shortcomings and weaknesses in the Ten-Year Plan. But these weaknesses had little to do with the fate of the Plan after the assassination of its chief political protagonist. The Plan was not 'put away' after a serious evaluation of its shortcomings. The Plan could not retain its central position more on account of other issues, and among them the 'ownership' of the Plan and the process of plan formulation which determined the ownership of the Plan were the overriding issue. This issue was integral to the whole structure of planning, to the way in which the specialty and professionalism of planning was related to the politics of planning. Here we go back to the point made about the political dimension of the Six-Year Plan.

The NPC we saw, was not vested with any executive responsibilities and its work was cast in an advisory role. This advisory character of planning however need not have rendered planning ineffective. The 'separation of functions' in which planning was expected to play the overall role of reflection, forecasting and envisioning the future could have been quite effective had there been mechanisms that enabled the NPC to function as a summit advisory body on economic and development decision-making. The system could have been so designed as to give the NPC a stature which could have made such an advisory role quite powerful and influential. Such a link between planning and economic management was not established, and the NPC itself was far removed from the processes of decision-making. This may explain, to some extent, why the Plan document conveys the impression of being remote from the far-reaching socio-political and economic changes which were taking place during the period of its preparation. Its avowed disregard of the institutional forms within which development takes place gave this professionalism' an apolitical tone. On hindsight, one could be critical of this 'remoteness of approach'. It neglected the complexity of the development process which was acknowledged in the last chapter of the Six-Year Programme of Investment.

For these reasons, despite Bandaranaike's own commitment, the product of such a process was unlikely to generate the wide political involvement that was needed, as had been possible in the case of Jayawardene's Six-Year Plan. The preface to the Ten-Year Plan refers to the 'manner of presentation' and the need for popular summaries and a nationwide discussion on the Plan. These were certainly innovative ideas and in certain circumstances could have given the Plan a broad popular base. But a process of national discussion by itself was not enough. To be credible and productive, part of the process at least should have taken place before the completion of the Plan. More importantly, the contents of the Plan should have had a visionary outreach to the future, a social and human content that could capture the imagination of the youth and win the involvement of people. The Ten-Year Plan is very much a document on 'economic development'.[10] The other strategic weaknesses of the Ten-Year Plan are found in some of the basic assumptions it makes regarding the availability of resources, both financial and human. The Plan blandly states that its implementation assumes that 'the terms of trade will remain stable as at 1957', and that the financial and monetary policy of the government 'would be geared to the implementation of the Plan'.[11]

Immediately after the completion of the Plan, the developments in the economy belied some of the basic premises on which the Plan had been formulated. There was a grave deterioration in the balance of payments; the budgetary situation had rapidly worsened and deficits were becoming intractable. The flows of both external and domestic resources were falling far below Plan expectations, making a critical part of the macroeconomic framework of the Plan wholly inapplicable in the emerging situation. It is surprising that the planners failed to recognize the emerging trend of a long-term decline in the terms of trade. It was similarly short-sighted in regard to the growing fiscal imbalances. In the diagnosis of Sri Lanka's development problem, the vulnerability of Sri Lanka's external sector and the need for diversifying it was not adequately addressed. Neither did the Plan recognize the dangers inherent in the rising public expenditure, especially the food subsidy. The preparatory work neglected these issues, and as a result the predictive capacity of the Plan on some vital aspects of the economy were undeniably weak.[12] This could be regarded as a fatal flaw in the Ten-Year Plan.

The authors of the Ten-Year Plan took the political conditions as given. They assumed that the Plan would be implemented successfully in a mixed economy in which the public sector would play the dominant role. The industrialization it envisaged was a public-sector-driven industrialization. The Plan was being prepared for a government with a mixture of ideologies, but with a dominant socialist orientation. Unlike the Indian planning process the Ten-Year Plan did not have a policy framework that clearly defined the spheres of enterprise for the public and private sectors. Finally, the Plan's strategy for the diversification of the economy and structural change concentrated solely on import substitution in agriculture and industry. This was a strategy that all governments were willing to accept. It resulted in creating sectors in both agriculture and industry which were highly protected, costly and inefficient.

At this point we need to recognize that it is easy enough to make some of these criticisms with hindsight. The analysis of world economic trends or of domestic economic policy were still not at a stage as to provide conclusive guidelines. Any critique of the Ten-Year Plan must keep in focus the state-of-the-art planning at the time it was produced. The Ten-Year Plan was drafted at a time when the socialist economy and socialist planning was well regarded by many economists, both in Sri Lanka and abroad. There was also no established certainties about the comparative efficiency of public-sector and private-sector enterprise. It would be fair by the Ten-Year Plan to say that the Sri Lankan planners could not have anticipated that the Sri Lankan experience of public enterprise and the variant of socialism it practised would be as disappointing as it proved to be. Even with regard to the terms of trade and import substitution, the international signals were not as clear as they were to become a few years later.

When the SLFP returned to power in 1960 after a brief interlude, the change in the country's economic prospects demanded a reappraisal of some of the basic assumptions of the Ten-Year Plan. To meet these needs, the government prepared the Three-Year Implementation Programme 1962–64. But curiously enough, this was not placed firmly within the framework of the Ten-Year Plan as had been the intention of the NPC.

The time span of the Programme does not qualify it to be in the category of a national plan. But it is a valuable document on its own right as its focuses clearly on the implementation of a plan, the supportive policies needed and the choice of investments on the basis of cost effectiveness and productivity. It presented a programme which emphasized investments with quick-yielding returns and reallocated resources away from projects with longer periods of gestation, such as major irrigation projects.[13] It set more modest targets for the Programme, reducing the growth targets of 5.2 per cent per year to 4.8 per cent. Yet even for this Programme, the forecasts of budgetary and external resources that were required left significant un-financed gaps.

During this period, the country's efforts to cope with its BOP crisis led to an elaborate system of exchange controls resulting in the rationing of foreign exchange. This activity became crucial for any meaningful development planning. The Ministry of Finance set up machinery to manage the allocation of foreign exchange for both the public and private sectors. An important feature of the Three-Year Programme was the preparation of a portfolio of projects for which external assistance was being obtained. The Three-Year Programme, therefore, focused on a component of economic management and planning which was to become critical in the years to come and act as the key determinant of economic growth—namely, the external sector of the economy and the availability of external resources for development.

The Three-Year Programme suffered an initial political setback when the Finance Minister, who was the principal sponsor of the Plan, resigned when his budgetary proposals for the reduction of the food subsidy were not accepted by the Cabinet. The programme however, remained an important frame of reference for resource allocation. Individual government investments were brought under closer scrutiny during this period.

Macroeconomic Management and Sectoral Planning: 1965–70

In 1965, the UNP was voted back to power. National planning underwent major changes and adaptations both in organizational form and content. Gamani Corea, who headed the planning organization during the period 1952–60, was brought back as the professional head of a newly created Ministry which took over the portfolio for national planning. The Prime Minister became the Minister of Planning and Economic Affairs. This change in structure was a response to the changing character of the economy and to the new and complex problems that had emerged in the first half of the 1960s. It had also demonstrated the type of macroeconomic coordination that was needed at the national level.

At the very outset, the planners had defined for themselves a set of tasks and responsibilities in which the formal exercise of preparing a national plan in the manner of the Ten-Year Plan was virtually excluded. Gamani Corea expressly indicated his intention not to devote the time of the Ministry to writing a plan document in the style of the Ten-Year Plan. The Ministry approached its new responsibilities on two levels: it set up four planning committees at the sectoral level to examine and evaluate ongoing public-sector programmes and future proposals in relation to short-term and long-term needs, and to prepare phased programmes of public-sector investment for the period 1966–70. At the macroeconomic level, it drew up a strategy for 'economic recovery' which aimed at mobilizing and augmenting external resources, restoring supplies, improving the depreciated capital stock in key sectors such as transportation to get the economy working at capacity, and increasing the efficiency of public sector investment. The Secretariat returned to the project and programme-based planning of the 1948–56 period. The main elements of planning during this period comprised the mobilization of foreign aid, the management of the foreign exchange budget and the preparation and supervision of the government capital budget in terms of sectoral programmes.

To perform these tasks, the Ministry of Planning and Economic Affairs took control of a few key decision-making levers. The concerns of foreign aid and foreign exchange budgeting were transferred from the Ministry of Finance to the Ministry of Planning and Economic Affairs. All important proposals of sectoral Ministries had to receive the comments of the Planning Ministry before they could be considered by the Cabinet. The government capital budget, both at the stage of formulation and negotiation of budgetary allocations as well as implementation, came under close supervision of the Planning Ministry. This Ministry was thus actively involved in obtaining as well as allocating the key resources of the economy on a continuing basis. It consequently acquired considerable decision-making power and authority over execution.

In this process, however, the short-term tasks of economic management and resource allocation took precedence over long-term planning. During this period, the Planning Ministry had a division concerned with perspective planning. It attempted to prepare an input–output matrix for the economy and develop a planning model, but this remained at the experimental level and never became an instrument for short-term forecasting or medium-term planning and decision-making.[14] While this division and its work had little influence on the central concerns of the Ministry, the collection and organization of sectoral data was carried out in close collaboration with other ministries and helped improve the quality of data.

In the 1965–70 period, the planning process acquired several new elements which were to influence and define its future role in the total structure of national decision-making. Organizationally, the planning apparatus was brought to the centre of economic decision-making, and the conventional planning functions, such as programming of investment, were linked firmly to economic management. This was reflected in the designation of the Ministry itself—Planning and Economic Affairs. It also introduced new disciplines of project evaluation for improving the efficiency and productivity of the public-sector investment programme and established systems of progress control for monitoring plan implementation. Some of its sectoral programmes were quite successful, particularly the programme in domestic agriculture. The 1965–70 government established a Cabinet Planning Committee which became the apex institution for discussion and decision-making in economic matters.

The period also witnessed the entry of major new determinants of economic policy. The government began to rely heavily on external aid and foreign borrowings. A large proportion of the government capital budget came to be financed with flows of foreign aid and foreign loans.[15] There was a sharp increase in foreign indebtedness. The major part of the gap was financed by short-term and long-term borrowing from abroad. This meant a set of adjustments to external factors very different from what was required in the period prior to 1960. The adjustments to short-term fluctuations in external transactions became an overriding demand. The implementation of medium-term plans in a relatively stable environment which was at all times doubtful was now a wholly unrealistic prospect. The presence of international institutions and the disciplines and policies promoted by them, which included non-inflationary budgets and realistic exchange rates, became increasingly important. The missions from international financing institutions began to provide regular inputs into the policy frameworks and short-term strategies in Sri Lanka.

The 1965–70 period also emphasized the differences in the economic policies between the UNP and the SLFP. The strategy of the UNP was directed towards creating conditions for a better functioning of the market mechanism. The response of the economy to this approach was fairly positive. The improvement in supplies and the flow of external resources initially resulted in a spurt of economic growth. But after achieving a high of 8 per cent in 1968, the growth rate fell to 5.1 per cent in 1969 and then 4 per cent in 1970. The planning process was caught in the dilemma of applying deflationary policies to meet short-term problems on the one hand, and sustaining an adequate rate of economic growth in the long term on the other. Certain measures that the government introduced such as the dual exchange rate and reducing the free food ration reflected this dilemma and the government's hesitant polices. At the end of the period, the government was formulating a strategy which would have imposed greater austerity on the economy if the government had been returned to power. It was, however, defeated in the general elections.

The planning process during this period was also grappling with another set of problems which were peculiar to the nature of the type of mixed economy that had grown. A large part of the economy, in both services and production, was managed by state enterprises. This constituted an administered part of the economy. Policies which were intended to make greater room for the operation of market forces were in conflict with the expansion of public-sector enterprises. The mixed economy and the coexistence of two systems of economic enterprise—the state and the private sector—each requiring a different set of incentives and policies, posed a host of complex problems for planners and economic managers which were not fully understood nor clearly conceptualized for the purpose of policy-making. A lack of a firm commitment to a mixed economy in which both the public and private sectors had well defined roles hampered the process of long-term investment and tended to demoralize both sectors. Some of these problems became more pronounced as Sri Lanka moved into the 1970s.

If the Ten-Year Plan was the high point of professional excellence in formal planning, the period 1965–70 was the phase in which national planning was most effectively linked to highest levels of decision-making on the economy and development. But with the exception of the annual exercises of the government capital budget and the foreign exchange budget, the Ministry prepared no plans as such, even of a short-term nature. Under the new dispensation, planning was moving into giving strategic policy direction for increasing investment, higher growth and expansion of output in the short, medium and long term. If this policy-making had been supported and supplemented by a more formal exercise in national planning, the direction and outcome of policies would have been more transparent and the vision of the future clearer. The planning-cum-policy-making that was being done would have had greater political and popular acceptance. It is difficult to speculate how planning would have developed if the UNP had returned to power.

The Alternations in Planning in the 1970s

With the change of the government in 1970 when Mrs Bandaranaike and the SLFP-led coalition, the United Front, came into power, national planning once again underwent the expected changes in the personnel as well in the type of planning. Planning retained its ministerial status and came under the Prime Minister. It continued to exercise its control over the government capital budget, the foreign exchange budget and the mobilization of foreign aid. In addition, the Ministry undertook the preparation of a Five-Year Plan. The Five-Year Plan was initially driven by a strong sense of national urgency. Unemployment had risen to nearly 15 per cent. Youth discontent had erupted in a violent insurrection. The crisis affecting the BOP was deepening. The Five-Year Plan therefore needed to give a central place to employment creation and export diversification. For the first time export diversification became a major objective of the planners, and an export promotion plan was included as a major component. The Five-Year Plan was thus in many ways more problem-oriented than previous plans. As it was directly related to major aspects of the prevailing crisis, the Plan could have become a useful instrument of decision-making. However, this did not happen.

In many respects the fate of the Five-Year Plan resembled that of the Ten-Year Plan. The unsettled conditions in the world economy in the first half of the 1970s, the world food shortage, the devaluation of the dollar and the steep rise in energy prices rendered the macroeconomic framework totally irrelevant almost immediately after the publication of the Plan. The sectoral programmes such as the export-development programme were, however, pursued within the limits of the resources available. The outcome of the development effort during this period was far short of Plan expectations. The impact on employment was negative. Unemployment continued to rise, and reached about 24 per cent by the mid-1970s. Growth rates, targeted for an annual average of 6.1 per cent, only reached an average of 2.5 per cent.

There were many reasons why the Five-Year Plan did not become an effective instrument for policy-making. Some are to be found in the inadequacies of the Plan itself. It lacked a well-defined policy component for macroeconomic management in the changing global economic environment. The political environment was also not favourable. The Plan offered little to satisfy political objectives. The Plan's commitment to a mixed economy did not have the full consensus of the coalition. Furthermore, with the youth insurrection in 1971, when the extreme left, the JVP attempted to overthrow the government which had failed to satisfy them, the social and political crisis became the centre of attention for the government. In this regard, the medium-term strategy of the Plan did not draw the involvement of policy-makers as had been expected.

In 1977, the political pendulum once again swung to the right, and the UNP returned to power. Soon after it assumed office, the government began rearranging the planning organization to bring it in line with its plans for liberalizing the economy. As a result of these policy changes, the planning process too had to undergo considerable adaptation. The planning function as it had developed after 1965, either as a cluster of functions and controls at the apex of government giving direction to the economy or as the process of plan preparation for the medium and long term, virtually ceased to exist.

The Scenario after Liberalization

The UNP governments had demonstrated an approach to planning which had generally avoided the centralized planning exercises of the socialist governments. This approach reflected policies which placed greater reliance on the market and private enterprise and which applied the planning process selectively to public-sector programmes and to specific sectors. These features in the planning approach became more pronounced in the post-1977 period. The tendency in the government was to decentralize decision-making to enable ministries and agencies to assume greater responsibility. The intervention of a planning agency in policy-making and investment tended to get diminished in the process. Agencies set up for specific programmes, such as the Mahaweli Development Authority and the Greater Colombo Economic Commission, as well as the sectoral ministries themselves, acted with greater autonomy and obtained their mandates directly from the Cabinet. A Committee of Secretaries from the development ministries and a Committee of Cabinet Ministers became the coordinating organs within the government for evaluation and approval of development programmes and policies.

Within this set-up, the role of the planning apparatus was considerably reduced. Planning became part of the Ministry of Finance. While this helped to make planning a service to the ongoing decision-making of the government and act in close association with the government budget and financial management, it pushed into the background the formal exercise of plan formulation and with it some of the essential tasks of planning. The main planning instrument in the post-1977 period has been the Five-Year Public Investment Programme, which is revised annually. These rolling plans, however, did not have the formal structure or the comprehensive coverage of national planning documents. They concentrated on public investment programmes, which were presented in summary form.[16] The IBRD which normally was not in favour of formal planning exercises commented on the need for a medium-term outlook that would enable the government to coordinate their policies better and act with greater foresight.

However, the term planning itself has fallen into disuse. Master plans for sectors and short-term strategies for the management of the development process, such as the poverty reduction strategy, have taken the place of national planning. 'Regaining Sri Lanka', and its precursor 'The Poverty Reduction Strategy' (PRS) which it incorporates, seek to fulfil some of the needs of a national plan. In terms of its methodology for sharpening the focus of planning on one critical problem, it is a new departure in planning and strategy formulation.

The PRS is by its very definition not a national plan for the improvement of the quality of life for the whole of society. It can be argued that the reduction of poverty by itself is an indicator of such an improvement. However, in the way that the PRS is constructed, it cannot give us the holistic vision of Sri Lanka's society in the long term; neither is each sector— health, education, industry—depicted in full as a well-formulated national plan does in its sector plans. Nevertheless, both in the processes that went into the formulation of the PRS as well as in its contents, the PRS is a very valuable input into the process of national planning in Sri Lanka. Its limitations when viewed in terms of its place within a planning process which provides the directions for the long-term future, and within it the medium term and short term, call for a more wide ranging debate on national planning in Sri Lanka than we presently have.

There was another critical development during this period. Constitutional changes had created a new set of challenges for national planning. The establishment of Provincial Councils and a system of devolution had posed new problems for national coordination of development on the one hand and the devolution of planning functions on the other. These issues of national planning, however, did not receive the attention of the political leadership and policy-makers.

PLANNING IN A MARKET ECONOMY

The story of national planning that has been briefly recounted in the foregoing sections is largely one of frustrated hopes and unfulfilled goals. It is in the two phases of planning in Gamani Corea's career as a planner—the Ten-Year Plan period and the 1965–70 phase—that we see Sri Lankan national planning at its brightest and best. It is also these two phases that typify the two different types of planning that provide the lessons that are most revealing—the long-term foresight to direct the economy towards desired goals and the aptitude for short-term economic coordination aimed at sustainable growth. One type of planning cannot be successful without the other. Both types must work together and be mutually reinforcing. Regrettably, Sri Lanka never enjoyed the full and effective combination of the two at any given time.

There has been no sustained and serious discussion in Sri Lanka on the role and nature of national planning. This applies to its role in a mixed economy such as what prevailed in Sri Lanka up to 1978, and more so to a market economy of the type towards which Sri Lanka is aiming to move. The mixed economy that evolved up to 1978 required a conceptual framework that could have led to the balanced coexistence of the public and private sector, the state and market, welfare and growth. Within such a social democracy, planning may have been able to design the right framework of incentives as well as the policies and institutions that would have enabled either the Ten-Year Plan or the Five-Year Plan to work. Neither the politicians, planners, professionals or other members of the intellectual elite were able to produce the right ideology that would have yielded such an outcome.

The situation has worsened for national planning after 1978. Whereas both in the advanced democracies in Europe as well as in the fast-growing capitalist countries of South East and East Asia the concepts and disciplines that are intrinsic to planning have been continuously adapted and applied to provide long-term and medium-term perspectives and give direction to their economies, in Sri Lanka the term 'national planning' and the activity associated with it fell into disrepute as the country moved in the direction of a market economy. Planning was perceived as a process of state intervention which was inherently antagonistic to the market and to private-sector initiative. There were some efforts on the part of professionals to challenge these misconceptions.[17] But regrettably, these efforts did not promote the systematic inquiry that was needed to restore to planning its essential role in charting the path of future development for the country.

At the start of the post-war period many developed economies showed a distrust of national planning similar to what we observe in Sri Lanka in the post-1977 period, with similar expressions in many other developed market economies. If there should be any doubt about the relevance and importance of planning for market economies, one need only refer to the post-war experience of planning in many of these countries, including Germany, Japan, France, Holland, etc. The basic rationale for planning in an open economy can be derived from these experiences.

First, the market mechanisms which are based on a multitude of micro-level decisions of households and enterprises do not automatically lead to the required macroeconomic performance which will produce sustained high employment and continuing growth with only a moderate degree of inflation. Second, the market will not yield an efficient allocation of resources when the market structures are imperfect, particularly when benefits and costs external to the enterprise, such as environmental costs and benefits, are not taken into account in the pricing. Third, market allocation of resources while they are economically efficient do not automatically meet the requirements of equity and social norms that override those of economic efficiency. These considerations become much more important in developing market economies and indeed provide a powerful rationale for planning.

It has to be pointed out that almost all successful plans in market economies were able to project a vision of change, for a higher quality of life and a better society, that was able to motivate various sectors and mobilize a broad-based national collective effort towards achieving the goals. This process of social mobilization towards clearly-conceived goals is perhaps the most vital function of the national planning process. However, when it is formulated in this manner planning activity becomes much more than a technocratic exercise confined to the conventional methodologies of plan preparation. These methodologies are no doubt indispensable, but in order to function as an instrument of social transformation, it has to have other dimensions of a political and social character.

Economic management limited to a short-term horizon as we have in Sri Lanka still falls far short of the national planning that we need. First, such management has to be extended over a long-term horizon. The extension of this framework of short-term management into a longer timeframe is essential in a developing market economy for a variety of reasons. Most important, the decision-making throughout the economy is influenced by future expectations. To the extent that there is a credible framework of future expectations in the medium term and long term, the choices relating to savings and investment are likely to be more rational, the confidence in future development greater and the propensity to defer present consumption for future returns higher. Second, macroeconomic goals of full employment, growth and moderate inflation have to be combined with larger societal goals of equity, participation and sustainability. Third, this planning framework with longer time horizons must be disaggregated to sectors and to various important components of the economy if it is to be effective in influencing the decision-making in different parts of the economy, and at the level of the firm and the household.

Planning in a market economy requires the active participation of all stakeholders, among whom the private sector and trade unions must play leading roles. The macro-economic framework for private sector development requires the involvement of both employers and workers in setting the development goals, designing the framework of incentives for growth and productivitiy as well as the distribution of the benefits of growth. In Sri Lanka's case, many contesting value systems contributed to the plural-istic socio-economic mix of state and market that has emerged, from the liberal demo-cratic tradition to Fabian socialism to revolutionary Marxism. In this mix there are many elements that cannot be discarded. These include a state and society which assume the basic responsibility for social welfare and a democratic system which tena-ciously survives and expands the scope for participation.

We therefore need to find the framework for the state-private sector-worker part-nership that would be better attuned to the participatory equitable social order that we must promote in Sri Lanka. There are at least three main value systems in today's global debate on development that such a planning process needs to take into account: first, the value system that has come out of the development policies of the international banking institutions, chiefly the IBRD and the IMF—a value system which is positivistic in which the distinguishing feature is the freedom and efficiency of the market; second, the value system that is normative and linked to the holistic approaches that have been defining human development and the expansion of human choice; third, the value system that is rights-based and derived from norms of good governance, social justice and the fulfilment of social and economic rights. Societies would be setting goals and shaping their futures in terms of all three value systems. Sri Lanka needs to envision its future in terms of all three value systems, and planning processes need to define the development path that leads to that future. We need to apply these criteria to our efforts at 'Regaining Sri Lanka'. What is perhaps the saddest part of our story of development is that when we started the journey we had elements of all three value systems, but still managed to lose our way. The chapter on planning is only a small part of that story.

NOTES

1. W. Arthur Lewis in his preface to the third edition of *The Principles of Economic Planning* takes us through six different meanings of 'planning' ranging from residential and town and country planning to the 'planned economy' and target setting for the economy as a whole.

2. This document was submitted by a group of Congress members in 1947 and should not therefore be seen as representing the mainstream thinking in the Congress.

3. J.A.L. Cooray and a few other younger members of Congress formulated a Bill of Rights to be included in the Constitution for independent Sri Lanka.

4. These were later published in 1949 under the heading 'Six Year Plan for Ceylon' in a series called *Building the Nation Series* and were later again reproduced in 1950 under the title 'The National Plan,' in a publication of the Government Information Department entitled *Ceylon Today—A Government by the People.*

5. 'The national income of Ceylon in 1944 was estimated at Rs 1,842 million and in 1947 at Rs 1,969 million' (for the Six-Year Plan), *Ceylon Today*, p. 29.

6. The relevant issues are discussed at length in the author's 'Planning in Uncertainty' in Urutia and Yukawa (1988).

7. Thomas Balogh refers to this mindset in the British Civil Service 'who were not trained for planning' and resisted the entry of professional planners—'Britain's Planning Problems' in Stuart Holland's *Beyond Capitalist Planning*, p. 124.

8. The Colombo Plan proposals which followed the Six-Year Plan and were formulated in reponse to the Commonwealth Conference held in Colombo were more ambitious in regard to the level of investment but made no major alteration in priorities. These proposals, while they covered most of the major sectors, were still a collection of projects and were not examined in depth for their macroeconomic implications nor were they fully integrated with the government budget and the external account.

9. 'The strategy of development ... would hold true irrespective of the institutional forms to be established ....', see National Planning Council (1959c), p. 3.

10. Out of the 484 pages in the Plan document only 16 pages are given to the social services which include health, education and housing. The sketchy analysis in these chapters does not bear comparison with the more thoughtful chapters of the IBRD report on the social sectors.

11. Myrdal, who visited Sri Lanka to advise the economists, had this to say: 'The choice seemed to be either to present what may be called an intellectual exercise in which no specific decisions are embodied or to prepare a more immediate document setting out clearly the specific decisions of government on a variety of fields.' National Planning Council (1959b), p. 121.

12. The language of the Plan was always 'hedging' and tentative when it makes macroeconomic or even sectoral conclusions. While this style may safeguard the professional integrity of the Plan, the reader would tend to lose confidence in the Plan's final outcomes.

13. One of the best chapters in the document was the chapter on irrigation and land development which provided a critical evaluation of the investment on irrigation and colonization.

14. The work of the Perspective Planning Division on developing a model for the Sri Lanka economy was never taken forward. The Perspective Planning Division ceased to exist shortly after the change of government in 1970 and the planning organizations which followed showed no sustained interest in the work.

15. The Rupee Account of commodity aid was used to finance the government capital budget which consequently recorded a very substantial increase of about 50 per cent.

16. The experience of the 1978–82 period brought to the surface a number of shortcomings and imbalances in both the investment programme and the management of the economy. These had serious macroeconomic consequences for both the government budget and the BOP. The diminution of the role of planning and the relative absence of a centralized, well-defined, and internally consistent framework with accepted national and sectoral targets, certainly contributed to this situation. Private consumption and investment in the liberalized regime were at times wasteful of scarce resources and neglectful of the long-term interests of the economy.

17. For example The National Conference of the Chartered Institute of Management Accountants in 1990 adopted as their main theme Effective National Planning—the Key to Developing Sri Lanka. The keynote addresses by the then Minister of Agriculture, Lalith Athulatmudali and the present author attempted to explore some of the critical issues of national planning in an open economy.

REFERENCES

Ceylon Fisheries Corporation (1965), *Draft 10-year Plan for the Development of the Fishing Industry*, p. III, Colombo.

Corea, Gamani (1975), *The Instability of the Export Economy*, Colombo: Marga Institute.

Department of National Planning (1962), *The Short-term Implementation Programme*, Colombo: Department of National Planning, p. 346.

Firmin, Oules (1966), *Economic Planning and Democracy*, Harmondsworth: Penguin Books.

GOSL (1946), *Post-war Development Proposals*, Colombo: Government Press, p. 22.

_____ (1998), *Poverty Reduction Strategy*, in draft form and consultation stage, 1998–2002.

_____ (2003), *Regaining Sri Lanka*, p. 182.

Gunatilleke, Godfrey (1980), 'A Pluralisitic Strategy of Development', *Marga Journal*, 6(1).

_____ (1991), 'National Planning in an Open Economy', *Marga Journal*, 11(6).

Holland, Stuart (ed.) (1978), *Beyond Capitalist Planning*, Oxford: Basil-Blackwell.

ILO (1971), *Matching Employment Opportunities and Expectations: A Programme of Action for Ceylon* Report of the Inter-Agency Team, 2 Volumes, Geneva: ILO.

International Bank for Reconstruction and Development (1952), *The Economic Development for Ceylon*, 2 Volumes, Colombo: Ceylon Government Press.

Kothari, Rajni (1977), 'Redesigning the Development Strategy', *Marga Journal*, 4(4).

Lewis, W. Arthur (1949), 'The Principles of Economic Planning', Unwin University Books, George Allen and Unwin.

Ministry of Agriculture and Food (1958), *Agricultural plan: First report of the Ministry of Planning Committee,* p. 381, Colombo.

———— **(1966),** *Agricultural Development Proposals,* p. 351, Colombo: Ministry of Planning and Economic Affairs.

Ministry of Finance (1950), *A Six Year Plan for Ceylon,* Colombo: The Department of Information.

———— **(1955),** *The First Six Year Plan—An Assessment,* Colombo: Department of Information.

Ministry of Finance and Planning (1978), *Five Year Public Investment Programme Issued Annually from 1978–2002,* Colombo: National Planning Division.

Ministry of Land, Irrigation and Power (1966), *Plan of Development of Ministry of Land, Irrigation and Power,* Colombo: Ministry of Planning and Economic Affairs.

Ministry of Planning and Economic Affairs (1966), *The Development Programme 1966-1967,* p. 52, Colombo.

Ministry of Planning and Employment (1965), *The Five-year Plan: Agriculture Sector Programme* (including Fisheries), p. 108, Colombo.

———— **(1968),** *Report of the Irrigation Programme Review,* p. 117, Colombo.

———— **(1971),** *The Five-Year Plan 1972–1976,* p. 137, Colombo.

Naqvi, Syed Nawab Haider (1989), 'For Morality's Sake', *Marga Journal,* 10(4).

National Planning Council (1957), *First Interim Report,* pp. 192, Planning Secretariat, Colombo.

———— **(1959a),** *Report of Committees and Technical Working Groups,* p. 102, Colombo: Planning Secretariat.

———— **(1959b),** *Papers of Visiting Economists,* Colombo: Planning Secretariat.

———— **(1959c),** *The Ten-Year Plan,* p. 490, Colombo: Planning Secretariat.

Pieris Ralph (1971), 'Towards Comprehensive Planning', *Marga Journal,* 1(1).

Planning Committee on Economic Overheads (1967), *Report of the Planning Committee on Economic Overheads,* p. 40, Colombo: Ministry of Planning and Economic Affairs.

Planning Committee on Education, Health, Housing, and Manpower (1967), *Report of the Planning Committee on Education, Health, Housing and Manpower,* p. 107, Colombo: Ministry of Planning and Economic Affairs.

Planning Committee on Industry (1966), *Report of the Planning Committee on Industry,* p. 17, Colombo: Ministry of Planning and Economic Affairs.

Planning Secretariat (1960), *Six-year Programme of Investment, 1954/55 to 1959/60,* p. 510, Colombo: Government Press.

Urrutia, Miguel and Setsuko Yukawa (eds) (1988), *Development Planning in Mixed Economies,* Japan: The United Nations University.

4

Understanding Reforms: 1960–2000

Lal Jayawardena

Introduction

This chapter seeks to review some aspects of Sri Lanka's economic experience from 1960 to 2000 and makes relevant comparisons with East Asia. In doing so, it attempts to indicate some of the challenges that lie ahead and makes suggestions for dealing with them in certain areas.

Sri Lanka's Human Development Achievements

Sri Lanka's principal economic achievement has been amply documented. This has been the achievement of a relatively high quality of life on a modest per capita income— a life expectancy of 73 years, an adult literacy rate of 91 per cent, and an infant mortality rate of 14 per 1,000, the lowest in the low-income developing world. The United Nations Development Programme's (UNDP's) Human Development Index, an aggregate measure of the quality of life, ranks Sri Lanka in its 1999 Human Development Report at 90 out of 174 countries, while the highest rank accorded to any other South Asian country is 132. Sri Lanka's human development achievements were based on massive investment in the social sectors, on free health care, universal free education and subsidised food. These expenditures during the decades of the 1960s and 1970s averaged around 9 per cent to 10 per cent of GDP, and as much as half this expenditure, 4 per cent to 5 per cent of GDP, was accounted for by an untargeted food subsidy.

Growth, Savings and Investment

Sri Lanka's most spectacular failure, however, has been its inability to translate this social sector achievement into rapid economic growth. As Table 4.1 shows, Sri Lanka's per capita income in 1960 was around US$ 150. This was the same as China's Province

Table 4.1

COMPARATIVE GDP/GNP PER CAPITA DATA

	1960[a]	1997[b]
Hong Kong	310	25,200
Indonesia	91	1,100
Malaysia	280	4,350
Singapore	443[c]	32,810
South Korea	152	10,550
Sri Lanka	152	800
China (Province of Taiwan)	149	12,797[d]
Thailand	82	2,740

Notes: [a] See Lakshman (1997: 15).
  [b] See UNDP (1999), Table 11.
  [c] See Yah et al. (1988: 7).
  [d] See IMF (1999).

of Taiwan and South Korea's, and significantly higher than Indonesia's and Thailand's. Only Hong Kong and Malaysia at around US$ 300 and Singapore at over US$ 400 had incomes that were higher. Today, Sri Lanka's Gross National Product (GNP) per capita is a little over US$ 800, Singapore's is over US$ 30,000, South Korea's over US$ 10,000 and Malaysia's is US$ 4,500. Sri Lanka's overall GNP has grown over the long haul at 4.8 per cent (1975 to 1995), while East Asian growth has averaged 8 per cent since 1960. Low growth has meant that Sri Lanka has never succeeded in eliminating its substantial backlog of overt unemployment. This has remained relatively stable for over 30 years from 1960 at 13 to 16 per cent of the labour force, and has only in the last few years fallen to an average of 11 per cent, due in part to a slowing down in the labour force growth.

The disparity in income growth between East Asia and Sri Lanka has a straight-forward explanation. Sri Lanka was consistently saving and investing much less than East Asia. Table 4.2 presents gross domestic savings and investment as percentage shares of GDP. As indicated therein, in 1965 Sri Lanka was investing 15 per cent of

Table 4.2

COMPARISON OF INVESTMENT AND SAVINGS IN SRI LANKA AND EAST ASIA

	Gross Domestic Savings/GDP		Gross Domestic Investment/GDP	
	Sri Lanka[a]	East Asia[b]	Sri Lanka	East Asia
1965[c]	12%	17%	15%	20%
1990	17%	38%	22%	36%
1994[d] to 1998	16%		25%	

Notes: [a] See CBSL (1998).
  [b] See World Bank (1993: 41).
  [c] 1960–69 Average for Sri Lanka.
  [d] 1994–98 Average. When migrant remittances are taken into account national savings average is 20.5 per cent.

GDP while saving 12 per cent, the difference being financed by foreign savings. East Asia was then investing 20 per cent of GDP, or 5 percentage points more than Sri Lanka, while saving 17 per cent. By 1990, according to the World Bank's East Asian Miracle study[1] of the seven East Asian high performers, East Asia's average savings rate had more than doubled to 38 per cent of GDP while their investment rate had nearly doubled to 36 per cent. Individual East Asian countries did considerably better than the average. By 1984, Singapore had the highest savings rate in the world at 42 per cent of GDP, and the highest investment rate at 49 per cent. Malaysia was, until the recent crisis, saving and investing over 40 per cent of GDP. Sri Lanka has recently been saving domestically at 16 per cent to 17 per cent of GDP, no more than East Asia was doing in 1965, and investing at 25 per cent of GDP, not a great deal more than East Asia was doing then. The difference in recent years is that remittances from Sri Lankans abroad have begun to make a modest contribution to financing investment by raising national savings by a few percentage points to an average of 20.5 per cent.

MAIN REASONS FOR LOW GROWTH

Why did Sri Lanka fail to make progress with regard to savings and investment? The principal villain of the piece during the 1960s appears to have been the food subsidy in contrast to the other social sector investments in health and education which were needed to underpin Sri Lanka's high quality of life. The late Professor Joan Robinson, the celebrated Cambridge economist, always lamented the fact that Sri Lanka 'ate of the fruit before growing the tree'. It is arguable therefore that if Sri Lanka had, for example, abandoned the food subsidy, running at nearly 5 per cent of GDP in the mid-1960s, it could have invested in plant and machinery at around 20 per cent of GDP as East Asia as a whole was then investing, instead of the 15 per cent it had succeeded in doing at the time. The extra growth resulting from the 5 percentage points of extra investment, perhaps an extra percentage point or so in GDP terms, would have been compounded over a 40-year period and the marginal savings reinvested. This would have undoubtedly accelerated Sri Lanka's economic growth to the point conceivably of permitting the high average levels of savings and investment that East Asia has now reached, provided fiscal discipline had been otherwise maintained. This unfortunately did not happen for reasons stemming from Sri Lanka's democratic political framework. There were altogether four developments that need to be noted, the first two having to do with the intensification of Sri Lanka's ethnic problem and its fiscal consequences.

The first development was the election pledge of the then leader of the Opposition, S.W.R.D. Bandaranaike, to make Sinhalese the sole official language, a pledge which won him a landslide victory in the 1956 elections. One of Sri Lanka's most eminent academic politicians of the day, Colvin R. de Silva, observed prophetically 'One language, two nations; two languages, one nation'. The second development was the introduction of 'standardization of marks' in the early 1970s—an euphemism for making it easier for children in rural areas, where the majority of votes lay, to enter university as compared with urban children. This resulted in a situation where, for instance, the students of the most important urban secondary school in Jaffna, the Jaffna College, who were denied a university education, became the leaders of the Tamil insurrectionary movement—of the Liberation Tigers of Tamil Eelam (LTTE), and the moderate Tamil Party, the Tamil United Liberation Front (TULF)—which came out with a call for a separate 'Eelam' state. The financing of the resulting internal civil conflict had, before the post-2001 peace process, risen to the equivalent of 6 per cent of GDP, which in effect replaced the food subsidy.

The third development was that there was a propensity to indulge in mega projects, for the sake of electoral reasons, whose costs had a habit of ballooning out of control and exacerbating budget deficits invariably financed by printing money, i.e., borrowing from the Central Bank. Aggregate demand was kept in check by tight monetary policies so that annual inflation averaged around 12 per cent. The BOP was also kept viable by a steady and substantial periodic depreciation of the rupee: from Rs 15 = US$ 1 in 1977 after the first attempt at economic reforms, to nearly Rs 100 = US$ 1 today. In other words, Sri Lanka has had the worst possible policy combination for high growth—a loose fiscal policy and a tight monetary policy. In the 1980s and 1990s overall budget deficits were invariably in excess of 10 per cent of GDP, and there were only 3 occasions when there was a current account budget surplus. In other words, there was consistent public dis-savings.

The fourth development was that there were the predictable consequences of a high level of literacy and of an oversupply of graduates and low growth. The government became the employer of first resort, accounting for 57 per 1,000 of the population in 1997, the highest rate in South Asia. India and Pakistan in contrast had each only 19 per 1,000 of their population in government employment.

ATTEMPTS AT REFORM

There were altogether three attempts at reform. The first was in 1977. Sri Lanka's growth experience in the dirigiste period of the 1960s and early 1970s was not a happy one with only 3 per cent GDP growth annually. The incoming UNP government, and in particular President J.R. Jayewardene, wanted to liberalize the economy, abandon import licensing and convert the food subsidy into investment. This also happened to be the advice given to him by his economic advisors. The optimal course of action from an economic standpoint would have been to cut the entire food subsidy, but there was always the risk of sparking off the classic IMF food riot. This is precisely the kind of situation when a country has a real opportunity to negotiate with the IMF because it is not suffering from a rapid erosion of reserves and therefore not under pressure. It was the author's task as the then Secretary to the Treasury and the Ministry of Finance and Planning, along with Anoop Singh of the IMF and Sarwar Lateef of the World

Bank who were the Resident Representatives of their respective institutions, to do just that. It was recognized that there were political risks that might be encountered and it was agreed to leave the matter in the hands of a leading nutritionist, Brightie de Mel, who worked out that between 1970 and 1977, average daily calorie consumption per head of the lower income groups had fallen well below the daily national nutritional needs norm of 2,200 calories which met the protein norm of 40 grams for growth.

The relevant extract from Brightie de Mel's report to the Treasury is worth citing because it illustrates the kind of detailed research and evidence that proved decisive then in working out a compromise on the food subsidy issue and has relevance to the kinds of evidence that may be needed today in a revived reform effort, to gain support from the donor community:[2]

> Since 1973 the government has imposed a ban on the import of certain foodstuffs. From 1972 to 1973 the importation of pulses fell from 30,600 metric tonnes (MT) to zero. In 1973 the importation of staple dried fish was reduced by nearly 50 per cent dropping from 35,000 MT in 1972 to 16,800 MT in 1973. In 1975 imports of dried fish fell to 15,300 MT and in 1976 this declined to 6,656 MT, a decrease of more than 60 per cent. The reduction of imports of pulses and fish, the principal protein staples of Sri Lanka, was initiated in 1972–73 concurrent with the world slump in grain production, and was an effort to conserve hard currencies for the purchase of wheat and rice, the prices of which achieved an all time high in that period.

	Food Balance Sheet—G/CAPUT/DAY						
	1969	1970	1971	1972	1973	1974	1975
1. Dried and salted fish	9.32	8.63	8.63	8.74	4.55	4.85	4.69
2. Pulses	18.52	16.20	7.91	7.32	3.97	2.15	5.4
Total of 1 and 2	27.84	24.83	16.54	16.06	8.52	7.00	10.09
3. Whole milk powder	2.55	2.74	2.22	1.40	2.14	1.89	2.32
Total of 1, 2 and 3	30.39	27.57	18.76	17.46	10.66	8.89	12.41

> Since then the ban has continued in effect as a means of stimulating domestic protein production. Although indigenous production of pulses and fish has increased, protein availabilities continue to lag behind national requirements. (All foods are produced locally now except for wheat, sugar, powdered whole milk and some rice.) Sri Lanka, during the last few years, has also been adversely affected as a result of changes in the world economy. High prices and general shortage of foods have intensified the problem of malnutrition, particularly among the lowest 43 per cent of the population who earn less than Rs 200 a month. In 1969-70 the Socio-Economic Survey indicated that those earning less than Rs 200 (about US$ 28) per month (43 per cent of population) were receiving 2,064 calories and 47 grams of protein daily while those under Rs 400 (about US$ 55) per month were getting 2,272 calories and 54 grams of protein, the national nutritional requirements being 2,200 calories and 40 grams of protein per capita per day. By 1973 (Consumer Finance Survey 1973) these nutrition levels had fallen to 1,931 calories and 34.5 grams of protein and 2,099 calories and 37.3 grams protein respectively, a fall of about 100 calories and 12.5 grams per capita per day for the lowest income group.

This evidence indicated that it would be both politically and nutritionally unwise to remove the subsidy in its entirety. The compromise agreed on was to target the subsidy to the bottom-half of the population while taking it away from the top-half. This was an administrative challenge which was satisfactorily met to the point of meriting a separate Annex on its modus operandi in the IMF Report on the programme.

This attracted the full range of IMF facilities then on offer, i.e., a four-tranche drawing and an Extended Fund Facility (EFF). This was followed by a predictable upsurge in growth. This growth impulse was rapidly lost as project costs escalated financed by ample recourse to the Central Bank printing money for accommodating the resulting fiscal deficits, leading to rising inflation. By 1989, reserves had predictably fallen to two weeks worth of imports resulting from the erosion of the real exchange rate that followed.

This was the background to the second attempt at reform which took the form of an ESAF programme in 1989, which the IMF staff prepared for Sri Lanka. As a result, growth accelerated between 1989 and 1994 to an average of 6 per cent. Once again, reforms fell victim to the usual Sri Lankan political cycle. The political process breached the ESAF conditionality with the government announcing on 1 May 1994 a package of relief measures in anticipation of elections later that year. The Opposition, which subsequently won the 1994 elections, countered by promising a subsidy on flour, which it went on to implement, against the advice of its economic advisors at a time when all World Bank projections pointed to a rise in world grain prices. The critical reform opportunity only available in the first year of a democracy was missed unlike in 1977. It took two years for the flour subsidy to be phased out, but by then defence expenditure had risen to 6 per cent of GDP and the budget deficit to 9.5 per cent of GDP.

The third attempt was in 2001 when the BOP was in a similarly parlous state as a result of enhanced military expenditure and a budget deficit of 10 per cent of GDP. The new element of IMF conditionality was a clean, as opposed to a managed, float of the exchange rate to restore competitiveness and rebuild reserves. Unfortunately, in the run up to elections in December 2001, the budget deficit ceiling of 8.5 per cent of GDP imposed by the IMF was breached as a result of predictable give-aways, the second occasion when the political cycle frustrated reforms.

LESSONS OF THE REFORM EXPERIENCE

What does the Sri Lankan experience imply for reforms? First, the right exchange rate accompanied by high literacy and market oriented reforms could imply the first stage of economic diversification propelled by foreign investment. Sri Lanka in the mid-1970s was a 90 per cent tea, rubber and coconut exporting economy. Today, more than 50 per cent of its exports are garments, as is typical of this first stage. This was essentially the product of the 1977 reforms and the inflow of foreign investment generated. Second, in order to reach the next stage of diversification, Sri Lanka needs to progress beyond mere literacy in the direction of skill development with appropriate educational reforms.

Third, while the peace process initiated in 2002 will, if successful, phase out the 6 per cent GDP spent on the military budget, it will not eliminate the overall budget deficit, let alone yield a current account surplus. It is difficult to see how this can happen without a major public sector reform and reduction of the substantial numbers in the public service.

Fourth, unless an incoming government embarks on reform at the outset of its tenure it will fritter away its political goodwill and be unable to ensure fiscal discipline and be forced to turn to reforms only when the foreign exchange reserves run out. Sri Lanka has had two such opportunities; the first was in 1977, when the new government was clearly committed to moving away from previous dirigiste policies, and the second was, as mentioned, in 1994. The third is the opportunity that Sri Lanka has in the wake of the 2002–03 ceasefire with the LTTE and the peace talks whose outcome will have to be favourable if Sri Lanka is to return to a high growth path.

REFORM ISSUES

Several important reform issues arise on which this account of Sri Lanka's experience sheds light. One of the first is, why do countries undertake major reform measures? The motivation in Sri Lanka was straightforward. The country sought to move from a dirigiste framework which had paralysed growth since independence in the direction of a liberal market oriented economy and, to the maximum extent possible, achieve a shift from consumption and subsidies towards investment. This in a democracy, as mentioned, has to happen in a government's first year of office in order to ensure political feasibility for the austerity package and to have a meaningful negotiation with the IMF which will be inevitably involved. On all other occasions, reform becomes compulsory when reserves run out and there is precious little room for manoeuvre. Under these circumstances, what tends to happen is that the IMF country staff writes the programme.

Another important issue concerns the relation between political reform and economic reform. In other words, what does a conventional parliamentary democracy imply for economic growth? Sri Lanka's experience is not an entirely happy one. It is doubtful that the country would have had free health care, free education and a food subsidy without democracy. On the other hand, Sri Lanka has had governments in power which had every incentive to announce wage increases and subsidies in the run up to elections in breach of understandings with the IMF, as happened in 1994 and in 2001, saddling an incoming government with entirely avoidable problems. Sri Lanka's experience with political opportunism within a democracy as regards the aggravation of the existing ethnic problem has been disastrous for fiscal policy, leading to a substantial increase in the military budget as mentioned, to 6 per cent of GDP or well over half the budget deficit. Within a democracy, one cannot think of any alternative to a constitutional provision which empowers say, the Supreme Court, to vet political party manifestos with a view to eliminating anything which is ethnically inflammatory.

Yet another issue listed on which Sri Lanka's experience has a specific contribution to make is the question of a threshold level of human development that must be reached before reform can be effective. The author would argue strongly for free education with revised curricula to familiarize students with information technology (IT) from the outset involving appropriate educational reforms, and would also argue for free health care involving, as in Sri Lanka's case, household visits by midwives to pregnant mothers, which together with high literacy have been the principal factors underlying Sri Lanka's high life expectancy and low infant mortality. There is a need as well, for subsidised nutrition to a target group of the very poor. These are issues which have achieved some prominence in the light of current concerns with international terrorism and market failure issues highlighted by Joseph Stiglitz in his WIDER lecture,[3] and in his most recent book,[4] and obviously where the state must play a prominent role. Ideally, these kinds of expenditure should be underwritten by the donor community in comprehensive enough fashion to counter market failures as in Ethiopia, according to Stiglitz. To cite his WIDER lecture:

> The experience of Ethiopia emphasizes another determinant of optimal deficits, the source of financing. For the last several years, Ethiopia has run a deficit of about 8 per cent of GDP. Some outside policy advisers would like Ethiopia to lower its deficit. Others have argued that the deficit is financed by a steady and predictable inflow of highly concessional foreign assistance, which is driven not by necessity of filling a budget gap but by the availability of high returns to investment. Under these circumstances— and given the high returns to government investment in such crucial areas as primary education and physical infrastructure (especially roads and energy)—it may make sense for the government to treat foreign aid as a legitimate source of revenue, just like taxes, and balance the budget inclusive of foreign aid.

Stiglitz's accounts both in his WIDER lecture and his book *Globalization and its Discontents* would mean that in Ethiopia, donors not only built schools but provided for curriculum development and teachers. Similarly, with health aid not only would hospitals be built by donors, but doctors' salaries paid. Rural roads would not only be built but maintained, thus ensuring that rural produce would at all times find ready access to urban markets. All this is explicitly discussed in his book:[5]

> Sometimes countries had used aid dollars to construct schools or clinics. When the aid money ran out, there was no money to maintain these facilities. The donors had recognized this problem and built it into their assistance programs in Ethiopia and elsewhere. But what the IMF alleged in the case of Ethiopia went beyond the concern. The Fund contended that international assistance was too unstable to be relied upon. To me, the IMF's position made no sense, and not just because of its absurd implications. I knew that assistance was often far more stable than tax revenues, which can vary markedly with economic conditions. When I got back to Washington, I asked my staff to check the statistics, and they confirmed that international assistance was more stable than tax revenues.

George Soros has also recently put forward a global solution to the problem of financing market failure and providing for public goods involving a special allocation of Special Drawing Rights (SDR).[6]

The relevance of the Ethiopian approach to financing deficits and the role of donors to Sri Lanka is that this may be the only way in which the momentum of the current peace process can be maintained and adequate resources found for rehabilitation and reconstruction in the conflict areas and for accelerating growth in general, involving both mechanisms for ensuring low inflation and prudent debt management. The mechanisms employed to these ends in Thailand and Indonesia have been described in detail in the World Bank's East Asian miracle study[7] and merit intensive study as possible models for Sri Lanka to follow today.

> To achieve the twin objectives of low inflation and prudent debt management, both governments created mechanisms to insulate their economic technocracies. In Thailand, the government's Budget Bureau has tight control of the budget drafting process and has maintained a stable exchange rate and low inflation. To draft the budget, the Budget Bureau consults with the National Economic and Social Development Board about proposed public investments and with the Finance Ministry about expected revenues. It then determines together with the Central Bank how much deficit financing the economy can tolerate without increasing inflation. Having determined aggregate allowable expenditure, it calculates how much each government agency may spend and forwards a broad outline of proposed expenditures to the Cabinet.
>
> Throughout, the Bureau draws support from budgetary laws that limit the government deficit to a small percentage of the year's total expenditures and that caps the percentage of the budget that can be spent servicing the foreign public debt (the current cap is 13 per cent). Parliamentary rules offer a further unusual guarantee against runaway deficit spending. Non-ministerial members of Parliament on the budget committee may propose only minimal changes and in any event may not revise the budget upward. The results have been impressive. Except for the disruptions caused by the 1972 and 1979 oil shocks, the annual inflation rate has been close to 5 per cent. Few developing economies can lay claim to such an achievement, and even more advanced HPAEs (High Performing Asian Economies) such as Hong Kong and Korea have had higher rates. This demonstrates how a small technocratic core, insulated from politics, can set a positive tone for an entire economy.
>
> In Indonesia, too, technocrats keep a tight rein on the budget. Under Suharto, a balanced budget has been the cornerstone of government financial policy. In 1967, the legislature approved a law limiting expenditures to domestic revenues plus foreign assistance. Since then, the finance ministry has institutionalized a review that requires each ministry to justify proposed expenditures on a line-by-line basis. In addition, parliamentary rules restrict the legislature's discussion of the budget to broad policy issues. Armed with these instruments, the finance ministry has established a macroeconomic environment favourable to growth. Inflation has dropped since the 1960s and has generally remained low and stable.

Perhaps the counsel of perfection is to be found in a law explicitly establishing a totally independent Central Bank. The Central Bank Law in Chile is probably ideal in this respect in its Article 27, which is reproduced below:

Article 27

The Bank may provide financing or refinancing only to banking and financial institutions. Under no circumstances may it provide them its guarantee, or acquire instruments issued by the State, its agencies or enterprises.

No public expenditure may be financed by means of funds coming directly or indirectly from the Bank.

Nevertheless, in case of foreign war or the threat thereof, which shall be so qualified by secret decision of the National Security Council, the Bank shall be able to obtain credit from, or grant it to or finance the State and public or private enterprises.

Finally again, if accelerated growth is desirable, when should a country like Sri Lanka liberalize its capital account? Common sense suggests that this should happen sooner rather than later, so long as Sri Lanka can insulate herself from the kind of asset bubble and the kind of trouble which sparked off the East Asian crisis. Liberalizing the capital account, while not strictly a necessary condition for enhanced foreign investment, will doubtless send a positive signal to get investment of the right kind. Indeed, Sri Lanka's Institute of Policy Studies[8] has argued that, as a result of the absence of peace, the 'hardest hit has been the flow of FDI to the economy.... The risky investment climate has been conducive only to investment in light industries where fixed capital costs are limited. This has in turn meant that the economy's employment structure continues to be dominated by low skill labour, whose real wage growth has been marginal.' Sri Lanka's preferential margin is bound to erode within 3 to 5 years as India's tariff reforms continue, and the question really is how soon the post-2001 peace process succeeds and donor support is mobilized.

FUTURE PERSPECTIVES FOR REFORM

Sri Lanka is in the early years of its political cycle once more and is poised for major reforms to be undertaken against, hopefully, the background of a successful peace process which will save on a substantial proportion of the military expenditure and to that extent reduce the fiscal deficit. The broad outlines of the reform package are to be found in the most recent World Bank Country Report on Sri Lanka, prepared by a task force led by Eric Bell, and appropriately entitled *Recapturing Missed Opportunities*.[9] What this report leaves out are the more radical suggestions made above as regards the need to ensure maintaining fiscal discipline and opening the capital account presumably because they belong to IMF territory.

In this effort a vital role is played by the Resident Representatives of the IMF and the World Bank. The author was fortunate with regard to the colleagues he had to work with in 1977. Until mid-2002 Sri Lanka had a truly outstanding IMF Resident Representative in Nadeem-ul-Haq who had gone well beyond the call of duty to build up a consensus within civil society on economic reform by, for example, organizing particular conferences on deregulation and financial sector reform. His presence in Sri

Lanka during 1999–2002 was, in the judgement of the government and certainly of the author, crucial if the reform efforts were to succeed. Yet the IMF turned down a request from the government, and from a reform minded Prime Minister no less, to have Nadeem-ul-Haq's term extended. Fortunately, in the present case, Nadeem's successor is familiar with Sri Lanka having led Fund missions to the country in recent years. Nevertheless, the IMF personnel policies as regards the tenure of its Resident Representatives clearly need revision if reform opportunities are to be captured in timely fashion, especially because there is an inevitable learning period for any new-comer, however competent that person may be.

Meanwhile, under the Sri Lankan Constitution, the President has the power to dissolve Parliament within a year of elections and call for fresh elections which the government can counter only with a two-thirds majority in Parliament, something which it has not yet been able to muster. Since one year has passed there is not much time left for implementing reform. Significant reform can mean compressing a reform into the next programme within this timeframe in Sri Lanka or a satisfactory mode of cohabitation will have to be worked out. Otherwise, Sri Lanka will fall victim to the populist political cycle once again.

Crude back-of-the-envelope calculations are presented in Tables 4.3 and 4.4 for a 20-year-period ending 2020 which indicate the enormity of the challenge Sri Lanka now faces. Despite eliminating a budget deficit of 10 per cent of GDP and attracting 5 per cent of GDP as foreign investment, Sri Lanka will still, by 2020, have a lower per capita income than Malaysia in 1997. These calculations involve the expository abstraction that the budget deficit is eliminated overnight to enable an average 8 per cent growth to be registered, which is of course impossible in fact. Even more ambitious growth targets such as 10 per cent have been mentioned in the Regaining Sri Lanka Policy document of the UNF government. This suggests that unless drastic reductions occur in Sri Lanka's capital-output ratio, which appears difficult to visualize in the short run, the time path for the reduction of Sri Lanka's budget deficit must be a more gradual one. This, however, could be accelerated if there is substantial aid linked to a successful peace process, even after taking account of the reduced military expenditure, i.e., if the Ethiopian model described by Stiglitz and recapitulated above is followed and donor support appropriately enlisted.

Table 4.3

SCENARIOS OF INVESTMENT AND GROWTH: THE CHALLENGE

	Investment/GDP	Annual GDP Growth Rate
(1) Present situation	25%	5%
(2) Desired situation	49%	8%
(3) =Investment gap	15%	
(2) – (1)		
Financed by		
(4) Eliminating budget Deficit	10%	
+		
(5) Foreign investment	5%	

Table 4.4

Comparative Per Capita GDP

Malaysia (1997)[a]	US$ 4,530
Sri Lanka (1997)	US$ 800
Feasible Optimum Scenario– Sri Lanka (2020)	US$ 3,200[b]

Notes: [a] GNP.
     [b] Annual 8 per cent GDP growth, and 1 per cent Population growth implying 7 per cent Per Capita GDP growth.

Donor support in adequate amounts to look after all market failures comprehensively and sustain rapid growth is especially important to Sri Lanka now. It is in fact virtually dictated by the need to sustain a rapidly ageing population, now 19 million, which will stabilise by 2025 at 23 million. This is the natural by-product of the country's high level of human development and literacy and the fall in the rate of population growth from nearly 3 per cent in the 1960s to 1 per cent today.

There is indeed a real opportunity for a deal between Sri Lanka and the donor community at present whereby Sri Lanka commits itself to the policies needed for low inflation and prudent debt management while the donors guarantee aid support adequate to look after market failures comprehensively and sustain rapid growth.

Notes

1. See World Bank (1993: 41, Figures 1–5).
2. See Jayawardena et al. (1986: 91).
3. See Stiglitz (1998).
4. See Stiglitz (2002: 25).
5. See Stiglitz (2002: 29).
6. See Soros (1998: 73).
7. See World Bank (1993: 170–72).
8. See IPS (1999: 40).
9. See World Bank (2000).

References

Central Bank of Sri Lanka (1998), *Annual Report 1998.*
Institute of Policy Studies (1999), *Sri Lanka—State of the Economy 1999.*
International Monetary Fund (1999), Staff Data Base—Provisional GNP estimate for 1999.
Jayawardena, Lal, Ann Marsland and P.N. Radhakrishnan (1986), *WIDER Studies on Stabilization and Adjustment Policies and Programmes,* Country Study 15, Sri Lanka.

Lakshman, W.D. (ed.) (1997), *Dilemmas of Development: Fifty Years of Economic Change in Sri Lanka*, Colombo: Sri Lanka Association of Economists.

Soros, George (1998), *George Soros On Globalization*, New York: Public Affairs.

Stiglitz, Joseph E. (1998), *More Instrument and Broader Goals: Moving Towards the Post-Washington Consensus*, WIDER Annual Lecture No. 2, Helsinki: WIDER.

——————— (2002), *Globalization and its Discontents*, New York: Norton.

UNDP (1999), *Human Development Report 1999*.

World Bank (1993), *The East Asian Miracle, Economic Growth and Public Policy*, Oxford 1003.

——————— (2000), *Recapturing Missed Opportunities*, Country Paper on Sri Lanka.

Yah, Lim Chong et al. (1998), *Policy Options for the Singapore Economy*, Singapore: McGraw-Hill.

5

THE IMPORTANCE OF THE PUBLIC SECTOR IN ECONOMIC AND SOCIAL DEVELOPMENT

J.B. Kelegama

INTRODUCTION

The developing countries are being constantly advised, in fact pressurized, by the International Monetary Fund (IMF) to emasculate the public sector—to prune government activities, reduce government expenditure and hand over government-owned enterprises to the private sector. It is alleged that state-owned business enterprises are generally inefficient, operate at a loss, crowd out private enterprise, necessitate government subsidies which enlarge the budget deficit and distort prices and misallocate resources. The state, it is argued, cannot manage business ventures and therefore these should be left in the hands of private enterprise. Private enterprise, it is further noted, needs a free environment to operate efficiently and consequently the state should remove obstacles and hindrances by deregulation, decontrol, liberalization and downsizing of the state. In other words, the state should not interfere with the operation of market forces—'the invisible hand'—which, if not interfered with, are assumed to increase production, allocate resources efficiently and promote growth and employment. The recipe for success, it is repeated, is downsizing the state and upsizing the private sector. The IMF Representative in Sri Lanka, for example, has echoed these views when he told Reuters recently: 'The one element holding back economic activity is the size of the public sector as well as the influence of the public sector.'

This 'one size fits all' formula first, ignores the stage of development of developing countries. Many developing countries, for example, do not have a capable domestic entrepreneurial class that could mobilize capital and develop the economy; there is therefore no alternative but for the state to fill the gap. Second, it ignores the inadequacy and shortcomings of the private sector, for example, its tendency to invest in businesses which yield high profits quickly and showing little interest in businesses which yield low profits and that too over a long period, even when they are necessary to build up a viable economy, such as roads, railways and harbours. Third, it does not pay attention to the social services which do not yield profits such as schools, universities, hospitals (except fee-levying schools, universities and hospitals), irrigation schemes and clean drinking water.

The crucial importance of public investment in a developing economy cannot be overemphasized. Developing countries like Sri Lanka lack modern and efficient infrastructural facilities which are an essential prerequisite to any economic development. It is beyond dispute that the country needs more and better roads and railways, harbours and airports, irrigation schemes, power supplies and communications for any production (economic activity) to take place, and more and better hospitals, schools and institutions for higher education to provide health, knowledge and skills to people to engage more productively in economic activity. It is the responsibility of the state to provide these infrastructural facilities which in turn require higher public investment. Thus, improvement of the infrastructure involves increased public investment and it is therefore necessary for public investment to rise in developing countries.

Public investment in infrastructure alone may not be enough to promote economic growth in some developing countries, particularly those which lack a capable domestic entrepreneurial class. In such countries, the state may have no alternative but to invest directly in productive enterprises such as factories and banks. Public investment is also necessary in nationally desirable enterprises which the private sector shuns, for example, building a glass factory which the private sector has failed to establish since independence in Sri Lanka. Public investment is also necessary in undertakings where public ownership is preferable to private ownership. For example, leaving vital necessities like electricity and natural gas to the mercies of the market is too risky, especially when giant private firms like Enron can vanish overnight. In all the rapidly growing economies of East and South East Asia, public and private enterprises co-exist without conflict in a complementary relationship.

Fourth, it does not take an overall view of the economy in the long term and provide manpower skills and training needed in the future. Fifth, it forgets that the private sector cannot provide such services as national security, food security, preservation of the environment and biodiversity and regulations and controls necessary to prevent business malpractices and to ensure competition. Sixth, the pace of development initiated by the private sector may be too slow to accelerate economic growth and create employment and public intervention would be needed to speed up capital accumulation and accelerate growth. Finally, it ignores the fact that in developing countries, there are several problems which cannot be solved by the private sector alone such as poverty, inequality in the distribution of benefits and unemployment and underemployment; if not solved, these problems could make things difficult for private enterprise and the free market to operate.

The crucial role played by the public sector was highlighted by the Report of the South Commission, of which Gamani Corea was a member, as follows:

> There has hardly been a historical case of sustained economic growth and development without the active participation of the state as a regulator and promoter. By their very nature, unregulated market systems pay little or no heed to such strategic areas as basic

industries, health and education services, scientific and technological research, and the preservation of the environment and natural resources. It is particularly unlikely that the free play of market forces would result in the growth with equity that a people-centered development strategy seeks to achieve. Excessive reliance on market forces can lead to concentration of economic power and wider disparities in income and wealth, to the underutilization of resources, to unemployment and to the wastage of the savings potential, with the result that the pace of development and technical progress is retarded.

Thus, contrary to the IMF, the South Commission states that it is essential that the state plays a leading role in the economy both as a regulator and promoter. In fact, Asian experience indicates that an active state which increases public investment and guides and regulates the private sector, far from reducing, increases economic growth.

Views of Joseph Stiglitz

Joseph Stiglitz, Nobel Prize winning former Chief Economist of the World Bank and Chairman of President Clinton's Council of Economic Advisers, has highlighted the need for government involvement in economic activity in his book *Globalization and its Discontents* as follows:

> The IMF policies in part based on the outworn presumption that markets, by themselves lead to efficient outcomes, failed to allow for desirable government interventions in the market, measures which could guide economic growth and make everyone better off.... I believe governments need to—and can—adopt policies that help countries grow but that also ensure that growth is shared more equitably .... Inequality, unemployment and pollution: these were all issues in which government had to take an important role.

> Over the past fifty years, economic science has explained why, and the conditions under which markets work well and when they do not. It has shown why markets may lead to underproduction of some things—like basic research—and the overproduction of others—like pollution. The most dramatic market failures are the periodic slumps, recessions and depressions, that have marred capitalism over the past two hundred years, that leave large numbers of workers unemployed and a large fraction of the capital stock underutilized. But while these are the most obvious examples of market failures, there are a myriad of more subtle failures, instances where markets failed to produce efficient outcomes. Government can, and has played an essential role not only in mitigating these market failures but also in ensuring social justice. Market processes may by themselves, leave many people with too few resources to survive.

Views of Amartya Sen and Jean Dreze

Amartya Sen, another Nobel Prize winner, and Jean Dreze in the updated version of their earlier book, *India: Economic Development and Social Opportunity,* argue that liberalization and market reforms alone are not enough to improve the quality of life; it is essential to tackle directly certain issues of equity such as in education, health and gender through a more active role by the government and people's participation:

We have emphasized the need to take the debates on economic policy well beyond the issues of economic reforms in their present form .... The concentration on attacking or defending liberalization as the central policy issue distracts attention from a broader understanding of social opportunities of which the use of the market can be an important yet quite incomplete part .... There are many other issues of great importance which have been thoroughly overshadowed by the focus on arguments—both for and against—the reforms .... The central issue, we have argued, is to expand the social opportunities open to people .... The creation and use of social opportunities for all require much more than the 'freeing' of markets... India has insufficient and ineffective government activity in ... areas—school education, health care, social security, land reform, environmental protection and promotion of social change ... and many of the relevant tasks call for more—not less—government activity and public action. There is a need for a radical change in the terms of the debate.

Private Investment Needs Public Investment

There will be little private investment without efficient infrastructural facilities. Expectation of private profits is as much related to infrastructural facilities as they are to tax and other incentives and infrastructure is most essential for private activity to take place at all. It is hardly necessary to point out that private investment will not be attracted by poor and inefficient infrastructure consisting of bad roads, railways, harbours and airports, frequent breakdowns in power and poor communications however attractive tax and other concessions are. Poor infrastructural facilities tend to raise the cost of production and lower the profit margin. A major reason why three-quarters of the world's foreign direct investment (FDI) flows into developed countries is the superior infrastructure of those countries. Africa receives only 1.0 per cent of world FDI mainly because of its poor infrastructure while Latin America receives 10.5 per cent and Asia 12.2 per cent by virtue of their better infrastructure.

Public investment does not, as some say, crowd out private investment. On the contrary, public investment is a sine qua non for private investment. Without public investment in infrastructure, there will be little private investment. Further, it stimulates private investment by involving private firms through contracts in the creation and improvement of infrastructural assets and providing them with new business through orders for materials and equipment required in infrastructural investment. In most countries including Sri Lanka, private firms are selected after floating tenders to build or improve roads, airports, seaports, irrigation and hydroelectricity and to construct buildings for schools, hospitals, administration and public housing. In addition, the equipment and materials needed by the government for these physical assets—machinery, spare parts, motor vehicles, ships, aeroplanes, railway engines, generators and other materials—are purchased from private firms on the basis of tenders. So, expanding public investment results in expanding private investment in a symbiotic relationship. This is taking place in all developing countries, particularly in the East Asian countries where high levels of public investment have created a favourable climate for private investment.

DECLINING PUBLIC INVESTMENT

Sri Lanka had a development-oriented interventionist state and a sizeable public sector since colonial times. Apart from the investment in roads, railways, harbours, airports, electricity generation, schools and hospitals which form the economic and social infrastructure, it was the state that wanted the pioneering financial institutions like the Bank of Ceylon, People's Bank, Development Finance Corporation, State Mortgage Bank and the National Development Bank as well as major irrigation schemes, land settlements and the major industries such as cement, paper, chemicals, wood, oils and fats, textiles, tyres and tubes, iron and steel, hardware, sugar, oil refinery and others to build the economic foundation for growth. It built an indigenous business community through state bank credit, protection of nascent domestic industries and Ceylonization of trade under which specific foreign markets for exports and imports were reserved for the indigenous citizens. Besides, the state played a crucial interventionist role in trade through the Food Commissioner who had the monopoly of importing and distributing staple foods, the Co-operative Wholesale Establishment (CWE) Pharmaceuticals Corporation, State Trading Corporation, Marketing Department, Paddy Marketing Board, state-aided cooperatives and guaranteed price schemes to offer competition to the private sector and to ensure a fair deal to the consumers. The state took special interest in social welfare and poverty alleviation through government owned Crown land alienation to landless peasants, colonization schemes, free education, free health services, subsidized food and relief for the poor. All governments until 1977—whatever the political affiliation—supported state involvement and intervention in economic activity to operate a mixed economy with a social welfare orientation, although some placed greater emphasis on state involvement than others.

A mixed economy is one where both private and public sectors co-exist in complementary harmony. While admitting the positive features of private enterprise, its competitiveness, initiative and creativity, it recognizes that business purely based on profit maximization tends to ignore social concerns and national priorities. When Sri Lanka's private sector was underdeveloped and weak, it was believed that the state had to play a crucial role in building up the economic structure and support and guide the private sector to grow in strength while also looking after social interests. It was none other than the former Prime Minister Sir John Kotalawala who stated in his Foreword to the *Six Year Programme of Investment 1954–1960:* 'The government and the private sector are therefore like oarsmen in a boat. While they must row together, they must ensure that they also row in rhythm, for it is only in a spirit of cooperative endeavour that they can reach the promised land of contentment and prosperity that will give us confidence in ourselves as a nation.'

The relative importance of public investment is, however, declining in the Sri Lankan economy with the adoption of free market policies of deregulation, liberalization, privatization and emasculation of the role of the state in economic activity. Public investment was 7.9 per cent of GDP in 1995 but it declined to 6.4 per cent in 2000 and to 5.9 per cent 2001 as shown in Table 5.1.

Table 5.1

PUBLIC INVESTMENT, 1995–2002

Year	Rs (billion)	% of GDP
1995	52.8	7.9
1996	46.0	6.0
1997	51.3	5.8
1998	68.3	6.7
1999	71.4	6.5
2000	81.0	6.4
2001	82.7	5.9
2002	72.0	4.6

Source: Annual Reports of the Central Bank of Sri Lanka (various issues).

The budget for 2002 continued this decline. Public investment for 2002 was estimated at 5.4 per cent of gross domestic product (GDP); the actual investment, however, tended invariably to be lower. In 2000, the actual public investment was 20.8 per cent lower than the estimate and in 2001 it was 22.2 per cent lower. According to the revised estimates in the Budget 2003 Speech, the actual public investment was around Rs 72.0 billion or 4.6 per cent of GDP. The Budget Speech of 2002 itself underlined the importance of public investment in increasing the productive capacity of the economy. Referring to the budgets of 2000 and 2001, it stated: 'in spite of the increase in expenditure, public investment declined to 5.9 per cent of GDP in 2001 from 6.5 per cent in the previous year impacting adversely the future productive capacity of the country'. Thus, the further reduction of public investment from 5.9 per cent of GDP in 2001 to 4.6 per cent of GDP in 2002 would have surely 'impacted adversely' on the productive capacity even more.

PUBLIC SECTOR IN DEVELOPED COUNTRIES

The developed countries have large public sectors although developing countries are advised to have small ones. The developed countries are basically private enterprise based economies or free market economies and yet they maintain sizeable public sectors. Government spending as a percentage of GDP is 52 in Sweden, 50 in Denmark and France, between 40 and 50 in Japan, Belgium, Italy, Germany, the Netherlands and Canada, between 30 and 40 in the UK, Spain and Australia and 29 in the USA as shown in Table 5.2. Sweden has the highest amount of government spending in relation to GDP while the US has the lowest. Strangely, Sri Lanka's government expenditure in 2000 was 27 per cent of GDP, even lower than that of the US and yet we are asked to emasculate the public sector.

Government spending in the 22 rich countries of the Organization for Economic Cooperation and Development (OECD) as a whole rose from 32.3 per cent of GDP in 1970 to 42.3 per cent of GDP in 1995. It is all right for them to increase government spending but bad for developing countries to do so!

Table 5.2

GENERAL GOVERNMENT SPENDING AS PERCENTAGE OF GDP, 2001

Sweden	52	Netherlands	41
Denmark	50	Canada	41
France	50	Norway	40
Greece	49	Iceland	40
Austria	47	New Zealand	39
Japan	46	UK	39
Belgium	46	Spain	38
Italy	45	Australia	33
Germany	45	Ireland	29
Finland	43	USA	29
Portugal	42	Sri Lanka	27

Source: OECD, *Economic and Financial Indicators,* in *The Economist,* 4 August 2001.

Public spending on such a large scale is financed by high taxation. Total tax revenue exceeds 50 per cent of GDP in Sweden, varies between 40 and 50 per cent in Denmark, Finland, Belgium, France, Italy, the Netherlands and Norway, between 30 and 40 per cent in Germany, Britain, Canada and Switzerland and 20–30 per cent in the US and Japan. In Sri Lanka, total tax revenue in 2000 was only about 15 per cent of GDP, much lower than in the developed countries. Corporate tax rates are 40 per cent or more in Canada, Japan, Italy, Belgium and US and 39 per cent in Germany— more than in Sri Lanka where it is 35 per cent. The top income tax rate is 60 per cent in the Netherlands, 50–60 per cent in Denmark, Finland, Sweden, Belgium, France and Germany and between 40 and 50 per cent in Spain, Italy and Britain as compared to 35 per cent in Sri Lanka. Yet, there are some who advocate a reduction in taxation to promote private investment when much higher corporate and individual income taxation has not discouraged private investment in developed countries.

State intervention in the developed countries takes several forms such as subsidies to agriculture and industry, protection of domestic industries by high tariffs and import restrictions, bail-outs of bankrupt big businesses, prevention of monopolistic practices, social welfare schemes and state ownership of assets. In fact, state subsidies are a major reason for the high level of government spending; agricultural subsides in the developed (OECD) countries amounted to $361 billion in 2001, equal to 40 per cent of the value of agricultural production. State aid to the manufacturing sector in the European Union (EU) alone in 1995–97 amounted to $48 billion or 2.8 per cent of value added; these subsidies are mainly to ailing industries such as shipbuilding, coal mining and automobiles. Subsidies to industry account for 5 per cent of German public spending. The US government has bailed out several large firms in difficulties such as Chrysler, Lockheed, Continental Illinois Bank and Long-Term Capital Management. In addition, there are export subsidies for agricultural products. Social welfare in Western Europe such as unemployment benefits, medical and health benefits and care of the aged account for a substantial part of general spending but it is much less in the US. This is the main reason for a more equitable income distribution in Western Europe than in the US.

All the developed countries protect their agriculture and industry. The US, for example, protects its sugar, tobacco, groundnuts, dairy products, textiles, garments, automobiles, steel, lamb, catfish, etc. The EU protects its dairy products, wine, tobacco, vegetable oils, tomatoes and citrus fruits and Japan restricts imports of rice and beef. Many seem to forget that the US through various trade restrictive measures such as the McKinley Tariff of 1890 and the Dingley Tariff of 1897 became the most protectionist country in the world at the beginning of the 20th century. Japan went even further by closing its doors to global market forces until its industries reached world standards. These countries also have legislation and mechanisms to prevent monopolies threatening consumer interests; the US court action to penalize Microsoft Corporation recently is a good example. Besides, they also intervene to protect the environment and biodiversity, to ensure food and fuel security and of course to guarantee national security.

State involvement in business activities is not unusual in the so-called free market, developed economies. France, for example, has over 3,000 state-owned and state-linked businesses; it has a majority stake in some 1,500 companies and minority stake in about 1,300. There are 6 million people in the public sector in France—a quarter of the workforce. The public sector contributes 10 per cent of the country's GDP. The state, for example, owns 44 per cent of Renault and majority stakes in Air France, France Telecom, Credit Lyonnaise and Caisse des Depots et Consignotions. Few know that Japan has 163 public corporations involved in everything from construction, to water works and airports—for example, Housing Loan Corporation, Japan National Oil Corporation, New Energy and Industrial Technology Development Corporation, Japan Highway Public Corporation, Japan Bank of International Cooperation and National Space Development Agency.

Norway is a country where state capitalism is working successfully. Almost all health care, education (including 80 per cent of the running costs of church schools), pensions, water, electricity, roads, railways and fixed-line telecoms are state provided. The state dominates in oil and gas and has big stakes in manufacturing; it owns 45 per cent of the country's industrial giant, Norsk Hydro (oil, gas, chemicals, fertilizers, aluminum) and 47 per cent of Den Norske Bank, the biggest commercial bank, 82 per cent of Statoil (oil), 78 per cent in Telenor (telecoms), 100 per cent in NSB (railways) and 100 per cent of Statkraft (power generation). Overall, the state holds about 40 per cent by value of the local stock market. One worker in three is in the public sector. State businesses operate on strict commercial lines, but the Norwegian authorities and the people oppose foreigners taking over Norway's natural resources. In fact, the government blocked a Finnish bid for a big Norwegian insurer recently. It is because of its fear of global market forces that it does not want to join the European Union (*The Economist*, 15 December 2001).

PUBLIC SECTOR IN EAST ASIAN COUNTRIES

The East Asian countries have for many years been the fastest developing countries in the world and indeed a model for other developing countries. However, many are not aware that a major factor in their success is the active role played by the state. The governments of these countries did not leave major economic activities to be determined by the invisible market forces; instead, they guided, supported and protected indigenous enterprises, sometimes in defiance of market forces, and actively participated in economic activity. They in fact selected those sectors in the manufacturing sector which should be developed into major future industries and supported them by subsidies, concessional credit, restriction of imports and other concessions. They imposed restrictions on foreign ownership of property, such as land in South Korea and banks in Malaysia and Thailand, and controlled foreign investments to discourage those which threatened or competed with them. None of these restrictions and discriminatory practices discouraged foreign investment; on the contrary, the East Asian countries received more FDI than all the other developing countries.

East Asian countries do not see any conflict between encouraging private enterprises and maintaining state-owned business undertakings. Malaysia, one of the most rapidly growing economies in the world, had more than 800 state firms in the mid-1980s, the largest of them being the Heavy and Industrial Corporation of Malaysia (HICOM) which established nine subsidiaries in areas such as steel, automobiles, cement and paper. Much of the growth in the early 1980s was due to HICOM. Indonesia had 164 state-owned firms worth $60 billion and employing 7,00,000 workers in 1997; state-owned Baden Urusan Logistic Nasional (BULOG) has the monopoly of import of basic food—rice, wheat, corn, sugar, soyabeans and fishmeal. South Korea has 141 state firms including banks and industries such as the Pohang Steel Works and Thailand has 67 state firms. In Taiwan some of the largest banks and industries are state-owned while in Singapore, about 60 per cent of its GDP is generated by state-owned and state-linked businesses such as Singapore Airlines—the most efficient airline in the world—Singapore Telecom, Development Bank of Singapore, Government Investment Corporation (GIC) and its subsidiary GIC Real Estate, which owns 125 real estate investments in 25 countries. The major listed companies owned and managed by the government's Temasek Holdings amount to 24 per cent of the total capitalization of the Singapore stock market. It is important to note that most of the state-owned firms operate efficiently and earn profits to feed government revenue.

Public investment in East Asia is nearly equal to private investment and plays a bigger role than in any other region. The IMF's pressure resulted in the shrinking of the public sector in most developing countries but not East Asia. In 1997, public investment constituted only 16 per cent of total investment in Latin America, 28 per cent in South Asia (25 per cent in Sri Lanka) and 32 per cent in sub-Saharan Africa but 45 per cent in East Asia. The rapid growth of East Asia, which exceeded that of other regions, owes much to its large and dynamic public sector. Latin America has the smallest public sector but its average annual growth of GDP per capita in 1990–99 was 1.7 per cent while East Asia, which has the largest public sector, achieved 5.9 per cent. It should not be forgotten that the country with the highest growth rate of per capita GDP in the world—China with 9.5 per cent—has the largest public sector in the world. The oft-repeated IMF statement that the public sector needs to be reduced to promote growth has no foundation.

The East Asian countries are the most rapidly growing countries of the world as a result of their high levels of domestic investment funded mainly by their equally high levels of domestic savings. They are also the biggest recipients of FDI among the developing countries. Some believe that investment is high in these countries because FDI is high, but actually it is the other way round—FDI is high because domestic investment is high. FDI, though substantial as compared with other developing countries, funded only a secondary part of their total capital investment. Thus, between 1988 and 1998, FDI accounted for about one-fifth to one-fourth of total investment only in three of the 10 East Asian countries; it was negligible in two and was moderate, 5–10 per cent, in the rest. In other words, the greater part of investment in these countries was financed by domestic savings and these high levels of domestic savings and investment attract FDI. Besides, domestic investment is high in these countries because public investment is high. It is the low ratio of public investment that results in lower gross domestic investment, little inflows of foreign capital·and lower economic growth in South Asia and Sri Lanka.

It is relevant to note that none of the developing countries which implemented free market policies and downsized the public sector achieved a significant breakthrough. As shown in Table 5.3, the annual growth rate of GDP per capita in the period 1975–99 was only 0.3 per cent in Argentina and Ecuador, 0.8 per cent in both Mexico and Brazil, 0.1 per cent in the Philippines, and Bolivia had a negative growth rate of –0.6 per cent. On the other hand, rapid growth has taken place in those countries with mixed economies, strong governments and large public sectors which were not as liberalized as those in East Asia. The average annual growth of GDP per capita in 1975–99 was 6.5 per cent in South Korea, 4.2 per cent in Malaysia, 5.7 per cent in Thailand, 4.6 per cent in Indonesia and 8.1 per cent in China. All these countries have mixed economies where private and state sectors co-exist complementing each other and economic activity is guided and controlled by the state in one way or another. China may not have western freedom and democracy but it has delivered on the essential economic demands of the Chinese people, namely food and housing, and achieved the highest economic growth rate in the world.

Table 5.3

AVERAGE ANNUAL GROWTH OF GDP
PER CAPITA, 1975–99

Free market	
Argentina	0.3
Mexico	0.8
Ecuador	0.3
Bolivia	–0.6
Peru	–0.8
Philippines	0.1
Mixed economies	
Indonesia	4.6
Malaysia	4.2
Thailand	5.7
South Korea	6.5
China	8.1

Source: *Asian Development Report,* 2001.

HIGH GROWTH FROM HIGH PUBLIC INVESTMENT

The relationship between public investment and growth and between public and private investment is illustrated by Sri Lanka's experience in 1978–81. The highest sustained average economic growth in the country was in the four years 1978–81 when it reached 6.5 per cent from the low level of 2.6 per cent of the previous four years 1974–77. The high growth of 1978–81 was caused mainly by the high level of investment: average annual gross total domestic investment rose from 15.5 per cent of GDP in 1974–77 to 26.9 per cent in 1978–81. Total investment rose so sharply because public investment rose significantly—nearly doubled—from the average annual level of 7.8 per cent of GDP in the previous four years to 14.4 per cent in 1978–81, mainly on account of the massive investment in the Accelerated Mahaweli Development Scheme and partly as a result of the new Parliamentary Complex, port development and expanded public housing. With the decline in public investment in these projects, average economic growth dropped to 5.0 per cent in 1982–85 and then to 2.7 per cent in 1986–89.

Increasing public investment in 1978–81 also stimulated expanding private investment as contracts for the state's Mahaweli multi-purpose project were awarded to specific private firms and purchases of equipment and materials were made direct from other private firms. In addition, the rise in employment and income from public investment resulted, through the multiplier effect, in increased business in the private sector. Thus, average annual investment in the private sector rose from 7.8 per cent of GDP in 1974–77 to 11.6 per cent of GDP in 1978–81 (Table 5.4). In the former period public and private investment were equal but in the latter, public investment exceeded private investment. This rise in public investment instead of 'crowding out' the private sector, boosted it and private investment increased by about 50 per cent.

Table 5.4

INVESTMENT AND GROWTH

Years of GDP	Average Annual Growth of GDP (%)	Gross Domestic Investment (%)		
		Total	Public	Private
1974–77	2.6	15.5	7.8	7.8
1978–81	6.5	26.9	14.4	11.6

Source: Estimated from the Annual Reports of the Central Bank of Sri Lanka (various issues).

The need to raise public investment to promote economic growth by improving the infrastructure and stimulating private investment is paramount. The current level of public investment is too low. In 1995–2000 for example, public investment amounted to 6.7 per cent of GDP—in contrast to 14.4 per cent in the highest growth years of 1978–81. Average private investment during 1995–2000 was 19.1 per cent of GDP and total domestic investment was therefore 25.8 per cent of GDP. In the same period, investment ratios of East Asian countries, despite the serious economic downturn of 1997–98, was much higher. For example, average annual investment ratio to GDP was 38.4 per cent in China, 34.5 per cent in Singapore, 34 per cent in Malaysia, 31 per cent in South Korea and 29.8

per cent in Thailand. The major reasons for this high level of domestic investment in these countries are the high level of public investment and high levels of domestic savings.

It is pointed out by some that Sri Lanka is unable to increase public investment even if it is necessary because it lacks resources. They fail to see that the government lacks funds because it has deliberately reduced its revenue by lowering taxes when the desperate situation demands higher taxation to finance rapid economic growth. Tax revenue has declined from 17.0 per cent of GDP in 1996 to 14.5 per cent of GDP in 2002. It is not too late for the government to take measures to raise public investment —both by higher taxation and foreign borrowing—for that is the best method, as proved by East Asia, of increasing total gross domestic investment, attracting more FDI and achieving high economic growth.

Need for the Public Sector

The state cannot entrust the task of economic development to the market forces and wait patiently for the free market to deliver the goods. In a developing country like Sri Lanka where private enterprise is still generally undeveloped, the state has a responsibility to regulate the market to prevent abuses and to undertake directly a good part of economic development. High economic growth and equitable distribution of opportunities and benefits require a dynamic public sector playing a leading participatory as well as interventionist role in the economy; without it, economic growth can never be pro-people, can never provide them with opportunities for economic and social advancement and can never safeguard the interests of future generations. We have to be conscious of the fact that markets have no conscience and do not promote social justice; it is only the government who can ensure it. This may sound as a heresy to those believing in the Washington Consensus, but as Joseph Stiglitz, the former Chief Economist of the World Bank and economic adviser to President Clinton, pointed out recently, the most successful developing countries are those which have not followed the precepts of the Washington Consensus.

The role of the state in the era of globalization is as important as ever for capturing new opportunities in trade, investment and migration, protecting people from the vulnerability and insecurity created by the market forces, insulating the economy from external shocks, reducing the inequalities in opportunities for human advancement, narrowing wide economic disparities in income and wealth and protecting indigenous culture and the environment. An open economy does not mean that the state should abdicate its crucial role in protecting its people and natural resources; it does not mean dismantling of subsidies, controls and regulations designed to protect, support and promote the country's economic and social interests—to increase domestic food and milk production, to uplift the rural economy, to encourage import substitution while promoting export-oriented industries, to channel foreign capital to nationally important sectors such as electronics, automobiles and heavy industries, to utilize resources of international institutions and transnational corporations without allowing them to dominate domestic trade, industry and economic policy. Increased public spending on education to improve skills and raise productivity, on health and welfare, raise living standards and output and a more content labour force are in fact necessary to attract foreign capital to a country.

It is true that several state-owned corporations are running at a loss; this is not because of state ownership but bad management, for nearly all state-owned firms in East Asia operate at a profit. The fact is that we have politicized public corporations by appointing all officers from the chairman to the labourer for political loyalty than for competence, overstaffed them with cronies and interfered with their policies so that inevitably they operate at a loss; when they are making losses we call them inefficient and call for privatization. Virtually all public corporations can be run efficiently if they are allowed to operate as commercial enterprises freed from political interference; then they can become assets providing revenue to the government as in East Asia.

Public ownership does not discourage foreign investment as the IMF argues. In fact, the *Economist* of 29 September 2001 emphasizes it as : 'As for public ownership, on balance, global capital doesn't much care. Investors lending to publicly owned enterprises may see advantages, in fact, notably government guarantees on the debt. China has many state-owned enterprises, and seems to have no trouble attracting inward investment.'

Critics of public business enterprises conveniently ignore the inefficiency of large private business enterprises. Enron, the 6th largest energy company in the world, crashed in the biggest corporate bankruptcy in US history in December 2001 amid accusations of abysmal mismanagement, dubious accounting, hiding true facts from shareholders and the public, bribing 'auditors' with excessive fees to project a false picture, lies and fraud, with many losing their life savings and jobs. Wall Street's credibility and faith in the free market were shattered. Deregulation suffered a severe blow: if a huge private company like Enron could go bankrupt due to mismanagement and dishonest practices, how could one trust other private companies to provide electricity, gas or water? The *Newsweek* of 10 December 2001 refers to the Enron crash as follows:

> It claimed it would revolutionize life and commerce by substituting the efficient hand of the market for the clumsy hand of government regulation. But Enron's leaders proved to be every bit as bungling as any government bureaucrat. Sift through the financial debris, and you see that Enron lost a total of about $7 billion on four dumb investments ....

As to deregulation/privatization of utilities the same *Newsweek* has this to say:

> But dereg has caused lots of problems. In 1998 the Midwest had huge electricity price hikes and rolling blackouts; some utilities had sold power outside their service areas and the traders they were relying on to replace that power didn't deliver. Upstarts have dropped in and out of retail markets in several states, sticking established players with big costs. And of course, there's California, which got caught with too little energy in the spring (helping Enron and others make big profits) and now is stuck with too much expensive energy. This has crippled the state's finances, driven its biggest utility into bankruptcy and clobbered customers. Leaving vital necessities like electricity and natural gas to the tender mercies of the market is too risky. Especially when a big player like Enron can vanish overnight. (Sloan, 2001)

Further, theoretical and empirical research on privatization does not provide clear and definite support to the IMF view that privatization of state enterprises increases efficiency and contributes to rapid growth. The evidence is mixed; some support it while others reject it. Studies by Martin and Parker conclude, 'Generally the great expectations for privatization evident in Ministerial Speeches have not been borne out.' In reviewing a number of other international studies that compared state and private sector enterprises, they find that the evidence is mixed; there are several studies that point to superior efficiency in the public sector. They conclude: 'In sum, the international studies do not provide unequivocal support for privatization programmes.' John Weiss who studied 500 of the largest enterprises in Mexico in 1985–90, concludes, 'In terms of the influence of ownership, which is the main focus of this analysis, there is no support for the view that state ownership *per se* implies poor performance .... What is clear ... is that the results give no support for privatization of the remaining enterprises on efficiency grounds.'

CONCLUSION

The crux of the matter is that both the public and the private sector are the engines of growth; one alone is inadequate. In a growing economy there is room for both to co-exist. There are enough projects which the private sector can undertake and there are many others, shunned by the private sector, which the state can undertake. Public investment in developing countries complements rather than displaces or crowds out private investment. Both are necessary. As Toynbee has pointed out, every social system in history has been a mixed system combining the public with private enterprise. In our own times, the highest economic growth rates have been achieved by the mixed economies of East Asia.

REFERENCES

Central Bank of Sri Lanka, *Annual Reports*, various issues, Colombo.

Economist, The, 4 August 2001 and 15 December 2001.

Martin, Stephen and David Parker (1997), *The Impact of Privatization: Ownership and Corporate Performance in the UK*, Routledge.

Ministry of Finance (2003), *Budget Speech*, Colombo: Government Printer.

Sen, Amartya and Jean Dreze (1995), *India: Economic Development and Social Opportunity*, New Delhi: Oxford University Press.

Sloan, Allan (2001), 'Free Lessons on Corporate Hubris, Courtesy of Enron', *Newsweek*, 10 December.

Stiglitz, Joseph (2002), *Globalization and its Discontents*, New York: W.W. Norton and Company.

The Government of Ceylon, *Six Year Programme of Investment 1954–1960*.

The Report of the South Commission, 1990, *The Challenge to the South*.

Toynbee, Arnold J. (1948), *Civilization on Trial*, London: Oxford University Press.

UN, *Asian Development Report 2001*.

Weiss, John, 'Mexico: Comparative Performance of State and Private Industrial Corporations'.

SELECT READINGS

Economic and Political Weekly.

Economist, The, September 29 2001.

World Bank (2000 and 2001), *World Investment Reports*, Washington D.C.: World Bank.

————— (2002), *World Development Indicators*, Washington D.C.: World Bank.

Part II

MACROECONOMIC POLICY

6

Current Fiscal Policy

D.D.M. Waidyasekera

Introduction

Sri Lanka's fiscal and tax revenue system is at a critical juncture. While government expenditure has been steadily increasing over time, government revenue has steadily declined creating recurrent fiscal deficits with all their attendant repercussions. During the last six years, total government expenditure and net lending has increased from Rs 268 billion in 1998 to Rs 402 billion in 2002, and Rs 417 billion in 2003, while total government revenue has only increased from Rs 175 billion to Rs 261 billion and Rs 275 billion respectively.

The overall deficits amounted to 9.2 per cent of gross domestic product (GDP) in 1998, 10.8 per cent in 2001, 8.9 per cent in 2002 and 8 per cent in 2003 with the total public debt increasing to an unprecedented 105 per cent of GDP (Central Bank, 2003). While this situation calls for the rationalization of government expenditure, it also calls for far-reaching policy measures to expand the revenue base. One important reason why taxation is essential in getting macroeconomic policies right is that alternative ways of financing government expenditure—money creation, mandating larger required reserves, domestic borrowing and foreign loans—can have very harmful effects on the economy. These required policy measures in respect of the fiscal and taxation system have evoked considerable controversy and debate. This chapter aims to focus on and analyse some of the main issues relating to the fiscal and taxation policies currently prevalent in Sri Lanka.

Functions of a Fiscal and Tax System in a Developing Economy

A fiscal and taxation system has several functions to perform in an economy, particularly in a developing economy like Sri Lanka. First, its primary function is to raise revenue for the government for its public expenditure, as well as for local authorities and similar public bodies. Its efficiency is therefore primarily judged by whether this function is performed adequately and satisfactorily. A second function is to reduce inequalities through a policy of redistribution of income and wealth. The equity principle in taxation implies that taxes should be imposed in accordance with the ability to pay. This has two dimensions: (*a*) horizontal equity, i.e., similar treatment of persons in similar circumstances and (*b*) vertical equity, i.e., different treatment of persons with different taxable capacity. Third, the fiscal system is also employed for social purposes such as discouraging certain activities which are considered undesirable. Excise duties on liquor and tobacco, the special excises on luxury and semi-luxury goods, the Betting and Gaming Levy in Sri Lanka are examples of such taxes.

The tax system can also be used to increase the level of savings and capital formation in the private sector. In addition, it can also protect local industries from foreign competition through the use of import duties, turnover taxes/value added tax (VAT) and excises. Taxation is also used as an instrument of demand management to eliminate an inflationary or deflationary gap in the economy. Taxation reduces the effect of the multiplier and so can be used to dampen upswings in a trade cycle.[1] Finally, the tax and fiscal system is used to achieve economic growth through its influence on the allocation of resources. This includes:

- transferring resources from the private sector to the government to finance the public investment programme;
- directing private investment into desired channels through such measures as regulation of tax rates and the granting of tax incentives;
- influencing relative factor prices for enhanced uses of labour and economizing the use of capital and foreign exchange.

These objectives may, however, to some degree, be in conflict. For example, the achievement of a more equitable distribution of income may conflict with growth objectives and in practice there are always some trade-offs or compromise.

How adequately and effectively has the fiscal and tax system in Sri Lanka performed these functions? How effective have the policy and administrative measures been in solving the problems that have arisen? These are some of the questions that have become issues in the current policy debate. The sections of the chapter that follow attempt to raise and throw some light on some of the major issues in this debate.

DECLINING TREND IN GOVERNMENT REVENUE

One of the alarming issues that has arisen is the continuing decline in the trend of government revenue. Table 6.1 indicates the trend in government revenue in terms of GDP from 1990 to 2002.

Table 6.1

TRENDS IN GOVERNMENT REVENUE, 1990–2002, AS PERCENTAGE OF GDP

	1990	1991	1992	1993	1994	1995	1996	1997	1998	1999	2000	2001	2002
Total revenue	21.1	20.4	20.1	19.6	19	20.4	19	18.5	17.2	17.7	16.8	16.7	16.5
Tax revenue	19	18.3	17.9	17.2	17.1	17	17	16	14.5	15.0	14.5	14.6	14
Non-tax revenue	2.1	2.2	2.2	2.4	1.8	2.7	2.1	2.5	2.7	2.7	2.3	2	2.5

Source: Central Bank of Sri Lanka, *Annual Reports*, various issues.

As indicated in the table, total government revenue has declined steadily from 21.1 per cent in 1990 to 20.4 per cent in 1995, 17.7 per cent in 1999 and 16.5 per cent in 2002. Tax revenue has fallen from 19 per cent in 1990 to 17.7 per cent in 1995, 15 per cent in 1999 and 14 per cent in 2002. Even non-tax revenue comprising profits and dividend transfers from public enterprises, interest, rent and social security contributions has shown a decline from 2.7 per cent in 1995 to 2.5 per cent in 2002.

The trend of government revenue is illustrated graphically in Figure 6.1.

Figure 6.1

TRENDS IN GOVERNMENT REVENUE AS PERCENTAGE OF GDP

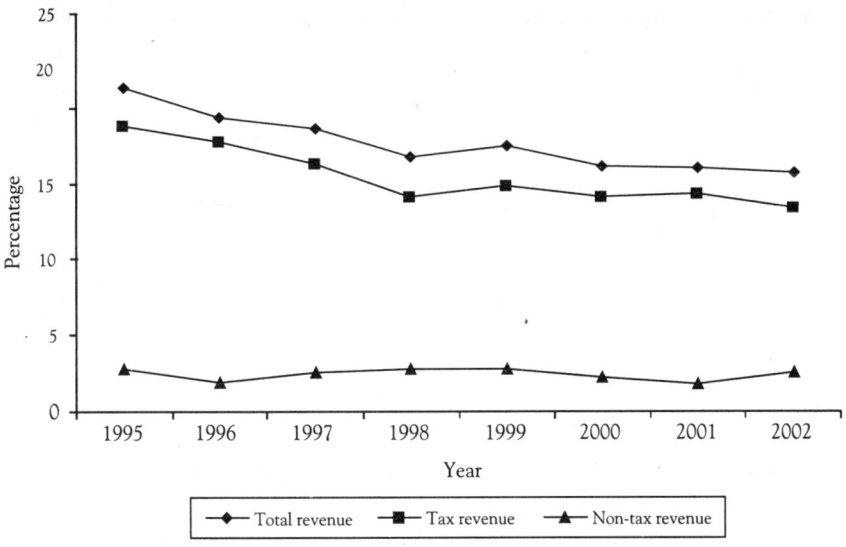

Source: Compiled from Table 6.1.

Component-wise there are two features noticeable in this trend. One is the relative insignificance of the direct taxes in relation to the indirect taxes and second, the declining trend in Goods and Services Tax (GST)/VAT and import duties. Only the excise duties and the National Security Levy (NSL) have shown an increase and held their own due largely to the periodic increases in their coverage and rates.

REASONS FOR THE DECLINE

These trends are a result of many factors both external and internal. In the external sphere, there was a decline in world economic growth. For instance, the growth of world output had slowed down to a dismal 2.3 per cent in 2001 and 3 per cent in 2002 with recessions in the US, the European Union and Japan and world trade, which had expanded in 2000 by about 12.5 per cent, slowed down to about 8 per cent in 2001. With the liberalization of the economy and the accent on export oriented growth, these trends had an adverse effect on the balance of payments and national income in Sri Lanka, with resultant impact on domestic tax revenues.

The endogenous factors are many and varied. Briefly, they include the following:

1. The variety of unplanned and ad hoc fiscal and tax exemptions, incentives, concessions and reliefs which have eroded and narrowed the fiscal base.
2. The increase in the exemption threshold and the reduction in income tax and duty rates.
3. Lack of elasticity and buoyancy in the fiscal system.
4. Complexity in tax legislation and lack of fiscal consistency.
5. The imposition of various ill-planned ad hoc fiscal policy measures such as the grant of regular tax amnesties.
6. Weaknesses in revenue administration.

However, it must be noted that the ability of governments to raise revenue is just one among many factors that influence growth. Economic growth is more closely associated with productivity growth and economic efficiency than with tax effort. It could very well be that growth is the cause and the revenue ratio the effect. Nevertheless, other things being equal, improved government finance is inevitably linked and is a sine qua non to improved economic performance.

ROLE OF INCOME TAXES

In developed countries, direct taxes such as the income tax constitute a significant portion of total tax revenues, while indirect taxes such as the taxes on international trade and on domestic goods and services play a relatively less significant role. By contrast, in the developing countries the opposite is the case with the bulk of government revenue coming from indirect taxes such as customs duties, VAT or sales taxes and excise duties, while direct taxes are of lesser importance.

In Sri Lanka income taxes comprise on average only 15 per cent of tax revenue or 2.3 per cent of GDP as compared to 65 per cent from taxes on domestic goods and services or 9.4 per cent of GDP. Table 6.2 gives the share of the income taxes both personal and corporate for the period 1998–2002.

Table 6.2

INCOME TAXES, 1998–2002

(rupees million)

	1998			1999			2000			2001			2002		
	Amount Rs	% of Tax Revenue	% of GDP	Amount Rs	% of Tax Revenue	% of GDP	Amount Rs	% of Tax Revenue	% of GDP	Amount Rs	% of Tax Revenue	% of GDP	Amount Rs	% of Tax Revenue	% of GDP
Personal	8,099	5.5	0.8	9,169	5.5	0.8	10,820	6	0.9	12,203	5.9	0.9	12,172	5.5	0.8
Corporate	11,788	8	1.2	18,362	11	1.7	15,757	8.6	1.3	18,673	9	1.3	13,934	6.2	0.9
Tax on interest	—	—	—	—	—	—	—	—	—	2,733	1.3	0.2	11,513	5.2	0.7
Total	19,887	13.5	2.0	27,531	16.5	2.5	26,577	14.6	2.2	33,609	16.2	2.4	37,619	16.9	2.4

Source: Central Bank of Sri Lanka, *Annual Report, 2002.*
Note: Excludes Save the Nation Contribution.

Should Income Tax be Abolished?

This paucity of the taxes on income relative to the indirect taxes such as VAT, excises and import duties has led to a policy debate as to whether it is worth having income tax at all and whether income tax should be abolished.

The main argument put forward for its abolition is that taxes on income act as a deterrent to saving, both personal and corporate, and that it penalizes both saving and investment. Its abolition would help to increase savings particularly in the corporate sector, which in turn would stimulate greater investment and economic growth. It is argued that in the context of a developing country where the primary focus should be on rapid economic development, the equity considerations inherent in the income tax should give way to economic growth as a priority. Further, collection and administration of income taxes is both cumbersome and dilatory, often with considerable litigation and harassment of taxpayers. The revenue yield is relatively small in comparison to the other taxes and the revenue loss from its abolition could be recouped through increase in the consumption taxes. The basic premise of this argument is that there should be a policy shift from direct taxation to indirect taxation in the interest of savings, investment and economic growth.

On the other hand, it is argued that the premise that increased disposable income would automatically lead to investment is not entirely valid. Investment depends on a number of factors and variables both endogenous and exogenous, and such disposable income may very well end up in increased consumption, particularly in a consumerist society, rather than on investment. Second, as economic development takes place, the role of income taxation becomes important as witnessed in all the economically developed countries where taxes on income represent the major source of government revenue. Third, income tax is a major tax handle in all fiscal systems in the world except in tax havens such as the Bahamas, Isle of Man, Cayman Islands, etc., which have been blacklisted for money laundering, smuggling, drug peddling, terrorist financing, etc. Abolition of income tax would put Sri Lanka into this blacklist with all its attendant consequences. Fourth, income tax is a progressive tax based on a person's ability to pay in contrast to the consumption taxes which are essentially regressive in character and impose a tax burden on the consumer irrespective of his ability to bear it. Equity purposes therefore demand that there should be some tax on income.

The Taxation Commission of 1990 which examined this issue very carefully concluded, 'Despite its diminishing contribution to government revenue, income tax has a positive role to play in Sri Lanka's tax system and we see very little merit in the suggestions made to abolish it altogether. It is a progressive tax based on a person's ability to pay, and its abolition would be a retrograde step. It will also deprive the country of a tax handle with important future potential' (GOSL, 1991: 93).

Abolition of Personal Income Tax

Consequently, the debate shifted to abolition of income tax only on personal income leaving the corporate sector intact. Personal income tax brought in only 5.5 per cent of the total tax revenue or 0.8 per cent of GDP. Its abolition would be a measure of relief to individuals already hard pressed by rising costs of living and would also relieve the revenue administration of a lot of routine work. Such a limited measure would not affect government revenue from the corporate sector. It would also remove the inequity of exempting one set of individuals, for example public servants, while taxing other sections.

This argument has considerable merit. Its imposition, however, could lead to a number of problems. Individuals do not mean only employees but include persons who receive profits and income from other sources such as agriculture, trade, businesses and professions. Sole proprietorships and partnerships are also taxable on an individual basis and all such traders and businessmen as well as professionals like lawyers and doctors, etc., would be entitled to tax exemption.

Second, taxing the corporate sector while exempting individual trades and businesses would tend to encourage companies to transform themselves into sole proprietorships or partnerships. The corporate form of business organization has several advantages over the non-corporate form, but whether such advantages would prevail over the attraction of not paying taxes on profits depends on the circumstances. While limited liability public companies would probably not be affected, private companies, many of which are family concerns, may be encouraged to do so. The number of companies registered for tax purposes as on 31 December 2002 was 19,186 resident companies and 246 non-resident companies. Out of this, there were only 240 public limited liability companies listed in the Stock Exchange.[2] The balance, the vast majority, are all private companies most of them being family concerns. Exemption of personal taxation would certainly lead to a majority of these private companies transforming themselves into sole proprietorships or partnerships for the purpose of avoiding taxation.

A third problem concerns directors' salaries. Directors of companies are, for tax purposes, considered employees. Exemption of such income could lead to a situation where company profits could be siphoned off by enhancing directors' salaries either nominally or otherwise, thereby avoiding or minimizing the company's tax liability.

Exemption of Public Sector Emoluments

At present, exemption from income tax is granted on the official emoluments and pensions of certain categories of persons. These include public officers, judicial officers, employees of provincial and local authorities, corporation employees, university employees, employees of Boards or Commissions appointed by the President or a Minister. The exemption also includes, apart from the President, Ministers, Parliamentarians and Governors of Provinces, members of Provincial Councils and local authorities.

The rationale advanced for this exemption when it was first introduced in 1979, was that the salaries of these categories of employees were much lower than those in the private sector, particularly for employees with similar qualifications and shouldering similar responsibilities in the managerial and professional grades. They were also not in receipt of the many benefits and perquisites which their counterparts in the private sector enjoyed. As an alternative to increasing the salaries of persons in the professional and managerial grades to a level equivalent with those in the private sector, the government exempted public sector salaries from income tax.

This situation has been a source of debate for quite some time and many are of the view that the present position is full of inequities and unjustifiable, particularly when employees in the other sectors are liable to tax under the Pay As You Earn (PAYE) system. In respect of government and corporation employees, the salary disparities have been considerably narrowed, while the salaries of employees of state banks are comparable to those paid to their counterparts in other commercial banks.

The inequity is compounded if both spouses are in receipt of exempt income. Further, the exemption of the salary makes it difficult to submit other incomes to the proper marginal tax rate. This latter anomaly has, however, now been rectified by means of a special employment tax credit from 1 April 2003 by the Inland Revenue Amendment Act No. 37 of 2003.

Though various International Monetary Fund (IMF) missions and the Taxation Commission Report 1990 itself recommended that the exemption be removed, so far it has not been done. Such removal would, however, necessitate a compensatory adjustment to ensure that the net of tax salary or pension would remain unchanged. The other option, for the sake of equity, would be to exempt the emoluments of all employees including private sector employees under PAYE. The total number of employees under PAYE as on 31 December 2001 was 2,21,003 and revenue collected from PAYE for 2001 was Rs 5,946 million and Rs 5,103 million in 2002 (DIR Administration Reports 2001 and 2002).

THE DEBATE ON THE RATE STRUCTURE

In the years following independence in 1948 when rapid economic development was the priority, the indigenous entrepreneurial sections in Sri Lanka had neither the resources nor the ability to undertake the lead role in development. It was thus left to the state to undertake the public investment programme necessary to lay the foundation for rapid economic growth, particularly in the areas of infrastructure, industries, agriculture and irrigation, banking and finance.

The development and maintenance of such public investment programmes necessitated a high level of savings and government revenue. This resulted in the recourse to high tax and duty rates, a variety of taxes and a complicated fiscal system. Sri Lanka has been a veritable guinea pig for tax experiments. Taxes and levies have been introduced and abandoned, some after a few years and one even after one day. There was the Kaldor scheme[3] in 1959 involving Expenditure, Wealth, Gifts and Land Taxes, the Capital Levy (1971), National Development Tax (1961–62), Surtax (1962), Registration of Businesses and Professions Levy (1961–62), Compulsory Savings (1971–75), Gifts Tax (1959–85) and even a Sales Tax on 1 August 1962 which lasted only one day. The marginal tax rates were high during this period, the corporate rate going up to 60 per cent in 1978 and the personal tax rate to 80 per cent in 1964.

With the economic liberalization of 1977 and a reversal of fiscal strategies, the taxation policies were changed to one of broadening the base and lowering the rates. The marginal rates were progressively reduced with the standard corporate rate from 1 April 2003 being 32.5 per cent (inclusive of 2.5 per cent contribution to the Human Resource Endowment Fund) and with a lower rate of 20 per cent for small companies.[4] The marginal personal tax rate has also been reduced from 1 April 2003 to 30 per cent, all under the latest Inland Revenue (Amendment) Act No. 37 of 2003.

The current debate revolves around whether the tax and duty rates have been lowered too far or whether they should be lowered still further. With the private sector deemed as the engine of growth and expected to take the lead role in economic development, it is argued that tax rates should be sufficiently low to attract private investment, both local and foreign, and that the standard rate should be lowered still further to the officially proposed rate of 20 per cent by 2004.

These arguments are based largely on supply-side economics as expounded by such economists as Milton Friedman and Jude Wanniski and based on what is known as the Laffer Curve, named after Alfred Laffer. Taxes, in this view, are a major constraint to economic effort and investment and if they are drastically reduced, production will expand and public revenues rise. Studies of selected countries also seemed to indicate that those that imposed a lower effective average tax burden achieved substantially higher rates of growth in real GDP than did their more highly taxed counterparts.

However, supply side economics and the Laffer Curve have had their critics like Paul W. McCraken, Paul Krugman and John Kenneth Galbraith. They have questioned the assumption and theory behind the Laffer Curve and proved that it is not as scientific as it appears. The supply side cuts of the early 1980s in the US do not appear to have raised work effort or saving and they unquestionably increased the deficit. As implied by David Stockman,[5] the supply side vision was simply a cover for the reduction of taxes of the upper income tax brackets. Further, empirical studies carried out in two countries, Jamaica and India where tax changes relevant to the Laffer Curve had been implemented, have also concluded that the assertion that tax reductions would lead to revenue increase should at best be treated with caution (Ebrill, 1987). It is therefore doubtful whether, as argued by some, tax cuts are a panacea or will serve as a 'quick fix' for a sick economy. A fiscal policy based on the 'trickle down' theory of development has its resultant defects. An analysis of the patterns of income distribution in Sri Lanka has shown that the upper income deciles have benefited more and the lower deciles have had their incomes reduced through these policies. This is also confirmed by the Gini ratio which measures the degree of income concentration.

As far as attracting foreign direct investment (FDI) is concerned, it is contended that the status of tax rates as compared to other variables is not appreciably relevant in attracting FDI. In developed countries tax rates are much higher than the 32.5 per cent rate in Sri Lanka as for example in Canada, Japan, Italy, Belgium, the US, France, Germany and the Netherlands. Yet three-quarters of the world's FDI flows to the developed countries while, in spite of low tax regimes, countries in Asia, Latin America and Africa receive relatively far lesser amounts. A publication by the South Centre on FDI states that 'the locational advantages such as market size and growth, production costs, skill levels, political and economic stability and the regulatory framework' are relatively more important and suggests that developing countries would have gained more had they focused on improving the general business environment.[6]

In Sri Lanka, in spite of the declared policy of lowering the tax and duty rates further, fiscal decline has led to the government taking recourse to ad hoc measures of increasing the effective tax and duty rates. A surcharge of 20 per cent on corporate tax was levied in 2001, in effect increasing the corporate tax rate to 42 per cent till it was abolished in 2002–03. A surcharge of 40 per cent effective from 21 February 2001 was imposed on customs duty which was reduced to 20 per cent from 15 April 2002 and 10 per cent from 1 January 2004.

Thus, in spite of the officially declared low tax regime, the government can and does raise the effective tax and duty rates if and when necessary by means of the surcharge. Apart from the surcharge, the government has also taken recourse to the imposition of new taxes and levies such as the Debit tax on bank transactions from 1 May 2002, the VAT on financial services from 1 January 2003, the Port and Airport Development Levy from 1 May 2002, the increase in the Embarkation Tax to Rs 1,500 from 1 September 2003 and the Economic Service Charge from 1 April 2004.

TAX RATES, CAPITAL FORMATION AND INVESTMENT

While overall fiscal strategy has an impact on private sector investment, taxes can be singled out as a key variable that affects private sector investment decisions. The debate in this area revolves round whether and to what extent marginal tax rates affect savings, capital formation and investment. Table 6.3 provides statistics relating to marginal tax rates, domestic savings, gross domestic capital formation and investment in Sri Lanka over a time period from 1960 to 2002.

It is difficult to establish a direct and precise statistical correlation between income tax rates and domestic savings, capital formation and private investment. This is due to several factors such as the time lag, changes in the tax base and other externalities and variables that determine savings, capital formation and investment. Nevertheless, the empirical and statistical trends tend to suggest that savings, private capital formation and private investment have been sensitive to effective tax incidence.

During the period 1960–78 when the marginal tax rates, both individual and corporate were high (the corporate rate ranged from 45 to 60 per cent and individual rate from 60 to 80 per cent) private savings, capital formation and private investment ratios were relatively low. The major part of the investment was public investment. With the progressive lowering of the tax rates from the 1980s onwards, all three ratios tended to pick up though with a time lag. However, too much significance cannot be attached to the movement of the marginal tax rates alone as there are a number of other important

Table 6.3

TAX RATES, SAVINGS, CAPITAL FORMATION AND INVESTMENT, 1960–2002

Year (i)	Marginal Tax Rate		Domestic Savings Ratio % of GDP[a] (iv)	Gross Domestic Capital Formation % of GDP[b] (v)	Investment Ratio % of GDP[c] (vi)
	Individuals (ii)	Companies (iii)			
1960	60	45	11.7	13.2	10.0
1964	80	57	12.3	14.2	9.9
1969	65	50	13.0	19.2	14.9
1978	70	60	15.3	13.9	13.6
1980	55	50	11.2	26.7[d]	25.2[e]
1988	40	50	12.0	16.9	16.8
1990	40	50	14.3	18.2	18.2
1995	35	35	15.3	22.2	22.1
1998	35	35	19.1	21.7	21.7
1999	35	35	19.5	24.1	24.1
2000	35	35	17.4	24.7	24.7
2001	35	35	15.8	19.0	18.0
2002	35	35	14.6	19.3	19.2

Sources: Central Bank of Sri Lanka, *Annual Reports*, various issues.
Department of Inland Revenue, *Administration Reports*, various issues.

Notes: [a] Includes government, public corporations and private savings.
[b] Private sector and corporations, excludes government and public sector enterprises.
[c] Private and state sponsored corporations, excludes government.
[d] Includes Mahaweli Development Schemes and other lead projects.
[e] The correlation coefficient between (iii) and (v) works out to −0.566, and between (iii) and (vi) to −0.617.

factors that affect savings, capital formation and investment. Correlation between variables do not prove causation. Nevertheless, it seems logical to conclude that to promote savings, capital formation and private investment, the avoidance of prohibitive rates of taxation and their reduction to reasonable levels is necessary, though not by itself a sufficient condition.

It may also be noted that the correlation coefficient between the marginal corporate tax rate and Gross Domestic Capital Formation (GDCF) ratio for this period works out to approximately −0.566 and the correlation coefficient between the marginal corporate rate and the Investment Ratio (IR) to −0.617. Both these coefficients are statistically significant.

ELASTICITY AND BUOYANCY OF THE FISCAL SYSTEM

One of the main reasons for the decline in government and tax revenue in Sri Lanka in spite of periodic recourse to a variety of taxes and levies, is the inherent lack of elasticity and buoyancy in the fiscal system.

Elasticity in a tax system reflects the built-in responsiveness of tax revenue to movements in national income or GDP. Buoyancy reflects the total response of tax revenues to changes in national incomes or GDP including the effects of an expansion in the tax base, increases in tax rates and other discretionary changes in fiscal policies over time. An elastic system will automatically raise revenue at the same or at a faster rate than the growth of national income (or GDP) and facilitate a sustained increase in necessary government outlays. These, in turn, tend to keep pace with the general economic growth. An elastic tax system also reduces the economic uncertainties associated with frequent discretionary changes in taxes, duties and levies.

An inelastic fiscal system, on the other hand, compels the government to rely on frequent ad hoc increases in order to maintain short-term revenue objectives. Such practices over a period of time produce a complex and economically unproductive fiscal system and lead to adverse economic effects and unintended distributional consequences. Frequent ad hoc changes in fiscal policies also create uncertainties among taxpayers and affect investment and production adversely.

In the Sri Lankan fiscal system the elasticity has been estimated at 0.7. The buoyancy coefficient is slightly higher, estimated at 0.9, but both coefficients are below unity. Overall, the tax and fiscal system is inelastic in Sri Lanka (GOSL, 1991: 75).

THE ROLE OF CONSUMPTION TAXES

The consumption taxes in the form of customs duties, turnover taxes, GST/VAT and the excises have increased in importance over the years and now comprise the preponderant part of government revenue. This is reflected in the figures given in Table 6.4 and illustrated in Figure 6.2.

Table 6.4

CONSUMPTION TAXES AND DUTIES 1998–2002 IN RS MILLION

	1998		1999		2000		2001		2002	
	Amt	% Share	Amt	% Share	Amt	% Share	Amt	% Share	Amt	% Share
Turnover taxes	16,166	10.9	1,799	1	1,708	0.9	1,119	0.5	733	0.3
GST/VAT	23,177	15.7	35,540	21.4	43,893	23.5	45,900	22.3	66,458	29.9
Excise duties	30,293	20.5	35,928	21.6	42,655	23.3	44,978	21.8	52,099	23.4
National Security Levy (NSL)	21,079	14.3	28,127	16.9	33,539	18.3	43,065	20.9	28,695	12.9
Import duties	28,154	19.1	27,720	16.6	23,970	13.1	26,156	12.7	28,307	12.7

Source: Central Bank of Sri Lanka, Annual Report, 2002.
Note: The NSL and the GST were amalgamated to form a VAT effective from August 2002.

Figure 6.2

REVENUE BY COMPONENT 2002

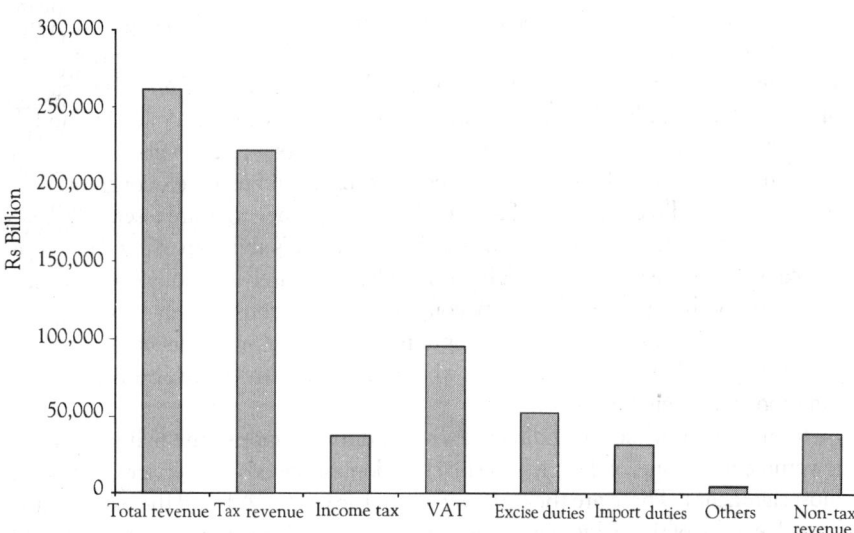

Source: Compiled from Central Bank of Sri Lanka, *Annual Report,* 2002.
Notes: VAT comprises the combined VAT inclusive of GST and NSL levied for part of the year. Others include Stamp Duties and Debit Tax.

As can be seen, the indirect taxes comprise over three-quarters, almost 80 per cent of government tax revenue. A further feature is the relative decline in the import duties from 19.1 per cent in 1998 to 12.7 per cent in 2002 and the growing importance of the taxes on domestic goods and services which bring in over two-thirds of the revenue.

The debate on the role of indirect taxes revolves round two basic issues. First, have the consumption taxes reached saturation point in the Sri Lankan fiscal system or can they be expanded further and to what extent? Second, has the VAT system proved effective and met the expected goals compared to the turnover taxes and the GST which it replaced? The answers to these questions require a detailed analysis of the problems involved and constitute a separate exercise by itself. This section of the chapter can only attempt to briefly highlight some of the issues in this debate.

Pros and Cons of Levying Consumption Taxes

First, there are pros and cons in levying indirect taxes. The main arguments in their favour are that their yield is substantial, individuals are given a choice and they reduce disincentive effects. There is also the added attraction that the public is less conscious of the tax burden as the taxes are generally hidden in the prices and their presence is not readily felt by the consumer. Since indirect taxes are paid piecemeal when a taxpayer enters into some transaction, it is convenient and less burdensome.

Consumption taxes avoid penalizing saving and investment and are generally neutral between savings and spending. Indirect taxes are also perhaps the only means of reaching the vast majority of the population whom the tax net often fails to capture and the informal or hard-to-tax activities. Indirect taxes are easily collectible and the proportion of administrative costs in collecting these taxes is relatively low. They are also often not affected by economic crises and thus remain relatively constant.

However, indirect taxes also have their demerits. Since they are essentially based on consumption they do not take into account a person's ability to pay and hence are basically regressive in character. They do not lend themselves readily to measures in progressivity though the regressivity could be reduced considerably by the use of a discriminatory rate structure and exemption of essential items. Indirect taxes are also generally passed on to the consumer, who ultimately bears the tax burden, and are inflationary in their effects.

In Sri Lanka, while the indirect taxes and duties comprise the major portion of government revenue, of these it is the taxes on domestic goods and services that are the most significant. These are the turnover taxes, the GST/VAT and the excise duties. The objectives of these different types of levies on goods and services are envisaged as the import duty being primarily the instrument of protection, the turnover tax/GST/VAT for revenue purposes and the broadened excise duty for both revenue and social purposes. Have these levies in their present form and content reached saturation point or can they be used further by either expanding their base or increasing their rates or both?

GST/VAT

The VAT system was an amalgamation of the NSL and the GST; it attempted to broaden the base by reducing the number of exemptions and introduced a differential rate schedule of 20 and 10 per cent apart from the zero rate. The dual rate was subsequently unified to a single rate of 15 per cent from 1 January 2004. It has, however, created several complications and increased prices on a number of items, thus adding to the cost of living. In this context, it is difficult to envisage a situation where the VAT rates could be further increased, particularly as any additional revenue by this measure would be considerably reduced by a corresponding increase of the input tax, which is deductible from the output tax payable.

As far as the tax base is concerned, some modifications such as the contemplated re-introduction of a 25 per cent mark up on calculation of output tax at import point may be feasible, but their net effects may not be appreciable. Since the VAT has already been extended to the hitherto exempted financial services sector, the only feasible area of expanding the base and coverage would be the wholesale and retail trading sector, which is presently exempt from VAT and which is liable only to the 1 per cent tax to Provincial Councils. The wholesale and retail trading sector comprise about 22 per cent of GDP of which the exempted domestic sector is about 10 per cent.

Its inclusion into the VAT system has been officially recognized but not yet implemented. It would, however, require some revenue sharing arrangement with the provincial authorities. It would also create some administrative problems with an anticipated 30,000 new tax files being opened.

Tariffs

As far as the tariffs are concerned, the prospects of expanding customs duties appears to be limited. In Sri Lanka, export duties were tailed off with the duties on tea, rubber and coconut abolished in 1992 and on all remaining items in 1993. The import duties are now used not so much for revenue as for protective purposes. A rationalization of the tariff system on the basis of the Tariff Commission recommendations has been in progress during the last 10 years, reducing it to a two-band structure of 10 and 25 per cent. However, the tariff regime has again become complicated with the 35 per cent band on some agricultural products, and two new tariff bands of 2 and 20 per cent introduced in November 2002 mainly out of revenue considerations. There was also a surcharge of 40 per cent imposed in February 2001, which was subsequently reduced to 20 per cent from 15 April 2002 and 10 per cent from 1 January 2004. The surcharge was, however, only partly a revenue measure and was more an attempt to curb the import of non-essential and sumptuous goods with a view to improving the trade balance and the balance of payments.

   The revenue from import duties has shown a declining trend from 19.1 per cent in 1998 to 12.7 per cent in 2002 (see Table 6.4). The average import duty (the effective rate)[7] without the impact of the surcharge in 2002 was 4.8 per cent. It is therefore argued that if no exemptions are given to importers, a flat rate of 5 per cent would be sufficient to maintain the level of revenue collected from import duties.

   The trend of lowering tariffs is also the result of international agreements like the World Trade Organisation (WTO), the South Asian Preferential Trade Arrangement (SAPTA) and the Indo-Sri Lanka Free Trade Agreement (ILFTA). In view of these developments, the further scope for expansion of import duties appears to be limited.

Excises

Of all the consumption taxes, the scope for further expansion appears to be mainly in the excise duties. Excise duty is one of the oldest taxes having been introduced by the Excise Ordinance No. 8 of 1912 and recently broadened by the Excise (Special Provisions) Act No. 13 of 1989. They are based partly on a specific basis and partly on an ad valorem basis. The share of excise duties has remained high in total tax revenues, second only to the GST/VAT and bringing in 23.4 per cent of tax revenue in 2002. Given the relative price inelasticity of demand for liquor and tobacco products on which most of the excise duties are levied, they have been subject to frequent rate increases and hence have proved to be an effective tax handle to generate government revenue. There is also greater scope for utilizing the Special Excises to include more items of a luxury or semi-luxury character.

Excise duties, if properly administered, could therefore be utilized to further expand government tax revenues without affecting incentives for savings, investment and production. However, its ultimate effectiveness would depend on several factors like the identification of excisable items, an appropriate rate structure, a rational system of classification and valuation and last, but not least, a properly organized effective administrative network.

THE VAT DEBATE

The other major issue in the debate on consumption taxes is the effectiveness of the VAT system in meeting its objectives and its impact on consumers. Sri Lanka originally had a multi-rate cascading turnover tax since 1964, which was amended in 1981 to include imports and with a partial credit system on inputs used in manufacturing to reduce cascading effects. The regressivity of this tax was mitigated by exempting basic items of mass consumption and charging higher rates on luxury items and lower rates on essential items. The turnover tax regime was flexible as it could be changed by means of gazette notification, thereby enabling policy planners to readily adjust the tax to suit changing fiscal conditions. As a revenue earner, it produced the revenue the government expected of it without difficulty.

The turnover tax was abolished in April 1998 with the introduction of a value added system in the form of a GST which was later transformed into a VAT in August 2002. There is no doubt that in principle a VAT system is superior to other forms of sales taxation. It achieves neutrality between methods of production and between propensities to save and consume. It permits lower and fewer rates, minimizes distortions in resource allocation and is transparent, thereby enabling the tax content of a price to be known. Above all, a VAT system eliminates the cascading effects of a turnover tax and through its in-built, self-enforcing and cross-checking mechanism is more suitable for administrative purposes. For these reasons, about 120 countries have adopted this system as one of the main sources of revenue.

The VAT system in the form of the GST was a consumption type tax with full credit given for all inputs including capital goods. It was levied on an invoice basis with input tax separately specified and was based on the destination principle. A single rate of 12.5 per cent was applied to all goods and services except exports which were zero-rated. It had a high threshold of Rs 5,00,000 per quarter or Rs1.8 million per annum. However, the revenue yield of the GST was disappointing due to several reasons. These included the exclusion of the wholesale and retail trading sector and the financial services, the large list of exemptions, the less than neutral rate of 12.5 per cent, the refund mechanism and a myriad administrative problems. To compensate for this, the government made use of another turnover tax, the NSL whose coverage and rates were periodically increased as and when required by fiscal conditions.

These two levies were amalgamated in August 2002 and termed the VAT under the VAT Act No. 14 of 2002. It was expected that this modified form of the VAT would eliminate the weaknesses in the GST and bring in the required revenue expected. The main differences between the GST and the VAT are:

1. The VAT had two positive rates (apart from the zero rate) instead of the single 12.5 per cent in GST. This was subsequently unified into a single rate of 15 per cent from January 2004.
2. The VAT exemption schedule is much more limited than the GST schedule with several items being taxable, thus broadening the VAT base to include items such as sugar, dried fish, maldive fish, etc., which were made taxable.
3. Under VAT the excess of input tax is refunded instead of carrying it forward as in the GST.
4. There were a number of additions to zero rating.
5. The deferment provisions were extended to certain other transactions and situations.

The other principles and provisions enumerated in the VAT are basically the same as under the GST. The debate revolves round how effective the VAT has been in removing the distortions of the GST, in meeting its revenue goals and relieving the burden on the consumer.

Price Impact

On the one hand, although there were changes in relative prices, the introduction of VAT has had a favourable impact on the general price level. One of the basic reasons was that several essential commodities such as rice, wheat flour, pharmaceuticals, etc., that form a major portion of the consumption basket that were subject to either GST or NSL or both, were exempted under VAT. Another reason was that the base of the VAT at import point was not computed with the addition of a 25 per cent markup that was levied under the NSL on imports. As a result, the effective rate of tax under VAT is less than under the GST and NSL system on imports.

On the other hand, it is pointed out that with the broadening of the VAT base, a number of items that were hitherto exempted under GST or NSL or both had been made taxable, either at 10 per cent or even at the 20 per cent rate band and 15 per cent from Jauary 2004. These include such items as tea, coconut poonac, rock phosphate, electricity between 30 and 90 kWh, thus increasing the prices of these commodities and services.

In respect of financial services which were originally exempt under both the GST and VAT, a VAT was imposed from 1 January 2003.[8] This was not based on the output less input method but on the addition method of profits plus wages in computing value added.[9] Under this method there is no deduction for input taxes paid. Though the government explicitly indicated that financial institutions are not supposed to pass the tax on to the consumers, it is highly unlikely that banks and financial institutions will refrain from increasing their finance charges and passing this liability on to their customers.

Revenue

In terms of revenue, the VAT has not shown any improvement over the GST. Tax revenue from GST, NSL and VAT on domestic goods and services fell from 3.3 per cent of GDP in 2001 to 3.1 per cent in 2002, while the combined revenue (including imports) collected from GST, NSL and VAT fell to 6 per cent in 2002 from 6.3 per cent in 2001 (Central Bank Report, 2002: 181). In 2003 while the estimated VAT revenue was Rs 120 billion, the actual collection was only Rs 97 billion (Central Bank Report, 2003: 170).

The main reasons for the shortfall in VAT revenue include:

1. The structural changes made in the VAT in contrast to the GST as, for example, granting refunds of excess input tax instead of carrying it forward as under GST; additions to zero rating and extension of deferment procedure.

2. Anomalies in the application of VAT. For example, some sectors such as the construction industry became liable to lower rates under VAT than under GST and NSL. Certain final goods and services such as construction and leasing were liable to VAT at 10 per cent, while inputs into those sectors were liable at 20 per cent. This enabled suppliers to claim higher input credits on purchases than VAT payable on sales. This anamoly was reduced to some extent by limiting the input credit to the rate of output tax payable in October 2003 and subsequently rectified by changing to a single rate of 15 per cent from 1 January 2004.

3. Leakages arising from the grant of refunds. Excess input tax under VAT is not carried forward as under GST and all excess taxes have now to be refunded in time. Thus, there is a large refund element particularly in respect of exporters, tea factories, garments, hotels, leasing and construction sectors. The proportion of refunds to total tax collection increased from 12 per cent under GST to 20 per cent under VAT. The revenue estimates have been drastically affected by these refunds.

Compliance and Administration

VAT is a complicated system for both taxpayers and the administration. There are complex procedural obligations for registered VAT payers such as registration, keeping of records, issue of tax invoices, calculation of output tax, etc. Hence compliance rates are low and there are many large firms who deduct the input taxes but do not remit the tax due to the DIR, hence affecting the departmental revenue performance.

VAT type of taxes are not easy to administer. It necessitates effective start up requirements and the maintenance of critical levels of administration. The much vaunted self-policing system inherent in a VAT structure has been found wanting in most countries including Sri Lanka.

Due to all these problems, there is a school of thought that contends that the introduction of a VAT system in Sri Lanka in 1998 was too hasty and premature a measure. The turnover tax system in spite of its cascading nature was working effectively, was sufficiently flexible to adjust to changing fiscal situations and brought in the revenue

Table 6.5

COUNTRIES WHICH ABOLISHED AND RE-INTRODUCED VAT

Country	Introduced	Removed	Re-introduced
Vietnam	1973	1973	1999
Grenada	1987	1999	–
Ghana	1995	1995	1999
Malta	1995	1997	1999
Belize	1996	1999	–

Source: Liam et al. (2001).

estimated without difficulty. Since the tax was included in the price and was not transparent, it evoked little public criticism. In the context of the ethnic conflict when defence expenditure was 7 per cent of GDP and even in its aftermath, when rehabilitation and reconstruction would require as much expenditure if not more, the imposition of a complicated and sophisticated VAT system suitable for developed countries, presumably at the behest of multilateral lending agencies,[10] was both ill advised and premature. For example, in Singapore, VAT was introduced only at the time when its economy was strong. 'The GDP growth rate had been very high since the early 1990s. There had been full employment. People were in a position to afford a new tax. The budget surplus allowed the government to make a reduction in other taxes, which were expected to generate less revenue than the GST' (Jenkins and Khadka, 1998).

Hence, some of the countries which introduced VAT found it expedient to suspend or abolish it temporarily and re-introduce it after adequate preparation and once the economic conditions became more conducive to its implementation. About five countries abolished it after introduction; three of them re-introduced it in a modified form after some time when conditions became more suitable, while in two, Grenada and Belize, it still remains abolished (Table 6.5).

It is thus contended that the VAT should be temporarily abolished or suspended and the turnover tax be reverted to during the interim. Once a final peace settlement to the ethnic conflict is reached, rehabilitation and reconstruction are well under way and the economy is brought back to a sustainable level, then a VAT system appropriately modified to suit Sri Lankan conditions may be re-introduced.

ROLE OF FISCAL INCENTIVES—PROS AND CONS

In Sri Lanka, fiscal incentives have become an integral part of the development strategy. They were originally used from 1951 onwards and after 1977 became a major instrument of development policy. Though an attempt was made to reduce their scope and coverage in the late 1980s and early 1990s, fiscal incentives continued to be a major instrument in Sri Lanka's development strategy.

The debate on the use of a wide ranging fiscal incentive framework revolves round the issues of how effective they are in stimulating private investment and attracting

FDI and whether their benefits outweigh their costs. The rationale advanced for the use of fiscal incentives is that they constitute an important, if not a major, element in determining investment behaviour. It is generally assumed that fiscal incentives have an influence as they increase the net rates of returns and thus reduce the need for large capital investment and also reduce risk. The availability of incentives tends to make otherwise unpromising and risky ventures more attractive. Tax incentives in the form of income tax reliefs benefit concerns which are profitable. To that extent, they do not involve government subsidies or public guarantee to loss makers. Further, even in cases where relief may seem unnecessary, well conceived incentives may help ventures to build their reserves and embark on expansion. Tax and fiscal incentives are also valuable as an indirect stimulant to investment because they publicize and enhance the country's investment climate.

The role of fiscal incentives in determining investment behaviour has, however, been controversial. According to current studies, incentives by themselves do not play a major role in determining investment vis-à-vis other factors such as infrastructure facilities, cheap and easy credit, access to markets, a reliable and skilled labour force, political and economic stability, etc. Investment responds to a multiplicity of factors and compared to these, fiscal incentives at best play only a marginal role.

They have also been called into question on several grounds. One is that they distort investors' decisions and thus produce a less than optimum allocation of resources. Tax holidays tend to attract investors who are more keen on making quick profits and exploiting temporary shortages rather than on making investments of a substantial nature, which take time to develop and whose profits may not be large in the initial stages. It is, however, the latter type of investments that are crucially required by developing countries such as Sri Lanka and it is precisely in these fields that fiscal incentives to private investment have rarely had the desired effect. Fiscal incentives also tend to attract 'fly-by-night' investors who use the generous incentives only to pull out when the time comes to be regular taxpayers.

Fiscal incentives in the form of exemptions, tax holidays, reliefs, duty waivers and other concessions erode the revenue base and provide a fertile ground for tax and duty avoidance through 'tax shelters'. Further, revenue forgone in granting fiscal incentives is a matter of concern. If a given investment would not have taken place but for the fiscal incentive, the revenue forgone could be regarded as nil. There would be no activity to tax but for the tax incentive. Where, however, fiscal incentives confer benefits to investors who would, in any event, have undertaken the investments, the incentive involves an unnecessary revenue sacrifice. In reality, fiscal incentives are costly in revenue terms. It has not been possible to compute accurately the loss of revenue resulting from the grant of the wide range of incentives in Sri Lanka largely because most exempt firms do not, in practice, send their tax returns. The revenue forgone is, however, estimated to be substantial. The cost of fiscal incentives, it is felt, outweighs their benefits.

In view of the above, it is felt that fiscal incentives if offered at all, must be exceptional and given only for specified periods, their cost benefit ratio must be properly examined and they must be subjected to continuous review. With a sufficiently low rate of tax there would be no need for a complicated system of fiscal incentives.

TAX EVASION, THE BLACK ECONOMY AND TAX AMNESTIES

The large incidence of tax evasion in Sri Lanka is a cause of great concern. While the most immediate concern is the loss of revenue, in the long run such evasion tends to reduce the built-in elasticity of the tax system to the extent that the evaded income is spent on goods and services, generates inflationary pressure and raises the prices of real property. It also distorts the fundamental objectives of a fair fiscal system.

Tax evasion takes many forms such as non-filing of returns, under-reporting of income or overstatement of expenses, allowances and exemptions and transfer pricing. It is difficult to estimate the extent of evasion in Sri Lanka on a definite basis but there is no doubt that it is very considerable.

The existence of large-scale tax and duty evasion is linked to the existence of a black economy. The build up of black money takes place with the opportunities that are available for persons to evade taxation and to effectively conceal the profits and wealth that they earn. The main sources of black money include smuggling, the gem industry, terrorist activities, narcotics, illicit liquor, gold, commissions, bribes and pay-offs in tenders, the activities of such persons as brokers, auctioneers, land dealers, bookmakers and, not least, professionals.

The debate in this area takes the form of assessing to what extent the measures taken by the government have been effective in reducing tax evasion and bringing the black money into the open, so that such resources may be used productively for economic development. Ultimately, no money lies idle and even black money flows into investment somewhere although, from the national point of view, not to the most beneficial or ideally suited areas.

Measures to remedy this situation have generally taken three forms:

1. Closing loopholes in the tax, customs and excise laws.
2. Stricter enforcement in revenue administration.
3. The grant of tax and foreign exchange amnesties.

Legislation

A number of amendments to the tax, duty and excise laws have been made periodically to close any legal and procedural loopholes which persons can make use of to avoid taxes and duties. Nevertheless, at the same time, legislative loopholes have been created to minimize liability and assist tax evasion due presumably to pressure from various vested interests. Such instances include the generous expansion of various deductible expenses, various concessions and reliefs, ad hoc customs duty waivers and the inclusion of such clauses as the mandatory provision of specific reasons as to why a taxpayer's return is not accepted, etc.

Enforcement

The enforcement powers in the revenue laws are wide and include such measures as heavy penalties for non-compliance and default, powers of seizure and sale of movable or immovable property, proceedings before a Magistrate, fines and imprisonment, powers of search and inspection and powers to prevent defaulters from leaving the country. However, in practice, most of the drastic powers are rarely used and the effective use of powers such as raids on suspected evaders have been, since 1977, severely curtailed by various rules and guidelines making them virtually non-functional. Similarly, some powers have been whittled down, for example, the limiting in the recent Inland Revenue (Amendment) Act No. 37 of 2003, the powers of an assessor to make an additional assessment to five years by the end of the year of assessment, even in the case of fraud, evasion, or wilful default, powers which existed earlier under Section 134 of the Inland Revenue Act.

The Tax Amnesty Debate

Another policy response that has been used in reducing tax evasion and black money is the grant of tax and foreign exchange amnesties. The debate on this issue is whether such amnesties are justified and whether they have been effective in meeting the declared objectives.

There are a number of perceived advantages and disadvantages in operating a tax amnesty. In terms of the advantages, tax amnesties allow taxpayers to comply in respect of past breaches of revenue laws and allow tax evaders to come back into the system. A second benefit to tax agencies is the collection of outstanding taxes. A third advantage is that tax amnesties may increase future voluntary compliance as taxpayers who have evaded in the past (for whatever reason) may be ready to turn over a new leaf and become compliant taxpayers in the future. A final advantage of tax amnesties is that they allow for a transition period prior to a strengthened enforcement regime. Tax evaders who are detected after the amnesty have only themselves to blame if they face more severe penalties as a result of not accepting the amnesty offer.

However, there are also a number of obvious disadvantages with tax amnesties. They discriminate against honest taxpayers and in the long run affect taxpayer morale. Tax amnesties may well work once, but when they are offered with regular frequency, they undermine the equity objective in taxation and lower the society's respect for the revenue administration. A third disadvantage is that taxpayers may expect amnesties to be offered again in the future, possibly resulting in a reduction of compliance. The success of an amnesty cannot be measured by the number of declarants or the amount of revenue collected during the amnesty. What is of crucial importance is the compliance effects in the long run and any amnesty offer, no matter how well designed, could potentially have an impact on future levels of compliance. Finally, an amnesty may not be economically viable. Although the concept of net amnesty revenue is simple, the actual calculation of the final figure could be quite complex.

In Sri Lanka, tax amnesties have been granted with monotonous regularity in the past few decades commencing from 1964. Further, in order to draw unreported incomes into the country's development efforts, a scheme of bearer certificates of deposit has been in operation since 1982, enabling tax evaders to purchase these certificates with undeclared incomes and to derive a return.

The latest amnesty under the Inland Revenue (Special Provisions) Act No. 10 of 2003 was the eleventh such amnesty granted since 1964 and it generated much controversy both for and against its provisions. It was wide, ranging across the board amnesty exonerating offences in no less than 26 Acts including Inland Revenue, GST, NSL, Stamp Duty, Betting and Gaming, Exchange Control, Import and Export Control Act, the Excise Ordinance and the Customs Ordinance among others.

Almost all the amnesties granted in the past have been failures. Table 6.6 gives some results of these amnesties.

All these previous amnesties suffered a basic common drawback. They were not across the board amnesties, each one being restricted to either income tax or foreign exchange. The 2003 amnesty was an attempt to overcome this basic defect with the object of commencing a new tax regime from the year 2003. The concessions were not available from 2003 onwards and all tax liabilities were strictly enforced thereafter. 'We trust, Mr Speaker, that the present Bill will be an improvement on the previous ones and in this way the State in the future will be able to collect its just dues by way of taxes and also the number of tax defaulters will decrease. We hope to decrease the number of tax defaulters and increase the number of those who would be legitimately paying tax' (former Minister of Finance K.N. Choksy).[11]

Table 6.6

RESULTS OF AMNESTIES SINCE 1964

Year	No. of Declarants	Amount Recovered (Rs Million)
1964	78	21
1965	595	38
1970 (demonetization)	n.a.	n.a.
1978	160	30
1989	9	4
1990	n.a.	0.96
1992	n.a.	n.a.
1993	n.a.	n.a.
1997	100	285
1998	7	223
2002	592	n.a.
2003*	51,000	n.a.

Source: Compiled from Minister of Finance K.N. Choksy's statement in Parliament, Hansard, 19 February 2003, and Keynote address to the International Fiscal Association (Sri Lanka Branch), 29 May 2003.

Note: *Provisional declarations at end of amnesty period 31 August 2003.

While the government was confident that it was a step in the right direction with an unprecedented number of declarants, there was criticism in granting such a wide-ranging exoneration of fiscal offences in as many as 26 Acts and Ordinances including for the first time, Customs offences. Further, since the sources of income or the assets declared include both local and foreign, and since the declarations are accepted at face value without verification with apparently no discretion to reject them, they could, according to some analysts, be possibly used as cover to avoid legitimate tax liabilities in the future. It has also affected morale among customs and revenue officials in that they feel that long and painstaking investigations conducted against influential big time defaulters have abruptly come to nought. Some estimate the loss of customs duties and fines alone to be around Rs 27 billion and a total revenue loss to the government of over Rs 50 billion or more. Due to this controversy the Amnesty Act is to be subsequently amdended and hence for a realistic evaluation of the results of the amnesty it would be more appropriate to await the final outcome.

FISCAL DEVOLUTION

Another important fiscal issue currently being debated in the country arises from the ongoing ethnic problem and the attempt at reaching a settlement through negotiations. While a system of decentralized units in the form of village Councils or 'Gam Sabhas' existed in Sri Lanka from ancient times, prior to independence the system of local government was essentially dependent on the central government. Even after independence, what continued to prevail was administrative decentralization with local bodies only enjoying limited revenue powers.

The 13th Amendment to the Constitution led to the creation of Provincial Councils under Section 154A of the Constitution and enactment under the Provincial Councils Act No. 42 of 1987. This was the first attempt to formulate some form of devolution giving powers to these Councils to plan, execute and manage the totality of selected functions. However, in Sri Lanka, compared to other countries where multi-level systems of government prevail, the sub-national units were introduced into a state explicitly unitary in character. The debate in this area revolves round the question as to how far the fiscal powers devolved to these units are adequate in securing sufficient revenue for provincial expenditure, their dependence on the centre and the inherent weaknesses in the currently devolved system.

Provincial Finance

The main sources of revenue devolved to the provinces are enumerated in Sections 36.1 to 36.20 of List I of the 9th Schedule to the 13th Amendment. While at first glance these sources appear formidable, a closer scrutiny reveals that the main sources consist only of the turnover taxes and stamp duties while licence taxes, motor vehicle licence fees and court fines are the other substantial revenue sources. These devolved sources, however, account for less than 4 per cent of the government total revenue and hence only a relatively insignificant proportion of the country's revenue has been devolved on the provinces.

It is also clear that there is a serious imbalance between provincial revenue collection in relation to provincial expenditure. Some vertical imbalance is unavoidable in any devolved revenue system but in Sri Lanka, because of too little internal revenue of the provinces, the imbalance is severe. Only around 23 per cent of recurrent expenditure is secured from own revenues, and 77 per cent is secured from transfers from the Central Government. The nature of the fiscal imbalance also has a horizontal dimension particularly with reference to the Western Province, which accounts for almost two-thirds of the entire revenue collection of all the provinces.

While provincial revenue is only around 4 per cent of government revenue or 0.6 per cent of GDP, in contrast, provincial expenditure is around 10 per cent of total government revenue or about 3 per cent of GDP. These disparities necessitate the recourse to equalization measures in the form of grants which constitute mainly the Block Grants (80 per cent of total transfers), the Matching Grants and the Criteria Based Grants. In addition, there is a grant for specific regional development projects called the Provincial Specific Development Grant (PSDG) which constitutes about 10 per cent of the total transfers. These grants have been considerably reduced recently resulting in provincial units being hard pressed to meet their expenditure requirements.

Weaknesses of the Provincial Council System

The present decentralized Provincial Council system has, both in concept and practice, serious inherent weaknesses and contradictions. Beset with institutional and financial constraints, it is neither a purely administratively decentralized system nor a fully devolved system of government.

The 13th Amendment has been a hastily drawn up document with the objective of solving a political and ethnic problem rather than a well thought out and well conceived scheme of decentralized governance within the Sri Lankan context. Further, little attention has been paid to the fiscal and financial aspects, monitoring and supervising mechanisms or inter-governmental relations that underpin a multi-level system of government. To quote Richard Bird, 'The process currently under way appears to assume that the extent, nature and timing of devolution is essentially a political question that will be resolved on political grounds. Any economic and fiscal questions relating to devolution seems to be viewed as simply details to be cleared up later, once a political solution is reached. The premise of this argument is sound. Devolution is essentially a political matter. The conclusion is mistaken. Careful attention must be paid to the economic and fiscal aspects of devolution from the beginning' (1996).

CONCLUDING REMARKS

The current issues and debates discussed in this chapter are of importance not only at a macroeconomic level to policy planners and administrators but to entrepreneurs and the general public at large who ultimately bear the burden of economic and fiscal policies. These current issues are discussed in the background of low economic growth, dwindling government revenue and in the background of attempts to resuscitate and rebuild the economy by programmes such as the Regaining Sri Lanka (RSL) initiative of the government. To quote: 'The truth is that Sri Lanka is in the thick of an economic crisis—a crisis born out of deep and deadly indebtedness .... Therefore, we need to act prudently and with a renewed vision to stop the country from going down the slope of ruin .... There is only one way ahead. That is achieving substantially higher economic growth .... Not just for the short term, but over a number of years—a sustained growth that will free the country from the tentacles of accumulated debt.'[12] The debate on the various fiscal issues currently prevalent has to be viewed in this context.

The relative decline in the direct taxes and the increasing preponderance of the levies on goods and services has led to a debate as to whether the direct taxes on income should be abolished or the rates further reduced in favour of greater reliance on the consumption taxes. This in turn has led to a debate as to whether the consumption taxes have reached saturation point and to what extent further taxation is possible in this area, particularly in relation to the excise duties which apparently provide the only major source of additional revenue from the indirect taxes. The VAT which replaced the GST has presumably not led to achieving its objectives and due to its complicated structure and administrative weaknesses has not realized the estimated revenue targets.

Due to the inherent inelasticity of the fiscal system, government revenue has not kept pace with increasing GDP and per capita income. While it is difficult to establish a precise correlation between taxation, savings and capital formation, the evidence points to the fact that prohibitive levels of taxation act as a disincentive to savings, capital formation and investment. Nevertheless, the importance of tax and fiscal incentives in stimulating investment both domestic and foreign appears to be overrated and their utilization has only a marginal effect. Their ad hoc and unplanned use erodes the fiscal base and the rationale for their utilization appears to be controversial.

The measures used to reduce tax evasion and black money do not appear to have had much effect, particularly the regular use of tax amnesties which have proved controversial and so far not led any to appreciable results. The final results of the latest amnesty are still subject to realistic evaluation. Finally, the debate on fiscal devolution has led to the realization that in devising any form of political devolution, it is essential that careful attention be paid to the economic and fiscal aspects of devolution right from the beginning.

NOTES

1. The size of the multiplier in an open economy is $(1/[S + M + T])$
   where
   S   = Marginal propensity to save
   M   = Marginal propensity to import
   T   = Marginal rate of taxation
2. Department of Inland Revenue and Securities and Exchange Commission.
3. Prof. Nicholas Kaldor, a Cambridge economist in 'Comprehensive Reform of Direct Taxation', GOSL Sessional Paper No. IV of 1960.
4. Small companies are defined to mean those whose taxable income is less than Rs 5 million for the assessment year.
5. Director of the Office of Management and Budget in President Reagan's Administration in the US.
6. 'Foreign Direct Investment, Development and the New Global Economic Order', published by the South Centre.
7. The average duty or effective rate is the ratio of import duty collection to total adjusted imports.
8. Due to the difficulty in computing value added of financial transactions, most countries have exempted the financial sector from VAT other than, for instance, Israel.
9. Value added can be looked at from the additive side (wages plus profits) or from the subtractive side (output minus input). Value added = wages + profit = output − input.
10. It is part of the tax reforms which constitutes one element of what is known as the 'Washington Consensus'.
11. *Hansard*, 19 February 2003.
12. GOSL (2003), 'The Future—Regaining Sri Lanka', http://www.regainingsrilanka.org/

REFERENCES

Bird, Richard M. (1996), 'Fiscal Aspects of Devolution in. Sri Lanka,' April 1996, (mimeo).
Central Bank of Sri Lanka, *Annual Report*, 2002, Colombo.
_____, *Annual Reports*, various issues, Colombo.
Department of Inland Revenue, *Administration Reports*, Colombo.
Ebrill, Liam P. (1987), 'Evidence on the Laffer Curve: The cases of Jamaica and India', in *Supply Side Tax Policy: Its Relevance to Developing Countries*, Ved P. Gandhi (ed.), Washington D.C.: IMF.
Ebrill, Liam et al. (2001), *The Modern VAT*, Washington D.C.: IMF.
GOSL (1991), Report of the Taxation Commission 1990, Government of Sri Lanka Sessional Paper No. 1 of 1991.
Jenkins, Glen P. and Rup Khadka (1998), 'Value Added Tax Policy and Implementation in Singapore', Working Paper 1001, *International Tax Program*, Harvard, March 1998: 44.

SELECT READINGS

Ramanujam, T.C.A. and T.C.A. Sangeetha (1997), 'Do Tax Rate Reductions Result in Higher Revenue Mobilisation?', *Income Tax Reports 1997*, Vol. 226, Chennai: Company Law Institute of India Private Ltd.

Stella, P. (1991), 'An Economic Analysis of Tax Amnesties', *Journal of Public Economics*, 46: 383–400.

Tait, Alan A. (1988), 'Value Added Tax: International Practice and Problems', Washington D.C.: IMF.

Waidyasekera, D.D.M. (1993), 'Tax Reform in Sri Lanka: Implementation of the Tax Commission's Recommendations', *Tax Notes International*, 6(22).

_____ (1995), 'Should the goods and services tax be postponed or not?', *Daily News*, 18 August.

_____ (2000), *Decentralization and Provincial Finance in Sri Lanka*, Colombo: Institute of Policy Studies.

_____ (2001), 'The Role of Taxation in Development Strategy: The Sri Lankan Experience', *Asia-Pacific Tax Bulletin*, 7(4).

Waidyasekera, D.D.M., D.M. Ariyasena and A.B. Wijayapala (2002), *Provincial Revenue Performance Improvement Programme*, Colombo: UNDP—Finance Commission.

7

PUBLIC DEBT: INSTITUTIONAL ISSUES

Nihal Kappagoda

INTRODUCTION

Public debt and its management are important public policy issues for Sri Lanka. This chapter deals with them in two main sections. The first deals with the importance and requirements for the effective management of public debt. The principal debt management functions that should be performed and a possible structure for public debt management are discussed. The present institutional arrangements for public sector borrowings are reviewed. The second section analyses various aspects of the current external and domestic public debt situation in Sri Lanka during 1992–2001. This includes a discussion of the status of external indebtedness and the use of some vulnerability indicators to assess the risks to the economy. The way out of the present public debt situation from an institutional and policy point of view is discussed in the final section.

PUBLIC DEBT MANAGEMENT

Public debt management has become a priority for many developing and transition economy countries. This is a change from the early 1980s. When the debt crisis emerged in 1982, governments that undertook debt management focused their attention on controlling and recording medium- and long-term external public debt. Less attention was paid to controlling and monitoring private non-guaranteed debt including short-term debt. Different institutions within governments dealt with domestic and external loans. These obligations were consolidated only when debt service payments of governments had to be estimated for the preparation of their budgets and the payments were accounted for audit purposes. The management of domestic debt was handled separately and not considered to be a priority at that time.

This approach changed in the 1990s—particularly during the latter half of the decade—as a result of factors that altered the international financial environment. These changes and the new requirements for debt management are leading countries to review the institutional arrangements for public sector borrowing and its management. Emerging markets and developing countries that are liberalizing their capital accounts need to undertake these reviews as a matter of priority, cognizant of the fact that public debt management covers all the activities of a loan cycle as before. Debt management requires a higher level of sophistication than it did in the past due to the greater complexity of the loan portfolios, covering both domestic and foreign loans and the availability of more advanced techniques some of which are used by multinational investment institutions.

A publication of the World Bank and International Monetary Fund (IMF)[1] *Guidelines for Public Debt Management* states that an effective governance structure for public debt management requires a clear legislative framework and well-defined organizational arrangements with the mandates of different agencies being articulated to ensure that there is no overlapping. Debt management operations need to be supported by an accurate management information system (MIS) which would enable analytical work to be undertaken as loan portfolios become more complex and governments begin to undertake debt and risk analyses.

Requirements for Effective Debt Management

The experience of countries that encountered debt service problems over the past 20 years 1982–2002 has provided guidance on the steps that debtor countries should take to improve debt management. The first is the adoption of clear objectives for public debt management. The second is the introduction of a transparent institutional framework and procedures for borrowing, on-lending and the issue of loan guarantees by the government and better surveillance of loan performance. At the same time, a framework for approving borrowing by the private sector[2] and monitoring transactions arising from these is necessary. Third, an effective monitoring system for loans must be established to track the accumulation and maturity structure of all debt contracted by the government, the central bank, state corporations, joint stock companies and the private sector. In a partially liberalized economy such as Sri Lanka, the compilation of debt incurred by joint stock companies and the private sector requires the monitoring of private flows through a combination of reporting by exchange control authorities, the banking system and borrowers directly. Fourth, countries must adopt a sound macroeconomic framework which includes fiscal, monetary, interest and exchange rates, reserve management and pricing policies, a transparent governance structure in the public and private sectors and policies to protect vulnerable groups in society from the adverse impact of adjustment policies. Fifth, countries need to establish an MIS including the development of a set of early warning indicators of any impending debt service payments problems to enable policy makers to take timely action. Sixth, a borrowing policy and multi-year/annual plan based on estimates of sustainable borrowing levels following a debt sustainability analysis and a strategy for implementing the plan should be formulated. Seventh, explicit guidelines for lending and on-lending and the issue of guarantees by the government should be introduced. Eighth, the capacity for assessing risks to the country's loan portfolio and managing the risks identified should be developed. Finally, at a micro level, borrowed funds should be channelled to high priority projects and programmes.

Effective coordination of debt management with fiscal and monetary policies while maintaining separate responsibility for each is an important aspect of debt management. It will be difficult to implement the macroeconomic policies of the government in the absence of or with poor coordination. Borrowing policies should ensure the long-term sustainability of the fiscal deficit. Cash flows arising from a given debt structure should be consistent with the long-term fiscal projections of the government. However, debt management policy should not be subordinated to monetary policy. If it is, decisions on debt management may not be made to achieve sound portfolio management. In some instances, the monetary authorities may prefer to issue debt that is index-linked to inflation with a view to preserving price stabilization, but debt managers may take the view that the domestic debt market is not developed adequately to mobilize the required resources using the type of debt instrument chosen. Similarly, the monetary authorities may prefer to borrow in foreign currency to bolster foreign currency reserves while those responsible for debt management policy may not agree with this due to the higher risks associated with foreign currency debt. The institutional arrangements should clarify the implementation of policy in the three areas and the separate accountability of the agencies responsible for them.

Objectives for Debt Management

It is reported that the objectives for public debt management are not clearly defined[3] in many developing countries. The same is true of the governance structure and legal basis for public sector borrowings making it difficult for those responsible for debt management to function effectively. The Organization for Economic Cooperation and Development (OECD), in a survey of debt management structures conducted among its members in 2000, identified several overall objectives for public debt management some of which are relevant to developing countries. These are to:

- ensure the financing needs of the government;
- minimize borrowing costs;
- keep risks at an acceptable level; and
- support the development of domestic markets.

These objectives are appropriate for any country with a well-developed domestic capital market when it accesses international capital markets. Many developing countries will give priority initially to obtaining the financing needs of the public sector at a low cost. In the early stages of development, countries have little choice in the sources and currencies of funding as the borrowing is mostly from official sources. As access to international capital markets increases and governments begin to borrow from them—as Sri Lanka is poised to—the objectives should also take account of the government's risk preferences and tolerances. The development of the domestic debt market is also a priority for Sri Lanka. There will be a push to strengthen and deepen domestic capital markets and develop secondary markets if and when the capital account of the balance of payments is liberalized and borrowers are able to convert local currency into foreign exchange freely. At such a time, borrowers may wish to exercise a choice between the domestic and international capital markets. Another objective could be to ensure that public sector borrowing levels keep selected public debt indicators within ceilings adopted by the government.

Organizational Structure for Public Debt Management

Debt management covers more functions than the mobilization of foreign and domestic resources, the recording of this debt and making timely debt service payments. There is a range of analytical functions that need to be performed for effective debt management. When a Public Debt Management Office (PDMO) is set up by the amalgamation of the domestic and foreign borrowing activities, two bureaucratic cultures merge. It is normally difficult to achieve institutional change. In such situations capacity building requires a great degree of patience and tolerance. Legislative and regulatory amendments are also necessary to bring about these changes. It always takes time in any country, suggesting the need for a long preparation period. In considering the requirements for public debt management, it is useful to review the full range of debt management functions that should be performed by a PDMO for public sector borrowing at various stages of the loan cycle.

Many emerging markets are beginning to coordinate their external and domestic borrowings and have established or are considering establishing PDMOs with varying levels of legal authority. While lessons on the organizational structure can be learnt from developed countries that have established PDMOs, the financing requirements in emerging markets are different. One important difference is the continuing need for project financing by the government and state corporations from bilateral and multilateral institutions at varying degrees of concessionality. There is still a need for borrowing to meet the foreign exchange needs of the public sector, be it by the Central Bank or other agencies of the government. Domestic capital markets are being strengthened and new instruments introduced to mobilize domestic capital. But many countries are at some distance from exercising a real choice between the domestic and international capital markets for mobilizing resources for the public sector.

The functional organization for public debt management could be similar to that of an investment institution. While the agencies responsible for debt management may not be structured as in these institutions, three operational offices can be set up to correspond to the three principal categories of debt management functions. These could be referred to as the Front, Middle and Back offices. The Front Office will be responsible for Loan Mobilization and Management and make the major decisions on foreign and domestic borrowings based on the approved borrowing plan. It will also take responsibility for on-lending and guarantee operations and hedging and derivative transactions of the government. The Middle Office will be responsible for Debt and Risk Management. It should undertake portfolio analyses, develop a risk management strategy and borrowing scenarios and compare the emerging debt indicators with agreed benchmarks. This would enable sustainable levels of public sector borrowing to be estimated and a borrowing policy and plan for the public sector to be prepared. The Front Office should formulate a strategy for implementing the borrowing plan by mobilizing resources from domestic and foreign sources with the assistance of the Middle Office. The Back Office will be responsible for Debt Service Payments and the MIS. It will make debt service payments based on creditor invoices that are crosschecked with its own database, be responsible for monitoring on-lending and guarantee operations of the government, and the preparation of accounting and other reports required by creditors and the government. Straddling all three offices will be a legal group whose principal function will be to support the activities of the Front and Back offices. The three offices will be interdependent and exercise checks and balances over each other in the interests of transparency and accountability.

The organizational structure for public debt management should include a Public Debt Policy Committee. It should be a high level Committee chaired by the Minister of Finance or the Governor of the Central Bank and comprise the Secretary of Finance, heads of relevant departments in the Ministry of Finance and Central Bank and representatives of private sector groups such as banks and exporters. The membership should be broad-based to function in a transparent and effective manner. It should be able to provide technical direction to the PDMO, oversee and approve the broad parameters of loan operations of the public sector and approve guidelines for the private sector.

In most emerging markets, many of the Front and Back Office functions are currently performed by the agencies dealing with foreign and domestic borrowings for the government but the same is not true of the functions of the Middle Office. A strong analytical capability for public debt management should be built up in the Middle Office to support the borrowing activities of the public sector. This is a long-term process requiring a combination of appropriate staffing, relevant technical assistance and on-the-job training.

The organizational structure suggested for a PDMO is illustrated in Figure 7.1 which sets out the institutional framework that is necessary for public debt management. It corresponds to the three groups of debt management functions that have been identified. It is the ultimate structure that should emerge in a PDMO when all the functions are brought into one office instead of being scattered among different agencies of the government.

Figure 7.1

Organizational Structure for a Public Debt Management Office

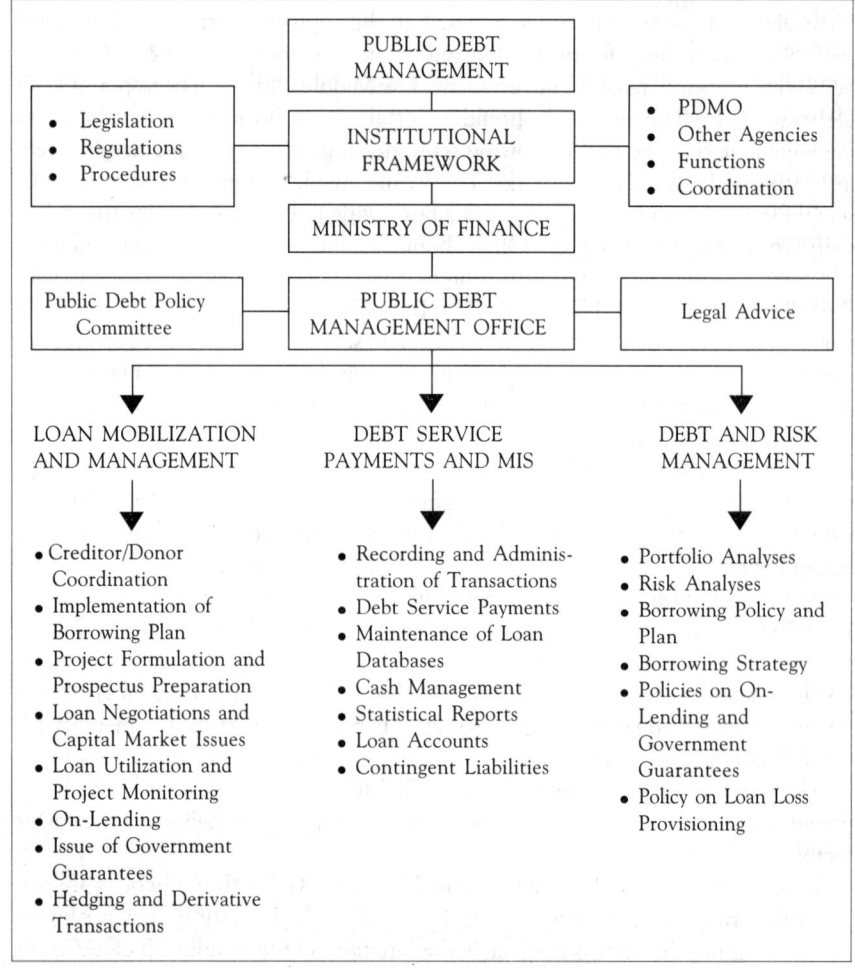

Current Institutional Framework in Sri Lanka

There are many laws[4] in Sri Lanka that have an impact on external and domestic borrowings of the public sector. The Foreign Loans Act of 1957 and its subsequent amendments (1962, 1963, 1980 and 1984) cover external borrowing and guarantees issued by the government for foreign loans. The laws that enable domestic borrowing by the government are the Local Treasury Bills Ordinance (1923, 1953, 1992 and 1995), Registered Stock and Securities Ordinance (1937, 1949, 1983, 1985 and 1995), Treasury Certificates of Deposit Act (1989) and Tax Reserve Certificates Act (1957, 1961 and

1981). These acts empower the Minister of Finance to authorize the mobilization of the foreign and domestic resources required for government operations. The Monetary Law Act of 1949 makes provisions for the Central Bank to act as the fiscal agent and banker to the government, thereby enabling it to issue and redeem domestic debt and make debt service payments on foreign borrowings of the government. The Act holds the Central Bank responsible for the management of public debt and for providing its views on the terms and conditions of new loans or issues. The annual Appropriations Act limits the extent of foreign and domestic borrowings that are permitted to meet the expenditures that are authorized by Parliament when the Budget is approved.

At present, many of the Front Office functions relating to external borrowing are performed by the External Resources Department (ERD) of the Ministry of Finance. These are principally loans on concessional terms from bilateral and multilateral sources. Borrowings from capital markets have been handled by other Departments of the Ministry in the past. Domestic borrowing through various borrowing instruments is undertaken by the Public Debt Department (PDD) of the Central Bank while the Treasury raises funds through overdraft facilities. The responsibility for the issue of government guarantees is divided between the ERD and the Fiscal Policy Department (FPD) of the Ministry of Finance. The Back Office functions of settlement for both domestic and external borrowings of the government are performed by the PDD. The database for external loans is maintained by the ERD using the CS-DRMS software of the Commonwealth Secretariat while several databases are used by the PDD to store data on domestic borrowing of the government. The Back Office functions of loan accounting and cash management are the responsibility of the Department of State Accounts of the Treasury. The analytical functions required for effective resource mobilization and debt management that would normally be done by a Middle Office are not being performed in a systematic manner with the exception of some ad hoc debt analyses being done by the PDD.

The Central Bank has a Domestic Debt Management Committee to coordinate the mobilization of domestic debt. There is no similar coordination mechanism for external debt or for public debt as a whole.

ANALYSIS OF THE PUBLIC DEBT OF SRI LANKA

External Debt

Debt Outstanding[5]

Long- and medium-term public sector external debt outstanding of the government and state corporations (guaranteed and unguaranteed) with an original maturity exceeding one year increased from $5,711 million at the end of 1992 to $8,382 million at the end of 1999, an increase of 47 per cent. The highest level was in 1999. It declined in 2000 and 2001. When private sector debt and IMF drawings are also included the stock of debt grew from $6,308 million at the end of 1992 to $8,988 million at the end of 1995—an increase of 41 per cent. It then fluctuated in the $8,000–9,000 million range but was below the level reached in 1995. When short-term debt is included, the total stock of external debt outstanding increased to $10,067 million in 1995 and fluctuated in the range of $8,600–9,400 million thereafter.

Another feature of the long and medium-term external debt outstanding was that the government accounted for 81–86 per cent of the total. Public and publicly guaranteed debt outstanding accounted for a larger share and was in the range of 89–95 per cent during the 10-year period.[6] The public sector was the dominant sector for external borrowing. The share of multilateral sources in the total stock of long and medium-term debt outstanding was in the range of 44–50 per cent while the share of bilateral sources was slightly lower. On the other hand, commercial sources which are poised to increase their share of lending to Sri Lanka accounted for 11–13 per cent of the total. They include lending from capital markets, commercial banks, export credit agencies and other non-concessional sources. The level of short-term debt outstanding was below 10 per cent of the total external debt outstanding during the entire period with the exception of 1995.

Debt Service Payments: 1992–2001[7]

External debt service payments increased significantly in 1994 and 1995 and were above $700 million after 1994. The payments exceeded $800 million during 1999–2001 with the highest level of $952 million being reached in 2000. Despite this increase in absolute terms, the debt service ratio[8] declined from 17.1 per cent in 1992 to 13.3 per cent in 2001. At these levels, the ratio is in the range for less indebted countries though the indebtedness of a country has to be determined along with other indicators. The share of the government in total external debt outstanding was in excess of 80 per cent of the total, while the share of the government in total external debt service payments was approximately two-thirds of its share in external debt outstanding during this period. This was due to the higher level of concessionality associated with government borrowing compared to state corporations and the private sector.

External Debt Indicators[9]

Following the international debt crisis of the 1980s, the World Bank and IMF developed some external debt indicators to classify the indebtedness of developing countries. Based on inter-country analyses, the World Bank determined critical values for some of the external debt indicators for countries classified as highly, moderately and less indebted. Initially, the indicators were based on the nominal values of debt. As the methodology developed, these were replaced by indicators that measured the present value of debt service payments as they take account of the concessionality and term structure of debt outstanding which the nominal value of external debt does not. The critical values of six indicators used for classifying indebtedness are summarized in

Table 7.1

Critical Values of External Debt Indicators[10]

Indicator	Highly Indebted	Moderately Indebted	Less Indebted
DOD/GNP	> 50%	>30% and <50%	<30%
DOD/XGS	>275%	>165% and <275%	<165%
TDS/XGS	>30%	>18% and <30%	<18%
INT/XGS	>20%	>12% and <20%	<12%
PV/GNP	>80%	>48% and <80%	<48%
PV/XGS	>220%	>132% and <220%	<132%

Sources: Global Development Finance, 2002 and earlier issues, the World Bank.

Table 7.1. Although gross national product (GNP) has been used for these critical values, it should be noted that the World Bank now uses Gross National Income in estimating the levels of the indicators.

The debt indicators illustrate Sri Lanka's external debt position. The interest ratio was at or under 7 per cent and the debt service ratio was in the range of 13–17 per cent during 1992–2001. The debt outstanding to gross domestic product (GDP) ratio exceeded 50 per cent for the entire period although it declined from 69 per cent in 1992 to 53 per cent in 2001. The ratio comparing debt outstanding to exports of goods and services declined from 207 per cent in 1992 to 132 per cent in 2001; it was below 165 per cent after 1995. The decline was similar to that observed for the ratio which compared the stock of debt to GDP. Given that two of the four indicators were in the range for a less indebted country while a third was in this range after 1995, Sri Lanka clearly falls into the category of countries classified as less indebted. This classification is confirmed when the present value indicators are used. Both were in the range for less indebted countries.

These external debt indicators are not an exhaustive list. They do not capture the difficulties that could be encountered in making government debt service payments caused by budget constraints, making it necessary to estimate other indicators related to the budgetary position. Payments may not be made because of liquidity problems which are not forecast by a stable structure of external indebtedness as it is in the case of Sri Lanka. Further, rising external debt may coincide with an increase in debt service payments capacity and does not necessarily lead to balance of payments difficulties. Thus the benchmarks based on inter-country analyses should be modified in the context of the country specific situation.

Average Terms of Assistance and Concessionality[11]

One reason for Sri Lanka's low level of external debt indicators was the concessional terms on which official creditors who accounted for 85–90 per cent of the debt outstanding in the 1990s made loans available. The average interest rate on new loan commitments made in the 10 years under review was in the range of 1.9–3.8 per cent. Grace periods averaged 4.1–9.7 years and the total repayment periods averaged 19.5–34.9 years. These terms led to an average grant element that fluctuated in the range of

31.6–66.6 per cent. The concessionality of these averages was due to the terms extended by official creditors that resulted in the grant elements for these loans to fluctuate between 42.5 and 76.3 per cent. The average grant element for private creditors shows that these loans were non-concessional. The ratio of concessional[12] loans to total external debt outstanding increased from 71.9 per cent in 1990 to 77.5 per cent in 2000.[13]

Another reason for the favourable external debt position was the high level of grants received by Sri Lanka in the past. Unfortunately the absolute levels have declined during the 1990s from a high of $207 million in 1991 to $56 million in 2000. The annual decline has been consistent since 1995. In 2001 grant receipts were of the same order of magnitude as in 2000.

Currency Composition of Debt[14]

There has been a greater dominance of the main loan currencies in the composition of medium and long-term public external debt outstanding during 1992–2001. Three loan currencies—the US dollar, Special Drawing Rights (SDRs) and yen—accounted for the bulk of the debt outstanding. Their share increased from 81 per cent in 1992 to 91 per cent in 2001. The SDR is the dominant loan currency and accounted for 36 per cent of debt outstanding in 2001. Its share increased from 31 per cent in 1992. This is mainly due to the designation of all loans from the Asian Development Bank (ADB), International Development Association and, to a lesser extent, the International Fund for Agricultural Development in SDRs and their dominance in multilateral lending which accounted for over 40 per cent of debt outstanding. The SDR is followed by the US dollar whose share increased from 27 to 30 per cent as many loans from non-US sources were also designated in US dollars. The share of the yen also increased from 22 to 25 per cent during this period. The increased share of the three dominant currencies accounted for two-thirds of the reduction in the combined share of the currencies of five of the bilateral donors, i.e., Canada, France, Germany, Netherlands and the UK, from 17 to 2 per cent. The rest of the decline was accounted for by the euro which had a share of 6 per cent of external debt outstanding in 2001.

Any action that is taken by the authorities to manage currency risk would require the statistics of debt outstanding to the ADB on its concessional loans to be estimated on the basis of currencies of obligation rather than the loan currency which is the SDR. The Bank practice is to make disbursements on these loans in multiple currencies and repayments are required in the same currencies. The loan database in the ERD maintains the amounts outstanding in the loan currencies.

The movements in the exchange rate of the SDR and the yen (and to a lesser extent the other currencies) against the US dollar has implications for managing currency risk. It also has an impact on aggregating statistics of the debt outstanding in US dollars which is the practice followed in Sri Lanka. Figure 7.2 shows the magnitude of the fluctuations in the exchange rate of the US dollar to the yen that took place during 1991–2001. Any debt service payments that were made in yen in 1992 and 1998 could have had a favourable impact on the balance of payments position if they were made with reserves held in US dollars. The position could have been reversed in 1995.

Figure 7.2

YEN/US DOLLAR EXCHANGE RATE

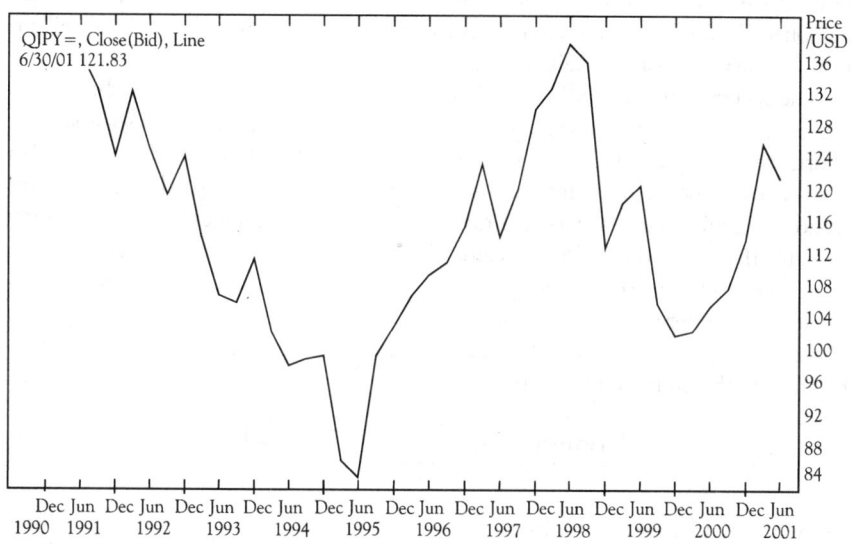

QJPY=, Close(Bid), Line
6/30/01 121.83

Price /USD
136
132
128
124
120
116
112
108
104
100
96
92
88
84

Dec Jun Dec Jun Dec Jun Dec Jun Dec Jun Dec Jun Dec Jun Dec Jun Dec Jun Dec Jun Dec Jun Dec Jun
1990 1991   1992   1993   1994   1995   1996   1997   1998   1999   2000   2001

Source: Bloomberg.

The choice of loan currency will become an important component of debt management as Sri Lanka moves towards more commercial borrowing.

Net Transfers and Flows[15]

Aggregate debt data show that net transfers were positive for seven years during 1992–2001. They were above $300 million in 1994 and 2001, between $200 and 300 million in 1992, 1993 and 1998, and less than $50 million in 1995 and 1997. The transfers were negative in the three remaining years, i.e., –$12 million, –$384 million and –$203 milion in 1996, 1999 and 2000 respectively. The breakdown of this aggregate data by creditor source shows that net transfers from multilateral sources were positive in all the years except in 1999 and 2000. They were $327 million in 1992, $282 million in 1993 and between $100 and 200 million in 1994–96 and 2001. The position with bilateral creditors was different. Net transfers were negative in 1992, 1993, 1996, 1997, 1999 and 2000 and positive and below $100 million in the other years. Available data on private creditors show that net transfers were negative for half the period while they were positive and under $100 million in 1994, 1995, 1997 and 1998 and $155 million in 2001. This pattern of net transfers is captured in the three-year averages.

Committed Undisbursed Balances[16]

The build up of committed loan funds that remained undisbursed continued during the 1990s and reached its highest level in 1999 when it was $2,817 million. It declined to $2,547 million at the end of 2001 which was of the same order of magnitude as that at the end of 1992. The average level of disbursements achieved during the period under review was $638 million with a high of $1,003 million in 2001 and a low of $409 million in 1999. Loan commitments averaged $765 million with a high of $1,457 million in 2001 and a low of $375 million in 2000.

The accumulation of undisbursed balances at the end of 2001 was over three times the average annual level of commitments during the 10-year period. This suggests that efforts are needed to reduce the level at least in respect of the major lenders. While this was the overall position, bilateral and multilateral lenders as a group exhibited different trends. Actual disbursements as a ratio of undisbursed balances were consistently higher in the case of the multilateral group of lenders compared to the bilateral lenders. This is a reflection of the large undisbursed balances in projects financed by Japan—the leading lender to Sri Lanka—which accounted for the largest component in the bilateral group. The ADB and World Bank accounted for the bulk of the undisbursed balances in the multilateral group.

Domestic and Total Public Debt

Growth of Domestic Debt[17]

The extraordinary growth in domestic debt that took place during 1992–2001 had several features. Domestic debt became a larger share of government debt outstanding in 1997 and remained so for the rest of the period. The annual increases were above 20 per cent in 1993, 1996, 1998, 2000 and 2001. The domestic debt outstanding increased over 100 per cent between 1992 and 1996 and again between 1996 and 2001. Short-term financing—mainly treasury bills—which was a larger share of total domestic debt in 1992 and earlier became smaller. In 2001 the share was 34.1 per cent. The high share of domestic debt in government debt service was another feature. It was in the range of 71–82 per cent for the entire period. The ratio was significantly higher than the share of domestic debt outstanding in total government debt as domestic debt was of short to medium-term maturities while foreign borrowings by the government was, as stated earlier, mainly on concessional terms.

Marketable and non-marketable borrowing instruments are used by the government to mobilize resources from the domestic market.[18] Treasury Bills and Treasury Bonds are in the former category and Rupee securities, Central Bank advances, loans from commercial banks and Development Bonds are in the latter. In the marketable category, Treasury Bills are zero-coupon instruments issued for maturities of three, six and 12 months. Treasury bonds pay a coupon rate with maturities of two, three, five and six years. They were issued for the first time in 1997. In the non-marketable category, Rupee securities account for the largest amount of domestic debt. These are fixed rate instruments that pay interest semi-annually. They could have maturities from one to 30 years though maturities on outstanding issues are less than 10 years. Central Bank advances which are limited to 10 per cent of the budgeted revenue and available interest free are short-term borrowings by the government. Overdrafts are also made available by commercial banks. These, along with Central Bank advances, are used essentially for cash management purposes. Development bonds designated in US dollars were issued for the first time in 2001. These were sold to domestic and foreign institutions and have a maturity of two years.

There are other features in the growth of domestic debt. The first is that marketable instruments accounted for 51.2 per cent of domestic debt in 1992 when they were made up entirely of Treasury Bills. This share declined to 39.8 and 36.4 per cent in 1995 and 1998 respectively but increased to 42.3 and 50 per cent in 1999 and 2000 respectively following the government's strategy to move towards marketable instruments while mobilizing resources at the lowest possible cost. The share declined in 2001 to 49 per cent due to the larger borrowing requirement from the domestic market and the resulting higher cost of borrowing. The smaller increase in the amount of Rupee securities outstanding observed in 1998–2000 compared to earlier years was reversed in 2001 when there was an increase of over 10 per cent.

The share of marketable securities increased once again in 2002. Treasury bonds outstanding have increased in importance since they were first issued. They became larger than Treasury Bills in 2000 when the amount outstanding increased by the order of 100 per cent in both 1999 and 2000 and larger than Rupee securities in 2002.[19] The three instruments accounted for 84.9 per cent of domestic debt outstanding in 2001.

The Employees' Provident Fund and National Savings Bank continue to be the leading investors in Rupee securities and Treasury Bonds. The reliance on the banking system for both short and longer-term financing has been in the range of 24–42 per cent. The share declined from 42 per cent in 1993 to 24 per cent in 1998 and increased thereafter to 32 per cent in 2001. Commercial banks accounted for about 20 per cent of total debt outstanding.

Growth of Total Public Debt[20]

At the time of independence, the public debt of Sri Lanka was made up of Rs 125.4 million of foreign loans and Rs 391.5 million of domestic loans. There were significant milestones in the growth of public debt. One was the commencement of borrowing from the World Bank in 1959. The next was the establishment of the Aid Group for Sri Lanka in 1965 which provided the framework for mobilizing international assistance for the country's development on an enhanced and systematic basis. This led to significant increases in foreign borrowing over the years up to the present. Foreign debt in local currency terms became larger than domestic debt in total public debt outstanding for the first time in 1984. It remained larger until 1997 when domestic debt once again became a larger component of public debt outstanding. This position continued until the end of 2001. Total public debt outstanding as a share of GDP has increased over the years. It increased to above 60 per cent in the second half of the 1970s and was over 90 per cent during the entire 1990s, with the exception of 1997 when it was 86 per cent. It was above 100 per cent for the first time in 2001.

Debt Sustainability and Vulnerability Analyses

Debt sustainability of a country is its ability to service its borrowings—foreign and domestic; public and publicly guaranteed and private non-guaranteed; and short and long-term debt—without compromising its long-term goals and objectives. Countries estimate sustainable levels of borrowing using critical levels or benchmarks of various debt indicators that are relevant. There are no values of debt indicators that can apply across the board to all countries at various levels of development. Sustainability is a dynamic concept that has to be judged using numerous indicators.

When judging debt service problems it is necessary to distinguish those of liquidity from insolvency. This is easy in the case of corporate entities though difficult in the case of sovereign borrowers. Firms that have a positive net worth, i.e., those whose assets exceed liabilities, but face difficulties in meeting their financial obligations have a liquidity problem. Those that have a negative net worth are insolvent. It is difficult to extend the concepts of solvency and liquidity to a sovereign borrower as measuring the net worth of a country's present problems. Countries do not disappear or are not taken over because of financial problems. Accordingly, creditors and investors tend to judge liquidity and solvency by analysing a country's debt indicators.

International financial institutions use ceilings or benchmarks of debt indicators to assess a country's debt situation. These are averages determined by inter-country analyses. In view of this, it is best that a country develops its own early warning signals of a possible debt crisis as critical levels tend to vary from country to country and even within a country over time. Some vulnerability indicators are defined in the following section and should be estimated if they are considered to be appropriate for Sri Lanka. These are additional indicators that enable a more comprehensive assessment of a country's capacity to cope with external debt service problems.

The methodology for determining external indebtedness is better developed than for domestic indebtedness. External debt and vulnerability indicators are applicable to the whole economy and therefore to the total external debt of a country. There are no ceilings for the external debt of the public sector or central government. On the other hand, fiscal indicators are applicable to the central government only. There is no basis to expand these indicators to the entire public sector.

Vulnerability Indicators

There are several vulnerability indicators which supplement the analysis of indebtedness using debt indicators and enable a more comprehensive assessment of the country's ability to cope with debt service problems. They are the following:

(a) Concentration of exports which is the percentage share in total exports of the main export and the three main export products. It provides a measure of export diversity and the extent to which the country is reliant on a narrow range of products. The assumption is that a lower diversity will result in a greater volatility of exports.

(b)   Variability of exports which is the standard deviation of export values over the latest 10-year period for which information is available as a percentage of the average export level. This provides a measure of the extent to which export earnings have fluctuated over the past 10 years.

(c)   Current account deficit[21] excluding interest and net official transfers as a share of the GDP. This provides a measure of the extent to which the country would continue to be reliant on external resources even if its debt service burden was eliminated.

(d)   Foreign exchange reserves coverage is the proportion of reserves to the annual level of imports of goods and services in the latest 12-month period. A higher reserves coverage indicates a greater capacity to cope with adverse shocks to the economy.

(e)   Aid dependency is the extent of reliance of the current account deficit on net official financing. A higher figure indicates less exposure to volatility in private capital flows but greater sensitivity to the terms of official financing including policy implementation.

(f)   The fiscal burden as determined by the share of government external debt service in government revenue and expenditure and the shares of tax revenue and foreign grants in GDP. The higher the share of external debt service, the lower the flexibility of the government to respond to adverse shocks. Higher levels of tax revenue to GDP (and less reliance on grants) is an indicator of a more developed tax base which should enable the government to respond effectively to adverse shocks.

(g)   The policy track record of the government is an indicator of the stability of both official financing and private flows in the future and the ability to undertake policy adjustment.

Sri Lanka's Indicators[22]

External debt indicators show that Sri Lanka is a less indebted country. Some vulnerability indicators have been estimated from among those proposed in the earlier section. These are intended to assess Sri Lanka's capacity to withstand liquidity problems and other shocks to the economy. The foreign exchange reserves cover ratio—which is relevant in a country that has only liberalized its current account—has been below the three to four months level (the minimum below which it should not be allowed to drop) during 1992 and 1999–2001. It has been around the threshold level for the rest of the period. This indicator and the absolute level of official foreign exchange assets should be closely monitored because they are low. Short-term debt as a ratio of total external debt has been below 10 per cent during the entire period. Its level as a ratio of official foreign exchange assets has been around 24–29 per cent except in 1992–93 and 2000–2001 when the ratio was in the range of 40–60 per cent. These higher levels at the beginning and end of the period were due to the low level of official foreign exchange assets. Although this ratio is more relevant to a country that has liberalized its capital account, it is not at a critical level.

The government debt service to government revenue ratio was above 50 per cent for the entire 10- year period. It was 60 per cent and above for half the period and 83 and 76 per cent in 2000 and 2001 respectively. There is no internationally agreed critical level for this indicator. It should be closely monitored when it is in the range of 15–30 per cent and urgent action taken when it goes above 30 per cent. Since Sri Lanka's levels have been much above this for the past 10 years, urgent and sustained action is long overdue. The comparison of government debt service to government expenditure shows that it has been in the range of 36–52 per cent during the 10 years. It does not provide any fiscal space when it is at a level of the order of 50 per cent, which it was in 2000 and 2001 and crowded out other critical expenditures.

Another issue of concern has been the declining trend of government tax revenue to GDP ratio. Total government revenue as a ratio of GDP of Sri Lanka compares favourably with the ratios for other South Asian countries except in the smaller countries and some South East Asian and Mekong region countries. However, when tax revenue collections in Sri Lanka were reviewed, the ratio declined from 17.9 per cent in 1992 to 14.6 per cent in 2001. The decline is sharper, from 17 per cent to 11.5 per cent during the same period if the National Security Levy is deducted. This shows that the development of the tax base is urgent and should be given serious attention. Revenue constraints may cause difficulties in making both domestic and foreign debt service payments.

Future Action

Public debt management has become a priority in Sri Lanka as it has in some other Asian countries. The government has decided to establish a PDMO to deal with all aspects of debt management. The activities currently undertaken by various departments of the Ministry of Finance and Central Bank at various stages of the domestic and external loan cycles, which are principally the Front and Back Office functions, need to be reviewed and rationalized, gaps identified and activities recommended to deal with them. An appropriate institutional structure should be proposed to build on the existing capacities. Further, the laws dealing with public sector borrowing should be reviewed with a view to consolidation and drafting a new public debt management law covering both domestic and external borrowings and their management. The new law should enable the preparation of regulations and procedures relating to mobilizing resources for the public sector from both domestic and external sources, and the issue of government guarantees and on-lending.

It is recognized that public debt management activities are presently performed by many departments of the Ministry of Finance and Central Bank. It is not imperative that these be transferred to the PDMO immediately in the new organizational arrangements. It may be more efficient for some of them to remain where they are initially. It is more important to ensure that all debt management functions are performed and establish firm institutional links to one or more divisions or units of the PDMO in their execution or the use of its output. In the long term, however, they should be brought under the umbrella of the PDMO.

Sri Lanka should adopt annual borrowing plans which will ensure that selected debt indicators remain below the maximum levels that have been adopted as government policy. Given that Sri Lanka is classified as a 'less indebted' country, it is recommended that the maximum level of debt service and the two present value indicators (PV/GNP and PV/XGS) be set at the ceiling for the ratios for less indebted countries. Based on Table 7.1 the ceilings for these should be 18, 48 and 132 per cent respectively. The nominal value debt indicators, i.e., DOD/GNP and DOD/XGS, should be used if the present value indicators cannot be estimated. In this case the ceilings for these two indicators should be 30 and 165 per cent respectively. Other indicators that can be controlled by policy action should also be kept under frequent review. The minimum foreign exchange reserves cover should be set higher than the minimum range of three to four months, perhaps at six months, and the maximum level of government debt service to government revenue ratio should be set at 30 per cent. It is recognized that this ceiling is academic in the present context given that the current ratio is much higher. It may take five to 10 years of sound budget management and a concerted effort to extend the short-term maturities of domestic debt when they fall to reduce this ratio below the ceiling. While a borrowing policy can be formulated which initially uses ceilings for indicators that are based on inter-country analyses, Sri Lanka should over time revise them based on experience gained in using them.

Effective budget management measures should be introduced to support the fiscal consolidation initiatives of the government. It would involve a combination of policies to increase government revenue, including tax reforms, improved collection procedures and measures to reduce current expenditures. The fiscal consolidation by the government will be directed towards meeting the targets set out in the Fiscal Management (Responsibility) Act of reducing the budget deficit from the 2002 level of 8.9 per cent to 5 per cent by 2006 and maintained at that level thereafter to reduce the borrowing requirements. It is expected that these measures will reduce the government debt outstanding to GDP ratio from the current level of over 100 per cent to 85 per cent by 2006 and 60 per cent by 2013.

A borrowing policy covers both quantitative targets and qualitative issues. It is important for any borrowing plan that loan funds be used for high priority development activities that are productive or build essential social and physical infrastructure. Individual borrowing decisions should be based on responsible behaviour of the government without which borrowing ceilings will be ineffective. The rates of return—financial or economic—should be adequate to generate surpluses to make debt service payments. Loans for the social sectors and environmental protection would not be able to meet this condition. In this event the government should meet the debt service payments from general revenue.

It is necessary to recognize that arrears on debt service payments could accumulate due to bad loan and investment decisions even though the borrowing is within the approved ceiling. These should be closely monitored particularly in the case of borrowings by state corporations and corrective action taken in a timely manner. Technical arrears should not be allowed to arise due to delays in making debt service payments. A policy on the accumulation of domestic arrears by the government should be adopted.

It should cover the total value of arrears and the maximum period after which they should be cleared.

The policy will not be complete without monitoring loan implementation on government borrowing including those that are on-lent to state corporations. The extent to which the PDMO should become involved depends on the effectiveness of the monitoring activities of the operating ministries. Borrowings are made on behalf of the government by the Ministry of Finance and accordingly, the ministry is accountable to the lender for the use of borrowed funds.

NOTES

1. 21 March 2001.
2. Private sector borrowing can be subject to approval and monitoring only when the capital account has not been liberalized.
3. International Monetary Fund and World Bank, *Developing Government Bond Markets, A Handbook*, 2001.
4. Annual Report 2002, Central Bank of Sri Lanka
5. Tables 1 and 3 of Appendix.
6. In view of the large share of the public sector in total external debt outstanding, the comments made in regard to the external debt of the country apply to the public sector as well.
7. Tables 1 and 2 of Appendix.
8. Total debt service payments as a ratio of exports of goods and services.
9. Table 4 of Appendix.
10. Interest (INT), Debt outstanding (DOD), Total debt service (TDS), Exports of goods and services (XGS), Present value of debt service payments (PV).
11. Table 5 of Appendix.
12. Defined as loans with a grant element of 25 per cent or more.
13. *Global Development Finance*, Vol. 2, The World Bank, 2002.
14. Table 6 of Appendix.
15. Table 7 of Appendix. Net flows are defined as disbursements minus repayments while net transfers are defined by reducing interest payments from net flows.
16. Table 8 of Appendix.
17. Tables 9, 10 and 11 of Appendix.
18. Draft Report of the First Mission: Central Government Debt Management and Domestic Debt Market Development in Sri Lanka, World Bank and IMF, 2003.
19. Table 9, 10 and 11 of Appendix.
20. Table 12 of Appendix.
21. Balance of Payments Manual (Fifth Edition), IMF, 1993.
22. Table 13 of Appendix.

References

Central Bank of Sri Lanka (1993, 1997, 2000, 2001, 2002), *Annual Report*, Colombo, Sri Lanka.

International Monetary Fund (1993), 'Balance of Payments Manual (Fifth Edition)', Washington, USA.

International Monetary Fund and The World Bank (2001), *Developing Government Bond Markets, A Handbook*, Washington, USA.

——————— **(2001),** 'Guidelines for Public Debt Management', Washington, USA.

The World Bank (2002), *Global Development Finance*, Vols I and II, Washington, USA.

Select Readings

Kappagoda, Nihal (2001), 'Public Debt Management: A New Priority' in *Bulletin on Asia-Pacific Perspective 2001/02*, New York: ESCAP, United Nations.

——————— **(2002),** *Institutional Framework for Public Sector Borrowing*, Geneva: UNITAR.

International Monetary Fund and The World Bank (2002), 'Guidelines for Public Debt Management: Accompanying Document', Washington, USA.

——————— **(2003),** 'Central Government Debt Management and Domestic Debt Market Development in Sri Lanka: Draft Report of the First Mission', Washington, USA.

Appendix

The statistics provided in the tables cover the period 1992–2001 except in Table 12. Unless otherwise indicated, statistics relate to medium and long-term debt. Statistics of external public debt cover public and publicly guaranteed debt.

Abbreviations used in the tables

CUB	Committed Undisbursed Balance
DI	Disbursements
DOD	Debt Outstanding
GDP	Gross Domestic Product
GDS	Government Debt Service
GE	Government Expenditure
GNP	Gross National Product
GR	Government Revenue
M&LT	Medium and Long-Term
P&PG	Public and Publicly Guaranteed
PNG	Private Non Guaranteed
PV	Present Value
XGS	Exports of Goods and Services

Table 7.1A

TOTAL EXTERNAL DEBT OUTSTANDING

(US$ million)

	1992	1993	1994	1995	1996	1997	1998	1999	2000	2001
Government	5,288	6,307	6,960	7,303	7,134	6,791	7,468	7,438	7,077	7,184
State corporations and private sector with govt. guarantees	423	437	740	783	643	670	718	944	1028	744
P&PG debt	5,711	6,744	7,700	8,086	7,777	7,461	8,186	8,382	8,105	7,928
PNG debt	191	235	348	372	267	270	277	286	278	248
IMF drawings	465	615	596	530	530	433	367	258	161	209
Total M&LT external DOD	6,368	7,594	8,644	8,988	8,574	8,164	8,830	8,926	8,544	8,385
Short-term debt	580	639	893	1079	498	478	484	475	575	557
Total external DOD	6,947	8,233	9,537	10,067	9,072	8,642	9,314	9,401	9,119	8,942
Share P&PG debt in total M&LT Debt (%)	89.7	88.8	89.1	90.0	90.7	91.4	92.7	93.9	94.9	94.5
Share of short term in total external DOD (%)	8.3	7.8	9.4	10.7	5.5	5.5	5.2	5.1	6.3	6.2

Sources: Central Bank of Sri Lanka, *Annual Reports,* 1993, 1997, 2000 and 2001, and External Resources Department for Government DOD.

Table 7.2A

EXTERNAL DEBT SERVICE PAYMENTS

(US$ million)

	1992	1993	1994	1995	1996	1997	1998	1999	2000	2001
L&MT debt principal	244	195	277	419	392	364	387	451	524	480
Interest	198	139	242	304	300	297	282	291	326	249
IMF										
Repurchases	74	18	13	33	47	66	83	100	97	78
Charges	11	2	7	8	7	6	7	5	5	4
Total payments	526	354	540	764	746	733	759	846	952	811
Debt service ratio	17.1	13.7	13.7	16.5	15.3	13.3	13.3	15.2	14.7	13.3
Share of govt. debt service payments	51	63	60	45	51	54	55	53	46	55

Sources: Central Bank of Sri Lanka, *Annual Reports*, 1993, 1997, 2000 and 2001.

Table 7.3A

BREAKDOWN OF EXTERNAL DEBT OUTSTANDING BY CREDITOR CATEGORY

(US$ million)

	1993		1995		1997		1999		2001	
	Amount	%	Amount	%	Amount	%	Amount	%	Amount	%
Bilateral	3,062	41.4	3,532	41.0	3,063	37.6	3,661	43.7	3,276	41.7
Multilateral	3,499	47.3	4,062	47.2	4,078	50.1	3,710	44.3	3,545	45.1
Commercial	837	11.3	1,021	11.8	1,001	12.3	1,010	12.0	1,038	13.2
Total	7,398	100.0	8,615	100.0	8,142	100.0	8,381	100.0	7,859	100.0

Source: External Resources Department.

Table 7.4A

EXTERNAL DEBT INDICATORS (PER CENT)

	1992	1993	1994	1995	1996	1997	1998	1999	2000	2001
Total external DOD/GDP	69	69	63	66	59	53	55	56	54	53
Total external DOD/XGS	207	194	197	176	164	140	145	154	131	132
Debt service ratio	17	14	14	17	15	13	13	15	15	13
Interest/XGS	7	5	6	7	6	6	4	5	5	4
PV/GNP	41	41	41	43	41	38	43	46	44	n.a.
PV/XGS	103	107	109	101	97	89	97	103	98	n.a.

Source: Central Bank of Sri Lanka, various years, and World Bank (for PV indicators).

Table 7.5A

AVERAGE TERMS OF NEW COMMITMENTS

	1993	1995	1997	1999	2001
Interest (%)	3.1	3.6	2.6	1.9	2.7
Maturity (years)	27.2	24.1	26.5	34.9	19.5
Grace period (years)	8.1	7.3	9.7	8.5	4.1
Grant element (%)	55.0	31.6	55.9	66.6	39.3
Official (%)	69.4	42.5	65.1	73.3	52.6
Private (%)	9.2	15.1	6.0	12.5	11.7

Source: External Resources Department.

Table 7.6A

CURRENCY COMPOSITION OF P&PG EXTERNAL DOD (PER CENT)

	1993	1995	1997	1999	2001
Canadian dollars	1.6	1.3	1.2	1.0	0.9
Deutsche marks	7.3	7.1	5.9	4.7	0.1
Euro	—	—	—	0.6	5.6
French francs	2.1	2.0	1.6	0.7	0.4
Netherlands guilders	1.4	1.4	1.1	0.7	0.1
Pounds sterling	2.1	1.4	1.2	0.6	0.2
SDR	33.7	36.0	38.8	35.5	36.1
US dollars	25.9	24.4	26.2	26.5	29.6
Yen	24.0	24.7	22.6	28.2	25.4
Others	1.9	1.7	1.4	2.1	1.6

Source: External Resources Department.

Table 7.7A

AVERAGE NET TRANSFERS ON P&PG DEBT

(US$ million)

	1993–95	1996–98	1999–2001
Bilateral	12.6	−1.8	17.5
Multilateral	194.6	94.4	−24.9
Private	−19.0	−14.3	−79.9
Total	188.2	78.3	−87.3

Source: External Resources Department.

Table 7.8A

LOAN COMMITMENTS, DEBT OUTSTANDING, COMMITTED UNDISBURSED BALANCES AND DISBURSEMENTS ON P&PG EXTERNAL DEBT

(US$ million)

	1992	1993	1994	1995	1996	1997	1998	1999	2000	2001
Multilateral										
DOD	2,593	2,885	3,231	3,428	3,512	3,423	3,653	3,452	3,302	3,336
CUB	1,460	1,300	1,058	915	904	774	836	963	902	1,001
DI	373	338	253	199	259	180	224	155	128	267
Loan commitments	114	222	77	102	343	135	284	345	143	413
Bilateral										
DOD	2,925	3,062	3,382	3,532	3,319	3,063	3,444	3,661	3,463	3,276
CUB	961	1,185	1,476	1,445	1,509	1,484	1,583	1,805	1,410	406
DI	104	128	220	243	164	162	252	216	227	289
Loan commitments	286	324	411	263	465	385	236	290	111	471
Private										
DOD	797	837	995	1,021	941	1,001	1,149	1,010	855	1,038
CUB	33	57	93	140	153	32	28	48	55	140
DI	169	141	282	185	94	241	285	39	114	447
Loan commitments	183	170	319	235	161	125	278	60	122	573
Total										
DOD	6,315	6,784	7,608	7,981	7,772	7,487	8,246	8,122	7,619	7,649
CUB	2,453	2,541	2,626	2,499	2,566	2,290	2,440	2,817	2,367	2,547
DI	646	608	755	627	517	584	761	409	469	1,003

Source: External Resources Department.

Table 7.9A

Growth in Total Government Debt Outstanding

(rupees million)

	1992	1993	1994	1995	1996	1997	1998	1999	2000	2001
Domestic debt	1,70,020	2,13,685	2,49,119	2,85,759	3,56,703	3,87,740	4,63,426	5,43,465	6,76,660	8,15,965
Short-term	97,924	1,01,845	1,08,725	1,27,470	1,49,798	1,37,494	1,63,253	1,75,886	2,08,017	2,78,624
M&LT term	72,096	1,11,840	1,40,394	1,58,289	2,06,905	2,50,246	3,00,173	3,67,579	4,68,643	5,37,341
Foreign debt	2,35,538	2,70,224	3,01,812	3,46,286	3,59,685	3,76,331	4,61,273	5,07,866	5,42,040	6,36,741
Total DOD	4,05,558	4,83,909	5,50,931	6,32,045	7,16,388	7,64,071	9,24,699	10,51,331	12,18,700	14,52,706
DOD/GDP	95.4	96.9	95.1	94.6	93.3	85.8	90.8	95.1	96.9	103.2
Share of domestic debt		44.2	45.2	45.2	49.8	50.7	50.1	51.7	55.5	56.2

Source: Central Bank of Sri Lanka, *Annual Reports*, 1993, 1997, 2000, 2001 and 2002.

Table 7.10A

Government Debt Service (GDS) Payments in Rupees Million

	1992	1993	1994	1995	1996	1997	1998	1999	2000	2001
GDS-external	12,694	12,065	13,117	14,639	17,230	19,943	25,651	30,192	32,297	37,668
GDS-domestic	39,324	46,873	50,476	63,024	64,933	63,786	89,215	73,693	1,43,429	1,41,404
Total GDS	52,018	58,938	63,593	77,663	82,163	83,729	1,14,866	1,03,885	1,75,726	1,79,072
Government revenue (GR)	85,781	98,339	1,10,038	1,36,258	1,46,279	1,65,036	1,75,032	1,95,905	2,11,282	2,34,296
Government expenditure (GE)	1,16,973	1,41,660	1,70,764	2,03,483	2,18,659	2,35,097	2,68,179	2,79,159	3,35,823	3,86,518
Total GDS/GR (%)	60.6	59.9	57.8	57.0	56.2	50.7	65.6	53.0	83.2	76.4
Total GDS/GE (%)	44.5	41.8	37.2	38.2	37.6	35.6	42.8	37.2	52.3	46.3
Share of domestic debt in GDS	75.6	79.5	79.4	81.2	79.0	76.2	77.7	70.9	81.6	79.0

Source: Central Bank of Sri Lanka, *Annual Reports*, 1993, 1997, 2000, 2001 and 2002.

Table 7.11A

Growth in Government Domestic Debt by Maturity, Instrument and Institution

(rupees million)

	1992	1993	1994	1995	1996	1997	1998	1999	2000	2001
Total domestic	1,70,020	2,13,685	2,49,119	2,85,759	3,56,703	3,87,740	4,63,426	5,43,465	6,76,660	8,15,965
Debt maturity										
Short term	97,924	1,01,845	1,08,725	1,27,470	1,49,788	1,37,494	1,63,253	1,75,886	2,08,017	2,78,624
M&LT	72,096	1,11,840	1,40,394	1,58,289	2,06,905	2,50,246	3,00,173	3,67,579	4,68,643	5,37,341
Instruments										
Rupee securities	69,180	1,05,707	1,37,554	1,57,928	2,05,975	2,39,475	2,50,570	2,62,056	2,63,888	2,92,813
Treasury bills	87,096	97,196	98,896	1,13,771	1,24,996	1,14,996	1,19,996	1,24,996	1,34,996	1,70,995
Sri Lanka development bonds	—	—	—	—	—	—	—	—	—	14,749
Treasury bonds	—	—	—	—	—	10,000	48,915	1,04,867	2,04,124	2,29,174
Other	13,744	10,782	12,669	14,060	25,732	23,269	43,945	51,546	73,652	1,08,234
Institution										
Central Bank	34,932	16,480	21,345	28,684	34,303	19,770	27,179	48,867	97,778	92,871
Commercial Banks	23,179	73,665	78,698	84,671	67,461	80,776	85,875	90,804	1,01,252	1,63,937
Total for banks	58,111	90,145	1,00,043	1,13,355	1,01,764	1,00,536	1,13,054	1,39,671	1,99,030	2,56,808
National Savings Bank	30,782	37,767	46,407	48,406	47,794	62,498	67,260	79,555	87,263	95,976
Employees Provident Fund	54,563	65,645	79,745	95,000	1,13,236	1,34,867	1,57,711	1,81,581	2,11,742	2,45,028
Other	26,564	20,138	22,923	28,998	93,909	89,839	1,25,401	1,42,658	1,78,625	2,18,153

Source: Central Bank of Sri Lanka, *Annual Reports*, 1993, 1997, 2000 and 2001.

Table 7.12A
TOTAL GOVERNMENT DEBT OUTSTANDING (RUPEES MILLION) — INDEPENDENCE TO 2000

	1948	1950	1955	1960	1965	1970	1975	1980	1985	1990	1995	2000
Domestic debt	392	515	889	1,937	3,697	6,295	10,859	29,070	62,611	1,33,897	2,85,759	6,76,660
Foreign debt	125	125	205	294	489	1,578	3,705	22,277	69,452	1,76,883	3,46,286	5,42,040
Total DOD	517	640	1,094	2,230	4,185	7,873	14,564	51,347	1,32,064	3,10,779	6,32,045	12,18,700
Share of domestic debt	75.8	80.4	81.3	86.8	88.3	80.0	74.6	56.6	47.4	43.1	45.2	55.5
GDP	n.a.	n.a.	n.a.	6,711	8,084	13,664	26,577	66,527	1,52,375	3,21,784	6,67,772	12,57,634
DOD/GDP	n.a.	n.a.	n.a.	36.4	51.8	57.6	54.8	77.2	86.7	96.6	94.6	96.9

Source: Central Bank of Sri Lanka, *Annual Reports*, 1993, 1997, 2000 and 2001.

Table 7.13A
VULNERABILITY AND OTHER INDICATORS

	1992	1993	1994	1995	1996	1997	1998	1999	2000	2001
Vulnerability Indicators										
Gross official foreign exchange assets coverage* (months)	2.7	4.3	4.5	4.1	3.8	3.7	3.6	2.9	1.5	2.3
Short term to total external debt (%)	8.3	7.8	9.4	10.7	5.5	5.5	5.2	5.1	6.3	6.2
Short term external debt to official foreign exchange assets (%)	60.4	42.7	25.2	26.3	25.7	23.6	24.4	29.0	54.8	41.6
Current account balance**/GDP (%)	–6.4	–5.3	–7.8	–6.5	–5.2	–2.9	–1.8	–3.7	–6.6	–1.7
Government debt service/ government revenue (%)	61	60	58	57	56	51	66	53	83	76
Government debt service/government expenditure (%)	45	41	37	38	38	36	43	37	52	46
Government tax revenue/GDP (%)	17.9	17.6	17.2	17.8	17.0	16.0	14.5	15.0	14.5	14.6
Other										
Exchange rate to US$ (Rs at year end)	46.00	49.56	49.98	54.05	56.71	61.29	67.78	72.12	82.65	93.16
Official foreign Exchange assets ($ Mn at year end)	936	1675	2022	2063	1937	2029	1984	1639	1049	1338
CSE all share Index (year end)	605	979	987	664	603	702	597	573	448	621
Market capitalization (Rs Bn) (year end)	65	124	143	107	104	129	117	113	89	124

Source: Central Bank of Sri Lanka, various years.
Notes: * Months of imports of goods and services.
** Excluding grants.

8

Exchange Rate[1]

Sisira Jayasuriya

Introduction

Exchange rate policies in developing countries, including Sri Lanka, have been an area of interest for Gamini Corea throughout his professional career, both as a senior government planner and Central Bank officer in Sri Lanka and as an international development economist. His views on this issue, as on many others, reflected the 'internationalism' of his overall perspective: he combined an appreciation of the usefulness of exchange rate policies for stimulating export growth in individual countries with concerns about their potential impact on aggregate global supplies and prices, when many developing countries simultaneously depreciate their currencies in response to downturns in global commodity markets.

In Sri Lanka, Gamini Corea was an influential participant in the discussions that led to the setting up of a multiple exchange rate system—the Foreign Exchange Entitlement Certificates (FEECs) scheme in 1968—which aimed to provide enhanced incentives for exports through a more favourable (depreciated) exchange rate. Though the initial aim of moving to a market responsive rate was quickly abandoned, this particular measure was significant in that it was the first attempt in Sri Lanka to deliberately use the exchange rate as a policy tool for export promotion. From that time onwards, the twin effects of an exchange rate change—its impact on export performance on the one hand, and on inflation on the other—have dominated public debates about the appropriate exchange rate policy. Both public interest and confusion about exchange rate issues remain alive in Sri Lanka, with politicians claiming that even a small rupee appreciation against the US dollar is a sign of the strength of the economy and the success of government economic policies, while exporter lobby groups are calling for currency depreciation, claiming that they are experiencing major difficulties as a result of appreciation. In reality, the rupee, despite a minor appreciation against the US dollar since June 2003, actually experienced a significant overall effective depreciation in 2003, due to its sharp falls against the euro and yen (Central Bank, 2003).

This chapter looks at some of the main issues related to exchange rate policy and the surrounding debates during the last decade or so. During this period, the exchange rate regime as well as the broader policy environment have changed in quite fundamental ways, with the shift to a floating exchange rate regime in 2001 marking the culmination of a series of measures towards a market responsive exchange rate regime. The chapter first outlines the changes in exchange rate regimes and the behaviour of the exchange rate and then moves on to an analytical discussion, highlighting some key issues and challenges that monetary authorities face.

BACKGROUND

The shift to a multiple exchange rate system in 1968 marked the first major change in exchange rate policy since the setting up of currency arrangements in the post-independence era that saw Sri Lanka operating a unified 'fixed but adjustable' exchange rate system as part of the Bretton Woods system. Until then, the fixed exchange rate had been maintained in the face of mounting payments difficulties from the mid-1950s onwards with resort to ever more stringent import restrictions and exchange controls.[2] The 1968 changes proved quite inadequate to overcome the payments problems and the early 1970s saw draconian exchange rate and trade restrictions put in place. Popular dissatisfaction with these controls and resulting shortages were key factors that paved the way for a change in government in 1977.

Shortly after coming to power in early 1977, the new government of J.R. Jayawardene abandoned the dual exchange rate system and established a unified exchange rate system as part of a broader package of policy reforms. The rupee was initially allowed to float following the unification with only limited Central Bank intervention. But interventions soon intensified, particularly from the first half of 1981, and the float was eventually abandoned in November 1982. The exchange rate regime became a (quite tightly!) 'managed float' and remained so until the shift to a floating regime in 2001. Though the Central Bank claimed that the exchange rate regime was market responsive, the rupee was permitted to depreciate only marginally until 1989, despite a steadily widening current account deficit. Clearly, the Central Bank used the exchange rate primarily as a nominal anchor to contain inflation, rather than as a tool for export promotion. In 1989, persistent macroeconomic imbalances generated a payments crisis that led to the adoption of a major structural adjustment programme. A key component of the adjustment programme was implementation of a more flexible exchange rate policy, which involved a significant devaluation at the very outset; the Sri Lankan rupee depreciated 17.4 per cent in 1989 vis-à-vis the US dollar, the intervention currency.[3]

Throughout the 1990s, the Central Bank made daily adjustments to the exchange rate, responding to developments in the foreign exchange market, and implemented what was in practice a crawling peg exchange rate regime. The overall effect of the adjustments was a steady depreciation. Immediately following the implementation of the adjustment programme, there was a significant revival in foreign investment (in both foreign direct investment [FDI] inflows, particularly into the garments sector, and some portfolio capital), in export growth and in overall economic growth. The capital inflows were facilitated by measures towards current account convertibility and the relaxation of some capital controls. As a result of these capital flows, some of which were interest rate sensitive, the monetary authorities confronted the novel problem of coping with the inflationary impact of large private capital flows.

Though it is difficult to estimate the direct contribution of the exchange rate change to this improved economic performance, the exchange rate adjustment did help to revitalise export performance and favourably influenced capital flows. But the role of the exchange rate adjustment is sometimes over emphasized and is unlikely to have this effect in the absence of other components of the adjustment programme, such as more liberal and investor friendly policies, and the general feeling of optimism among both domestic and foreign investors generated by the restoration of political stability. Athukorala and Rajapatirana (2000) have demonstrated that the exchange rate adjustment was not the primary driver of the improved export performance. Export growth came from foreign investment attracted by the combination of trade and investment liberalization and the very high quota rents associated with Sri Lanka's preferential access to developed country textile and garments markets.

By the mid-1990s, however, these large private capital flows had dried up and export growth too started to slow down. There were several factors that impacted on overall investor sentiment and broader economic performance, such as the change in the government in 1994, the Mexican crisis in 1994 and the re-eruption of the civil war in early 1995. But some analysts focused on the Central Bank policies as the main culprit for this faltering export performance, alleging that its policies aimed at maintaining the nominal exchange rate at too high a level, tended to appreciate the real exchange rate (particularly during 1994–95), raise the cost of capital and erode competitiveness of exports.

These views found a receptive audience in certain quarters and generated a considerable amount of public debate.[4] In fact, there was no significant real appreciation during 1994–95 and, in any case, analysis of Central Bank intervention during this period indicated that it actually 'leant against the wind' to achieve a greater degree of depreciation than would have been warranted solely by the foreign exchange market fundamentals, despite the Bank's own refusal to publicly admit that it had done more in the market than merely intervene to smooth fluctuations.[5] Indeed, the Central Bank's exchange rate strategy involved some degree of real exchange rate targeting, with systematic depreciation of the nominal rate in an attempt to resist appreciation of the real rate. This was not an easy task because there were forces outside the control of the monetary authorities that generated persistent pressure for real appreciation.

The domestic policy environment during the second half of the 1990s was dominated by the escalating costs of the war and the government's fiscal deficit rose to 9–10 per cent of gross domestic product (GDP). But the pressure that such a fiscal deficit would have normally placed on the current account was mitigated by an unusually long-lived boom in international tea prices. This, in combination with a strong expansion of output, enabled export revenues to be sustained well into the second half of the decade. Even the 1997 Asian economic crisis initially appeared to have no major impact on the Sri Lankan economy or its export revenues. The Central Bank, concerned that a large depreciation would destabilize the foreign exchange market in the wake of the East Asian currency collapses, successfully resisted incipient speculative pressure on the rupee. Ministers made political capital out of this, claiming that the maintenance of the value of the rupee was evidence of the competence and success of the government's economic management. A slowdown in manufactured export growth and a major downturn in many commodity exports was already clearly visible, and it was obvious that exports would face greatly intensified competitive pressure in the aftermath of the Asian crisis. However, the rupee was permitted to depreciate by less than 10 per cent in 1998 against the US dollar and only 6 per cent in 1999. Not surprisingly, it did not take long before serious external sector imbalances developed.

Once the tea boom ended, the trade and current account balances deteriorated rapidly, producing a sharp fall in the country's foreign assets by 2000. A further increase in the fiscal deficit in 2000—driven by election related pork barrelling expenditures— aggravated macroeconomic instability. A payments crisis loomed—during the second half of 2000, official reserves (excluding the Asian Clearing Account) dropped by more than $600 million—putting pressure on the exchange rate (IMF, 2002). External funding support became imperative. Discussions with the IMF led to a floating exchange rate regime in January 2001 and a standby arrangement was signed in April 2001. Despite clear signs of a slowing economy, interest rates were raised in late 2000 and maintained in the first half of 2001. These high interest rates heightened political instability and a poor external environment pushed the economy into the largest contraction since the Great Depression of the 1930s. The maintenance of high interest rates until well into the second half of 2001 is, at first glance, puzzling but not surprising when placed in the political context: from the viewpoint of the government, a large depreciation of the currency in an election year was politically very unattractive and anything that could stabilize the currency level in the all important short run was clearly the lesser evil.[6]

The change in government, with the UNF under the leadership of Ranil Wickremesinghe coming to power the cessation of active military conflict, prospects of a lasting peace and an improved external environment led to restoration of growth (albeit moderate) and the slowing of both inflation and the depreciation of the currency. It is too early yet to judge the performance of the 'free float' exchange rate regime. However, as the following discussion will hopefully make clear, it can be said with confidence that there is no guarantee of long-term stability in the exchange rate regime without changes in some of the economic fundamentals. This requires no highly sophisticated or complex analysis. What the story of Sri Lanka's monetary policy experience in recent years demonstrates is the simple point that, monetary authorities have only limited capacity to affect the course of the economy in the long run when fiscal policy systematically undermines macroeconomic stability. Before we look at the Sri Lankan experience, some of the basic underlying theoretical and measurement issues are discussed.

The Exchange Rate, External Balance and Competitiveness

The role and importance of the real exchange rate as an instrument of external sector balance has been a subject with a relatively long history in economics literature. But interest in the role of exchange rate policy as a tool for export promotion over a sustained period is rather more recent. It owes much to analyses of the East Asian export growth performance that have highlighted the role of the competitive (even 'undervalued') real exchange rates in their export successes. In practice, the measurement of the real exchange rate poses several problems. Arriving at a consensus on even the conceptual definition of an equilibrium rate has proved surprisingly difficult; estimating such an equilibrium rate, even more so.

There are two broad approaches to defining and measuring the real exchange rate. The most widely used is the real effective exchange rate (REER) (or the 'External' RER) defined as the ratio of foreign prices to domestic prices. It is usually measured as the ratio of an index of the foreign trading partners' representative price levels expressed in domestic currency terms using bilateral exchange rates, with appropriate weights for the relative importance of each country—typically 'trade weights' that reflect the share of each country in the overall trade of the home country. Thus, the real effective exchange rate is given by:

$$REER = \frac{EP^w}{P^d} \qquad (1)$$

where, E is the nominal exchange rate defined as the number of home currency (rupees) per foreign currency, P^w, foreign (world market) price level and P^d, domestic price level. E is the nominal effective exchange rate (NEER) measured as the weighted averages of bilateral exchange rates and P^w is the weighted average of individual country price indices relating to the trading partner countries.[7] The way that RER changes in response to changes in its component variables can be expressed in the form of proportional changes, with a ^ sign representing the proportional change in that variable, as:

$$R\hat{E}ER = \hat{E} + \hat{P}^w \qquad (2)$$

Thus, movements in the real exchange rate index bring together changes in the nominal exchange rates and the inflation differentials between the home country and its trading partners. If, because of changes in E (a nominal currency depreciation), foreign prices, in domestic prices or an amalgam of them, the numerical value of the REER rises (falls) the real exchange rate depreciates (appreciates) and foreign goods become more (less) expensive relative to domestic goods. In other words, a real depreciation (appreciation) is tantamount to an improvement (decline) in competitiveness of the home produced goods in both domestic and world markets. A real depreciation tends to improve the country's trade balance as both domestic and foreign demand switches to domestic goods, while a real appreciation has the opposite effect.

In its simplest form, the above measure treats all goods as internationally traded goods and has serious theoretical and empirical limitations. For example, if barriers to trade are non-existent, arbitrage would ensure that prices at home and abroad are identical, i.e., the 'law of one price' holds, which implies that the REER is always unity. Even if trade costs are positive, unless they changed over time, inter-country price level changes would be identical. As such, the concept of a real exchange rate defined in this way lacks any real value. But if we allow for the existence of both tradeable and non-tradeable goods, the measure acquires more content as international price differences between non-tradeables, by definition, cannot be arbitraged away.

A theoretically appealing and empirically useful real exchange rate concept can be defined for a small economy using the framework of the 'dependent economy' or Salter model. The country produces and consumes two goods, tradeables (T) and non-tradeables (N), with non-tradeable price (P_n) and tradeable price (P_t). Then the ratio, P_n/P_t, can be defined meaningfully as a real exchange rate— the 'internal' real exchange rate (IRER). Domestic resources move between tradeables and non-tradeables in response to changes in IRER and its movements can be interpreted as changes in the relative profitability or 'competitiveness' of tradeables.[8]

In this chapter, we will use the definition of the long-run equilibrium real exchange rate (LRER) as the rate that prevails when the economy is in internal and external balance given sustainable values of fundamentals including policy, exogenous and predetermined variables.[9] The importance of capital flows is now recognized in defining the concept of an equilibrium exchange rate, which is implicit in statements about currency overvaluation. If in the past, the generally accepted view of an equilibrium real exchange rate was one which maintains current account balance in the medium term; the appropriate definition in the context of substantial capital inflows is a real exchange rate which maintains a current account deficit just equal to the expected rate of capital inflows. A country which can, for whatever reason, expect to experience a certain level of capital inflows over a given time period will have a higher equilibrium rate than one which has a lower inflow.

This makes it important to distinguish between 'permanent' or sustainable levels of net capital flows from 'transient' flows in discussions of real exchange rate misalignment; it is the former which is relevant for determining the equilibrium rate. This is a difficult task and a degree of subjective judgement is unavoidable. In any case, such an equilibrium real exchange rate is not directly observable in the foreign exchange markets, and the fact that the market clears at a given nominal exchange rate (without Central Bank intervention) at a given point in time does not signify that the prevailing real exchange rate is a longer term equilibrium rate.

A deviation from this in any direction is regarded as a misalignment of the real exchange rate. In practice, overvaluations are considered of greater policy concern because the external sector disequilibrium associated with a persistent overvaluation, if not rectified, will generate an external sector crisis. For countries that are attempting to stimulate exports as part of an export-oriented development strategy, it becomes imperative that the real exchange rate is not permitted to become overvalued as that would erode the competitiveness of the export (or more generally, the tradeables) sectors.

FISCAL DEFICITS AND THE REAL EXCHANGE RATE

Standard national income identities imply that, starting from a point of internal and external balance, there will then be an excess of national expenditure over national income, unless there is an exact offsetting reduction in private sector expenditures.[10] At a given national income and a fixed exchange rate, this will produce a current account deficit (or widen the existing deficit). The real exchange appreciation is the associated relative price change and it is rooted in the demand and competition for real resources.

Consider the case of a fixed exchange rate regime and how a fiscal expansion affects relative prices (ignoring cross border capital flow issues).[11] So long as the exchange rate is kept unchanged and some part of the higher government expenditure goes on non-tradeables, their prices (which depend on domestic supply and demand) will increase; but higher demand for tradeables will have relatively minor effects on their prices (because for a 'small economy', like Sri Lanka, changes in its domestic consumption are too small to affect world prices of its traded goods). This implies an increase in relative prices of non-tradeables to tradeables (i.e., an appreciation of the real exchange rate) and an increase in the general price level. Profitability and production of non-tradeables will increase in response to the relative price change. Non-tradeables producers can offer higher prices than before to primary factors and thereby take some of them away from tradeables producers. Producers of tradeables (both exports and import-competing) experience this resource competition in the form of higher costs with no offsetting increases in prices, so their profitability and production will fall.

On the other hand, the relative price change will tend to increase demand for tradeables for consumption. The resulting excess demand for tradeables, resulting from lower domestic production and higher domestic demand, will generate a current account deficit and loss of foreign reserves or higher foreign debt. These are the familiar effects of a fiscal expansion under a fixed exchange rate. Sri Lanka has experience of such fiscal deficits and their implications for balance of payments; it was such payments problems that pushed governments to impose severe import and exchange controls in the pre-1977 period. In the final analysis, a fundamental imbalance between national income and national expenditure has to be overcome, either through the markets or through administrative controls on trade and payments.

If the currency is permitted to depreciate (or devalued) sufficiently, domestic relative prices change so that tradeables prices increase, thus producing a real exchange rate depreciation. The higher tradeables prices attract resources away from non-tradeables while expenditures switch away from tradeables to non-tradeables. Producers in the tradeables sector experience this as an improvement in their output price. However, unless this is accompanied by a cut in real national expenditure, higher demand and reduced supply in the non-tradeables market will push non-tradeables prices upwards until the initial relative price change is fully reversed. In other words, the initial depreciation of the real exchange rate will be fully eroded in the absence of expenditure reductions and the expenditure switching effects of the nominal depreciation will not result in a *real* depreciation. This process whereby the initial real exchange depreciation is eroded is experienced by tradeables producers as an increase in costs that erode the higher profitability from higher output prices.

Costs increase as a direct result of currency depreciation (devaluation) because some inputs are imported, but this increase is always lower than the improvement to profitability given by the depreciation so long as there is some domestic value added. But costs also increase because domestic input prices may increase in response to the general price level increase that results from the depreciation. The response of wages—the price of labour, the main component of domestic inputs—is crucial. If wages are linked to prices, a rise in wages will offset the positive effects of the devaluation on profitability, reversing the real depreciation. If higher prices are not compensated for by higher wages, there will be a real wage cut and the nominal depreciation would become a real depreciation. Thus, successful real exchange rate depreciation to correct an existing imbalance is achieved at the expense of workers' real wages. In other words, *the costs of government's fiscal profligacy—caused increasingly by expenditures on non-productive activities—are paid for by workers through lower real wages.*

This emphasizes the fundamental point that currency depreciations are not painless solutions to poor export performance and associated external imbalances arising from real exchange rate misalignments. They are a mechanism for passing the costs of wasteful government expenditures on to workers. *This is of course not an argument for maintaining overvalued exchange rates but a warning about how, at the end of the day, it is the poor who end up by paying for the fiscal deficits generated by wasteful or destructive expenditures.* The political temptation to obscure this fact is understandable, but the fact that this hardly ever figures in any of the discussions and analyses of this issue, underlines the hypocrisy and cynicism (mixed with ignorance) that pervades public debates about the merits and demerits of exchange rate depreciations. We now look at the actual behaviour of nominal and real exchange rates in Sri Lanka in recent years.[12]

BEHAVIOUR OF THE REAL EXCHANGE RATE IN SRI LANKA

In this chapter, we use a measure of the real exchange rate based on a measure of the REER as defined in Equation (1).[13] We measure movements in foreign prices by an index of the wholesale price indices (WPIs) of the major trading partners, US, UK,

Figure 8.1

The Real Exchange Rate, 1980–2002

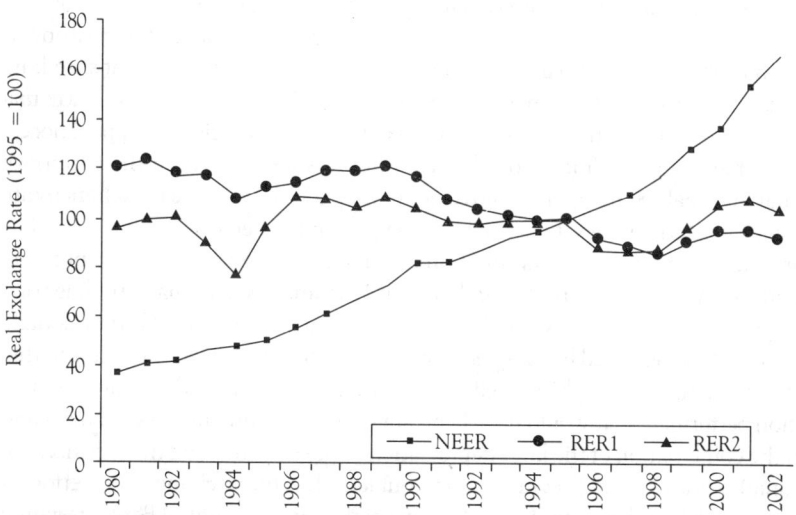

Source: Computed from data in Annual Reports of the Central Bank of Sri Lanka, various issues.
Note: An increase in the index represents a depreciation.

Japan, India and the European Union (EU), weighed by their 1995 export shares and adjusted by the changes in bilateral exchange rates, and changes in domestic costs by Sri Lanka's consumer price index (CPI). The rationale for this is that a real exchange rate constructed with the domestic CPI—which has a higher weight of non-tradeables than the WPI—is a better proxy for non-tradeables prices and hence closer to the ideal theoretical construct.[14] We also computed a REER measure with Sri Lanka's WPI as the domestic price index for comparison and this gives an indication of how domestic tradeables prices have behaved relative to foreign tradeables price levels. The differences between them provide a guide (albeit imperfect) to the differences in the price movements of tradeables and non-tradeables in the domestic economy. Figure 8.1 shows NEER as well as both RER indices.

There are several striking features about the behaviour of the NEER and RER indices. First, the NEER has depreciated throughout this period, with the pace of depreciation quickening until 2001. It continued to depreciate through 2003, though this was masked by the slight appreciation of the rupee against the US dollar. Second, comparison of the two indices shows clearly that CPI has risen faster than WPI. Bearing in mind that if there were any politically induced biases in measurement they would have been in the direction of underestimating CPI (the more politically sensitive measure of inflation), it is fair to conclude that *domestic non-tradeables prices have certainly increased faster than tradeables prices during the 1990s*.[15] This suggests an appreciation of the (internal) real exchange rate.[16] Third, turning to the direction of movement in the RER indices during the 1990s both indicate some overall appreciation though with alternating phases of appreciation and depreciation. Finally, and perhaps most importantly, looking at the long-run behaviour of the nominal rate and the real rate, nominal rupee depreciations appear to have restrained significant real exchange rate appreciation, but by steadily *accelerating* the pace of depreciation.

Figure 8.1 suggests that adjustments to the nominal rate—almost always downward—have been (at least partially) effective as a tool to avoid significant sustained appreciation. However, the general steepening slope of the time path of the nominal exchange rate suggests that progressively larger nominal depreciations appear necessary to achieve a given impact on the real rate. It is apparent from the pattern of nominal and real exchange rate movements that the driver of real exchange rate appreciation is Sri Lanka's domestic inflation, which has been well above that of its major trading partners. In a low inflation global environment, Sri Lanka's inflation performance has been strikingly poor. Between 1995 and 2002, its major trading partners experienced price increases of about 8–10 per cent in their tradeables prices while Sri Lanka's WPI increased by 71.4 per cent and CPI almost doubled. There is no need to resort to complex or sophisticated analyses to locate the immediate causes of this inflation performance. It would have been amazing if the outcome was any different, given the combination of the large depreciation of the currency and the expansion in (nominal) money supply (M2 more than doubled). But the exchange rate depreciations are not the fundamental cause of inflation; they are the Central Bank's response to continuing upward pressures on the real exchange rate, the instrument used to avoid serious real exchange rate misalignment. The fundamental causes of the underlying inflationary pressures, as discussed in the following section, lie elsewhere.

The presence of a relatively stable real exchange rate of course does not indicate that there is no misalignment. The equilibrium rate can vary depending on the behaviour of its underlying determinants, such as fiscal policy, terms of trade, capital inflows, productivity improvements in the economy and demographic factors. Factors that enhance national income, such as positive terms of trade movements or higher productivity, generally appreciate the equilibrium rate. Negative shocks to the economy have the opposite effect. Since the equilibrium rate itself fluctuates, in some circumstances, an appreciation of the real exchange rate is not necessarily a problem, but in other circumstances depreciation may be essential. The success of policy is measured by the extent to which the real exchange rate is maintained at a level close to an equilibrium rate, so that systematic long-term misalignment is avoided.

A recent study, reported in IMF (2002), has analysed the behaviour of the equilibrium real exchange rate in Sri Lanka and found no evidence of a serious real exchange rate misalignment during the mid-1990s.[17] However, misalignment emerged in 1999 and widened in 2000. It was largely eliminated by 2002, through a steep depreciation, and at a very high cost in terms of economic growth and employment. The developments in 2000–2001 were a major warning that any significant misalignment may be seriously destabilizing in the present environment and that relatively high foreign reserves are no longer a guarantee of stability as capital flight can be rapid even without full capital account convertibility. According to the IMF (2002), during the second half of 2000, official reserves (excluding Asian Clearing Account) dropped by more than $600 million, even though the capital account was not fully liberalized. If the sources of persistent pressure on the real exchange rate are not addressed, the price will be destabilising capital movements and currency crises. This takes us to the discussion of the role and implications of fiscal deficits in Sri Lanka.

The Fiscal Deficits and Financing

During the early 1990s, the Sri Lankan economy experienced both large budget deficits and large private capital inflows, both of which tend to raise the domestic price level and appreciate the real exchange rate, thereby generating current account deficits.[18] But several analyses have shown that since 1994, private capital inflows have been of minimal significance as a source of inflationary pressure. It is the large budget deficits that are the primary cause of inflation, real exchange rate appreciation and current account deficits (Athukorala and Jayasuriya, 1996; IMF, 2002).

Fiscal deficits reflect the imbalance between government expenditures and tax revenues. In principle, higher government expenditure can be financed by higher taxes in which case there is no fiscal deficit but produces a direct and transparent resource transfer from the households and firms to the government. In this case, there is no net increase in overall demand for resources.[19] But the existence of a higher budget deficit implies that direct resource transfers are insufficient to meet the demands of the government. Indirect means of financing have to be used. But, except in the case where foreign savings (available in the form of loans or grants) are used to finance purchases of foreign goods and services, higher fiscal expenditures inevitably mean that the government is grabbing a higher share of domestic resources.

If, as is the case in Sri Lanka, continuing fiscal deficits are generated by socially unproductive expenditures, in the final analysis, competitiveness of exports and other tradeable sectors are eroded and private investments are crowded out because the government is pulling resources away from productive sectors. Fiscal policy then systematically undermines the positive effects of measures such as trade liberalization on the profitability of potential internationally competitive productive sectors. *To the extent that the resources drawn away by the government are diverted to socially unproductive activities and sectors, it has a direct negative impact on growth.* The method of financing determines only the specific channels through which the government takes away resources from other sectors.

Monetization of deficits ('printing money') and obtaining low interest finance from 'captive' sources, together with foreign aid and loans—mostly at concessional rates— were the main instruments of deficit financing in the past. In the case of monetization, the government obtains real resources through seignorage (the 'inflation tax') as inflation erodes the real value of money held by the public. Low interest finance from captive financial institutions is a form of taxing financial intermediaries using financial repression. Institutions such as the National Savings Bank and the Employees' Provident Fund (EPF) were compelled to lend to the government at artificially low, often negative, interest rates and to thus subsidize government expenditures. (In the case of the EPF, this was a direct tax on workers' savings and, ironically, was intensively exploited by the supposedly 'leftist' United Front government during the 1970s.) Though the monetization of part of the deficit generated major payments problems that, in turn, led to the control regimes of the 1960s and 1970s, these sources of domestic finance, together with cheap foreign finance, enabled the cost of financing the deficit to be kept under 'control'. Thus, past fiscal policy was, in a sense, 'sustainable', irrespective of the efficiency and distributional consequences.

But this is no longer the case. These methods of financing deficits have proved quite inadequate to finance the increasingly larger deficits of the 1990s. Borrowing from domestic residents—bond financing—has become more and more important in recent years. Such bond financing raises domestic interest rates and thereby the cost of capital to the private sector and crowds out private investment. Persistence of relatively high inflation has meant that higher nominal interest rates have to be offered to the public to induce them to buy bonds and lend to the government. The share of domestic public debt as a proportion of total government debt has increased from 42 per cent in 1990 to 60 per cent in 2002, and servicing the debt has entailed increasingly larger interest payments. Interest payments on domestic public debt now constitute the single largest item of government expenditure.

If the government borrows in domestic markets, induced upward pressure on the domestic interest rate may pull in foreign funds, weakening the impact on domestic interest rates and the extent of crowding out of the private sector. This has become relevant to Sri Lanka to some degree in recent years, even though foreign investment flows have been quite low since the early 1990s. Though the capital account has not been fully liberalized, current account liberalization and related relaxations in exchange controls have significantly enhanced de facto international capital mobility. In this situation of partial or imperfect international capital mobility, domestic capital markets are only partially insulated from the international capital market. Higher domestic interest rates generate some capital inflows (or reduce outflows, including capital flight), as long as they are not offset by expectations of faster currency depreciations. This is an indirect way of accessing foreign savings to finance the deficit.

Unfortunately, none of these financing methods can be sustained in the long run if fiscal expenditures grow in a manner that makes it impossible to pay back borrowings in the future by running surpluses. Rigorous statistical analysis of the Sri Lankan fiscal deficits and simulation experiments based on time paths of expenditure and revenue growth over time and implied future repayments, confirms what even a simple glance at the time series plots of the relevant variables suggests: *unless drastic changes are made to fiscal policy, excessive accumulation of the stock of public liabilities will be such that the criterion of intertemporal solvency will be violated and future liabilities cannot be met* (Cashin et al., 1999; IMF, 2002). The situation, already very serious by 1997, has been aggravated by developments in late 2003.[20] This may have profound implications for both internal and external balance. We shall return to this after discussing the impact of fiscal deficits on the real exchange rate.

Unsustainable Fiscal Deficit, Inflation and the Currency

As shown in Figure 8.1, depreciations of the nominal rate have been the chosen mechanism over the past two decades for adjusting the real exchange rate to avoid serious misalignment. The fact that this strategy has required (on a trend basis) accelerating nominal depreciation suggests that the persistent pressure exerted by the fiscal deficit on the inflation front has been entrenching inflationary expectations among the public. Recent political developments have reinforced concerns about the viability of optimistic scenarios of foreign capital flows and faster economic growth and the political feasibility of reining in expenditures or increasing revenues. In this context, it seems useful to sketch out a 'pessimistic scenario' that highlights the dangers inherent in the current policy setting. Like many developments in Sri Lankan political and economic life that have already come to pass, this is a scenario that is, of course, best avoided. Though this is termed a 'pessimistic' or 'worst case' scenario, it should be stressed that this is the logical outcome of present trends and it will be avoided only if there is a fundamental change in either the fiscal policy stance and/or the external economic environment.

If the optimism about growth and capital inflows that promised a peace dividend proved a transient aberration and the current fiscal policy stance were to continue unchanged, options for financing the fiscal deficit will inevitably narrow. Without a significant increase in yields, the public will become increasingly reluctant to purchase government bonds without a significant rise in yields. Even then, as rates go up, the risk premium may increase even faster. On the other hand, with interest payments on current debt already a severe drain on expenditure, higher interest borrowings become a very limited option. If large foreign inflows or rapid growth do not provide the resources to finance the deficits, the Central Bank will become the lender of last resort to the government. The repeated pledges to avoid the money printing path to deficit financing, like most other government pledges, can be safely discounted. Recall that when the fiscal deficit enlarged in 2000 due to election-related expenditures, the government had no hesitation in resorting to Central Bank credit and monetized a large part of the deficit, with predictable and disastrous consequences. When all other options run out and political considerations constrain deficit reduction, the inflation tax will have to become the financing instrument.

This is not a new experience for Sri Lanka; what is new is the context. The opening up of the economy over the past two decades, particularly since the early 1990s, has transformed the environment in which economic agents operate their methods of operation and the sophistication of their responses. Trade is liberalized. The exchange rate has been depreciating over a long period and is now floating. Its capacity to be a credible nominal anchor in a crisis situation is already significantly compromised. If the deficit is monetized and the currency continues to float freely, the resulting pressure on the current account deficit will lead to continuous declines in the nominal exchange rate. Any attempt to arrest this process by slowing down the depreciation through Central Bank intervention will appreciate the real exchange rate and aggravate current account deficits and accelerate loss of reserves. This suggests a scenario of steady and gradual accumulation of problems. But this process will not go on for ever.

Both economic theory and global experience, including recent East Asian experience shows that agents will anticipate these effects of a ballooning fiscal deficit and the consequences of monetization of the deficit. This anticipation generates responses that will short circuit the process of steady deterioration and instead precipitate a sudden and sharp currency crisis. As the government raises interest rates to bond-finance the deficit, informed, sophisticated agents see beyond the short term; they will 'rationally' anticipate where these developments are headed in the longer term. High interest rates, rather than being a magnet to attract foreign funds, will be seen as an indicator of unsustainable deficits. (Indeed, there is anecdotal evidence that this occurred in 2000 in an incipient form.) They will see that bond financing is reaching its limits and that any further shifting of the costs of the deficit to the future is becoming untenable. In such a situation, 'given the unsustainable deficit, speculation on the possibility of default and depreciation is inevitable' (Corden, 2002: 111). Inflation and currency depreciation will be on the agenda, irrespective of anyone's wishes or statements. A full blown Latin American/East Asia 1997 scenario will become a reality with capital flight, currency collapse, financial sector crisis, fall in private investment and economic recession.[21] The political consequences and associated economic effects can be imagined.

This is, of course, a 'worst case' scenario and the present downward spiral may be cut short and Gamini Corea's vision of a prosperous Sri Lanka may become a reality. But in the absence of a fundamental change in policy or some particularly benign unanticipated shock, the longer the delay in implementing fundamental policy changes, the more the odds would lessen that this pessimistic scenario becomes the realistic scenario.

NOTES

1. Without implication, the author thanks Prema-chandra Athukorala and Max Corden. This chapter draws on joint work with Prema-chandra Athukorala.
2. The mini-devaluation of 1967 was essentially an attempt to maintain the status quo relative to the Indian rupee.
3. Based on an end-of-year comparison.
4. See Econsult (1995), Herath (1995), Ratnayake (1995).
5. See Athukorala and Jayasuriya (1996).
6. What this suggests about the political independence of the monetary authority is left to the readers to ponder.
7. The numerators and denominators are often reversed, as for example in many IMF documents, in which case the interpretation of an increase or decrease of the index is the opposite of what follows.

8. All these measures have limitations as tools for assessing the overall international competitiveness of an economy and particularly for that of a particular commodity (or group of commodities). Factors influencing competitiveness clearly differ from commodity to commodity. When a large proportion of domestic costs of tradeables are accounted for by imported (tradeable) intermediate goods (e.g., the garments sector), the IRER is not a good guide to changes in competitiveness of that industry. Trade liberalization-induced price changes can affect the competitiveness of importables quite differently from those of exportables. In cases where there is interest in the changing competitiveness of a particular commodity (or a group of commodities), it is useful to construct commodity specific real exchange rates. See Athukorala and Jayasuriya (1996) for real exchange rate indices computed for several commodity groups.

9. For discussions on the concept and measurement of equilibrium real exchange rates, see the papers in Williamson (1994), Hinkle and Montiel (1999). This clarifies and further extends earlier discussions of this issue in the literature such as that of Edwards (1989).

10. The assumption that the private sector will reduce its expenses to exactly offset fiscal expansions is the so-called Ricardian equivalence conjecture which has little or no empirical support in developing countries (or even in most developed countries).

11. See Corden (1994) for a clear and non-technical exposition of this analysis.

12. Exchange rate behaviour in the pre-1990 period is discussed in Athukorala and Jayasuriya (1994).

13. The basic pattern indicated in this figure is similar, but not identical, to the REER estimated by the IMF (noting that an increase in their index corresponds to a fall in our index); see Figure IV.1 in IMF (2002). The differences are due to differences in country coverage, base year and weights and the price indices used.

14. Another candidate for domestic non-tradeables prices is the GDP deflator. How various measures of the real exchange rate—including the REER—can be related to the theoretical construct of the tradeables/non-tradeables relative price, and meaningfully interpreted, is discussed in Appendix 8A in Little et al. (1993) and in detail by Hinkle and Nsengiyumva (1999).

15. This conclusion is also supported by comparing the rate of inflation indicated by the GDP deflator, which rose at a broadly similar rate to CPI since 1990. Some of the falls in tradeables prices may reflect impact of trade liberalization.

16. This may also be partly due to the impact of trade liberalization on domestic prices of imports but note that the imported goods have a large weight in CPI.

17. The findings based are consistent with the conclusion of a previous study, which looked at the period up to 1995 without explicit estimation of an equilibrium rate (Athukorala and Jayasuriya, 1996). The IMF study used the 'macroeconomic balance approach' to estimate the equilibrium rate, which involves the determination of the real exchange rate that will ensure simultaneous current account and internal balance. As with all methods used to estimate equilibrium real exchange rates, this has several weaknesses and limitations.

18. If the exchange rate is floating, real appreciation is not inflationary because capital inflows appreciate the nominal exchange rate and lower the domestic price level.

19. In principle, even this may have some effects on the real exchange rate, depending on how different the expenditure pattern of the government (i.e., the split between expenditure on tradeables and non-tradables) is from that of the private sector.

20. The Cashin et al. (1999) analysis indicated that public debt was already 53 per cent of GDP higher than was sustainable in 1997. The IMF (2002) analysis along similar lines suggests that, without a major improvement in growth and reduction in the fiscal deficit, debt to GDP ratio will increase from 104 per cent in 2001 to 127 per cent in 2006.

21. If capital controls are removed in the near future and full capital account convertibility is implemented, the possibility of such a crisis would increase several fold.

REFERENCES

Athukorala, Prema-chandra and Sisira Jayasuriya (1994), *Macroeconomic Policies, Crises,and Growth in Sri Lanka*, 1969–90, Washington D.C.: World Bank.

_____ (1996), *Macroeconomic Policies and Export Competitiveness in Sri Lanka*, Colombo: The National Development Council of Sri Lanka.

Athukorala, P. and S. Rajapatirana (2000), *Liberalisation and Industrial Transformation: Sri Lanka in International Perspective*, Oxford and New Delhi: Oxford University Press.

Cashin, Paul, Nadeem Haque and Nilss Olekalns (1999), *Spend Now, Pay Later? Tax Smoothing and Fiscal Sustainability in South Asia*, IMF Working Paper WP/99/63, Washington D.C.: IMF.

Central Bank of Sri Lanka (2003), *Monetary Policy Review*—October 2003, Press Release, http://www.lanka.net/centralbank/press_161003.doc

Corden, W. Max (1994), *Economic Policy, Exchange Rates, and the International System*, Oxford: Oxford University Press.

_____ (2002), *Too Sensational: On the Choice of Exchange Rate Regimes,*Cambridge, Massachusetts and London, England: MIT Press.

Econsult (Pvt) Ltd. (1995), 'The Central Bank's Defence of Government's Exchange Policy' *Daily News*, 11 April, p. 31 and 18 April, p. 26.

Edwards, Sebastian (1989), *Real Exchange Rates, Devaluation, and Adjustment: Exchange Rate Policy in Developing Countries*, Cambridge, Mass.: MIT Press.

Herath, P.W.R.B.A.U (1995), 'The External Value of the Sri Lankan Rupee', *The Island*, 2 April, p. 18. (Reproduced in *Ceylon Daily News*, 4 April and *The Sunday Observer*, 21 May, p. 12.)

Hinkle, Lawrence E. and Fabien Nsengiyumva (1999), 'The Two-Good Internal RER for Tradables and Non-tradables', in Hinkle, Lawrence E. and Peter J. Montiel (eds), *Exchange Rate Misalignment: Concepts and Measurement for Developing Countries*, Oxford and New York: Oxford University Press.

Hinkle, Lawrence E. and Peter J. Montiel (1999), *Exchange Rate Misalignment: Concepts and Measurement for Developing Countries*, Oxford and New York: Oxford University Press.

IMF (2002), Sri Lanka: Selected Issues and Statistical Appendix, IMF Country Report No. 02/208, Washington D.C.: IMF.

Little, I.M.D., Richard N. Cooper, W. Max Corden and Sarath Rajapatirana (1993), *Boom, Crisis and Adjustment: The Macroeconomic Experience of Developing Countries*, New York: Oxford University Press.

Ratnayake, Kishan (1995), 'Devaluation: Pros and Cons', *Achievers* (NDB), reproduced in *Sri Lanka Business Review*, April, pp. 7 and 17.

Williamson, John (1994), *Estimating Equilibrium Exchange Rates*, Washington D.C.: Institute for International Economics.

Part III

AGRICULTURE, INDUSTRY AND
TECHNOLOGY DEVELOPMENT

Part III

9

AGRICULTURAL DEVELOPMENT: CONTROVERSIAL ISSUES

Nimal Sanderatne

INTRODUCTION

Independence in 1948 did not mark a new era of agricultural policies in Sri Lanka. The agricultural policies adopted after the Donoughmore Constitution of 1931 continued to dominate agriculture. The main thrust of these policies in the early post-independence period was to attain self-sufficiency in food, mainly rice, through extensive land settlement of the dry zone. Other factors that influenced agricultural policy formulation in the post-independence period were a belief in agricultural fundamentalism, the interest and influence of key political personalities, a response to the insurgency of 1971 and the failure of land reforms resulting in a heavy burden on the public finances of the country. Multilateral international agencies have had an increasing influence on the country's agricultural policies since 1977.

The first change in agricultural policy strategy came about after the political change in 1956. The new government placed an emphasis on institutional changes and government support for paddy farming in particular. The Paddy Lands Act of 1958 that sought to regulate tenancies on paddy lands was the most significant policy to support peasant agriculture. The earlier policy of land settlement in the dry zone also continued. The other significant change came about largely as a response to the serious foreign exchange crisis that had engulfed the country in the late 1950s. From 1960 onwards the government commenced an import substitution programme with a new emphasis on the cultivation of subsidiary food crops and livestock. The import substitution strategy was reinforced during the 1970–77 period, when the government banned the import of most food items.

The early 1970s witnessed land reforms. The Land Reform Law of 1972 placed a ceiling on the ownership of land at 50 acres per individual, with a lower limit on paddy land at 25 acres. It however exempted company-owned estates. These were subsequently nationalized by the Land Reform Law of 1974.

The key agricultural development policy of the 1977 regime was the Accelerated Mahaweli Development Programme (AMDP) that enabled a further large extent of land to be settled by the diversion of the Mahaweli river. The debates on the Mahaweli centred on environmental concerns, the high cost of the scheme, its inflationary impact on the economy and the ethnic dimensions of the settlement.

The poor performance of estates under state ownership and a large fiscal burden owing to huge losses in state plantation corporations resulted in their management being handed over to 24 private companies in 1992. This was followed by the sale of most of the estates to companies in 1995, ironically by the same party that headed the coalition government that had nationalized them 21 years before. Neither the nationalization of the estates nor their privatization generated much controversy, except for the Marxist parties' traditional opposition to private ownership of the estates.

Debates and controversies regarding agricultural policy issues have been rather limited, perhaps even muted. There has been some controversy regarding land settlement policies pursued from a period prior to independence. They were both political and economic. They centred on the costs and benefits of land settlement, the protective tenure conferred by the Land Development Ordinance, the ethnic implications of land settlement and the environmental impact of the Mahaweli diversion.

The tenancy reforms of 1958 evoked considerable political controversy. Subsequently, several evaluations of these reforms have been critical of their implementation. The usual controversies with respect to land reform were largely absent prior to, and immediately after, the land reforms of 1972 and 1974. Criticisms were levelled after the reforms about the mismanagement of the lands taken over. Even the privatization of the estates in 1995 attracted little criticism, except for the ideological stances of the Marxist parties. More recently, there have been controversies regarding the liberalization of trade in agricultural produce, the removal of production subsidies and the imposition of a water tax.

The discussion of the controversies is necessarily selective. The earlier debates are discussed in greater detail than the more current issues. The next section describes the most important agricultural development policies. The controversies surrounding these are captured in the third section. The fourth section makes some concluding reflections on the controversies.

Evolution of Policy

Land Settlement

Land settlement in the dry zone was the key agricultural development policy in the first decade after independence. Post-independence land settlement was a continuation of government-sponsored colonization that commenced under the Land Development Ordinance of 1935. However, the progress of colonization was slow till 1947. Between 1931 and 1947 only 13 colonies involving 3,145 settlers had been established. Peasant colonization gained momentum after independence as the spraying of DDT (dichlorodiphenyltrichloroethane) drastically reduced malarial deaths from 12,500 to

4,500 between 1946 and 1947. The impact of this on colonization was unmistakable. Between 1948 and 1953, 16 colonization schemes were inaugurated and 10,426 colonists settled (Farmer, 1957: 147–67).

Until 1953 peasant families were resettled on an agricultural holdings of eight acres that consisted of five acres of wet or irrigated land for rice cultivation and three acres of dry land or 'highland' for a homestead and cultivation of other crops. The reduced availability of irrigated land and the need to settle more peasants on the available land necessitated a reduction in land holding. It was also contended that a five-acre paddy holding was too large for cultivation solely with family labour. Therefore in 1953, the government reduced the area of land holding per family to three acres of wet paddy land and two acres of dry land or highland (Sanderatne, 1974: 321–23).

In 1956, the allotment was further reduced to two acres of wet paddy land and one acre of dry land or highland. Together with the change in the size of allotment was a new policy known as 'advanced alienation'. Hitherto, the colonist was brought to the scheme only after irrigation facilities were provided, the land made suitable for cultivation and the allotees' houses constructed. Under the new policy of 'advanced alienation', the colonists were brought into the settlement two or three years prior to the availability of irrigation facilities.

The colonists were paid cash subsidies for jungle clearing and land preparation, given work for wages on irrigation works and road building and encouraged to undertake *chena* (slash and burn) agriculture at this stage. Allotee participation in preparing the settlement from its earliest stages was thought of as a means of evoking greater commitment to the project and of decreasing costs. However, inability of the irrigation plan to keep up with the schedule created considerable hardship as farmers had to face a period of unemployment. In response to this problem, the date of arrival of a colonist on the site was reduced to a year prior to the provision of irrigation (ibid.: 323).

Highland Colonization

Apart from the aforesaid land settlement programme, there were several other land settlement and land development schemes. In 1955, Highland Colonization Schemes for growing cash crops on smallholdings were begun. Till 1966, about 31,500 acres were cultivated with tea, rubber and coconut (Land Utilization Committee Report, 1967: 34). In 1968, cultivation of tea and rubber was abandoned on these schemes owing to uncertainties in the international market for these products, and cinnamon and coffee schemes commenced. In recent years, there has been less expansion of these schemes (ibid.: 27).

A colonist in these schemes was given two acres of tea, or 22 acres of rubber or five acres of coconut. The cost to the government of settling a colonist was about Rs 7,500 in the case of the tea and rubber schemes and Rs 7,000 for the coconut scheme. This expenditure included expenditure on clearing the jungles and subsidies for seeds, fertilizers, implements, and other cultivation needs as well as housing.

Middle Class Alienation

Land was also alienated to 'middle-class' individuals for development. A middle class individual was defined for this purpose initially as one with an income of less than Rs 12,000 per annum, and later as one with an income of less than Rs 24,000 per annum. The government did not meet any expenses, but the recipient of the land was entitled to a loan. Nearly 75,000 acres were alienated until 1955 to about 6,000 allottees. From 1956 to 1966, about 73,000 acres were alienated to about 8,000 allottees. This scheme was later abandoned, as its objectives were not attained (Land Utilization Committee Report, 1967).

Village Expansion Schemes

The largest extent of land alienation has been under the Village Expansion Schemes. Land surrounding old villages is allotted to villagers in blocks of one to three acres as a means of reducing the extreme population pressure on available village land. Subsidies were provided for house construction and the digging of a well but financial assistance was much more modest than under the major colonization schemes. The number of recipients of land under these schemes exceeded 7,00,000. These beneficiaries out-number those under all other settlement schemes (Farmer, 1957: 174–76).

Youth Settlement Schemes

The increasing incidence of unemployment among educated youth in the country and the limited absorptive capacities in traditional agriculture and other sectors led to the formulation of a new policy of Youth Settlement Schemes in 1965.

The basic idea underlying these schemes were that the youth should be assured a minimum monthly income by the cultivation of profitable food and cash crops on a scientific basis. Ancillary income sources from poultry and livestock were also envisaged. These schemes were expected to generate high incomes for the youth, and be adequate incentives for them to remain in agriculture. Between 1966–69, 40 youth settlement schemes were established. These 40 schemes covered an area of about 9,500 acres of which about 2,100 acres were devoted to homesteads. This scheme was abandoned in the 1970s (Ministry of Land, Irrigation and Power, 1966a: 133–36; and 1966b).

Accelerated Mahaweli Development Programme

Another significant thrust in land settlement occurred in 1978 with the AMDP. It was the centrepiece of the agricultural development policy of the 1977 regime. The AMDP sought to bring under cultivation about 2,65,000 hectares of new land and the cultivation of about 1,00,000 hectares of land that had been developed but lacked adequate irrigation facilities in the dry zone. In addition, it was designed to supply 600 megawatt (MW) of electricity through generation of hydroelectricity within a short period of seven years (Chandrapala, 1986: 269–70). The accelerated programme was completed in 6 years between 1978 and 1983. By the end of 1985, 47,278 farmers were settled in systems H, C, B and A.[1] The cost of the project is estimated at around Rs 35 billion. The increase in paddy production and yields in the post-1977 period were mainly due to the lands brought under cultivation under the AMDP. However, after 1988 the project lost steam owing to the political changes that occurred in that year. The progress in human settlements left much to be desired owing to resource constraints.

Tenancy Reforms on Paddy Lands: The Paddy Lands Acts of 1953 and 1958

Tenancy reforms on paddy lands perhaps evoked most controversy with respect to agricultural policy. There were two attempts to regulate tenancy conditions on paddy lands. The initial attempt in 1953 was a limited reform that had almost no effect. The Paddy Lands Act of 1958 was a far more comprehensive effort at regulating tenancy conditions.

The Paddy Lands Act of 1953

In 1951, the UNP government presented a Paddy Lands Bill, ostensibly to solve some of the tenure problems on paddy lands. The reasons for the introduction of this bill are somewhat obscure. It was perhaps a means of facing some of the criticisms that came from a few Opposition members who advocated the abolition of tenancy. It may also have been an international demonstration endeavour to keep up with other countries in Asia which were enacting land reforms. However, the voluminous 'World Bank Report on the Economic Development of Ceylon' in 1952 only made mention of the need to consolidate small sized holdings in the paddy sector.

The Bill was finally passed in 1953 after a two-year delay. Its applicability was restricted to the two districts of Hambantota and Batticaloa, which had certain unique conditions and peculiar problems. Strangely, the then Minister of Agriculture himself admitted that this Bill was not meant to benefit the tenants but to increase productivity on paddy lands. In a parliamentary debate he mentioned that the Bill was introduced solely with a view to obtaining greater production, and though the tenants did obtain certain advantages, the fact was that these advantages were incidental to the main purposes underlying the introduction of the Bill, which was achieving greater productivity from paddy lands.

The Paddy Lands Act of 1953 required tenancy arrangements to be written and registered. During the period of such an agreement, ejection of a tenant was permitted only for certain specified causes, and for such ejection a court order was required. A five-year period was laid down as a minimum period of secure tenancy and a maximum rent stipulated.

The characteristic feature of the Hambantota district was that large extents of paddy lands were owned by absentee landlords and managed by middlemen called *gambarayas*. The latter often managed the lands of more than one owner. The 1953 Act in effect reduced the rent paid by these middlemen to the landlords and improved their security as 'tenants'. Those who tilled the land were still treated as labourers and did not benefit from the reforms at all.

Similarly, in the Batticaloa district landowners rented their land on a leasehold basis to managers who farmed a number of small sized ownership units in a single operational unit. Similar to the experience in Hambantota, the reform benefited these managers by providing them with a degree of secure tenure and rent reduction. The applicability of the Paddy Lands Act of 1953 to these districts either indicated ignorance and disregard for actual conditions prevailing in them or was designed purposefully to discredit reforms by not conferring any benefits to tenants (Sanderatne, 1974: 344-46).

The Paddy Lands Act of 1958

The change of government in 1956 had important repercussions on agricultural policy. The Mahajana Eksath Peramuna (MEP) government was a coalition of several parties under the leadership of S.W.R.D. Bandaranaike's SLFP. An important constituent party was the Viplavakari Lanka Sama Samaja Party (VLSSP) under the leadership of Philip Gunawardena. The MEP also had electoral support and no-contest agreements with other Left parties, notably the Lanka Sama Samaja Party (LSSP) and the Ceylon Communist Party (CCP). The MEP platform consisted of a very large number of issues including the nationalization of foreign owned estates. However, the critical issues which resulted in its victory were language, culture and religion, and a general dissatisfaction with the previous regime. Although agrarian reform as such was not an issue in the elections, the SLFP had a strong rural base.

There were two aspects of the new leadership which had an influence in them espousing land reforms. First, the government had a substantial rural support base, and second, the leader of the VLSSP, Philip Gunawardena, who became the Minister of Agriculture, had a deep interest in agrarian issues. His own university education in agriculture and the social sciences in Wisconsin and Iowa in the US, and active involvement in Mexican revolutionary politics provided a background and enthusiasm for agrarian reform. The portfolio of Lands and Irrigation rested with C.P. de Silva, who had been involved with land settlement as a civil servant. He turned out to be an opponent of the Paddy Lands Act from within the cabinet.

Philip Gunawardena's term of office as Minister of Agriculture resulted in a new direction on agrarian reform. For the first time, the need for comprehensive policies covering marketing, credit, crop insurance and land tenure reform with village-level farmer organizations was recognized and policies formulated to establish these. A new Department of Agrarian Services was established to administer these programmes. Although the significance of these years lay in the formulation of all these policies and the new direction they gave to peasant agriculture, Gunawardena is best remembered for introducing the controversial Paddy Lands Act of 1958 (Sanderatne, 1974: 347-48).

The main objectives of the Paddy Lands Act of 1958 and its subsequent amendments were to regulate the authority that landlords could exercise over tenants, regulate the rents paid by tenants and to provide security of tenure of a permanent and heritable nature. It also had provisions to prevent further fragmentation of paddy lands and provide measures for the consolidation of small sized holdings. An important objective was to establish Cultivation Committees for the organization of paddy culti- vation. It also had provisions for regulating interest rates on cash loans made to paddy cultivators, charges made for the hire of implements and draft animals by cultivators, and the fixing of wages for agricultural labourers (Sanderatne, 1974: 350–57).

The control of tenancy rents stipulated in the Act was designed to alter tenurial conditions towards an incentive-oriented rental structure. The two important aspects of the control were regulation to an equitable level and the introduction of a form of payment which would remove disincentive effects with respect to the adoption of improved practices.

Import Substitution

The post-1956 agricultural policies attempted to broaden the emphasis on food crop production beyond paddy cultivation to subsidiary food crops and to livestock. The Guaranteed Price Scheme (GPS) was extended to cover red onions, chillies, green grams, *kurakkan*, maize and a few other crops. There was a new emphasis on research and extension for other crops. Yet this attempt had limited success owing to fairly free imports at the time. The exceptions were perhaps potato production, which nearly doubled from about 6,78,000 pounds in 1958 to 12,50,000 pounds in 1961, and poultry and egg production, which more or less met the domestic requirements. This thrust in agricultural policies continued into the 1960s and achieved a degree of success.

A significant change in agricultural policies was brought about in 1970 by compel- ling economic circumstances. The foreign exchange reserves were depleted to such low levels that the government was more or less forced to ban the import of a wide variety of consumer goods, including most food imports. This ushered in a regime of import substitution for agriculture as well as industry, in contrast to the post-independence period of liberal trade. A wide variety of agricultural produce that could be cultivated in the country continued to be imported, and the foreign exchange crisis deepened. For instance in 1964, Sri Lanka spent Rs 151 million, or nearly 8 per cent of the import bill, on the import of subsidiary food crops (chillies, grams, onions, potatoes and pulses). The new policy attempted the curtailment of these imports and institutional support and production subsidies for their cultivation. The rise in domestic prices owing to the import ban was perhaps the biggest incentive to increasing production of these crops. Import substitution in agriculture continued to be a policy till 1977, though some degree of protection continued even after 1977.

Land Reforms and Privatization

As a response to the insurgency of April 1971 the government enacted the Land Reform Law of 1972. This was the first attempt to alter the land tenure structure of the country by a redistribution of privately owned land. For the first time, it placed a limit on the extent of land that could be privately owned. Hitherto, land policies were confined to the redistribution of government owned lands, the expropriation of small extents of marginal estate lands for village expansion schemes and the regulation of share rentals of paddy lands.

The Land Reform Law of 1972 placed a ceiling on the individual ownership of land at 50 acres, except in the case of paddy land where the ceiling was 25 acres. Lands held by public companies and religious institutions were exempt from this law.

Lands in excess of the ceiling were vested in the Land Reform Commission and alienated in several different ways to individuals and cooperative farms. The total extent of land expropriated amounted to a little less than one million acres, over one-half of which were coconut lands. Only 56,000 acres of paddy land were available for redistribution. Although owners were compensated, the method of compensation and delays in payment resulted in the lands being virtually expropriated with very minimal compensation.

There was a certain amount of displeasure and criticism over the fact that the 1972 Law did not apply to company estates, many of which were foreign owned. In 1974, the Land Reform Law of that year took over the company owned estates. These estates were distributed among several organizations, the Sri Lanka State Plantations Corporation (SLSPC) and the Janatha Estate Development Board (JEDB) managing the bulk of the estates.

Owing to fluctuations in prices of tea and rubber, poor management of the estates and high costs of production, the state corporations incurred heavy losses and productivity declined. Ultimately in 1992, the government decided to hand over these estates to 22 regional private companies. This experiment did not yield the expected results due to the insecurity of tenure of the management contract. Consequently, in 1996, the government decided to divest the ownership of estates to private companies. This measure in effect reversed the land reforms enacted in 1974.

Economic Liberalization

November 1977 marked a watershed in economic policies. It is generally assumed that the liberalized policies pursued since then resulted in a removal of restrictions on agricultural imports and that the protection offered to farmers, particularly in respect of food crops, was removed. This however is not a correct representation of agricultural policies. In fact, even after liberalization in 1977, several food crops were heavily protected by tariff and non-tariff barriers. For instance, chillies, big onions and potatoes were under import licensing till July 1996. Red onions were totally banned during this period. An import duty of 35 per cent and a further tax of 20 per cent were applicable to food imports (Central Bank of Sri Lanka, 1998: 98). It was as late as 1996 when all import restrictions were removed. However, despite protective measures, liberalized economic and trade policies resulted in cheaper imports and consequent depressed prices at the farm level. This resulted in poor progress in food production in the 1990s.

The post-1977 governments adopted different policies with respect to production subsidies, largely at the insistence of the multilateral agencies. The fertilizer subsidy was an important policy that came under scrutiny. The fertilizer subsidy for paddy and other crops was introduced in the 1960s and continued till 1989. This subsidy amounted to 40–50 per cent of the cost of fertilizer. The removal of this subsidy in 1989 proved a politically unpalatable policy that the government was compelled to undertake at the insistence of the IMF and the World Bank. Therefore, with a change of government in 1994, a subsidy of 30 per cent in the retail prices of the main fertilizers was introduced. There is clear evidence that fertilizer usage was much higher during periods of fertilizer subsidy. For instance, when the subsidy was reintroduced in 1994, the use of fertilizer increased by 17 per cent in the cultivation year 1994–95 (Ranaweera, 1998: 97).

CONTROVERSIES

This section deals with six of the most controversial issues in agricultural policies. These controversies were at the political, technical and academic levels.

Cost and Benefit of Colonization

The high cost of colonization and the low productivity of land settlement in relation to its capital investment have been recurring themes of reports of government commissions and committees, international organizations and visiting specialists.

The Land Commission of 1955–58 estimated the average unit cost of a settler at Rs 10,500. The Committee on Utilization of Crown Lands in 1953 estimated the cost to be Rs 14,000. B.H. Farmer estimated the capital cost in 1951 at Rs 12,750, and in 1953 at Rs 6,535. Large components of this expenditure are the costs of irrigation, land-clearing and housing.

A study made in 1962 estimated the benefit and cost ratios of two schemes to be 0.56 and 0.67. The Report of the Committee on the Gal Oya Scheme, 1966–68, estimated an overall benefit and cost ratio of 0.5 on its project and estimated that discounted costs exceeded benefits by Rs 277 million. An FAO–IBRD (Food and Agricultural Organization–International Bank for Reconstruction and Development) team that visited the country in 1966 drew the government's attention to the high capital and output ratio, which they estimated at over 17:1. In 1987 Thorbecke and Svejnar pointed out that benefit and cost ratios of irrigation projects were 'much lower than anticipated at the outset' (Thorbecke and Svejnar, 1987: 101).

Whatever the precise calculations, there is little doubt that although a large expenditure had been incurred in bringing new land under cultivation, the productivity on these lands was not significantly higher than in the rain-fed paddy lands in the early years. Given the considerably higher infrastructural expenditure and traditional agricultural practices, it follows that the capital and output ratio of these schemes was extremely high (or the benefit and cost ratio low). Does this imply that the expenditure on colonization was too much, or the that such expenditure should not have been incurred?

Another contention advanced was that the expenditure incurred was not adequate in terms of the supporting services required for modernized agriculture. The lack of an efficient well-trained and committed extension service, inadequate availability of credit and inputs, and unsatisfactory marketing facilities, it was contended, were responsible for these colonization schemes not developing a highly productive agriculture.

The findings of 'The Socio-Economic Survey of Nine Colonization Schemes' in 1967–68, conducted by the University of Peradeniya, demonstrated the lack of adequate services to support settlement agriculture. The proportion of farmers reporting dissatisfaction with government services in the nine schemes ranged from 55 to 96 per cent with a median level of discontent of 86 per cent. In the nine schemes between 34 to 54 per cent of farmers complained of poor management of cooperatives, while 45–66 per cent complained of a lack of supplies and facilities in cooperatives (Jogaratnam and Schickele, 1969). Schickele conveyed this inadequacy of supporting services forcefully:

> It is, of course, unrealistic to expect settlers transplanted from old traditional villages on to newly developed land to modernize their farming methods spontaneously. Why should they, and how could they? There was no one to demonstrate the new techniques to them, to guide them in the adoption of innovations, to help them in organizing multipurpose cooperatives and cultivation committees. Roads and general communications were often worse than where the settlers came from; but the sizeable land allotment made it easier for them to subsist than on the much smaller units in the old village.
>
> In short, the colonization policy has been to assign settlers their land allotment; the rest was up to them. (Schickele, 1971: 32)

The very restricted exploitation of highlands in the allotments was also responsible for depressing the total productivity of the colonization projects. The average cropping index of highland in the nine colonization schemes surveyed in 1967–68 was only 53 per cent. It ranged from a low of 30 per cent (Hakwatuna Oya) to a high of 75 per cent (Rajangana and Minipe [temple]) with a median cropping index of 50 per cent. Even this may be an overstatement of cropping, as the area rather than the intensity of cultivation is measured. The lack of an irrigation system for the highlands, inadequate knowledge for cultivating dry zone highland crops and an extension service not geared to providing the know how for highland crops (and in any case inadequate in numbers and training) were among the primary causes for the very inadequate exploitation of these lands. Settlers often attempted to grow crops like coconut, which were dictated by their food needs and experience in the wet zone rather than soil-climatic suitability of the area. Successive seasons of failure to grow crops led to an ultimate abandonment of growing any crops whatsoever (Jogaratnam and Schickele, 1969).

Protective Tenure

One of the areas of considerable controversy is with respect to the protective tenure on colonization schemes under the Land Development Ordinance of 1935. The merits and defects of the restrictions imposed on land held under this Ordinance has led to controversy till today. The controversy has been rekindled recently with efforts at making land marketable so as to improve its utilization and productivity.

The form of tenure granted under the Land Development Ordinance of 1935 followed the third form of restricted tenure recommended by the Land Commission of 1927–29. Land granted 'in perpetuity on a restricted tenure' contained restrictions and conditions which rendered it less flexible in its ownership rights than land held under fee simple or freehold. Among these restrictions were the inability to mortgage the land with the concomitant prohibition of seizure or foreclosure of land for collection of debts, and limits on the fragmentation of the land through inheritance. Further, the grantee could not lease the land for cultivation by others, and had to maintain certain conditions of cultivation and his house in a state of good repair (Land Development Ordinance, 1935).

The intent of these conditions was to protect the newly settled farmers from a loss of their land to more resourceful interests which might purchase such land or obtain it through moneylending activities, to preserve a peasant-proprietor form of land-holdings and prevent share and other forms of tenancy, and maintain a viable size of holding.

The experience of many countries, as well as experience in other areas in Sri Lanka, had suggested the advisability of such protective limitations. Where such protection had not been afforded, land so alienated had been sold or foreclosed after a few years to landlord interests, money lenders and others, or fragmented. Such developments ended up reproducing the unsatisfactory tenure conditions existing in the traditional villages and defeated a fundamental objective of settlement policy. Schickele expressed the merits of these restrictions well:

> There are grave drawbacks in a free market for farm land, particularly in newly developing countries where traditional peasant farming is becoming transformed into modern production processes and management methods, and where most farmers are in a very weak bargaining position in the market of land as well as goods and services vis-à-vis a small, powerful local elite. Under such conditions, the right of a small farmer to dispose of his land freely, to mortgage it and sell it, makes him highly vulnerable to pressures from investors, moneylenders, and merchants to mortgage his land for any loans he may urgently need, and to be forced to sell it when he is unable to repay the loan at the rate it gets in default. (Schickele, 1968: 2)

Schickele was, however, careful to point out deficiencies of the restricted tenure in certain cases. One example was where a farmer was incapacitated by age or illness and wanted to move into another area permanently or temporarily, or turn it over to his son after a few years. He also suggested that subdivision of certain units could be permitted till a minimum size, as some holdings in the colonization schemes were somewhat larger than a minimum viable unit (ibid.).

B.H. Farmer issued a memorandum of dissent on the restriction of fragmentation recommended by the Report of the Land Commission, 1955–58. He contended that while fragmentation could be disadvantageous in estate agriculture, there was no evidence to suggest that small units of paddy cultivation or tree crops were less efficient. Further, he cited evidence of consolidation of fragmented units through sale, inheritance and marriage. He also suggested a social undesirability of a control of fragmentation owing to its conflict with the customary practice of inheritance which, could, in turn, lead to familial disputes (Report of the Land Commission, 1958: 175–79). Farmer argued: 'The immediate effect of really efficient measures to prevent fragmentation, would be the creation of a large class of landless, jobless and embittered people ...' (ibid.: 177). He pointed out that, in practice, it was not possible to enforce the legal prohibition of fragmentation as various means of circumventing the law could be found.

The Land Commission of 1955–58 recommended a change in the restricted tenure granted under the Land Development Ordinance of 1935. They were of the view 'that after a certain stage there should be freedom of disposition subject only to the condition governing fragmentation' (ibid.: 86). They recommended a three-stage tenure as follows:

- 1st stage: A probationary supervised tenure of about three years.
- 2nd stage: A phased purchase of the developed allotment by the colonist.
- 3rd stage: A freehold subject only to a condition preventing fragmentation.

The premises of this recommendation were: that the restricted tenure was often conceived of as leased land (*badu-idam*) and therefore a disincentive to full exploitation; that the restricted tenure prevented access to credit sources; that the prevention of a transfer or sale resulted in inefficient cultivators continuing to hold land; that the saleability of the land was not likely to lead to a large scale transfer of land from peasants to other classes; and that agricultural productivity could be better maintained by legislation to acquire unsatisfactorily cultivated land (ibid.: 82–96).

In 1969, the Land Development (Amendment) Act No. 16 framed regulations to give effect to the suggested changes in tenure of alienated land. However, this legislation was not implemented. One purpose of permitting colonists to purchase their holdings was to fund further settlement projects with the finances so obtained. Quite apart from the question of the merits of a protective tenure as against a freehold tenure, had colonists undertaken to purchase their holding over a time period by paying the cost of developing their settlement, there would have been a continuous source of funds for further land development.

The payment of the costs of housing and land development by the settler would reduce the public costs of colonization and thereby enable expenditure on new colonization projects as well as provide much needed investment in supporting services. On the other hand, it can be argued that infrastructural expenses should not be borne by the colonists but by the public at large.

The purchase of holdings by the colonists does not invalidate the need for protecting the deterioration of tenure conditions by mortgage and foreclosure to more resourceful interests. Even with the existing legal limitations, it is not uncommon to find colonists as de facto tenants or labourers despite their de jure status of protected ownership rights or leasehold in perpetuity.

It has been argued that the disadvantage of the inability to offer these holdings as collateral to obtain credit should be met by institutional credit policies not requiring such collateral but offering credit on the basis of production needs. Recovery should be ensured through the supervision of lent funds, the strengthening of village level institutions and the dovetailing of all agricultural policies at the village level. In fact, institutional credit offered through cooperatives and rural banks do not require collateral. However, private traders, moneylenders, merchants and other non-institutional sources who provide most credit needs in the rural sector sometimes ask for collateral. It is precisely such commitment of the agricultural holding as collateral that must be avoided if the objective is that of preserving an owner-cultivating peasantry in the settlement areas (Sanderatne, 1970).

Paddy Lands Act 1958

The introduction of the Paddy Lands Act of 1958 was preceded and followed by considerable discussion and political controversy all over the country. Although the Bill did not even abolish tenancy but merely regulated the conditions of paddy tenancy, those opposed to it interpreted it as a communist plot to abolish private property. The clause which provided for the possibility of establishing collective farms was used as evidence of this hypothesis. The powers vested in the Minister of Agriculture were considered dictatorial and contrary to the need to have judicial control of government action (Sanderatne, 1974: 348–49).

The introduction of the Bill threw open the contradictions in the policies and principles of the coalition government. The Cabinet and the government parliamentary party began to split into a Rightist group led by C.P. de Silva, the Minister of Lands and Irrigation, and a Leftist group led by Philip Gunawardena. The issues were of course not confined to agricultural policies but encompassed several other economic issues, especially those involving nationalization and state ownership of industries. The Right also viewed the growing activities and vigour of the Minister of Agriculture as a threat to their influence in the government and popularity in the country. The Prime Minister attempted to reconcile the two groups or at least to keep them together by various compromises (ibid.: 1974: 349).

The Prime Minister, an owner of paddy lands himself, was a keen supporter of the Bill. A year after the passing of the Paddy Lands Act, he wrote:

> Vested interests are still trying to defeat the purposes of the Act. They are trying to bring the peasant back into a dark age. This government which people thought would break on the issue of the Paddy Lands Bill will never allow this type of resistance. If necessary, the law will be made more effective. Let there be no doubt this government will do everything in its power to make this far-reaching legislation a real boon to the cultivators for promoting paddy production. For if we fail, it will be the greatest set-back to our Socialist Programme (quoted in ibid.).

Yet, the opposition to the Minister of Agriculture continued to grow within the government and various pressures such as an organized campaign against the Paddy Lands

Act were exerted. When Gunawardena proposed a cooperative credit bill designed to substantially increase credit for peasant agriculture, the opposition within the government grew to such an extent that the Prime Minister himself undertook to administer the proposed bill, and Gunawardena and his small group left the government. In September 1959, the Prime Minister was assassinated (Sanderatre, 1974: 350).

Soon after the enactment of the Paddy Lands Act its strongest supporters were no longer in the government. Besides, the years after the enactment were some of the most troublesome years in the country. The passage of the Sinhala Only Official Language Act in 1956 led to communal riots in May 1958. The assassination of the Prime Minister in September 1959 was followed by a period of considerable political uncertainty. The indecisive election in March 1960 ushered in another period of an unstable government till July 1960. Consequently, the implementation of the Paddy Lands Act of 1958 lacked political initiative and enthusiasm almost from its inception. The implementation was largely left to the bureaucracy (ibid.).

The opposition to reform at the macrolevel and the inadequate provision of services, and weaknesses of tenants vis-à-vis their landlords, rendered this reform largely ineffective. The implementation of the Paddy Lands Act of 1958 illustrates the difficulty of attempting to regulate tenancy conditions in a context where the interests adversely affected wield considerable power and influence (ibid.).

Land Reforms

There was very little controversy regarding the two land reform bills of 1972 and 1974 though the UNP opposed them. Some of those who supported the Land Reform Bill of 1972 expressed concern in the limitation of the land ceiling to private lands and the exemption of the land ceiling for company owned estates. The Marxist parties that were a constituent element of the government and had throughout advocated the nationalization of estates expressed this concern. Mounting criticism that foreign-owned company estates were not taken over led the government to take these over by the Land Reform Act of 1974. However, except for the opposition of landed interests to these reforms, there was an absence of serious opposition to the land reforms. In contrast, there was considerable criticism of the management of state lands and the decreasing productivity on estates (Fernando, 1980).

Privatization of Estates

The privatization of the estates, first through a management contract with companies, and then the outright sale of a large shareholding, too evoked little controversy. The fact that state ownership and management of these estates had led to a fall in productivity and huge losses was no doubt the reason for this relative reticence. The criticisms were mostly with respect to the manner in which the privatization took effect.

Protection, Subsidies and Environment

The issue of whether Sri Lanka's agriculture should be protected, and if so the extent of protection that should be conferred, is a continuing debate. There appears to be a divergence in the views held by economists and politicians. Even political views on agricultural protection are schizophrenic as politicians are torn between the interests of consumers and producers. The SAFTA (South Asian Free Trade Area) and SAPTA (SAARC Preferential Trading Arrangment) agreements and the Free Trade Agreement with India disclose protectionism for agriculture in an overall thrust to free trade.

Other controversial issues have been the question of production subsidies and the need to impose a water tax. Interestingly, these controversies are, owing to multilateral agencies insisting on the removal of the fertilizer subsidy, imposition of the water tax and freeing of trade in agricultural produce.

Environmental issues with respect to agricultural policies emerge from time to time. These have included environmental concerns in the cultivation of certain crops under particular soils and terrain. These debates have been particularly focused on potato cultivation in the up-country and tobacco cultivation. However, these environmental concerns have had little impact on changing agricultural policy.

CONCLUDING REFLECTIONS

Although several aspects of agricultural policies since independence have had an important bearing on the agrarian structure, controversies regarding agricultural development issues have been limited. Land reform figured as an important political issue on two occasions. The first occasion was when the Paddy Lands Bill was debated in 1958 and the second was the enactment of the Land Reform Law of 1972. Between the enactment of these pieces of legislation—1958 to 1972—there was little discussion of land reform issues. Significantly, it has not been an issue in any of the elections since independence and neither of the main political parties advocated land reform as an important plank in its programme during this period.

This reticence with regard to land reform is striking when one considers the high dependence of the population on agriculture and the very competitive nature of Sri Lankan politics, with every election since 1952 till 1977, and the elections of 1994 and 2001, resulting in changes in government and shifts in political power between the two major parties with their respective coalitions. What were the reasons for this reticence? One of the important factors may have been the extensive land settlement programmes. Land settlement or colonization too attracted little controversy except that Marxist parties were against these programmes for ideological and political reasons. They saw in these policies a means by which the governing party entrenched themselves in power. A land-owning peasantry was hardly conducive to gaining support for their Marxist ideologies. Colonization of the dry zone offered a good opportunity for governments to gain political support both in the wet zone areas where the settlers would be chosen from, and in the dry zone where they were settled.

The possibility of out-migration from the densely populated regions reduced political pressures that could have led to more radical land policies. The resettled peasants, owing to their newly acquired vested interest in land, were likely to support the existing political structures and institutions. The oligarchy, which ruled the country during the early post-independent period, viewed colonization as a useful long-run basis for ensuring political stability. This was particularly so with D.S. Senanayake, the first Prime Minister who had very strong agricultural-fundamentalist views.

Several reasons account for this approach towards agrarian policies. The legislature was overwhelmingly composed of landed interests and had an elitist approach to politics. They conceived of society as consisting of distinct classes and saw no need to break these class barriers. The peasants who were resettled on new land were not expected to be different in their economic or social status, only somewhat better economically than before owing to their larger land holdings.

The prevailing economic conditions too reinforced this approach to agricultural development. There was a substantial amount of land available and the prosperity of the country during the war years enabled the government to bear the costs of land settlement. The perceived need for a greater degree of self-sufficiency in rice was a strong motivating factor to expand cultivation by bringing in new areas. At this time, the technological breakthrough to achieve very high yields was not available. Therefore, the strategy for agricultural development necessarily implied an extensive strategy of increasing the area cultivated. Also, the concept of agrarian reform based on tenure changes and institutional developments at the village level was not a widespread body of opinion. Agrarian reform, essentially a post World War II, development in Asia, took time to reach Sri Lanka's shores.

The government formed after independence consisted of a landed oligarchy led by D.S. Senanayake, the Prime Minister, who was the Minister of Agriculture in the pre-independence period. Another factor was that the first few years after independence were a period of relative economic prosperity dependent on the plantation exports of tea, rubber and coconut. The war years followed by the Korean boom resulted in large foreign exchange surpluses and continuous BOP surpluses.

This prosperity enabled the government to undertake several welfare measures, which were perhaps a distraction from the agrarian issues mentioned earlier. The high cost of colonization too did not come into question at this time owing to the strong conviction of land settlement being the means of achieving self-sufficiency, as well as the general economic conditions being such as to place no immediate burden on the public finances of the country.

Colonization had another political significance in pluralist Sri Lanka. It gave the majority ethnic community the opportunity to resettle Sinhalese in the ancient historical capitals and ancient kingdoms and thereby confirm the area as a Sinhalese rather than a Tamil region. The land settlement issue has been a most controversial issue and was an underlying cause for the ethnic conflict. The opposition Marxist parties advocated the nationalization of the foreign owned estates, but their position did not influence the government. These parties concentrated their attention on urban labour conditions and trade union activities rather than peasant agricultural problems. Many of the Marxist leaders were themselves owners of substantial tracts of rubber and coconut lands.

The change of political leadership in 1956 resulted in only a minor difference in the class composition of the legislature. The leading members of the several political parties and the governing SLFP continued to have significant landed interests in coconut, rubber and paddy lands. The composition of the political elite from among the landed elite was one reason for the reticence and inactivity on issues of agrarian reform.

Competitiveness among political parties led to strong positions on issues likely to find favour with large sections of the community. This included promises of subsidies and welfare measures as well as emotional appeals on language, religious and racial issues. The country has not been lacking in social welfare measures and socialist legislation encompassing a large arena of the economy such as the nationalization of transport, insurance, port facilities, several big private-manufacturing companies, the state monopoly of big industries, state control of several items of the import–export trade and government ownership of about 80 per cent of the country's banking. Welfare measures have included free or subsidized rice, free medical facilities, free education through university and subsidised transport. However, land reform and agrarian reform did not figure prominently in this competition. In fact, these other issues may have submerged agrarian issues.

While political and public debate on agricultural policy has been rather limited, there has been a reasonable amount of discussion and controversy at the academic level. As the previous section disclosed, there has been considerable controversy regarding the high costs and limited benefits of investment on land settlement. The protected form of land tenure confirmed by the Land Development Ordinance has been a controversial issue, more so today than a few decades ago. A freer form of tenure is currently argued to be needed for a free market in land that is, in turn, considered a prerequisite for a more productive agricultural sector. However, vestiges of the earlier arguments for a protective tenure still prevail, though muted now. The ethnic dimension to land settlement has also been resuscitated in recent years.

The discussion on the Paddy Lands Act of 1958 has been mostly with respect to the efficacy of its provisions. These discussions too have been quite limited and mostly confined to research reports, journal articles and academia. Similarly, the land reforms of 1972 and 1974 have been critically evaluated mostly in academic writings. However, the general conclusion that these reforms failed in their objectives has been recognized. This recognition was no doubt the reason for the ultimate privatization of the plantations by the government led by the party that carried out the reforms in 1974.

It is interesting to note that current controversies in agricultural policies have been generated by the policies recommended by, and often insisted upon by international institutions. The liberalization of trade in agriculture, the removal of production subsidies and the imposition of a water tax are among these controversial issues. The interplay of international pressures and domestic political considerations would no doubt determine the ultimate set of agricultural policies. Economic and environmental considerations are likely to assert a lesser influence on agricultural policies.

NOTE

1. The downstream regions of the Mahaweli Basin and adjacent basins fed by the Mahaweli river have been broken up into irrigation areas called Systems. Each of the Systems is again broken up into Blocks, which share the water from an irrigation control point.

REFERENCES

Chandrapala, H.A. (1986), 'Performance in Agricultural Sector', pp. 219-290 in Ministry of Finance and Planning, *Facets of Development in Independent Sri Lanka*, Colombo.

Farmer, B.H. (1957), 'Pioneer Peasant Colonization in Ceylon: A Study in Asian Agrarian Problems', London: Oxford University Press.

Fernando, Nimal (1980), 'Continuity and Change in Plantation Agriculture: A study of Sri Lanka's Land Reform Program on Tea Plantations', University of Wisconsin, Madison.

Government of Sri Lanka (GOSL) (1935), Land Development Ordinance No. 19 of 1935, Colombo: Department of Government Printing.

————— (1958), Report of the Land Commission, Sessional Paper X, Colombo.

Jogaratnam, T. and Rainer Schickele (1969), 'Summary Report of the Socio-Economic Survey of Nine Colonization Schemes in Ceylon', Agricultural Economics Research Unit, University of Peradeniya.

Ranaweera, N.F.C. (1998), 'Fifty Years of Agriculture in Sri Lanka', in A.V. de S. Indraratna (ed.), *Fifty Years of Sri Lanka's Independence: A Socio-Economic Review*, Colombo.

Land Utilization Committee Report (1967), 'Sessional Paper XI of 1968', Ceylon Government Press.

Sanderatne, Nimal (1970), 'Agricultural Credit: Ceylon's Experience', in *South Asian Review*, 3(3): 215-26.

————— (1974), 'The Political Economy of Asian Agrarian Reform: A Comparative Analysis with Case Studies of the Philippines and Sri Lanka (Ceylon)', University of Wisconsin, Madison.

Schickele, Rainer (1968), 'Protection of Cultivator-Ownership in Farm Settlement Schemes: Ceylon as a Case Study', in *Land Reform, Land Settlement and Co-operatives*, Vol. 2, Rome: FAO.

————— (1971), 'Ceylon Papers 1967-70', New York: Agricultural Development Council.

Thorbecke, Eric and Ian Svejnar (1987), *Economic Policies and Agricultural Performance in Sri Lanka*, 1960-1984, Paris: OECD.

SELECT READINGS

Central Bank of Sri Lanka (1998), 'Economic Progress of Sri Lanka', Colombo.

Ministry of Land, Irrigation and Power (1966a), 'Plan of Development 1966-70', Colombo.

————— (1966b), 'Implementation Programmes and Targets for 1967-68', Colombo.

10

INDUSTRIAL POLICY

Sarath Rajapatirana[1]

INTRODUCTION

Policy debates inform the public; they should provide at least two sides to an issue. Even more importantly, they should provide the grist for policy making. One exception to the observation is the case between industrial policy and neutral policy towards industry in Sri Lanka. Sri Lanka moved from neutral policies towards industrial policy in the late 1950s without a debate. The government of the day, the SLFP under S.W.R.D. Bandaranaike simply adopted industrial policies due to the prevailing ideology and economic circumstances (deteriorating balance of payments situation) with state owned enterprises as the instrument. Similarly, in the 1977 reform package, the then government switched to a more neutral policy towards industry partly due to ideology and partly due to the failure of industrial policy with state owned enterprises as the focus of industrial policy. Again there would no debate. In the early 1990s, the case for industrial policy was made by Sri Lankan economists and debate began. This time the focus shifted to the private sector for carrying out industrial policy unlike the previous occasions. But there has not been a proper debate. This chapter examines the new case for industrial policy today. It is hoped that it would provide a little balance to the debate.

By industrial policy is meant policies aimed at raising the share of a particular component of output, most commonly the share of manufacturing output in gross domestic product (GDP) in the case of Sri Lanka. This could be done by raising productivity (output per unit of input) and value added by diverting resources to the sector or activity. It could be manufacturing, exports or any other component of GDP or an activity that is considered to have strong growth potential. This leads to the claim that public support is needed for a particular dynamic activity or sector. The main rationale for such intervention is that if it is left to the market or, in common parlance, to the private sector, such an activity will not come about and be a future source of output growth. Thus, industrial policy implies targeting or selective intervention in a particular sector or activity. It is based on the infant industry argument. There is of course a strong case for infant industry intervention in economic theory going back to the time of List, Hamilton among others (Baldwin, 1969). Sri Lankan economists have, by and large, espoused this argument as necessary for the country to achieve high rates of growth of manufacturing output and exports and to match the performance of East Asian economies.[2] Putting these two positions together, a majority of Sri Lankan economists have denigrated the industrial achievements of the country to date.

By policy towards industry is meant an approach that does not target any particular activity as a public policy, but maintains a neutral stance towards all activities through uniform incentives. But neutral policy towards industry does not mean an abdication of the government's role. It means that the government has an onerous role to play in promoting growth but it is done at a more general level and where intervention in any particular activity is the exception rather than the rule. Under this policy stance, public policy addresses only those distortions that prevent the emergence of a viable long-term industry or activity. Thus, the difference between these two types of policy stances can be described as selective intervention in the economy in contrast to the pursuit of neutral policies in general. The government provides a trade regime that is neutral and produces for the domestic market and the foreign market, stable macro-economic policies and exchange rates, and legal and regulatory frameworks that will allow easy entry and exit from different sectors or activities. With a few exceptions, it lets the market make the decisions as to where to invest.

Some Sri Lankan analysts have attempted to draw a distinction between trade policy and industrial policy. When trade policies are deliberately articulated to favour one particular activity over others, they become instruments of industrial policy. However, it is well known that in the presence of domestic distortions, trade policy is not the appropriate instrument to address the distortion. It leads to an unnecessary consumption cost (under some circumstances to a production cost) and could be avoided by using a domestic subsidy for the intervention. Of course, if the purpose is to discourage the expansion of an activity or a particular output that has negative externalities (such as the production of a pollutant), then the appropriate policy is a targeted domestic tax. This chapter does not consider interventions on optimal tariff or strategic trade theory grounds given the small country assumption for Sri Lanka. It has no monopoly or oligopoly power to influence foreign demand or supply.

The debate between industrial policy and policy towards industry assumes special significance in Sri Lanka for several reasons. First, by and large, it has been a one-sided debate. The majority of Sri Lankan economists have favoured industrial policy over neutral policy towards industry. Second, many who advocate selective intervention to raise manufacturing output and exports have not made a rigorous attempt to examine the validity of the arguments on either side, but have taken market failure as a given fact and one that obviously leads to industrial policy.[3] Most often, neutral policies have been denigrated by Sri Lankan economists as those that would not lead to rapid industrialization. They are characterized as 'market fundamentalist', 'neo-classical' in approach or what some have called 'a low growth trajectory'. Often, neutral policies are attacked as an element of the ' Washington consensus', even though economic policies could originate anywhere in the world and they have. In fact, those countries that have achieved great economic success do not owe a penny to any particular capital city except their own.

Those who favour neutral policy towards industry accuse the other side of 'picking winners', 'statist' who prefer maintaining the dominance of the public sector beyond its comparative advantage or are unable to let go of control of various aspects and activities of the economy due to a particular political ideology or bureaucratic interest to extract rents from a control regime. They are also said to be unaware of what has happened in the world in the last two decades when there has been greater use of market based allocation of resources (read 'neutral policy towards industry') from Beijing to Moscow and from Delhi to Kampala. Third, the debate assumes special significance because Sri Lanka's manufacturing output growth has slowed since the late 1990s and a reassessment of Sri Lanka's strategy to achieve high growth has been suggested. Fourth, with large and new foreign assistance resources available from donors in 2003, there will be a reassessment of economic policy. Finally, while the majority of Sri Lankan economists have argued for industrial policy, policy makers have not followed their advice, especially after the 1977 liberalization of the economy.[4]

In this discussion, an attempt has been made to keep out the 'noise' elements of the debate so that one can look at the issues per se and not characterize each position or denigrate the opposite side. It examines the debate in terms of the issues and does not focus on any particular individual author or authors. This has been done in the interest of space and is not meant to deny any credit or assign any blame to any individual author or authors.

To anticipate the conclusion, the chapter finds that the risks and costs associated with industrial policy have not been sufficiently recognized in the Sri Lankan debate. The main ingredient of the success of East Asian countries is not industrial policy but proper economic fundamentals. Their 1997–2000 crises were in part due to the attempt to use financial policies as an instrument of industrial policy and the neglect of fundamentals such as macroeconomic stability. This chapter presents an alternative to industrial policy, namely to have neutral policies towards industry but intervene in particular activities when it is justified on proper infant industry grounds. It would also require an institutional set-up to ensure that the determination and implementation of such intervention minimizes the costs of intervention and avoids capture by vested interests.

This chapter is structured as follows. After the introduction, sections 1 and 2 examine the main elements of the case for industrial policy, which is based on the infant industry argument. Section 3 evaluates the case put forward for industrial policy based on the East Asian countries' experience, especially following the crisis faced by them during the 1997–2000 period. Section 4 examines Sri Lanka's manufacturing export experience to consider whether one would be better informed by looking at actual experience, rather than conjectures as to what would have happened if one type of policy was followed rather than the other. Section 5 provides conclusions.

THE CASE FOR INDUSTRIAL POLICY

As referred to earlier, industrial policy derives its theoretical support from the infant industry argument. It is a very respected argument in neoclassical economics and has been examined by leading economists from Corden (1974, 1994), Grubel (1966), Johnson (1965), Kemp (1960) to Krueger and Tuncer (1982). In contrast to these authors, Amsden (1989), Lall (1990) and Wade (1990) advocate industrial policy both on grounds of their heterodox position on economic theory and their interpretation of the East Asian experience. They were later supported by Stiglitz (1989) in his critique of globalization.[5]

The main elements of the infant industry argument can be summarized in four propositions.[6]

(*a*) New industries and activities have high costs compared to foreign enter-prises and they require some time period to become competitive.

(*b*) It is not profitable for any new firm to enter that industry without assis-tance due to the reason that the firm that is willing to invest in technology, labour training and similar learning activities cannot appropriate the ben-efits of that investment to itself.

(*c*) With assistance from the government, the firm may be able to become competitive in the future and be able to turn out net profits following initial losses that justify the initial investment.

(*d*) Assistance is required for a temporary period over which costs would fall and it would enable the firm to compete with foreign firms without further public assistance.

Sri Lankan economists have argued that there are a host of reasons why initial costs of firms would be high. They include many 'supply side market failures' in both product and factor markets, limited ability to create technological capability, the absence of necessary labour and managerial skills, weak backward and forward linkage creation and weak institutions that could promote industry.[7] Individual entrepreneurs overesti-mate the costs and risks and underestimate the benefits from their investment in this milieu. Sri Lankan economists cited in this chapter see market failures and the absence of markets as leading to a weak industrial performance all around and the country's inability to duplicate the success of East Asian countries, according to their own inter-pretation of the ingredients of East Asian countries' industrial success.

It is necessary to examine the arguments for intervention on infant industry grounds to see what elements support the case for industrial policy. With reference to (*a*), high costs of new industries would arise from the reasons given by those who advocate industrial policy. But while agreeing that the initial costs of industries may be high for a variety of reasons, industrial policy cannot be the sweeping answer that has been put forward by the majority of Sri Lankan economists. To be sure, developing countries like Sri Lanka will have high costs of capital, weak institutions that raise transaction costs and make initial costs of establishment and operation high. The main contention of those who advocate industrial policy is that these deficiencies have to be addressed by targeting these activities for public support on a wide scale. It would imply a subsidy of some type to the firm or activity, either to raise profitability of the industry through raising domestic output prices (through a guaranteed price to the producer or through protection) or reduce costs through a subsidy to the particular factor of production or input, if it is overpriced due to a distortion (such as a monopoly in the supply of the input). It could be a subsidy to capital or to skilled labour or to some intermediate input. However, the optimal intervention theory holds that the intervention has to go to the origin of the distortion directly. It is well known that trade protection is not the answer in the presence of domestic distortions, since it leads to a lower welfare outcome than an optimum subsidy.[8] A targeted subsidy to address the high cost is superior to trade protection since the former does not involve a consumption cost. But it could involve costs in terms of the producer surplus in the manner in which the subsidy is financed (e.g., raising taxes on other efficient producers). It is essential that there is a time element involved in the process to give it the required dynamic character, namely that over time costs decline and profitability increases. The initial high costs must fall over time for the industry or activity to become profitable. However, it is important to make the point that the initial cost disadvantage is temporary and not a permanent state of affairs. If the latter were the case, the country has no static or dynamic comparative advantage in the production of the item, so that no amount of subsidy will help to overcome the cost disadvantage. The infants supported then become a geriatric ward needing permanent sustenance.

With respect to (b), the presence of an externality, it is essential that the benefits of investments are not internal to the firm but to the industry. This means that a private entrepreneur would not be able to recover the investment costs in future profits because the benefits of his investment (such as training labour or acquiring technological capability) could not be appropriated by that entrepreneur. If the benefits are internal to the firm, it can make initial losses but recover them over time and in fact become a profitable venture without public support. In this sense, these losses are an investment and, as any investment, it must have a high rate of return compared to other investments.[9] Thus, it is essential that there is an externality, namely the firm that makes the investment cannot appropriate the returns to it because other firms (in the industry) that benefit from it (such as a lowering of their supply curves) keep the benefit to themselves.

With respect to (c), it is necessary that industrial policy based assistance leads to the creation of returns over and above what would be possible if there were no intervention. What is even more important is that the returns to the activity must rise above all other activities for it to be optimal. Otherwise, the resources used to support one activity imply an opportunity cost to other activities. Thus, if manufacturing and export activities are supported for reasons of raising a particular component of GDP, it must be such that there is no reduction in output of other activities beyond a reasonable period of support. In other words, the return to the supported activity must be such to pass a test of returns over and above other activities. The real reason for the promotion is to raise GDP and its growth rate rather than some particular component of GDP. Thus, measuring success as equal to an increase in exports due to promotion of exports is not the appropriate way to measure success. The simple test is whether support for an activity raises overall GDP, or in a dynamic sense raises the GDP growth rate.

Finally, with respect to (d), the issue of the time period of support needed for an infant to grow up has to be determined. What is the cut off period for support? It should be intuitively clear that all activities requiring support may not have the same period and extent of support, because cost structures, degrees of learning, the extents of market power and technological capabilities differ. This then leads to the issues of how to determine what activities to support, what form must the support take and for what period is support to be provided? These are intrinsically difficult questions.

The above generic (or could even be described as naive) requirements for viable industrial policy are more demanding than commonly recognized in the Sri Lankan debate on industrial policy. Moreover, other considerations not captured above come into play making the advocacy of industrial policy a questionable proposition. These considerations also arise from the received theory of policy intervention. They may sound easy on the surface, but are eminently difficult to implement. These considerations are:

(i)   The choice of which activities to support—activities that have long-term dynamic comparative advantage—is not easy to determine. Why would fixed income earning bureaucrats have better knowledge of products and markets than those in the market themselves, those whose decisions as to where to invest are subject to their own individual risk evaluations so that they would be careful in choosing the investment in the first place? The exceptions to this rule are few and hard to come by.

(ii) What is the optimal form of intervention, given that received theory tells us that the policy must be targeted to the particular deficiency or distortion that prevents a country from realizing greater returns to its resources from supporting a particular activity?

(iii) For what period is support needed and could it be fixed in advance?

(iv) What is the exit policy from support in the absence of a fixed period when a highly political choice is involved in giving or taking away support? The latter is more difficult given that the political processes are not often capable of withdrawing support once it is given; since groups or coalitions are built to preserve the support.

(v)   It is not the case that bureaucrats and administrators are neutral actors in allocating support; they could be seeking rents themselves, as public choice theory tells us, through rent and revenue seeking activities.[10]

(vi) It is also not clear whether the firms which receive public support will actually put it to the use for which it is requested. This is a difficult area to monitor due to the principal-agent problem encountered in decision making for optimal outcomes. The public is the principal and the bureaucrats are the agent. It is not the case that their interests coincide even among, presumably, the best of the world's bureaucrats as one saw in the East Asian countries.

(*vii*) The firms that receive the support will pursue lobbying to maintain that support. It may also be rational for the firm receiving the support not to make the investment in fact, but window dress in order to satisfy some bureaucratic performance criterion. As Baldwin (1969) has noted, it is not even clear that the firms will make the appropriate investment of the funds it receives in public support. Their incentive to maximize profits would prevail over making some uncertain long-term investment. If the investment in knowledge that industrial policy has supported is easily duplicable by other firms, then the returns to it will fall, and firms will be reluctant to make the investment even if public funds were to be available.

(*viii*) Finally, private markets can create mechanisms to preserve the knowledge to ensure returns to such investment through technology agreements with foreign firms that have the technology protected by patents. Alternately, domestic firms (if there is a small number involved in the industry) can come to an agreement to use technology on a cost-sharing basis. Thus an externality is internalized through the use of the market.[11]

In Sri Lanka the past record of the various public enterprises that received huge targeted subsidies is hardly encouraging. They became a veritable geriatric ward rather than infants who grew up to adulthood to fend for themselves. This must have a sobering effect on those who advocate industrial policy for Sri Lanka. They must be careful to recognize the difficulties in formulating, implementing and monitoring industrial policies. They would of course argue that the support of public enterprises was wrong because even a prima facie case for infant industry could not be made in those cases. But the fact is that nobody tried. It was a political decision based on ideology at the time when the governments of the day followed the model of state ownership as a panacea for handling all manner of perceived social evils. These enterprises wasted public resources on a tremendous scale and impacted adversely on both GDP growth and equity. However, the proponents of modern day industrial policy would argue that support for the private sector would be more viable on grounds that private enterprises will have to pass market tests ultimately, even if they were to receive handsome subsidies initially. Thus, those who say that Sri Lanka should follow the East Asian model are implicitly making that argument. That case is examined in the following section.

East Asian Countries' Experience and Its Relevance for Industrial Policy in Sri Lanka

A large number of Sri Lankan economists emphasize the role of industrial policy (i.e., the use of selective intervention to promote manufacturing exports) as the main ingredient that led to the stellar performance of East Asian countries. This demands careful analysis to establish what really worked and what did not, if these countries are to serve as a model for Sri Lanka.

The debate has become even more important due to the 1997–2000 East Asian crisis. The crisis that began in Thailand spread to Malaysia, Indonesia and to the four Tigers. While Hong Kong, Taiwan and Singapore experienced much reduced GDP growth compared to their past, these countries did not face a crisis. South Korea, Indonesia and Thailand, on the other hand, underwent tremendous economic crises. Some countries lost more than 10 per cent of their GDP in a single year. Even before the crisis there had been doubts about the nature of the performance of these countries and a vast majority of the mainstream (orthodox) economists were sceptical about the role of industrial policy as the main reason for their success. Following the crisis, even greater doubts began to emerge on whether the approach was viable. East Asian countries had been held in such esteem before, that the World Bank called their performance 'the East Asian Miracle' and compiled evidence of the manifestation of the miracle and elements that were responsible for it (World Bank, 1993). This view came to be challenged even before the East Asian crisis. Some began to doubt whether there was ever was a miracle after all. Moreover, it is noteworthy that these economies have recovered remarkably well, some five years after the crisis. The main antidote to the crisis that led to the recovery has been more neutral policies towards industry, eschewing selective interventions through industrial policy.

By any objective standard, the East Asian countries have performed better than any other group of developing countries. They achieved the highest rates of GDP growth during the period 1967–97, averaging around 7.5 per cent per year. They had high GDP growth and associated employment growth and the most rapid growth in exports for any group of countries. Korea was able to raise its real exports at the pace of more than 20 per cent per year. Taiwan had a similar or near similar record. Despite reduced demand for exports during world recessions in the early 1970s and early 1980s, Hong Kong was able to increase its exports at double-digit rates.

With exports, imports also increased and East Asian economies became more open economies. There were low levels of protection all around save in a few areas. Over time these countries became more integrated with the world economy. Following the crisis these countries resolved to open their economies even more.

Interpretation by Different Schools

As expected, analysts from different camps provided their own interpretations of the success of East Asian countries.

At an international level, two broad schools can be identified for analytical purposes, as supporting one view or the other. A conventional school's interpretation associated with Bhagwati (1978), Dollar (1995), Krueger (1978), Lawrence and Weinstein (2001), Little (1981), Sachs and Warner (1995) among others, is that the East Asian countries began to grow faster following a period of economic reforms of the mid-1960s when these countries began to use neutral and more market driven policies rather than administrative mechanisms to allocate resources. This school, contrary to the opinion of some economists in Sri Lanka, did not associate the success of the East Asian countries with laissez faire policies. Nor was there a Washington Consensus at the time.[12] Except for Hong Kong, all other countries intervened in the markets in one way or another. But these interventions were less than in their own past. They intervened to move towards neutral policies.[13]

With respect to the trade regime in particular, East Asian countries' interventions led to more or less neutral incentives between producing for the domestic and the export market. They maintained good fundamentals such as sound fiscal policies, avoidance of inflation and allowed only mild financial repression. This view is the mainstream view, not only because of the avowed leadership of the main contenders in the economic profession, but also due to the vast amount of empirical work they themselves had undertaken and inspired others to undertake. Little (1981), who pioneered the examination of the link between trade and development, holds that the presumed increase in productivity from industrial policy, even if it were true, would be a necessary condition but not a sufficient condition for success since the returns to intervention must be high enough to offset the cost of intervention. It also needs to be shown that the private sector was incapable of undertaking the investments needed in the first place, as discussed earlier, in order to justify industrial policy. Furthermore, Little holds that there is no empirical evidence to show that the East Asian countries were able to realize high rates of social return from industrial policies. The purported evidence is anecdotal and not empirically well established (see in particular Amsden [1989], Lall [1990] and Wade [1990]).

While agreeing that East Asian countries have achieved stellar success Krugman (1997), Young (1995) as well as by Kim and Lau (1994) showed that there was no miracle in East Asia but the success was result of increased use of resources, both labour and capital and not through increased efficiency. They also made the important observation that East Asian countries were different in their growth experience compared to Japan in the 1950s and 1960s, even though it is claimed that the countries followed the Japanese approach. For one thing, compared to Japan, the four Tigers except Hong Kong had low (and sometimes negative) total factor productivity (TFP) growth. For another, the highest TFP was observed for Hong Kong, the country that did not follow the industrial policy intervention model of Japan.[14] Further, slowing growth in such cases is inevitable when growth is not due to increasing efficiency but increased use of factors. They offer the slow down in Japan in the decade 1993–2003 as confirmation of their point of view. Japanese growth had to come to an end as its TFP growth levelled off. In addition, it is found that East Asian countries were well behind the technological frontier reached by the advanced industrial countries, even though they were able to reach high levels of technical efficiency.[15] Thus, industrial policy did not meet one of the strongest cases made for it by its proponents.

In contrast to the conventional view, the supporters of industrial policy (associated with Amsden, Lall, Stiglitz and Wade—referred to earlier) claimed that the East Asian countries were successful in reaching high levels of efficiency and also in reaching the technological frontier. The success of the East Asian countries was more due to 'getting the prices wrong' through industrial policy interventions and 'Governing the market' (Wade, 1990). Their evidence is much less systematic than that of the neutral policy towards industry school's conventional view. The industrial policy school's evidence tends to be anecdotal, using mostly South Korean and Taiwanese data. Amsden is the main protagonist in using the Korean example. She treated it as an unqualified success prior to the crisis. It is noteworthy that this claim has never been examined in terms of the analytical requirements for infant industry presented earlier in this chapter. There are some oblique references to them but their main plank is based on their interpretation of empirical evidence from East Asia. In sharp contrast, the policy towards industry school or the conventional view holds that these countries succeeded not because of industrial policy but in spite of it (Little, 1981).

As to be expected, industrial policy advocates do not attribute the failure of the countries in the late 1990s as arising from anything to do with the failure of industrial policy. However, the subjugation of the financial market to implement industrial policy through directed credit led to the loss of financial discipline, weak commercial banks, macroeconomic disequilibrium and huge moral hazard and financial collapse.

Industrial Policy Issue and East Asian Countries' Performance

The industrial policy school gained ground in the 1980s in the debate on the factors responsible for the success of East Asian economies, i.e., prior to the East Asian crisis. Their main point of contention was that in addition to getting the fundamentals right, the East Asian economies selectively intervened in the economy through industrial policy in order to depart from the neutral incentives. Those who espouse this view argue that the success of these economies confirms the importance of dynamic factors such as the learning effects and externalities, and that by substituting for the market these countries were able to achieve success in industrialization. Some, Amsden in particular, claim that the success of East Asian economies was not due to neutral incentives but due to factors that are yet to be understood well.

Amsden and Wade contend that what they describe as the neoclassical position is not relevant to developing countries given that the concern should not be with static but dynamic comparative advantage.[16] Sanjay Lall, another advocate of industrial policy, has influenced the majority of the Sri Lankan economists who contend that industrial policy intervention was the reason for the success of the East Asian countries. Abeyratne (1996), Kelegama and Wignaraja (1991), Rodrigo (2001), Vidanapathirana (1993) and Wignaraja (1992) argue for industrial policy in Sri Lanka.

Following Lall, they base their position on the need to promote technology in Sri Lanka through industrial policy. However, they do not deny that incentives are important for industrialization. They claim that government intervention is necessary to lead firms in developing countries like Sri Lanka to acquire technology capability. According to their view, East Asian countries succeeded due to building technological capability through industrial policy. They claim that economic liberalization has to be supported by industrial policy, which means that they do not support neutral incentives. Accordingly, they believe that the trade regime should have different rates of protection to reflect different degrees of support for different activities. Some go to the extent of recommending quantitative restrictions to achieve this degree of dispersion of incentives.[17]

Other Asian countries except Hong Kong and Singapore (at least up to a point) provided extra incentives to the export sector through a plethora of special incentives comprising duty drawbacks, duty exemptions, bonded warehouses, Export Promotion Zones, tax concessions, direct transfers, subsidized credit. Bhagwati (1988) has called these efforts as those aimed at creating an 'ultra export bias'. The bias is measured by the excess domestic currency received by producers in exporting activities compared to producers in import substituting activities. Some analysts have argued that exports have special externalities (such as non-pecuniary externalities in which, as the industry expands, long-run supply curves would fall) and their promotion could enhance productivity (Wesphal, 1990). Others have argued for them on pure 'learning by doing grounds'. Whatever the rationale for these policies, it is clear that East Asian countries did follow a Mercantilist strategy of valuing export growth over import growth at the earlier stages of opening their economies. A definite sequencing was followed; exports were promoted before imports were liberalized. The issue is whether this was the appropriate policy in terms of maximizing the growth rate of GDP, which is the final test of success and not maximizing a specific component of output, as described earlier in this chapter.

East Asian countries' interventions included trade policies (both protective tariffs and export subsidies), tax incentives, credit subsidies, direct transfers and moral suasion. Many of these countries established programmes to accelerate advanced industries. Financial market policies played a decisive role in these interventions in the case of Korea, Indonesia and Thailand and to some extent in Taiwan. Mild financial repression that resulted from the low deposit rates and ceilings on lending rates in the early years was not considered to be harmful. There was also the theoretical justification for intervention in financial markets (Stiglitz and Weiss, 1981) based on asymmetric information related issues between lenders and borrowers that created moral hazard and adverse selection. These attributes of the financial market were said to preclude the market forces from allocating financial resources optimally.[18]

Emphasis on Exports and Postponing Import Liberalization

Some analysts have identified the slow growth of productivity in East Asian countries as arising from industrial policy that led to the slow rate of import liberalization. Rapid import liberalization would have helped in two ways. It would have helped to create a competitive environment for domestic producers on the one hand, and acted as an effective conduit for acquiring technology to move to the technology frontier on the other. A study by Lawrence and Weinstein (2001) shows that productivity growth is closely associated with import liberalization. They find that East Asian countries were successful in exports because imports associated with these exports allowed them to increase productivity. Thus, exporting is the result of productivity increase and not the other way round. Looking at Japan over some 40 years of GDP of exports and import growth, they conclude that Japan could have grown even faster had it liberalized its imports faster. They come to the same conclusion on Korea.

Exporters were provided.'free trade status' while keeping import growth low. However, the system relied on highly efficient administrative mechanisms, tolerant international competitors who did not challenge export subsidies used to offset the bias against exports arising from import restrictions. There are inherent difficulties in offsetting the bias both in terms of the administrative arrangements and lack of tolerance for export subsidies in the world today. These factors militate against the sequencing of export promotion before import liberalization. Moreover, other empirical work (Panagariya, 2000) showed that exports of countries that provided export subsidies have not grown faster than countries that did not provide export subsidies.

Coordination failures, incomplete markets and asymmetric information issues could well lead to departures from optimal resource allocation under the price mechanism. Government interventions in this case were consistent with optimal policy. There were risks and difficulties that arose in the East Asian countries to question whether the interventions were optimal per se or whether the bureaucrats who were entrusted with substituting for the market were capable of carrying them out without resisting the incentives to seek rents. Public Choice Theory (Buchanan and Stubblebine, 1962; Tullock, 1969) has sounded a sceptical note on the reliance on bureaucrats to act optimally. They could intervene in such ways either to make a personal financial gain or increase the power of the bureaucracy for its own purposes. In the event, most would agree that the interventions in East Asia turned out to be excessive and harmful particularly in the financial sector. Some would argue that it was the financial sector that led to the undoing of the strong performance of the East Asian economies and there was nothing wrong with interventions in the real sector per se (Ito, 2001). But this dichotomy is somewhat strained, artificial and not possible to sustain in real world policy making, for the financial sector problems can and did have serious effects on the real sector and vice versa.

Results of Industrial Policy

Beason and Weinstein (1996) found that subsidies granted to different industries were negatively correlated with their efficiency in Japan, which is regarded as the paragon of success of industrial policy. They showed that the industries that were found to be least productive received the highest subsidies per unit of their value added. Moreover, earlier research had also shown that selection of industries on infant industry grounds was not an easy task even if the bureaucracy was not seeking rents. Zinsmeister 1993 wrote that, 'many of its strongest businesses—such as home electronics, cameras, robotics, precision equipment, pianos, bicycles, watches and calculators, numerically controlled machine tools, and ceramics—developed without help from MITI or other agencies'. Perhaps, the highly praised bureaucracies of East Asia resisted the temptation to seek rents. But it became clear during the crisis in East Asia that this assumption was no longer valid. There was a capture of the bureaucracy by politicians and industrialists. The most acute cases were seen in Indonesia, Thailand and South Korea where there was rampant corruption and misuse of funds arising from a symbiotic relationship among the three groups—bureaucrats, industrialists and politicians.

The success of bureaucracies of Japan and in the early period of the South Korean performance may have been the exception rather than the rule. Moreover, this approach led a few families to dominate particular industrial activities, as was the case in South Korea and Indonesia. It led to the growth of monopoly and the lack of contestability in goods and credit markets. The capture of bureaucracy by industrialists and politicians has been found in the allocation of subsidies of various kinds. Instead of promoting contests among the different groups, the bureaucracy entered the contests themselves leading to corruption on a wide scale.

One important lesson from the East Asian experience is that the industrial policy-making process can be easily captured and corrupted, as was the case in South Korea. It would entail heavy costs at the firm level but also have economy-wide and large macroeconomic effects that would operate via the credit and banking systems, as happened in South Korea, Thailand and Indonesia.

A study by Pack (2000), which carefully documents the experiences of Japan and South Korea, finds that industrial policy's contribution to the industrial success of these countries was small at best and advocates neutral policies towards industry for developing countries at large. His finding is important for two reasons. First, in the past Pack has been a strong advocate of industrial policy and following the East Asian crisis, he has re-examined the case to come to the present conclusion. Second, his analysis is done carefully, using four counterfactual calculations to examine the case for industrial policy based on TFP estimates. He finds that only one third of 1 per cent of growth in the two countries could be attributed to industrial policy. While this is not trivial, it is hardly the secret of success. In addition, the conduct of industrial policy requires an exceptionally capable and non-corrupt bureaucracy and the political ability to withdraw support from non-performing firms. One finds that the risks of using industrial policies when these conditions are not present outweigh their expected benefits.

Relevance for Sri Lanka

The above discussion leads to a number conclusions regarding the lessons for Sri Lanka from the experience of East Asian countries.

(i)   No one has established the case rigorously for East Asian countries' use of industrial policy on infant grounds described in the earlier section of this chapter titled 'The Case for Industrial Policy'.[19]

(ii) The stellar performance of East Asian countries can be ascribed to getting the fundamentals right and not to industrial policy per se. What little empirical evidence exists supports that position. The findings of Krugman, Young and Kim and Lau show that there was no stellar TFP growth, but overall GDP growth was based on factor augmentation attributable to high savings and investments, supported by a stable macroeconomic environment, strong property rights and political stability, at least up to the time of the 1997–2000 crisis.

(*iii*)   The pursuit of export promotion at the expense of import liberalization turned out to be less successful than realized earlier, as found by Lawrence and Weinstein (2001).

(*iv*)   The crisis calls into question the viability of the industrial policies that led to weak financial systems, the over-dependence on bureaucratic decision making leading to large moral hazard and ultimate collapse of the financial system, weakened by decades of lack of scrutiny and failure to meet basic prudential and regulatory standards.

(*v*)   Industrial policies in other countries have fared worse as those of India, Argentina and Turkey among others. They provide a strong counterfactual test of East Asia's experience. Unlike East Asian countries, they did not have good fundamental economic policies.

(*vi*)   The contribution from industrial policy has been modest by Pack's estimate and should be contrasted with the risk of capture and rent seeking. It must be precluded as a viable option for Sri Lanka.

(*vii*)   Finally, the recovery in East Asian countries has been good, largely due to the reversal from industrial policy towards more neutral policies toward industry.

SRI LANKA'S MANUFACTURES EXPORTS EXPERIENCE

Sri Lanka's manufactures export experience has been the main bone of contention for those who advocate industrial policy for Sri Lanka. The experience is denigrated strongly by them on several grounds. It is for this reason that one has to examine the experience as the main arena of the debate of industrial policy versus policy towards industry in the country.

Manufactures Export Performance

Two broad periods could serve to show contrasts in manufacturing export performance. The period 1960–77 when Sri Lanka was a highly inward oriented economy and the period from 1978–2002 when, following the economic liberalization beginning in 1977, it became a more outward oriented economy.

During the first period, manufactures export growth was low, some 3–5 per cent per year in current dollars and its share was only 5 per cent of merchandise exports. During the latter 1978–95 period, manufactures exports grew by 32 per cent per year in current dollars. Their share rose to 70 per cent of total merchandise exports. The value of manufacturing exports increased from a mere $5 million to over $2.4 billion in current US dollars by the mid-1990s. During the 1980–95 period, Sri Lanka was among the top five low income countries with respect to average growth in export earnings from manufactures exports and was increasing its share of manufacturing in total merchandise exports. The labour intensive factor content of Sri Lankan exports rose from a low 2.6 per cent in the 1962–77 period to nearly 60 per cent during 1990–95 and it may have risen in the remaining years to 2002.[20] There was a corresponding decline in the share of land or resource intensive factor content in exports over the same period from 96 per cent to 32 per cent by 1990–95. It may have fallen below 32 per cent by 2002. The important point here is that with the economic liberalization and the related movement towards more neutral policies, the economy responded strongly not only in terms of the rate of growth of exports but its composition to reflect the country's comparative advantage in labour intensive manufactures.

In addition, with a return to more neutral policies during the latter period, the bias against exports reduced. The overall efficiency of the economy improved. This is indicated by the total manufacturing TFP growth. TFP growth was negative during the period 1966–74 and 1977–81. It became positive during the 1981–88 period and rose to a remarkable 9.17 during 1988–93.[21] Similar high TFP growth is observed when manufactures excluding textiles and clothing are considered. Many Sri Lankan economists consider the concentration on textiles and clothing as a weak characteristic of Sri Lanka's manufacturing experience due to the low value added in the activity and increased competition from China, once Multi Fibre Arrangement (MFA) quotas are rescinded following the Textile and Clothing Agreement of the Uruguay Round. But specialization is what leads to gains from trade and commodity composition changes over time, as comparative advantage changes.

Despite the success of Sri Lanka's manufacturing exports as seen in the above performance, the majority of Sri Lankan economists found this performance as wanting in many respects. A variety of criticisms were levelled against this performance by those who espoused industrial policy.

Criticisms of Sri Lanka's Manufactures Export Performance

First, the growth rates achieved by Sri Lanka was seen as wanting in comparison to the East Asian countries. The latter grew faster on a sustained basis over some special periods in their development. Second, the value added in Sri Lanka's manufactures exports is considered to be low and hence is described as 'shallow industrialization' by the advocates of industrial policy. Third, it is said that there were no strong forward or backward linkages in the manufacturing sector. Fourth, commodity composition of Sri Lanka's exports is said to be narrow. Fifth, industrialization has only resulted in a low rate of labour absorption. Finally, Sri Lanka's exports use less technology compared to the East Asian countries.

Evaluation of the Criticisms

Several issues arise from these criticisms and the advocacy of industrial policy as the antidote to the alleged poor performance.

(i)   As seen in the earlier section titled 'The Case for Industrial Policy', by looking at one component of GDP, namely manufacturing exports, one cannot pass judgement on the success or failure of a policy towards industry even though the advocates of industrial policy argue in that vein. The proper criterion should be whether it raised the GDP level and its growth rate. Increasing manufacturing exports is not equivalent to maximizing national income. It is possible to raise manufactures exports by various means through subsidies and other special incentives but that is not equivalent to raising overall efficiency or improving welfare. Besides, such policy is not sustainable and will not be tolerated by trading partners in the current international trading environment.

(ii)   Increasing exports by keeping import controls (as suggested by those who advocate industrial policy and claim that Sri Lanka liberalized too rapidly) has many flaws. It would increase the bias against exports and lead to an appreciation of the exchange rate. Empirical evidence from Japan and Korea (see Lawrence and Weinstein, 2001) show that these countries could have grown even faster had they liberalized their imports along with the export promotion measures they adopted in the 1960s and 1970s.

(iii) The idea of linkages, both forward and backward, is flawed. It ignores incentives faced by the producers. In other words, maximizing domestic value added as advocated by industrial policy proponents could lead to lower levels of efficiency and competitiveness and reduce Sri Lanka's share in world trade. A simple example would illustrate this point. If a country uses imported inputs but the government insists that those should be domestically produced, it would hurt the competitiveness of the activity. There is no guarantee that these inputs would be produced at low costs domestically compared to imports. Besides, since imported inputs tend to be produced with more capital intensive technology, this would amount to a substitution of capital for labour and would go against the country's comparative advantage. In fact, countries' comparative advantage is determined in terms of value adding and not producing the whole value chain in the country. During the import substitution phase (1960–77), Sri Lanka attempted this strategy with disastrous results.

(iv) There is little or no economics involved in the advocacy of raising the level of technology. Investment in technology is like any other investment. The investor in technology has to look at costs and returns. In doing so, the investor adopts the most viable technology unless he or she faces constraints in the choice of technology. To insist that technology upgrading has to be attempted through industrial policy is to argue on non-economic grounds. Thus, for example, the school which claims to be the 'neo-technology school' (Lall, 1990; Pack, 2000; Westphal, 1990) is valuing technology for its own sake. The bottom line is whether the use of 'low level' technology is due to a distortion or not, in which case a correction is appropriate. But that need not be industrial policy. When one applies the infant industry argument to this situation there is no general justification for technology upgrading through public intervention. Besides, the textiles and garments sector was able to adopt high level technology on its own as indicated by Wignaraja (1998).[22] There is of course another alternative to industrial policy based technology upgrading, which is to remove any barriers to foreign direct investment (FDI) so technology upgrading takes place in a viable way. This is what has happened in the textiles and garments sector.

(v)   The commodity composition of Sri Lanka's exports reflects the country's comparative advantage. In fact this has changed from resource intensive to more labour intensive goods as economic policy became more neutral. It could have happened faster had policy reforms not been delayed until 1977.

(vi)   The charge that labour absorption was low cannot be sustained given that employment increased rapidly following the economic liberalization and also because the factor content of exports changed to more labour intensive products. In any case, the conjecture that industrial policies could have led to higher labour absorption is not demonstrated by anyone. It is merely a matter of conjecture.

(vii)   Sri Lanka's export performance is not as poor as it is made out to be by industrial policy enthusiasts. It has been achieved under adverse circumstances. First, there has been continued bias against exports despite the 1977 liberalization (Abeyratne, 1996; Ratnayake, 1988). Second, during most of the post-liberalization period the exchange rate remained appreciated adding to the bias, with some respite following the adoption of a floating exchange rate. Third, there were substantial macroeconomic imbalances in the early 1980s due to the undertaking of the Accelerated Mahaweli and other lead projects. That led to a Dutch disease problem. Other activities were put at a disadvantage including manufacturing. Third, there were two periods of political uncertainty during the JVP uprising in 1989 and the ethnic conflict that plagued the country since 1983. This was hardly the environment to foster high export and GDP growth.

(viii)   Finally, the blanket advocacy of industrial policy neglects the political economy problems associated with such a policy in Sri Lanka. It could be easily captured by different interest groups, including state owned enterprises, due to widespread political patronage and would also open the door to wide-scale rent seeking. One very important reason for neutral policies towards industry is precisely to avoid a situation where different activities are provided different incentives. Departing from neutrality invites lobbying efforts to attempt to capture rents through this process. Yet many of industrial policy enthusiasts lament the fact that structure of protection is not adopted to provide what is called a 'functional role'.[23]

An Alternative to Industrial Policy

As described earlier, evidence from East Asia's and Sri Lanka's own experience and theoretical reasons suggest that neutral policy towards industry is more likely to maximize national income than industrial policy. It is also clear that there is no merit in concentrating on a particular component of GDP as manufacturing output or manufactures exports, given the need to maximize income growth. This chapter focused on manufactures exports to highlight the main issues in the debate on industrial policy versus neutral policy towards industry since it is the arena in which the majority of Sri Lankan economists have advocated industrial policy.

As stated at the outset, there are specific cases in which selective interventions are needed when there are sizable distortions, such as capital and labour market distortions, constraints to profit maximizing technology (as against adopting sophisticated technology for its own sake), lack of complementary investments among others. Here, the issue is to address the distortion directly by appropriate policy measures. By and large, neutral policy towards industry along with getting the fundamentals right (sound macroeconomic policy, stable prices, wages and exchange rates, well established property rights) will go a long way to provide the proper environment for strong GDP growth with industrial output as an important component of it.

But this may not be sufficient and that is why some specific interventions may be necessary. The important point is that the answer is not industrial policy. Thus, for example, where there are capital market distortions such as the lack of appropriate collateral for entrepreneurs to finance their investment, the intervention would be focused on the specific nature of the distortion. The absence of an efficient mortgage instrument or the limited ability to use movable property as collateral could lead to constraints on capital. Another example is one in which an entrepreneur finds that he or she has no access to technology needed for the activity. The answer would be to remove barriers to FDI and let cost sharing arrangements take place among entrepreneurs in the activity.

In the case of a labour market problem such as the inability to retain workers once they are trained, the answer is to have an apprentice period in which the entrepreneur can finance the cost of the training through appropriate wages that lead to the recovery of the training cost and subsequently pay high wages to attract the best talent. Many Sri Lankan firms are known to do this with success. In the event that there is still an inability to appropriate the training costs, public policy could intervene by providing a tax credit or a direct subsidy for labour training on a cost sharing basis. The infant industry argument provides for theoretically sound and practically enforceable arrangements such as these. The conditions under this type of assistance that could be provided are discussed below.

Finally, many of the reasons that were given earlier in the chapter for intervention must satisfy certain criteria to avoid replacing one distortion with another and making matters worse in the bargain.

The appropriate way to formulate the intervention is to ensure that the following conditions are met:

(i) Domestic distortions that have been identified as warranting interventions should not be addressed through trade policies. The proper antidote is a domestic subsidy because it avoids the consumption loss associated with protection.

(ii) The subsidy should be appropriately targeted and not be a blanket subsidy.

(iii) Such a subsidy should be the exception (that is a departure from neutral incentives) rather than the rule.

(iv) It is necessary to isolate the evaluation of the need for subsidy or policy measure from any line ministry or group that has a vested interest in the subsidy or policy change. It could be done by an independent body such as a public commission.[24]

(v) The work of such a body must be done in the public domain and be subject to light and transparency. A request for assistance must be heard and the decision made public. All interested parties could be invited to give evidence whether the particular intervention is necessary or not.

(vi) All assistance must have a sun-set provision with no possibility of extension beyond the initial support and the same party cannot ask for support for the same purpose again.

(vii) Special funds could be administered to support such activities such as support for small and medium-scale enterprises with fixed resources based on the same principles as above for one-time grants.

CONCLUSIONS

Sri Lankan economists have argued for industrial policy on many grounds. These include many 'supply side market failures' in both product and factor markets, limited ability to create technological capability, the absence of necessary skills, managerial skills, weak linkage creation and weak institutions that could promote industry.

The case for intervention through industrial policy on infant industry groups is more stringent than commonly recognized by the majority of Sri Lankan economists.

(i) Identification activities to support on the basis of long-term dynamic comparative advantage is not easy.

(ii) The determination of the optimal form of intervention is similarly not easy.

(iii) The period of support needed cannot be fixed in advance.

(iv) Bureaucrats and administrators are not neutral actors in allocating support, they could be seeking rents.

(v) Firms, which receive public support, may not put it to the use for which it is requested. This is a difficult area to monitor due to the principal-agent problem.

(vi) The firms that receive support will pursue lobbying to maintain that support as long as possible.

(vii) Finally, private markets can provide the proper mechanism to acquire the knowledge through patents and technology arrangements with foreign firms that have the technology protected through patents. Alternately, domestic firms (if there is a small number involved) can come to an arrangement to use technology on a cost-sharing basis.

A number of conclusions were reached on the lessons for Sri Lanka from the experience of the East Asian countries. The stellar performance of East Asian countries can be ascribed to getting fundamentals right and not to industrial policy per se. The issue of whether the East Asian model is duplicable in Sri Lanka, given that the contribution from industrial policy has been modest, should be contrasted with the risk of capture and rent seeking. The recovery in East Asian countries has been largely due to the policy reversal towards more neutral policies toward industry.

Once it is realized that industrial policy is not the proper response to market distortions, it behoves one to suggest an alternative, which is to formulate specific interventions through appropriate institutional arrangements. The way to formulate the intervention is to ensure that the following conditions are met: (a) domestic distortions that have been identified as warranting intervention should not be addressed through trade policies. The proper instrument is a domestic subsidy because it avoids the consumption loss associated with protection; (b) the subsidy should be appropriately targeted and not be a blanket subsidy; (c) it should be the exception (that is a departure from neutral incentives) rather than the rule; (d) it is necessary to isolate the evaluation of the need for subsidy or policy measure from any line ministry or group that has a vested interest in the subsidy or policy change by an independent body such as a public commission; (e) the work of such a body must be done in the public domain and subject to light and transparency; (f) all assistance must have a sun-set provision with no possibility of extension beyond the initial support; and (g) special funds could be administered to support such activities as small and medium-scale enterprises using fixed resources based on the same principles as for one-time grants.

NOTES

1. The author wishes to thank Prema-chandra Athukorala (Australian National University) for initial discussions and Migara de Silva (World Bank) and Nimal Sanderatne (University of Peradeniya) for valuable comments. Jill Mitchell of the American Enterprise Institute provided excellent editorial and processing assistance. Saman Kelegama deserves special thanks for his encouragement to get this work done and for his understanding and patience with the delivery of the completed chapter. It is a singular honour to participate in a tribute to Dr Gamini Corea whose contributions to Sri Lankan economic policy making have been invaluable, not to mention his contributions to international policy making. The author alone is responsible for any mistakes that remain.

2. Why the majority of Sri Lanka's economists have favoured industrial policy over neutral policy towards industry is an interesting research question in its own right.

3. Wignaraja (1998) may be the exception. But his argument cannot be sustained on the conditions required for the infant industry argument, among other reasons discussed in the section 'Sri Lanka's manufactures exports experience' of this chapter.

4. Industrial Policy Statement put out by the Ministry of Constitutional Affairs and Industrial Development, see http://www.saarcnet.org/newsaarcnet/govtpolicies/srilanka/POLICY/sir.htm 1994. Also, a major policy report led by Sanjay Lall 'Building Sri Lankan Competitiveness: A Strategy for Manufactured Export Growth' in 1966, done at the behest of the National Development Council has been shelved.

5. Stiglitz is perhaps the exception because his espousal of industrial policy arises mostly on grounds of the pure theory of information that markets do not carry information efficiently and markets are altogether absent in others. He uses this view to interpret the East Asian Experience (1996).

6. Krueger and Tuncer (1982).

7. These reasons have been put forward by many but prominent among them are Abeyratne (1996), Kelegama and Wignaraja (1991), Rodrigo (2001), Vidanapathirana (1993) and Wignaraja (1991).

8. Corden (1994) was a pioneer in the ranking of trade interventions since 1957. He was followed by others including Bhagwati and Ramaswamy (1963) and Johnson (1995).

9. A simple test is whether, over time, the present value of the benefits (appropriately discounted) exceeds the losses including the investment (similarly discounted) that are to accrue over the lifetime of the investment. This is necessary but not sufficient. The returns must be better than any other investment that could be undertaken for it to be sufficient. Otherwise, the intervention is not optimal.

10. It is extraordinary that only a fleeting reference is made by those advocates of industrial policy to the possibilities of capture of industrial policy by those who want to maximize private returns in terms of rent and revenue seeking. This is not confined to Sri Lanka but applies to all leading advocates such as Amsden (1989), Lall (1990), Stiglitz (1989) and Wade (1990). Yet the theory of public choice has clarified the issue of capture of decision-making processes involved in formulating, implementing and monitoring industrial policy.

11. Coase (1960) made this point and it was the basis for the extension of externality issues in the work of Buchanan and Stubblebine (1962).

12. The term 'Washington Consensus' was coined by John Williamson in the mid-1980s following the debt crisis in Latin America. Later he retracted the term and remarked that it was neither Washington based nor was there a consensus to speak of.

13. Lal and Rajapatirana (1989) showed that trade incentives were closer to neutrality in the case of South Korea compared to India, using Little-Mirlees type of accounting prices (ratio of shadow prices to market prices).

14. See World Bank (1993). The Hong Kong TFP growth data kept the Miracle Study from tilting towards support for industrial policy.

15. Technical efficiency is reached when the frontier (the production possibility curve determined by the given level of technology) is achieved. The technological frontier lies outside the production possibility curve determined by the world state of technology. Sustained growth involves technological change to move the technology frontier forward.

16. Keynes provides the best explanation of neoclassical economics as a method, a way of examining issues and not a given body of thought, in his introduction to the Cambridge Economics Handbooks series. This was published jointly by Cambridge University Press and Nisbet Company and was started by John Maynard Keynes (1922) who was the editor of the series. Thus, what is alleged to be neoclassical is the use of marginal economic analysis method or the main toolbox of economists. Like value, costs and returns-economics decisions are made a margin.

17. But it is now well known that Quantitative Restrictions (QRs) lead to chaotic incentive structures, encourage rent seeking and break the link between domestic and foreign prices in ways that makes macroeconomic management difficult by introducing structural rigidities.

18. One theoretical objection to Stiglitz and Weiss (1981) is that their model applies to a single game in a game theoretic world and does not apply to repeated games where the parties learn through subsequent rounds. Thus, a commercial bank may not be able to monitor borrower behaviour in the first round of the 'lending game', but would certainly learn to evaluate risks well in a particular market and among particular borrowers. In that case the Stiglitz-Weiss model fails to show the non-optimality of financial markets.

19. Wignaraja (1998) makes an attempt to provide an analytical basis for industrial policy, noting that export growth is positively correlated with technological capability at the firm level. But this is hardly an infant industry test. It is more of a statistical artifact based on a limited sample and not a proper empirical test. Merely raising technological capability does not lead to an improvement in resource use. The proper test is whether increasing technological capability raised TFP growth overall and not one component of GDP such as manufactures export growth. Neither test was done in the study.

20. Athukorala and Rajapatirana (2000).

21. Ibid.

22. It behoves the advocates of technology capability to ask the question why textiles and garments were able to upgrade their technology while others were not able or willing to do so.

23. Kelegama (1989).

24. Australia has such an institution called the Productivity Commission. It reports to the Prime Minister but remains independent in its evaluation. Some of the best economists of the country work with the Commission as consultants or staff members to advise formulation of appropriate policy.

REFERENCES

Abeyratne, Srimal (1996), 'Trade Strategy and Industrialization', in W.D. Lakshman (ed.), *Dilemmas in Development*, Colombo: Sri Lanka Economists Association.

Amsden, Alice (1989), *Asia's Next Giant*, New York: Oxford University Press.

Athukorala, Prema-chandra and Sarath Rajapatirana (2000), *Liberalization and Industrial Transformation: Sri Lanka in International Perspective*, Oxford and London: Oxford University Press.

Beason, Richard and David E. Weinstein (1996), 'Growth, Economics of Scale and Targeting in Japan, 1995–1990', *Review of Economics and Statistics*, 72(2): 286–95.

Bhagwati, Jagdish (1978), *Foreign Trade Regimes and Economic Development: Anatomy and Consequences of Exchange Control Regime*, Mass: Ballinger Press.

————— (1988), 'Export Promotion State Strategy: Issues and Evidence', *World Bank Research Observer*, 3(1): 27–57.

Bhagwati, Jagdish and V.K. Ramaswamy (1963), 'Domestic Distortions, Tariffs, and the Theory of Optimum Subsidy', *Journal of Political Economy*, February, 71(1): 44–50.

Baldwin, Robert E. (1969), 'The Case Against Infant Industry Tariff Protection', *Journal of Political Economy*, May/June, 77, 295–305.

Buchanan, J.M. and W.C. Stubblebine (1962), 'Externality', *Economica*, XXIX, 371–94.

Coase, R.H. (1960), 'The Problem of Social Cost', *Journal of Law and Economics*, October, III: 1–44.

Corden, W.M. (1994), *Trade Policy and Economic Welfare*, (second edition) (revised edition 1997), Oxford: Oxford University Press.

Dollar, David (1995), 'Outward Oriented Developing Economies Really Grow More Rapidly: Evidence from 95 LDCs 1976-85', *Economic Development and Cultural Change*, 40(4): 523–44.

Grubel, Herbert (1966), 'The Anatomy of Classical and Modern the Infant Industry Arguments', *Weltwirtschaftliches Archiv*, XCVII(December): 325–42.

Ito, Takatoshi (2001), 'Growth, Crisis and the Future of Economic Recovery in East Asia', in Joseph E. Stiglitz and Shahid Yusuf, (eds), *Rethinking the Asia Miracle,* World Bank and New York: Oxford University Press.

Johnson, H.G. (1995), 'Optimal Trade Intervention in the Presence of Domestic Distortions', in R.E. Baldurin and G. Haberler (eds), *Trade, Growth and Balance of Payments,* Chicago: Rand McNally.

———— (1995), 'Optimal Intervention in the Presence of Domestic Distortions in Trade Growth and Balance of Payments' (Essays in honour of Gottfried Haberler), Chicago: Rand McNally.

Kelegama, Saman (1989), 'The Speed and Stages of Trade Liberalization Strategy: The Case of Sri Lanka', *Marga Quarterly Journal,* 10(1).

Kelegama, Saman and Ganeshan Wignaraja (1991), 'Trade Policy and Industrial Development in Sri Lanka', *Marga Quarterly Journal,* 2(4): 27-53.

Kemp, M.C. (1960), 'The Mill-Bastable Infant Industry Dogma', *Journal of Political Economy,* LXVIII: 65-67.

Kim, Jong Il and Lawrence Lan (1994), 'The Sources of Economic Growth of the East Asian Industrial Countries', *Journal of Japanese and International Economics,* 8(3): 235-71.

Krueger, Anne O. (1978), *Foreign Trade Regimes and Economic Development: Liberalization Attempts and Consequences,* Mass: Ballinger Press.

Krueger, Anne O. and Baran Tuncer (1982), 'An empirical Test of the Infant Industry Argument', *Amercian Economic Review,* 72(5).

Krugman, Paul (1997), 'What Ever Happened to the Asian Miracle?' *Fortune,* 136(4): 26-29.

Lal, Deepak and Sarath Rajapatirana (1989), *Impediments to Trade Liberalization in Sri Lanka,* Thames Essay No. 50, London: Aldershot.

Lall, Sanjay (1990), *Building Technological Capability,* Paris: OECD.

Little, I.M.D. (1981), 'The Experience and Causes of Rapid Labour-Intensive Development in Korea, Taiwan Province, Hong Kong, and Singapore, and Possibilities for Emulation', in Edy Lee (ed.), *Export-led Industrialization and Development,* Geneva: ILO (Reproduced I.M.D. Little, 1999), *Collection and Recollections: Economic Annexes and their Provenance,* Oxford: Clarendon Press, 213-40.

Lawrence, Robert Z. and David E. Weinstein (2001), 'Trade and Growth: Import-Led or Export Led? Evidence from Japan and Korea', in Joseph E. Stiglitz and Shahid Yusuf, (eds), *Rethinking the East Asia Miracle,* New York: Oxford University Press.

Pack, Howard (2000), 'Industrial Policy: Growth Elixit a Poison?', *The World Bank Research Observer,* 15(1): 47-67.

Panagariya, Arvind (2000), 'Evaluating the Case for Export Subsidies', World Bank Policy Research Working Paper No. 2276, Washington D.C.: World Bank.

Ratnayake, Ravi (1988), 'Trade Policy and the Performance of the Manufacturing Sector: Sri Lanka', *The Developing Economies,* March, XXVI(1).

Rodrigo, Chris G. (2001), 'Does Sri Lanka Need Industrial Activism ?', *Sri Lanka Economic Journal,* New Series.

Sachs, Jeffery and Andrew Warner (1995), *Economic Reform and the Process of Global Integration* , Brookings Papers on Economic Activity, No. 1 Brookings Institution, Washington D.C.

Stiglitz, Joseph E. (1989), 'On the Economic Role of the State', in A. Heertje (ed.), *Economic Role of the State,* Oxford: Basil Blackwell.

Stiglitz, Joseph E. and Andrew Weiss (1981), 'Credit Rationing in Markets with Imperfect Information', *American Economic Review,* June, 71(3): 393-410.

Tullock, Gordon (1969), 'Social Cost and Government Action', *American Economic Review,* 59(2). Papers and Proceedings of the Eighty-first Annual Meeting of the American Economic Association, pp. 189-97.

Vidanapathirana, Upananda (1993), 'A Review of Industrial Policy and Industrial Potential in Sri Lanka', Sri Lanka Economic Association.

Wade, Robert (1990), *Governing the Market: Economic Theory and the Role of the Government in East Asian Industrialization,* Princeton: Princeton University Press.

Westphal, Larry E. (1990), 'Industrial Policy in an Export-Propelled Economy', *Journal of Economic Perspectives,* 4(3): 41–59.

Wignaraja, Ganeshan (1992), *Trade and Industrial Policies in Sri Lanka,* Prepared for the Trade and Industrialization Reconsidered Conference, United Nations University and WIDER, Helsinki.

—————— **(1998),** *Trade Liberalization in Sri Lanka: Exports, Technology and Industrial Policy,* London: Macmillan.

World Bank (1993), *The East Asian Miracle,* New York: Oxford University Press.

Young, Alwyn (1995), 'The Tyranny of Numbers: Confronting the Statistical Realities of the East Asian Growth Experience', *Quarterly Journal of Economics,* 110(August): 643–80.

Zinsmeister, Karl (1993), 'MITI Mouse: Japan's Industrial Policy Doesn't Work', *Policy Review,* Spring(64).

SELECT READINGS

Athukorala, Prema-chandra and Sisira Jayasuriya (1994), *Macroeconomic Policies, Crises and Growth in Sri Lanka 1969–1990,* Washington: World Bank.

Kelegama, Saman (1990), 'Open Economic Policy and Its Impact on Domestic Industrialization in Sri Lanka', *Upanathi,* 1 and 2.

Krueger, Anne O. (1997), 'Trade Policy and Economic Development: How We Learn', *American Economic Review* (Presidential Address), 87: 1–22.

Krugman, Paul (1987), *Learning to Industrialize,* London: Macmillan.

Lal, Deepak (2003), 'Free Trade and Laissez Faire: Has the Wheel Come Full Circle?', in Sarath Rajaptirana and James Riedel (eds), *The World Economy* (Feschrift to Honour Max Corden), 26(April).

Little, I.M.D., Tibor Scitovsky and Maurice Scott (1970), *Industry and Trade in Some Developing Countries,* London: Oxford University Press.

Rajapatirana, Sarath (1989), 'Foreign Trade and Economic Development: Sri Lanka's Experience', *World Development,* 16: 1143–57.

—————— **Estudios de Economia (1993),** 'Policy Recommendations for Export Promotion', University of Chile, Faculty of Economics and Administration, June, 1–27.

Stein, Herbert (1995), *On the Other Hand: . . . Essays on Economics, Economists, & Politics,* Washington: The AEI Press.

Stiglitz, Joseph E. (1996), 'Some Lessons of the East Asian Miracle', *World Bank Research Observer,* 11(2): 151–77.

—————— **(2001),** 'From Miracle to Crisis to Recovery: Lessons from Four Decades of East Asian Experience', in Joseph E. Stiglitz and Shahid Yusuf (eds), *Rethinking the East Asia Miracle,* New York: Oxford University Press.

Wignaraja, Ganeshan (1995), 'Outward Oriented Trade Policy and Industrial Performance in Sri Lanka', *Marga Quarterly Journal,* 13(4).

11

Technology Development: Key Issues in Productivity

Chandana Perera and Sarath Dasanayaka

Introduction

Technology, innovation and research and development (R&D) are widely recognized as important factors in the economic growth and development in any country. It has been reported that economic growth draws its vital nourishment from technology, innovation and R&D without which—no matter how favourable all other factors might have been—modern economic development and industry competitiveness would have been unattainable. This chapter discusses various aspects of technology development and related issues in Sri Lanka.

Brief History of Science and Technology Development in Sri Lanka

---

Sri Lankan technological history can be divided into a number of periods. Technologies in different sectors were developed in these periods and these technologies determined the main economic base of the country. However, a study of the present status of technology can be divided into two major periods: pre-independence period (both before colonial and after colonial), and the post-independence period.

Pre-Independence Period

The Sri Lankan technology level before the 16th century was comparable to most societies of the time. It is believed that in ancient times advanced knowledge of trigonometry, some practical geometry and astronomy were well known to Sri Lanka. The Spinning Jenny was used in the traditional weaving industry even in the 16th century and Portuguese writers reported that Sri Lankan guns were the best in the world at that time. In the health sector, a number of hospitals were built by many kings (e.g., Parakramabahu and Dutugemunu) and therefore, most writers reported that Sri Lanka was very advanced with respect to contemporary Ayurveda. Further, Sri Lankans were excellent in irrigation technology including many trans-basin diversions, multi-purpose irrigation, drainage, flood control and conservation. Some writers reported that Sri Lankan 12th century irrigation technology was unique and was not seen in the rest of the world till the 17th century (Goonatilake, 1976; Mendis,1974; Needham, 1956).

With the colonial incursion from the 16th century, Sri Lanka was increasingly exposed to western technology. This western technology was introduced as a package without any interaction with the existing local technology. The Portuguese did not introduce much technology into Sri Lanka but the Dutch introduced some technology with respect to construction of water canals, roads and harbours.

The modern technology era, however, began in Sri Lanka in the 19th century with the British colonization of the country. The British idea was to develop Sri Lanka as an agricultural base for them and as a market for their industrial products. Therefore, they produced tea, rubber and coconut as the main exports from Sri Lanka to the world market. In order to facilitate these, they developed a major rail and road network and the Colombo port, and set up associated engineering departments such as the Ceylon Government Railway (CGR), Public Works Department (PWD), Government Factory, Colombo Port Workshop and the private sector owned Walker Sons & Co. Ltd, Walker & Greig, Brown and Co. Ltd and the Colombo Commercial Company.

At the beginning, all the key positions of these organizations were manned by the British who later trained technical people for these organizations. The Ceylon Technical College was founded in 1893, which was elevated to the Faculty of Engineering in the University of Ceylon in 1950. In order to eradicate tropical diseases and to improve the health of the settlers, the British established the Bacteriological Institute in 1900 (now called the Sri Lanka Medical Research Institute), the Ceylon Medical College in 1870 and the Nurses Training School in 1939. In addition to this, a number of hospitals, clinics and dispensaries were established and due to all these measures, substantial advances were made in the field of health. This created various implications for demography in Sri Lanka. In the field of agriculture, the Department of Agriculture, the Tea Research Institute, Rubber Research Institute and the Coconut Research Institute were set up in the 1930s, but little attention was paid to the R&D of rice, subsidiary crops and spices.

The British attempted the restoration of major ancient irrigation works mainly due to the pressure from Sri Lankan representation in the legislature. The Gal Oya Multi-purpose Project was the first modern irrigation work started with the assistance of USA Consultants. The Irrigation Department also commenced developing and repairing most of the irrigation works by using Indian and other war displaced national engineers. The Irrigation Department mainly used local technology and talent with labour intensive methods. In the industrial sector, the British pioneered the establishment of several factories such as coir (1937), steel-rolling (1937), plywood (1941), leather (1941), acetic acid (1942), paper (1942), glass (1944) and ceramics (1944) due to the war situation. During this period, an Industrial Research Laboratory was established in the Department of Commerce and Industries to serve local industry. Some technological achievements were also made in hydropower electricity generation, transport and telecommunications and broadcasting fields during the British occupation of Sri Lanka.

Post-Independence Period

After political independence in 1948, a number of R&D institutions were established in order to develop Science and Technology (S&T) in Sri Lanka. The Ceylon Institute of Scientific and Industrial Research (CISIR) was the first of its kind. But this institution failed to deliver its objectives as reported by many publications (APCTT, 1986; Wijesekera 1976) due to inadequate staff, lack of research groups and expertise in different fields, too wide an area of coverage and lack of linkages with industry. In 1966, the Industrial Development Board (IDB) was set up to provide various technical services to small and medium-scale industry (SMI). Its principal functions were the preparation of feasibility reports, technical services, surveys on industries, documentation and publications, loan arrangements, management information and advice to SMI. It was expected that the IDB would inform other R&D organizations about the technology needs and capabilities of other industries, but this did not happen and there was no significant contribution to indigenous technology development.

In 1956, a Ten-Year Plan was formulated by the Planning Secretariat with the help of famous economists but it ignored the R&D community in developing S&T in Sri Lanka (APCTT, 1986). In 1965, the National Science Council (NSC) was set up after intense lobbying by the S&T community in Sri Lanka. At the beginning, the NSC tried to formulate a national science policy for Sri Lanka which, however, could not be completed. In 1974, the National Engineering Research and Development Centre (NERDC) was set up to carry out and promote research, innovation and commercialization. This organization accomplished some research and innovation activities but their commercialization was not very satisfactory. In 1976, an UNCTAD mission to Sri Lanka reported that Sri Lanka had the machinery for screening imported technology but it was incomplete and considerable R&D sector development was required. This mission recommended that a Centre for Transfer and Development of Technology be established as a focal point to link R&D institutions with the national economic planning apparatus. But so far no action has been taken on this.

R&D efforts in the private sector are confined to local subsidiaries of multinationals and their joint ventures and some Sri Lankan companies. Some specialized R&D work is carried out by some state corporations such as ceramics, tyre and mineral sands. During the 1960–77 period, much R&D work did not take place in the private sector due to heavy state involvement in the economy. During this period, most of the technology transfers occurred as donations from the erstwhile Soviet bloc in the form of setting up mega factories. Most of these industries were for import substitution and they showed inefficiency at the outset. Later, politicization almost wiped out the competitiveness of these industries and they became a burden to the public.

After the 1977 policy reforms, the private sector was given a leading role in the economy. Thereafter, private R&D activities showed positive growth in some industry and firm levels. Technology transfer and R&D work took place in sectors such as infrastructure, construction (housing and dams, etc.), garments, communication, ceramics, rubber products and information technology through sub-contracting, outsourcing or private R&D work. With the escalation of the ethnic conflict from 1983, government expenditure was diverted to war rather than to industrial development. Furthermore, foreign or local private sector investment did not take place to the extent expected. Therefore, it is obvious that much development in S&T did not take place after 1983.

As the above brief historical note shows, Sri Lankan R&D history was not much of a success. Prior to independence, it is seen that the state deliberately ignored technology issues which were not within the domain of plantation agriculture. But after independence, the most significant reason for the failure was lack of high level political commitment and support for R&D activities. Furthermore, the need to develop technology and associated skills and motivate the S&T community within the country was not sufficiently recognized. Lack of recognition and lack of active liaison with the international S&T community and S&T developments elsewhere in the world are other reasons for this gloomy picture. An overall well defined technology policy should be in place at national, sectoral and firm levels to put Sri Lanka on the world technology map.

Non-existence of an industrial capitalist class may be another key reason for the low industrial base in the country. During the past century, the involvement of the majority of the Sri Lankan capitalist class was limited to plantation and service sector based activities. Presently, their main involvement can be observed in the financial sector such as banking, leasing, insurance, etc., and trading where not much technology progression is taking place.

GOVERNMENT RECOGNITION AND COMMITMENT FOR TECHNOLOGY DEVELOPMENT

Government recognition of the importance of technology and commitment to technology development are very important factors in the technology development of a country. In the recent history of Sri Lanka, the following initiatives/events taken by different governments highly influenced the technology development of the country.

- President J.R. Jayawaradene elected in 1978 was the pioneer in understanding the importance of S&T and R&D for Sri Lankan economic growth and development.
- In June 1982, the National Science Council was taken under his direct purview and the main role of this body was to advise the President on S&T issues.
- In May, the President requested the formulation of a National Science Policy Plan and Implementation Document. This was done in April 1985. This Committee was headed by Cyril Ponnapperuma and it formulated S&T policies for eight economic sectors.
- From 1984 onwards, various science and technology agreements were signed with various governments and various bodies such as CINTEC, the Arthur C. Clarke Centre were set up, etc.
- In 1994, a Cabinet level Ministry of Science and Technology was established giving due recognition to the importance of S&T.
- The Ministry of Science and Technology has focused on 10 identified thrust areas of industry in which Sri Lanka has the potential to become competitive in the world market. An Asian Development Bank Science and Technology Personnel Development (ADB/STPD) project covering seven universities and five R&D institutes was initiated in 1998 to train S&T personnel in these thrust areas. The creation of technology watch is also part of this project.
- The National Science and Technology Commission (NASTEC) was formed by an Act of Parliament which started operations in August 1998. It has been designed as the Apex Policy Formulating and Advisory body to the government of Sri Lanka on S&T matters.
- The post-2001 Government has taken initiatives to develop Small and Medium Enterprises (SMEs) through various policy measures and incentives. A number of foreign funded programmes are going on with respect to this SME technology capacity building.　•

Among the ongoing activities of S&T development, the Science and Technology Personnel Development Project under the Ministry of Science and Technology and activities of the Ministry of Enterprise and Industrial Development for the development of SMEs are important milestones.

Even though successive Sri Lankan governments have taken various steps in technology development, there is much more to be done to bring Sri Lanka's technological status to a satisfactory level. One of the major drawbacks is the lack of a proper technology policy framework integrated with the industrial development framework. Sound macroeconomic policies are critical in order to allow the introduction of tax and other incentives to encourage faster innovation. The APCTT Report (1986) sets out three major types of instruments which can be used to formulate an effective technology policy; these are legal instruments, financial instruments and fiscal instruments. To ensure the sustained development of both industry and technology, it is vital that parallel policies are implemented on both fronts. In this context, it is worthwhile to consider the framework developed by Gunawardane (2000), which stresses the need for a Centre for Transfer and Development of Technology (recommended by the UNCTAD Mission in 1976) and an Industrial Development Bank.

To enhance technology development, improving the awareness of both the public and business enterprises about the technological and marketing forces/changes and the necessary structural changes needed to respond to them is important. At present, a part of this requirement is fulfilled by the Technology Watch Centre of the National Science Foundation by providing information on technology development in other parts of the world. At the same time, technology development can also be enhanced by directing efforts towards creating an S&T culture. Programmes at both the school level and national levels, government rural lab programmes, media (television, radio and newspapers), publications (books, journal, websites), etc., are some of the means by which an S&T culture can be promoted.

Implementation of policies geared to technology development will be more effective if there is representation at the decision-making level of government. In Sri Lanka, for example, representation of the Science and Technology Ministry at the level of the Cabinet will ensure that the attention of policy-makers to technology development remains a key priority. Technology development is mainly influenced by the country's education and industry. These subjects are governed by the various administrative bodies and thus continuous dialogue at the ministerial level is an important means through which progress of technology is addressed.

Human Resource Aspects

There are four major ways of getting human resource for S&T. These are:

- Technical Institutes,
- Universities,
- Migration of qualified people to the country,
- Use of foreign technical personnel and consultancy services.

According to the Statistical Abstract of Sri Lanka, more than 20,000 are enrolled for middle-level technical courses and about 30,000 are enrolled for vocational training programmes directly related to technology. Sri Lankan universities produced only about 1,000 graduates in natural science and about 650 graduates in engineering in 2001. Even though the Sri Lankan education system produces limited human resources for S&T, Sri Lankan industry is not capable of providing satisfactory jobs in S&T disciplines. Due to the lesser demand for the S&T disciplines in Sri Lanka, many graduates from technical colleges and universities leave the country for foreign employment while some are employed in non-technical disciplines. Unattractiveness of employment in S&T disciplines is noticed by the inclination of S&T students in following professional management and business courses like CIMA and CIM. (For example, about 30 per cent of engineering undergraduates of the University of Moratuwa follow CIMA or other professional management courses.) The most unfortunate aspect is that almost all the brilliant students (top 10 per cent of the batch) are enrolled in professional management courses in addition to their regular degree programme, and will be employed in management, business and banking disciplines after graduation without giving much technology input for the progress of the country.

The status of the scientists and technologists is poor compared to the professionals in the other disciplines and S&T professionals are generally beset by the following problems:

- Poor income standards and living conditions.
- Inadequate facilities to do research.
- Constraints to update their knowledge.
- The tendency to devalue the importance of Sri Lankan S&T personnel by relying excessively on foreign experts.
- Low social status in comparison with other professions.
- S&T personnel are not given due place in decision making.

This situation results in high mobility of the S&T professionals from Sri Lanka to developed countries. In the long run, such asymmetric mobility is likely to widen the gap between rich and poor nations, offsetting all efforts to bridge the disparity in S&T capacities between developed and developing countries. A study conducted by the Committee on Science and Technology in Developing Countries (COSTED) of the International Council for Science (ICSU) involving three Asian countries, Bangladesh, India and Sri Lanka, revealed that migration of S&T professionals is a serious issue in Sri Lanka and Bangladesh for many reasons. Government funding of education up to the Bachelor's degree in Sri Lanka results in significant loss to the government as a result of out-migration. Allowing for such mobility, countries can gear policies towards the following:

- keeping a systematic global watch on trends in the movement of S&T professionals that may help developing countries to evolve their national framework of human resource development;
- introducing mechanisms for retaining and making the best use of exceptional talents within the country;
- creating a favourable environment for attracting resources for world-class education and research institutions in developing countries to retain talented professionals;
- introducing measures and programmes to attract nationals overseas either temporarily or permanently.

R&D AND TECHNOLOGY CAPABILITIES

R&D Expenditure

According to a National Science Foundation (NSF) survey, the total R&D expenditure in the country was Rs 1,492 million in the year 2000 compared to Rs 1,410 million in 1996. Hence, the R&D/GDP ratio for the year shows a fall to 0.17 per cent. However, this figure needs adjustments to accommodate under-presentation of figures in certain areas/sectors in the national S&T system. With these adjustments, the total expenditure on R&D can be estimated as Rs 1,810 million, which is 0.19 per cent of the GDP in the year 2000. From these figures, it can be seen that Sri Lanka is still struggling to achieve the R&D/GDP ratio of 0.2 per cent, which is far below the recommended figure of 1 per cent of the national GDP for the developing countries.

The R&D expenditure according to the type of expenditure shows that more than 69 per cent was spent as recurrent. The R&D institutions, which contribute to more than 67 per cent of total R&D expenditure in Sri Lanka, show that more than 67 per cent of recurrent expenditure is spent on salaries and wages. From these figures one can categorize that the R&D in Sri Lanka is a labour intensive research-based one.

Table 11.1

R&D EXPENDITURE (RS MILLION)—BY NATURE OF RESEARCH ACTIVITY

Year Nature of Activity	1984 Amount (Rs Mn) (per cent)	1996 Amount (Rs Mn) (per cent)	2000 Amount (Rs Mn) (per cent)
Basic research	24.75	446.30	363.60
	(10%)	(32%)	(24%)
Applied research	185.16	867.30	743.90
	(72%)	(61%)	(50%)
Experimental development	46.89	96.00	385.20
	(18%)	(7%)	(26%)
Total	256.80	1,409.60	1,492.60
	(100%)	(100%)	(100%)

Sources: Science and Technology Statistical Handbook, 1996 and NSF unpublished report.

As shown in Table 11.1 it can be seen that the R&D activities in the year 2000 were more oriented towards experimental development activities than in 1996—from 7 per cent in 1996 to 26 per cent in 2000. The above change in the nature of R&D activities can be considered as a reflection of the economic policies of the country towards industrialization and the response of the public sector research institutions to these industrialization policies by expanding their R&D activities at the cost of basic and applied research.

Table 11.2

R&D EXPENDITURE (RS MILLION)—DISCIPLINE AND TYPE

Discipline	1984	1996	2000
Natural sciences	30.70	318.30	441.90
	(12%)	(22.60%)	(30%)
Agriculture	153.40	669.20	341.10
	(59.80%)	(47.4%)	(28%)
Engineering	32.80	164.30	255.90
	(12.80%)	(11.60%)	(17 %)
Medical sciences	13.30	136.60	159.80
	(5.20%)	(9.70%)	(11%)
Social sciences	26.50	121.20	238.10
	(10.20%)	(8.60%)	(16%)
Total	256.70	1,409.60	1,492.60
	(100%)	(100%)	(100%)

Sources: Science and Technology Statistical Handbook, 1996 and NSF unpublished report.

According to Table11.2, it can be seen that percentage of R&D expenditure dropped in the agriculture sector and increased in natural science. The above changes are due to the significant changes in R&D expenditure by the private sector industrial organizations carrying out research in natural sciences and engineering and technological research.

Patents in Sri Lanka

According to the NSF survey (Amaradasa et al., 2002), a total of 461 patents had been registered with the National Intellectual Property Office of Sri Lanka (see Table11.3). The growth trend of patents is a clear indication of rising interest of innovators in protecting intellectual property. A significant conclusion of the NSF study was that the smaller contribution of patents both by commercial organizations (22 per cent) and by public research institutes (6 per cent), as compared to the contribution of 72 per cent by individual inventors, was a reflection of the weak innovative character of the organized sector. This could be observed by the comparatively higher amount of patents in dryers and dehydration technologies, food and beverage processing, agricultural systems and energy conservation.

Table 11.3

DISTRIBUTION OF PATENTS ACCORDING TO NSF CLASSIFICATION

NSF Classification	No. of Patents Granted																	Total
	1982	1983	1984	1985	1986	1987	1988	1989	1990	1991	1992	1993	1994	1995	1996	1997	1998	
Dryers/dehydration technologies	3		1			2		1		2	1		4	1	3	2		20
Food and beverages process technology	2				1	1	2	5					2	2	4	4	1	24
Rubber production and processing technology		3	1	3	3	6	2	1	1		1				1	1	2	25
Agricultural systems and development		1		2	1	3	1	4	2	2		1	4	1	1	6	6	35
Construction technology and materials	3	3	1	1	1	2				2	1	2		2			3	21
Packaging and packing materials			2	2	1	1	2	1	3	4	1		3		3	1	1	25
Energy saving/generating devices	1	1		3	1	3	2	2	2	9	2	4	3	8	7	8	2	58
Process technology—manufacturing sector				2		2		1	1	3	2	2	1	1	5	3	7	30
Process technology—miscellaneous			1	1	3	3	1	5	1	1	3	6	3	3	4	6	5	46
Innovations—domestic appliances/utilities		1	1		1	2	2	1	1	2	2	5	3	2	12	3	1	39
Innovations—miscellaneous	4		2	3	5	3	1	1	5	4	2	4	3	3	17	9	13	79
Product development			4	1		1	3	4	4	1	4	1	3	10	8	12	3	59
Total	13	9	13	18	17	29	16	26	20	30	19	25	29	33	65	55	44	461

Source: Amaradasa et al., 2002.

Future Directions of R&D

The majority of the R&D activities related to traditional industries are limited to assisting the existing technologies to improve productivity and diversification or improvement of the quality of existing products. There are limited R&D for developing innovative value added products. For example, R&D related to the tea industry concentrates mainly on new machinery and new flavours even though there are possibilities for developing cosmetic applications for tea, such as perfumes and facials.

Utilization of local raw materials is essential for the industrial development of a country. Sri Lanka is rich in natural resources (e.g., industrial minerals, plants, animal products, sea water). All these natural resources can be exploited to obtain valuable commercial products (e.g., silica and quartz mineral for electronic grade silicon, sea water for chemicals). Given that most of the natural resources are non-renewable, alternative practices to the present policy of exporting these resources without value addition need to be explored in order to maximize benefits. In the final analysis, this would require that product and process technologies are developed to yield maximum value addition to local raw material.

Harvests are wasted because produce cannot be or processed. In this situation, R&D for high yield is counter productive. Parallel development of technologies for high yield and post-harvest food processing, packaging and transport have to be paid due attention. This situation is not different even in the other sectors and requires improved coordination between technology development activities.

Figure 11.1

TECHNOLOGY DEVELOPMENT DIRECTIONS

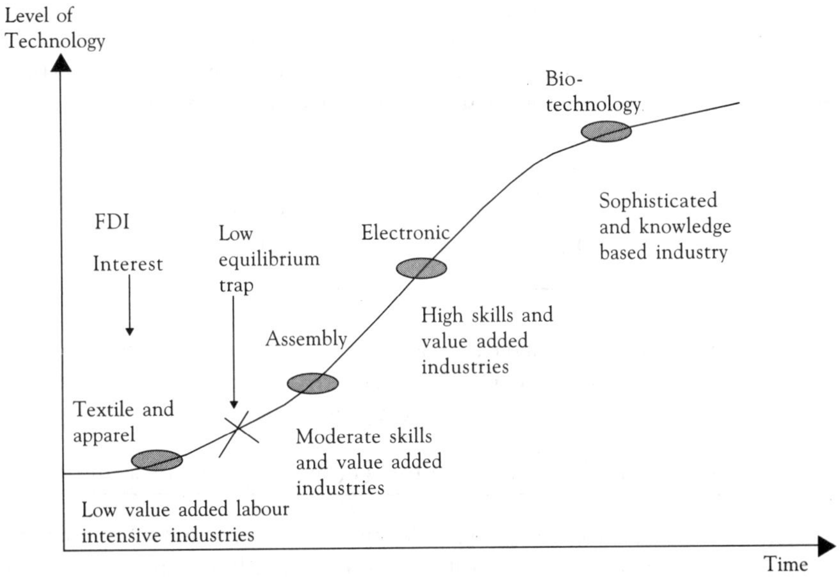

For a developing economy, it is vital to encourage high quality industrial jobs that enable people to learn new, adaptable technological skills. However, at present, the majority of industries in Sri Lanka do not use very advanced technologies while adding low value to the product. Most of the foreign direct investment (FDI) flows to these industries provide employment without much enhancement of the quality of life. Non-availability of adequate technological capabilities is one of the major reasons for Sri Lankan industries to be caught in this low equilibrium trap. Gearing future technology development activities to attract industries like automobile assembly, electronics and biotechnology would provide opportunities for skills development in the country.

Inter-firm relationship in technology development activities is at a very low level in Sri Lanka. Cooperation in R&D activities will help to reduce the high level of risk and R&D expenditure. Technology Management literature shows three levels of cooperation as follows:

(a) Research and development cooperation: Cooperative activities can be carried out in the pre-competitive stage in different forms. These include university based cooperation research financed by associated firms, government-industry cooperative R&D projects with universities and public research institutes and R&D cooperation on a private joint venture basis.

(b) Technological cooperation: Cooperation agreements can be formed to transfer and share the technology between firms in the competitive stage. Corporate venture capital in small high-tech firms is another form of cooperation.

(c) Manufacturing cooperation: Firms can build up partnerships to manufacture the end product.

The availability of S&T indicators is important to measure the S&T capability of the country. While the NSF maintains a fairly comprehensive tabulation of such data, extending its work programme to the analysis and provision of benchmarks by examining the performance of organizations in other countries would prove helpful. In turn, this can assist R&D organizations to set targets and measure performance.

UNIVERSITIES, R&D INSTITUTES IN TECHNOLOGY DEVELOPMENT

R&D activities of universities and R&D institutes provide a major contribution to the technology development of the country. In addition to R&D activities, universities contribute to technology development by producing the required human resource base.

Contribution of Universities for Technology Development

Even though Sri Lankan universities provide valuable human capital for the country's technology development, their contribution is at a lower level compared to other developing and newly industrialized countries. Only three Sri Lankan universities have engineering faculties (excluding the Open University). According to statistics of the University Grants Commission, about 60 per cent of graduates are from non-science/technical disciplines.

The major emphasis in Sri Lankan universities is given to undergraduate teaching while less priority is given for research (see Table 11.4). The majority of the postgraduate courses are part time courses which do not produce valuable research output. Even though there are some research activities carried out in the universities, R&D output is at a very low level. This situation is evident from the universities' share of the patents which has been less than 1 per cent. In order to bring university research to acceptable levels, universities should successfully face the following challenges:

- Difficulty in retaining and recruiting the best graduates in the academic staff.
- Doctoral degree holders from the West not returning (brain drain).
- Red tape and bureaucratic hurdles.
- Lack of research funding.
- Less opportunities for publications.

Until very recently, the interaction between universities and industry has been fairly limited. This may be one of the reasons for the low level of research in the universities. During the past few years some initiatives have been taken to build up the relationship between the two. Some of the examples are:

- University Industry Interaction Cell, University of Moratuwa;
- Design Centres (University of Moratuwa, University of Peradeniya);
- Ruhuna Business Incubator (Collaboration with University of Ruhuna);
- Faculty/department-industry consultative boards.

Presently, these bodies are at their infant stage and mainly provide existing knowledge of the university academics to industry in the form of solutions for some industrial

Table 11.4

GRADUATE OUTPUT OF SRI LANKAN UNIVERSITIES BY ACADEMIC STREAM

Graduate Output (Faculty/Academic Stream)

Year	Arts	Management	Commerce	Law	Science	Medicine	Dental	Veterinary Medicine	Agriculture	Engineering	Architecture & Quantity Surveying	Computer Science & IT	Total
1995	1,590	62	285	140	844	442	66	37	226	458	56		4,206
2000	3,656	1,646	802	173	1,264	904	77		249	548	55	–	9,374
2001	3,256	1,601	766	182	1,052	801	71	70	365	653	79		8,896

Source: University Grants Commission, 2002.

problems and continuous education rather than developing new technologies for the industry. By recognizing the importance of university–industry interaction, the Science and Technology Personnel Development project funded by the ADB has funded many of these university–industry interaction bodies. Other means of strengthening university–industry partnerships in the future might take the form of Science/Technology Parks.

Technology Management Education

Improper management of technology is one of the key reasons for retarding the technology management of any country. Neither engineering education nor management education in Sri Lanka recognized the importance of technology management until 1998. In 1998, the University of Moratuwa under the Department of Management of Technology (MOT) took the initiative to train future technology managers of the country.

Management of Technology has been introduced as a subject at the undergraduate level. A specialized MBA degree programme in Management of Technology has been started in 2001 and now this programme has two batches. This programme comprises a number of Technology Management subjects such as Technology Transfer, R&D and Innovation Management, R&D Commercialization, Technology Policy and Social Shaping of Technology. Research degree programmes (MSc, MPhil and Ph.D) in Technology Management, short courses and executive diploma (proposed) are some of the activities carried out by the Department of Management of Technology, University of Moratuwa to disseminate the knowledge in Technology Management.

Contribution of R&D Institutions for Technology Development

There are about 20 R&D institutions in Sri Lanka according to the NSF listing. In addition to these R&D institutions, about 10 professional and S&T support institutions are operating in the country. Even though these professional and S&T support institutions are not directly involved in R&D activities, they make a valuable contribution by providing research funding and operating S&T journals for the publication of research outcomes.

About a quarter of the R&D institutions are mainly dedicated to agriculture based industries. Only a few research institutions are dedicated to engineering and modern technologies. According to NSF statistics, during the 1994–97 period, there were 94 international publications from Sri Lankan R&D institutions; 45 of these were published by the Industrial Technology Institute (ITI—former CISIR). Public funded research institutes own only 6 per cent of the patents registered at the National Intellectual Property Office (NIPO) between 1980-98. Again, it could be noticed that the majority of the patents are owned by ITI (Amaradasa et al., 2002). The Rubber Research Institute of Sri Lanka (RRISL) is another contributor of innovations for rubber production and processing technologies. The World Intellectual Property Organization has awarded the 'Scientist of the Year 2000' Gold Medal to the Director of RRISL in the recognition of the number of implementable patents produced by him and his colleagues. Looking at the R&D performance of the institutions, it could be noted that a few orgnizations are dominating the scene. Lack of commercialization is another weak area of the local R&D institutions.

The following common problems can be identified as the major factors which affect the performance of local R&D institutions:

Factors hindering local R&D activities—

- Limited funds for R&D;
- Poor access to knowledge (lack of IT facilities);
- Non-empowerment of researchers.

Factors hindering commercialization—

- No clear commercialization policies;
- Lack of information about market signals;
- Slow response due to bureaucratic structure and rigid policies;
- Lack of commitment of top management;
- Poor relationship with industry.

CONCLUSIONS

Sri Lankan history in technology development is not marked by much success. Prior to independence it is seen that the state deliberately ignored technology issues which were not within the domain of plantation agriculture. But after independence, the most significant reason for the failure was lack of high level political commitment and support for R&D activities.

After the 1977 economic reforms, the government has taken considerable effort to develop the country as a newly industrialized country based on S&T. However, due to reasons such as the lack of improvements in the conditions of the S&T community, non-development of a proper S&T policy framework, lack of an S&T culture and uncertainties brought about by the ethnic conflict, the effort for S&T development was not very successful.

Sri Lanka's initiatives to develop its S&T capabilities continues to suffer from several critical constraints. R&D remains a labour intensive exercise while expenditure is well below the recommended value for developing countries. In addition, while interest in obtaining patents has been on the increase, the organized sectors remain weak in acquiring such patents.

Due to the poor remunerative condition of the S&T community, many graduates from S&T disciplines seek employment in other fields and qualified S&T professionals often prefer to leave the country. To compound the problem, the majority of university graduates are still to be found in non-S&T disciplines. The emphasis on research at the university level remains low, although in the recent past some initiatives have been taken to strengthen university–industry interaction. In terms of technology indicators, some R&D institutions tend to a dominate. Nevertheless, the lack of commercialization of R&D is a major problem that cuts across all the institutions.

Sri Lanka needs to focus attention on developing the acquisitive, adaptive, operative and innovative capabilities in line with the country's factor and resource endowments. When acquiring technology, all the components of technology such as technoware (machine embodied form of technology), humanware (human embodied form), inforware (information embodied form) and orgaware (organization embodied form) must be assessed in order to gain the maximum benefits and to enhance national technology capabilities.

REFERENCES

Amaradasa, R.M.W., M.A.T. de Silva and R.P. Pathirage (2002), 'Patents in a Small Developing Economy: A Case Study of Sri Lanka', *Journal of Intellectual Property Rights*, 7(5): 395–404.

Asian and Pacific Centre for Transfer of Technology (APCTT) (1986), *Technology Policies and Planning in Sri Lanka*, New Delhi: APCTT.

Goonatilake, S. (1976), 'Technology and the Societal Context', *Engineer*, March, 4(1): 30–40.

Mendis, D.L.O. (1974), 'Technology of Development and the Underdevelopment of Technology in Sri Lanka', *Proceedings of the 31st Annual Sessions of the Sri Lanka Association for the Advancement of Science*.

Needham, J. (1956), 'Mathematics and Science in China and the West', *Science and Society*, 20(3): 320–43.

National Science Foundation (NSF), Unpublished Reports.

Science and Technology Statistical Handbook, 1996.

Sri Lanka University Statistics, University Grants Commission, 2002.

Wijesekera, R.O.B. (1976), 'Scientific Research in a Small Developing Nation—Sri Lanka', *Economic Review*, 2(3): 9–13.

SELECT READING

Gunawardane, R.P. (2000), 'Master Plan for Industrial Development—a welcome move', *Daily News*, 28 January 2000.

Part IV

EMPLOYMENT AND LABOUR

12

LABOUR PRODUCTIVITY GROWTH AND EMPLOYMENT GENERATION

Ravindra A. Yatawara

INTRODUCTION

The dual goals of productivity growth and employment generation are tantamount to the development process. Productivity growth reflects greater efficiency, enhances competitiveness of a nation and leads to higher living standards, while job creation is a powerful tool to eliminate poverty and stem social unrest. However, there has been a traditional belief of a trade-off between these two goals, and hence an implicit debate over the preference of goals. That rising labour productivity and decreasing employment are inextricably linked is easily seen in the definition of productivity growth (i.e., growth in value added per worker). If valued added can be held constant while shedding labour, there is positive productivity growth.[1] The government's emphasis on each of the goals of productivity growth and employment generation has also tended to vary over time. For example, President Premadasa's '200 Factories Programme' aimed at promoting industrial employment in rural areas in the apparel industry, with no emphasis on productivity. The year 1996 was declared the Year of Productivity, followed by a declaration of the Decade of Productivity in 1997 (albeit followed up by a lacklustre initiative), but with little talk of job creation.

Today, productivity growth is crucial to remain competitive in the international market in the face of increased global competition in the market for goods, services and capital. The dramatic opening to trade of many developing and transitional economies has eroded Sri Lanka's traditional competitiveness based on cheap labour. Thus, it is an opportune time to revisit this 'implicit' debate. In fact, this chapter argues that no such debate should exist. Productivity growth and employment generation should be dual goals in a single policy package. In the context of achieving these goals, is chapter also addresses the issue of labour market regulations in Sri Lanka, which is another ongoing debate in the country.

The calculation of labour productivity growth lends itself to understanding why productivity growth is important and its relationship to employment generation. Labour productivity drives economic growth and material living standards, as measured by income per capita. Growth in income per capita is equal to growth in labour productivity plus the growth in the employed population ratio.[2] Thus, an acceleration of labour productivity growth from 1 per cent to 2 per cent (holding demographics constant) would double national living standards approximately every 36 years, instead of every 72 years. In the context of profit maximizing firms, productivity gains can lead to real cost reductions per unit of output, filtering down to lower prices and thus increased real incomes and greater global competitiveness. Further, as Sri Lanka faces an ageing population, the workers to population ratio is likely to fall and there will be a greater burden on productivity growth to improve living standards.

Whereas the extent of job growth per se may simply reflect demographic trends and thus not be a policy priority, given the high level of unemployment in Sri Lanka, particularly among the educated, employment generation is very important. It is a key to reducing poverty in rural areas and curbing socio-political unrest.

The conventional belief that labour productivity growth is associated with decreasing employment was clearly witnessed in the US manufacturing sector in the 1980s. Some argue that layoffs occur because technological progress leads to a mismatch between the new required skills and the prevailing skills of the existing labour force, or due to rigidities in wages or prices. Alternatively, others argue that productivity growth happens as a result of downsizing, making firms 'lean' by shedding redundant labour in the face of competitive pressures.

However, this negative relationship does not necessarily have to hold. Insofar as labour productivity gains lead to cost reductions and profit increases, job growth may in fact increase. First, high profits may induce new firm entry which would increase employment. Second, technology driven increases in labour productivity that lead to increased relative wages will encourage greater job applications, stimulating job growth and putting some downward pressure on wages. Thus, the relationship between these variables remains an empirical matter.

Aggregate data over the 1963–2000 period show positive productivity growth in all sub-sectors of the economy[3] (see Figure 12.1). It is only in the agriculture sector that the rise in productivity is associated with a fall in employment. The largest productivity gain has been in the services sector, which currently contributes the largest value-added per worker and employs 41 per cent of those employed. The lowest value-added is in agriculture, which has a 36 per cent employment share.

However, it is can be misleading to draw inferences from aggregate data to characterize what has been happening at the micro-level to specific industries or individual plants. This chapter focuses on the connection between employment growth and productivity growth at the disaggregated level for the manufacturing sector, and the associated implications for aggregate employment and productivity growth. As with similar studies for different countries, the paper finds substantial heterogeneity among industries. While there are industries where downsizing is associated with increases in productivity, the paper identifies many industries where (i) productivity growth accompanies increases in employment, and (ii) downsizing is associated with reductions in productivity.

Figure 12.1

VALUED ADDED AND EMPLOYMENT BY SECTOR

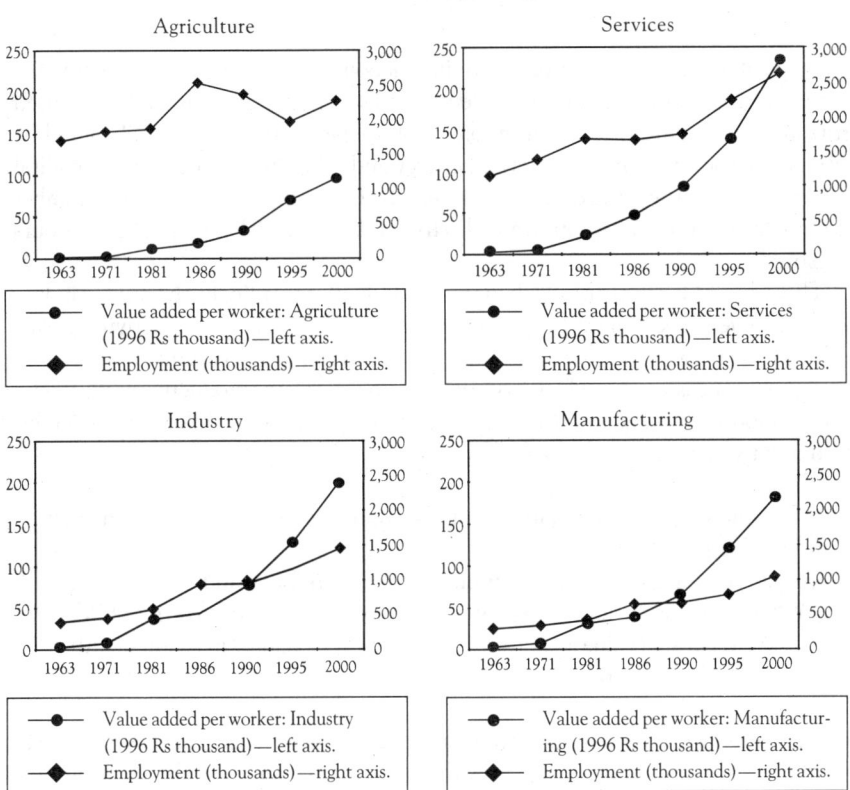

Source: Central Bank of Sri Lanka, *Annual Report*, 2000.
Note: Employment data for 1963, 1971, 1981 come from the Census of Population. In the later years, they come from the Labour Force Surveys.

This may provide useful information as to which industries need productivity enhancements, and the importance of removing barriers to growth of dynamic industries that are undergoing productivity enhancements and providing new jobs. Given that there are many cases where productivity growth and job growth coincide, this makes a case for the government strategies to think of these two policy objectives together-strategies that remove obstacles to both productivity growth and employment generation. The chapter then identifies some such policies that would promote productivity growth and job growth. Section 2 defines the notion of productivity used here and discusses the data. Section 3 analyses the disaggregated manufacturing data in employment/ productivity quadrants. Section 4 looks at the relationship of productivity and employment to wages. Section 5 discusses policies that would promote greater productivity growth and generate more employment opportunities. Section 6 concludes.

MEASUREMENT AND DATA

The typical measure of factor productivity is labour productivity measured as value added in production (at constant prices) per labour input.[4] Value added is used instead of gross output to avoid problems of double counting. It is calculated by subtracting the value of raw materials, energy and other inputs (other than capital and labour) from the gross output measure. The labour input measure is the number of employees although, when available, the preferred variable is number of hours employed.

The value added measure of labour productivity is, accordingly, the ratio of industry level value added to industry level employment. Thus, labour productivity growth is the residual growth in value added after accounting for growth in employment. The focus on this measure of productivity, rather than total factor productivity, affects the interpretation of results. From a growth accounting framework (Solow, 1962), labour productivity growth could be broken down to:

(a) capital deepening (changes in the extent of capital per worker in each industry),

(b) increasing educational attainment of the workforce, and

(c) 'true' technological change or total factor productivity growth (TFPG— the change in value added after accounting for changes in labour quantity, labour quality and capital).

The measure used here cannot differentiate between these alternatives. For instance, it cannot distinguish productivity growth due to investments in labour saving machinery and due to technological change. However, given the unreliability of the Sri Lankan capital stock data, its omission is not a huge limitation and in fact does prevent making misleading pronouncements.

Aggregate sectoral data are obtained from the *Annual Reports* of the Central Bank. Disaggregated data are restricted to the manufacturing sector (defined as production activities under Division 3 of the International Standard Industrial Classification [ISIC]) and comes from the Survey of Industries carried out by the Department of Census and Statistics. Data on number of firms, gross output, inputs, employment and wages were extracted at the four-digit ISIC level of industry classification. Output data was deflated by the gross domestic product (GDP) deflator, material inputs by the Wholesale Price index (WPI), energy costs by the energy component of the WPI and salaries and wages by the Colombo Consumers' Price Index (CCPI). The focus here is on establishments with 25 or more persons employed, which accounted for 90 per cent of value added in manufacturing covered under the survey, 80 per cent (3,62,000 of 45,400) of the employment and 17 per cent (2,035 of 12,132) of the establishments in the survey of 1999.

PRODUCTIVITY AND EMPLOYMENT QUADRANTS

The manufacturing industries at the four-digit level of ISIC disaggregation are divided into four groups or quadrants in the spirit of Davis et al. (1996). Quadrant I consists of the 'successful upsizers', industries that were able to increase productivity growth and job growth over the 1990–99 period. Quadrant II contains the 'successful downsizers', which are industries that managed to increase productivity but did so at the expense of employment generation. Quadrant III industries are 'unsuccessful downsizers', which are industries that witnessed declines in both productivity and employment, while Quadrant IV consists of industries that exhibited declining productivity but increasing employment—so-called 'unsuccessful upsizers' (see Figure 12.2).

Figure 12.3 charts the average annual percentage change in labour productivity, employment and value added for total manufacturing, and for the average industry in

Figure 12.2

PRODUCTIVITY AND EMPLOYMENT QUADRANTS

Quadrant I *Successful Upsizers* Productivity growth > 0 Employment growth > 0	**Quadrant III** *Unsuccessful Downsizers* Productivity growth < 0 Employment growth < 0
Quadrant II *Successful Downsizers* Productivity growth > 0 Employment growth < 0	**Quadrant IV** *Unsuccessful Upsizers* Productivity growth < 0 Employment growth > 0

Figure 12.3

PRODUCTIVITY GROWTH, EMPLOYMENT GROWTH AND VALUE ADDED GROWTH

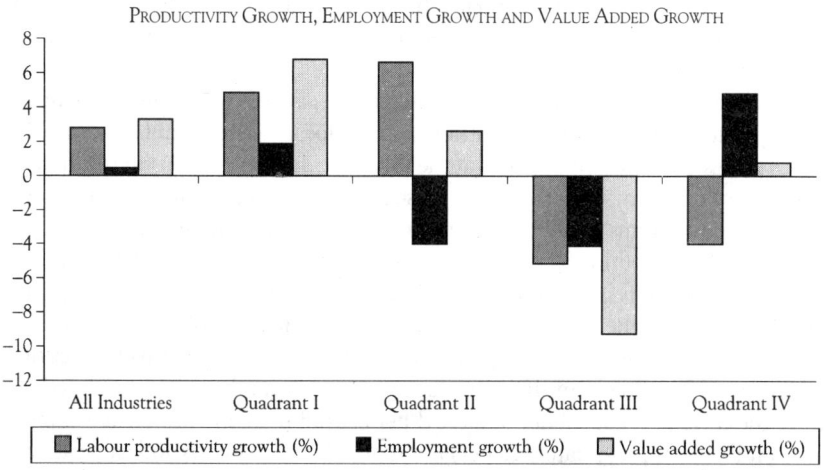

each quadrant. It shows that productivity growth can occur by industries increasing or decreasing employment (Quadrant I and Quadrant II), that shedding labour does not necessarily lead to successful increases in productivity (Quadrant II and Quadrant III) and symmetrically that employment increases can be associated with both productivity increases and decreases (Quadrant I and Quadrant IV).

Figure 12.4 lists the Sri Lankan manufacturing industries (at the four-digit ISIC level of classification) according to their performance in productivity and job growth over the 1990–99 period. There is no obvious pattern in the quadrant allocation and there appears to be considerable heterogeneity within broader industry classes (say within the two-digit ISIC classification). Industries in Quadrant I reflect dynamism where productivity and employment are expanding, while Quadrant III industries are declining in size and competitiveness.

The placement of industries in each quadrant may be consistent with more than one story. Quadrant I industries, which increased productivity and employment, are consistent with a story of technological innovation that increased productivity and an elastic demand curve for their products that allowed the industry to expand and increase employment. It is also consistent with an increase in product demand, combined with increasing returns from technology (which allows average cost to fall as output expands). Quadrant II industries reflect the traditional story of raising productivity by shedding labour. Alternatively, it could reflect industries experiencing technology growth but facing falling demand for their products.

The falling productivity and employment, seen in Quadrant III industries, reflect declining industries facing a negative technology shock, reduced competitiveness and an elastic demand curve which leads to loss of market share. It is also consistent with falling demand for the products coupled with increasing returns technology. Increased employment and reduced productivity of Quadrant IV industries could reflect an increase in the labour intensity in the production process (reduced capital deepening), or a shift to lower quality workers which could be observed by falling wages. The outcome is also consistent with a negative technology shock that reduces productivity but an inelastic demand for their product that allows them to continue hiring workers. Alternatively, these industries may face increasing demand for their products but diminishing marginal returns to labour.

The relative importance of each quadrant can be gauged by the number of firms, their employment share and their contribution to value added in manufacturing. Figure 12.4 places Sri Lanka's industries (at the ISIC four-digit level of classification) into the respective quadrants and Table 12.1 presents some summary statistics of the data. Over 75 per cent of firms in 1999 are in Quadrants I and II, employing 75 per cent of the employed and contributing 85 per cent of manufacturing value added. They also had the highest number of entrants and exits. The second quadrant contains most of the firms and contributes the most to value added. However, in terms of employment, they absorb only 22 per cent of the employed, compared to 55 per cent by Quadrant I industries in 1999. Quadrant III, with falling productivity and employment has 8 per cent of the firms and contributes a mere 3 per cent of manufacturing value added. Quadrant IV has approximately 12 per cent share of firms, workers and value added.

Figure 12.4

SRI LANKA MANUFACTURING IN PRODUCTIVITY AND EMPLOYMENT QUADRANTS*

	Quadrant I			Quadrant IV	
3111	Slaughtering & Preserving Meat		3213	Knitting Mills	
3214	Carpets & Rugs		3521	Paints, Varnishes & Lacquers	
3522	Drugs & Medicines		3909	Industries nec	
3530	Petroleum Refineries		3812	Metal Furniture & Fixture	
3903	Sporting & Athletic Goods		3551	Tyre & Tube Industries	
3902	Musical Instruments		3412	Containers, Boxes & Paperboard	
3116	Grain Mill Products		3819	Fabricated Metal Products	
3559	Rubber Products nec		3513	Synthetic Fibres, Plastic Materials	
3825	Computing & Accounting Machinery		3420	Printing & Publishing	
3831	Electrical Industrial Machinery		3529	Chemical Products nec	
3134	Soft Drinks & Carbonated Waters		3829	Machinery & Equipment nec	
3117	Bakery Products		3112	Dairy Products	
3231	Tanneries & Leather		3699	Non-metalic Mineral Products nec	
3852	Photographic & Optical Goods		3312	Wooden & Cane Products nec	
3233	Leather & Leather Substitutes		3839	Elect. Apparatus & Supplies nec	
3114	Canning & Processing Fish		3901	Jewellery & Related Articles	
3511	Basic Industrial Chemicals		3813	Structural Metal Products	
3853	Watches & Clocks		3320	Furniture & Fixture	
3220	Wearing Apparel		3720	Non-ferrous Metal Basic Industries	
3832	Radio, TV & Communication Equip.		3512	Fertilizers & Pesticides	
3215	Cordage, Rope & Twine		3132	Wine Industries	
3240	Footwear Except Rubber or Plastic		3849	Transport Equipment nec	
3560	Plastic Products nec			(Single Firm Closed in 1995)	
3319	Wood & Cork Products nec		3844	Motorcycles & Bicycles	
	Quadrant II			**Quadrant III**	
3692	Cement, Lime & Plaster		3610	Pottery, China & Earthenware	
3122	Prepared Animal Foods		3710	Iron & Steel Basic Industries	
3133	Malt Liquors & Malt		3119	Cocoa, Chocolate & Confectionery	
3115	Vegetable, Animal Oils & Fats		3833	Elect. Appliances & Housewares	
3311	Saw Mills & Wood Mills		3212	Made-up Textile Goods	
3118	Sugar Factories & Refineries		3691	Structural Clay Products	
3620	Glass & Glass Products		3823	Metal & Wood Working Machinery	
3419	Pulp, Paper, Paperboard Items nec		3851	Professional Equipment nec	
3211	Spinning, Weaving & Finishing		3113	Canning Fruit & Vegetables	
3841	Ship Building & Repairing		3411	Pulp, Paper & Paperboard	
3140	Tobacco		3811	Cutlery & General Hardware	
3131	Distilling, Rectifying Spirits		3843	Motor Vehicles	
3822	Agricultural Machinery & Equip.		3821	Engines & Turbines	
3523	Soap, Perfumes & Other Toilet Items				
3121	Food Products				
3824	Industrial Machinery & Equipment				
3219	Textile nec				
3842	Railroad Equipment				

Note: Ordered in each quadrant by highest productivity growth.

Overall labour productivity grew in the manufacturing sector by 2.8 per cent annually over the 1990–99 period. Quadrant I and Quadrant II industries grew by 4.8 per cent and 6.6 per cent respectively, while Quadrants III and IV plants registered negative growth rates of –5 per cent and –4 per cent respectively. Employment growth (as well as growth in average firm size) has been the highest in Quadrant IV industries (unsuccessful 'upsizers'), while value added growth was highest in Quadrant I (successful 'upsizers') industries.

Over the 1990s, there has been some rationalization with the total number of firms dropping from 2,401 to 2,035. This is reflected in all quadrants but the most dramatic drop is in Quadrant II, from 1,191 firms to 890 firms. The impact on average firm's size varies with a substantial increase in Quadrants I and IV industries (the 'upsizers') and

Table 12.1

SUMMARY STATISTICS BY QUADRANT, 1990–99

	All Industries	Quadrant I	Quadrant II	Quadrant III	Quadrant IV
No. of establishments 1990	2,401	721	1,191	190	299
(share)	100	30.03	49.60	7.91	12.45
No. of establishments 1999	2,035	683	890	166	296
(share)	100	33.56	43.73	8.16	14.55
Average firm size 1990	136.7	212.1	90.0	123.0	149.5
Average firm size 1999	177.9	290.6	88.1	116.7	222
Number of net entrants 1990–99[a]	771	256	236	87	192
Number of net exits 1990–99[a]	1,137	294	537	111	195
Employment 1990	3,28,187	1,52,897	1,07,219	23,376	44,695
(share)	100	46.59	32.67	7.12	13.62
Employment 1999	3,61,935	1,98,495	78,369	19,367	65,704
(share)	100	54.84	21.65	5.35	18.15
Employment growth (%)[b]	0.49	1.93	–3.99*	–4.11*	4.79*
Value added share 1990	100	28.27	49.63	6.78	15.44
Value added share 1999	100	39.95	45.76	2.54	11.86
Average value added per firm 1990 (1982 Rs Mn)	8.3	7.8	8.3	7.1	10.3
Average value added per firm 1999 (1982 Rs Mn)	12.7	15.1	13.3	3.9	10.3
Value added growth (%)[b]	3.31*	6.79*	2.64*	–9.25*	0.80
Labour productivity growth (%)[b]	2.81*	4.86*	6.63*	–5.15*	–3.99*
Initial (1990) wage level (1982 Rs)	10,177.13	9,024.73	10,330.87	13,343.57	12,202.91
Real wage growth[b]	0.63**	00.92*	1.04*	–0.37	–0.09

Source: Department of Census and Statistics.
Notes: [a]Gross number of entrants and exiters were not available. Instead, the net entrants or exit numbers were reported annually.
[b]Growth rates estimated by fitting a logarithmic trend equation.
*Statistically significant at the 1% level.
**Statistically significant at the 5% level.

a marginal decrease in average employees per firm in Quadrants II and III (the 'downsizers'). Quadrant II has the smallest average plant size, with about 80 workers per firm, while the largest average plant size is 290 for Quadrant I plants. Interestingly, Quadrant IV industries had the highest initial value added per firm, but over the decade, industries in Quadrants I and II (successful in registering positive productivity growth) have added value to their production process and by 1999 had higher value added per firm than Quadrant IV. The value added in the average plant in Quadrant III actually declined.

PRODUCTIVITY–WAGES NEXUS

The data from Table 12.1 indicate that the unsuccessful industries in terms of productivity had the highest initial (in 1990) real wages. The successful upsizers (Quadrant I) had the lowest initial real wages. The industries that increased productivity (successful upsizers and downsizers) had the highest real wage growth over the decade, with the larger increase coming from Quadrant II which had a higher productivity growth (accompanied by a reduction in employment). The industries that experienced productivity declines exhibit zero real wage growth. Although the coefficients

Figure 12.5a

PRODUCTIVITY GROWTH AND WAGES GROWTH IN QUADRANT I AND QUADRANT II INDUSTRIES

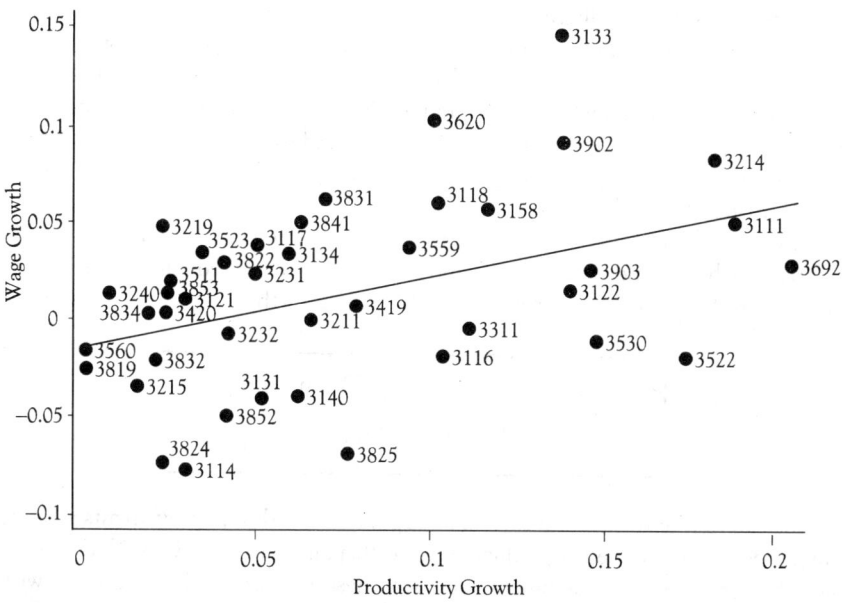

Figure 12.5b

Productivity Growth and Wages Growth in Quadrant III and Quadrant IV Industries

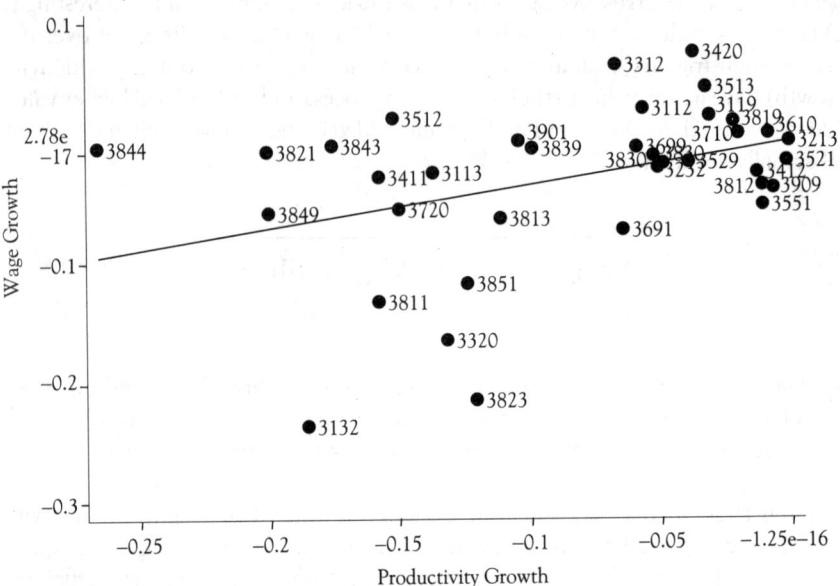

on real wage growth are marginally negative for Quadrants III and IV industries, they are statistically no different from zero.

These results point to an interesting asymmetry. Productivity increases lead to real wage increases, but productivity declines do not lead to real wage decreases (see Figures 12.5a and b). This brings into focus the issue of rent sharing between plant owners and labour. In industries with declining productivity, workers are still able to secure nominal wage increases to maintain their real wages. In industries with rising productivity, a fraction of the productivity gains is indeed shared with labour, in the form of higher real wages. However, the magnitude of the wage increases are significantly smaller than productivity increases.

A second interesting observation is that real wage growth does not appear to be related to whether industries are expanding employment or reducing employment. Instead, the key to real wage growth is productivity growth.

POLICIES TO PROMOTE PRODUCTIVITY GROWTH AND EMPLOYMENT

To the extent that the data reveal real wage growth, and thus improvements in living standards, are determined by productivity growth, policies to improve productivity are vital for Sri Lanka's development. Further, these polices can be consistent with employment generation. However, a multi-pronged approach is needed to stimulate both productivity growth and job creation.

Macroeconomic Environment

The government must be an enabler of economic growth, productivity growth and job creation. First, this involves effective macroeconomic management and policy consistency. The traditional challenge facing many governments has been the continued expansion of budget deficits and domestic financing of these deficits, which have pushed up interest rates and crowded out private investment. In response, governments have curtailed (potentially productivity enhancing) public investment (such as infrastructure development), while maintaining non-productive current expenditures (including subsidies and wages, pensions and interest payments). New macromanagement challenges are also likely to arise with greater inflows of foreign aid, and their tendency to lead to appreciating real exchange rates.

Policy consistency is a key factor because it reduces the element of uncertainty in an unstable global economy and sends a signal to businesses and labour upon which long-term investment commitments are made. Fluctuations in policy lead to greater uncertainty and fear of investing in the country.

A great source of uncertainty and deterrent to investment and productivity enhancements in the island has been the ongoing conflict with the Liberation Tigers of Tamil Eelam (LTTE). A well-designed peace will lead to reduced budget deficits, greater economic activity, more foreign investment and technology transfer and a stimulated tourist industry. However, an ill-conceived peace would only postpone the burden to a later generation, bequeathing them with perhaps a far graver crisis.

Regulatory Environment

The regulatory environment must be revamped to remove burdensome laws and streamline procedures for regulations that need to remain. Excessive regulations in product and factor markets have shown to have a negative impact on productivity and employment generation. Regulations on product markets that inhibit competition tend to reduce incentives to innovate and improve productivity. Factor market regulations often inhibit firms from expanding or new firms from emerging, because they fear that employment expansion in good times, for example, may not be reversed in bad times (see labour market flexibility). The government also needs to review and eliminate unnecessary or burdensome laws, permits, licences and rules that impose obstacles to investment and economic activity.

Further, the government should streamline procedures for those regulations that are necessary (e.g., health, safety, taxes, etc.). The maintenance of law and order is also crucial so that there is appropriate respect for individual and property rights, as well as contract enforcement. An immediate concern that needs to be remedied is that of dispute resolution; it should be dealt with in a speedy manner. The current tendency for a prolonged wait for decisions from tribunals and courts creates uncertainty and unnecessary burden for both worker and employer. This points to a larger issue of increasing public sector efficiency. Low levels of public sector productivity impede productivity growth in the private sector.

Labour Market Flexibility

An oft-cited obstacle to productivity growth and job growth is the level of excessive labour regulations in Sri Lanka. While the problems in the labour market cannot be blamed squarely on the labour laws, laws such as the Termination of Employment Act of 1971 and political interference in wage bargaining do reduce the flexibility of employers to respond to changing market conditions, and to move from low productivity sectors to high productivity sectors. For example, a firm facing increased demand for its product, may resist hiring new workers in fear that if the demand increase is temporary, they would be unable to retrench the new employees once demand drops. Further, some laws have skewed incentives in a direction away from productivity and employment, as is the case with the Gratuity Act of 1983. The Act requires employers to pay their workers who remain on the job for more than five years, half of their last monthly salary multiplied by the number of years employed. Although this system was designed to reward workers for staying on the job, many workers take advantage of this bonus and leave their jobs after five years. As a consequence, the Gratuity Act has created an incentive for employers not to invest in training their workers, thus retarding productivity growth.

Although there has been no robust empirical work on Sri Lanka's labour regulations, empirical work on Europe has shown that high employment protection laws lead to reduced employment (see, for example, Bertola, 2001). More relevant for Sri Lanka, such as the recent work on Indian states (Besley and Burgess, 2002), show that states that amended the Industrial Disputes Act in favour of workers experienced lower productivity, employment, investment and output, as well as increased poverty.

The issue of labour market regulations is more easily understood by characterizing a job, for simplicity, as essentially having two features—(*i*) wages, and (*ii*) some degree of permanence or job security. Both aspects of the job are costs to the employers, because providing job security limits the employers' ability to adapt to exogenous changes in the market environment. Thus, there is a trade-off between wages and job security. Figure 12.6 contrasts the distribution of wages under two equilibria: Equilibirum 1—low wage/high job security (low variance of wages) outcome and Equilibrium 2—high wage/low job security (high variance) outcome. One equilibrium is not clearly superior to another, the choice depending on the country's socio-cultural stance. In fact, the US situation could be characterized as Equilibrium 2 (greater return/greater risk) while Europe has opted for Equilibrium 1, with lower wages and greater employment protection. Sri Lanka has also chosen Equilibrium 1 and in the predictable economic environment of the 1950s and 1960s, performed well. However, the current unstable global environment raises the opportunity cost of this job security.

Figure 12.6

DISTRIBUTION OF WAGES UNDER TWO DIFFERENT REGIMES

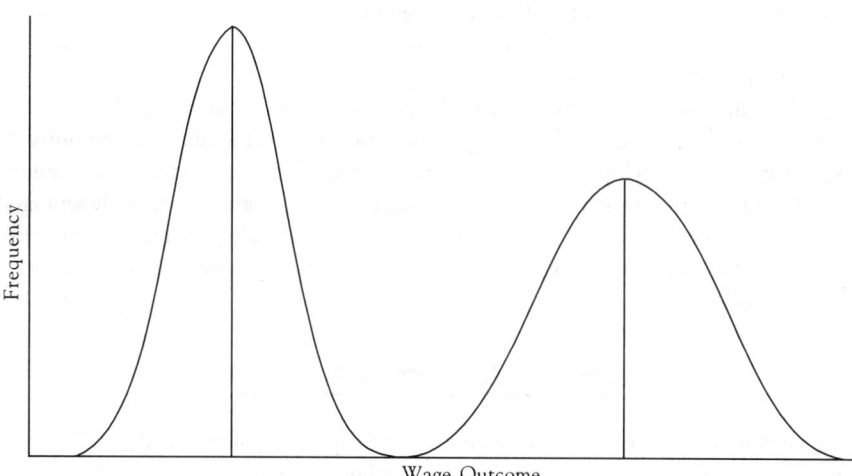

Eqm 1: low average wages/high job security   Eqm 2: high average wages/low job security

mean wage outcome

Embracing the opportunities arising from globalization could lead to even higher mean average wages (pushing the Equilibrium 2 distribution out to the right). Missed opportunities, taken up by other countries, may in fact reduce our average incomes (pushing the Equilibrium 1 distribution to the left).

Evidence suggests more labour market flexibility is desirable but the movement to it should involve two features. First, less job security should be compensated with higher wages to workers. Second, Sri Lanka should develop an unemployment insurance system that would ease the ill effects of job insecurity. Developing a credible system of worker adjustment assistance, which includes income support, worker training and job search assistance, would be an appropriate accompaniment to any major changes in existing labour laws. Given the cost and administrative requirements, a programme may be gradually built up with appropriate financing, beginning with limited coverage.

Workforce Development

Investing in human capital is key to productivity growth, employment generation, labour market flexibility and income generation. As mentioned earlier, some labour regulations create a disincentive to firms to invest in their human capital. Further, firm innovations to circumvent rigid labour laws have the side effect of reducing incentives for on-the-job training. For example, due to the difficulties involved in termination on non-disciplinary grounds, firms have resorted to using temporary workers, contract workers and sub-contracting parts of the production process to units not covered by the

Termination of Employment Act. All these developments have negative impacts on incentives to train workers on the job and creates distrust among the permanent cadre. In the short term, this may be addressed by giving tax incentives to firms that provide on-the-job training. If a durable peace is established, additional incentives should be given to firms that train ex-combatants.

The education system also must re-orient itself towards the needs of the private sector. As such, there should be more interaction with the business community in school curricula development and more programmes should bring together students and businesses prior to graduation, such as internships and other work-study arrangements. Investing in the young, compared to mid-career adults, will bring the highest return because the young have a longer working life and hence a greater incentive to acquire skills.

Labour–Management Relations

Successful firms in Sri Lanka have developed cooperative and consultative labour-management relations. The traditional distrust between management and labour can only be countered by greater communication throughout the chain of command in the firm, thus generating a sense of shared destiny. This needs to be augmented with a fair sense of rent sharing. Compensation schemes need to be simplified and be more closely linked to productivity. When instituted, shop floor improvement programmes such as '5S', Total Quality Management, Total Preventive Management and Just-in-time, have been largely successful.

Capital Accumulation and Technology Transfer

The development of local and foreign capital, as well as technological innovation, increase productivity. However, channeling local savings into productive investment that generates employment has been problematic. One reason is that most of the savings in the Employees' Provident Fund (EPF) and the Employees' Trust Fund (ETF) are captured to finance the government's budget deficit. Further, high intermediation costs of the inefficient state banks have kept interest rates high for the remaining loanable funds, as other commercial banks tend to use these rates as a benchmark. Thus, better macromanagement (with lower fiscal deficits) and greater bank efficiency would release local savings at lower cost to investors.

As local resources are scarce, foreign investment is a good source of investment funds and technology transfer. In fact, affiliations with foreign investors have led to more innovative management techniques, improved productivity and greater penetration of foreign markets by utilizing the resources of the foreign parent company.

Currently, there are also insufficient resources put into technology development (or at least localizing licensed technology) and technology dissemination. Technology extension must also go beyond the Western Province to promote both productivity and employment generation in rural areas.

Encouraging Entrepreneurship

A source of job growth is developing entrepreneurs and revitalizing small and medium enterprises (SMEs). Although some argue that the average Sri Lankan is culturally risk averse, the existing regulatory framework also provides disincentives towards entrepreneurship. Besides labour and product market regulations, the government should simplify corporate organization and registration laws, provide technical assistance on starting a new business and promote venture capital. Further, assistance to commercial banks to develop a comprehensive electronic credit background search system would expedite the loan application process and lead to firm and job growth.

The government or the aid community also needs to play a role in revitalizing the SME sector, which could be an active source of employment generation, particularly in the rural sector. SMEs need information on best industrial practices because they are too often described as being low in productivity and poor in quality, employing old machinery and equipment, with inadequate management skills. This results in poor working conditions, low wages and a failure to meet contractual agreements. More support should be given by government ministries, research institutions, universities, vocational training institutions and local chambers of commerce to small businesses on production design, productivity and quality improvement, engineering, business management and marketing.

CONCLUSIONS

This chapter has shown that productivity growth and job creation are compatible objectives. In fact, in the current competitive global environment, productivity growth is the likely key to employment generation. The 21st century global environment is characterized by fluctuations and the need for flexible responses. The source of this variability comes from the entry of many new countries into world trade and production. On the one hand, this leads to the emergence of new consumer and financial markets and partners in trade. On the other hand, it also increases the number of rivals in world trade and production. Non-responsiveness to new competitive pressures results in a loss of markets that a small open economy like Sri Lanka cannot afford. Thus, maintaining competitiveness involves maintaining productivity growth.

The dynamics of the new economy are such that many idiosyncratic opportunities arise as potential trading and production partners seek each other out. Those who gain from the globalized environment are those who are able to respond quickly to these new opportunities. Therefore, anything that limits the ability of firms to adapt to changed circumstances is a possible source of inefficiency and impedes productivity growth, job creation and income enhancement.

NOTES

1. Likewise, productivity falls as employment growth increases beyond value added growth.
2. Let Q = national output or valued added; P = population size; L = employed population. Then income per capita $Q/P = Q/L$ (labour productivity) $\times L/P$ (employed to population ratio). This implies growth of income per capita $(Q/P) = (Q/L) + (L/P)$
$$= \text{labour productivity growth}$$
$$+ \text{growth in employed share of population.}$$
3. Industry includes manufacturing, mining and quarrying and construction.
4. $\Pi = Q/L$, where Π = labour productivity, Q = real value added in production, L = labour input.

REFERENCES

Bertola, G. (2001), 'Aggregate and Disaggregated Aspects of Employment and Unemployment', European University mimeo.

Besley, T. and R. Burgess (2002), 'Can Labour Regulation Hinder Economic Performance? Evidence from India', London School of Economics mimeo.

Davis, S., J. Haltiwanger and S. Schuh (1996), *Job Creation and Destruction*, Cambridge: MIT Press.

Solow, Robert M. (1962), 'Technical Progress, Capital Formation and Economic Growth', *American Economic Review*, 52(2): 76–86.

SELECT READINGS

Athukorale, P. (1996), 'Labour Productivity in Manufacturing Sector in Sri Lanka', Ministry of Finance and Planning.

Baily, M.N., E.J. Bartelsman and J. Haltiwanger (1996), 'Downsizing and Productivity Growth: Myth or Reality', in D.G. Mayes, (ed.), *Sources of Productivity Growth in the 1980s*, Cambridge: Cambridge University Press.

Heckman, James (2002), 'Flexibility and Job Creation: Lessons from Germany', NBER Working Paper 9194.

Ministry of Employment and Labour, Sri Lanka (2002), 'Productivity Policy—Private Sector Component'.

Yatawara, Ravi A. (2003), 'Productivity Growth in Sri Lankan Manufacturing: Evidence from the 1990s', University of Delaware mimeo.

Appendix

Table 12.1A

		Growth of Valued Added	Labour Productivity Growth	Employment Growth	Wage Growth
3111	Slaughtering & Preserving Meat	34.80	18.75	16.05	4.87
3112	Dairy Products	−5.67	−5.75	0.08	2.93
3113	Canning Fruit & Vegetables	−16.83	−13.73	−3.10	−2.36
3114	Canning & Processing Fish	18.95	2.92	16.03	−7.53
3115	Vegetable, Animal Oils & Fats	1.87	11.50	−9.62	5.67
3116	Grain Mill Products	14.92	10.32	4.60	−1.89
3117	Bakery Products	7.65	4.96	2.69	3.74
3118	Sugar Factories & Refineries	−7.54	10.19	−17.72	5.80
3119	Cocoa, Chocolate & Confectionery	−4.78	−3.16	−1.62	2.27
3121	Food Products	2.86	2.88	−0.02	1.01
3122	Prepared Animal Foods	7.94	14.01	−6.07	1.46
3131	Distilling, Rectifying Spirits	0.59	5.11	−4.53	−4.20
3132	Wine Industries	−2.55	−18.50	15.95	−23.34
3133	Malt Liquors & Malt	9.72	13.72	−4.00	14.55
3134	Soft Drinks & Carbonated Waters	7.38	5.82	1.55	3.38
3140	Tobacco	3.66	6.08	−2.42	−4.01
3211	Spinning, Weaving & Finishing	0.93	6.55	−5.63	−0.03
3212	Made-up Textile Goods	−14.69	−5.10	−9.60	−1.74
3213	Knitting Mills	1.41	−0.15	1.56	0.32
3214	Carpets & Rugs	51.45	18.15	33.30	8.19
3215	Cordage, Rope & Twine	2.50	1.52	0.98	−3.40
3219	Textile nec	−4.07	2.21	−6.27	4.63
3220	Wearing Apparal	2.79	2.27	0.51	0.37
3231	Tanneries & Leather	5.94	4.89	1.05	2.51
3233	Leather & Leather Substitutes	10.17	4.10	6.08	−0.76
3240	Footwear except Rubber or Plastic	5.10	0.74	4.37	1.29
3311	Saw Mills & Wood Mills	−3.27	11.13	−14.40	−0.50
3312	Wooden & Cane Products nec	8.22	−6.71	14.93	6.62
3319	Wood & Cork Products nec	12.00	0.03	11.97	−2.45
3320	Furniture & Fixture	9.89	−13.20	23.09	−16.28
3411	Pulp, Paper & Paperboard	−25.05	−15.76	−9.29	−2.63
3412	Containers, Boxes & Paperboard	7.56	−1.32	8.88	−2.46
3419	Pulp, Paper, Paperboard Items nec	4.38	7.80	−3.42	0.62
3420	Printing & Publishing	−2.20	−3.79	1.59	7.64
3511	Basic Industrial Chemicals	4.03	2.49	1.54	1.84
3512	Fertilizers & Pesticides	−3.74	−15.24	11.49	2.25
3513	Synthetic Fibres, Plastic Materials	8.62	−3.30	11.92	4.75
3521	Paints, Varnishes & Lacquers	3.48	−0.17	3.65	−1.56
3522	Drugs & Medicines	20.55	17.32	3.23	−2.01
3523	Soap, Perfumes & Other Toilet Items	3.18	3.38	−0.20	3.40
3529	Chemical Products nec	5.52	−3.97	9.49	−1.35
3530	Petroleum Refineries	26.24	14.72	4.21	−1.12
3551	Tyre & Tube Industries	8.39	−1.11	9.50	−5.00
3559	Rubber Products nec	9.87	9.33	0.54	3.65

(Contd. on next page)

		Growth of Valued Added	Labour Productivity Growth	Employment Growth	Wage Growth
3560	Plastic Products nec	6.71	0.06	6.65	−1.73
3610	Pottery, China & Earthenware	−2.03	−0.85	−1.18	0.59
3620	Glass & Glass Products	3.24	10.06	−6.82	10.15
3691	Structural Clay Products	−11.09	−6.46	−4.63	−7.05
3692	Cement, Lime & Plaster	10.61	20.41	−9.80	2.77
3699	Non-metallic Mineral Products nec	−3.34	−5.91	2.58	−0.34
3710	Iron & Steel Basic Industries	−11.23	−2.06	−9.17	0.88
3720	Non-ferrous Metal Basic Industries	−13.08	−15.03	1.95	−5.32
3811	Cutlery & General Hardware	−35.02	−15.83	−19.20	−13.03
3812	Metal Furniture & Fixture	−0.27	−1.09	0.82	−3.37
3813	Structural Metal Products	−3.16	−11.15	7.99	−6.18
3819	Fabricated Metal Products	−1.38	−2.22	0.85	1.67
3821	Engines & Turbines	−22.77	−20.06	−2.71	−0.54
3822	Agricultural Machinery & Equip.	−10.52	4.06	−14.58	2.83
3823	Metal & Wood Working Machinery	−20.18	−12.13	−8.06	−21.20
3824	Industrial Machinery & Equipment	−13.49	2.25	−15.74	−7.40
3825	Computing & Accounting Machinery	51.53	7.60	43.93	−6.88
3829	Machinery & Equipment nec	−0.51	−5.20	4.68	−0.99
3831	Electrical Industrial Machinery	17.55	6.90	10.64	6.21
3832	Radio, TV & Communication Equip.	21.05	2.04	19.01	−2.17
3833	Elect. Appliances & Housewares	−11.46	−4.86	−6.60	−1.64
3839	Elect. Apparatus & Supplies nec	−1.51	−9.98	8.47	−0.20
3841	Ship Building & Repairing	5.33	6.26	−0.94	4.93
3842	Railroad Equipment	0.27	1.85	−1.58	0.34
3843	Motor Vehicles	−18.85	−17.60	−1.25	−0.05
3844	Motorcycles & Bicycles	−13.85	−26.58	12.72	−0.17
3849	Transport Equipment nec	−15.25	−20.00	4.75	−5.72
3851	Professional Equipment nec	−14.90	−12.46	−2.45	−11.47
3852	Photographic & Optical Goods	7.47	4.16	3.31	−4.83
3853	Watches & Clocks	10.93	2.40	8.53	1.52
3901	Jewellery & Related Articles	−3.19	−10.44	7.24	0.24
3902	Musical Instruments	57.22	13.76	20.19	9.03
3903	Sporting & Athletic Goods	36.72	14.59	22.13	2.48
3909	Industries nec	5.14	−0.85	5.99	−3.52

13

Youth Unemployment: An Exploratory Study*

W.D. Lakshman

Introduction

Youth unemployment is a worlds wide phenomenon and academic and policy interest in the subject today is immense.[1] High rates of youth unemployment are seen as a tremendous waste of an important national resource. The sheer volume of statistical information, study reports, conference papers, newspaper articles and policy documents and their critiques that is found on the World Wide Web is testimony to the enormous interest that exists today on the subject. Reporting the deliberations of a conference held in Washington D.C. in February 1999 on youth unemployment, the Organization for Economic Cooperation and Development (OECD) presented the following conclusion:

> Unemployment rates among young men aged between 20 to 24 range from around 9 per cent in the U.S. in 1997 to more than 25 and 28 per cent in countries like France and Spain.[2] Throughout the industrial world, governments acknowledge that youth unemployment is one of the most serious social and political challenges they confront. To date, however, little progress has been made in dealing with the problem. In 1979, average unemployment rates for men of this age group in OECD countries were 8 per cent. In 1997, they had risen by 5 percentage points to 13 per cent.

High levels of youth unemployment impinge adversely on the economic performance and social welfare of any nation. Conditions pertaining to youth unemployment in developing countries are, on impressionistic evidence, perhaps even more alarming than in advanced countries. From a number of important angles, this problem affects developing country economies and societies differently from the advanced countries. There are no publicly funded schemes of assistance either to help the affected persons tide over the period of unemployment or to help them acquire the skills and training to

---

*This is a revised version of a conference paper. An earlier draft of the paper was published in S.T. Hettige and Markus Mayer (eds) (2002), *Sri Lanka Youth: Challenges and Responses*, Colombo: Friedrich Ebert Stiftung, pp. 57–88.

find employment. The families of the persons concerned are therefore forced to support the unemployed youth. Youth unemployment is prevalent mostly among low income families. The phenomenon therefore, leads to further deterioration of the living conditions of the poor. Most importantly, as the experience of many a developing society illustrates, extensive youth unemployment leads to revolutionary upheavals with substantial social, political and economic costs.

Sri Lanka offers an interesting case study of youth unemployment in developing countries. According to available statistical evidence, Sri Lanka has had, over the last three to four decades, a rate of open unemployment which is among the highest in the South Asian region. The 1960s can be described as the period when the earliest systematic attempts were made in Sri Lanka to measure the rate of unemployment in the country. This period also witnessed widespread recognition of the problem of unemployment as one of major social, political and economic significance. Over time, there were ups and downs in the country's rate of unemployment but throughout the period it remained above 10 per cent. It varied from over 20 per cent in the early 1970s (Central Bank, Consumer Finance Survey of 1973) to 10–14 per cent during 1990–97 (Department of Census and Statistics).

Another characteristic feature of Sri Lankan unemployment has been that the numbers unemployed have been higher among the young and the educated members of the labour force and among first time job seekers. It has also been found that most of the first time job seekers usually had to wait long before they eventually found a job. This characteristic of the country's unemployment problem, combined with certain observed features of the labour market, led the International Labour Organization (ILO) mission headed by Dudley Seers to Sri Lanka in the early 1970s to highlight a number of structural elements of unemployment in the country. It has been fashionable since this mission to highlight the mismatches between existing labour skills and the needs of the employers, and between aspirations of those waiting for jobs and employment opportunities that are available.

There are also issues of under-employment of labour. This is a condition found extensively in sectors like domestic agriculture, cottage industry and various informal service activities. There is impressionistic evidence to suggest that part of the recorded youth unemployment is more under-employment than open unemployment strictly defined. The production losses resulting from the under-utilization of available labour services have been significant. This has been so particularly in the case of qualified personnel who, after 9 to 13 years of school education and some times even after another three to four years of university education, are unemployed for not only months but times even for years. Unemployment, particularly among the country's youth and the more educated, has been exceedingly destabilizing from the point of view of the society at large. Politically, the problem of widespread unemployment has influenced election results and has given rise to extra-parliamentary political conflict of a very serious nature.

Given these economic, social and political implications of heavy unemployment and under-employment the governments in Sri Lanka, irrespective of the political parties they belong to, have considered the search for solutions to these problems as of utmost policy significance. Economic policy making since the 1960s in Sri Lanka has been very heavily motivated by a desire to find a lasting solution to this problem.

A strong database is not, however, available to make a comprehensive and defini-
tive study of youth unemployment in Sri Lanka. The available labour force surveys
are subject to various limitations.[3] There is adequate information, however, to undertake an exploratory study. The problem is of sufficient specific and general significance to warrant such an initial exercise at this stage. The present study therefore attempts:

(a)   to analyse and assess the nature and extent of prevailing youth unemploy-
      ment in Sri Lanka;
(b)   to explore economic, social and political factors causing this important and
      volatile segment of the country's overall problem of unemployment;
(c)   to identify the strengths and inadequacies of recent government policies
      and programmes earmarked to meet the persistent challenges of this
      problem; and
(d)   to develop ideas for future policies and programmes.

This chapter consists of four sections. The next section sets out the background for the
study of youth unemployment by examining the extent of overall unemployment in
the country and its changes over time. The following section examines the nature and
extent of youth unemployment in the country during the last two decades or so. This
is followed by an exploration into major causal factors behind high rates of youth
unemployment and the observed structural characteristics of this problem. This exploration is inter-disciplinary and goes into economic, social and political spheres.
Some comments are made here on the strengths and weaknesses of general and
employment-oriented policies under the programme of liberalization carried out in the
country since 1977. The final section attempts briefly to cull out the policy lessons of
the foregoing analysis for the future.

THE BACKGROUND: UNEMPLOYMENT IN SRI LANKA

During the post-independence period,[4] Sri Lanka witnessed 'the emergence of a
chronic large scale unemployment ... due to the contrast between the fast growth of
population and the inertia of the economy in the face of adverse trends in the
economy' (ILO, 1971: 17). Open unemployment has been identified as a major
problem in the country since around the end of the 1950s, implying that the problem
was not seen as of major social, political and economic significance prior to this
period. By the beginning of the 1970s, extensive open unemployment had become a
major political issue affecting not only democratic electoral processes but also spawn-
ing extra-parliamentary struggles for political power. The incumbent government,
whatever its political ideology, has been compelled to take a keen interest in the
behaviour of unemployment and its pattern of distribution among different social

strata and regions. Emphasis came to be placed on the problem of unemployment in major development plans of successive governments.[5] The assistance of foreign expert missions was sought to analyse and to recommend policy measures to alleviate the problem (e.g., ILO, 1971).

Table 13.1 presents a data series of overall numbers in unemployment and the rate of unemployment in the country from 1959–60.[6] The available data from a number of surveys indicate that open unemployment during various years in the 1960s was estimated at between 7.6 per cent at the lowest and 15 per cent at the highest. To the extent that the data for different years in the 1960s are comparable, the rate appears to have increased, reaching 15 per cent of the labour force at the end of the decade.

As compared to the 1960s, the following decade witnessed a significant increase in open unemployment. The extent of unemployment in the first three quarters of the

Table 13.1

ESTIMATES OF UNEMPLOYMENT IN SRI LANKA

Year/Source	Number Unemployed (thousands)	Unemployment Rate (%)
1959–60 ILO Survey (ILO, 1963)		
Low estimate	349	10.5
High estimate	450	12.8
1963 Census		
Low estimate	264	7.6
High estimate	390	10.8
1963 Consumer Finance Survey, CB*	457	13.8
1968–69 Labour Force Survey	450	11.0
1969–70 Socio-economic Survey, DCS*	550	15.0
1971 Census	839	18.7
1973 Survey of Labour Force Participation Rates	793	18.3
1973 Consumer Finance Survey, CB*	1,000	24.0
1975 Land & Labour Utilization Survey, DCS*	984	19.7
1978–79 Consumer Finance Survey, CB*	874	14.8
1981 Census of Population	897	17.9
1981–82 Consumer Finance and Socio–economic Survey, DCS*	609.6	11.7
1985–86 Labour Force and Socio–economic Survey, DCS*	840.3	14.1
1986–87 Consumer Finance and Socio–economic Survey	967	15.5
1990 (4th quarter). Sri Lanka Labour Force Survey, DCS[a]*	954	15.9
1991 (4th quarter). Sri Lanka Labour Force Survey, DCS[a]*	862	14.7
1992 (4th quarter). Sri Lanka Labour Force Survey, DCS[a]*	846	14.6
1993 (4th quarter). Sri Lanka Labour Force Survey, DCS[a]*	831	13.8
1994 (4th quarter). Sri Lanka Labour Force Survey, DCS[a]*	797	13.1
1995 (4th quarter). Sri Lanka Labour Force Survey, DCS[a]*	749	12.3
1996 (4th quarter). Sri Lanka Labour Force Survey, DCS[a]*	709	11.4
1997 (4th quarter). Sri Lanka Labour Force Survey, DCS[a]*	645	10.3
1996–97 Consumer Finance and Socio–economic Survey[b]	656	11.5

Notes: [a]Data exclude Northern and Eastern Provinces.
    [b]'Certain areas' in the North and the East were excluded also in the Survey.
    *CB refers to the Central Bank and DCS to the Department of Census and Statistics.

1970s was particularly bad. The beginning of the 1970s witnessed the first attempt in the 20th century in Sri Lanka to capture state power through an armed insurrection. Though it, failed, all analysts of this insurrection would agree that it was planned and carried out basically by the country's youth and that a major part of its socio-economic explanation must be sought in the conditions of widespread unemployment which prevailed among the youth.

The relatively poor economic performance of the country during 1970–77, reflected in this increase in unemployment, was widely attributed to the weaknesses of the contemporary economic policy regime—one of import substitution under protection and extensive state controls. The government elected in 1977 overhauled the country's economic strategy, moving toward de-regulation, liberalization and outward-orientation. The priority was the alleviation of unemployment when these policy reforms were undertaken. In terms of the employment objective, the country had fared better under policies of liberalization than under the preceding policies of state control, state sector dominance and self-reliance-orientation. The rate of unemployment declined slowly

Table 13.2

AVERAGE ANNUAL RATES (%) OF EXPANSION OF LABOUR FORCE AND EMPLOYMENT AND THE AVERAGE
ANNUAL RATE OF ECONOMIC GROWTH, SELECTED PERIODS, 1946–97

| Period (1) | Rate of Expansion of Labour Force[a] | | | Rate of Expansion of Employment[a] | | | Rate of Growth of GDP[b] (8) | Employment Elasticity (9) = (5)/(8) |
	Total (2)	Male (3)	Female (4)	Total (5)	Male (6)	Female (7)		
1946–53	2.1	1.6	3.9	2.0	1.5	3.5	4.2[c]	0.47
1953–63	1.5	2.1	−0.1	0.8	1.2	−0.8	2.6	0.29
1963–71	3.8	2.6	8.0	1.8	1.5	3.0	3.9	0.46
1971–81	1.2	1.3	0.9	1.3	1.4	0.7	4.5	0.29
1981–1985/86	3.8	1.5	10.6	4.9	2.1	15.6	4.9	1.00
1985/86–90	0.1	−0.9	2.3	−0.4	−1.0	1.0	3.1	−0.13
1990–91	−2.1	−2.0	−2.2	−0.6	−0.6	−0.7	4.6	−0.13
1991–92	−1.2	4.0	−10.6	−1.1	3.0	−9.7	4.3	−0.25
1992–93	3.9	1.3	9.3	4.8	2.4	10.7	6.9	0.70
1993–94	0.8	2.1	−1.8	1.5	2.1	0.2	5.6	0.27
1994–95	0.4	−0.1	1.6	1.4	0.6	3.3	5.5	0.26
1995–96	2.3	3.2	0.3	3.3	4.1	1.5	3.8	0.87
1996–97	−0.2	−0.6	0.5	0.8	0.1	2.4	6.4	0.13
1991–97	1.0	1.7	−0.3	1.9	2.2	1.3	5.4	0.35
1992–97	1.5	1.2	2.0	2.5	1.9	3.8	5.6	0.44

Sources: DCS, Census of Population, 1946–81; DCS, Labour Force and Socio-economic Survey, 1985–86; DCS, Labour Force Survey, 1990, First Quarter; Central Bank Annual Reports for information in Column (8).

Notes: [a] In the case of periods involving more than one year, the average annual rate of expansion has been computed by dividing the per cent rate of expansion over the period as a whole by the number of years involved.

[b] In the case of periods involving more than one year, the average annual rate of growth is the average of annual rates of growth during such periods.

[c] Average for 1951–53.

till about the second half of the 1980s when there was a temporary reversal of this declining trend. Although firm data are not available, there were informed guesses that around 1988–89 the unemployment rate had risen to as high as 18 per cent. After 1990, however, the earlier downward trend in the rate of unemployment resumed and continues to date.

The rapid creation of jobs also resulted in changing job aspirations of the people, particularly the youth, and raising labour force participation rates among women. However, as will be shown later, the strength of demographic and other socio-economic and political developments was such that the rate of expansion of the labour force was low and mildly declining (see Table 13.2). Nevertheless, the rate of expansion of employment opportunities was inadequate to bring the country anywhere near full employment in spite of several specific employment creation programmes. The rate of unemployment, though declining, remains above 10 per cent. At no time during the last two decades did it fall below 10 per cent.

Youth Unemployment

The employment problem in the country has had certain peculiar characteristics that made the economic and political costs of unemployment particularly heavy. The objectives of this chapter require that three of these characteristics are adequately highlighted. These are, indeed, aspects essentially of unemployed youth. Unlike in the earlier section, the discussion in this section is based predominantly on information from the Quarterly Labour Force Surveys. For comparative purposes, the data for 1985–86 from the Labour Force and Socio-economic Survey of that year are also presented.

Concentration among the Youth

Unemployment is heavily concentrated among the young age groups. The relevant information for a few recent years is presented in Tables 13.3 and 13.4. The rate of unemployment among the two age groups, 15–19 and 20–24, was generally about 2.5 times that for the overall rate. According to Table 13.4, more than 75 per cent of total unemployment is found among the three age groups, 15–19, 20–24 and 25–29. In fact, the percentage of persons in the age range of 15–29 years within total unemployment has gradually increased over the years—76 per cent in 1985–86, 78 per cent in 1991, 79 per cent in 1994 and 83 per cent in 1997.[7]

The following are some of the features in the composition of unemployment among young age groups.

First-time job seekers constitute a very large proportion of total unemployment—82 per cent for the 4th quarter of 1997. The relevant proportions for men and women were

Table 13.3

UNEMPLOYMENT RATE BY AGE

(per cent of labour force)

Age Group	1985–86			1991: 4th Q			1994: 4th Q			1997: 4th Q		
	Total	Male	Fem	Total	Male	Fem	Total	Male	Fem	Total	Male	Fem
All ages	14.1	10.8	20.8	13.7	9.6	21.2	12.1	9.8	17.0	10.3	7.7	15.4
10–14	9.9	12.5	5.4	33.3	12.5	51.9	7.1	6.5	8.3	**	**	**
15–19	31.7	28.5	38.0	31.2	32.8	28.9	32.3	29.3	38.5	34.8	30.9	40.1
20–24	30.4	23.4	42.5	35.8	27.3	47.7	31.3	27.5	37.9	28.0	23.5	35.0
25–29	16.7	10.6	27.7	16.0	11.5	23.0	13.1	7.4	22.7	15.3	11.6	21.5
30–39	8.0	5.7	12.6	8.7	3.7	18.2	7.9	5.7	12.0	4.9	2.9	8.9
40–49	4.6	4.3	5.2	3.8	3.4	4.6	2.3	2.8	1.1	1.3	1.0	1.9
50–59	3.4	3.5	2.9	0.2	0.3	0.0*	3.5	4.5	0.0*	0.4	0.5	0.0*
60 & above[a]	2.6	2.0	4.9	0.6	0.7	0.0*	1.5	1.8	0.0*	0.1	0.2	0.0*

Sources: DCS, 1987; QLFS (various).
Notes: [a] Age 55 & above for 1985–86.
*Less than 0.05.
**Statistical practice has changed after 1994 in how this age group is treated. Recognizing the reality that a proportion of children of this age is employed, the recorded number employed from this age group has continued to be included in the labour force. But the practice of indicating a number falling into this age category as unemployed has been abandoned after 1994. Hence the absence of a rate of unemployment among those in the 10–14 age group in 1997.

Table 13.4

PATTERN OF DISTRIBUTION OF UNEMPLOYMENT BY AGE GROUP: SELECTED YEARS

Age Group	1985–86	1991[a]	1994[a]	1997[a]
15–19	22.3	19.3	22.4	22.6
20–24	36.7	42.2	41.2	40.4
25–29	17.4	16.7	15.6	20.3
30–39	13.6	15.8	15.5	12.7
40–49	5.1	4.8	3.9	3.0
50 & above	3.8	1.2	1.6	1.0
	100.0	100.0	100.0	100.0

Sources: DCS, 1987; Quarterly Report of the Sri Lanka Labour Force Survey (various).
Note: [a] Average of the data for the four quarters of the given year.

80 and 84 per cent respectively. As Table 13.5 shows, in 1991, the numbers of the unemployed in this category were distributed between the rural and urban sectors roughly in correspondence with the population proportions of these sectors, 75 and 25 per cent respectively. By the 4th quarter of 1997, these proportions have changed to 91 and 9 per cent respectively. A few data points are inadequate to surmise that the rural youth are finding it increasingly difficult to secure the 'first' job in their working lives but the time trend shown in Table 13.5 should not be ignored.

Table 13.5

PATTERN OF DISTRIBUTION OF THE UNEMPLOYED WHO NEVER HAD A
JOB BY RESIDENTIAL SECTOR: SELECTED YEARS

(per cent of total unemployment)

Residential Sector	1991: 4th Q	1992: 4th Q	1994: 4th Q	1997: 4th Q
Urban	24.4	25.1	23.5	9.2
Rural	75.6	74.9	76.5	90.8

Source: Quarterly Report of the Sri Lanka Labour Force Survey (various).

Table 13.6

PATTERN OF DISTRIBUTION OF THE UNEMPLOYED BY DURATION OF
UNEMPLOYMENT: SELECTED YEARS

(per cent of total unemployment)

Waiting Period	1991: 4th Q	1992: 4th Q	1994: 4th Q	1997: 4th Q
Less than 6 months	14.4	7.4	16.9	10.3
6 to less than 12 months	9.4	14.0	10.0	11.1
12 months & more	76.2	78.6	73.1	78.6

Source: Quarterly Report of the Sri Lanka Labour Force Survey (various).

Another significant aspect of youth concentration in the country's unemployment is brought out in Table 13.6. Not only was the overwhelming bulk of them first-time job seekers, a very large proportion of them had been waiting for long periods to secure their first job.

A third characteristic is that among the youth, women find it more difficult than men to secure employment. The rate of unemployment for women in the young age categories is substantially higher than for men (see Table 13.3). Most of the job openings in the export-oriented industry after liberalization were for young women. Young women also form the bulk of migration for overseas employment. Yet, the economy's rate of creation of employment opportunities appear to have fallen short of demands created by the rise in women's rate of labour force participation.

Education and Unemployment

A continuing characteristic of Sri Lanka's unemployment problem over the last several decades has been its overwhelming concentration among those with more than six years of schooling (Table 13.7). The largest concentration is among those with 6 to 10 years of schooling. The percentage of the unemployed who passed the General Certificate of Education (Ordinary Level) examination is also quite high—the second highest in the five education attainment levels shown in Table 13.7. The proportion of the unemployed with the highest level of educational attainment shown in the table is also disturbingly high and has increased in the course of the 1990s.[8]

Table 13.7

DISTRIBUTION OF THE NUMBERS UNEMPLOYED BY LEVEL OF EDUCATION

								(per cent of total unemployment)
Level of Education	1990	1991	1992	1993	1994	1995	1996	1997
No schooling	1.3	1.9	1.5	1.3	1.2	0.8	1.2	0.6
Years of schooling: 1–5	7.2	7.1	7.7	7.0	7.4	4.7	6.7	4.8
Years of schooling: 6–10	49.7	45.7	50.5	44.9	44.9	47.1	42.3	45.3
GCE (O Level)	26.5	30.3	27.0	28.7	28.3	29.1	23.5	28.2
GCE (A Level) and above	15.4	15.1	13.7	18.0	18.2	18.4	18.9	21.0
Total	100.0	100.0	100.0	100.0	100.0	100.0	100.0	100.0

Source: Quarterly Report of the Sri Lanka Labour Force Survey (various).

Table 13.8

RATE OF UNEMPLOYMENT AT DIFFERENT EDUCATIONAL ATTAINMENT LEVELS, 4TH QUARTER OF 1994 AND 1997

		(per cent of labour force)
Level of Education	1994: 4th Q	1997: 4th Q
No schooling	1.8	2.1
Years of schooling: 1–5	0.2	2.6
Years of schooling: 6–11	12.2	10.8
GCE (O Level)	20.2	16.7
GCE (A Level) and above	20.1	16.7
Total	12.1	10.3

Source: Quarterly Report of the Sri Lanka Labour Force Survey (various).

Table 13.8 shows that the highest rates of unemployment are found among the two groups with the highest educational attainment, namely GCE (O Level) and GCE (A Level) and above. The relevant percentages have gone down between 1994 and 1997, along with the decline in the overall rate of unemployment, but even in 1997 the rates for these two groups were about 6 percentage points higher than the overall rate of unemployment.

In terms of educational categories, women are again more disadvantaged than men. The proportion of those with high levels of educational qualifications has generally been higher among unemployed women than among their male counterparts.[9] The relative disadvantage of educated women in the labour market operates more strongly in rural than in urban areas.

The social, political and economic implications of unemployment, concentrated among the relatively educated youth, are quite serious. In addition to the frustration this causes among the unemployed youth and their families, the entire phenomenon is destabilizing from the point of view of society at large. The country has gone through extensive political unrest in the recent past in two separate theatres of conflict, North and East, on the one hand, and the rest of the country, on the other. The violent conflict in the latter theatre has been brought under control but in the former, a civil war continues unabated. It is noteworthy that the youth have played and are playing the dominant role in these political conflicts. It is natural to surmise that there has been a close causal relationship running from the pattern of unemployment highlighted above to these political processes. Even without its political repercussions, extensive unemployment among the educated youth implies enormous loss to the economy by way of foregone production. When its political repercussions are added, losses to the economy and society from such unemployment become even more substantial.

Structural Mismatches

On the one hand, unemployment has been found to exist side by side with shortage of labour in different segments of the economy. On the other hand, there has been a mismatch between existing labour skills and the needs of the employers, as well as between aspirations of those waiting for jobs and employment opportunities that are available. Table 13.9 sets out the 1997 data on the distribution of actually employed persons by occupational groups and the distribution of the unemployed by occupations desired and indicates the existence of a huge mismatch between what is available and what is desired. The labour market mismatch in agriculture and fisheries, clerical jobs and 'elementary' occupations is particularly striking. The more educated a job aspirant is, he/she appears to desire agricultural and manual jobs less and office jobs more.[10]

Job aspirations are conditioned by the existing disparities among different categories of occupations. These disparities are caused by factors like wage rate and social rating differentials as well as between different occupations. The educational system in the country, moreover, has been known to distract new entrants to the labour force from manual pursuits in agriculture, fishing, animal husbandry, services, etc. The incompatibility between what the employers are looking for in the persons they would like to

Table 13.9

ACTUALLY EMPLOYED BY MAJOR OCCUPATIONAL GROUP AND THE UNEMPLOYED
BY DESIRED OCCUPATIONAL CATEGORY, 1997

Occupational Category	Per cent of Actually Employed in Each Group	Per cent of the Unemployed Desiring an Occupation in the Category
Managerial	1.68	0.32
Professional	5.60	10.85
Technical & related	4.15	2.42
Clerical	4.55	18.30
Sales & services	11.88	5.12
Agricultural & fisheries	22.43	0.86
Craft & related work	14.98	15.41
Plant & machinery operator	6.08	4.38
Elementary occupations	26.08	14.66
Others	2.53	27.69

Source: QLFS, 4th Quarter 1997.

recruit and the characteristics—qualifications and training, experience and overall quality—of the manpower that is looking for jobs has been noted. Human values and skills, and the institutional arrangements (e.g. , in education) which influence them, do not appear to change as rapidly as the economy and its structure. There is hardly any manpower planning to guide the employers or those training the youth for life skills or those looking for jobs.

There is yet another mismatch about which information is not available in the statistical surveys referred to. This concerns the aspiration-availability mismatch in respect of public and private sector jobs. The public sector in Sri Lanka, following the practices which the British colonial system had left behind, operates on the tenet of permanent or lifetime employment. Jobs in the public sector have come to be considered permanent and more secure than those in the private sector. Over the last several decades, there has been a process of gradual shrinkage of the public sector in terms of employment opportunities opening up therein. The private sector has expanded in both absolute and relative senses. Along with these structural transformations of the economy, attitudes of job aspirants also have changed, though slowly. Yet, in spite of these changes, it appears that on the part of the educated youth there is still a greater desire to seek public sector jobs in preference to private sector jobs. Hence the tendency for them to wait until they either succeed in finding a desired type of occupation or realize the futility of waiting any more and decide to take on what is available.

REASONS FOR HIGH RATES OF YOUTH UNEMPLOYMENT

This exploratory study commences by referring to a debate between two points of view regarding the nature and causes of youth unemployment in Sri Lanka. A mission sponsored by the ILO in 1971 laid strong emphasis on the structural characteristics of youth unemployment in Sri Lanka and considered it very important that the structural mismatches were given special attention in the country's employment policy. As against this viewpoint, an argument has been articulated recently that the stress on structural characteristics of youth unemployment is misleading and that the causality behind all forms of unemployment has to be explored in inadequate accumulation. It has been argued that low levels of accumulation and sluggish growth and the consequent inadequacy in labour demand can explain high levels of unemployment without resorting to structural types of explanations (Kelly and Gunasekera, 1990). Unemployment, these critics argue, has persisted because the increase in the overall demand for labour consistently fell short of the increase in the overall supply of labour.

The argument relating accumulation and growth on the one hand, and unemployment on the other, from an overall point of view is generally correct. This implies that policies must place priority on eliminating the obstacles to rapid accumulation. Every time overall unemployment dropped significantly, rates of unemployment for almost all the different segments of the labour force too have declined (e.g., the data in Table 13.8). Though generally valid, if this viewpoint is accepted to the total neglect of real structural conditions of unemployment, then it can also lead to misleading policy inferences. The relationship between economic growth and employment expansion is not always a straightforward one. The exploration of reasons for youth unemployment adopted in this study, therefore, assumes the importance of both types of explanation and is strongly inter-disciplinary in approach.

Labour Force, Accumulation and Employment

Table 13.2 presents information about growth of labour force, employment and gross domestic product (GDP) during the last five decades. The annual average rates of growth are indicated for several identified sub-periods, the choice of the sub-periods dictated by the availability of labour force related data. Subject to the limitations of data,[11] one would observe from Table 13.2 that the rate of labour force growth during the period covered in the table has been low, when the two bulges in the rate in the 1960s and the first half of the 1980s are ignored.[12] If these two very high rates are disregarded, one might even seen a mild and gradual tendency toward a fall in the rate over time.

Apart from demographic and economic transformations, there were certain other reasons which moderated labour force growth in the 1990s. The 'disappearance' of several thousands of youth during the heightened civil disturbances of 1988–90 was one such factor. Also to be noted are large numbers of deaths that have continued to take place in the civil war of the North and the East, among combatants on either side as well as among the civilians. The accelerated privatization of state industrial and commercial enterprises and the cadre reduction in the public services during this period also led to large numbers of voluntary retirements. The actual expansion of labour force during 1990–97 (Table 13.2) was marginal.

The conditions of female labour supply, in contrast to those for males, have changed in many ways over time, particularly over the last two decades. The share of females in the total labour force increased from 22 per cent in 1946 and 26 per cent in 1981 to 33 per cent in 1997. The expansion in the proportion of women in the labour force was accompanied by significant changes in the age pattern of their labour force participation as well. This was due largely to the rise in literacy as well as education levels of women. Along with the structural changes in the economy, there has been an expansion of occupations considered acceptable for women. The surge in job opportunities for women in the 1980s and the 1990s within the increasing number of export-oriented industries in the country's free trade zones and elsewhere was responsible for raising the female labour force participation rate.

Growth of employment opportunities during the past half century was subject to marked fluctuations. The negative employment growth figures during 1985/86–1990 reflect the extent of disruption of economic activities during 1987–90 due to political disturbances and widespread violence. Limitations in data, particularly their non-comparability, may explain part of the fall in employment during 1990–92. That there was some drop in the economy's capacity to create employment opportunities can also be seen from the behaviour of unemployment rates in Table 13.1. The fluctuations in the rate of growth of employment over time followed changes in economic policies and strategies—the employment elasticity of growth varying according to the prevailing strategy of development. In the following account it is proposed to focus on more recent times.

One of the most important objectives sought through the economic policy reforms of 'opening up' and 'liberalization' was rapid creation of jobs. The early stage of these reforms, i.e., until about the beginning of the 1980s (see the data for 1971–81 in Table 13.2), witnessed the beginnings of export-oriented industrialization through foreign direct investments (FDI) and the commencement of a number of large construction projects through foreign assistance that was then abundantly available. Although the full potential of export-oriented industrialization was yet to be realized, these construction projects created a large volume of jobs. These early years of adjustment, however, also witnessed the loss of a large volume of jobs in sectors which had been opened up for competition from imports. The overall employment impact of these policy reforms during this early phase was rather insignificant. The employment elasticity had dropped to 0.29. The full employment generation impact of liberalization and export-oriented industrialization can be seen in the following sub-period, 1981–85/86, when employment elasticity had gone up to 1. Most of the jobs created were for women; female employment rose by 15.6 per cent per annum. This had its corresponding natural impact of raising the rate of labour force participation among women as well. Female labour force grew by 10.6 per cent per annum while the total labour force rose at the rate of 3.8 per cent. The economy was able to cope with the problem satisfactorily, with the rate of unemployment dropping from the Census figure of 18 per cent for 1981 to the DCS, 1987 figure of 14 per cent for 1985–86 (Table 13.1).[13]

Sri Lanka has maintained the liberal framework of economic management since 1977, in spite of several changes in leading political personalities and the change of political party in power in 1994 when the Peoples Alliance under Chandrika Bandaranaike Kumaratunga came into power. One policy objective, namely rapid creation of jobs, continued to dominate. The economy has remained capable of creating jobs reasonably well, with the employment elasticity at 0.44 (1992–97).

The relationship between GDP growth and employment growth would depend on the nature of the economic growth process that was in place at any particular period of time. The period 1992–93, for example, which exhibited a strong growth momentum in the economy, was also a period when certain strong employment promotion mechanisms were in operation. Two examples for these strong employment promotion mechanisms were the district garment factory programme[14] and self-employment promotion schemes. These and other special employment promotional measures were implemented after 1993 as well. Similarly, the process of economic growth in the first half of the 1980s was characterized by strong growth of certain labour-absorbing sectors like construction and export processing zone industries. It seems that if strongly favourable impacts on employment are to be generated, the growth process needs to be carefully guided to make it more labour absorbing.

What Sri Lanka's experience over the last five decades or so shows is that the most fundamental factor behind the phenomenon of heavy unemployment in the country is inadequacy of accumulation and consequent sluggishness in economic growth. Extensive youth unemployment is a facet of this general problem. During a few years in the late 1970s and the early 1980s, high rates of accumulation—28–32 per cent— were temporarily achieved. This led, however, to inflation and balance of payment problems, as domestic savings consistently remained around 17–18 per cent of GDP. In the 1990s, the country could only maintain an investment rate of around 25 per cent. Still, the domestic saving rate failed to go beyond 16–18 per cent. The resulting gap was met through foreign savings.

The global integration model of growth and development in Sri Lanka over the last two decades has depended on FDI to play a major role in employment creation. FDI and domestic investments both, however, have failed to expand at sufficiently high rates to be able to eliminate unemployment and thereby, to substantially improve real wages and working conditions during these 20 years. Reasons for this failure are varied and complex. The factors most widely cited are limited natural resource endowments of the country, conditions of political instability and insecurity, weaknesses in physical infrastructure and so on. The nature of political instability and certain institutional and other peculiarities in the system, giving rise to high rates of unemployment among the youth, are explored in the rest of this section.

Political Instability

The gradual evolution of the country's long standing ethnic problem into a bloody separatist war since the early 1980s has been the most damaging for economic growth and employment creation. In addition, since around the mid-1980s, there were the operations of the underground political movement[15] of the Janatha Vimukthi Peramuna (JVP) whose cadres came from the country's majority Sinhala community. The activities of the JVP were militarily contained and suppressed by the end of the 1980s. Until then, this movement had exercised an enormously disruptive influence on the processes of economic and social development in the country. One sees a familiar vicious circle here. Extensive unemployment, particularly among the first-time job seekers was a major factor, among others, behind both these political movements. These political movements in turn have been responsible to a large extent for the failure of economic processes that were put in place to accelerate job creation in the economy.[16]

The combined influence of these two political movements, the JVP and the LTTE, in the second half of the 1980s was economically disastrous. Capital accumulation in general and FDI in particular dropped. The rate of unemployment, which had dropped substantially to 14–15 per cent by the mid-1980s, increased to around 18–19 per cent by the end of the decade according to informed opinion. Once the JVP insurrection was suppressed by the end of 1989, the regions affected by that insurrection returned to some normalcy. Investment and economic activity picked up. The post-1990 period has also been characterized by certain policies specifically designed to address the unemployment problem, e.g., the district garment factory scheme and various self-employment promotional programmes. The gradual decline in the rate of unemployment during the 1990s has also reduced unemployment among the youth and the educated. The ethnic war in the North and the East of the country has continued unabated, however, with its adverse effects on accumulation, growth and employment.

Labour Institutions and Investment

Economic management under policies of liberalization is guided by the perception that Sri Lanka's comparative advantage lies in labour intensive lines of manufacturing industry, as labour is seen as the most abundant factor resource. In FDI-promotion policies, investments in labour intensive product lines have been encouraged. This, it was believed, would be the fastest route to full employment, real wage increases and improvement of working conditions.[17] Institutional conditions shaping the labour market processes would, in this scenario, acquire great significance as a determinant of the investment climate.

Employers' organizations have consistently presented the argument that legal institutions in the country, particularly those affecting capital–labour relations, tend to discourage long-term private investment.[18] The disincentive effect of such legal institutions, it is argued, has been especially strong on FDI. The employers have consistently viewed the Termination of Employment (Special Provisions) Act,[19] introduced in the early 1970s, as particularly obnoxious. The labour laws in operation assign a significant role to the ministry and the Department of Labour in monitoring, arbitrating and adjudicating in matters of conflict between capital and labour. The employers complain that these government agencies are generally conciliatory towards the employee, even when fair play demands a decision in favour of the employer (Amerasinghe, 1998). Sri Lanka has signed almost every ILO Convention, making the environment in the country further labour friendly and perhaps not so capital friendly. Employers and extreme right wing politicians have often argued that Sri Lanka has built up a social democratic labour regime much before building up the strong economic foundations to sustain such a regime.

The nature of trade unionism that has developed in Sri Lanka is also referred to as introducing significant institutional impediments to investment. The proportion of the country's total workforce that is unionized is small but these unionized workers are in key economic sectors like plantations, port operations and large enterprises. Trade unions, therefore, can and do exercise significant power in the national economy. The bulk of the unionized workforce is in nationally integrated trade unions whose mother union is often affiliated to a national political party. Not infrequently, trade union action has been taken on national political issues, without identifiable trade union demands to be met by enterprise management. Moreover, following perhaps the British practice, the trade union movement has developed an exceedingly antagonistic approach to dealing with owners and managers of enterprises. The perception would be rather alien to both employer and employee that, within an enterprise, labour and capital both stand to gain from success as well as to lose from failure. Insofar as the entrepreneur class views the prevailing structure of labour institutions with suspicion, these institutions will retard the accumulation process. Such institutional barriers to the emergence of a vibrant investment culture would operate particularly strongly in the case of more labour absorptive types of investments.

Inadequate Accumulation in Agriculture

In Sri Lanka, the proportion of agriculture in the GDP declined from 29 per cent in 1970 to 25 per cent in 1980 and 18 per cent in 1997. Its proportion in the country's total employment also declined from around 50 per cent in the 1960s to 37 per cent in 1997. The proportion of agriculture in employment was consistently higher than its GDP proportion, implying low productivity conditions of agriculture.

From the mid-1950s, the plantation sector has suffered from problems of falling commodity prices and increasing production costs. The worsening conditions of profitability and pressures of political idelology led to nationalization of privately owned plantations in the mid-1970s. Rightly or wrongly, the state ownership and management were blamed for a variety of ailments of this sector of agriculture after nationalization. During the 1990s, therefore, most of the large plantations were re-privatized. Whatever else has happened in this sector through changes in economic and management conditions, nationalization and re-privatization, investment remained low and the technology of plantation production has not changed to any significant extent. It has continued to be substantially a manual operation.

Over time, however, there was gradual expansion of education among the children of the plantation workers, thus raising their life aspirations and job preferences. Some of them have managed to obtain other jobs, in urban centres around plantations or after migrating to other locations. The majority, however, would remain unemployed for some time, either till they find non-agricultural jobs or till they are eventually compelled, by lack of alternatives, to accept occupations in the plantations.

Work conditions in the rural, small farm segment of agriculture are even worse than in estates. In plantations, at least wages have increased over the last two decades due to intervention of trade unions in the plantation sector.[20] In plantation agriculture, the predominant form of employment has been wage labour. But small farm agriculture in rural areas operates on hired labour in combination with unpaid family labour. Wage rates in this sector have not increased as much as in the plantation sector. Due to low productivity, caused by low capitalization and technological backwardness, incomes earned even by owner cultivators in this sector are low. Given these conditions, it is not surprising that agricultural pursuits do not entice young members of the rural labour force who have, in fact, enjoyed even better educational opportunities than the estate sector youth.

Unemployment: Structural Conditions

One important structural aspect is the diversity of the sectoral incidence of the problem of unemployment. This is attributable partly to disparities in the sectoral distribution of investment and partly to labour market segmentation. In contrast to large-scale industry and modern financial services, investment in agriculture and fisheries, small industrial and other enterprises was limited. One sees a technological dualism in the economy, related to a large extent to this disparity in sectoral distribution of investment. The totality, or at least large segments, of the slowly modernizing, low investment sectors continue to be traditional in terms of production technology and low on the scale of social acceptability. The young and educated members of the labour force are therefore not attracted to these sectors under the prevailing social conditions. While sectors with high levels of capitalization and, therefore, more modernized in terms of technology experience labour surpluses, the under-capitalized sectors continuing with traditional technology face labour shortages.

As Table 13.10 shows, the primary sector consisting mainly of agriculture and fishing has contracted over the recent past, not only relatively but also absolutely in terms of employment. This was not due to any significant improvement of either labour productivity or average yields from land in agriculture. There has been absolute contraction in the extent of land cultivated with food crops, like paddy, in many areas. These conditions arose from several inter-related reasons—adverse trends in farm gate prices for outputs and market prices for inputs, under-capitalization of agriculture and effects of the ongoing civil war on a large agricultural area of the country. There has been an increasing tendency of the youth to abandon agriculture.

There is also a regional element in the structural unemployment under discussion here. In regions where economic activities of traditional types (for example, agriculture and fishing) are predominant, the rate of unemployment is very high among the youth

Table 13.10

NUMBERS EMPLOYED BY ECONOMIC ACTIVITY AREA AND ANNUAL AVERAGE
GROWTH RATES: SELECTED PERIODS, 1985/86–99

Economic Activity Area	1985–86	1990	1993	1997	1986–90	1990–93	1993–97	1986–97
	(number: in thousands)				(annual % rate of growth)			
Agriculture	2,531	2,361	2,159	2,069	−1.7	−2.9	−1.0	−1.7
Mining & Quarrying	67	80	81	78	4.9	0.4	−0.9	1.5
Manufacturing	648	669	684	870	0.8	0.7	6.8	3.1
Electricity, Gas & Water	21	32	33	32	13.1	1.0	−0.6	4.9
Construction	227	197	227	301	−3.3	5.1	8.1	3.0
Trade, Restaurants & Hotels	514	485	577	716	−1.4	6.3	6.0	3.6
Transport, Storage & Communications	220	206	212	270	−1.6	1.0	6.8	2.1
Insurance & Real Estate	65	64	82	92	−0.4	9.4	3.0	3.8
Community & Personal Services	631	793	912	960	6.4	5.0	1.3	4.7
Not defined	207	160	235	192	−5.7	15.6	−4.6	−0.7
Total	5,131	5,047	5,202	5,580	−0.4	1.0	1.8	0.8

Source: Labour Force and Socio-economic Survey, 1985–86 and QLFS.

in general and among the educated youth in particular. The labour market in these regions is, however, not integrated with that of other regions where modern sector economic activities are flourishing. This labour market segmentation arises from limitations in information flows or from various social and other impediments to interregional migration. Modern sector job opportunities in 'more developed' regions are therefore closed to the unemployed from the remote 'less developed' regions looking for such opportunities. Discussions with the authorities in the Board of Investment indicate that there are many vacancies in modern factory industry under its administrative jurisdiction without takers.

Another aspect in the structure of employment in Sri Lanka, as shown in Table 13.11, is the large proportion of workers in the self-employment ('own account workers') category. This is partly related to agriculture dominance of the employment structure, as much of agricultural employment is self-employment. Recent economic policy, realizing that the country's unemployment is too large to be completely absorbed by formal sector enterprises, has placed an increasing emphasis on the expansion of the informal sector and self-employment in its employment strategies. Because of the adverse political implications of an urban-biased growth path, some of the programmes of informal sector development and self-employment promotion have been designed with a rural focus. Various credit schemes were used, among others, to encourage small informal sector businesses and small enterprises.

Table 13.11

DISTRIBUTION OF EMPLOYMENT BY EMPLOYMENT STATUS, 1990–97

(percentages)

Year	Employee	Employer	Own Account Worker	Unpaid Family Worker	Total
1990	55.2	1.8	29.2	13.8	100
1991	62.4	2.2	25.4	10	100
1992	60.1	1.6	27.1	11.2	100
1993	60.0	2.0	27.4	10.4	100
1994	60.7	2.3	27.2	9.8	100
1995	59.8	2.5	28.3	9.4	100
1996	61.1	2.4	26.8	9.9	100
1997	59.3	2.4	29.1	9.3	100

Source: QLFS.

An extensive study (Lakshman et al., 1995) of a participatory development programme based on the promotion of self-employment in rural areas in a region with a heavy incidence of youth unemployment has shown the following:

- The self-employed are among the poorest, with serious limitations in funds that can be allocated for their economic activities.
- Very rarely do the educated youth get involved in these activities.
- There is a non-entrepreneurial housewife bias among the self-employed.
- The self-employment activities are under-capitalized and are in technologically weak conditions.

- They are commenced without any forceful business orientation.
- They operate under severe market limitations.

These characteristics show that these activities are merely domestic household activities carried out on their own account, basically for a little extra family income. Except for a handful of activities undertaken by a few relatively more enterprising persons, these serve as stop gap mechanisms until the operators are absorbed into the market economy as wage earners. A common experience with own account workers, particularly those of a relatively young age with a few years of schooling, whether men or women, is that no sooner did they receive a formal sector job, they would abandon their self-employment. In relatively more developed societies with institutionally well-integrated markets, the concepts of 'self-employment' and 'small enterprise' denote respectable modes of remunerative engagement. In the case of perhaps over 75 per cent of the relevant cases in Sri Lanka, this would be a totally misleading notion of 'self-employment' and 'small enterprise'. Naturally, this sector of the economy requires a complete transformation if the educated youth looking for employment, particularly the male youth, are to start thinking seriously of moving into such activities.

Another significant structural aspect of Sri Lanka's employment problem is that the first-time job seekers continue to indicate an unrealistic predilection for government sector jobs in spite of the gradual shrinkage of the government vis-à-vis the private sector. The average educated youth has preferred to wait for long periods hoping that such a job would come on his/her way.[21] On the basis of data collected in the Quarterly Labour Force Survey (4th quarter, 1997), one could see that as much as 94 per cent of assistance to the unemployed during the period of unemployment had come from parents, spouses or children.[22] Weaknesses in the country's educational system have been widely criticized for being unresponsive to domestic and global changes and for its irrelevance to the needs of the economy and society (e.g., World Bank, 1994, 1998). Weaknesses in the system of education are thus blamed for the creation of unrealistic job aspirations among the educated youth. By neglecting technical education, it is also argued, the system of education failed to provide the needed manpower for higher technological levels of growth.

Social Exclusion in the Labour Market

Due to various social and political factors, large segments of the labour force fail to secure jobs for which they otherwise have requisite skills and qualifications. Some are excluded because of gender preferences of employees and some because they lacked control over resources like financial assets, land, information and, most importantly, social and political connections. Most of the excluded are indeed constrained by various structural and institutional characteristics of their social existence.

A striking feature is the expansion of employment opportunities more rapidly for female than for male workers. This is shown by the employment pattern of most free trade zone factories in general, and garments factories in particular, whether inside or outside these zones.[23] The same applies to the opportunities created by the growing phenomenon of labour migration for employment overseas. In the area of self-employment, promoted through numerous initiatives of 'participatory' development, there was an extreme form of female bias. The above pattern of creation of employment opportunities has excluded male workers from much of the opportunities generated. With the female rate of labour force participation increasing, the limited growth achieved could not exhaust even the female supply of labour. Hence the general pattern of relatively higher rate of unemployment for women of all age groups and at all educational levels.

Most of gender neutral jobs created (e.g., agricultural wage work created by agri-businesses, construction sector jobs or numerous industrial activities of self-employment type) were not in great demand among the relatively educated males in lower age groups looking for jobs. The rate of expansion of jobs in demand among the relatively educated and young members of the workforce, particularly the males, was limited as the country failed to move up to higher technological stages of growth due to inadequate capital accumulation.

Further, one observes a regional element in the process of social exclusion. Most jobs were available in Colombo and other major urban locations and a few other 'growth centres', e.g., the locations where the free trade zones were set up and major development projects like the Mahaveli Scheme[24] were implemented. A large proportion of the unemployed and the under-employed from remote rural areas was thus overlooked in the distribution of the limited available opportunities.

Even when the government offered various opportunities through poverty alleviation schemes, specifically for the weak and the vulnerable in society, all such groups did not gain easy access to those opportunities because of institutional and structural characteristics surrounding them. Of significance here were institutional characteristics like traditional power structures in village life and political party affiliations.

Certain elements of social division and disintegration have alienated large segments of the society from the processes of modernization. These are divisions based on ethnic, linguistic, religious and caste differences. Even among those having common ethnic origins speaking a common language, the hierarchical stratification of society has remained strong. Markets, operating in these disintegrated and stratified social conditions, have failed to be neutral in respect of different segments of the society, particularly because available opportunities have expanded slowly.

Another point to be noted is the fact that, in conditions of inadequate growth of opportunities, people have tended to use the political mechanism, in addition to the market mechanism, to obtain their share of the limited resources and opportunities. This has turned out to be to the disadvantage of the Northern and Eastern Provinces with a concentration of minority communities—a point worth noting in any attempt to explain the ongoing ethnic war in the country.[25]

The conclusion one may arrive at then is that macroeconomic policies of liberalization cannot be depended upon solely to find speedy and effective solutions to the country's problem of youth unemployment through a process of accelerating accumulation and growth.[26] There are areas in which intervention is required if solutions to this problem are to be found at the speed demanded by the population.

Quantity versus Quality in Employment

The bulk of FDI in Sri Lanka in general, and in its three free trade zones in particular, is in labour intensive production lines. There were signs of gradual diversification of FDI into capital and technology intensive industrial lines, but this transformation has been very slow. The manufacturing sub-sector of textiles, wearing apparel and leather products has remained the lead sector in the portfolio of FDI. This has meant that the bulk of employment opportunities created in export-oriented industry, financed by both FDI and domestic capital, in the country's three free trade zones as well as outside these zones, have gone to young women. The wage employment opportunities opened up in export-oriented industry, though quantitatively large, have remained low in 'quality'. As the diversification of industrial investments into capital and technology intensive areas is relatively slow because of relatively sluggish rate of accumulation, itself a reflection of relatively slow inflow of FDI, no significant gradual increase in real wages is observed. This remains so even after two decades of FDI-dependent export-oriented industrialization.

The bulk of the ordinary workers in modern industry continue to be paid low wages and are made to serve under unattractive working conditions. The policy establishment considers it inadvisable as yet to introduce regulations to improve quality of jobs created by FDI-funded industry on the following arguments. First, the dynamics of population and labour force growth in Sri Lanka ensure availability of a sufficient labour supply on terms and conditions offered by industry.[27] Processes of modernization of society and continuing technological backwardness of agriculture strengthen this tendency, pushing young people out of agriculture. Second, overall industrial accumulation has remained sluggish, making structural transformation in industry, including diversification, rather slow. Third, FDI flows into developing countries are determined under highly competitive world conditions and Sri Lanka would outcompete itself if stronger regulations are introduced in respect of FDI.

The really effective long-term improvement would depend on the speed of accumulation itself and institutional development on the labour market front. But some regulation of the processes involved could address the 'quality of factory jobs' issue, thus making them more attractive to the young and more educated members in the labour force looking for acceptable types of jobs.

Conclusions

Every developing country has its peculiar structural elements in respect of the employment problem. In spite of these, the fundamental solution to problems of extensive unemployment in general, and youth unemployment in particular, must be sought in factors which determine the rates of saving, capital accumulation and technological modernization. Currently, the most widely recommended as well as adopted policy framework for raising growth and employment in developing countries consists of (*a*) deregulation and liberalization and (*b*) promotion of closer integration with the process of globalization. In addition to this general policy framework, Sri Lanka has, in the recent past, adopted certain peripheral policy measures in the form of numerous initiatives to stimulate small enterprise development, self-employment and informal sector activities. As the job creation process within the programme of liberalization turned out to be highly urban-biased, the country also promoted setting up of garments factories in rural and semi-urban areas through active state intervention in market processes. These generated large numbers of factory jobs in semi-urban and rural settings. Such peripheral measures, it appears, would substantially improve the employment impact of a package of liberalization and global integration, though it involves action going against libertarian ideologies.

In the liberal policy framework for development, the reliance placed on FDI is very significant. In spite of extensive as well as expensive promotional efforts, Sri Lanka remains handicapped, from a number of different angles, in the competitive struggle to attract FDI. Such handicaps include (*a*) conditions of political instability and insecurity, (*b*) weaknesses in political, legal and labour-related institutions, (*c*) remaining weaknesses in physical infrastructure conditions and (*d*) low industrial skills of the available labour force. Furthermore, domestic capital, at its current level of development, is incapable of providing adequate numbers of joint venture partners to FDI. All these underline the importance of building up and strengthening domestic capital, even if it requires reviving the lost confidence in 'industrial policy'.

The outward looking strategy has shown its greater potential to achieve objectives of growth and full employment than a package of inward looking policies. Such outward orientation, however, does not necessarily require liberalization in the form it is advocated today. Nor does it mean that the minimalist state is the best recipe for accumulation, growth and employment creation. A significant lesson is that adjustment through market forces, without well-thought out intervention to help the labour surplus sectors, would take a long time to achieve near-full-employment conditions in a developing economy. The same set of policies does not appear to be able to achieve the employment-related objectives in different segments of the economy. The issue of the quality of jobs created, discussed in this chapter, further highlights the regulatory role of the state. This is of special significance as the quality issue is likely to be a legitimate question in the minds of the young and educated job seekers in every developing society.

The relative ineffectiveness of neoliberal policies of global integration in agriculture in Sri Lanka has been noted. Commercialization, modernization and technological transformation of agricultural practices through increased capital formation in agriculture are needed to utilize the full employment potential of this sector, in conformity with the needs of enhanced productivity. Agriculture continues to be an area requiring special attention from the state almost everywhere in the world. That the measures to achieve greater labour absorption in agriculture must be combined with measures to promote non-farm employment and rural industry cannot be over emphasized. Here lies the significance of small industry promotion measures and regional development initiatives.

The Sri Lankan experience highlights the need for effective and ongoing systems of manpower planning in developing countries. This is of particular significance where the types of structural unemployment discussed in this chapter are present. It would help both policy makers and job aspirants in the labour market by making information about the sector-wise distribution of available employment opportunities as well as the pattern of available skills in the economy readily available. As part of, or along with, manpower planning exercises, the state can intervene for the promotion of employment in a number of areas like (*a*) collection and dissemination of labour market information, (*b*) provision of training and retraining facilities and (*c*) suitable regional policy measures to alleviate the regional inequalities in the distribution of employment opportunities.

For the success of any policy package of market liberalization, there must be the appropriate institutional arrangements. This is particularly important in respect of small enterprises, whose significance in employment policy is highlighted in this chapter in several respects. For the achievement of their full development potential, these small enterprises need improved access to resources like information, technological knowledge and credit. They need access to marketing channels. They ought to be able to benefit from the results of ongoing research and development work. Improved facilities for technological and management training are essential for them to be able to effectively compete in the market. These facilities are not supplied adequately and at affordable prices by markets. The state has a very crucial and catalytic role to play in building up and strengthening required institutional arrangements to help markets achieve the employment-related objectives of developing societies.

NOTES

1. Historically, the rate of youth unemployment has generally been higher than the national rate of unemployment in almost every country. It always takes time for young people to gain work experience and to get into regular employment. Today's conditions in youth unemployment are, however, considered as requiring special attention because the numbers involved are very large and economic, social and political implications of such high levels of youth unemployment are serious.
2. The quotation refers to the age group 20–24. Some would include the age group 15–19 as well among the category of the youth in the labour force. In the UK, the rate of unemployment among 15–19 years old is as high as 29.9 per cent, giving a total number close to 90,000 people. (Sarah Peart on the Internet: www.greenleft.org.au/back/1998/333/333p96.htm) In an NBER Working Paper, Sanders Korenman and David Neumark have noted that between 1970 and 1994, unemployment rates for the 15–24 years old age group in 11 European countries rose, on average, by 16 percentage points, from 4.2 to 20.6 per cent. By comparison, the US rate moved only 1.5 points over the same period, from 11 to 12.5 per cent. In Canada, the unemployment rate among workers under 25 (in 1996) was about 17 per cent, nearly twice the national rate of 9 per cent. In 1996, an average of 3,91,000 youths were unemployed in Canada (Foot, 1997).

3. It is useful to comment briefly on some of these data limitations. (*a*) Concepts and definitions used in surveys of different vintage lack uniformity and comparability. (*b*) These surveys have used different reference periods for information collection. (*c*) The Quarterly Labour Force Survey (available from 1990), which is extensively used in this study, is based on a very small sample of 2,500 households. (*d*) In more recent times, no survey has been conducted in all parts of the country, as the Northern and the Eastern Provinces of the country have remained inaccessible due to the on-going civil disturbances there. (*e*) Finally, there is a lack of innovation with respect to concepts, definitions and methodologies used in information gathering. Internationally developed concepts and their measurement guidelines would not always be adequate for particular circumstances prevailing in an individual country.

4. After about 150 years of British colonial rule, Sri Lanka (then Ceylon) gained political independence in 1948.

5. See, for instance, GOSL (1959), p. 60 and GOSL, (1972), p. 12.

6. Attention has already been drawn to some inconsistencies in the data presented in Table 13.1.

7. Although not highlighted at this point in the chapter, the reader may also note that for these young age groups, the rate of unemployment has almost consistently been higher for women than for men. More generally too, the incidence of unemployment has been greater among females than among males. Available information, not presented in Table 13.4, shows that this differential in the unemployment rate between women and men has widened as total unemployment reached high levels in the 1970s. Although the labour force participation rate for women has consistently been substantially lower than for men, the female share of total unemployment remained between 45 and 55 per cent throughout the 1980s and the 1990s respectively.

8. A special sub-category in this group, not separately shown in Table 13.7, consists of those with a Bachelor's degree from the 12 universities that exist in the country. Through a special analysis of QLFS data, the Labour Market Information Bulletin of the Tertiary and Vocational Education Commission (June 1998, p. 16) estimates that in the first and second quarters of 1997, 1.4 per cent of total unemployment in the country consisted of graduates.

9. The percentages of those with (A) GCE (O Level) and (B) GCE (A Level) respectively among the unemployed men and women during the 1990s were as follows:

	1990	1991	1992	1993	1994	1995	1996	1997
For Men								
(A)	23.3	25.0	25.1	28.0	27.0	29.4	23.8	23.9
(B)	8.4	10.5	7.9	12.9	11.3	10.9	10.4	13.6
For Women								
(A)	29.5	34.5	28.9	29.4	29.6	28.8	28.1	32.4
(B)	21.9	18.8	19.4	22.5	24.9	25.5	26.9	28.4

Source: Quarterly Report of the Sri Lankan Labour Force Survery (various).

10. The reader has to be cautioned of the treacherous nature of these survey data on the desires of the unemployed. It is not known whether adequate checks were applied in the collection of this information from the unemployed to ensure that the desires expressed are realistic in terms of their abilities and competencies.

11. All the sample surveys used in this study as data sources are household surveys. The accepted definition of a household results in non-enumeration of members of a surveyed household, who 'have usual residence elsewhere', thus living away from the family 'most of the time'. Up to five boarders and lodgers in a household are included as members, if they 'live and have their meals or share other essentials of living with the family'. Households having more than five boarders and lodgers, however, are treated as 'an institutional unit' and excluded (DCS, 1987). The available data from these surveys under-report, both in the labour force and employment numbers, the following important categories of workers:

- Members of armed forces, usually living in barracks and other types of quarters.
- Workers in free trade zones, usually living in boarding houses.
- Workers who have migrated overseas temporarily for employment.

These categories are important because it was within these categories that the most rapid expansion in employment opportunities occurred in recent times. If they are included, the employment rate is likely to be higher and the unemployment rate lower than are estimated using available statistics without any correction.

12. The peak in the 1960s was the delayed labour force impact of high rates of population growth observed in the late 1940s and the early 1950s following the successful anti-malaria campaign of the mid-1940s. Had the labour force participation rates for women remained constant, after this peak, the rate of expansion of labour force would have continued to drop slowly, along with the gradual decline in the country's birth rates. However, after the changes in economic policy at the end of the 1970s, employment opportunities for women expanded rapidly, pushing up their labour force participation rates. The second peak in labour force growth (early 1980s) was a result of this socio-economic transformation.

13. The conflicting nature of the evidence in the publications of the two principal agencies, which provide labour force related information is to be noted here. The Central Bank data indicate a drop in the rate of unemployment from 15 per cent in 1978–79 to 12 per cent in 1981–82, followed by a rise in 1986–87 to 16 per cent. There is no compelling reason to accept the Central Bank's figure of 12 per cent for 1981–82, in preference to the Census of Population figure of 17 per cent for 1981.

14. This was a programme with a very attractive government-funded package of incentives for private enterprises to set up garment factories in areas remote from the metropolis. Over 100 such factories were set up during 1993–94 and a similar scheme, smaller in scale, is being operated at the time of writing.

15. In the early 1980s this group operated as a legitimate political party and contested the presidential elections of 1982. Subsequently, for reasons which space does not permit here to discuss, the group was declared illegal by the government, pushing them to go underground.

16. One can argue, quite justifiably, that the economic policy processes of the post-1977 period and their visible economic as well as socio-political impacts were responsible, to a significant extent, for the emergence of these militant political movements. Although the writer shares this view, there is no room here for a detailed discussion of this point.

17. The fastest growing sector of the economy during this period indeed was manufacturing and as anticipated, a large volume of jobs was created in this sector. Table 13.10 provides the relevant data for 1985/86–1997. In regard to employment in the manufacturing industry, what this table shows is the net aggregate result of a process. Liberalization has had both positive and negative effects on industrial employment. Also its employment impact on different segments of the manufacturing sector has been different. The sharp reduction in protection provided earlier to domestic industry has led to closure or contraction of some industries, with adverse employment impacts. To what extent those who lost employment in such declining sectors obtained jobs in expanding BOI and other industries, or remained unemployed or moved out of the labour force is not known. The country is, however, still a long distance away from the objectives listed in the sentence in the text to which this footnote relates.

18. In an emerging capitalist system like in Sri Lanka, there should clearly be a regulatory framework to safeguard the legitimate rights of the workers. Labour laws will invariably be a part of that framework. The enlightened segments of the employer class do not deny the desirability of such a legal environment. But their argument is that Sri Lanka's labour laws are too constraining and inhibiting from the point of view of capital.

19. This Act makes the lay-off of workers extremely difficult even when necessitated by financial conditions of an enterprise.

20. Trade union pressure in this sector was particularly effective as the leader of the principal trade union of estate workers S. Thondaman remained a member of the Cabinet of Ministers over the entirety of this period.
21. It has been noted that over 75 per cent of the first-time job seekers were found to have waited for over one year looking for an acceptable job. Having waited for a year or so with family assistance, the jobless educated youth would change his/her aspirations gradually and would eventually take up whatever was available. The social and economic cost of this practice is quite obvious.
22. The other sources of assistance in this statistical tabulation are the following: (*a*) government, (*b*) charitable institutions, (*c*) property income, and (*d*) savings withdrawals. Two other categories are also shown: (*e*) those requiring no assistance, and (*f*) those for whom no assistance was available.
23. A significant proportion of employment created in manufacturing industry in general, and in BOI industries in particular, has been for young female workers. Because of the known interest of free trade zone investors everywhere in recruiting docile and easily trainable workers, young women workers dominate the workforce of such industries. The overwhelming majority of the jobs provided have been of the manual or simple machine operator type. The absorption of the more educated youth, particularly male, in these industries has therefore been insignificant. Another important point to be noted in respect of these industries is that they depended heavily on imported raw materials and intermediate products and, therefore, the indirect employment created by them through backward linkages was insignificant (Lakshman, 1996).
24. This refers to a large infrastructure project involving the construction of several reservoirs along the country's longest river, Mahaweli, with irrigation and hydro-power objectives.
25. As already noted, an interesting case of the use of political bargaining to secure an increasing share of resources and opportunities for a minority community is presented by the leadership of the Tamil estate workers in the Central Province.
26. No doubt, policies of liberalization were able to achieve these objectives more effectively than policies of a closed economy.
27. Some discussions with BOI officials, however, indicate that this argument is not quite correct as there appear to be many unfilled vacancies in the country's free trade zones.

REFERENCES

Amerasinghe, Franklin (1998), 'The Role of State in the Era of Globalisation', ILO: National Tripartite Seminar on the Effects of Globalisation on Industrial relations, mimeo.
Department of Census and Statistics (DCS) (1987), *Labour Force and Socio-economic Survey— 1985/86 Sri Lanka*, Preliminary Report, Colombo: Department of Census and Statistics.
Foot, David K. (1997), *The Globe and Hail*, 14 October 1997.
Government of Sri Lanka (GOSL) (1959), *National Planning Council, Ten-Year Plan*: 60, Colombo: Government Press.
_____ (1972), *Ministry of Planning and Employment, Five-year Plan*: 12, Colombo: Government Press.
International Labour Organization (ILO) (1963), 'A Survey on Employment, Unemployment and Underemployment in Ceylon', *International Labour Review*, 87(3).
_____ (ILO) (1971), *Matching Employment Opportunities and Expectations: A Programme of Action for Ceylon: Report and Technical Papers*, Geneva.

Kelly, T.F. and H.M. Gunasekera (1990), 'A Critical Re-assessment of the Mismatch Unemployment Hypothesis for Sri Lanka', *Upanathi*, 5(1 and 2): 39–56.

Lakshman, W.D. (1996), 'Globalization, Economic Growth and Employment in Sri Lanka', *The Indian Journal of Labour Economics*, 39(3): 673–704.

Lakshman, W.D., S.S. Vidanagama and S.M.P. Senanayake (1995), Self-employment Within a Framework of 'Structural Adjustment': A study in the Light of Social Mobilisation Programme Experiences in the Matara District, mimeo.

Shehzard, Mohammed (2004), 'The Challenge of Unemployment', *Frontline*, 21(7), 27 March–9 April.

World Bank (1994), *Sri Lanka: Education and Training Sector Strategy Review*, Report No. 12460 CE.

————— (1998), *Sri Lanka Social Services: A Review of Recent Trends and Issues*, Report No. 17748-CE.

Select Readings

Colombage, S.S., 'Current Sources of Information on Labour and the Gaps and Deficiencies in the Information System', Conference Paper, mimeo.

Kiribanda, B.M. (1997), 'Population and Employment', in W.D. Lakshman (ed.), *Dilemmas of Development: Fifty Years of Economic Change in Sri Lanka*, Colombo: Sri Lanka Association of Economists, pp. 223–49.

Kelly, T.F. (1992), 'A Strategy for Skills Development and Employment Policy in Sri Lanka', mimeo.

Lakshman, W.D. (1997), 'Income Distribution and Poverty', in W.D. Lakshman ed., *Dilemmas of Development: Fifty Years of Economic Change in Sri Lanka*, Colombo: Sri Lanka Association of Economists, pp. 2171–22.

Lakshman, W.D., Philippe Regniér and S.M.P. Senanayake (1994), *Small and Medium Industry in an Intermediate City: A Case Study of Kurunegala in Sri Lanka*, Colombo: Faculty of Graduate Studies (University of Colombo) and Modern Asian Research Centre (Graduate Institutes of Development and International Studies in Geneva).

Richards, P.J. (1971), *Employment and Unemployment in Ceylon*, Paris: OECD.

14

Migration and Brain Drain

Raja B.M. Korale

Introduction

This study attempts to make an assessment of the dimensions of brain drain and its impact on Sri Lanka, and to review existing policies and analyse appropriate interventions to deal with its possible adverse effects.

Overseas employment opportunities for skilled and unskilled labour has alleviated the unemployment problem and has also created a new source of much needed foreign exchange in the form of private transfers. Migrant remittances are now the largest source of foreign exchange coming into the country other than earnings from apparel exports. The remittances made by migrant workers have not only contributed to easing the balance of payments difficulties, but it has also been an important source of income support for lower and middle income households. The government through the Sri Lanka Bureau of Foreign Employment (SLBFE) has been actively promoting the migration of skilled and unskilled workers as temporary contract labour, adding new destinations such as Cyprus, Greece, Italy, Malaysia, Singapore, South Korea, etc., by entering into bilateral agreements. At present, overseas migration has encompassed practically the entire range of skills, from unskilled to highly skilled, and the annual outflow has been estimated at over 2,00,000 migrants. Accordingly, the socio-economic impact of migration is known to be widespread on consumption, savings and investments and on family bonds.

The main source of data on migration is the SLBFE which compiles data on temporary contract migration for foreign employment. Highly skilled migrants who make their own arrangements to find employment and travel to the host countries are not monitored by the SLBFE. Similarly, there is hardly any information on refugee migration and illegal migration to the developed countries. There are no formal arrangements to receive information on migration from host countries on a routine basis. The information on brain drain is too weak and fragmentary to undertake research.

MIGRATION DIMENSIONS

Post-Independence Period

In the post-independence period, emigration has exceeded immigration and international migration has contributed negatively to population growth in Sri Lanka. In the period immediately after independence, net migration was negative because of repatriation of Indian estate labour to India. This repatriation of Indian labour continued until the 1980s. In addition, a number not exceeding 2,000 Sri Lankan citizens had also immigrated annually in the 1950s and 1960s. Immigration of Sri Lankan nationals which started to increase at the beginning of the 1970s rose approximately to 40,000 per year by 1980. The growth of migration in the 1970s was mainly because of the outflows through brain drain and through temporary migration of labour to the Middle East and to West Africa. The number migrating in the 1980s rose to about 45,000 per year. During this decade, net outward migration had peaked at 64,000 in 1983 at the time of communal violence in Sri Lanka. In the aftermath of the political instability and social unrest, the net outward migration peaked at 81,000 in 1992. Communal violence, political instability and social unrest contributed to a large number of highly skilled persons leaving the country.

It is known that a large number of academically and professionally qualified persons left the country during this period; however, as immigration statistics are not disaggregated by occupation, it is not possible to derive the composition of these flows. This outward migration continued at high levels in the early 1990s at about 40,000 per year but declined to a lower level of 35,000 per year at the end of the 1990s (see Appendix Table A-1). Sri Lankan outward migration in the 1980s and 1990s comprised of three or four channels: (*a*) the temporary migration for employment to the Middle East and other destinations, (*b*) more permanent migration arising from brain drain mainly to Western Europe, North America and Australia, (*c*) refugee migration also mainly to the same destinations where refugees are accepted sympathetically, and (*d*) illegal migration to destinations such as Japan, Italy, South Korea, Australia and Western Europe via former Soviet block Central Asian Republics. Information on residency status, length of stay and purpose of travel is essential to identify different categories of residents, visitors, short-term and long-term migrants (United Nations, 1985). This information is not compiled by the immigration authorities.

SLBFE Placements

The main source of data on migration for employment were those initially compiled by the Ministry of Plan Implementation (Korale et al., 1985a) and, from 1985 onwards, by the SLBFE. The SLBFE has placed over 1,50,000–1,80,000 persons in employment annually during the past few years (Table 14.1).

Table 14.1

FOREIGN EMPLOYMENT PLACEMENTS REGISTERED WITH THE SLBFE

Year	All Migrants	Professional	Middle Level	Clerical	Skilled	Unskilled	House-maids
1995	1,72,489	878	2,495	4,594	27,165	23,497	1,13,860
1996	1,62,576	599	1,945	3,371	24,447	21,735	1,10,479
1997	1,50,283	573	1,639	3,579	24,578	20,485	99,429
1998	1,59,816	695	2,980	4,896	31,787	34,109	85,349
1999	1,79,114	1,217	3,155	6,196	37,187	43,649	87,710
2000	1,81,370	923	3,734	5,802	36,370	35,905	98,636
2001	1,83,856	n.a.	n.a.	n.a.	36,758	33,026	1,02,791

Source: Sri Lanka Bureau of Foreign Employment.

The numbers placed by SLBFE do not include migrants who secured employment and travelled abroad on their own. A majority of persons who enter developed countries travel on their own without reference to the SLBFE. Available information including receiving country information indicates that 15,000–25,000 persons migrate annually on their own. A further 5,000–10,000 appear to be leaving the country through undocumented and illegal channels. In addition, an increasing number of students who travel abroad for higher education, estimated at about 5,000, eventually decide to secure employment and residence abroad. Immigration and emigration records documented a negative migration difference of about 30,000–40,000 per year at the end of the 1990s (net negative migration average to 43,600 per year for the period 1991–98). Some of the illegal migration is not captured in these records. These rough calculations indicate that 2,00,000–2,30,000 persons migrate annually for employment and residence abroad.

Illegal Migration

There is no information on illegal migrant transfers and on refugee migration. Information relating to both illegal immigrants and refugee migration will have to be compiled through cooperation with receiving countries. The spate of illegal migrations reported in the press is also indicative of the growing interest and unfulfilled demands amongst those leaving the country for employment and residence. 'Illegal migration is well organized at the demand end. Illegal migrants who go to Italy and Japan are readily absorbed through networks which have been formed to receive them. The networks studied suggest that in all three areas there is an active labour market with a relatively strong demand in the host country' (Appleyard, 1998). According to reports, illegal job agents charge Rs 1,00,000 –5,00,000 to ferry them to their destinations. As some of the asylum seekers and illegal migrants are skilled migrants, it is essential to monitor these flows.

Migration to Selected Countries Based on Host Country Data

Sri Lankan migrants now have access to a wider range of destinations for employment and residence. During the recent past, many new destinations were added which included Malaysia, Singapore, Hong Kong, South Korea, Japan, Taiwan, Maldives, Southern Africa, Cyprus, Greece, Italy, Lebanon and Israel, etc. Migration to Western Europe, Canada, USA, New Zealand and Australia has also increased. Yet, the number migrating to the Middle East will continue to remain high and the Middle East will remain the main source of migrant remittances to Sri Lanka.

Australia

Australia has been a destination for long-term migrants from Sri Lanka. The Australian Census of Population 1991 had disclosed that there were 32,292 Sri Lankan born persons aged 15 and over residing in Australia of whom 19,233 had been employed, 3,326 unemployed and the balance of 9,332 were not in the labour force. Of the employed, 1,565 were administrators and managers, 4,010 were professionals and a further 1,366 were para-professionals. Thus, 6,941 or more than 36 per cent of the employed had been skilled migrants or persons who had acquired professional skills in Australia. A breakdown of the skills background of the unemployed is not available. It is known that a large number of Sri Lankan skilled migrants who have been admitted to settle down are unemployed or under-employed. Australian immigration statistics for 1999–2000 show that 1,280 Sri Lankan migrants have been admitted during the year as settlers. Of them, 700 were skilled migrants, 304 were under the family migration programme and others were refugees and non-programme migrants. The statistics provided in Table 14.2 show that the migration difference of 4,419 is more than thrice the number admitted as immigrants under the settlement programme. Illegal migration to Australia has also increased and several unsuccessful attempts were detected and reported in the press. Thus, the total annual migration to Australia could be about 4,500–5,000 of whom one-third to half are those with professional and sub-professional qualifications.

Canada

The data presented in Table 14.3 shows that 66,535 immigrants have entered Canada during the period 1990–99 at an average rate of 6,650 persons per year. The table shows that the number admitted was high as 12,635 in 1992 which had declined to 3,328 in 1998. The immigrants classified by class of immigrants for the period 1997–99 presented in Table 14.4 shows that 7,300 persons had entered as refugees leaving Sri Lanka. Generally, Sri Lankan migrants are single persons or families with spouse and one child. On this assumption, not less than 1,500 persons who migrated to Canada annually by the end of the 1990s are economically active persons in the prime of their working lives and the majority of them would be those with university degrees who would be classified as skilled migrants (Table 14.5).

Table 14.2

AUSTRALIAN IMMIGRATION STATISTICS—FINANCIAL YEAR 1999–2000: TOTAL MOVEMENTS

	Settler (Arrival/ Departure)	Long-term Resident (Return/ Departure)	Long-term Visitor (Arrival/ Departure)	Short-term Resident (Return/ Departure)	Short-term Visitor (Arrival/ Departure)	Total (Arrival/ Departure)
Arrivals	1,280	484	1,439	21,619	13,892	38,714
Departures	99	448	1,066	19,699	12,983	34,295
Migration	1,181	36	373	1,920	909	4,419

Persons Conferred Australian Citizenship
1990–91	3,271 (2.7%)
1998–99	1,707 (2.2%)
1999–2000	1,832 (2.6%)

Permanent Arrivals
1999–2000	1,089
2000–20001	1,321

Sri Lankan Students Present in Australia
31 December 2000	1,155
30 September 2000	1,144
31 December 2001	926

Source: Department of Immigration and Multicultural Indigenous Affairs, Australia and Australian Bureau of Statistics websites.

Table 14.3

SRI LANKAN IMMIGRANTS ADMITTED TO CANADA, 1990 –99

Year	1990	1991	1992	1993	1994	1995	1996	1997	1998	1999	Total
Number of immigrants	3,106	6,826	12,635	9,103	6,671	8,926	6,151	5,070	3,328	4,719	66,535

Source: Citizenship and Immigration Canada website.

Table 14.4

SRI LANKAN IMMIGRANTS TO CANADA BY CLASS OF IMMIGRANTS, 1997–99

Category	1997	1998	1999	Total
Principal applicants and dependants	5,070	3,328	4,719	13,117
Family class	1,732	643	1,485	3,860
Refugees	2,564	2,130	2,606	7,300
Other class	174	125	49	348

Source: Citizenship and Immigration Canada.

Table 14.5

SRI LANKAN IMMIGRANTS ADMITTED TO CANADA, 1996: AGE PROFILE OF IMMIGRANTS

Age Group	Both Sexes		Male		Female	
	Number	%	Number	%	Number	%
0–4	197	3.1	104	3.4	93	2.8
5–9	515	8.0	267	8.7	248	7.4
10–13	513	8.0	254	8.2	259	7.7
15–19	525	8.2	279	9.0	246	7.3
20–24	636	9.9	297	9.6	339	10.1
25–29	874	13.6	382	12.4	492	14.7
30–34	770	12.0	372	12.1	398	11.9
35–39	621	9.7	317	10.3	304	9.1
40–44	459	7.1	241	7.8	218	6.5
45–49	326	5.1	163	5.3	163	4.9
50–54	232	3.6	92	3.0	140	4.2
55–59	243	3.8	87	2.8	156	4.6
60–64	208	3.2	82	2.7	126	3.8
65+	322	5.0	147	4.8	175	5.2
All ages	6,441	100.0	3,084	100.0	3,357	100.0

Source: Citizenship and Immigration Canada.

New Zealand

Immigration statistics extracted from the New Zealand website shows that 7,217 Sri Lankan migrants entered New Zealand between 1982–98 (see Table 14.6). Of them, 5,743 migrants entered the country during the period 1992–98. The number of refugees that entered during this period was 424. The number of migrants exceeded

Table 14.6

SRI LANKAN IMMIGRANTS TO NEW ZEALAND, 1982–98

Year	Number of Immigrants	Number of Refugees
1982	16	—
1983	16	—
1984	48	—
1985	49	—
1986	84	—
1987	185	—
1988	277	—
1989	210	—
1990	278	51
1991	311	54
1992	353	18
1993	638	18
1994	1,006	40
1995	1,343	39
1996	1,131	89
1997	541	132
1998	731	88
Total	7,217	529

Source: New Zealand Immigration Service website, http://www.immigration.govt.nz

Table 14.7

Sri Lankan Immigrants Admitted to New Zealand, 2000–2001:
Residence Approvals by Category of Approval

Category of Approval	Number
Business	4
Family	130
General skills	514
Humanitarian	23
Other	1
Refugee	103
Total	775

Source: New Zealand Immigration Service website, http://www.immigration.govt.nz

Table 14.8

New Zealand: Applications for Refugee Status

				Applications				
Year	1990–91	1991–92	1992–93	1993–94	1994–95	1995–96	1996–97	1997–98	1998–99
No.	39	41	14	14	22	18	62	81	51
				Persons Included				
No.	51	54	18	18	40	39	89	132	88

Source: New Zealand Immigration Service website, http://www.immigration.govt.nz

1,300 in 1995 and the annual average for the seven-year period 1992–98 is 820 migrants. Table 14.7 and 14.8 illustrate the position of Sri Lankan migrants to New Zealand. In some families that migrate, both husband and wife are professionals. In the absence of other data for reasons stated earlier, it is possible to assume that approximately 2,000–2,500 migrants who were academically and professionally qualified had taken up residence in New Zealand between 1992 and 1998.

United States

As shown in Table 14.9, during the period 1990–98 nearly 10,000 Sri Lankan immigrants were admitted to the US. Of the 1,085 admitted in 1998, 635 persons had been new arrivals and 450 migrants were adjustments from previous years. Of the 450 admitted in 1998, 39 had entered as students and 130 as temporary workers,

Table 14.9

Sri Lankan Immigrants Admitted to the United States of America

Year	1990	1991	1992	1993	1994	1995	1996	1997	1998	Total
Number of immigrants	976	1,377	1,081	1,109	989	960	1,277	1,128	1,085	9,982

Source: US Department of Justice, and US Immigration and Naturalization Service website, http://www.usdoj.gov

confirming that 39 Sri Lankan students had not returned to Sri Lanka after completing their studies. The occupational background of these immigrants admitted in 1998 show that 185 were professionals and 54 were administrators and managers and others were those in sales, administrative support and craft level occupations. Thus, 240 skilled migrants had obtained domicile in the US in 1998 according to these records.

Table 14.10

IMMIGRANTS ADMITTED TO THE UNITED STATES, 2000

Occupational Group	Number
Professional specialty and technical	199
Executive, administrative and managerial	69
Sales	10
Administrative support	54
Precision, production, craft and repair	12
Operation, fabrication and labourer	8
Farming and fishing	1
Service	56
No occupational information	714
Total	1,123

Source: US Department of Justice, and US Immigration and Naturalization Service website, http://www.usdoj.gov

The information provided in Table 14.10 that about two-thirds of the Sri Lankan immigrants who were admitted to the US had gained admission not on the basis of their occupational and professional backgrounds. The data shows that 268 persons were those with professional, technological, administrative or managerial qualifications. The spouses of most of these persons could themselves be professionally or academically qualified persons which is not reflected in the records. They would have been treated as spouses or other close relatives of the immigrants admitted to the US.

Table 14.11 shows that the number of persons who had been deported from US had increased significantly in the 1990s.

Table 14.11

SRI LANKAN MIGRANTS DEPORTED BY THE UNITED STATES

Year	Total	Criminal	Non-Criminal
1993	9	—	9
1994	13	—	13
1995	13	—	13
1996	45	—	45
1997	119	3	116
1998	135	3	132

Source: US Department of Justice, and US Immigration and Naturalization Service website, http://www.usdoj.gov

Norway

Tables 14.12 to 14.15 indicate the position regarding the Sri Lankan immigrants to Norway.

Table 14.12

SRI LANKAN IMMIGRANTS ADMITTED TO NORWAY AS ON 1 JANUARY1999 AND 1 JANUARY 2000

Immigrant Category	1999	2000
Total Immigrant Population	9,141	9,826
First Generation Immigrants	6,806	7,128
Foreign Born	6,871	7,275
Foreign Citizens	3,662	3,405

Source: Norwegian Directorate of Immigration website, http://www.udi.no

Table 14.13

SRI LANKAN IMMIGRANTS ADMITTED TO NORWAY AND NET MIGRATION, 1997–99

Year	Immigrants	Emigration	Net Migration
1997	366	81	285
1998	418	75	343
1999	403	56	347

Source: Norwegian Directorate of Immigration.

Table 14.14

ASYLUM SEEKERS FROM SRI LANKA ADMITTED TO NORWAY, 1991–2000

Year	1991	1992	1993	1994	1995	1996	1997	1998	1999	2000	Total
Number of asylum seekers	556	403	255	233	90	413	196	173	112	165	2,596

Source: Norwegian Directorate of Immigration.

Table 14.15

NATURALIZATIONS OF SRI LANKAN IMMIGRANTS ADMITTED TO NORWAY, 1977–2000

Total	Annual Average							
1977–2000	77	81	86	91	96	1998	1999	2000
	80	85	90	95	00			
5,977	10	29	34	411	714	531	650	454

Source: Norwegian Directorate of Immigration.

Others

In addition to these destinations and the UK, skilled Sri Lankan workers have migrated in significant numbers to many countries in Western Europe including France, Germany, Italy, Switzerland and the Scandinavian countries. Recently they have migrated to Singapore and West and South African states. There are no reliable sources of data on the dimensions of migration to these countries. The fact that Sri Lanka has a net migration difference of 35,000–45,000 migrants annually, and only a fraction of this can be accounted for as an increase in temporary contract migration which has now practically stabilized, shows that about 25,000–30,000 have been annually seeking long-term employment, employment and residence mainly in the developed countries. Of this number, it is not optimistic to assume that about one-thirds to one-fourth comprise academically and professionally qualified persons who left the country. This means that 6,000–8,000 academically and professionally qualified persons have been taking up employment and residence in the developed countries annually.

BRAIN DRAIN

Adverse effects of migration are the loss of the employed with good skills and experience and the difficulty in filling vacancies in institutions that require high level talent such as universities and research organizations. The loss of high level skills in critical positions not only affect the planned programmes for which they are responsible, they have other adverse effects of loss of employment in complementary skills.

As far as the impact on the receiving country is concerned, the skilled migrants are admitted on the basis of demand for skilled labour and it is usually described as brain gain. In the case of the sending country, it could take the form of brain overflow if the country has reacted to the effects of brain drain and increased the supply and resorted to policies of allowing persons to seek employment abroad. Yet, the sending country should at least receive compensation of the capital invested and recurrent costs incurred in education and training in the production of skills. If there is compensation for the loss of skills produced by the country from the immigration of trained manpower, then it may be worthwhile to attempt to train persons for foreign employment. In the Indian example, the large number of engineers leaving the country has been described as brain overflow.

MIGRATION FROM SELECTED OCCUPATIONS

A few occupations were selected such as engineers, accountants and medical doctors in order to examine the growth in stock of human capital with the additions of output from education and training institutions while emigration and other losses are taking place. These assessments are summarized in the following paragraphs.

Engineers

The outflow of engineers has been continuing since the 1960s at which time the migration was mainly to work and for residence in the UK, the US, Canada and Australia. In the 1970s, migration increased to include developing countries. This was one of the occupations on which the Cabinet Committee on Brain Drain, 1974 focused on and the report disclosed that 275 engineers had left the country between May 1971 and June 1974 causing acute scarcities, especially in the public sector. The prospects for migration increased further in the 1980s and 1990s with opportunities for short-term contract migration in the Middle East and other destinations.

The total number of professionally qualified and graduate engineers registered with the Institute of Engineers Sri Lanka in 1995 was 3,623 and this number had increased to 5,056 by 2000, an increase of 1,433. The output of graduate engineers from the universities in Sri Lanka during this period was 2,641. In addition to these graduates who had qualified in Sri Lanka, there were others who had obtained their qualifications in foreign universities and returned to Sri Lanka. Further, there were others who had completed institution examinations and had been upgraded as engineers. Even if an allowance is made for labour force separations due to retirements and deaths and if that number is equivalent to the output from the latter two sources, it is evident that the migration losses exceed 1,200 engineers during the five-year period 1995–2000, approximately 250 engineers per year.

Accountants

Accountants have been one of the most mobile groups moving out for employment and residence to many destinations. The SLBFE records show that 1,393 accountants had migrated for foreign employment between 1995 and 1999. The Sri Lanka Institute of Chartered Accountants had 2,172 full members enrolled in the Institute in March 2001 and of this number, 600 were Chartered Accountants working abroad. During the period 1995–2000, 653 Chartered Accountants had qualified and entered the profession (Table 14.16).

According to the records there were 1,628 Chartered Accountants in 1995. This shows that over 100 Chartered Accountants had migrated from Sri Lanka during this period assuming that a similar number of accountants (600) were working abroad in 1995 too.

Table 14.16

OUTPUT OF ACCOUNTANTS

	1995	1996	1997	1998	1999	2000	Total
Output ACA	72	89	100	100	179	113	653
Output ICMA	—	110	133	162	153	209	767
Total	72	199	233	262	332	322	1,420
SLBFE migrants	348	201	183	246	415	n.a.	1,393

Sources: (a) Institute of Chartered Accountants of Sri Lanka.
        (b) Sri Lanka Institute of Cost and Management Accountants.
        (c) Sri Lanka Bureau of Foreign Employment.

The registered membership of the Sri Lanka Institute of Cost and Management Accountants increased from 905 members in 1995 to 1,420 members in 2000. Thus, the membership increased by 515 members whereas the total number that qualified during this period amounted to 767 accountants, which means that 252 fully qualified cost and management accountants left the country for overseas employment. Thus, at least 350 fully qualified accountants left the country during the above period. The statistics compiled by SLBFE include partly qualified accountants of these two institutions who had worked in the capacities of assistant accountants and junior accountants. Inclusive of these groups, the total number that migrated is substantially higher, rising to nearly 1,400 during the five-year period 1955–99.

Medical Doctors

A high proportion of medical doctors who have graduated from Sri Lanka had migrated for employment abroad. According to Brain Drain Committee Report of 1974, between 1971 and 1974, 558 medical doctors had left the country which amounted to 17 per cent of the total number of medical doctors in the country. The out-migration of medical doctors for employment has recently declined from these high levels (Table 14.17). According to the records of the Sri Lanka Medical Council the number of medical doctors registered with the Council had increased from 4,182 in 1995 to 7,266 at the end of year 2000. The total number of medical doctors who had graduated from universities in Sri Lanka between 1995–2000 amounted to 3,820. If one were to assume that the inflow of medical doctors who graduate from foreign universities is equivalent to the losses due to deaths and retirements, about 750 medical doctors had been lost through migration between 1995 and 2000. Recently, the Government Medical Officers' Association (GMOA) complained that about six medical doctors were leaving for the developed countries per week and raised the issue of the amount invested in the training of medical doctors which is over Rs 1 million per medical doctor.

Table 14.17

ACADEMICALLY AND PROFESSIONALLY QUALIFIED MIGRANTS, 1995–2000

Occupation	1995	1996	1997	1998	1999	2000	Total
Accountants	348	201	183	246	415	248	1,641
Architects	13	7	12	15	20	10	77
Doctors	34	15	5	9	17	3	83
Engineers	326	202	203	253	333	229	1,546
Librarians	2	1	5	1	6	3	18
Managers	156	134	167	145	242	182	1,026
Programmers	68	67	42	68	100	56	401
Scientists	257	125	115	207	270	—	974
Total	1,204	752	732	944	1,403	731	5,766

Source: Sri Lanka Bureau of Foreign Employment.

LONG-TERM PHENOMENON

International migration was assumed to be a temporary phenomenon. Current population projections had assumed that migration would tail off within 15–20 years. Population projections had assumed that net migration would decline from 45,000 in the 1980s to 35,000 by the end of the 1990s to 25,000 in 2000 and would decline further to 15,000 by 2010. Current migration trends show that the migration flows are unlikely to tail off in the medium term.

A number of factors will contribute towards maintaining high migration flows from Sri Lanka.

- Increase in disparity between employment incomes and earnings in local and foreign employment.
- Slow growth in wages, rising cost of living and poor savings.
- Employment and income insecurity—privatization, restructuring and downsizing resulting in increased job insecurity.
- Inadequate access to higher education—severe competition for degree programmes in engineering, computer science, medicine, law, etc.; delayed admission to university programmes; and students having to accept a field of study other than what they had chosen, etc.
- Government promotion of temporary migration as a short-term measure for reducing unemployment and also to benefit from migrant remittances.
- Social and political unrest in the country.

These and other push factors, combined with the increased opportunities for migration to skilled migrants through relaxation of entry criteria in receiving countries, will maintain high levels of migration. Since the country's future population size would primarily depend on migration assumptions, the population projections should be reviewed.

IMPACT OF MIGRATION

International migration from Sri Lanka has assumed such proportions as to have an impact on many socio-economic conditions. These effects are briefly discussed below.

Demographic Effects

The net migration from Sri Lanka has been negative during the past several decades. Migration has contributed in reducing population growth. A decline in fertility and external migration taken together has contributed in reducing the population growth rate to 1.1–1.4 per cent per annum. The current population projections have assumed that the net outflow would average 25,000 per annum during the years 2000–2005 and would decline to 15,000 per annum between 2006–15. Because of illegal migration, the available statistics are not comprehensive and reliable. Examination of data from other sources show that large numbers are migrating annually to a few selected countries such as Canada, the US, the UK, Australia and New Zealand. It is known that large numbers migrated to Italy and Germany through undocumented channels. Migrants to these destinations are long-term migrants and the majority obtain residence in those countries. In addition to the direct effect of reducing the population, their families would also join them eventually further reducing the population.

Impact on Labour Force

The labour force is estimated to increase annually with net additions of 1,35,000 workers. The current level of new entrants is estimated at 2,75,000 per year and the withdrawals at 1,40,000 (Table 14.18). The present dimensions of migration amounting to 1,90,000–2,20,000 per year with a return migration of 1,70,000 per year are quite large and significant in relation to the components of the labour supply. The majority of female migrants, being reckoned as housewives, would have been out of the labour force. In numerical terms, the annual outflow through migration amounts to 70 per cent of new entrants to the labour force, but net migration which is reckoned to be approximately 30,000–40,000 amounts to about 25 per cent of the net additions to the labour supply.

Table 14.18

LABOUR FORCE COMPONENTS

Labour Force Components	Both Sexes	Male	Female
New entrants	2,75,000	170	105
Withdrawals	1,40,000	80	60
Net additions to the labour force	1,35,000	90	45
Total migrants	1,90,000	75,000	1,15,000
Total return migrants	1,70,000	65,000	1,05,000

Source: Abeykoon (1998) and author's estimates.

Impact on Employment

The principal beneficial impact of migration is withdrawal of surplus labour. In a situation of chronic educated unemployment and under-employment, migration has reduced the pressure on the labour market. There were over 13,500 unemployed graduates who sought entry to the Graduate Placement scheme the government launched in 2000. Labour Force Survey, 2000 data show that 25.8 per cent of the unemployed were GCE O Level qualified and a further 25.3 per cent had GCE A Level or higher qualifications. Migration therefore is a good safety valve. If persons possess skills, then they should be able to find work. Migration reduces the employment creation burden through the following ways:

- Placements vacated by migrant workers become available.
- There is withdrawal of persons who were in employment or actively seeking employment.
- Labour mobility is increased through a replacement of mature workers by younger workers.
- Current levels of wages and salaries are supported and maintained by withdrawal of skilled labour and wages would have suffered without migration.
- Strengthening and expansion of skills development capacities are supported on the basis of migration losses.

The employment policy which is being formulated has accepted foreign employment as a strategy for employment promotion. The current levels of gross outflow for foreign employment of around 1,80,000 annually has contributed to lower intensity of the unemployment problem through withdrawal of surplus labour and also reduction of public protests over the educated unemployment problem. The large-scale outflow of skilled and semi-skilled workers had increased the opportunities for absorption of the unemployed and under-employed to the positions left behind by the migrants. The migrants' earnings have also helped to soften the lack of employment incomes of the unemployed from remittances effected by parents and siblings.

Impact on Households

Unlike in the case of temporary migration for employment, the impact of brain drain on the family and the household is mainly negative in Sri Lanka. The degree of the negative impact depends on the extent to which family resources were utilized in the education and training of the migrant and the degree to which the household was dependent on his earnings. Where the migrant had mainly utilized the resources of the state for his education, which is the position in a majority of cases, the state has to bear the costs and wastage. The parental burden depends on where the migrant obtained his education; if he had had his education in a private school or abroad, in fee charging institutions then the family would have had to use their savings or even proceeds from sale of assets for his education. Except for those families that could support the education of their children abroad without an adverse impact on their welfare, which is only a small proportion of parents, other households that educate their offspring abroad are generally disadvantaged by this investment without any immediate returns by way of remittances.

Migrant Remittances

The principal benefit the country receives from external migration is through migrant remittances. The total value of remittances recorded as private transfers had amounted to Rs 87,697 million or US $1,160 million in 2000. About 95 per cent of private transfers are composed of migrant remittances. The total value of private transfers have grown from US $136.7 million in 1980 to US$363.6 million in 1990 to $727 million in 1995 to the current level of US $1.16 thousand million. These numbers in fact underestimate the total value of migrant transfers. The amounts excluded the value of goods and articles brought in by the returning migrants who now exceed 1,50,000 per year as well as the value of money in the form of foreign currency and bank drafts brought in by them when they return to Sri Lanka. These amounts are recorded as receipts from tourism. In US dollar terms, migrant remittances have grown at the rate of 10.3 per cent per year in the 1980s and 12.3 per cent per year in the 1990s.

The Middle East has contributed to more than 60 per cent of the remittances. The European Union and the far East are relatively new sources and taken together, they contribute to around 20 per cent of the total value of the remittances. With the increase in migration to Korea, Hong Kong, Japan and Taiwan, which are more recent destinations, the remittances from far East Asia has increased. Similarly, there has been large-scale migration, some of it through illegal channels, to Italy, Cyprus and Greece in addition to the other European countries which have raised the volume of remittances from the European Union region.

Despite there being a large migrant, skilled, professional population in North America, the contribution of North America in total remittances amounts to 7 per cent. This amount includes the amounts sent in by migrant residents elsewhere through their bank accounts in North American banks and the private transfers effected by private institutions and organizations resident in North America to the non-governmental organizations(NGOs) in Sri Lanka. The private transfers from Australia had amounted to US $12 million or 1.2 per cent of total remittances (Table 14.19).

Table 14.19

PRIVATE REMITTANCES BY REGION OF ORIGIN

Origin	US Dollars (million)		Rupees (million)		Percentage Share	
	1995	2000	1995	2000	1995	2000
Middle East	423	730	23,567	55,252	58.2	62.9
North America	58	78	3,233	5,893	8.0	6.7
South and Central America	7	11	405	834	1.0	0.9
EU 108	156	5,991	11,782	14.8	13.5	
Eastern Europe	4	4	202	333	0.5	0.4
Europe Other	37	59	2,065	4,458	5.1	5.1
South Asia	5	8	262	606	0.6	0.7
South East Asia	15	22	810	1,655	2.0	1.9
Far East Asia	55	68	3,086	5,118	7.6	5.9
Australia	7	12	400	894	1.0	1.0
North Africa					0.0	
Central Africa					0.0	
South Africa	0		15		0.0	
Other	8	12	446	872	1.1	1.0
Total	727	1,160	40,482	87,697	100.0	100.0

Source: Central Bank of Sri Lanka.

As much as 75 to 80 per cent of remittances have been sent by migrants who had obtained temporary employment abroad. The need to support the families left behind and because of the short duration of stay abroad, these migrants have not had other options but to repatriate their savings. The current facilities offered which include non-resident foreign currency (NRFC) accounts, customs duty concessions and opportunity to purchase goods and articles at duty free shops have been effective in mobilizing the savings from temporary migrants. The temporary migrants have no opportunities for integration and domicile in the countries of migration in the Middle East and the far East, etc. Therefore, they have no option but to repatriate their savings as remittances on the conclusion of their travel abroad. These inducements had made it possible to raise migrant remittances to the current level of US $1.1 billion.

The facilities offered that are currently available locally are insufficient to attract investments from long-term migrants. The facilities available to them in their countries of employment and residence are more attractive than what is available here. In view of the change in the profile of migration it would be possible to attract private transfers if appropriate policies are established and inducements are offered to them.

As stated earlier, the principal benefits the country could receive from migration are migrant remittances. In the case of Sri Lanka, there is no evidence to confirm that there are significant inflows of remittances from migrants employed and domiciled in developed countries. It is those who leave for the market economies of Europe, North America and Australia that have had the privilege of receiving free tertiary education and training in Sri Lanka. In fact, some of these persons have also had the privilege of receiving further education and training in the developed countries supported by technical assistance or by their employers. The strengthening of academic and professional education to current levels was necessary to meet the local demand and migration losses. Although the additional output may not have been fully utilized, the opportunity costs of the investments and expenditure incurred in producing high level manpower lost through brain drain or brain overflows has been considerable. It had not been hitherto possible for the country to receive benefits in the form of remittances or investments from the migratory flows of the highly skilled, academically, professionally or technologically qualified persons who had left the country.

First, there are no on-going programmes which have attempted to utilize their services and investments for the benefit of the country. The needs and aspirations of these migrants are different from those who migrate on short duration contracts as temporary migrants to the Middle East and more recently to Singapore, Hong Kong, Malaysia, Maldives, South Korea, etc. The migrants to the market economies in the west expect at least equally favourable, if not more favourable, terms for their investments than what they could receive in their countries of migration. It had not been possible to match even the low rates of interest in foreign currency deposits that they could receive in the countries of domicile for investing in Sri Lanka. These migrants have not been interested in rupee investments for several reasons including the devaluation of the rupee, unattractive returns on investments and the uncertain economic, political and security situation. There has been no attempts made to ascertain the type and kind of investments that the Sri Lankan migrants would agree to consider to invest a part of their savings in Sri Lanka. They are likely to ask for some guarantees on transfer of capital and profits out of the country depending on their needs. Assets such as land in urban centres which appreciate and agricultural land could be some investments the migrants may favourably consider.

The profile of migration has also changed recently with the large-scale migration of skilled and semi-skilled workers to many countries including Italy and traditional countries of migration such as Canada, the US and Australia. Unlike in the migration flows which occurred in the 1970s and 1980s, the large majority of migrants are drawn from low and lower middle income households who have the responsibility of meeting some of the expenses of their families and close relatives left behind. There is evidence that migrant remittances from Western Europe had increased recently.

In view of budgetary constraints and public debt, it is opportune to explore the possibilities of attracting part of the savings of these migrants for investments in Sri Lanka. They might be interested in acquiring land in strategic places where land prices would remain buoyant. They might also accept high yielding investments with government guarantees. As this large group has hitherto remained untapped, it is essential to review inducements and incentives offered to the migrants. In order to mobilize these long-term migrants, it will be necessary to establish contact with the migrant communities. Such a dialogue would show the avenues and facilities that would be attractive to them. It is evident that these migrant communities who are mainly professionals would look for certain forms of investment. They may not be attracted by investments which would require regular and constant attention on their part with the services of investment advisers. It is possible to assume that even at present, they are able to achieve returns at the upper end of the spectrum generally with the help of good investment advisory services. This will require a review of tax and fiscal policy relating to investments by nationals resident abroad and an identification of issues and constraints that currently discourage repatriation of their savings.

Prospects for Migration

The external environment has changed in favour of migration of skilled labour. The US immigration policy, which allowed inflow of talent, is viewed as having contributed towards its recent continued economic growth and prosperity. Many developed countries are in the process of relaxing immigration controls to admit highly skilled labour. Canada, Australia and the UK have allowed entry on the basis of industry needs. Singapore provides tuition free education on the condion that students, on completion of their studies, work in Singapore for a contracted duration.

The events of 11 September 2001 in the US and the slowing down of economic recovery have currently lowered the demand for skilled manpower in the countries of migration. The screening of migrants from developing countries could also affect the pace of migration. Once the demand picks up, the opportunities for the migration of a wide range of skills will continue. Therefore, opportunities for migration for employ-ment and residence are likely to increase in the medium term.

The manpower demand projections in countries of migration which can be ac-cessed show that the range of skills have widened to encompass categories that include middle and craft level skills. The occupations which will be considered for visa pur-poses released by the immigration authorities of Canada and New Zealand include bricklayers, carpenters, plumbers, drain layers, nurses, pharmacists, hospital assistants to professionals and managers.

The Sri Lankan migrants to these countries have by and large been restricted to professionals and a smaller proportion of middle level technicians. Prospective migrants from Sri Lanka in craft level occupations and middle level administrative and techni-cal occupations have not been able to gain access to these opportunities for two main reasons—inadequate English language skills and trade certification.

As there are also plans to utilize foreign employment as a strategy for alleviating unemployment and under-employment, it would be cost effective to upgrade the skills of craft and middle level technician categories to meet the level of skills required in the countries of migration. Until recently, skill formation at these levels have been mainly on the job. The arrangements made for skill upgrading and certification to match the occupational requirements of the skill importing countries would help to open up the already existing opportunities at a much higher level of remuneration than those that are available in the Middle East. The opening up of these opportunities would also reduce the need to leave the country through illegal channels undertaking hazardous journeys.

Clandestine Migration

The issue of clandestine and illegal migration was recently highlighted in the press after the heads of foreign missions in Sri Lanka raised it with the government. Accord-ing to press reports, the foreign missions had requested the government to take action against the persons engaged in smuggling migrants and had named some of the persons engaged in large-scale human smuggling operations. The number of illegal migrants had increased substantially during the past few years, but no data is available on the dimensions of illegal migration.

Clandestine migration can be categorized under two broad groups. The first cat-egory comprise persons who enter countries utilizing false or forged travel documents. Sri Lankan migrants had been using false travel documents to enter the countries of destination for about one-and-a-half decades. They often travel to an intermediate destination or destinations to sort out the documentation needed to enter and legit-imize their stay in the host country. Thus, there are a large number of Sri Lankan migrants who have entered West European countries through these means. Persons having contacts with human smuggling operators abroad have assisted these illegal migrants.

Migrants utilizing the services of human smuggling operators for illegal entry are a relatively new phenomenon in Sri Lanka. Agents who have contacts with human smuggling operators in the countries of migration arrange illegal migration in fishing trawlers and other vessels. Italy, Greece and Australia have been the more popular destinations. (Migrants are required to pay the total fees up front which amounts from Rs 3,50,000 to Rs 5,00,000 to destinations such as Italy and Australia.) These attempts have come to light when they were caught before departure and in seaports enroute to the destinations. Lives have been lost at sea in attempting these journeys. There are many cases pending against smugglers and those who attempted to migrate and were caught in their attempts to leave the country.

These clandestine migrations have continued and expanded due to two or three reasons. First, low incomes and savings, and poor job prospects have fuelled migration flows. The earlier easy entry as refugees and acceptance of claims of refugee status had given the impression that migrants could get admitted easily to the country of migration. Industry was willing to accept workers without checking their immigration status as the demand for these skills had outstripped the supply of nationals willing to take up these jobs at the operating wage levels. The demand for skilled and semi-skilled workers, which outstripped the supply, had created openings for human trafficking operators to procure workers and supply them to industry. In Italy, the mafia are said to be involved in the procurement of immigrant workers. In fact, it is said that illicit immigrants enter Italy illegally, but are able to gain legitimacy and after some time obtain rights for domicile. What had been observed is that the number of destinations has also increased recently. Initially the destinations were mainly to Europe and North America and to a lesser extent to Japan and South Korea. The unfulfilled demand for migration opportunities will continue to support illegal migration. The failed attempt to smuggle 123 illegal immigrants to Italy reported in the press revealed that the particular smuggler had successfully carried out the transfer of six previous boatloads to Italy (*Daily News*, 16 April 2001 and *Lakbima*, 16 April 2001). *Daily News* of 19 April 2001 reported another case of 15 illegal immigrants who had landed in Western Australia. On 30 May 2001, it was reported that 24 Sri Lankan illegal migrants who were on their way to Germany were taken into custody by Russian authorities in Kazakhstan.

Falsification of travel documents and personal identification documents is carried out on a large scale to support illegal migration. Birth and marriage certificates are falsified to lower the age of the migrant and fresh travel documents are processed to hide duration of residence in countries where such restrictions exist. As these prospective migrants do not want to contradict themselves, personnel records and identification data maintained by government institutions would also be falsified.

As mentioned earlier, the heads of foreign missions have urged the government to take action against these smugglers operating here. Apart from the risk taken by the migrants and infringement laws, there are several other concerns. First, a significant part of the fee paid by the migrants that comes to around $5,000 is remitted out of the country to the shippers and the human smuggling operators abroad. Second, these illegal migrants affect the employment prospects, social recognition and acceptance of those who had migrated to the countries of employment and are domiciled as expatriate workers. Third, this illicit human trafficking also tarnishes the government's image.

RETURN MIGRATION

Return migration can be grouped as (a) temporary migrants returning home after a brief period of overseas employment and (b) long-term migrants returning home for personal reasons. There is no system of monitoring return migration and data on return migration and re-integration of migrants are particularly poor. Earlier studies (conducted in the 1980s) have shown that the average duration of employment abroad was about two to two-and-a-half years for temporary migrants. Assuming that the duration of stay has increased say to about three years, the dimensions of returned migration would be about 1,70,000 annually. According to available information, re-entry to employment and type of employment depends on the skill category.

Approximately 60 per cent of migrants were females who had migrated for domestic employment. There is no reliable data on the proportion of the females who sought employment on their return to Sri Lanka. Many female migrants who returned become housewives; others seek re-employment as domestic workers and a significant proportion attempt to re-migrate. The majority of semi-skilled and skilled workers re-enter the crafts and trades they practiced before migration. Most persons in professional, technical, and clerical occupations who migrated were from the public sector. They cannot re-join the state sector unless they had been granted leave, because qualification restrictions on re-entry etc. As a result, many of them continue to work abroad as long as they can and attempt to engage in self-employment on their return. The prospects for entering into business and service activities are relatively more attractive to returning professionals.

Most skills acquired by migrants are not used on their return, which is wastage of new skills acquired. The differences in technologies used abroad often make it difficult to adopt them in the work place.

In view of the present job situation, where the private sector could still draw its high level personnel from the state sector and from those returning after their higher education abroad for the positions that arise which has hitherto not been large, the opportunities that would be available to returning migrants are limited. There will not be any significant return migration of professionals employed in the developed countries until the jobs and income situation improves. There is a new interest in utilizing the investment funds with the Sri Lankan migrants abroad and such a programme could yield better results.

The return migration of long-term Sri Lankan migrants who had retired from employment and receive pensions or investment incomes do not exert pressure on the labour market. Many countries operate schemes for the admission of migrants who have access to investment funds. In view of the country's foreign exchange situation, the promotion of return migration of those with access to regular foreign incomes is beneficial.

PROTECTION OF MIGRANT WORKERS ABROAD

The protection of migrant workers employed abroad has been a major issue. The active involvement of the government in promoting labour migration, with the objectives of lowering unemployment and gaining access to migrant remittances, casts a greater burden on the government. The large-scale migration of women for domestic work and other unskilled work, where working conditions are unregulated, have resulted in the continuous reporting of a large number of cases of infringement of terms and conditions, harassment and abuse of workers. The SLBFE has introduced a number of measures to assist the temporary migrant workers including registration with the Bureau, appointment of labour attaches in the receiving countries, intervention in labour disputes and repatriation.

Contract labour migration is different from permanent emigration. The labour contracts specify, among other things, the duration of stay in the country and some migrants have been prosecuted for over staying, even though they had secured re-employment. Many cases have been reported of migrants being stranded as their contracts have not been honoured. Several countries have imposed restrictions on recruitment of females for domestic employment abroad. The severe competition for available placements by foreign employment agencies in the labour exporting countries had resulted in a deterioration of terms and conditions and reduction of remuneration. The recruitment of women for domestic employment and unskilled work through reputed agencies that guarantee good terms and conditions of employment would reduce the current problems of harassment and their being stranded.

POLICY TO MANAGE THE BRIAN DRAIN

Current Government Policy

Government policy has been modified from the earlier regulatory phase and now promotes migration for foreign employment. Sri Lanka thus assumes the role of a skills exporting country. The current government policy initiatives on migration and brain drain are based primarily on two or three considerations:

(a) a need to minimize the impact of an acute unemployment problem especially afflicting educated youth;

(b) a need to maximize migrant remittances through export of surplus labour; and

(c) difficulties of adopting a separate policy for the migration of highly skilled professionals from unskilled and low level skills that have been leaving the country mainly for short-term employment to the Middle East and other destinations.

The current policies have been formulated to promote temporary migration of un-skilled and semi-skilled labour and it has become difficult for the government to adopt a contrary policy towards highly skilled workers on the grounds of equity or any other considerations.

There are two main considerations which make it disadvantageous to encourage migration of academically and professionally qualified persons. It is generally the most skilled persons who are either in senior positions or in lucrative employment who leave the country for foreign employment. The migrations of such persons do not help in the absorption of any small surpluses that currently exist in the professions, who could only be employed at the recruitment grade. Second, it is the general perception and under-standing that highly skilled persons who migrate to developed countries do not ordi-narily repatriate their savings as migrant remittances. Thus, from the point of view of employment and migrant remittances, there are no direct benefits accruing to the country through the migration of professionals to developed countries, except possibly to improve the labour market situation where there are some labour surpluses that had arisen in some specific skill categories.

The current policies on return migration are, for all practical purposes, directed towards temporary contract oversees migration. The government has however intro-duced several incentives to mobilize migrant remittances, which are of special interest to highly skilled migrants who return to Sri Lanka, though they may not be so attrac-tive to those who are residents in developed countries. These include permission to maintain NRFC accounts in commercial banks in Sri Lanka, the provision of tax free interest on such accounts and their utilization for the purchase of any item without exchange control approval.

There are also ad hoc incentives to encourage return migration of talent. The provision of dual citizenship to Sri Lankan nationals who relinquished their Sri Lankan citizenship when they obtained citizenship in the host countries is one such facility specially directed towards professionals who emigrated. The avoidance of double taxa-tion agreements entered into with many countries including the UK, the US, Canada, Australia, etc., is another incentive provided to the returned migrants. This concession allows the returned migrants to benefit from the lower tax regime in Sri Lanka. Fur-ther, the rupee has been devalued frequently, so residing in Sri Lanka is attractive for returnees who are in receipt of income in foreign currency from their oversees invest-ments and employment incomes.

Concluding Remarks and Suggestions

Sri Lanka has accepted the position that it would be difficult to retain its high level manpower in a situation where there is an international demand and market for highly skilled personnel as it cannot compete and offer comparable remuneration and other terms and conditions available in the host countries. The free market economic policies adopted since 1977 and globalization have also contributed to the migration of highly skilled persons.

The ongoing conflict in the North and the East, political instability and governance issues along with unattractive wages have been push factors which have made it difficult to retain skilled persons who can find alternative overseas employment. These conditions have operated as negative influences on the return of young persons who proceeded overseas for higher education and skill acquisition. In these circumstances, brain drain from Sri Lanka will have to be accepted as a medium-term phenomenon. Accordingly, the country will have to formulate strategies to meet the effects of skilled migration. Some of these strategies are given below.

Strengthening Higher Education

The strengthening of higher education and training and increasing the capacities in university degree programmes have minimized the adverse effects of brain drain and prevented skill shortages from disrupting development programmes. However, the losses at the upper middle and senior positions as well as in scarce specializations will continue to remain an issue.

Compiling Labour Market Information and Adjusting Skilled Manpower Supply

Among the other strategies to minimize any adverse impact of brain drain are the obtaining and assessing of information on emerging markets, the skill requirements in demand, location, dimensions and timing. The government should respond to them quickly by adjusting training capacities (Hoffman, 1997).

Strengthen Migration Data Base

The statistics compiled by SLBFE exclude the large numbers who travel on their own without reference to the SLBFE, having organized their employment through recruiting agents in the receiving countries. SLBFE also does not cover those persons who travel for education and residence abroad. The current border control documents used by the Department of Immigration and Emigration do not contain information to categorize persons by purpose of travel and to identify migrants who leave the country. By the inclusion of a few particulars into the embarkation and disembarkation cards on residency status, purpose of travel, final destination, type of visas endorsed, intended duration of stay abroad, highest educational and professional attainments, anticipated date of return and other details, it will be possible to compile valuable data including information on brain drain (United Nations, 1985).

Bilateral Arrangements to Share Migration Data with Host Countries

Assistance and cooperation from receiving countries are essential to compile statistics on international migration. As Sri Lanka has already entered into agreements with a number of West European countries for the return of Sri Lankan nationals who do not have the right to enter or remain in the country of migration, the contacts already established would facilitate information sharing on an ongoing basis on the number of migrants that arrive in the host country and the numbers processed and those waiting at different stages of processing of their applications for residence and domicile. Sri Lanka as a skill losing or exporting country should arrange to have better bilateral arrangements to receive such information from host countries on a routine basis.

Remittances

The current volume of migrant remittances exceeds US $1 billion and it is therefore important to have reliable data on migrant remittances which is a major source of foreign exchange to the country. The system of records that are maintained in commercial banks on the advice of the Central Bank of Sri Lanka will have to be reviewed, and information required for policy purposes should be collected by strengthening the system.

Mobilizing Remittances from Skilled Migrants

Unlike in the case of labour migration for contract employment where the migrant repatriates savings in the form of remittances, the general impression is that skilled migrants to developed countries do not repatriate significant migrant remittances. Transfers of remittances by skilled migrants to developed countries have not been investigated. In view of the increasing importance of high level migration and because of the scale of their employment earnings, savings and investments and the remittances they could make, their investment behaviour should be the subject of study and research.

Enlisting Support of Sri Lankan Expatriate Communities

Some ad hoc attempts have been made by the government to mobilize Sri Lankan expatriate communities to support development initiatives and to contribute to selected projects. But these contacts have not been maintained and continued. Suitable schemes will have to be worked out in consultation with the Sri Lankan expatriate communities to involve their participation in schemes that will be mutually beneficial.

REFERENCES

Abeykoon, A.T.P.L (1998), *Demographic Projections for Sri Lanka,* Colombo: Population Information Centre.

Appleyard, Reginald (1998), *Emigration Dynamics in Developing Countries: Volume II: South Asia,* Geneva: International Organization for Migration.

Central Bank of Sri Lanka (1998), *Economic Progress of Independent Sri Lanka 1948–1998,* Colombo.

Hoffman, Eivind (1997), 'Administrative Records and Surveys as Basis for Statistics on International Labour Migration', *International Statistical Review*, 65(2): 221-246.

Korale, Raja B.M., G.D.C. Gunapala, I.M.K. Ilangasinghe, S. Weerasinghe, N. Rajapakse, P.S. Mathucumarana and I. Premaratne (1985a), *Foreign Employment: Sri Lanka Experience*, Colombo: Ministry of Plan Implementation.

Sri Lanka Bureau of Foreign Employment (1999), *Statistical Handbook of Migration 1999*, Colombo: The Bureau.

Sri Lanka University Grants Commission (2000), *Sri Lanka University Statistics 2000*, Colombo.

United Nations (1985), 'Consolidated Statistics of All International Arrivals and Departures', *A Technical Report*, New York: UN.

SELECT READINGS

Beine, Michel, Frederic Docquier and Hillel Rapoport (1999), 'Brain Drain and Economic Growth: Theory and Evidence', Seminar 19th-20th March, University of Versailles, St Quentin en Yvelines.

Central Bank of Sri Lanka (2000), *Annual Report 1999*, Colombo.

Egerton, Muriel (2000), 'Monitoring Contemporary Student Flows and Characteristics: Secondary Analysis Using the Labour Force Survey and the General Household Survey', *Journal of the Royal Statistical Society Series A* 163, Part 1: 63-80.

GOSL (1974), *Report of the Cabinet Committee Inquiring into the Problem of Technologically, Professionally and Academically Qualified Personnel Leaving Sri Lanka*, Govt. Printer, Colombo (Sessional Paper X-1974).

Gunawardena, C. (2001), 'Faculty Culture as a Framework for Analysing the Quality of University Teachers in Sri Lanka', Colombo: J.E. Jayasuriya Memorial Foundation.

ILO (1991), *Employment, Manpower and Labour in Sri Lanka: A Sectoral Review Report*, Geneva: ILO.

Jayatissa, R.A. (1986), 'Worker Remittances into Sri Lanka from Abroad: A Preliminary Study', *Upanathi*, 1 July: 239-256.

Korale, R.B.M. and I.M. Karunawathie (1981), *Migration of Sri Lankans for Employment Abroad*, Colombo: Ministry of Plan Implementation.

Korale, Raja B.M. et al. (1985b), *Dimensions of Sri Lankan Returned Migration*, Colombo: Ministry of Plan Implementation.

Marga Institute (1996), *A Study on Brain Drain from Sri Lanka: Final Report*, Colombo: Marga Institute.

Ministry of Finance and Planning/Asian Development Bank (2000), *Advancing Knowledge and Skills for Development and Competitiveness: The Tertiary Education Strategy*, Colombo.

Nigam, Shyam B.L. (1988), *Data requirements and Sources of Information on International Labour Migration: A Review of Existing Situation and Suggestions for Improving Data Base*, New Delhi: ILO/ARTEP.

Resources Development Consultants Ltd (1995), *Study 3: Migrant Workers: Literature Survey and Identification of data needs and policy actions*, Draft report, Colombo: Ministry of Finance, Planning, Ethnic Affairs and National Integration.

Rodrigo, Chandra and R.A. Jayatissa (1988), *Maximising Benefits from Labour Migration: Sri Lanka*, New Delhi: ILO/ARTEP.

Sri Lanka Ministry of Health, *Annual Health Bulletin 1997*, Colombo.

Sri Lanka Parliamentary Debates, *Official Report*, 2001. Volume 134, No. 1, Colombo: Government Publication Bureau.

Sri Lanka, Friedrich-Ebert-Stiftung (1989), *Sri Lankan Migrant Labour: Report of Workshop held at the Sri Lanka Foundation Institute,* 4-6 April 1989, SLFI, Colombo.

Sri Lanka, Department of Census and Statistics (1999), *Quarterly Report of the Sri Lanka Labour Force Survey: Third Quarter, 1999,* Colombo.

Philip, Martin, Andrew Mason and Toshikazu Nagayama (eds), (1996), 'The Dynamics of Labour Migration in Asia: Special Issue 1996', *Asian and Pacific Migration Journal,* 5: 163-366.

United Nations (1986), *National data sources and programmes for implementing the United Nations recommendations on statistics of international migration,* New York: UN.

Wickramasekara, Piyasiri (1993), *The Gulf Crisis and South Asia: Studies on the Economic Impact,* New Delhi: UN/ARTEP.

Appendix

Table 14.1A

ARRIVALS AND DEPARTURES AND MIGRATION DIFFERENCE

Year	Arrivals	Departures	Migration Difference	Indians Repat./Dep.	SLBFE Est Total
1952	16,230	17,587	−1,357		
1953	14,061	14,400	−339		
1954	14,031	14,467	−436		
1955	13,946	14,426	−480		
1956	16,320	17,917	−1,597		
1957	18,024	17,902	122		
1958	17,445	19,689	−2,244		
1959	22,443	22,885	−442		
1960	22,041	22,047	−6		
1961	19,386	20,518	−1,132		
1962	15,436	16,617	−1,181		
1963	14,786	15,970	−1,184		
1964	12,582	13,417	−835		
1965	11,385	13,088	−1,703	409	
1966	21,190	23,098	−1,908	1,276	
1967	28,008	29,665	−1,657	2,585	
1968	29,775	32,157	−2,382	1,484	
1969	28,153	30,979	−2,826	4,842	
1970	26,989	28,015	−1,026	9,125	
1971	21,049	24,756	−3,707	24,077	
1972	26,624	32,971	−6,347	31,249	1,705
1973	35,188	42,305	−7,117	39,138	
1974	38,874	44,833	−5,959	42,687	
1975	46,999	53,865	−6,866	22,867	1,039
1976	46,442	53,322	−6,880	44,249	529
1977	52,992	66,900	−13,908	38,148	5,633
1978	1,02,142	1,17,075	−14,933	28,112	8,074
1979	1,00,603	1,22,197	−21,594	22,360	25,875
1980	98,736	1,37,797	−39,061	17,831	28,644
1981	1,42,427	1,85,035	−42,608	24,058	57,447
1982	1,62,036	2,14,466	−52,430	28,272	61,468
1983	1,80,729	2,44,955	−64,226	22,327	65,771
1984	2,27,389	2,83,290	−55,901	32,019	70,375
1985	2,19,401	2,38,577	−19,176	38,034	75,303

Year	Arrivals	Departures	Migration Difference	Indians Repat./Dep.	SLBFE Est Total
1986	2,20,130	2,28,925	−8,795	31,557	80,572
1987	2,16,635	2,57,207	−40,572	15,817	86,212
1988	2,44,356	2,97,677	−53,321	19,063	93,109
1989	2,58,221	2,84,765	−26,544	11,665	1,00,558
1990	3,04,011	2,96,080	7,931	12,199	1,09,608
1991	2,90,512	3,70,371	−79,859	2,909	1,59,505
1992	3,39,109	4,20,749	−81,640	3,639	1,24,494
1993	3,71,510	4,13,548	−42,038	4,134	1,29,076
1994	4,22,367	4,48,437	−26,070	n.a.	1,30,027
1995	4,59,441	5,04,420	−44,979	n.a.	1,72,489
1996	4,88,055	4,94,258	−6,203	n.a.	1,62,576
1997	4,82,487	5,11,827	−29,340	n.a.	1,50,283
1998	4,81,793	5,18,050	−36,257	n.a.	1,59,816
1999	5,09,761	4,96,964	12,797	n.a.	1,79,114

Source: Labour Economics Series (1992), Colombo: Institute of Policy Studies, Department of Immigration and Emigration and SLBFE.

Table 14.2A

OCCUPATIONAL DISTRIBUTION OF THE EMPLOYED POPULATION 1953–86

(figures in thousands, percentages in brackets)

Major Occupational Groups	Census 1953	Census 1963	Census 1971	LF &SES 1981/82	LF & SES 1985/86
Professional, technical	113.6	142.7	178.5	269.2	272.9
& related workers	(3.8)	(4.5)	(4.9)	(5.5)	(5.3)
Administrative and	28.8	32.9	14.0	25.4	26.4
managerial workers	(0.9)	(1.0)	(0.4)	(0.5)	(0.5)
Clerical and related	103.3	110.4	186.1	274.1	280.5
workers	(3.5)	(3.7)	(5.1)	(5.6)	(5.5)
Sales workers	221.2	212.2	272.4	396.0	442.0
	(7.4)	(6.6)	(7.5)	(8.2)	(8.6)
Service workers	439.5	359.6	198.0	265.4	241.5
	(14.7)	(8.1)	(5.4)	(5.5)	(4.7)
Agricultural, animal	1,536.1	1,653.6	1,782.1	2,191.2	2,438.3
husbandry & forestry	(51.3)	(51.7)	(48.8)	(45.2)	(47.5)
workers, fishermen					
& hunters					
Production & related	488.3	739.7	926.4	1,415.4	1,420.9
workers, transport	(16.3)	(23.1)	(25.4)	(24.2)	(27.7)
equipment operators &					
labourers					
Workers not classified	62.5	40.6	91.5	14.0	9.2
	(2.1)	(1.3)	(2.5)	(0.3)	(0.2)
All occupational groups	29,93.3	3,199.7	3,649.0	4,851.4	5,131.7
Percentage	(100.0)	(100.0)	(100.0)	(100.0)	(100.0)

Source: Korale, A Statistical Overview of Employment & Unemployment Trends.

Table 14.3A

ESTIMATES OF CURRENTLY EMPLOYED SENIOR OFFICIALS AND MANAGERS
AND PROFESSIONALS, 1990–2000

Year	Total Employed	Senior Officials and Managers	Professionals	Technicians and Associate Professionals
1990	5,047,354	22,360	2,32,655	1,60,716
1991	5,015,519	39,753	2,29,843	1,60,509
1992	4,962,105	1,20,852	2,54,983	1,58,049
1993	5,201,474	74,362	3,09,453	1,94,130
1994	5,281,273	70,855	2,78,979	1,71,716
1995	5,357,109	81,871	2,96,289	1,80,941
1996	5,537,402	70,829	3,10,985	2,16,449
1997	5,607,881	92,763	3,05,298	2,38,049
1998	6,049,238	88,334	3,25,520	2,61,607
1999	6,139,713	89,410	3,50,440	3,10,846
2000	6,307,794	76,223	3,22,844	3,05,606

Source: Department of Census and Statistics, Sri Lanka Labour Force Surveys.

Table 14.4A

STATISTICS ON CONTRACT MIGRATION

Year	All Migrants	Professional		Middle Level		Clerical + Related		Skilled		Unskilled		Housemaid	
		Both Sexes	Female	Both Sexes	Female	Both Sexes	Female	Both Sexes	Female	Both Sexes	Female	Both Sexes	Female
1991	64,983	155	7	898	80	1,293	101	16,249	8,894	11,431	2,537		34,857
1992	44,652	271	10	2,475	431	0		11,348	4,530	8,466	2,096		22,092
1993	48,753	479	14	1,030	77	1,813	206	12,364	4,652	8,827	2,411		24,240
1994	60,168	262	18	833	46	1,559	151	12,586	5,433	8,824	2,019		36,104
1995	1,72,489	878	41	2,495	421	4,594	506	27,165	7,734	23,497	3,906		1,13,860
1996	1,62,576	599	43	1,945	309	3,371	477	24,447	4,888	21,735	3,268		1,10,479
1997	1,50,283	573	39	1,639	251	3,639	571	24,578	8,723	20,485	3,718		99,429
1998	1,59,816	695	40	2,980	383	4,896	842	31,787	9,665	34,109	9,670		85,349
1999	1,79,114	1,217	78	3,224	433	6,196	940	37,346	12,926	43,421	13,523		1,79,114

Source: Sri Lanka Bureau of Foreign Employment, 1999.

Table 14.5A

INTAKE AND OUTPUT OF UNIVERSITY GRADUATES BY PROGRAMME

Intake and Output in University Programmes: 1995, 1999 and 2000

Programme/ Course	Intake			Enrolment			Output		
	1995	1999	2000	1995	1999	2000	1995	1998	1999
Arts	2,589	3,993	3,865	10,492	13,230	15,305	1,590	2,764	3,613
Management	633	1,433	1,425	—	5,797	6,865	62	997	741
Commerce	810	924	935	5,211	3,653	4,278	285	571	530
Law	210	193	846	798	140	161	325		
Science	1,103	2,764	2,671	5,257	6,315	8,021	844	1,160	1,418
Medicine	839	893	896	4,314	5,280	5,556	442	897	1,049
Dental	66	78	91	424	366	358	66	68	70
Vet. Medicine	33	82	91	298	324	387	37	50	35
Agriculture	279	670	646	1,365	1,896	2,281	226	384	298
Engineering	653	738	875	2,703	3,632	4,129	458	615	631
Architecture	53	58	56	331	140	158	23	63	46
Quan. Surveying	24	53	61	0	153	163	33	64	31
Total	7,279	11,896	11,805	31,241	41,584	48,296	4,206	7,794	8,787

Source: University Grants Commission, 2000.

Table 14.6A

OUTPUT OF UNIVERSITY GRADUATES OF THE UNIVERSITIES IN SRI LANKA

Year	Arts	Commerce	Management	Law	Science	Medicine	Dentistry	Vet. Med.	Agriculture	Engineering	Arch.	Quan. S.	Total	CBSL
1990	1,759	772	494	88	814	360	27	34	175	454	39		4,522	4,522
1991	1,983	602	318	98	1,030	401	42	31	217	355	61	15	5,379	5,386
1992	1,620	302	533	89	1,055	334	48	32	188	379	49	22	4,436	4,564
1993	1,868	626	457	139	958	447	69	29	220	396	40	46	5,386	5,056
1994	2,219	610	62	216	1,285	399	41	31	190	670	47	21	6,186	5,393
1995	1,590	285	663	140	844	442	66	37	226	458	23	33	4,206	5,342
1996	2,226	515		316	1,427	555	58	27	190	441	31	14	6,489	5,216
1997	2,513	1,219		182	882	1,022	56	36	201	496	58	72	6,738	6,738
1998	2,764	571	997	161	1,160	897	68	50	384	615	63	64	7,794	6,758
1999	3,613	530	741	325	1,418	1,049	70	35	298	631	46	31	8,787	

Sources: University Grants Commission, 2000 and the Central Bank of Sri Lanka, 1998.

Table 14.7A

Unemployed and Under Employed Graduates Recruited to the Graduate Training Scheme, 1999

District	B.Sc. (Phy)	B.Sc. (Bio)	B.Sc. (Agri)	LLB	B.Sc. (Mgt)	B. Com	B.A. (Gen)	B.A. (Econ. Sp)	B.A. (Socio)	Others	Total	%
Colombo	122	195	65	10	119	242	309	16	26	32	1,136	8.2
Gampaha	68	197	69	8	146	113	320	55	23	19	1,018	7.3
Kalutara	96	100	35	6	71	82	350	26	29	15	810	5.8
Kandy	54	116	48	2	81	98	674	46	29	29	1,177	8.5
Matale	7	31	14	3	17	26	201	12	2		313	2.3
N'Eliya	6	9	16	1	19	17	107	7	3	4	189	1.4
Galle	53	90	42	3	131	90	364	21	20	99	913	6.6
Matara	46	109	60	3	83	59	658	24	17	23	1,082	7.8
Hambantota	27	45	39	7	41	49	400	24	29	5	666	4.8
Jaffna	71	29	29	3	49	98	239	35		20	573	4.1
Kilinochchi	1		1		4	6	14	2	1		29	0.2
Mannar					7	11	19	5			42	0.3
Vavuniya	6	3	5		8	17	25	3	1	35	103	0.7
Mullativu	3		1		5	11	17	7			44	0.3
Batticaloa	19	9	9		45	34	237	14		10	377	2.7
Ampara	21	25	12	4	68	42	150	4		8	334	2.4
Trincomalee	9	12			24	17	59	2		5	130	0.9
Kurunegala	45	61	45	8	69	76	1,233	120	51	18	1,726	12.4
Puttalam	11	9	17	1	18	32	148	21	3		260	1.9
A'pura	16	39	30	6	52	36	249	36	18	6	488	3.5
Polonnaruwa	5	26	11	3	22	21	84	15	9	12	208	1.5
Badulla	22	29	26	3	33	58	333	23	33	11	571	4.1
Moneragala	9	9	8		15	23	150	6	7		227	1.6
Ratnapura	35	70	36	4	60	44	332	24	28	9	642	4.6
Kegalle	46	50	29	4	80	38	500	35	26	23	831	6.0
All districts	798	1,263	647	79	1,267	1,340	7,172	583	357	383	13,889	100.0
Per cent	5.75	9.09	4.66	0.57	9.12	9.65	51.64	4.20	2.57	2.76	100.00	

Source: Department of National Planning.

Table 14.8A

UNIVERSITY ACADEMIC STAFF: APPROVED CADRE AND UNFILLED POSITIONS BY STAFF CATEGORY

University	Professor		Associate Professor		Senior Lecturer I		Senior Lecturer II		Lecturer/Asst Lecturer		Total	
	Approved	Present	Approved	Present	Approved	Present	Approved	Present	Approved	Present	Approved	Present
Colombo	45	35	31	33	112	64	97	111	207	164	492	407
Peradeniya	82	71	44	44	13	84	160	188	453	240	752	627
Sri Jayawardenepura	35	17	28	17	n.a.	53	114	86	221	126	398	299
Kelaniya	33	22	14	16	79	65	80	70	162	115	368	285
Moratuwa	17	13	7	12	31	34	58	57	113	86	226	202
Jaffna	38	18	9	8	35	28	88	28	118	108	288	190
Ruhuna	25	18	1	9	18	30	85	62	117	121	246	240
Eastern	8	2	—	—	6	8	16	16	121	73	151	99
Open University	12	7	—	2	—	37	25	33	138	53	175	132
South Eastern	—	—	—	—	1	1	—	1	41	18	42	20
Rajarata	11	2	—	—	—	2	33	14	3	25	47	43
Sabaragamuwa	9	3	—	—	—	1	24	4	2	32	35	40
All universities	315	208	134	141	295	407	780	670	1,696	1,161	3,220	2,584

Source: University Grants Commission, 2000.

Table 14.9A

PRIVATE REMITTANCES BY REGION OF ORIGIN

Origin	US Dollars Million					Rupees Million					Percentage Share				
	1995	1996	1997	1998	1999	1995	1996	1997	1998	1999	1995	1996	1997	1998	1999
Middle East	423	484	562	611	651	23,567	26,728	33,202	39,466	45,766	58.2	58.1	61.0	61.2	61.6
North America	58	70	72	76	77	3,233	3,864	4,259	4,888	5,442	8.0	8.4	7.8	7.6	7.3
South and Central America	7	8	9	10	11	405	468	521	646	782	1.0	1.0	1.0	1.0	1.1
EU	108	122	127	135	144	5,991	6,762	7,499	8,720	10,152	14.8	14.7	13.8	13.5	13.7
Eastern Europe	4	3	4	4	4	202	187	253	258	281	0.5	0.4	0.5	0.4	0.4
Europe Other	37	43	45	53	55	2,065	2,392	2,692	3,423	3,882	5.1	5.2	4.9	5.3	5.2
South Asia	5	7	8	8	8	262	374	478	517	567	0.6	0.8	0.9	0.8	0.8
South East Asia	15	17	16	19	20	810	925	972	1,227	1,414	2.0	2.0	1.8	1.9	1.9
Far East Asia	55	61	61	62	64	3,086	3,358	3,603	4,005	4,514	7.6	7.3	6.6	6.2	6.1
Australasia	7	8	9	10	11	400	468	501	656	758	1.0	1.0	0.9	1.0	1.0
North Africa											0.0	0.0	0.0	0.0	0.0
Central Africa											0.0	0.0	0.0	0.0	0.0
South Africa	0					15	3				0.0	0.0	0.0	0.0	0.0
Other	8	9	8	11	11	446	473	465	711	784	1.1	1.0	0.9	1.1	1.1
Total	727	832	921	999	1,056	40,482	46,003	54,445	64,517	74,342	100.0	100.0	100.0	100.0	100.0

Source: Central Bank of Sri Lanka, 1998.

Table 14.10A

Private Transfers in Relation to Exports and Imports and Related Variables

Year	Private Transfers Rs100 Mn	Private Transfers US $Mn	Exports Rs Mn	Exports US$	Imports Rs Mn	Imports US $Mn	GDP (Rs Mn)	Exchange (Rate US$)
1950	−0.69	−14.5	1,563	296.5	1,167	246.3	3,822	4.77
1951	−0.77	−16.2	1,904	387.0	1,559	317.9	4,171	4.78
1952	−1.04	−21.8	1,502	309.3	1,702	352.0	4,107	4.75
1953	−0.59	−12.4	1,568	314.4	1,608	342.9	4,390	4.75
1954	−0.67	−14.1	1,809	362.0	1,397	290.6	4,696	4.78
1955	−0.78	−16.4	1,940	397.5	1,460	310.4	4,914	4.76
1956	−0.83	−17.4	1,735	372.1	1,629	331.0	5,028	4.79
1957	−0.66	−13.9	1,682	350.5	1,804	370.4	5,349	4.76
1958	−0.78	−16.4	1,711	341.0	1,717	359.7	5,721	4.75
1959	−0.56	−11.8	1,754	372.3	2,005	411.2	5,930	4.76
1960	−0.31	−6.5	1,832	377.2	1,960	421.3	6,331	4.75
1961	−0.30	−6.3	1,733	358.5	1,703	376.7	6,353	4.76
1962	−0.30	−6.3	1,808	370.2	1,660	400.3	6,549	4.76
1963	−0.30	−6.3	1,731	358.7	1,490	392.5	6,849	4.76
1964	−0.36	−7.6	1,876	371.1	1,975	411.6	7,326	4.78
1965	−0.24	−5.0	1,949	400.9	1,474	403.6	7,499	4.78
1966	−0.26	−5.5	1,700	351.5	2,028	423.8	7,741	4.78
1967	−0.29	−4.9	1,690	339.4	1,738	408.4	8,319	5.93
1968	−0.13	−2.2	2,035	332.0	2,173	395.8	9,930	5.93
1969	−0.07	−1.2	1,916	320.7	2,543	446.1	10,834	5.96
1970	−0.05	−0.8	2,033	338.7	2,313	391.8	13,187	5.96
1971	−0.20	−3.4	1,947	325.4	1,986	373.7	13,674	5.96
1972	−0.29	−4.4	2,009	317.9	2,064	360.6	14,720	6.70
1973	0.02	0.3	2,617	366.4	2,715	412.9	17,920	6.75
1974	−0.02	−0.3	3,472	511.2	4,564	701.1	23,302	6.69
1975	0.21	2.7	3,933	563.4	5,251	767.3	25,691	7.71
1976	0.59	6.7	4,815	558.8	4,645	643.1	28,032	8.83
1977	2.13	13.7	6,638	767.1	6,007	726.2	34,684	15.56
1978	3.40	21.9	13,206	845.1	14,687	1,025.4	40,479	15.51
1979	7.48	48.4	15,279	981.4	22,541	1,449.4	49,782	15.45
1980	24.61	136.7	17,595	1,064.7	33,942	2,051.2	62,246	18.00
1981	41.68	202.8	21,043	1,065.5	36,582	1,876.9	79,337	20.55
1982	56.50	265.0	21,454	1,013.7	41,946	1,994.1	94,679	21.32
1983	68.43	273.7	25,096	1,064.1	45,558	1,921.3	1,13,878	25.00
1984	72.74	276.8	37,347	1,462.3	47,541	1,928.1	1,40,039	26.28
1985	72.91	266.0	36,207	1,315.3	54,049	2,044.3	1,48,321	27.41
1986	80.97	283.9	34,072	1,209.7	54,559	1,973.2	1,63,713	28.52
1987	96.13	312.5	41,133	1,395.7	60,528	2,075.1	1,77,731	30.76
1988	105.66	319.9	46,928	1,477.2	71,030	2,240.2	2,03,516	33.03
1989	132.28	330.7	56,175	1,547.1	80,225	2,226.5	2,28,138	40.00
1990	146.31	363.6	79,481	1,978.0	1,07,729	2,681.0	2,90,615	40.24
1991	170.70	400.9	82,225	2,040.0	1,26,643	3,034.0	3,37,399	42.58
1992	212.52	462.0	1,07,855	2,459.0	1,53,555	3,501.0	3,86,999	46.00
1993	278.18	561.3	1,38,175	2,858.0	1,93,550	4,010.2	4,53,092	49.56
1994	313.42	627.1	1,58,554	3,199.8	2,35,576	4,759.0	5,23,300	49.98
1995	367.00	679.0	1,95,092	3,799.0	2,72,200	5,311.0	5,98,327	54.05
1996	405.25	714.6	2,26,801	4,096.0	2,99,424	5,415.0	6,95,934	56.71

Source: Central Bank of Sri Lanka, 1998.

Part V

INSTITUTIONAL AND GOVERNANCE ISSUES

15

ECONOMIC LIBERALIZATION AND INSTITUTIONAL REFORM

David Dunham

INTRODUCTION

Mark Twain once quipped rather dourly that 'nothing so needs reforming as other people's habits'—a view all too familiar in debate on institutions and institutional change in the liberalization process. In Sri Lanka (as in many other countries), opposing positions have emerged, based on neoliberal economics on the one side and political science and sociology on the other. The discussion has been inward-looking with strong ideological undertones and it has been largely ungenerous, in the sense that there has been reluctance to build on work of the other camp. Replacing pre-existing organizations, rules and working procedures with others considered more efficient has, at times, been advanced on little more than a doctrinal belief that they were necessary—regardless of whether they were likely to be effective, given local politics and history. On the other side, emphasis has been placed on politics and political economy, with need for reform incidental and often portrayed more as a part of the problem than part of a possible solution. If Twain could have listened to discussions on institutional change in Sri Lanka over the last 20 years, there would have been attitudes he would have recognized.

This chapter looks at the discussion on institutions and institutional change in relation to economic policy reforms in Sri Lanka since it opened up its economy in the late 1970s. There have been at least three strands, all of which can be located in very much wider traditions. First, there has been the mainstream position where the driving force is need for greater efficiency in the economic reform process. Second, there has been a 'politics first' position in which reform is seen as part of the broader (economic and political) programme of particular governments, stressing political leadership, path dependence and macroinstitutional change. The point of entry of the first is from the side of economic policy and received ideas, that of the second through an interpretation of local politics and history. A third, partly overlapping strand that might best be described as a 'constitutional' approach, sets out from the erosion of democratic institutions and rise of ethnic conflict and emphasizes the need for a political solution, restoring a functioning democracy through greater accountability to civil society, decentralization and devolution or federalism. Since the latter is not explicitly concerned with economic reform, this chapter concentrates on the first two.

GETTING POLICIES RIGHT

Macroeconomic stabilization, economic liberalization and a downsizing and re-definition of the role for the state have been major pillars of mainstream economic policy prescriptions since the early 1980s. However, it soon became clear to advocates of reform that the outcome they had expected was not automatic. The problem was not seen to lie in the policies themselves so much as the policy context. The fact that policy making and were policy implementation were embedded in (and heavily de-pendent on) organizational arrangements and ways of operating that were carried over from the past and were inefficient and inappropriate, was increasingly emphasised. Early claims that 'lack of political will' on the part of government leadership was the main reason for slippage gave way to a more nuanced analysis, tempered by growing awareness of the starkly a-institutional nature of much of the early reform thinking and the enormous complexity of the process. Creating or upgrading weak institutional arrangements so that they were more responsive to reform began to be acknowledged as an essential ingredient of any effective policy package.

In this context, the discussion of institutional reform was driven by the need for more effective management of the economic policy agenda. The need for strong public sector organizations was clear and it was voiced relatively early. The fact that many government agencies lacked the capacity to formulate and carry through nec-essary reforms was seen to highlight the debilitating effect of weak organizations, unfocused objectives and poor coordination. Prominence was given to technical lead-ership, transparent procedures and accountability under the guise of good governance. Unwieldy bureaucracies and administrative rules, rent-seeking and corruption and a lack of strong bureaucratic leadership were seen as major constraints on reform. Re-ducing the size and role of the state and the upgrading of key cadres became promi-nent policy prescriptions as emphasis was placed on reducing corruption, democratic good governance and the policy management capacity of the government (World Bank, 1992, 1994). A range of measures—autonomy for the Central Bank, the cre-ation of a Securities and Exchange Commission and the creation of independent legal institutions—were also advocated to reduce external interference and political influ-ence.

Over time, experience with reform inevitably set in motion a learning process, drawing attention to other institutional dimensions. There was mounting sensitivity to the wider policy environment (the influences at work, where they impinged and how they influenced decision making), drawing on the theory of public policy manage-ment and on the burgeoning economic literature on institutions. Discussion was ex-tended to other microinstitutional arrangements that affected economic policy and (in the wake of the disastrous early experience in the former Soviet Union and later the East Asian Crisis) to macroregulatory institutions and the question of corporate governance. Recently, it has been broadened to non-market microinstitutions that affect the growth of an economy. The *World Development Report 2002: Building Institutions for Markets* pointed to the importance of social networks, participatory organizations and other non-market institutions that could facilitate interchange of information, promote competition and speed up the adoption of norms and values functional to market development (World Bank, 2002).

In practice, this rethinking was spurred on by increasingly ambitious perceptions of development needs and reform possibilities in the wake of the collapse of the Soviet superpower. In the late 1970s, economic policy reform comprised a series of partial reforms, usually involving trade liberalization, associated changes to the exchange rate and some removal of subsidies. At that time it was new and it was contentious and there was need to win over both governments and electorates. Fears were voiced that, in the wake of major reforms, massive popular unrest could bring in populist or left-wing governments, undermining the prospects of sustained success. The reform process was as a result episodic, and since deregulation or exchange rate depreciation could be formulated and implemented 'with the stroke of a pen' by the Central Bank or the Ministry of Finance, longer-term concern with institutions (beyond the efficiency of the agencies involved) was not a major issue.

With the demise of the Soviet Union and the introduction of pro-market policies in China, the credibility of a state-led alternative had effectively evaporated. Economic liberalization and broader policy reforms were widely accepted and advocates envisaged a transformation of the whole society. Economic reform became more or less synonymous with a pro-development strategy. As 'second generation reforms' turned to privatization, regulation, labour market liberalization, the redesign of social security, health and education systems or pro-poor growth initiatives, the significance of institutional arrangements became more obvious and the importance of consultation, negotiation and politics much more apparent. In a number of countries (Argentina, Poland, Mexico, Russia), responsibility for health and education delivery was already seriously decentralized (Nelson, 1996). Elsewhere, NGOs and civic organizations undertook much work in these areas (Tendler, 1997). Line ministries and government agencies found themselves seriously ill-equipped to deal with these messier policy environments and institutional issues were thrust to the fore almost as a matter of necessity.

The response was in essence an exercise in institutional design (Grindle, 2001), identifying characteristic problems (typically control and incentive problems) and prescribing structures, rules and organizational principles designed to revamp the situation and get key actors committed. These solutions were then advocated and passed on to governments as received wisdom, becoming part of the development ideology of the International Financial Institutions (IFIs) (see Chapter 2 in this volume). By their nature, however, they were acontextual and apolitical, suggesting that history and process were unimportant and that path dependence was irrelevant. Politics was not ignored. Reform was frequently seen to have been derailed by politics. Politicians and political parties were seen to be competing for votes in a political market place, pulled and pushed by interest groups and by groups in civil society, and it was recognized that there was a major problem securing sufficient support to sustain the process (Haggard and Webb, 1993). But no interest was shown in alternative interpretations of what was going on.

Putting Politics First

The alternative position questions the notion that, in a country like Sri Lanka, politicians respond to the interests of voters and that this shapes policy. Policy making in developing and transition economies is seen to be extremely closed, concentrated in the hands of the political leadership, top administrators and key advisors. Both sides would argue that the main interest of national leaders is retaining power (and often getting rich), preferring 'more power to less, survival in office to defeat, re-election to loss, and influence to irrelevance' (Grindle, 2001:349). Both would agree that state resources are often used for personal gain or to build and strengthen coalitions by rewarding loyal supporters (Grindle, 2001; Manzetti and Blake, 1996; Schamis, 1999; Walle, 2001), and it is seen as no surprise when the media, the judiciary and the police serve the interests of the leadership (or the ruling party), or when state institutions and public policy bolster cronyism and patronage.

The difference is that, in the 'getting policies right' model, a coalition in favour of reform will vote these people out of office, and rent-seeking will be eliminated through the institutional reform process (á la Kreuger, 1974). In the 'politics first' model, initial conditions, political culture and macropolitical institutions emerge as qualifying factors. History and context are important and when political and the institutional checks on it are weak, the leadership is more or less autonomous, with discretionary control over policy and the allocation of resources. Policy making is neither transparent nor accountable, with resources opened up by economic reform serving personal interests and patronage. Interest groups and civil society are then not the countervailing force the first position anticipates but always reacting—either poorly organized (and therefore weak politically) or else co-opted and unable to exert sufficient pressure to force a change in policy. Politicians compete for power in elections, but the electorate has limited influence on policy or on the way that it is implemented.

In such a context, reforms may be adopted as part of the economic and political programme of a particular government (sometimes just to please donors and secure funding), but they are vulnerable to manipulation, selective adoption and discriminatory implementation in ways that are advantageous to groups in power and those who can exert influence on them. The leadership controls the agenda of the liberalization process and also the way that it is implemented—which sectors are liberalized (and in what order), what activities are privatized, how tendering is dealt with, the terms of eventual sale to the private sector and then competition policy. Major state assets (such as telecommunications, energy and transport) are sold off, often with little transparency. If patronage is already a major characteristic of the way politics operates, all this can provide enormous scope for rent-seeking and cronyism and, as the stakes get higher, holding on to political power becomes that much more important—not just for the gains, but because of the cost of marginalization with a loss of power. Incumbents are more likely to subvert political institutions to stay in power and the temptation to suppress public scrutiny and dissent increases considerably. The government's capacity to implement reforms can often begin to be constrained by the nature of its own support structures and by the personal, social and political commitments that lie behind them (Hellman, 1998; Schamis, 1999). When regimes change, powerful vested interests and the expectations of supporters can then make it extremely difficult to change direction.

Reform and Institutional Change: The Sri Lankan Case

When Sri Lanka embarked on economic reform in 1977, it was a peaceful and stable democracy with an already impressive record of human development. The most significant changes since independence had been a shift from a multi-ethnic to a Sinhalese-Buddhist state and a sharp increase in the involvement of the state in the economy and social life (Athukorala and Jayasuriya, 1994; de Silva, 1993). Politics was dominated by a westernized landed and professional elite that led the main political parties (the United National Party [UNP]and the Sri Lanka Freedom Party [SLFP]) that competed for the elected right to distribute state patronage (Moore, 1990). There had been a continuing history of friction between the majority Sinhalese community and Tamil and Muslim minorities over access to jobs, land and other resources and, amongst the Sinhalese, between the urban elite and a rural educated youth. By the mid-1970s, the country was an almost classic case of an inward-looking, state-dominated economy.

A UNP government then came to power in 1977 on a ticket of economic change. Over the next quarter century, the economy was to record an average annual growth rate of 5 per cent. But there was also a marked deterioration in the country's governance, democratic institutions and political culture. To the 'getting policies right' school, the latter were serious destabilizing factors that were quite unrelated to the change in economic policy. Administrative reforms and reforms in policy management received high priority to give reform a boost. To those who put 'politics first', the government's policies were part of the problem because of the selective way they were used to serve political purposes and macroinstitutional changes that followed to generate that stability. This section looks at what was happening over successive governments.

The Jayawardene Government, 1977–89

The UNP had always been conservative and pro-business and it came to power in 1977 with a massive majority, promising to open up the economy and provide a just and righteous (*dharmista*) society. At the time, there was widespread support for the removal of domestic marketing restrictions (especially those on rice) and a generally favourable response to the opening up of the economy. The policy package it adopted was projected as a major liberalization effort (and indeed it brought about a momentous change in the Sri Lankan economy and society), but much depends on whether the period is viewed purely from the standpoint of economic policy or in a broader context. Even in terms of economic policy, it contained not only significant trade, exchange rate reforms and expenditure cuts (on food subsidies in particular) but a massive donor-supported public sector investment programme—the Accelerated Mahaweli Development Programme (AMDP), a new national capital and large-scale public housing—that was not, technically speaking, a liberalization measure (and soon by far the more prominent). But the differences went further.

No one who lived through the Jayawardene years would consider them adequately characterized by its economic policies. They were also coloured by a series of highly-charged and controversial political measures—constitutional changes, repression of opposition and dissent and the muzzling of unions. Clearly, there was need for political stability if the post-reform economy was to flourish, but from a 'politics first' perspective the new government went further. The changes were part of the distinctive political-and-economic programme of the Jayawardene government in which economic reform was no more than a part, and indeed of declining importance. The UNP was seen to be trying to revamp the economic and political landscape. Policy reforms contributed (lifting domestic market restrictions and opening up trade had always been part of Jayawardene's political agenda) but they were seen to be instrumental to very much broader objectives. A far more pressing concern was to benefit supporters, reshape political institutions to prevent anyone derailing his vision and entrench his own and his party's domination over the longer term.

Thus, seen from this point of view, implementation revealed priority for the Sinha-lese constituency, the need to create and preserve important sources of patronage and a determination to marginalize once and for all an already weak opposition. Trade liberalization was applied in a way that was highly discriminatory (Cuthbertson and Athukorala, 1990). The AMDP, the centrepiece of the Public Sector Investment Programme (PSIP), benefited mainly Sinhalese farmers. Heralded by the government as a revival of the ancient Sinhalese heartland, it touched deep-seated nationalist and religious sentiments in the Sinhala-Buddhist community. The PSIP in general pro-vided state land and housing and generated contracts, employment and other sources of political patronage. Cuts in food subsidies (which Jayawardene had consistently advocated since the 1950s) were used to provoke and crush the opposition trade union movement and to bolster party support in the farming community, hurting urban workers who traditionally supported his opponents.

Equally importantly, there were major changes in the macroinstitutional environ-ment to achieve the same objectives. The Westminster-style parliamentary system was replaced by an all-powerful Executive Presidency (with minimum accountability to Parliament) and, with proportional representation, party lists beholden to the centre replaced responsibility to constituencies—part of a pattern of increasing centralization that was to play a major role in reshaping Sri Lankan society. There was steady erosion of civil and electoral rights, increasingly high-handed treatment of ethnic minorities, refusal to hold parliamentary elections and eventual extension of parliament by means of a highly flawed referendum (Manor, 1984; Wijesinha, 1991).

In this context, how one looks at the history of institutional reform depends on the position adopted. From the point of view of economic policy, the reform process had faltered and had been increasingly undermined by weak policy management, urgent need for administrative reform and decentralization and the social tensions that had heightened sharply after 1983. A Presidential Administrative Reform Committee (ARC) was set up in 1986. It found an over-sized, inert and dysfunctional administrative system managing government policy and it advocated a holistic approach to reform and rationalization of cadre management, giving it a greater regulatory and facilitatory role (Wanasinghe, 1994; World Bank, 1988). However, its advice ran counter to the centralizing effects of the macroinstitutional changes that people on the other side would argue were essential and instrumental to Jayawardene's vision. Reforms aimed at 'good governance' and at decentralization (as response to 'the ethnic problem') were to fail persistently, suggesting limitations in a purely administrative approach that was trying to revamp institutional structures independent of historical and societal processes (Bastian, 1994). For the 'politics first' group, selective liberalization, the massive scale of donor aid to the PSIP (with its weak accountability) and the growing authoritarianism (and decreasing transparency) was helping create an environment in which corruption could flourish, exacerbating the all-too-obvious problems of effective policy management.

Certainly, the authoritarian nature of the regime was increasingly resented by the populace and by its opponents in the second half of the 1980s, forcing the government to arm its cadres, requiring a firmer hand to retain control and in the process provoking further resentment and mounting violence. Liberalization stalled (though it was not reversed). By the late 1980s, the country faced civil war in the north and east and insurrection in the south, a full-blown balance of payments crisis and a paralyzed economy, forcing Jayawardene to leave the presidency and call fresh elections.

The Premadasa Government, 1989–93

Elections of 1989 were held in an atmosphere of violence and alleged electoral fraud against a deliberately weakened and extremely disorganized opposition. The incoming President, Premadasa, was faced with economic and political crises and his response was firm and effective—establishing a virtual dictatorship. Agreement was signed with the International Monetary Fund (IMF) (which was in a strong position to exert influence) and a second generation of reforms was introduced, bringing privatization and income-transfers to the poor on to the policy agenda. The economy recovered strongly and a general sense of optimism emerged within the business (and donor) community as the reform agenda was implemented.

But much of what was to occur hinged on the exercise of centralized power that had been made possible by the institutional changes introduced by his predecessor. It entailed a strong element of command. Garment factories were steered into rural areas, there was reluctance to condone measures that could be read to imply labour retrenchment and when job creation failed to take off, the pace was forced by pressurising the Sri Lankan business community to make the necessary investment. Power and decision making were concentrated in very few hands, dictatorial practices of the President became increasingly blatant and corruption was institutionalized, but there was also policy clarity and predictability. The business community was only too aware that political rewards could be secured by opening factories, creating jobs and cooperating closely with the government. Favours would be granted, with almost immediate redress of grievances or administrative encumbrances, but unswerving support would be expected (Dunham and Kelegama, 1997). In contrast, to be blacklisted was seem by many as almost tantamount to business suicide.

As a result, Premadasa's rule in the early 1990s was probably the most dynamic period of the post-reform period, but it was also one that sadly went awry when it came to democratic good governance. When it came to 'getting policies right' institutional reform was obviously necessary. There was a United Nations Development Programme (UNDP) mission in 1990 on Enhancing Public Sector Reform and a Restructuring Management Unit was established in the Ministry of Policy and Plan Implementation. There was also a procession of the World Bank and Asian Development Bank (ADB) missions on related themes, arguing that investment and growth would be even higher if only policy management was stronger. However, from the other side, it was argued that it was precisely the lack of good governance—the ability of the President to supersede normal process and dictate decisions—that made the strong economy a reality. Indeed, policies of institutional reform were not taken up seriously. Neither were the proposals of the ARC nor those of later initiatives seriously implemented (Wanasinghe, 1994). On the contrary, it became increasingly clear that micro-institutional adjustments were always going to be insufficient to counter political will and a political culture that were moving in the opposite direction.

In practice, an already centralized political system and an already politicized bureaucracy were reinforced by Premadasa's determination to intervene politically 'to get things done' and to exert partisan political control over public officers. His personal power was such that institutions were created, used or adapted to serve his political purposes—as was the case, for example, with 'mobile secretariats' where top-ranking officials were directed into the field to deal with local problems. Privatization was carried out with little transparency, institutions were adjusted to give political direction to policy and a new trajectory took shape as cronyism, connections and corruption became standard operating policies.

The process led to further macroinstitutional changes as he sought to exert ever tighter control over the polity and society. When the funds that could be extracted from the PSIP had dried up in the mid-1980s, the scope for large-scale corruption in direct state economic activities had shrunk, only to be revived by privatization in the early 1990s. Both Jayawardene and Premadasa used 'liberalization' to serve their own purposes, adopting and implementing selectively what was useful to them. The potential gains could be high, providing resources that could finance, nurture and sustain their tight hold on power. However, increasingly under Premadasa, they were a source of political advantage that also needed to be protected. Political violence, thuggery and assassination increased, eliminating competitors within the party, intimidating opponents and resulting in a brutalization of Sri Lankan society. As protest and opposition mounted, first via a failed impeachment motion and then spilling over into extra-parliamentary action, it was met by repression and more authoritarianism, generating even less transparency and allowing more corruption—in turn generating a greater need and a continuing demand for institutional and administrative reform. Social tensions built up to breaking point and corruption and repression began to be seen by the population at large as a major national problem.

The Kumaratunga Government, 1994–2001

Premadasa was assassinated in May 1993 and a year later a centre-left coalition came to power with an anti-corruption and pro-peace agenda. There was at the time enormous pressure for institutional change—for an end to corruption and abolition of the Executive Presidency in particular. But it was not to be. The coalition of the in coming President, Kumaratunga, only held a tenuous one seat majority in the Sri Lankan Parliament and the accommodation needed to keep it together saw a further increase in the number of ministries and a division of responsibilities that defied all logical management. Such was the fragmentation that the Executive Presidency was retained as the focus of power and national policy making. Patronage and the necessary resources to keep together the coalition were also crucial and the government (reversing its initial stand) surpassed the efforts of its predecessor when it came to privatization. The national airline, telecommunications, plantation management and ports were all privatized, again with little transparency or accountability, and regulatory powers to control competition in particular markets were used as a source of additional rents (Jayasuriya and Knight-John, 2002). Again, her predecessors had created the macroinstitutional context to make this possible and the new government exploited the opportunities that were available to help it stay in power. There was in every sense 'path dependence': the problems continued, institutional reforms were advocated but fell on deaf ears because they paid little account to the political context, and critics analysed the context but offered no clear viable solutions.

There were also, however, other forces that were making change difficult—the escalation of military expenditure since the mid-1980s. Large-scale military purchases offered opportunities for brokerage, yielding 'commissions' for military personnel and for the politically-favoured civilians who managed to get involved in it. Domestically, the expansion of the military and security-related activities presented other opportunities for gain through the tendering and state purchase of necessary goods and services. This had been building up in the Jayawardene and Premadasa years but, with outbreak of almost open war in the mid-1990s, the military, state security and private security business acquired new dimensions. It spawned a pro-war lobby that put pressure on government to push for a military solution or maintain the status quo. Shared economic incentives converged in shared political interests and, for both, continued access to political power was essential. This created the economic basis for a coalition within the government's ranks (with some outside participants) to stifle any initiatives to establish transparency in government purchases, contracts and other commercial dealings.

The state enterprise sector had shrunk and with it the scope it offered to dispense employment and other sources of patronage. This posed a problem for a fragile coalition, but it was one that could be circumvented by funding from privatization and defence expenditures, by the expansion of the ministerial posts and privileges and, more generally, of the already-extensive privileges of politicians. Both sides in the debate were aware of this but, together, these processes were reinforcing changes in institutional culture, entrenching a system of political corruption, eroding democratic institutions and independence of the judiciary and making the whole problem more intransigent.

The Wickremasinghe Government, 2001 Onwards

A UNP government under Prime Minister Wickremasinghe returned to power in the parliamentary elections of 2001 as the coalition of its predecessor began to crumble—heralding in a difficult period of cohabitation with an Executive President, Kumaratunga, who had been re-elected. There was a strong undercurrent of discontent with a weakening economy, continuing corruption and with the ongoing war. Peace talks were initiated and, in such a situation, there were obvious interests in changing the political rules of the game so that checks and balances were in place to control an all-powerful Executive President. Neither have been easy and the jury is still out on this, but there do not appear as yet to have been significant changes in political culture or the institutional framework of policy. On the contrary, there is a widely held view that once the war is in the past (if that can actually be realized), the persistent problems of corruption and policy management will fast come to the fore again. That does not change the alternative views that have been conveyed in this chapter—the picture seems at the moment to be one of an established national trajectory and fairly established responses from the two approaches that have been identified. Neither has clear ideas about the way out of the impasse.

CONCLUDING REMARKS

This chapter has looked at alternative views in the discussion of institutional reform and economic liberalization in contemporary Sri Lanka. The first, described for convenience as a 'getting policies right' approach, emphasizes the importance of microinstitutional reforms in the economic policy environment and the way markets operate so that mainstream economic policies are much more effective. There can be no doubt that, from reports of the ARC to contemporary discussions of the need for administrative and policy management reform, it touches on an area of policy that is of profound importance. Many of the problems, in particular the underlying culture of patronage and corruption, are recognized widely as such in Sri Lankan society.

However, it is also clear that many of the specific policy measures that have been proposed run squarely counter to strategic thinking of the political leadership and to the changes that it has introduced in the macroinstitutional environment. Institutional reform has been an uphill struggle, be it reform of administrative arrangements or effective decentralization. In retrospect, it seems clear that while key areas have been identified—some (as with problems of corruption) agreed, others (such as necessary changes in labour market) much more contentious—the solutions prescribed have often seemed more a statement of received wisdom than a result of a broad-based analysis of the local context. This is one main reason why so many of the findings have failed to be taken up by the other side.

On the other hand, context has been the focus of the 'politics first' group. Reform is located in the broader political agenda of particular governments, adopted and implemented selectively to serve its ends. But it, in turn, would seem more concerned with explaining the weaknesses of a generalized application of mainstream thinking than devising alternative solutions or the ways in which they might work. It has been strongly analytical but much less policy prescriptive. It seems to be argued that, in Sri Lanka, where checks and balances have been eroded and the polity is structured to a large extent around political patronage, almost any policy runs the risk of being viewed and implemented to serve the leadership's purposes. At times it suggests a political leadership and a coalition of supporters with a strong vested interest in the status quo who do not want, or are unable, to initiate change without jeopardizing their position—and this is clearly difficult to accept for those who see their task as helping initiate policies.

The last 25 years, since Sri Lanka embarked on its reform agenda, has seen major changes in political ideology and in political culture and institutions that have shaped the country's development trajectory. That would seem incontestable. Corruption, for example, is qualitatively different and it is now acknowledged to be pervasive: it is widely condemned and the need for a change of direction is publicly recognized. There is therefore, a pressing need for effective institutional reform policies. But corruption has, at the same time, also been increasingly accepted. Many actions (such as using ministerial property for private purposes), that would once have been roundly condemned in the past, have come to be seen in the public eye as just normal perks. And that too is important. Pressure for institutional change, if it is to be effective, requires that what is happening is known and is understood and that it is seen as wrong. It needs perceived legitimacy. It remains part of the tragedy of Sri Lanka that discussions of policy and analysis of context remain far apart.

References

Athukorala, P. and S. Jayasuriya (1994), *Macroeconomic Policies, Crises and Growth in Sri Lanka, 1969–90*, Washington D.C.: World Bank.

Bastian, S. (ed.) (1994), 'Devolution and Development in Sri Lanka', Delhi: Konark Publishers.

Cuthbertson, A.G. and P. Athukorala (1990), 'Sri Lanka', in D. Papageorgiou, M. Michaely and A.M. Choksi (eds), *Liberalising Foreign Trade: Indonesia, Pakistan and Sri Lanka*, Oxford: Basil Blackwell.

de Silva, K.M. (ed.) (1993), 'Sri Lanka: Problems of Governance', Sri Lanka: International Centre for Ethnic Studies, Kandy.

Dunham, D. and S. Kelegama (1997), 'Does Leadership Matter in the Economic Reform process? Liberalization and Governance in Sri Lanka, 1989-93', World Development, 25(2): 179–90.

Grindle, M.S. (2001), 'In Quest of the Political: The Political Economy of Development Policy-Making', in G.M. Meier and J. Stiglitz, (eds), Frontiers of Development Economics: The Future Perspective, New York: Oxford University Press.

Haggard, S. and S. Webb (1993), 'What Do We Know About the Political Economy of Economic Policy Reform?', World Development, 18(2): 143–68.

Hellman, J.S. (1998), 'Winners Take All. The Politics of Partial Reform in Postcommunist Transitions', World Politics, 50(January): 203–34.

Jayasuriya, S. and M. Knight-John (2002), 'Sri Lanka's Telecommunications Industry: From Privatization to Anti-Competition?', in M. Hossain, A. Brown and T. Nguyen (eds), Telecommunications Reform in the Asia Pacific: Economic and Regulatory Experiences, London: Edward Elgar.

Kreuger, A. (1974), 'The Political Economy of the Rent-Seeking Society', American Economic Review, 64(3): 291–303.

Manor, J. (ed.) (1984), Sri Lanka in Change and Crisis, London: Croom Helm.

Manzetti, L. and C.H. Blake (1996), 'Market Reforms and Corruption in Latin America: New Means for Old Ways', Review of International Political Economy, 3(4): 662–97.

Moore, M. (1990), 'Economic Liberalization Versus Political Liberalism in Sri Lanka?', Journal of Modern Asian Studies, 24(2): 341–83.

Nelson, J. (1996), 'Promoting Policy Reforms: The Twilight of Conditionality?', World Development, 24(9): 1551–59.

Schamis, H.E. (1999), 'Distributional Coalitions and the Politics of Economic Reform in Latin America', World Politics, 51: 236–68.

Tendler, J. (1997), Good Government in the Tropics, Baltimore: Johns Hopkins University Press.

Twain, M. (1974), Pudd'nhead Wilson's Calendar, Avon Conn: The Limited Editions Club.

Walle, N. van de (2001), African Economies and the Politics of Permanent Crisis, 1979–99, Cambridge: Cambridge University Press.

Wanasinghe, S. (1994), Activating the Reform Process in Sri Lanka, Governance Research Series No. 1, Colombo: Institute of Policy Studies.

Wijesinha, R. (1991), Sri Lanka in Crisis 1977–88: J.R. Jayawardene and the Erosion of Democracy, Colombo: Council for Liberal Democracy.

World Bank, (1988), A Break With the Past: The 1987–90 Program of Economic Reforms and Adjustment, Washington D.C.: World Bank.

———— (1992), Governance and Development, Washington D.C.: World Bank.

———— (1994), Governance: The World Bank's Experience Washington D.C.: World Bank.

———— (2002), World Development Report 2002: Building Institutions for Markets, New York: Oxford University Press.

SELECT READINGS

Dunham, D. and S. Jayasuriya (2000), 'Equity, Growth and Insurrection: Liberalization and the Welfare Debate in Contemporary Sri Lanka', Oxford Development Studies, 28(1): 97–110.

Grindle, M.S. (1991), 'The New Political Economy: Positive Economics and Negative Politics', in G.M. Meier, (ed.), Politics and Policy Making in Developing Countries: Perspectives on the New Political Economy, San Francisco: ICS Press.

16

CONSUMER AFFAIRS AUTHORITY ACT IN THE OVERALL CONTEXT OF COMPETITION POLICY

A.D.V. de S. Indraratna

INTRODUCTION

Competition exists where there is free play of market forces. There is free play of market forces when there is a large number of buyers and sellers of a particular homogeneous product and there is no barrier for any one to enter, or exit from, the market for that product. Under such perfect competition, resources would be allocated most efficiently, or most productively used, thereby maximizing production. It would also maximize consumer welfare as prices settle at the lowest average cost to the producer or entrepreneur or the provider of goods, allowing him only his normal profit/opportunity cost. In such markets, prices would reflect social desires, the consumer is sovereign and his interest is protected.

Perfect competition, however, is an ideal situation. It does not exist anywhere. The real market is imperfect and the degree of imperfection ranges between perfect monopoly at one end and perfect competition at the other. In such imperfect markets, consumers have limited, or no power, to influence the market price. They are no longer sovereign and their rights are in jeopardy.

NEED FOR COMPETITION POLICY

In the absence of perfectly competitive market conditions, there must be a competition policy to promote competition in order to enhance both allocative efficiency and consumer welfare. For example, a provider of goods or services enjoying monopoly power can, depending on the degree of market imperfection, exploit the consumer through unfair or anti-competitive practices, such as misinformation, misleading advertisement, packaging, hoarding and predatory pricing. In such circumstances, there should be competition legislation to prevent such exploitation by the unscrupulous manufacturer or trader.

Competition policy is a process of implementation of competition legislation and other policies to promote competition through institutional arrangements/mechanisms in order to enhance both allocative efficiency and consumer welfare. This entails the existence of a number of firms or organizations, the rivalry between them helping to promote productivity and growth.

THE GOAL AND OBJECTIVES OF COMPETITION POLICIES

The ultimate major objective of an effective competition law and policy would be to preserve and promote competition as a means of maximizing efficiency with optimal allocation of resources and to ensure the production of quality goods and their availability to the consumer at the lowest possible price. This would result in a high or even rising standard of living for the people, which is the ultimate aim of all policies of a benevolent government.

It is within the aims of such policy to prevent manufacturers and traders or providers of goods and services from protecting or expanding their own dominant position or market share at the expense of consumer welfare. It would be part and parcel of this policy to establish competition agencies who would use competition advocacy and competition education to achieve the desired objectives. Apart from the overall goal of promoting growth and productivity and enhancing competitiveness, competition policies have certain specific objectives. They include:

- the maintenance of the competitive process or of free competition;
- the protection or promotion of effective competition;
- associated objectives such as freedom to trade, freedom of choice, and access to markets.

The Competition Act, 2002 of India, for example, states as its objectives the prevention of practices having adverse effects on competition, promoting and sustaining competition in markets, protecting the interests of consumers and ensuring freedom of trade carried on by other participants in markets in India.

The Competition Act of 1998 in South Africa states as its objectives:

- to promote the efficiency, adaptability and development of the economy;
- to provide consumers with competitive prices and product choices;
- to promote employment and advance the social and economic welfare of South Africans;
- to expand opportunities for South African participation in world markets and recognize the role of foreign competition in the Republic;
- to ensure that small and medium-sized enterprises have an equitable opportunity to participate in the economy; and
- to promote a greater spread of ownership, in particular to increase the ownership stakes of historically disadvantaged persons.

Interface with Other Policies

An effective competition policy, however, cannot be achieved by competition law and agencies alone. Competition legislation may be narrow in its scope, but competition policy is much broader and comprehensive and tries to bring harmony in all public policies that may encourage or adversely affect competition, consumer welfare and economic development.

In other words, competition policy has to be harmonized with the other agricultural, industrial, trade, investment, financial and labour policies of the country. For instance, the relationship between trade and competition policy is one of ensuring that the benefits of trade liberalization are passed on to consumers through effectively operating markets, rather than allowing them to be captured by anti-competitive behaviour or agreements. That is why trade and competition together was listed as one of the subjects for discussion at the Ministerial Summit at Cancum in September 2003.

The harmonization has become all the more important in view of the rapid globalization of the economies of the world, particularly of unequal partners working on a non-level playing field. For availing of the opportunities, and facing the challenges of globalization, competitive advantage through productivity gains is essential. It is accepted that government policies must aim at this in order to survive in the process of globalization. This can be achieved without stifling competition and jeopardising the interest of the consumer.

As a detailed analysis of this is not within the scope of this chapter, a few examples are cited in illustration. Just three years after the enactment of the Fair Trading Commission Act of 1987, an Industrial Promotion Act was passed. Industrial development does not depend upon the creation of monopolies, mergers or cartels. Competition can be safeguarded by encouraging small and medium-scale enterprises (SMEs) in manufacturing as well as in agriculture, through various incentives, without prejudice to the provisions of this Act.

Another example relates to the area of tariffs. Removal or reduction of tariffs is imperative for trade liberalization within globalization. This, however, does not mean that dumping should be allowed. Anti-dumping legislation, as contemplated upon by developing countries including Sri Lanka, should be complementary to competition legislation.

Foreign direct investment (FDI) is a necessary ingredient of sustained development of developing countries. It should be part of the investment policy of the country to encourage it by formulating a package of incentives. There must, however, be safeguards or safety nets against the formation of cartels or multinational investors acting against the national interest. Privatization, a derivative of globalization, is also undertaken on the ground that it increases efficiency. Privatization or 'restructuring' of Government Owned Business Undertakings (GOBUs), however, does not mean conversion of government monopolies to private monopolies. Privatization must be accompanied with broad ownership in order that competition may not be stifled.

Another instance that may be cited is regarding globalization. Globalization requires financial deregulation. This need not necessarily lead to complete convertibility of Sri Lanka's currency. Control of capital account, for instance, has to be continued, as is done today, until the country has fully taken off into sustained growth and adequate foreign exchange reserves have been built up to avert any financial crisis of the like which affected Asian economies in mid-1997.

Harmonization with labour policies may be equally significant. Free mobility of labour is a necessary condition for competition. Labour laws of the country must not hinder this.

The conclusion that emerges from the above illustrations is that other policies of a country relating to agriculture, industry, trade, investment, finance and labour need not hamper competition. They can be harmonized, as shown earlier, with competition legislation in order to promote both competition and development, the ultimate or eventual goal of which is the enhancement of the quality of life of the people.

HISTORICAL BACKGROUND TO COMPETITION POLICY IN SRI LANKA

Though the question of competition policy and consumer protection has engaged the attention of developed countries, and for that matter even some developing Asian countries, for quite some time, competition law and policy has been of relatively very recent origin in Sri Lanka. Although Sri Lanka gained independence in 1948, until 1977 the governments which ruled the country alternately did not follow a policy of promoting competition through competition law and policy. Instead, they followed a policy of consumer protection through consumer subsidies and price control.

Because of this policy of welfarism, the economy of the country began slowing down. It got into dire straits in the 'closed' (inward-looking) regime of 1970–77, with unemployment recording an unprecedented level of nearly a quarter of the labour force by the end of the period. Subsidies were nevertheless maintained, with administered prices of essential consumer articles. To scrutinize and review these prices from time to time, a National Prices Commission was established under the National Prices Commission Act of 1975. The objective of this Act, however, was far from making any legal provision for promotion of competition by preventing monopolies, mergers or anti-competitive practices which were against the public or consumer interest.

BEGINNING OF COMPETITION LEGISLATION

With the opening of economy in November 1977, trade was liberalized with tariffs considerably reduced and quotas and licencing lifted, doors were opened wide for foreign investment, and all other controls and restrictions were removed. Market forces were expected to operate freely and competition to grow with trade liberalization, finance deregulation and privatization, the derivatives of globalization which came in the wake of the opening of the economy. This was far from happening. On the contrary, privatization of public enterprises and GOBUs made the situation worse.

Realising this, two years after liberalization, the government came out with the Consumer Protection Act of 1979, the first piece of legislation enacted in the country for consumer protection. Its avowed objective was to ensure that the liberalized economy was not exploited to the detriment of the consumer. It addressed the questions of regulation of internal trade, regulation of prices and unfair and anti-competitive trade practices such as hoarding, exclusive dealing and price discrimination. Nevertheless, it had failed to protect the consumer through its effective enforcement or even to lay the foundation for an effective competition policy in the country due to the lack of resources and also perhaps due to lack of commitment.

However, to revert to state intervention with measures such as price control or administered prices was unthinkable in the context of the open economy, to which the government was committed as a matter of policy. Nonetheless, it took 10 years after liberalization for the government to think of introducing legislation in order to promote competition and protect the consumer. This was the passing into law of the Fair Trading Commission (FTC) Act of 1987. This Act repealed the National Prices Commission Act of 1975 and certain sections of the Consumer Protection Act of 1979, thereby establishing the present Fair Trading Commission. An amendment to this Act was brought in by Act No. 57 of 1993 and in between, the Industrial Promotion Act of 1990 was passed which could, among others, cushion any adverse effect on domestic industry that might be caused by competition legislation.

FAIR TRADING COMMISSION

The Fair Trading Commission (FTC) is a statutory government corporation managed by a board of seven directors headed by a full-time Chairman and a Secretary-General who functions as the Chief Executive Officer. It comes under the aegis of the Ministry of Commerce and Consumer Affairs. The primary objectives of this Commission are to control monopolies, mergers and anti-competitive practices, and to help formulate and implement a national price policy.

To begin with, several essential articles were listed under the jurisdiction of the FTC for purposes of price review. However, after the launching of the open market reforms from the end of 1977, all of them, except pharmaceuticals, were gradually taken out of control. Even pharmaceuticals were decontrolled with effect from 1 November 2002, but only for six months on an experimental basis. The FTC was asked to monitor the movement of prices during this period on the basis of which a decision could be taken at the end of the period whether to continue with the decontrol or not.

The overall objective of the Commission still remained the ensurement of a competitive business environment, which was the driving force of a market economy and was congenial for consumer protection. In the spirit of the FTC Act, competition was to be achieved by controlling monopolies, mergers and anti-competitive practices that were operating against the public interest.

FUNCTIONS AND ACTIVITIES OF THE FTC

The main function of the FTC in the recent past had been the conduct (under Section 11) of investigations on its own motion or on a complaint or request made to it by any person or body of persons. At the end of such investigation, an appropriate order (under Section 15) could be issued, in respect of the following: (*a*) existence or possible existence of a monopoly; (*b*) creation or possible creation of a merger situation; (*c*) the prevalence of an anti-competitive practice.

For the purpose of the Act, a monopoly was defined as one whose market share exceeded a prescribed percentage (Section 12). These percentages of market shares were prescribed in respect of 47 commodities (Appendix 1). In the year 2002, the Commission investigated 12 complaints coming under the above three categories. Among them were two interesting cases relating to anti-competitive practice and monopoly respectively. The first, was a complaint that the respondent company was using an unauthorized falsified advertisement to boost its market for herbal soap at the cost of the market of the complainant. On the evidence provided, the Commission concluded that the advertisement was misleading and hence distorting the market and was an anti-competitive practice against the public interest under Section 15(C) of the FTC Act. The respondent company was issued an order to refrain from using this advertisement in the future with which it complied.

The second, was the case of Shell using its 'dominant' position to charge the consumer a price higher than what he should justifiably pay, as well as tie him down to Shell by agreeing to refund only Rs 1,400 of the Rs 2,500 cylinder deposit and that too on surrender of the receipt of payment of the original deposit. Both of these were deemed to be against the public interest. An order was issued by the FTC directing Shell, by 15 January, to bring down the price by the specific amount which the Commission thought was being unjustifiably overcharged, and also to correct the practice which was tying down the customer to the Shell Company. The Shell Company appealed to the Court of Appeal to have the order quashed. The new Consumer Affairs Authority which came into being in April (see below) signed an memorandum of understanding (MOU) with Shell coming to an out-of-court settlement by which the latter has agreed to refund Rs 1,400 to any customer who returns the cylinder as well as reduce the price of LPG gas by a certain amount. This settlement was not at all in keeping with the spirit of the order given by the FTC. First, Shell has agreed to refund only that part of the deposit which it was in any case refunding even earlier on surrender of the receipt. Second, the price of LPG gas is being reduced only as demanded by the fall of world market oil prices. In other words, with this, Shell has won its case outside court.

Weakness of the FTC Act

The FTC Act of 1987, at its inception, was a mixture of competition and consumer protection legislation. The provisions, Sections 18–26, dealing with consumer protection, were repealed. By and large, consumer protection thereafter fell within the ambit of the Department of Internal Trade (DIT), except for pharmaceuticals. Any increase in the price of pharmaceuticals was subject to scrutiny and approval by the Commission, until 1 November 2002 as referred to earlier. The FTC Act thus became more the country's competition legislation.

Even as a piece of competition legislation, the FTC Act was weak in several respects. One relates to the question of definition or interpretation. Though it had power to investigate and issue orders in respect of monopolies, mergers and anti-competitive practices, investigations were often delayed or hampered due to problems in regard to their definition or identification. For example, as a monopoly was defined on the basis of a prescribed percentage of market share, difficulties arose when there were several categories of the same 'article'. An instance of this was Liquor/Spirit, in respect of which a percentage of 40 per cent had been prescribed. When a particular company or companies manufactured several categories of this article ranging from beer and wine to hard liquor and liqueur, the calculation of the market share for the purpose of monopoly under the Act became problematical. A classic case of this was found in the investigation, DCSL vs W.M. Mendis.

Similar was the case in regard to anti-competitive practices. Anti-competitive practices were not specified but were deemed to occur 'where a person in the course of business, pursues a course of conduct which of itself or when taken together with a course of conduct pursued by persons associated with him, has or is intended to have or is likely to have the effect of restricting, distorting or preventing competition' (Section 12).

Another weakness was the question of discrimination. Only articles, and not services, were brought within the provisions of the Act. Enterprises registered under the Board of Investment (BOI) Law were also kept outside the purview of investigation by the Commission. So were the enterprises or projects which had entered into agreements with the government.

Yet another weakness might be in regard to transparency and procedural fairness. Even though every attempt might have been made to adhere to these principles, both in respect of formulation and implementation of the law, there might have been a slight setback due to the dearth of resources and lack of commitment or political interference.

NEW LEGISLATION—CONSUMER AFFAIRS AUTHORITY (CAA) ACT

To alleviate the weaknesses and limitations of the existing legislation on competition and consumer protection, the new Consumer Affairs Authority (CAA) Act, No. 9 of 2003 (certified on 17 March 2003) was promulgated repealing the existing Fair Trading Commission Act, the Consumer Protection Act and the Control of Prices Act (Chapter 173). This Act is also based on a combination of competition and consumer protection legislation but with greater weightage given to the latter than in the FTC Act. As stated in the preamble to it, as part of government policy, the CAA Bill aims, by way of its broad objectives, to 'provide for the better protection of consumers through the regulation of trade and the prices of goods and services and to protect traders and manufacturers against unfair, and restrictive trade practices', and for 'promoting competitive pricing wherever possible and ensure healthy competition among traders and manufacturers of goods and services'.

With the coming into force of this Act, the present FTC and the DIT were amalgamated into the new CAA. There is provision within CAA for an investigative authority, comprising a Chairman, three working and seven non-executive Directors and an adjudicative Council consisting of three members. Section 7 of the Act specifies its objects and Section 8 spells out its functions under 15 broad categories (see Appendix 2).

This Act is in several ways an advance or improvement on the preceding legislation. As mentioned earlier, it has provided for both an investigative authority and an adjudicative body. It is less discriminatory in that it brings under its surveillance all goods as well as all services including professional services. It does not, as under the FTC Act, exempt from investigation enterprises either approved under the BOI Law, or which will enter into agreements with the government. To be more non-discriminatory, it should not have exempted even those which have already entered into agreements with the government. It also will be more effective in that the authority has to complete an investigation within 100 days of its initiation (Section 34[2]) and the penalties of fines and imprisonment prescribed for errant traders and manufacturers have been enhanced several fold and made very deterrent (Section 60). The absence in the Act of provision for appeal to the Court of Appeal against an order of the Council within a specified period would also make the authority very effective, though this may be considered by some as a violation of procedural fairness.

Another striking feature of this Act, which gives it more teeth, is the provision which enables the minister, in consultation with the authority, to declare as 'specified' any article or service 'essential to the life of the community', the price of which cannot be increased without the written approval of the authority (Sections 18[1] and [2]). This provision would be very useful if a trader or manufacturer, using his dominant position, persists in increasing the price of a 'good or service essential to the life of the community'. This provision has also come under criticism on the alleged ground that it gives arbitrary power to the minister.

CRITIQUE OF THE CAA ACT

Inadequacy as Competition Legislation

While the CAA Act may be more powerful than the earlier legislation in some respects, it would be less effective as competition legislation without the provision to investigate monopolies and mergers (and maybe cartels also) which act against the public interest. This provision which was in the FTC Act was excluded from the CAA Act, as the government is presumably contemplating separate legislation in respect of them.

The inclusion of the provisions to investigate any anti-competitive practice may somewhat fill this vacuum. Nevertheless, the government must soon introduce the legislation in respect of monopolies, mergers and cartels (M&M legislation) to work complementary to the CAA Act in order to effectively implement competition policy.

There should not be any fear that M&M legislation is a deterrent to foreign direct investment (FDI). If it were so, countries like China and India would not have attracted as much FDI as they have done and are doing now. For, despite opening their economies to FDI, China still has many controls and regulations and India has in place strict M&M legislation.

M&M legislation also does not imply that monopolies and mergers cannot exist or be created under them. On the contrary, it would not interfere but encourage them so long as they do not inhibit productivity and growth and do not act against the public interest. Furthermore, M&M legislation would be necessary to prevent the emergence of business tycoons, both local and foreign, who through cross-holdings and interlocking of directorates, etc., and using their dominant position undercut their rivals. This is certainly not healthy for an open market economy.

Some may think that the present Securities and Exchange Commission (SEC) Act may fulfil this need. This is erroneous thinking, for SEC covers only 274 or less than 10 per cent of the 3,000 public companies registered. Moreover, the SEC is concerned only with the shareholders' interest and not with the public or consumer interest with which M&M legislation is concerned.

OTHER WEAKNESSES

This Act is also subject to criticism in several quarters for other reasons. Apart from the lack of procedural fairness referred to earlier, it has been criticized for giving far too much power to the minister. The appointment of members to the authority and the Council by the minister, for instance, it is alleged, would deny the autonomy and independence, which a competition and consumer authority like this needs every much. Even though the minister's discretion in this regard is circumscribed by Sections 3(1) and 39(2) of the Act which specify the requisite qualifications of the members of these two bodies respectively, there is fear that this may be abused because of the weightage given to political considerations in the appointment to high posts in the public and corporate sectors. Because of this fear, it has been suggested that a body like the Constitutional Council makes these appointments instead.

The Act has also been criticized for not specifying anti-competitive practices (Section 34), as this would leave unnecessary room for contesting the orders of the authority.[1] The Act may also be criticized for not exactly spelling out the interface between itself and the regulatory authorities. For instance, the Public Utilities Commission (PUC) of Sri Lanka Bill to provide for the establishment of the Public Utilities Commission of Sri Lanka for the purpose of regulating utility industries to be gazetted from time to time, saw its passage through Parliament even before the CAA Act was passed. The Bill initially applies to only two public utility industries, viz., electricity and water as are set out in the Schedule to the Act itself.[2]

All powers and functions of competition promotion and consumer protection in respect of specific goods or services covered under these industries are vested in the PUC (Parts V and VI). While they are similar to those under the CAA in respect of all goods and services, the CAA does not specify how it would interface with the PUC when it comes to utility goods or services gazetted under the PUC Act.

The PUC Act has, of course, placed itself superior to the CAA (and other relevant Acts) by making PUC 'provisions and the regulations and the rules or orders made thereunder' having 'effect notwithstanding anything inconsistent therewith contained (in other acts)'. There is also provision in the PUC Act for cooperation and harmonization in respect of the Central Environment Authority, the Urban Development Authority, the Telecom Regulatory Commission (TRC) and other regulatory bodies to be designated as such from time to time under the PUC itself (see Section 35 of the PUC Act).[3]

These are not enough. There must be specific provision for interface between the two bodies governed by these respective Acts. Amendments would be necessary to both the CAA and PUC Acts to avoid any conflict in their respective functions on competition promotion and consumer protection in regard to utility industries, or this interface could be provided by MOUs between them.

Notwithstanding what has been stated before, one may admit that any new legislation when it is first introduced may be found wanting. It is only after its working for some time that its weaknesses and strengths could be tested. So it is in the case of the CAA Act. After its working for a few months, amendments could be brought in, in order to streamline it in the light of that experience, taking into consideration deficiencies pointed out here as well as the three core principles of transparency, non-discrimination and procedural fairness of competition policy accepted by the Doha Declaration of the World Tade Organization (WTO) and the United Nations (UN) set guidelines.

SUMMARY AND CONCLUSIONS

Under perfect competition, not only are resources allocated efficiently but consumer welfare is maximized. Since this ideal condition does not exist in practice and markets are imperfect in varying degrees, a Competition Policy backed by legislation is necessary to promote competition. To make this policy very effective, however, other government policies must be in harmony with it.

Competition legislation is of relatively recent origin in Sri Lanka. Until 1977, consumer protection was ensured through subsidies and administered prices. However, with the opening of the economy and privatization that followed in its wake, legislation became imperative for promotion of competition and consumer protection. The first piece of legislation for consumer protection was passed in 1979, but the implementation was not effective enough to protect the consumer, leave aside laying the foundation for a competition policy.

The FTC Act No. 1 of 1987 was passed to fill this vacuum. The FTC had powers for consumer protection as well as for promoting competition. However, powers regarding the former were gradually removed under the pressures of globalization and its derivatives, marketization, privatization and financial deregulation.

In order to remedy this, the CAA Act was passed in Parliament in January 2003. This amalgamated the powers and functions of the FTC and the DIT which was phased out. This Act too is a mixture of competition and consumer protection legislation. It may be weaker in some respects, particularly with the removal of the provision to investigate monopolies and mergers, but stronger in other respects than the preceding legislation.

The CAA Act needs immediate amendment to provide for interface between it and the PUC Act. Improvement may also be needed in conformity with the three core principles of transparency, non-discrimination and procedural fairness of competition legislation accepted by the Doha Declaration of the WTO and the UN set guidelines on competition policy. It is, of course, after the implementation of the Act, that its weaknesses and strengths can be really assessed. The Act could be then be streamlined with the necessary amendments in the light of this experience. It must also be complemented by M&M legislation to have an effective competition policy.

NOTES

1. The FTC has had, in fact, the experience of a respondent company challenging the Commission that what it has posed as anti-competitive practice was, in fact, an act to safeguard competition. The Australian Competition and Consumer Commission Act has specified the anti-competitive practices, as a result of which it has been able to uphold in Court its orders against anti-competitive practices.

2. An Industry Specific Act has already been passed for the PUC to be operative in respect of the electricity industry.
3. In addition to the TRC, there are other regulatory bodies, such as the National Transport Commission in respect of land transport and the Civil Aviation Authority in respect of aviation services.

REFERENCES

National Prices Commission Act of 1975.
Consumer Protection Act No. 1 of 1978.
Fair Trading Commission Act No. 1 of 1987.
Industrial Promotion Act No. 46 of 1990.
Consumer Protection (Amendment) Act No. 34 of 1992.
Fair Trading Commission (Amendment) Act No. 57 of 1993.
Consumer Protection (Amendment) Act No. 17 of 1995.
Public Utilities Commission of Sri Lanka Bill (2002), An Act to provide for the Establishment of the Public Utilities Commission of Sri Lanka.
Consumer Affairs Authority Act No. 9 of 2003.
Indraratna, A.D.V. de S., 'Strengthening Consumers' Rights a Concerted Initiative' in the Report on the Conference held on 6 February 2002 at Hotel Lanka Oberoi, Colombo, Sri Lanka– Inaugural Address.
Knight-John, Malathy (ed.) (2002), *Competition Policy and Utility Regulation: The Sri Lankan Experience*, Colombo: Law & Society Trust.
Public Utilities Commission of Sri Lanka Bill, An Act to provide for the Establishment of the Public Utilities Commission of Sri Lanka.
Strengthening Consumers' Rights, A Concerted Initiative, Report on the Conference held on 6 February 2002 at Hotel Lanka Oberoi, Colombo, Sri Lanka—A special reference to the Inaugural Address of Prof. A.D.V. de S. Indraratna.
Law & Society Trust and Institute of Policy Studies, *Towards a New Competition Policy in Sri Lanka* (2002), Colombo.
United Nations Conference on Trade and Development, *Report of the Intergovernmental Group of Experts on Competition Law and Policy* on its fourth session held at the Palais des Nations, Geneva from 3 to 5 July 2002.

Appendix 1

PRESCRIBED MONOPOLY PERCENTAGE

(By Gazette No. 535/11 of 7 December 1988)

Goods	Percentage
1. Aerated Waters	40
2. Asbestos Cement Sheets	50
3. Accumulators for Motor Vehicles	50
4. Aluminium Foil & Lining	50
5. Biscuits	45
6. Ball Point Pens	45
7. Cement	40
8. Crown Closures	50

9.	Collapsible Tubes	50
10.	Canvas Shoes	50
11.	Dry Cell Batteries	45
12.	Lead & Coloured Pencils	50
13.	Margarine	50
14.	Mathematical Instruments Sets	50
15.	Safety Matches	50
16.	Soap Products for Washing Clothes and Detergents	50
17.	Sewing Machines	50
18.	Bicycle Tyres	50
19.	Bicycle Tubes	50
20.	Toilet Soaps	50
21.	Water Pumps	50
22.	Razor Safety Blades	50
23.	Electric Motors	50
24.	Edible Fats	50
25.	Laundry Soap	50
26.	Toothpaste	50
27.	Condensed Milk	50
28.	Tin Cans and Closures	50
29.	Cigarettes	50
30.	L.P. Gas	50
31.	Pastels	50
32.	Crayons	50

Services		*Percentage*
33.	Building Maintenance and Janitorial Cleaning service	50

(By Gazette No. 747/16 of 31 December 1992)

Goods		*Percentage*
34.	Milk (Pasteurized and Sterilized)	50
35.	Glass Bottles/Containers	50
36.	Oxygen	50

Goods		*Percentage*
37.	Poultry Food	50
38.	Rubber Slippers	40
39.	Full Cream Milk Powder	40
40.	Beer	40
41.	Electric Bulbs	40

(By Gazette No. 753/11 of 11 February 1993)

Goods		*Percentage*
42.	Industrial Gases in all forms	50

(By Gazette No. 785/3 of 20 September 1993)

Goods		*Percentage*
43.	Salt	50
44.	Spirits/Liquor	40

Services	Percentage
45. Electricity	50
46. Water	50
47. Telecommunication	50

Appendix 2

Functions of the Consumer Affairs Authority

(a) Control or eliminate:

    (i) Restrictive trade agreements among enterprises;

    (ii) Arrangements amongst enterprises with regard to prices;

    (iii) Abuse of a dominant position with regard to domestic trade or economic development within the market or in a substantial part of the market; or

    (iv) Any restraint of competition adversely affecting domestic or international trade or economic development;

(b) Investigate or inquire into anti-competitive practices and abuse of a dominant position;

(c) Maintain and promote effective competition between persons supplying goods and services;

(d) Promote and protect the rights and interests of consumers, purchasers and other users of goods and services in respect of the price, availability and quality of such goods and services and the variety supplied;

(e) To keep consumers informed about the quality, quantity, potency, purity, standards and price of goods and services made available for purchase;

(f) Carry out investigations and inquires in relation to any matter specified in this Act;

(g) Promote competitive prices in markets where competition is less than effective;

(h) Undertake studies, publish reports and provide information to the public relating to market conditions and consumer affairs;

(i) Undertake public sector and private sector efficiency studies;

(j) Promote consumer education with regard to good health, safety and security of consumers;

(k) Promote the exchange of information relating to market conditions and consumer affairs with other institutions;

(l) Promote, assist and encourage the establishment of consumer organizations;

(m) Charge such fees in respect of any services rendered by the authority;

(n) Appoint any such committee or committees as may be necessary to facilitate the discharge of the functions of the authority; and

(o) Do all such other acts as may be necessary for attainment of the objects of the authority and for the effective discharge of the functions of the authority.

17

PRIVATIZATION AND REGULATION

Malathy Knight-John

INTRODUCTION

Policy reforms intended to bring about a shift away from a state-centred economic regime have been on the agenda of a number of developing countries since the 1980s. This change in policy direction came about both because of a realization on the part of governments that interventionist development strategies had failed to live up to their promises and a concerted effort on the part of the Bretton Woods institutions to promote market-oriented reforms.

The promulgation of this neoliberal agenda is seen in the wave of privatization[1] across the developing world in the 1980s and 1990s, following the trends set by Margaret Thatcher in the UK and Ronald Reagan in the US in the late 1970s. For most developing countries, privatization was a means to address the budgetary crunch imposed by loss-making entities. Whilst there has been extensive debate in the literature on the extent of external pressure to reform,[2] it is evident that this varied depending on the political economy circumstances of individual countries.

Privatization in Sri Lanka became a part of the country's reform agenda more than a decade after the liberalization of the economy in 1977. Since then, however, Sri Lanka has gained the reputation of being the most vigorous amongst its South Asian neighbours in pursuing privatization, with both internal and external factors driving the reform process. As in other countries at a similar level of development, privatization remains controversial due to its questionable distributional impacts and at times, as in the early 1990s for instance, the government has had to move cautiously due to various allegations relating to the lack of transparency in the process. In general, however, the relatively subdued nature of debate on the reform process has facilitated an essentially smooth implementation of privatization since the late 1980s, with little pressure on successive governments to evaluate the broader social effects of the exercise.

The move away from state-dominated development is parcelled with the notion of a regulatory state in the neoliberal reform agenda. The regulatory state is linked to second stage reforms, such as a competition policy framework and rules-based regulatory systems without which the benefits of first generation reforms, such as privatization, cannot be realized. The experience so far indicates that these second stage reforms require careful planning and consideration of the costs and benefits of alternative approaches to change, as they tend to face significant resistance from entrenched institutional structures and processes.[3]

In spite of the policy rhetoric espoused by international donor agencies,[4] commitment to reforms such as privatization has tended to overshadow the creation of effective regulatory structures, with ideology prevailing over a pragmatic consideration of the political economy milieu within which institutional change must take place. Similarly, on issues of governance integral to the dialogue on institutional change, the policy advice espoused by these aid agencies is guided by the constricting principle that the political components of governance are important only to the extent that they contribute to economic efficiency.

These issues and dilemmas of reform have been experienced by Sri Lanka with varying degrees of intensity as it progressed along its market-oriented development trajectory. In general, challenges of development have been addressed in a rather ad hoc manner influenced by the short-term outlook, linked to the electoral cycle that permeates the policy-making process. Policy debate, where it exists, has been largely confined to the academic realm with little interaction between the academic and policy-making communities.[5]

The objective of this chapter is to focus on some key elements of the policy debate with regard to privatization and regulation that have a direct bearing on Sri Lanka's development path. The next section of this chapter traces the evolution of policies and institutional changes with regard to privatization and regulation in Sri Lanka since the opening up of the economy. This is followed by analyses of some 'big picture' questions and controversies on privatization and regulation as they relate to policy, process and outcome issues faced by reformers, in an attempt to gain a better understanding of the dynamics of institutional change in Sri Lanka's political economy milieu. The final section focuses on the theme, what we have learned and what we need to learn for successful reform, based on the preceding analysis.

PRIVATIZATION AND REGULATION: POLICY AND INSTITUTIONAL CHANGE

Since independence, Sri Lanka has witnessed a series of economic policy shifts, influenced by changes in global thinking on development strategies, domestic political economy factors and the advice of international financial institutions, often as a part of loan conditionality. This section focuses on a particular period of the country's political economic history—the post-1977 years—and on a particular genre of policy and institutional change—reforms relating to privatization and regulation.

Sri Lanka pursued economic policies that were largely [6] nationalistic and inward-looking after gaining independence from the British, perhaps as an indirect backlash against colonial rule. An important part of these strategies was a strong reliance on state-owned enterprises (SOEs), with successive governments establishing new public enterprises, nationalizing a number of private entities and creating state monopolies. The state secured public support for these reforms by emphasizing populist elements such as employment creation, price controls on essential goods and services, distributional equity and regional development, in the operations of SOEs.

According to Kelegama (1997), the public enterprise sector expanded from around 5.7 per cent of gross domestic product (GDP) in 1961 to 12.2 per cent in 1974 and to over 15 per cent in 1977; by 1977, the public sector accounted for over one-third of investment and for around 40 per cent of formal sector employment. Many of these SOEs were loss-making and plagued with problems of overstaffing, mismanagement and corruption, inefficient procurement systems, excessive government intervention and politicization.

In spite of this inefficient and financially unsustainable state of affairs, the liberalization of 1977 brought little change to the status quo for almost a decade. Over the years, the SOE sector had provided a relatively easy avenue for rent-seeking and disbursement of political patronage through the creation of job opportunities well in excess of what was economically efficient. The massive influx of concessionary aid that came with the 1977 reforms—in particular a billion dollar land settlement/hydro-electric project—eased resource constraints and made it possible for the government to continue its practice of political patronage. In addition, the 1977–89 period—the first wave of liberalization—was one of mounting macroeconomic instability and political violence and was not conducive to any rigorous reforms.

In view of the fact that the United National Party (UNP) government that came to power with a four-fifths majority in Parliament and with executive power centralized in the Presidency under a new Constitution had a strong political mandate for economic reform, the slow pace of privatization was not so much one of an inability to manage the reform process. Instead, as argued by Dunham and Kelegama (1997), this unfinished agenda of the first wave of liberalization is best understood as a rational policy response to the political viability and sustainability of the reform process in the face of domestic social pressures.

By 1989, the start of the second wave of liberalization, the financial situation with regard to loss-making public enterprises had become unsustainable with budgetary transfers to these entities averaging around 10 per cent of GDP. International donors who had tended to overlook these problems in the early years of reform were no longer willing to ignore such glaring irregularities and aid was made contingent on a series of liberaliztion and stabilization measures, including the implementation of a privatization programme. As such, privatization was formally announced as a state policy in 1987 with the primary objectives of easing the fiscal burden and improving the efficiency of enterprises through the infusion of private sector norms.

The second wave of liberalization, the period that coincided with the first stage of privatization, saw the election of a new UNP government that gave little priority to institutional structures and good governance practices. In a sense, this was a trend that had been observed earlier during the first wave of liberalization when there were serious issues of transparency and accountability. However, the scale of the problem increased during this period given the unprecedented opportunities for rent-seeking in the privatization programme.

The adoption of privatization as a state policy was accompanied by the enactment of two pieces of legislation designed to facilitate the commercialization of SOEs. The institutional framework for privatization reflected the particular tensions between economic objectives and political imperatives that shaped policy formulation and outcomes during this period. The privatization programme was handled by a number of entities—the Presidential Commission on Privatization, the Public Investment Management Board, the Commercialization of Public Enterprises Division of the Ministry of Finance and the Plantation Restructuring Unit, to name the most prominent.

The involvement of these various institutions in the privatization programme, although clearly not expedient from an economic efficiency point of view, was designed to satisfy specific political needs of the time. With the President Ranasinghe Premadasa facing an impeachment and coalition management being a crucial element for political survival, it was vital to secure the support of a number of line ministries. The participation of these individual institutions with their own political agenda resulted in a systemic politicization of the privatization process.

Coalition building was a major concern of the new President for other reasons as well. Having entered into mainstream politics from a social background that differed vastly from the traditional English-speaking, professional, urban elite that had dominated the UNP in the past, he cultivated strong ties with the urban underclass, the rural poor and a new political business class to secure political support. As such, this was also a period when crony capitalism was at its peak, with privatization expanding the opportunities for excessive rent-seeking and contracts being offered on the basis of political connections rather than on economic competence in several instances.[7] Although the claim that a loss of transparency was the trade-off for speed of execution required by the donor agencies is valid to some extent, the scale of rent-seeking and corruption that prevailed during this period suggests that the political leadership's preoccupation with consolidating its support base was more significant in shaping the process.

A marked feature of the new government that differentiated it to some extent from the previous UNP regime was its ultra-populist stand with regard to policy formulation. In the case of privatization this was reflected in the form of the President dubbing the process 'peoplization', meaning handing back public assets from the bureaucrats to the people. A Presidential decree was also issued that no workers should lose their jobs as a result of privatization, indicating that job creation was key, regardless of economic costs. This was also a part of the Government's political strategy, in the face of allegations of cronyism, to placate trade unions that were being manipulated by opposition parties to oppose the reform process.

This phase of the privatization programme, from 1989 to 1994, saw the partial and full divestiture of around 43 commercial enterprises, with gross receipts of approximately

Rs 11.6 billion. The entities that were sold during this period could be typified as 'easy picks' in contrast to the more complex utility and service sector privatizations that were taken on in the next phase of the programme, from 1995 to 2001. The default modality for divestiture was the '51:30:10' formula where a majority shareholding of 51–60 per cent was sold to corporate investors, 30 per cent was offered on par to the public and 10 per cent was given free of charge to employees under an Employee Share Ownership Plan (ESOP).[8] The reasoning here was that corporate investors would have an incentive to transfer technology and invest productive capital in the enterprise if they had a majority stake, that the public share offering would help to boost the stock market and diversify share ownership and that ESOPs would win over trade unions ideologically opposed to privatization.

Increasing popular disenchantment with the civil war, authoritarian rule, political violence and spreading corruption created the conditions for political change. In late 1994, 17 years of UNP rule came to an end with the election of the People's Alliance (PA) government, made up of a coalition of the left-of-centre Sri Lanka Freedom Party (SLFP), the traditional left parties and splinter groups from the UNP. Contrary to expectations that the ideology of this group would lead to a reversal of the liberalization process, the actual course of policy under this regime was quite the opposite, particularly in the early years of PA rule. Privatization, for instance, was given high priority in the government's policy agenda, with several of the complex divestiture exercises in the pipeline during this period. As documented in Knight-John (2004), the gross receipts from privatization under the PA Government was about Rs 46.2 billion, with roughly the same number of entities as in the first phase being sold.

The institutional structures for privatization demonstrated better principles of governance than those that functioned under the previous UNP regime, at least in the initial years of operation. The PA Government had highlighted the corruption associated with the privatization programme of its predecessor as a key issue in their election campaign. As such, a new institution the Public Enterprise Reform Commission (PERC)—was established in 1996 to assume sole responsibility of the privatization process and to promote a structured and transparent culture with regard to the sale of state assets. Admittedly, transparency and access to information did improve with the establishment of this institution and the publication of Annual Reports and other materials, frequent press notices and the posting of pertinent transaction details on a designated PERC website (www.perc.gov.lk).

Progress in this area of governance, however, started to decline as the political priorities of coalition management began to dominate the policy-making process. The PA Government's ability to take resolute policy decisions was greatly undermined by the fact that it lacked an adequate majority in Parliament and had to consider the often contradictory view points of the various parties in its coalition. The political climate was one in which various interest groups vied for favours and rent-seeking activities—this time on a much larger scale given the size of the enterprises being privatized—re-emerged as a means of consolidating political power.

The new government also attempted to create the impression that it was more labour-friendly than the previous regime. A special piece of legislation, the Public

Enterprise Rehabilitation Act, was enacted in 1996 to address the interests of workers in privatized enterprises that had to be closed down and to limit the occurrence of industrial disputes. Seven entities were re-vested with the government under this Act at a cost of nearly Rs 1 billion to the treasury.[9] However, this legislation was operational only for short period of six months due to the fact that the private Chambers of Commerce had already begun to voice concerns that the PA Government was moving towards re-nationalization and policy makers wanted to avoid sending the wrong signals to investors.

As mentioned earlier, progress on the governance front achieved during the early years of PA rule began to wane over time. Exclusivity provisions without adequate monitoring and regulatory arrangement, in the divestiture of key utility and service sector entities such as telecom, gas and airlines for instance, and under-pricing of assets became a part of the Government's privatization strategy—ironic in a sense given the criticism that it had levelled against the previous regime for adopting similar practices. Explanations for these policy choices vary from the pragmatic to the rather more insidious political economy issues that are intrinsically linked to institutional change in the Sri Lankan context.

The rather more harmless explanation—what may be classified as 'pragmatic' from the view point of negotiators attempting to attract investors (particularly of the Fortune 500 type) in the midst of a civil war and a generally unsettled political climate—is as follows. Both the gas and the telecom transactions, for example, were negotiated at a time when terrorist attacks were rampant in the country and there were only three takers for the national airline, of which only one was a company that had experience in running an airline. It was also mandatory for all new owners of privatized companies to provide an ESOP and to retain all workers. It is not uncommon, moreover, for multinational companies to drive a hard bargain with developing country governments that face hard budget constraints and are in dire need of foreign investment. A case in point is that of the telecom privatization where the investor set out what was inherently a political choice of scenarios for the Government, with a three year monopoly and an immediate price hike or a five year monopoly and a phased out price hike. Such conditions were not uncommon even in the case of other major privatizations negotiated during this time.

What is more troubling, however, is a more insidious trend in governance practices—one that has been a hallmark of all political regimes since liberalization—namely, the ineffective regulatory framework that has accompanied the privatization process. A closer look at regulation and regulatory governance in Sri Lanka indicates that a number of factors contributed to this state of affairs. At times, the government took a deliberate policy decision to adopt a hands-off approach with respect to regulation in order to attract private investment. This trend was most marked under the 1977–88 UNP regime when the President J.R. Jayawardene went to the extent of indicating that what was important was investment even if it originated from 'robber barons'. Another factor that was especially prevalent in the first phase of privatization was that, the pace of asset sales required by the international aid agencies prevented a proper sequencing of the reform process where the establishment of effective regulatory structures would predate the divestiture exercise.

All these accounts, however, pale in comparison to the rent-seeking hypothesis set out in Jayasuriya and Knight-John (2002).[10] Privatization, according to this line of argument, created huge opportunities for rent extraction for politicians and their supporters, with a positive correlation between potential future profits and the size of rents. Moreover, rent extraction from state assets is not necessarily a one-off opportunity if regulatory restrictions hindering post-privatization competition are in place. This was precisely the situation with the telecom privatization, where the incumbent retained a dominant position in the market and anti-competitive practices were rampant in the absence of sound regulatory intervention. In short, the regulatory authority became a source of longer term rent extraction as the profitability of firms depends strongly on the regulatory structure in place. This argument is also consistent with the view put forward in Knight-John (2004) that revenue maximization was given priority over distributional concerns in asset sales, as it is inevitable that investors would be willing to pay more for an entity if regulatory restrictions hinder competition.

With the election of a new UNP Government in 2001 came a renewed commitment to private sector-led growth. The national policy statement of the government contained in a voluminous document incorporating action plans in seven key areas—'Regaining Sri Lanka'[11]—sets out an acceleration of the privatization process and reform of the legal foundations of the economy as two of its three main themes. The involvement of donor agencies in the policy-making process, both in an advisory capacity as well as in terms of scrutinizing progress on the reform front, is perhaps more overt now than under any previous regime.

Whilst it is still too early to make any conclusive assessments with regard to privatization and regulation under the new regime of President Chandrika Kumaratunga and Prime Minister Ranil Wickremesinghe, initial developments indicate a potential for institutional change with a more positive flavour than in the past. The final outcome it must be emphasized, however, rests on the Government's ability to get and sustain sufficient political capital to carry out its reform programme. This is not an easy task given the difficulties in managing the ongoing peace process, the climate of confrontational politics with the Executive President coming from the PA and the Prime Minister from the UNP and the need to accommodate the requirements of the minority parties in the government.

Although there were some initial hiccups with respect to the privatization programme, allegations of non-transparency and corruption have been considerably few, taking the past phases of privatization as a point of reference. The area in which there has been increased activity and marked progress is that of regulation. Significant progress has been achieved in the move away from sector-specific regulation towards multisector regulation, with the centralization of policy development functions under the Prime Minister and the creation of a separate entity—the Public Interest Program Unit (PIPU)—solely to address competition and regulation issues. Plans are currently under way to institutionalize a multisector regulator for public utilities (water, electricity, petroleum, transport, with flexibility to add on other sectors as the reform process gains momentum), one for financial and banking services and another for telecom, broadcasting and related communication industries, to replace the current telecommunications sector regulator.

The principles of regulation adopted by decision makers in the current regime are designed to increase private investment whilst at the same time safeguarding the public interest. The base modality, therefore, is competition wherever possible and regulation where necessary, with direct price controls being a third best option in the absence of less interventionist forms of market regulation. The framework also embraces the concept of an independent regulator, with accountability, transparency, consistency and legitimacy becoming embedded institutional values. Given that this style of independent regulation is relatively new in the South Asian context and that the reform process is very much one of learning by doing, the task for reformers has not been an easy one. The redesigning of regulatory structures and the elimination of the old style command and control, opaque models have also provoked considerable resistance from vested interests that had derived power and rents from the status quo.

Reforms were also undertaken to replace the competition and consumer protection legislation that had been introduced in 1987 and 1979 respectively, by bringing both these functions under one institution—the Consumer Affairs Authority (CAA). The key criticisms levelled at CAA's predecessors—the Fair Trading Commission (FTC) and the Department of Internal Trade (DIT)—was that there was a duplication of responsibilities and that they lacked teeth to effectively draw on their statutory powers due to a plethora of reasons ranging from political interference to inadequate financial resources and expertise.

The structure of the new authority does little to address these concerns of greater independence, particularly in view of the powers given to the Minister of Trade, Commerce and Consumer Affairs—in relation to the appointment of members and with regard to price control, for example. Another issue of contention is the removal of the power to investigate monopolies and mergers from the ambit of CAA. However, as will be discussed further in the next section, this policy decision is linked to a larger debate on facilitating efficiency enhancing mergers and is justifiable to some extent, given that there is some provision for merger control in the economy under the Takeovers and Mergers Code of the Securities and Exchange Commission (SEC) and the multisector regulator for utilities.

A notable improvement in the new legislation is the provision for concurrent jurisdiction with the multi sector regulators. What is apparently lacking, however, is the articulation of a clear and comprehensive competition policy framework as a result of which competition concerns still tend to be dealt with in a piecemeal fashion in response to a particular sector requirement. The tendency appears to be to sideline the formulation of a generic competition policy framework in favour of a sectoral approach for reasons that will be dealt with in the next section of this chapter.

POLICY QUESTIONS AND CONTROVERSIES

The debate on 'big picture' policy issues with respect to privatization and regulation has been relatively minimal compared, for example, to India and a number of Latin American and transitional economies that adopted similar reforms. The relatively inconspicuous response to the reform process was in part due to the fact that the more vocal antagonists such as trade unions had been placated by the various safeguard measures described in the previous section. This modest level of discourse on key policy issues is also linked to a more widespread problem in Sri Lanka—the absence of a cohesive civil society that actively participates in the development process.

In spite of the fact that the policy debate has been rather limited and that discussion, where it has existed, has been confined to academic circles with little interaction between decision makers and the academia, policy makers have had to, inevitably, confront some 'big picture' questions in the reform process. This section looks at some of these policy questions and controversies from the perspective of policy formulation, the implementation process and reform outcomes.

A fundamental question, and one that provides useful insights to other aspects of the reform process as well, is why did successive policy regimes choose privatization as a development strategy? With respect to the period from liberalization up to December 2001,[17] perhaps the most obvious answer, as mentioned elsewhere in this chapter, is budgetary considerations, with donor pressure coming in a close second. But is this all? It is argued that whilst these other considerations had an important role in the decision to enter into a privatization programme, the overriding factor is linked to the dynamics of interest group behaviour as set out in public choice theories.[13] The argument here is that agents within the government pursue their own interests and those of favoured groups at the expense of the public interest. This explanation rejects the notion of an altruistic and disinterested government, leans on rent-seeking behaviour and is consistent with the realities of political (and regulatory) capture that are rampant in the reform process.

In the Sri Lankan case, this argument is exemplified in a number of ways. As mentioned earlier in this chapter, corruption was widespread in the SOE sector prior to privatization. Although mopping up wastage and inefficiency and revamping these entities through the infusion of private sector norms was a stated objective of privatization, the exercise turned out to be one of crony capitalism where under-priced state assets were sold to political favourites. Rent-seeking was further institutionalized as a long-term feature of the reform process, in the absence of effective regulatory structures. An excellent example of this is that of the telecommunications privatization described in the previous section of this chapter. In sum, policy makers did not move away from the rent-seeking mindset that had prevailed in the SOE era; there was little reform in an institutional sense. Instead, decision makers in the government had discovered that there were more rents to be had through privatization than through the collection of monies under state ownership.

How does this relate to the role played by the donor community during these years? As mentioned earlier, the primary concern of aid organizations was the huge budgetary drain imposed by SOEs. What was important to these institutions was getting Sri Lanka's macroeconomic fundamentals right, with governance being a mere buzzword, useful only insofar as it contributed to economic efficiency. The donors wanted a speedy implementation of the privatization process, with transparency concerns being placed on the back burner. In a sense, this rather single-minded attitude of the aid agencies provided decision makers with the policy space to pursue their rent-seeking agenda under the guise of a 'speedy' reform process. The involvement of the international agencies also allowed the Government to justify the entire process to the general public as an externally imposed condition to receive assistance.

A second important policy question relates to the actual results of the privatization programme. As stated earlier on, the fiscal burden and improving the efficiency of entities were emphasized as key objectives of the programme. In addition, distributional objectives such as broad-basing share ownership, enhancing employment opportunities and improving the quality and access of goods and services were also cited as being important, to elicit public support for the reforms. In general, the efficiency of privatized entities has improved over the two stages of privatization. Whether these improvements are due to ownership change or to the introduction of competition, however, is an issue for debate and for further study.

The argument put forward by Nellis (1994), for example, is that ownership change is essential to 'lock in' the gains from the reform process and to sustain improved performance in the long term. However, how valid is this hypothesis in a political economy setting such as that in Sri Lanka, where ownership change is linked to cronyism? As argued in Knight-John (2004), whilst performance indicators such as network expansion have improved after privatization in the case of the gas and telecommunication sectors (where the incumbent operators were given five year exclusivities in the Liquefied Petroleum Gas business and in international telephony, respectively), these benefits of reform have been negligible in the non-urban areas. It is relevant in this context to note that the incumbent telecom operator (privatized in 1997) had no legally binding universal service obligations (USOs), although these were built into the licence agreements of its competitors. Moreover, in the absence of a counterfactual it is not possible to draw a firm conclusion on whether the improvements in the telecommunications sector were due to privatization in 1997 or due to the introduction of direct competition in 1996. Also, in the gas sector, the fact that prices did come down with the entry of another player consequent to the ending of the exclusivity period, supports the premise that it is competition rather than ownership change alone that holds the key to development-oriented reform.

According to Knight-John (2004), the results with respect to the distributional objectives of privatization have been less than satisfactory, with the relatively poor and those lacking political clout gaining little from the reform process. Again, this brings us back to the underlying reasons for privatization in Sri Lanka—rent-seeking and embedded cronyism—that precludes these 'less favoured' groups of society from enjoying the benefits of reform. These aspects of the reform process have contributed to the perception that the privatization process was biased towards vested interests. As mentioned earlier, the more vocal antagonists such as labour have been pacified with ESOPs and expensive retrenchment packages while consumer groups lack the critical mass to make a big impact in this regard. Privatization is enthusiastically supported by the well-connected who have the opportunity to purchase, often under-priced, state assets as well as the promise of continued rents, with the various exclusivity agreements that have been entered into. The burning question, however, is for how long and to what extent can this process continue before it irreversibly undermines itself? The answer to this question lies in the dynamics of institutions and institutional change in Sri Lanka, as will be analysed shortly.

A third policy issue relates to regulation, which, as emphasized throughout this chapter, has been ineffective and not tuned to the needs of an economy that had entered into a fairly extensive privatization programme. In several instances, privatization has preceded sound regulatory reforms, leading to the entrenchment of vested interests that have tended to resist competition-oriented change. The problem was compounded by the lack of a comprehensive competition policy framework and the emasculation of the existing regulatory and competition institutions through political interference. Again, one might argue that a strong regulatory and competition policy framework was antithetical to the goal of rent maximization by way of privatization.

The relevant question here is to what extent has the status quo with regard to regulation changed, given the spate of regulatory reforms in the recent past, and to what extent can it contribute to genuine institutional change? As mentioned in the previous section of this chapter, multisector regulation has been adopted as the new model for regulation in Sri Lanka. In addition to the economic advantages of scope and scale inherent in this structure, it has the potential to reduce political interference by severing direct links between a sector minister and the regulatory agency. Principles of good governance have also been incorporated into the new regulatory structures, with the involvement of the Constitutional Council, for example, in the appointment of commissioners—a move away from partisan politics and an attempt to add objectivity and independence to the regulatory process. Another important feature of the new genre of regulation is the provision of financial independence to the regulatory authority by way of levies and licensing fees—in stark contrast to the old style regulation where the agency depended on Treasury funds for its activities.

Despite the fact that these reforms have been in place for a relatively short period and that they are yet to be put into practice (the multisector authorities are still not fully functional), the indications are that there is a marked improvement in the thinking on regulatory strategies under the current regime. The principal problems of regulatory capture, insufficient coordination between different agencies and clear definition of their respective competencies, and inadequacies in the design of anti-trust legislation have been dealt with in the new regulatory legislation, perhaps not to the best possible extent—as will be discussed next—but with definite improvements over previous legislation.

What then are the remaining challenges in this regard? One key area that has not received adequate attention is the need to develop a generic competition law. As of now, anti-competitive business practices are dealt with under the new consumer protection legislation as well as under some of the sector regulation statutes, while mergers and monopolies are dealt with only under the public utilities regulation law and the Take Overs and Mergers Code of the SEC as mentioned earlier. The stated rationale for stripping what was originally meant to be a competition cum consumer protection authority of the powers to investigate mergers and monopolies, was that provisions to deal with such practices existed in sectors of the economy that needed them and that the new competition/consumer agency lacked the capacity to deal with these complex practices—going by the record of its predecessor. Decision makers also maintained the view that a small economy like Sri Lanka should not impose controls on efficiency enhancing mergers. However, it is noteworthy that no distinction was made in this regard between horizontal mergers (potential for abusive business practices) and vertical (potential for enhancing efficiency) ones. There are indications, however, that the tendency to sideline the formulation of a generic competition law and policy in favour of sector specific legislation may change, given the need to have a generic competition framework in place by a particular date, to meet the requirements of the planned Free Trade Agreement with the US.

A second important issue with respect to the current wave of regulation is that the new legislation is inconsistent in several instances with the devolution of power to local government bodies under the Constitution. An illustration of such irregularities is the centralization of licensing functions under the multi-utility regulator—the Public Utilities Commission (PUC), when these powers ought to have been vested with the relevant local authorities—thus depriving these local agencies of their due revenue. The absence of a dialogue between the PUC and the local authorities in regard to public–private partnerships could also be a stumbling block in the reform process given the need to obtain local authority approval for all building and other permits required for infrastructure development. What emerges from this analysis is that there has been a tendency to centralize the regulatory reform process in PIPU with inadequate interaction with other relevant bodies. As such, whilst the early indications are that the new wave of regulation is promising in terms of effectiveness, efficiency and legitimacy, there appears to be a parallel tendency towards centralized control in the regulatory process—a trend that needs to be corrected if the reform process is to derive maximum benefits from local expertise, avoid reinventing the wheel and be a truly development-oriented exercise.

Finally, we return to a recurring theme in this chapter, the dynamics of institutions and institutional change in Sri Lanka. As conceived in New Institutional Economics, rent-seeking is a result of policies and institutions that create the wrong incentive structures—for example ineffective regulation—and the introduction of more efficient institutions is constrained by the high political transaction costs linked to institutional change. The final outcome of institutional change rests on the distribution of power in society, the relative political leverage of those who are pro-reform and those who resist change and the nature of patron–client networks.

Applying this analytical framework to the Sri Lankan context provides some useful insights into the reform process. Similar to other countries in South Asia, political power in Sri Lanka is concentrated amongst a small group from the more privileged segments of society. This has resulted in governance structures that largely discount the interests of a vast majority of the population, with the leadership deriving its support from patron–client networks that serve its narrow political agenda. Traditionally, UNP regimes have leant on the business sector while the PA has been more labour friendly, although the dissimilarities between the two major parties in this regard have narrowed considerably over time. Successive political regimes have bought the support of groups opposed to the reform process—groups that have the power to resist change—as evident in the case of privatization. To put it differently, these groups have bought themselves into the rent-seeking process and have become embedded in the prevailing governance structure.

In view of these circumstances, institutional change is only possible if the political leadership is willing to completely overhaul and rebuild the institutions that have perpetuated bad governance over the years and create new structures to support the needs of the reform process. This requires immense political will—as it involves uprooting entrenched vested interests—and political risk, given the nature of the electoral cycle. In an alternative scenario, institutional change could be the natural result of a deep crisis—a situation that may not be too far off given the irregularities that have pervaded the reform process. In the final analysis, the future direction of institutions and institutional change and of the reform process rests on the path chosen by the new regime: will it be path dependence or will it be a new genre of governance?

CONCLUSIONS

The analysis of privatization and regulation in the preceding sections of this chapter provides some useful insights on the dynamics of reform and of institutions in the Sri Lankan context. Reform—even in well-functioning political systems—is a messy exercise; and this has been painfully evident in the case of Sri Lanka. Whilst there is no crystal ball to indicate the outcomes of pursuing alternative development policies and processes, one clear message that emerges from the reform experience is that better results could have been achieved in a more efficient institutional setting.

A key aspect of the reform process with regard to privatization and regulation is a marked degree of path dependence spanning successive political regimes. The more blatant examples of this trend are rent-seeking behaviour, crony capitalism, weak regulation and a tendency to discount the distributional effects of privatization. That such problems are not unique to Sri Lanka is evident from the literature on the privatization experience of the transition economies (Nellis, 2002) or from that of other South Asian economies (Ahluwalia and Williamson, 2003). This does not, however, exempt the political leadership and key decision makers in the reform process from making committed efforts to learn from past mistakes and create an institutional milieu conducive to equitable development.

Following from the discussion in this chapter, a few lessons emerge as being integral to the success of future reform efforts. First, it must be recognized that any reform is essentially a political exercise; blindly following donor prescriptions that are built on the shaky foundations of an apolitical and ahistorical policy process is bound to be a recipe for disaster. It is vital that the reform process has national ownership if it is to be truly meaningful in terms of development. This notion of national ownership leads us to the core of the reform problem—the nature of the state in Sri Lanka.

A realpolitik argument for the dismal results of Russia's privatization programme is proposed in Nellis (2002)—that the government lacked the capacity and the will to follow alternative policy constructions and that what reformers achieved was as best as could be expected under the circumstances. Was this true for Sri Lanka as well? It is clearly not the case that Sri Lanka lacked the professional competence to implement more development-oriented reforms. What was apparent, however, was the absence of political will to shake up the system in view of the threats of resistance from vested groups that formed the political support base and the nature of the electoral cycle. Given the political system in Sri Lanka, policy reforms have tradition-ally been determined by a five or six-year electoral cycle, with the government only implementing a particular policy if its net benefits outweighed its net costs within this short time span.

As such, the state in Sri Lanka appears to have alternated from a captive state (political capacity circumscribed by pressures from vested interests) to a parasitic state (state actively engaged in capturing rents from the reform process) depending on the particular political settlement—the distribution of power between state and society—at the time. This is certainly a far cry from the developmental state that is said to have—see for instance, Syn (2002)—been the driving factor for the success of the East Asian nations. What then does the nature of the state in Sri Lanka indicate in terms of the capacity for better institutions, better governance and a development-oriented reform process in the future? Clearly, it is not feasible and possibly counter-productive to attempt replicating the experience of developmental states elsewhere, given that path dependence and historical factors inevitably play a vital role in shaping the nature of the state. What is required instead is to restructure state-society relations—institutions—to suit Sri Lanka's development needs. It is not sufficient to tinker with economic reforms alone; what is important is to get the political processes right—an effort which requires tremendous political will, given the inevitable loss of political support and hardships in the short term. The good news, however, as evidenced in a number of countries that have undergone similar processes, is that once the process is right and reforms are on the correct track, support is forthcoming from a broad segment of the population. The key question is, will the current regime take up this challenge, or will the opportunity for change be missed once again.

NOTES

1. Privatization is defined broadly as both a partial and total sale of state assets and as a transfer of management to private parties in the context of this chapter.
2. See, for instance, Nellis (2002) and Stiglitz (2002).
3. Institutions as defined in this chapter include 'social rules, conventions, and other elements of the structural framework of social interaction' (Bardhan, 1989) as well as organizations—political, economic, and social bodies—that function within the scope of these rules.

4. See, for instance, the World Development Reports of 1997 and 2002.
5. However, there are indications that this may be changing with the greater involvement of academics in the policy-making process under the current regime.
6. A brief and unsuccessful episode of liberalization was undertaken in collaboration with the international financial institutions from 1965–70.
7. See Kelegama (1992) for examples of such transactions.
8. There have been variations around this formula in the case of individual enterprises, as detailed for example in Knight-John (1995).
9. Three of these entities were subsequently re-privatized.
10. Although this paper deals specifically with telecommunications privatization, the analysis lends itself generally to the political economy of privatization and regulation in Sri Lanka.
11. See http://www.regainingsrilanka.org
12. It is still too soon to draw any firm conclusions in this regard with respect to the current UNP regime.
13. The rent-seeking thesis does not contradict the budgetary objectives of privatization: the greater the proceeds from asset sales, the larger the share that can be expropriated by vested interest groups.

REFERENCES

Ahluwalia, Isher Judge and John Williamson (eds) (2003), *The South Asian Experience with Growth*, New Delhi: Oxford University Press.

Bardhan, Pranab (1989), 'Alternative Approaches to Theory of Institutions in Economic Development', in Pranab Bardhan (ed.), *The Economic Theory of Agrarian Institutions*, Berkeley, California: University of California Press.

Dunham, David and Saman Kelegama (1997), 'A Second Look at the Sri Lankan Experience, 1977–93', *Developing Economies*, 35(2): 166–84.

Jayasuriya, Sisira and Malathy Knight-John (2002), 'Sri Lanka's Telecommunications Industry: From Privatization to Anti-Competition?', Centre on Regulation and Competition Working Paper Series No. 14, Manchester: Centre on Regulation and Competition, University of Manchester.

Kelegama, Saman (1992), *Privatization: The Sri Lankan Experience*, Institute of Policy Studies, Public Enterprise Series No. 1, Colombo: Institute of Policy Studies.

————— (1997), 'Privatisation and the Public Exchequer: Some Observations from the Sri Lankan Experience', *Asia Pacific Development Journal*, 4(1).

Knight-John, Malathy (1995), 'Privatization in a Developing Country: The Sri Lankan Experience', Paper presented at the Asia Productivity Organization symposium on Privatization, Bangkok.

————— (2004), 'Distributional Impact of Privatization: The Sri Lankan Experience', in John Nellis and Nancy Birdsall (eds), *Distributional Impact of Privatization*, Washington D.C.: Center for Global Development.

Nellis, John (1994), 'Is Privatization Necessary?', *Public Policy for the Private Sector*, Washington D.C.: World Bank.

————— (2002), 'External Advisors & Privatisation in Transition Economies', Working Paper No. 3, February 2003, Washington D.C.: World Bank,

Sri Lanka (2002), 'Regaining Sri Lanka: Vision and Strategy for Accelerated Development', at http://www.regainingsrilanka.org

Stiglitz, Joseph (2002), *Globalisation and its Discontents*, London: Penguin.

Syn, Tan Wooi (2002), 'Capital Accumulation, State Intervention and Privatisation', Centre on Regulation and Competition Working Paper Series No.29, University of Manchester: Centre on Regulation and Competition.

World Bank (1997), *World Development Report:* Washington D.C.: World Bank.

———— **(2002),** *World Development Report:* Washington D.C.: World Bank.

SELECT READING

Krueger, Anne (ed.) (2000), *Economic Policy Reform: The Second Stage,* Chicago: University of Chicago Press.

18

Banking Sector Reform

H.N.S. Karunatilake

Introduction

From 1950 onwards, the premier financial institution that has looked at banking and economic policy critically was the Central Bank. In the face of major changes in policies and political problems, it has endeavoured to look at policies critically and tender advice to the government objectively. Despite this, its views have been influenced by strict theoretical economic criteria, at times ignoring the needs of the people and the human and social aspects of development. The Bank has often found it difficult to be guided by the need to harmonize its advice with pragmatic social considerations, particularly to the issues pertaining to the welfare of the people. The public has very often expressed their views on economic issues through newspapers, both in the form of articles to journals and letters to the editors. From the 1990s to date, more attention has been given in the newspapers to debate and discussion on banking and economic issues, mainly because practically every newspaper has carried special sections devoted to finance and business matters. This has given an opportunity for the press to highlight banking, financial and economic problems and for the public to express their views. However, as far as economic policy debates are concerned, the proposal to establish a central bank itself became a controversial issue in the late 1940s and the public and politicians with different convictions had the opportunity of engaging in a public debate on the proposal.

Views on the Establishment of a Central Bank

The Finance Minister J.R. Jayawardene, in consultation with the Cabinet of the first pre-independence government, in 1947, had taken a decision to set up a central bank and this was announced in the Throne Speech on 25 November 1947. But the proposal to establish a central bank resulted in a controversy spearheaded by a few Members of

Parliament and some members of the academic community in the University of Ceylon. The Monetary Law Bill was presented in Parliament exactly two years after the announcement in the Throne Speech that a central bank would be set up. Finance Minister J.R. Jayawardene took a bold, and perhaps an unorthodox decision, to invite an economist from the Federal Reserve System in the US to report on the Central Bank, rather than an official from the Bank of England. He was aware that a favourable report would not be forthcoming from an expert from the Bank of England that has always been guided by orthodox thinking and tradition. Two Bank of England officials who reported on the prospects for new central banks in Ghana and Nigeria produced negative reports, confirming the worst fears of Ceylon's first Finance Minister.[1]

John Exter from the Federal Reserve System, who was assigned the task of preparing a report on the establishment of the Central Bank and a draft bill, accomplished his task within one year of his arrival on the island.[2] Exter's views that recommended a central bank were not well received by some left wing political parties and academic economists in Ceylon. The proposals became controversial and the object of the critics was to forestall the establishment of the Bank, or to defer it for a considerable period of time. Several articles appeared in the local press examining the pros and cons of central banking. The role of a central bank, particularly in developing economies, was not clearly understood at that time because the literature on central banking had just started to appear; there were only a handful of books on the subject and very few of them were analytical. The critics of central banking at that time were also influenced by the orthodox and tradition bound central banking practices in the developed countries in the West with which they were familiar.[3] No one cared to consider the medium and long-term impact on the country of the Central Bank. Moreover, most of the University Economics teachers who were critical at that time had British postgraduate degrees and their analyses were influenced very much by the tradition and practice of central banking in Europe, most notably in the UK.

H.A. de S. Gunasekera, who was at that time the Senior Lecturer in Economics at the University of Ceylon, was the foremost academic critic and he maintained that in a dependent economy, heavily biased towards international trade, there was very little that a central bank could achieve and the preceding Currency Board System was ideal for a dependent economy.[4] After the Central Bank was established, in a symposium published in 1952 edited by Professor R.S. Sayers, Gunasekera did not change his views and he argued, 'An export economy such as Ceylon cannot even with independent monetary institutions effectively pursue an independent monetary policy. Ceylon's level of prosperity is determined by foreign demand for its staple exports, ... its level of income is determined by the prices that these exports fetch in foreign markets ... a policy of compensatory spending cannot stabilize incomes or prices in a country so utterly dependent on foreign trade as Ceylon is'.[5] His doctoral thesis written and published subsequently, entitled *From Dependent Currency to Central Banking in Ceylon* saw no change in his thinking. These same ideas were reiterated by two British academics, Newlyn and Rowan in their study *Money and Banking in British Colonial Africa* when they stated, 'Unfortunately, however, though economic autonomy may be desirable it is not necessarily attainable. Any economy, which through international trade forms a part of the world economic system cannot enjoy complete freedom either to choose the economic policies it desires, or to control the domestic situation.' Most of the other critics of the Exter proposals were those who had graduated from the University of Ceylon under the tutelage of Professor Gunasekera.

However, the business community welcomed the proposal to establish the Central Bank and they expressed the view that a central bank was more necessary in Ceylon than in other less developed countries because there was a need to control the expatriate banks in the island. One of the charges made against the expatriate banks in the early 1930s was that they were not interested in financing the Ceylonese business community. In Parliament, former Professor of History S.A. Pakeman, an Englishman, expressed the nebulous view that 'the Minister of Finance is in some danger of putting too great value on a new central bank. The Central Bank can do a very great deal. One freely admits that it cannot do everything'.[6] N.M. Perera, who received two doctorates from the London School of Economics and a leading Trotskyite had certain reservations and cautioned, 'I want the Honourable Minister of Finance not to overestimate, particularly in the first instance, the importance of the power of the Bank as he intended to do. The first reason is this. We have no money market in Ceylon; we have absolutely no market in Ceylon, there is no call money market at all in Ceylon. There are no local bills in Ceylon. The result is that, the influence the Bank could have on the local market is very limited'.[7]

ESTABLISHMENT OF THE CENTRAL BANK

The Monetary Board of the Central Bank of Ceylon was appointed in July 1950 and the Bank commenced operations after the opening ceremony on 28 August 1950. At the outset, the Bank had six departments and a staff of about 60 persons, most of whom had been recruited to the Bank service from other government departments that included the Treasury, the Department of Commerce and the Inland Revenue Department. Gamani Corea and Tissa Jayakody were the first two staff officers who were directly recruited to the Bank service in September 1950 from among graduates who had recently passed out from the universities.

Outside the field of economic and monetary management, the Central Bank faced a major problem in 1954 relating to the Governor of the Bank, N.U. Jayewardena who succeeded John Exter as Governor on 1 July 1953. However, Jayewardena's tenure of office was short-lived as he was suspended from office on 2 July 1954[8] on the basis of the findings of a commission whose report was published as Sessional Paper No. 20 of 1954.[9]

The first *Annual Report* of the Central Bank for the year 1950 that was issued in March 1951 expressed very specific views on the prevailing monetary situation. A considerable part of the Report was devoted to the 'analysis of the inflationary situation'. The Report emphasized that inflation was caused by a sharp increase in the money supply and an increase in the Colombo Working Class Cost of Living Index.

The Bank was critical of government policy and in this context, it opposed the increase in subsidies on the grounds that most of the subsidized consumer items such as rice and flour were imported and that a rise in prices outside Ceylon would make subsidies unwieldy and impractical, affecting both the budget and the balance of payments. The Bank stated that a 'widespread system of subsidies has a tendency to hide real costs, to distort the country's economy and sometimes to act as a serious barrier to efficiency. An alternative to an extension of the system of subsidies is an adjustment to changes in living costs by permitting a rise in incomes through the mechanism of the cost of living allowance'.[10] The Central Bank argued that there are great advantages in a system of wage payments which gears wages rather closely to the cost of living. Though domestic price stability is the goal of every government and every central bank, there were difficulties in achieving this objective in Ceylon because the economy is so dependent on its international trade. It further added that the surest and the most effective cure in an inflationary situation was an increased supply of goods.

Following sound economic thinking, the Bank advocated that there should be no budget deficit. 'From a monetary point of view, therefore, it is most disturbing that in 1950 the government should have run a deficit, that on an average of more than Rs 6 million a month to the money supply, at a time when other factors were already causing private incomes to expand.' The Central Bank Report for 1950 further stated that the weakness in the fiscal structure of the government was that, despite the rise in the national income, there had been no tendency for the budget deficit to be eliminated and it was a widely recognized principle of fiscal policy that taxes and expenditure should be such that government taxes and expenditure should automatically operate in a compensatory way.[11]

The views expressed by the Central Bank on subsidies, inflation and budget deficits have been the position taken by the Bank since its inception and there has been no variation in its stand since then on these issues. It is remarkable that the Monetary Board had occasion to express these views in 1950, when the country was experiencing one of the greatest commodity booms of the post-independence era. What is more significant is that compared to the yearly economic scenarios since the 1970s, in 1950 inflation was only at a single digit figure of 4 per cent, the food subsidy was financed wholly out of government revenue and the net cash deficit was Rs 153.6 million. Even so, only half of this deficit was financed by methods that contributed to increase the money supply, while Rs 74.3 million of the deficit was financed by the non-inflationary method of borrowing from the current savings of the people.

THE CENTRAL BANK'S APPROACH TO MONETARY AND FISCAL MANAGEMENT AND GOVERNMENT POLICY

The Bank from the very beginning adopted a constructive approach to monetary and fiscal management. The greatest obstacle to sound economic management has been the continuing budget deficits that have been the high watermark of economic management since the mid-1950s. The *Annual Report* of the Central Bank for 1951, however, mentioned that the government had heeded the advice given by the Central Bank and that there had been a relatively high degree of coordination between the Bank and the government.[12] In fact, Ceylon's cost of living rose much less than that of its principal trading partners. At the London Conference of Finance Ministers in January 1952, it was recognized that Ceylon had maintained a stable economy through a very trying period and it had not contributed to the prevailing Sterling Area crisis. The Report for 1951 went on to say, 'For the Central Bank the virtually balanced budget for 1951 was a factor of great significance since it enabled the Bank to pursue other policies effectively.'[13]

By 1952, however, the Bank had to focus its attention on a different set of economic problems. After the end of the Korean War boom, external assets started falling sharply and the cost of living ceased to increase. The Ceylon economy was confronted with a different set of problems that constituted the typical phases of the trade cycle. After the Korean War boom, the economy had to readjust itself to deflation, the fall of export prices and an adverse terms of trade. The Central Bank accused the government of living beyond its means because expenditure was sustained at a high level despite a rise in import prices. The Bank was concerned about the budget deficit in 1952 that was financed largely from bank credit and much of this deficit was used to finance consumption than investment and the Bank attributed the drain of external assets. The Central Bank believed that this could be corrected by following sound 'monetary and fiscal policies'.[14] If subsidies had been eliminated, the Bank stated that the budget deficit and the expansion of credit could have been reduced considerably. The government put had into effect an Eight Point Austerity Programme, but that did not reduce the budget deficit sufficiently to stop the drain of external assets.

In the first three years, the Central Bank cautioned the government of the adverse consequences of subsidies, the increase in the money supply and the rise in the cost of living. As compared to the post-1977 period, the level of inflation at that time was relatively very small and strictly it was not an issue worth highlighting. But the Central Bank, in terms of its commitment to sound economic management, thought it fit that it should bring it to the notice of the government.

Referring to 1953, the Bank stated that the continuing decline in external assets was a fiscal problem and it was a monetary problem only in the sense that the government deficit had to be financed through credit expansion that caused the money supply to expand.[15] The year 1954 was accompanied by an economic and financial recovery. The terms of trade improved by 22 per cent and contributed to improve real income and for the first time in many years, the government had an overall budget surplus. The first five years of central banking operations therefore, witnessed a boom, recession and recovery.

The 1956 Change

Economic conditions in 1956 witnessed a sharp reversal with a fall in exports, the deterioration in the terms of trade, a decrease in domestic production and a considerable decline in the balance of payments surplus. The Bank emphasized that fiscal policy measures were needed to counteract instability.[16] In April 1956, there was a change of government that made it increasingly difficult for the Central Bank to make its advice have an impact on government policy. The new government of S.W.R.D. Bandaranaike was committed to socialist policies and its general approach to economic management was not in harmony with the views of the Central Bank. For the first time, the National Planning Council and a Planning Secretariat were established by statute. The head of the Planning Secretariat was Gamani Corea. The Bank had no option but to accept the policies of the new government that represented a significant departure from that of the previous government that was committed to free and open economic policies. However, the Central Bank in its *Annual Reports* did not look critically at the policies of the new government, especially in the early years when these policies first came into operation. In its *Annual Report* for 1956, the Bank stated that, 'the declared intention of the present government was to place high priority on industrial development, with state ownership and control of basic industries, while giving private enterprise every encouragement to play its part in the development process'.[17]

In the field of development finance, there was a major institutional breakthrough in 1956 with the establishment of the Development Finance Corporation (DFC) of Ceylon. The DFC was pioneered by the Central Bank and the Governor, Sir Arthur Ranasinha, played a leading role in its establishment. It was the first private sector specialized development finance institution to be established. Throughout, the DFC of Ceylon has made a valuable contribution to finance private sector industry, agriculture and the services sectors, despite the fact that it has had access to limited resources, not being a deposit taking institution and generally followed conservative lending policies. However, of all the leading financial institutions there has been very little public discussion about its role and activities.

The Central Bank's Relations with the Government, 1956–65

The Central Bank has maintained that, from 1956 onwards, the increasing budget deficits had contributed to worsen the economic outlook. The Central Bank frequently advised the government on the dangers of inflationary finance. The government for the first time adopted the procedure of borrowing from the Central Bank, mainly through the issue of Treasury bills to finance the deficits. As stated in the 1959 Report, the Central Bank could not 'abandon its role of cooperation with the Treasury to meet expenses as had been budgeted'.[18] Political changes had affected the Central Bank in the discharge of its functions because the new administrations were not committed to take the advice given as it stood in conflict with social policies that these governments were committed to.

The Central Bank in 1959 lamented that its ability to act effectively was severely restrained by the 'fiscal and other policies to which the government was committed' and it went on to add that 'owing to the unsettled political situation the government was unable to effectively support the aims of monetary policy'.[19] As financial adviser to the government, the Central Bank again repeatedly suggested the consideration of a number of remedial measures to reduce the budgetary gap, but for various reasons the government either postponed or could not carry out the suggestions. The Central Bank, mindful of its statutory obligations, repeatedly advised the government of the dangers inherent in the situation that was developing. The government, despite the floating of a Rs 25 million loan in October 1959, continued to increasingly resort to borrowing on three-month Treasury bills and on 15 December, the Treasury bill rate rose to 2.03 per cent. Thereafter, the Monetary Board taking into account the financial and economic situation and after seeking the approval of the Finance Minister, raised the bank rate from 2.5 to 3 per cent.

The conduct of the Minister of Finance soon after was unprecedented in the annals of central banking. On 23 December 1959, the Minister of Finance issued a directive to the Central Bank under Section 115(2) of the Monetary Law Act to restore bank rate to the previous level. The Bank was completely taken aback by the inconsistent stand of the Finance Minister. The Bank complied with this directive on 24 December 1959 and thereafter stated, 'in view of the Government's attitude on financial policy, the Central Bank had to abandon the plans of monetary control which it had contemplated'.[20] This was a unique episode in the history of the Central Bank and was the only occasion that a Finance Minister had issued a directive to reverse an important monetary policy measure.

The Parliament constituted after the general election of March 1960 was itself dissolved in April 1960. A second general election took place in July 1960 that resulted in Sirimavo Bandaranaike, heading an SLFP coalition, becoming the Prime Minister. The latter administration enabled the Central Bank to introduce certain measures to restrict imports. The Bank observed that in the context of a sharp decline in external assets, 'Monetary instruments at best be used to supplement the wider policies adopted by the government itself.'[21] Faced with a difficult situation, the Central Bank indicated that there were two major considerations that would determine the type of measures that would bring about a rapid reduction in imports and other outlays to stop the sharp decline in foreign reserves. Inflationary pressures emanating from monetary expansion also had to be controlled. The Bank stated that the government could apply quantitative controls on imports through licensing and similar devices, higher import duties and exchange controls on outlays abroad, while action by the Central Bank would primarily be the restriction of credit for imports, or on bank credit in general.

The Central Bank went on to examine the merits of different methods of restricting imports in depth and these involved both quantitative and monetary methods of control. The Bank said, 'A more selective approach to credit control is needed, where emphasis is placed on the direct reduction of credit for imports.' Due to the prevailing political circumstances, the government heeded the advice of the Central Bank and in 1960 sharply raised the import duty on a wide range of non-essentials. At the same time, exchange control measures restricted outlays on foreign travel, study abroad and capital transfers. The Central Bank for the first time introduced monetary methods of import control. On letters of credit for the import of certain goods, commercial banks were required to insist on a cash margin of 50 per cent. Banks were directed not to increase the amount of their advances for the purpose of importing selected goods. Restrictions were also applied on hire purchase transactions on specified goods. Simultaneously, bank rate was increased from 2.5 to 4 per cent and the Central Bank raised the reserve requirements against demand deposits from 10 to 12 per cent.

This period could be characterized as one where there was considerable coopera-tion between the Central Bank and the government. A contributory factor was that Governor Rajapatirana and the new Prime Minister had healthy personal relations and she was willing to take advice. In 1961, on account of the measures taken by the Government and the Central Bank, there was a significant reduction in the volume and value of imports and the government was able to reduce the external payments gap and the drain on external assets. The Bank pointed out that Ceylon was less successful in curbing the internal monetary expansion. In 1962, there was a further extension of restrictions on imports, which were widened to include certain categories of essential goods. This, however, helped to reduce the decline in external assets. With the intensification of controls on imports, the impact of monetary expansion fell on the domestic level of prices that resulted in growing scarcities and sharply rising prices. The Central Bank observed that import restrictions imposed for balance of payments pur-poses had imparted a stimulus to the growth of domestic manufacturing industry, both in the public and private sectors.[22]

The period 1961–64 was characterized by increasing budget deficits that were financed by inflationary methods, while external reserves continued to fall. The Cen-tral Bank made a wide range of observations on the ongoing import substitution and industrialization process. In 1964, the government introduced a controversial bill to nationalize the banking system. There was open opposition to this move by the finan-cial and business communities and the public. However, there was a major split in the SLFP on bank nationalization and a powerful group within the Party crossed over to the UNP resulting in the incumbent government losing its majority in Parliament.

The Bank stated that it was unlikely that Ceylon could, in the short term, find a solution to her external payments problems by bringing about a rising flow of essential imports by increasing her exports alone. The Bank remarked, 'Ceylon could econo-mize on her external resources not only by curtailing imports of luxuries and inessen-tials, as indeed she has done, but also by replacing imports by domestically produced substitutes. As mentioned, restrictions on imports had already resulted in the establish-ment of several domestic industries. It needs to be well recognized that that there are severe limits in a country like Ceylon to foreign exchange saving through a process of import substitution in the sphere of manufacturing industry.'[23] The Central Bank emphasized the need to intensify import substitution in agriculture as there was greater potential in it than in industry.

The Bank and Liberalization after 1965

After the UNP government came into power in 1965 under Dudley Senanayake, the government tried as far as possible to liberalize the economy. However, due to the prevalence of stringent controls and restrictions, the UNP government was not able to achieve very much in its efforts to liberalize the economy. The Central Bank, the business community and the people welcomed the liberal policies of the UNP govern-ment, but the government faced difficulties in speedy implementation.

In pursuance of the government's objective of progressive liberalization, on 6 May 1968 the government, on the recommendation of the Central Bank, introduced the Foreign Exchange Entitlement Certificate Scheme (FEECS). Under this scheme, FEECS were issued to those who surrendered foreign exchange against the export of certain goods and services. The foreign exchange receipts from traditional agricultural exports were not eligible for benefits under the scheme. Holders of Certificates were entitled, subject to import and exchange controls, to purchase foreign exchange from the commercial banks for the payment of certain specified imports and other remittances. The business community and the public in general welcomed the FEEC scheme as it contributed to both increased domestic production and supply of goods. The continued decline in exchange earnings had resulted in a considerable reduction in the ability of industry and productive economic activities to exploit existing capacity to the fullest extent.

In the *Annual Report* for 1969, the Bank stated, 'The benefits to Ceylon of import substitution in industry are, however, rather mixed. Expansion in manufacturing industry, which became one of the dynamic sectors of the early sixties, was to an appreciable extent impeded in the mid-sixties, mainly as a result of foreign exchange difficulties. The exchange reforms of May 1968 and the accompanying import liberalization enabled industry to utilize existing capacity to the fullest extent possible and also to increase capacity considerably on the basis of imports of raw materials and capital equipment. However, although in physical terms, there was a noteworthy increase in production, it cannot be said that the growth in industry was entirely in the right direction. This industrial activity developed under the shelter of a virtual ban on imports of competing products, leading to a growth of uneconomic industries operating largely under monopoly conditions. The prices of these manufactured goods continue to be high, whereas the quality standards of a great many of them are quite low.'[24]

Banking, Monetary and Other Economic Reforms, 1970–77

The UNP government that endeavoured to open up and liberalize the economy and the financial system was defeated at the general elections held in May 1970. With a new government once again committed to socialist policies coming into power in May 1970, there was a fundamental change in economic policy.

The first controversial economic measure launched by N.M. Perera, the Finance Minister, was to demonetize large currency notes of Rs 50 and Rs 100, the objective of which was to bring to the surface the large quantities of notes that were believed to be hoarded by capitalists. The Minister believed that people were evading taxes and that they had amassed large amounts of black money. The Finance Minister was instrumental in getting the new currency notes printed without the knowledge of the Central Bank that was the sole note issuing authority. What was even worse was that the signature of the Governor of the Central Bank was placed on the new notes without his knowledge and authority. Every person was allowed to present these demonetized notes to the Central Bank or to a commercial bank in exchange for new currency of the same denominations between 27 October and 2 November 1970.

For all intents and purposes, this exercise turned out to be a failure, as large numbers of individuals were engaged by big businessmen and hoarders to exchange small parcels of notes that were within the prescribed limits for the new currency. The attempt to demonetize large notes was not successful because, on the one hand, the amount of black money was heavily overestimated and, on the other, there was a loophole in the procedure used to unearth the black money. Subsequently, the Central Bank did not give estimates of the quantum of black money that had been brought to light by the demonetization. In fact, between 1971 and 1972, there was a sharp increase in the new Rs 100 and Rs 50 notes, showing that hoarding of notes of large denominations had continued. The business community was very critical of the demonetization exercise that was carried out by the Finance Minister and there was considerable adverse publicity as the endeavour turned out to be unsuccessful.

An important decision taken by the government in 1971 was the announcement of the Five-Year Plan 1972–76. Many expressed doubts and a controversy arose whether the Plan's targets would be achieved in the background of economic and financial restrictions and increasing controls on production and distribution. The aims of the Plan were to achieve a growth rate of 6 per cent annually. The Central Bank observed that a growth rate of 6 per cent was attainable as the country had achieved higher growth rates in the past. But the success of the Plan depended on the ability to finance the required imports.[25]

In the 1975 *Annual Report*, the Central Bank viewed the economic events even more critically and it remarked, 'If the growth rate of 6 per cent indicated in the Five Year Plan is taken as the minimum desirable rate of growth, the performance of the economy falls far below this level.[26] The Sri Lanka economy has remained sluggish despite the contribution of several new areas of economic activity such as industry, gem mining, tourism and other non-traditional exports. The economy has been unable to effectively accelerate economic growth mainly due to the continuing dominance of traditional sectors, the plantation and domestic agriculture and their inability to sustain their contribution to the Gross National Product.'

As far as the banking system was concerned, the SLFP government openly declared that no foreign bank branches would be permitted to operate in the island. Earlier, an unpopular debits tax was introduced on current accounts when N.M. Perera was the Finance Minister. The public was very critical of this tax but their views were not entertained, nor were its repercussions on the banking habit given consideration.

The Post-1977 Liberalization Reforms and Policies

In 1977, there was a fundamental reversal of the inward-looking policies adopted by the Marxist dominated governments since 1956. The newly elected UNP Government introduced these liberal policies. The Central Bank was, however, instrumental in expressing its views discreetly and made no direct references to the major political change that had taken place in 1977. The Central Bank welcomed the new policies and the removal of a wide range of restrictions.

As a first step, the exchange system of Sri Lanka underwent a complete change in the second half of 1977. On 15 November 1977, the basic rate and the premium rate (FEEC) was unified at the initial rate of Rs 16 to the US dollar and the rupee was allowed to float. Imports were comprehensively liberalized thereafter, except for a few items that continued to require licensing. A new tariff structure designed to protect local industry was put into effect and imports of capital goods up to Rs 7,00,000 were allowed freely. Exchange controls on payments were liberalized and various state monopolies were progressively eliminated and public and private sector competition was encouraged. Subsidies on consumer goods were reduced and initially, the food subsidies were withdrawn from those receiving an income of more than Rs 300 per month. In the *Annual Report* for 1977, the Central Bank observed, 'The success of these policies will depend crucially on the manner in which they are carried to their logical conclusion, given the social and political constraints and the speed with which such policies would yield the desired results, in terms of increased output incomes and employment.'

The economic reforms of 1977 resulted in the economy showing a growth rate of 8.2 per cent and that was an all-time record. Unlike in previous years, when growth was confined to a few sectors, on this occasion it was very broad based. The Bank said the major breakthrough in reforms was the adoption of a realistic exchange rate, although it did not elaborate on the characteristics of a 'realistic exchange rate'. On the whole, the Central Bank welcomed the liberalization measures along with the curtailing of consumer subsidies and confining subsidies to a target group of the most needy. The Bank concluded, 'These policies envisaged the sweeping departure from a tightly controlled, inward looking, welfare oriented economic strategy to a more liberalized outward looking and growth oriented one.'[27] The problem throughout has been that the Central Bank has not given adequate attention to any element of a welfare bias in the policies that it has advocated and supported. Being the principal advisor to the government, the question arises whether it can ignore the welfare and social aspects of policies and whether it is correct for the Bank to judge all policies in the light of strict economic criteria.

Nationalization of the Bank of Ceylon and Establishment of the People's Bank and the National Savings Bank

From an institutional standpoint, the early 1960s were of special significance because the leading domestic commercial bank, the Bank of Ceylon, was nationalized when the government decided to buy up the shares of the bank that were held by private individuals. This policy was consistent with the thinking of the MEP government that the ownership should be with the state in all types of major activity. Soon after in 1961, the government proceeded to set up another commercial bank, the People's Bank, because it was of the view that the Bank of Ceylon would not be able to devote considerable attention to financing the rural sector. At that time, rural financing was being coordinated by the Cooperative Federal Bank that had very limited resources and an unsatisfactory administrative set-up which made it unable to function in an effective manner. The People's Bank concentrated in taking banking to the distant towns and villages that hitherto did not have access to banking facilities. From the time it was established, it has played a key role in rural development. Small businessmen who earlier did not have access to credit facilities at reasonable rates of interest were able to obtain loans at relatively low rates of interest.

As a result of the nationalization of the Bank of Ceylon and the establishment of the People's Bank, firm foundations were laid for the expansion of domestic banking. These two commercial banks together had more than 900 branches and most of the new branches were opened for the first time in areas that did not have banking facilities. These two banks made the greatest contribution to the development and expansion of commercial banking in the island. Until 1977, the successive SLFP coalition governments in power gave these two banks monopoly rights to protect and develop their business. The entry of foreign banks and their branches were not permitted. However, after foreign banks were allowed to open branches, they confined their activities mostly to the towns. Therefore, even if foreign banking was permitted in the pre-1977 period it would not have threatened the business of these two major indigenous banks.

The government of 1970–77 wedded to socialist policies was committed to mobilize more resources internally than to depend on external aid. In any event, because of its restrictive and inward-looking policies it was not able to get foreign aid or attract foreign direct investment (FDI). One major policy decision was the restructuring of the savings mobilization organization. In 1971, the Post Office Savings Bank that had the largest number of savings accounts, the Ceylon Savings Bank and the Savings Certificate Fund were amalgamated to form an entirely new institution, the National Savings Bank. The concentration of savings in a single institution was welcomed by the general public, and they supported the new institution without reservation. For a long time since the establishment of the National Savings Bank, the Bank invested all the mobilized savings in medium and long-term government securities and it thus became a major mechanism for the mobilization of funds to finance budgetary needs. Latterly, it has given loans for the construction of houses and buildings. In terms of individual deposits, it is the largest financial institution with over 8 million depositors and funds in excess of Rs 43 billion.

EXPANSION OF PRIVATE COMMERCIAL BANKING AND DEVELOPMENT BANKING

After the economic reforms of 1977, the banking and financial system expanded considerably and it became much more complex and sophisticated. The two largest banks, the Bank of Ceylon and the People's Bank, were state owned and there where two other private banks, the Hatton National Bank and the Commercial Bank of

Ceylon. To liberalize the banking and financial system and to promote expansion, the Central Bank set up an internal Banking Committee to evaluate applications by local and foreign banks to set up branches. In 1978, the Committee received a large number of applications for evaluation. In 1979, on the recommendation of this Committee, the Finance Minister under Section 121B of the Monetary Law Act approved the Banque Indosuez, the Bank of Credit and Commerce International (Overseas) and the Citibank N.A. to open branches. The banking and the financial system between 1979 and 1982, expanded by leaps and bounds and more than 14 leading international banks opened branches in Sri Lanka. Thus, by 1988, there were 26 commercial banks operating in the island and the majority were branches of foreign banks

The Development Finance Corporation of Ceylon (DFCC) established in 1956 was a financial institution that mainly catered to the private sector. In the 1980s, the government found that more than one specialized institution was necessary to provide finance for development because the government that came into power in 1977 realized that financing new projects had to be undertaken on a broad front and that the DFCC was not equal to this task. Accordingly, a decision was taken to set up a new long-term financial institution, the National Development Bank, with the object of financing long-term projects in the private sector. This Bank commenced operations in 1983. These two institutions were precluded from accepting deposits from the public and they had to depend on lines of credit from overseas sources or through refinance from the Central Bank. However, in the early years of operation the National Development Bank found that it ran out of resources due to a heavy demand for credit especially from the tourism sector; by around 1987 a large number of new hotels were built to cater to the increasing influx of tourists. The National Development Bank also financed a wide range of manufacturing industries. The business community welcomed the establishment of the National Development Bank and it was praised for its dynamism and the new initiatives it had taken. In this period, a few local commercial banks also commenced business, notably the Sampath Bank and the Seylan Bank. A new development in domestic banking was the establishment of Regional Rural Development Banks by the Central Bank of Sri Lanka since 1985, to meet the credit needs of the rural sector.

SUPERVISION OF BANKS AND FINANCIAL INSTITUTIONS

The institutional and policy changes implemented by the Central Bank since the end of 1988 was the beginning of a new era in the regulation and supervision of banking and financial institutions. The Banking Act No. 30 was passed in 1988, giving the Central Bank more powers to regulate banking institutions. In addition, in December 1988, the Finance Companies Act No. 78 was passed, as the Central Bank needed more powers to control and restructure finance companies that had proliferated. The regulation and supervision of non-bank financial institutions was separated from bank supervision and a separate department, the Department for the Supervision of Non-Bank Financial Institutions was established with effect from 23 December 1988. The earlier Control of Finance Companies Act No. 27 of 1979 did not provide an adequate legal framework for the inspection and supervision of finance companies that was reflected in the failure of several large companies after 1983.

In the meantime, the prevailing liberal financial and economic policies provided opportunities for finance companies to expand and develop their businesses. It is reported that by 1985, there were more than 250 companies that were accepting various kinds of deposits from the public but of these, only 72 had registered with the Central Bank. Prior to 1978, there was no legislation to regulate these companies and the government, on the advice of the Central Bank, had to bring in a new legislation and the Finance Companies Act No. 27 of 1979 was passed. Reports were reaching the Central Bank that many of these finance companies were paying very high rates of interest on deposits and they were mismanaged and were engaged in a wide range of malpractices; some of the companies that had started businesses had misappropriated the funds placed with them by depositors. There were many factors behind the failure of finance companies. They included mismatch of borrowing and investment lending, adopting dubious accounting methods to show a false position to the public, indiscriminate lending policies and trying to outdo one another by offering attractive rates of interest without understanding the consequences of such action.

Several finance companies, due to bad business practice and weak management and corruption, failed in the early 1980s. Many of them were unable to carry on because of the increase in capital requirements under the Finance Companies Act No. 78 of 1988. The number of companies registered with the Central Bank grew smaller in number and by the end of 1990, 20 companies were licensed by the Central Bank to undertake finance business. At the end of 1995, there were only 24 registered finance companies.

From 1983, the Central Bank was confronted with the problem of the failure of several finance companies that were registered by the Bank. The regulation of finance companies through Central Bank controls and directions issued to them were found to be virtually ineffective since the finance companies were such a heterogenous group and could not be subject to financial discipline. Many of the finance companies were family concerns, where a few directors took key decisions and controlled the business. Their credit operations and methods of conducting business were different from the banks and did not conform to established financial and accounting procedures. Accordingly, directions issued by the Central Bank had little impact on them. While there was considerable opposition from those who were in the finance company business, the depositors welcomed the new legislation in the expectation that more effective controls would be introduced by the Central Bank thereafter.

The Finance Companies Act No. 78 of 1988[28] was made applicable to all institutions engaged in finance business. It prohibited any person from carrying on a finance business unless it was registered under the Companies Act No. 17 of 1982 and had an issued and paid up capital of not less than Rs 5 million. Among the provisions in the Act was that the Monetary Board had to be satisfied that the information made available to it would not be detrimental to the interests of the depositors and creditors. Another requirement was that the company had to have a satisfactory accounting system, internal controls and a management record. The new Act allayed the fears of the depositors by giving the Central Bank an opportunity to restructure the finance companies.

By 1986, nearly all the finance companies registered by the Bank were examined by the Department of Bank Supervision of the Central Bank. Since all these examination reports were highly confidential, the Bank could not give any indications about the viability of the finance companies to the public. The people had to depend on their good judgement when they deposited money with these companies. Between 1983 and 1991, 13 finance companies went bankrupt and ceased operations, leaving more than 3,00,000 depositors in difficulties. By 1992, among the companies that failed there were two very large companies, Union Trust and Investments and Mercantile Credit Ltd. Each of these companies had total assets in excess of Rs 1 billion. The failure of these companies could be attributed to certain common problems. First, there was mismanagement and even after 1977, one could register a finance company under the Companies Act, by merely inserting advertisements in the press and engaging in wide publicity campaigns, promising very high rates of interest. It is known that one company that had ceased operations in 1988 was paying an annual rate of interest of 32 per cent on deposits. Most of these interest payments were met out of new deposits that came into the companies through intensive advertising. Several companies used the public deposits to give loans to their subsidiaries that were not making profits.[29]

Most companies were heavily under-capitalized and had past dues running into over five years. Furthermore, companies registered with the Central Bank were bound by provisions in the Finance Companies Act and directives issued by the Monetary Board of the Bank and these were openly violated. An ongoing controversy after 1994 was that some failed companies where the directors wielded political influence were able to pay depositors with funds made available from the Central Bank. This caused a major controversy in the press and among the public. The largest company that failed was able to pay all its depositors in full by obtaining lines of credit from the Central Bank after 1994 that totalled Rs 1.74 billion. It has been reported that, up to now, of the above total only some Rs 5 million has been paid by the company to the Central Bank. It is not known whether the lines of credit provided by the Central Bank has been used to pay the depositors, or whether a part was used for other purposes. The question also arises whether the payments to depositors were monitored by the Central Bank? Such lines of credit were not given to some smaller companies that had failed leaving the depositors in the lurch. The problem with the Central Bank has been that it has not treated all the failed finance companies and their depositors equally. Political influence and the close relations with the party in power have been factors that determined the quantum of assistance that has been forthcoming from the Central Bank after 1992. The discriminatory treatment of depositors by the authorities has led to great disappointment and bitterness among them.

THE BANKING COMMISSION 1990

A major event in the history of banking in Sri Lanka was the appointment of the second Commission on Finance and Banking by a mandate dated 21 December 1990.[30] The Commission was headed by M.R.P. Salgado a former Central Banker and a senior International Monetary Fund (IMF) official and consisted of seven members and a Secretary. The public in general welcomed the appointment of a new Commission, after a lapse of more than 55 years. Since the appointment of the Ceylon Banking Commission in 1934, with Sir Sorabji Pochkhanawala as Chairman, the banking system had undergone considerable change and diversification primarily after liberalization and opening of the economy in 1977.[31] In particular, these included the establishment of branches of 14 international banks from Europe, the US, the Middle East and Pakistan. Two new local banks, the Sampath Bank and the Seylan Bank were established in 1987 and 1988, respectively. Earlier in 1979, Foreign Currency Banking Units were introduced primarily with the intention of providing off-shore banking facilities to investors in the Investment Promotion Zone. During the 1980s, the Central Bank established Regional Offices in Anuradhapura, Matale and Matara. After 1985, the Central Bank pioneered the establishment of some 16 Regional Development Banks with a network of over 160 branches. The object was to expand the availability of development banking services in the rural areas. Another institutional development was the introduction of merchant banking in 1982, with the setting up of the Merchant Bank of Sri Lanka, a subsidiary of the Bank of Ceylon. The Finance and Banking Commission in its report dealt with a wide range of issues and topics that included the Central Bank, the role of commercial banks, development banks and other credit institutions, finance companies, deposit mobilization, the capital market, the underground economy, the development of Sri Lanka as an international financial centre and credit to the poor.

BANKS AND FINANCE COMPANY FAILURES

The failure of 13 finance companies between 1983 and 1990 threatened the stability of some domestic banks. One reason for this was that the President of the largest finance company that failed, Mercantile Credit Limited, also happened to be the Chairman of the Sampath Bank that was established in 1987.[32] Towards the end of 1990, the Bank had to face a multitude of problems. From November 1990, the Sampath Bank was confronted with a steady withdrawal of deposits. In December 1990, the Bank declared an interim dividend of 5 per cent to its shareholders, without reference to the Central Bank and this was after the Central Bank had provided the Sampath Bank with a loan of Rs 260 million to tide over the liquidity crisis created by the loss of deposits. In the meantime, in 1990 the Bank also made a loss of Rs 6.7 million in its domestic operations. At this stage, the Central Bank had to step in and take measures to restore public confidence.

In regard to Central Bank assistance to finance companies, the Governor clearly stated that he was unwilling to use public funds to meet depositors' liabilities. This was in response to a request for Central Bank assistance of Rs 750 million for Mercantile Credit Limited. A Cabinet sub-committee, consisting of four ministers and the Treasury held the view that this request for accommodation should not be granted as it would aggravate prevailing inflationary trends. In the case of three smaller finance companies, Finance and Guarantee Company, Asian Finance and Home Finance, the Central Bank made arrangements to hand over these companies to a leading finance company that took them over very willingly.

The finance company crisis that dominated economic events in the midst of the second JVP uprising in 1988 and 1989 was followed soon after by the failure of the Colombo branch of a fast expanding international bank, the Bank of Credit and Commerce International (BCCI) Overseas. Although the local branch was financially sound and well managed, the parent bank in the UK was progressively heading for bankruptcy. The BCCI Bank, based in London, was not given a full licence by the Bank of England. At that time, the Bank had 47 branches in the UK and several branches overseas that included Bombay, Karachi and Hong Kong. The Governor of the Central Bank took a bold decision in entrusting the management of the BCCI Bank to the Chairman of the Seylan Bank Lalith Kotelawala. The Colombo branch was able to avert a crisis and continue banking operations without a break, honouring the claims of all depositors.

Financial institutions have been at the forefront of the ongoing economic controversies, emphasizing the need for banking reform and the need for strong independent action devoid of political interference, by the Central Bank. There has been a new dimension to this problem by the recent failure of the Pramuka Savings and Development Bank. The reports of the Director of Bank Supervision of the Central Bank had revealed that, as far back as August 1999, the Bank had continued to grant loans and advances without carrying out a proper credit evaluation and that the 'failure of the Bank may be inevitable'. On 25 October 2002, the Monetary Board made an order under the Banking Act directing the Pramuka Bank to suspend business. Since October 2002, in the financial columns of the press, the Pramuka Bank crisis has been the leading financial issue and not a day passes without reference to the problem. Depositors continue to agitate to reopen the Bank. The Pramuka Savings and Development Bank was the first specialized Bank to fail since independence.

The depositors of the Bank have filed petitions in court against the action of the Central Bank. There is no doubt that the blame has to fall squarely on the Central Bank for not properly monitoring the work of the Bank and not taking timely action to avert this major banking crisis. Principles and questions of policy are involved in this issue, because the Central Bank should have taken more time and evaluated the Pramuka Bank application thoroughly and taken up a strong stand against any political intervention in its approval. It is clear enough that, for various reasons, this was not done. In the past, the Central Bank had an early warning system in the two departments dealing with bank supervision that would have alerted the Central Bank to prompt action in the event that a financial institution was heading for a crisis. But all these measures seem to have fallen into a state of neglect, mainly due to political interference.

The plight of the Pramuka Bank highlights the predicament into which other commercial banks may fall in the near future.

RESTRUCTURING THE CENTRAL BANK

In the Central Bank itself, there are major problems that have to be highlighted in the national interest. The Bank has been subject to severe political pressure and interference. The Central Bank has retrenched more than 1,000 of its highly trained, experienced and qualified employees in the last one-and-a-half years. In an Aide Memoire dated 20 November 2001 it was stated that the Central Bank had developed a new institutional structure for the Bank and 'work is currently ongoing to phase out the non-core functions of the Central Bank; the human resource policies are being revised to emphasise mobility and merit'. It went on to further add 'The Central Bank is finalizing its new organization structure in order to refocus on its core Central Bank functions of price stability and financial sector system stability and the non-core functions of business and agency and corporate services.' In the debatable restructuring of management and policy that it has undergone, the Central Bank it would be seen, will be concerned primarily with monetary policy and would progressively divest most of the development functions that it had hitherto carried out in the last 50 years in terms of provisions in the Monetary Law Act. With regard to the non-core functions such as Exchange Control, Public Debt, Development Finance and the Employees' Provident Fund, they are to be transferred to other institutions or to subsidiary companies of the Central Bank.

A great emphasis has been placed in the World Bank Aide Memoire on the Human Resource Manager. It goes on to say, 'Critical to the success of the restructuring exercise at the Central Bank will be the revision of key Human Resource policies which place increased emphasis on performance, permit greater mobility and which provide for clear rewards linked to individual staff contributions.' It would appear that the foregoing is merely a device to justify irregular contractual appointments and to forestall the recruitment of permanent staff. Recently, the press has highlighted some of the irregular recruitments that have been made in the Central Bank since the implementation of 'reforms' in the Bank. In other words, what the international credit agencies like the IMF and the World Bank want is for the Central Bank to emulate its counterparts in the developed world like the central banks in the US, UK and Europe and to resort to policies of hiring and firing staff. No Central Bank in South and South East Asia has taken such steps. These changes have been brought about on the basis of a line of credit to restructure the administration and objectives of the Bank. The objectives of the Bank have been laid down presumably by a northern nation, Sweden, that has given a line of credit to fund the voluntary retirement scheme, jointly with the IMF and the World Bank and without reference to national objectives and needs.

Under the Voluntary Retirement Scheme of the Central Bank, the proceeds of this line of credit have been used to pay the retirement benefits of its employees that have included a handsome compensation package. Although a core function of the Central

Bank is Financial System Stability, recent events point to the fact that it has failed miserably in performing this function. The net result has been to diminish the national role of the Bank and to clip or effectively reduce, the powers the Bank has exercised in the past. Even in regard to the Pramuka Bank, the Central Bank was unable to effectively deal with the crisis because it had under its Voluntary Retirement Programme, dispensed with the services of the most experienced and competent senior officials and supervisors. After retiring its most competent employees long before the scheduled retirement dates, the Central Bank has been hiring employees on a contract basis for key positions in the Bank. Such employees have been given posts in departments such as the Currency Department that requires highly reliable persons with considerable integrity. In this process, the Bank has ignored the promotion prospects and rights of its highly qualified and long standing employees of exceptional ability.

The other components of the 'Central Bank Strengthening Project' are, a Real Time Gross Settlement System, the Scripless Government Securities System and the General Ledger. In a letter dated 3 December 2001, the World Bank has made the following remark. 'While understanding the Central Bank's desire to support poverty alleviation and grass roots development we feel that this can be best achieved by actively pursuing the two core objectives identified earlier, price stability and financial system stability. It is our strongly held view that this function should be confined to policy analysis and formulation with the development finance function completely phased out of the Central Bank by June 2005.' The one area where the Central Bank has failed very badly is in the area of financial institution stability as evidenced by the failure of Pramuka Bank and the licensing of several banks pioneered by personalities with chequered careers.

CONCLUDING REMARKS

The lines on which banking and financial reforms have taken place in the recent past, including that of the Central Bank, throws out a very dismal and pessimistic picture as to the real outcome of the so-called reforms that have been put into effect in the past. Theory, rather than pragmatic considerations, seem to be the determining factors behind these reforms. Going against central banking practice in other Asian countries, the role of the Central Bank itself has been badly mutilated by curtailing its most vital national functions. At the same time, the Central Bank has been heavily influenced by the ideology of free enterprise, private ownership, globalization and competitiveness.

With the weakening of the status of the Central Bank of Sri Lanka and its politicization and poor and incompetent management, the people cannot be hopeful that it would be in a position in the future to pioneer and introduce fundamental changes and reforms in the national interest. The politicians who are currently handling financial management and reforms do not have the capacity to think in national terms and they do not have the ability to formulate and implement meaningful reforms. What is required immediately is to strengthen the management capabilities of the Central Bank and to free its senior officials from their close links to politicians in both political parties and to build up a strong and independent Central Bank that is not dependent on advice from a multitude of foreign agencies. However, without a national orientation in policies that will have to be implemented by patriotic leaders and politicians, the net result of any future banking and financial reforms will only contribute to worsening the prevailing economic and financial crises and increase the country's dependence on external advice and foreign aid.

The current government, presumably on the directions of the IMF and the World Bank, has put forward proposals for the privatization of the two leading commercial banks, the Bank of Ceylon and the People's Bank. The trade unions in both these banks have vehemently opposed this move and they have threatened to take drastic trade union action to prevent such a move. Conflicting pronouncements seem to be made by the government on this issue. While interest is being focused on further increasing the capital of the Bank of Ceylon, the government is now talking about restructuring the People's Bank and it would now appear that privatization has been stalled, at least temporarily.

Privatization would mean that the shares of both these institutions would be sold to local or overseas private individuals or companies. The issue raised by the government and endorsed by the Central Bank is that the two commercial banks are administratively inefficient, they operate on high margins and they are overstaffed. But the adverse consequences of privatization have not been highlighted in the ongoing debate. The consumer who now gets satisfactory service from the two leading commercial banks is likely to be saddled with higher bank charges and a very high minimum deposit to open new accounts. These practices are now being followed by many of the locally owned or expatriate owned banks in the country. Furthermore, if the shares in the two banks have been purchased by foreign investors all the profits will be repatriated overseas. It is very likely that the Insurance Corporation of Sri Lanka that has been privatized will very soon revise upwards all its charges, including premium payments, and impose burdens on the people. It is unfortunate that the present government, on account of its so-called globalized policies, has to depend heavily on foreign aid and investment instead of making an endeavour to find more financial resources internally. The recent Tax Amnesty Law is a case in point where over Rs 50 billion in taxes due to the government will be written off under the law and will pave the way for hundreds of tax defaulters and notorious financial crooks to get away with the millions that they legitimately owe the government.

Notes

1. Sir Cecil Trevor in his Report examined the whole field of banking in the Gold Coast (Ghana) and he stated, 'It might be difficult to find suitable premises for having a fully fledged central banking institution.' He further stated, 'In order to operate the currency and credit system of a country to its advantage it is necessary that all the flexible instruments necessary to an advanced economy should be available.' J.L. Fisher, an advisor to the Bank of England on a central bank for Nigeria said, 'I conclude that it would be inadvisable to contemplate the establishment of a central bank at the moment. Moreover, it is hard to see how a central bank can function as an instrument to promote the development of the country.'

2. Exter, 1949.
3. Sayers, 1956, p. 14, stated 'Although it is theoretically possible for a Currency Board System to be unduly restrictive, in the practical circumstances of the international banking structure there is generally all the elasticity of all the reserve cash necessary to allow as much credit expansion as local banks are willing to sponsor.' Similar views were expressed by Greaves, 1953.
4. Gunasekera, 1961. Also see Newlyn and Rowan, 1954, p. 267. Sayers, 1952, states, 'Looking back it is impossible to resist the statement that the foundation of central banks has been partly a matter of fashion.'
5. Gunasekera, 1961.
6. House of Representatives, *Hansard*, 25 November 1949, 7(10).
7. Ibid.
8. *Ceylon Daily News* of 1 July 1954 carried a headline, 'Central Bank Governor's Conduct to be Investigated' and it was further stated, 'The Governor of the Central Bank, Mr. N.U. Jayawardena is to be Reported to the Governor General and Removed from Office under Provisions of the Monetary Law Act.' On 2 July 1954, the headlines were 'PM Confers with H.E. on Bank Chief.'
9. Sessional Paper XX of 1954, 'Report of the Commission Appointed to Enquire into the Affairs and General Conduct of Neville Ubesinghe Jayewardena, Governor of the Central Bank and his wife Gertrude Mildred Jayewardena.'
10. Central Bank of Ceylon, 1950, p. 5.
11. Ibid., p. 7.
12. Central Bank of Ceylon, 1951, p. 12.
13. Ibid.
14. Central Bank of Ceylon, 1952, p. 4.
15. Central Bank of Ceylon, 1953, p. 6.
16. Central Bank of Ceylon, 1956, p. 4.
17. Ibid., p. 10.
18. Ibid., p. 52.
19. Ibid., p. 53. The Ministry of Finance introduced a series of measures to reduce the flow of imports and these were supplemented by Central Bank action.
20. Ibid., p. 53.
21. Central Bank of Ceylon, 1960, p. 20. Monetary methods of import control were only partially effective because of increasing budget deficits.
22. Central Bank of Ceylon, 1962, p. 2.
23. The problem with the new industries was that they were manufacturing the very same goods that were prohibited, and all the inputs were imported.
24. Central Bank of Ceylon, 1969, p. 15.
25. Central Bank of Ceylon, 1971, p. 13.
26. Central Bank of Ceylon, 1975.
27. Central Bank of Ceylon, 1977.
28. Parliament, Finance Companies Act No. 78 of 1988.
29. One of the major problems of the large finance companies like Mercantile Credit Ltd was that more than one-third of the loans were given to its own subsidiaries like Lanka Carbons Ltd, Premier Managements, Allied Investments Ltd, and Ruhunu Hotels Ltd, that were incurring heavy losses.
30. Report of the Presidential Commission on Finance and Banking, Sessional Paper No. 4 of 1991, Government Publications Bureau, Colombo.
31. Ceylon Banking Commission Report, Sessional Paper No. 23 of 1934, Government Publications Bureau, Colombo.
32. Originally the aim of the founders of the Sampath Bank was to establish it as a Buddhist Bank. The idea of a Bank emerged at the International Buddhist Conference held in Colombo in 1984. However, Albert Edirisinghe, who was one of the pioneers of the Bank along with Palitha Kannangara, invited N.U. Jayawardena to head the Bank, while several others had declined the invitation.

REFERENCE

Central Bank of Ceylon (1950), *Annual Report*, Colombo.
_____ (1951), *Annual Report*, Colombo.
_____ (1952), *Annual Report*, Colombo.
_____ (1953), *Annual Report*, Colombo.
_____ (1960), *Annual Report*, Colombo.
_____ (1962), *Annual Report*, Colombo.
_____ (1969), *Annual Report*, Colombo.
_____ (1971), *Annual Report*, Colombo.
_____ (1975), *Annual Report*, Colombo.
_____ (1977), *Annual Report*, Colombo.
Exter, John (1949), 'Report on the Establishment of a Central Bank for Ceylon', Sessional Paper No. 14, Ceylon Government Press.
Greaves, Ida (1953), *Colonial Monetary Conditions*, London: HMSO.
Gunasekera, H.A. de S. (1961), *From Dependent Currency to Central Banking*, London School of Economics.
Newlyn, W.T. and D.C. Rowan (1954), *Money and Banking in British Colonial Africa*, Oxford.
Sayers, R.S. (1952), *Banking in the British Commonwealth*, Oxford University Press.
_____ (1956), *Central Banking after Bagehot*, Oxford.

SELECT READINGS

Ariyaratne, T.W. (1993), 'Changes in the Banking and the Financial Sector in Sri Lanka', *Sri Lanka Economic Journal*, April.
Aziz, Shibly (1989), 'The Origin and Scope of the 1988 Finance Companies Act', *Sri Lanka Economic Journal*, April.
Ceylon Banking Commission Report (1934), Sessional Paper No. 23 of 1934, Colombo: Government Publications Bureau.
de Silva, Pratapkumar (1997), 'Hire Purchase in Sri Lanka', *Sri Lanka Economic Journal*, Vols 1 and 11.
Jayasena, W. (1989), 'Some Reasons for the Failure of Finance Companies in Sri Lanka', *Sri Lanka Economic Journal*, April.
Karunatilake, H.N.S. (1988), 'An Examination of the New Banking Act', *Sri Lanka Economic Journal*, April.
_____ (1989), 'The Performance and Role of Finance Companies in the Economy of Sri Lanka', *Sri Lanka Economic Journal*, April.
_____ (1990), 'Financial Sector Restructuring for the Nineties', *Sri Lanka Economic Journal*, September.
Report of the Presidential Commission on Finance and Banking (1991), Sessional Paper No. 4 of 1991, Colombo: Government Publications Bureau.
Sirisena, N. L. (1989a), 'Powers of the Central Bank to Regulate and Supervise Non-Bank Financial Institutions in Sri Lanka', *Sri Lanka Economic Journal*, April.
_____ (1989b), 'Problems of Supervising Non-Bank Financial Institutions in Sri Lanka', *Sri Lanka Economic Journal*, September.

Part VI

SOCIAL WELFARE

Part VI

19

THE COLONIAL LINEAGES OF THE WELFARE STATE*

Laksiri Jayasuriya

INTRODUCTION

Sri Lanka has an enviable record of having evolved as a 'welfare state' in a non-industrialized developing country. It is ranked in development literature as an exceptional case of a middle-to-low income country which has attempted to satisfy basic needs, especially of the poorest, by incorporating economic growth with minimum standards of welfare. Admittedly, since the late 1970s Sri Lanka has undergone a political and economic crisis which coincided with the decline of the social democratic state and the welfare state. Nevertheless, for a country with a poor per capita gross national product (GNP), Sri Lanka (or Ceylon as it was known till the 1970s) still rates relatively high in comparison with other developing countries on a range of social indicators such as human development index (HDI). There is no doubt that Sri Lanka's achievement, relative to comparable countries on several social indicators (e.g., 87 per cent literacy rate, infant mortality rate of 17 per 1,000 live births, life expectancy of 70 years) is remarkable and warrants greater systematic scrutiny and scholarly understanding (Jayasuriya, 2000; Osmani, 1993; UNDP, 1990-96).

The intriguing and perplexing question that arises is, how did Sri Lanka, as a low-to-middle income country, come to embark on the complex task of creating a 'welfare state'? In the case of Sri Lanka, the 'welfare state' as a coordinated institutional system which emerged in the 1960s and 1970s, was a logical sequence to the welfarism of the late colonial state and had its own distinctive character. The few theorists, mostly economists, who have examined Sri Lanka's social policy developments, have concentrated on the complex relationship between welfare and growth in Sri Lanka, and the economic impact of these welfare policies (Kelegama, 1987; Marga Institute, 1974; Osmani, 1993). Given that Sri Lankan social policy has been unexplored in the literature, the significance of the long history in understanding contemporary policy developments warrants consideration.

*This is an edited text of a paper published in the *Journal of the Royal Asiatic Society of Sri Lanka*, XLVI, 2003.

The burden of the argument presented in this chapter is that the Sri Lankan welfare state that existed until its dismantling in the late 1970s was largely a legacy of Sri Lanka's British colonial past, extending from the 19th century to the ending of colonial rule in 1948. Adopting a distinctly historical focus, the chapter endeavours to highlight, without discounting domestic social and cultural influences, the impact of British colonial policy on the development of Sri Lankan social policy from its earliest days of British rule to the consolidation of the welfare state around the 1960s and 1970s, two decades after the grant of independence from colonial rule.

While political factors in the first two decades of independence were important in the expansion of welfare programmes, they are not sufficient in themselves to fully explain the emergence of the Sri Lankan welfare state. A key proposition of the chapter is that the origins of the Sri Lankan welfare state are located in the interstices of colonial social policy, in particular the prevailing ideas of social liberalism that were influential in Britain in the first half of the 20th century. It will be argued that the concept of diffusion, i.e., 'transmission of ideas, policies and practices' (Midgley, 1984a: 170) serves to clarify the dynamics of social policy making in Sri Lanka. In short, colonial policy cannot be completely separated from the intellectual milieu of British social policy. In this sense, the chapter, in addition to drawing attention to the colonial foundations of social policy, should also be seen as contributing to the expanding literature on the impact of ideas on public policy (Hall, 1986).

Focusing on the historical evolution of social policies, the chapter identifies the three main phases of social policy development from the early formative period in the 19th century (1833–1931) through to the late colonial state, 1931–70. The early phase, extending from 1833 to 1931, denotes the early colonial state in Sri Lanka and is marked by the development of a colonial export economy and the modernization of Sri Lankan society. The second phase, from 1931 to 1948, represents the late colonial state. This features a period of partial self rule which also serves as a developmental prelude to the emergence of the welfare state. The third, more recent phase, covers the first two decades of independence (1948–70) and stands out as a transitional phase in which the late colonial state moved into the post-colonial era. In the periodization of Sri Lanka's recent history, the second and third phases denote a highly significant period of political development, of transition from a colonial to an autonomous independent state. Furthermore, this third phase not only documents the consolidation of the welfare state, but also begins to manifest the tensions and contradictions of post-colonialism and the 'post-colonial state'.

Post-colonialism, as understood in the growing literature on post-colonial studies, is used in a broad sense to characterize the abandonment of the cultural attitudes, beliefs, and social practices of the colonial era. This pertains in Sri Lanka, among other things, to the emergence of new cultural narratives, a confusing mix of political ideologies and the search for alternative socio-political structures. Unlike elsewhere, in Sri Lanka post-colonialism is not synonymous with post-independence. Rather, in the Sri Lankan context, the advent of post-colonialism is associated with the socio-political reforms of the late 1970s (e.g., the rejection of Westminster style political institutions), a neoliberal market economy, a vibrant cultural nationalism and a culture of violence partly fuelled by a civil war waged against a militant ethnic minority (Tamils). In short, the post-colonial era bears witness to 'the process of decolonization (which) requires the rejection of the imperialist legacy and its substitution by an authentic indigenous perspective' (Midgley, 1998: 34).

The chapter is focuses mainly on examining social policy development and social policy as a legacy of British colonial rule, extending from the early to the late colonial state and the first two decades of independence (1948s–70s). The first two phases of social development identified in the chapter constitute well defined stages—the early and late colonial state. Each phase is associated with constitutional reform documents, embodying the logic and rationale of British colonial policy in Sri Lanka. Sri Lanka was not just regarded as 'the senior colony of the Empire ... (but also) a constitutional pioneer' (Wright, 1950), and in fact, 'only the French have shown a greater preoccupation with constitutional reform' (Russell, 1982: xvii).

Constitutionalism is, perhaps one of the distinctive features of the Sri Lanka polity (Coomaraswamy, 1993; Fernando, 1999; Wilson, 1973). But what is more significant is that each stage of constitutional development has had an important bearing on social policy developments. Thus, the political reforms of the early colonial state ushered in by the foundational constitutional reforms of the Colebrooke–Cameron Commission of 1833 had an indelible impact on all subsequent social policy developments. Similarly, the social policy climate of the late colonial state can be understood only in terms of the epochal political reforms initiated by the Donoughmore Commission of 1927–29 which led to partial self rule. In addition, the defining policy initiatives, characteristic of each stage of social policy, were clearly identified by policy documents, government reports, or statutes.[1]

However, the chapter itself is primarily devoted to an exposition of the nature and form of social policy evolution from the early to the late colonial state and the first two decaded of independence. A key proposition advanced is that the colonial legacy extended in substance after independence. The first two decades of independence constituted an extension of the late colonial state, a sort of transition to 'post-colonialism'. Although the social and political developments of the post-colonial era (i.e., after 1970) are not examined in the chapter, these more recent social changes need to be understood only in the context of the historical legacy of colonial rule. In contextualizing the evolution of social policy leading to the welfare state, the chapter concludes by speculating on some of the major factors that may have been responsible for the emergence of the Sri Lankan welfare state—the *how* and *why* of social policy.

THE EARLY COLONIAL STATE (1833–1931): FORMATIVE PERIOD OF SOCIAL POLICY

The first phase of social policy development (1833–1931) was heavily influenced by a major constitutional reform document, the Report of the Colebrooke–Cameron

Commission of 1833 (de Silva, 1965, 1981; Mendis, 1956, 1957) which had a defining influence on all subsequent policy developments—social, economic and political. Although total colonial rule was imposed on the whole country by the British only in 1815 after its annexation from the Dutch in 1796, the colony did not achieve a single unified system of administration until the reforms of 1833. The 1833 Reform Commission sought to reform the system of government mainly by introducing radical changes to the system of public and judicial administration. The thinking of Colebrooke and Cameron was markedly influenced by the utilitarianism[2] of the era, especially the writings of Jeremy Bentham and John Stuart Mill (Stokes, 1959). Whereas Colebrooke's distinctive contribution was towards establishing an efficient unified system of public administration, Cameron was primarily concerned with introducing a liberal political culture based on the rule of law and a new system of judicial administration (Mendis, 1956).

Colebrooke, by his public administration reforms, sought to incorporate in an alien colonial context British liberal principles and utilitarian values such as the merit principle and equality of treatment. Thus, on the question of staffing of, and recruitment for, the public service, Colebrooke made a strong case for the inclusion of Ceylonese (i.e., the local inhabitants) in the higher echelons of the public service, hitherto confined to British civil servants drawn from the élite universities in Britain. Similarly, he argued strongly for a competitive system of examinations as the basis of entry to the Civil Service—an idea borrowed from the Northcote-Trevelyan reforms of the British Civil Service (Warnapala, 1974). The opening up of the public service to local applicants—the Ceylonization of the public service—was in later years to gain in importance as an issue for political agitation and become a catalyst for other social policy reforms, especially those relating to higher education.

These measures of governance, indicative of the opposition to patronage (e.g., the hereditary privileges afforded to high caste persons such as headman), signifies the influence of the intellectual ideas and values of utilitarianism in Britain during the 19th century on British colonial policy (Evans, 1978; Goldthorpe, 1964; Sleeman, 1973). Utilitarian ideas were also markedly evident in another main reform proposal of Colebrooke, namely the abolition of the semi-feudal traditional practice of forced labour or compulsory service (rajakariya). With the recommendation for its abolition, the 1833 Reform Commission took a major step in modernizing society by liberating it from some of the constraints of its traditional semi-feudal heritage and helped to create a free wage labour force.

A free wage labour force working on the plantation economy was also conducive to 'the development of individualism ... a potent feature in the proposals of Colebrooke for economic reform' (Samaraweera, 1973: 86). There is no doubt that 'the introduction of capitalism to Sri Lanka around 1833 marks the beginnings of the modern period of Sri Lankan history' (Kannangara, 1988: 136). In this context, the Colebrooke reforms initiated an economic climate opposed to mercantilism and state monopolies, but steeped in laissez faire doctrines of individual enterprise and free trade, all of which helped the growth of a prosperous plantation economy from 1850 onwards (Snodgrass, 1966).

The colonial economy, based largely on overseas capital, was a classic example of an enclave economy built around three main commodities: first, coffee to about 1886, followed by tea, rubber and coconut. This left the rest of the economy based on traditional peasant agriculture relatively neglected by colonial policy (Bandarage, 1983; Snodgrass, 1966). In effect, this created a 'dual economy', 'a highly organized, foreign owned, capitalist plantation economy (alongside) a tradition bound, primitive, self-sufficing subsistence peasant economy' (Ponnambalam, 1980: 8). The new colonial export economy also helped to generate a significant commercial entrepreneurial culture, which in turn created a local capitalist class based on the mercantilist foundations of the export economy (Bandarage, 1983; Jayawardena, 2000). This new local bourgeoisie was destined to play a vital role in shaping subsequent political and social developments of the 19th and 20th centuries, especially in the campaigns for political reform and self-rule (Jayawardena, 2000; Jayasuriya, K., 2001).

Equally significant for social policy development were the far-reaching judicial reforms proposed by Cameron, a progressive liberal and a dogmatic utilitarian (Samaraweera, 1973: 87) who was more heavily influenced by Jeremy Bentham than his fellow commissioner Colebrooke. The *Charter of Justice* proposed by Cameron introduced a uniform system of judicial administration and helped to establish an independent judiciary as the basis of good government. These reforms were also intended to serve as an effective check on the abuse of executive powers. But, more significantly, they laid the basis for the rule of law and the protection of the equal rights of all individuals within an open and accountable judicial system.

The other major influence on social policy development during this early phase of colonialism, was the impact of Christian missionary enterprise through Evangelicalism of the British Colonial Office and colonial administrators, all of whom belonged to the British ruling class (Dicey, 1996; Stokes, 1959). The reformist zeal and 'civilizing mission' of Christianity was also evident in social policy enactments such as the action taken to mark the end of polyandrous marriage, the abolition of slavery and the non-recognition of caste in all areas of public policy. In general, missionaries were regarded as the representatives of the 'government religion'.

One lasting consequence of the 1833 reforms was that education, understood as the promotion of English education, became the cornerstone of colonial social policy (Jayaweera, 1969). However, access to English education was confined to the urban middle class and made available mainly through state assisted missionary secondary schools. Direct state involvement in education occurred only towards the latter part of the 19th century and was mainly confined to Elementary Schools or primary education, mostly in the rural sector where the medium of instruction was in the vernacular (Sinhalese or Tamil). This marked the beginning of a two-tiered educational system which led to marked social and cultural differentiation between the urban-centred English educated and the more rural indigenous/vernacular educated. As a result the 'dual society' (contrasting metropolitan and provincial culture) framed in the context of a 'dual economy', was a direct consequence of the use of education as an instrument of social policy to consolidate the political hegemony of colonial rule.

The 'Christianization' of the early colonial state, achieved mainly through education in state assisted missionary schools, was also no doubt markedly influenced by Evangelicalism. This Christiniazation also greatly helped the colonial administrators to

sever the traditional links between religion and the state that had existed in the pre-
colonial period. In the long term, the revolt against Christainization of the state was a
key feature of the Buddhist religious revival and nationalism and one which fuelled
the opposition to colonial rule (Houtart, 1974).

There is no doubt that all political and social developments during this early phase
of colonial rule were guided by two main factors: the need for stable, efficient and
orderly government and the effective use of public expenditure in the management of
the colonial economy. The constitutional reforms introduced by Colebrooke favoured
giving the Ceylonese a greater role in governance by creating a body entrusted with
legislative and executive powers This was a characteristic feature of British colonial
rule by which the British sought allies in the colonized territory as 'a class of collabora-
tors' (Mamdani, 1976: 42). To this end, the Colebrooke reforms also helped to introduce one of the guiding tenets of British colonial rule, viz., 'indirect rule' based on a
partnership with local élites.

Social policy development was, however, secondary to questions of political governance and economic growth. Colonial administrators endeavoured to promote social
welfare measures only insofar as they were likely to strengthen British rule by gaining
the compliance and good will of local inhabitants. For example, health policy
developments and housing legislation (Housing and Town Improvement Ordinance
of 1915) of this period are a good indicator of this rationale. Nevertheless, the benevolent
paternalism of colonial rule, among other things, included promoting social policies
which had a bearing on enhancing the well-being of the local inhabitants.

One of the distinctive and significant features of social policy development in the
late 19th century concerns the measures taken to protect the expanding colonial
export economy in the plantation sector, by providing for the social needs of indentured labour recruited from India for employment in the plantation sector on a contract basis. These social welfare measures, such as improving health care facilities, were
critical to the economic well-being of the country. In addition, much of the pioneering
social legislation introduced during this period, e.g., health care for Indian labour on
estates and minimum wages, were intended to facilitate the continued recruitment of
immigrant Indian labour (Pieris, 1967; Wickramaratne, 1973).

Yet, there is no doubt that the special treatment afforded to indentured Indian
labour for work on the plantations was largely instrumental in subsequently gaining
government intervention in industrial relations in Ceylon. Furthermore, the beginnings of trade unionism in Ceylon were greatly assisted by the British trade union
movement and the Labour Party (Jayawardena, 1972). The growth of local trade
unionism among the urban working class and the emergence of the labour movement
may well have been an unintended outcome of colonial policy in the early colonial
state relating to immigrant labour welfare. These policy initiatives, however, were
fraught with considerable significance for subsequent political developments even
after independence in 1948, though it was not until the early 1930s that organized
labour, through its association with Left parties, began to make any direct impact on
social and economic policy developments (Kearney, 1971; Jayawardena, 1972).

SOCIAL POLICY IN THE LATE COLONIAL STATE (1931–48)

The first three decades of the 20th century leading to the radical political reforms of 1931—the Donoughmore Commission Reforms—was a period noted for agitation for a greater degree of self-rule, the Ceylonization of the administration, the politicization of the urban working class, and the growth of a strong nationalist movement (Jupp, 1978; Kearney, 1971). The politics of this period was characterized by a loose alliance of influential sections of the nationalist movement, comprised of political nationalists drawn from the English educated élite and the political Left, and the cultural nationalists mostly Sinhalese Buddhists. They were, however, all united in their demand not just for self-rule but also for a stronger focus on social welfare in redressing social inequalities.

The nationalist movement spearheaded the agitation for constitutional reform and succeeded in persuading the Colonial Office to appoint a Reform Commission in 1927. It is perhaps significant that the implementation of the Reform proposals, emanating from this Reform Commission (the Donoughmore Commission) was the responsibility of Lord Passfield who was the Secretary of State for the Colonies in the Ramsay-MacDonald Labour government. Passfield, of course, was the redoubtable Sidney Webb—one of the most influential of the socialist intellectuals from the heroic period of the British labour movement (Russell, 1982). Not surprisingly, Passfield, who was more sympathetic to the political aspirations of the Sri Lankan people, played an important part in the implementation of the recommendations of the Reform Commission.

It was also fortunate that one of the Labour members on the Donoughmore Commission of 1927–29, Drummond Shiels, was Lord Passfield's Under-Secretary at the Colonial Office until 1931. Shiels had been one of the most active and influential members of the Commission and the one who was mainly responsible for the landmark recommendation—the grant of universal suffrage in 1931. This happened to be one of the Commission's path-breaking and historic recommendations. Besides this, one of the main concerns of the Commission was, interestingly, the need for collective action for social welfare. The Commission:

> found that in many provinces poverty and ill health were the lot of many villages … many sections of the people had not even decent housing or adequate facilities for primary education … no poor law system for relieving destitution, no system of compensation for injured workmen, no up to date system of factory legislation and no control over hours and wages in sweated trades. (Mendis, 1957: 118)

Confronted by these facts, the Commissioners wanted to make the elected representatives of government more accountable and responsive to the needs of the people. Governments so far, they argued, were more of 'an oligarchy or plutocracy, not a democracy' (Jeffries, 1962: 33). As a way of addressing the neglect of social welfare policies and legislation in the previous government, the Commission went on to recommend a unique form of government modelled on the London County Council, which conferred a great deal of responsibility and power to exercise legislative and executive powers. This semi-autonomous system of government (1931–48) was a halfway house between colonial office domination and complete self-rule.

One outcome of the democratization of the government and the new political structures was the passage of an extensive body of social legislation, but without any acknowledgement of how this legislation was to be implemented. The time lag between enactment of legislation and its implementation with programmes and services was to prove a major shortcoming. This was clearly evident in much of the enlightened child welfare legislation of this period, most of which was a replica of British legislation (Jayasuriya et al., 1985). Elected legislators, while being enthusiastic in passing social legislation and recommending various economic and social measures, were in the hapless position of not being able to implement this legislation as they had no financial responsibility. This was mainly because the control of, and responsibility for, finance remained with the non-elected Executive, all of whom were British civil servants. In short, this anomalous situation of power without financial control was a serious political imbalance, in that the democratically elected legislature was not able to exercise financial control over its decisions as this authority rested with a non-elected Executive.

Nevertheless, in spite of this political impasse, social legislation once placed on the statute book acquired a momentum of its own and led to further electoral pressures. As a result, the extensive progressive social legislation helped create a political culture of welfarism which was later adduced (and accepted) as one of the arguments for political independence. The linkage of welfare politics with electoral politics was to remain a heavy burden and a legacy of this period of colonial rule for most of the post-independence period of Sri Lanka until overtaken by economic liberalism and the 'ethnic politics' of the 1980s (Dunham and Jayasuriya, 2000; Jayasuriya, 2000).

The actual welfare politics of this late colonial state (1931–48) focused on two main areas of social policy—education and health, and to a lesser extent on public welfare. Education reform loomed large and was also associated with the nationalist and religious movements of this period. The field of health care gained in salience, particularly as a result of the need to mitigate the disastrous social effects of the Great Depression of the 1930s, the severe drought of the mid-1930s and the malaria epidemics (Jones, 2000).

Social policies relating to public welfare (e.g., unemployment relief, food subsidy) and social infrastructure, mainly housing and public utilities (e.g., electricity and transport), were less important as issues of competitive politics. Public welfare measures undertaken in this period were primarily concerned with alleviating social distress, poverty and unemployment. The government's measures to combat unemployment and poverty, again reflecting the 'dual society', were mainly on two fronts—one strategy for the urban areas and another for the rural sector. In the urban areas, it was mainly one of providing temporary short-term relief by expanding work opportunities, e.g., as casual labourers in public works (e.g., roadwork, flood protection, etc.). However, for the first time in colonial rule, considerable attention was given to the plight of persons in the village peasant economy who were adversely affected by the lack of employment.

A central feature of rural welfare policies was the development of peasant coloniza-tion schemes in sparsely populated and relatively neglected areas with potential for increased agricultural production (mainly rice and some subsidiaries). These schemes required the deployment of population to these new areas of colonization, and a great deal of public expenditure was devoted to the development of schemes of colonization as a rural welfare strategy (Farmer, 1957). Rural housing was seen largely as an essen-tial element of peasant colonization and not as an aspect of a national housing policy. The problems of the landless peasantry soon came to be regarded as an important element not just of economic development, but of welfare politics (Moore, 1985).

The welfare politics of the late colonial state in 1931–48 was heavily influenced by the adverse social and economic circumstances of the post-Depression period. The response of successive governments to social and economic disadvantage, contained in a number of official reports, was similar in tone to UK reports such as the Royal Com-mission on Poor Law (1905–09) or the poverty studies of Booth, Rowntree and others (Newnham Report, 1936). These reports represent the first systematic attempt in Sri Lanka to quantify the problems of poverty and unemployment and prescribe remedial measures. The state sponsored welfare relief measures adopted were reminiscent of the British Poor Law of the 1920s. This Poor Law orientation to poverty alleviation, by providing social assistance and relief for the needy and destitute, has continued to dominate welfare policies even to the present day (Jayasuriya et al., 1985).

These social assistance schemes based on the British Poor Law 'principle of less eligibility', indicating a selectivist approach to poverty alleviation (i.e., as a safety net for those most in need) is, nevertheless, one which stands in sharp contrast to the more universalist policies in other areas of social policy, e.g., health and education. The selectivist approach, as Midgley observes, was 'descended from poor law principles in European states which have been established in a number of developing countries ... (and) are a startling example of the maintenance of colonial welfare policies in the post colonial Third World', (1984b: 3).

In contrast to the selectivist policies relating to public welfare, the food subsidy[3] introduced in 1942 as an emergency measure of public welfare during the Second World War, was available to all persons without a means test. It was a wartime relief measure destined to become an institutionalized welfare measure for nearly three decades after the war. The rationale for this was similar 'to the development of services as well as the provision of help in cash or kind (was) an impressive aspect of the wartime evolution of welfare in Britain' (Bruce, 1961: 272). Indeed, it was this which prompted Sir William Beveridge—one of the architects of the welfare state in Britain—to pose the question: 'If for warfare, why not for welfare' (ibid.).

The food subsidy outlived its utility as a wartime welfare measure but remained a key element of social policy expenditures until the 1970s (Alailima, 1995). It was the single most important item of social expenditure, varying between 4 per cent and 5 per cent of GNP during the period 1970–81. This single welfare policy measure acquired social, economic and political importance as the principal anti-poverty measure of all post-independence governments until it was abandoned in 1977 (Gunatilleke, 1993; Lakshman, 1989).

Without doubt, the social policies of the emerging Sri Lankan welfare state were clearly shaped by the British tradition of linking citizenship with social rights and favoured overall a universalistic rather than a residual or selective approach to welfare. The main exceptions were, of course, as we have seen, social security and public welfare, which were highly selective and based on a social assistance model. Overall, social welfare policies were responsible in 1947 for approximately 56 per cent of total government expenditure, and represented nearly a 50 per cent increase since 1871 when it was only 24.5 per cent (Warnapala, 1974). This was, in short, the legacy of welfarism which was largely a product of democratic electoral politics in the late colonial state and was central to the new political ethos of a fully independent Sri Lankan state after the grant of self-rule in 1948.

Looking back over this period of partial self-rule, it is difficult not to overestimate the importance of the 1931 reforms. The extension of the franchise, in a sense, partially democratized the colonial state while at the same time presenting the unelected local colonial executive—who had control of the purse strings—with significant problems of legitimacy. The evolution of social policy during this period is in no small way a product of this complex dynamic of enhanced democratization and the search for legitimacy. Moreover, the reforms promoted electoral competition in which welfare politics was to loom large in both late colonial and post-independence politics. From this perspective, the social policies of this period laid the groundwork for the future political and social developments in Sri Lanka.

EMERGENCE OF THE WELFARE STATE (1948–70)

With the achievement of independence in 1948, Sri Lanka adopted a new Westminster style constitution in 1948, modelled on the British constitution. From the outset, the newly independent Government of Sri Lanka embraced the welfarism it had inherited from the late colonial state, and proceeded to develop the welfare state on the basis of the earlier social policy initiatives. The Sri Lankan welfare state was built mainly around three major social documents, two of which were inherited from the pre-independence era, and ensuing Acts of Parliament: Education Act of 1945 (Kannangara Report, 1943); the establishment of the Department of Social Services, 1948 (Jennings Report, 1947); and the Health Act of 1953 (Cumpston Report, 1950). In this regard, the foundations of the emerging Sri Lankan welfare state bear comparison with the 'three pillars' of the British welfare state, viz., Education, National Insurance, and National Health (Marshall, 1973).

As in Britain, the principle of collective provision for common human and social needs through state intervention was firmly embedded in the logic and rationale of these reports. The importance attached to social welfare initiatives arising from the three reports in Sri Lanka is revealed by the fact that during the first two decades of independence (1948–68) social expenditure relating to education, health, transport, food subsidies and public welfare assistance, hovered around 40 per cent of total public expenditure or 10–12 per cent of gross domestic product (GDP) (Alailima, 1995; Gunatilleke, 1999; Osmani, 1993).

First and foremost, the Kannangara Report, by recommending a system of *universal* and *compulsory* free education from Kindergarten to the University, confirmed that welfarism in Sri Lanka was based on universalistic principles. The latter was a distinctive feature of the Sri Lankan welfare system until the advent of neoliberal social policies in the post-1977 era (Dunham and Jayasuriya, 2000). By adopting a bold and radical approach, the Kannangara Report ranks as the single most important social policy document in Sri Lanka's social and political development. This Report outlined what the erudite Left wing politician, N.M. Perera (a student of Harold Laski at the London School of Economics and Political Science), described as 'amazing revolutionary objectives' (Perera, 1944). Among the social objectives sought by the far-reaching reforms proposed were:

> the prevention of unemployment, the raising of the standard of living of the masses, increased production, a more equitable system of distribution, social security of co-operative enterprise, etc. But none of these things can be fully realized without mass education. We are of the opinion that free education must come first and foremost. (Perera, 1944: 5).

All educational policies of this period (e.g., change in the medium of instruction and a national system of education), were highly significant in that they opened up opportunities for greater social mobility on the part of significant social groups; in principle, opening up access to occupations (such as medicine and law) previously monopolized by the Western educated middle class. This probably rates as the single most important factor in determining the transformation of Sri Lankan society in the latter part of the 20th century.

The second pillar of the Sri Lankan welfare state relates to the health services. Here, the vital social policy document is the Cumpston Report, which led to the Health Services Act of 1952.[4] The major achievement of the Cumpston Report was threefold: the abolition of private practice for doctors in the state sector; enabling the development concurrently of preventive and curative services; and outlining the rationale for an equitable universal health service as a matter of right.

Its most significant recommendation, reflecting the egalitarian ideology of welfarism was undoubtedly the abolition of private practice for doctors in the public sector. This policy recommendation was regarded as being central to the establishment of a state funded equitable system of national health. This later led to the progressive introduction of Western medical services through a wide network of free medical institutions, including key elements of the total needed for a comprehensive integrated system of health services (Gunatilleke, 1985). Admittedly, the bulk of these services were located in the urban areas, but it should be borne in mind that this rapid expansion existed alongside a well developed system of indigenous medicine which was mainly responsible for catering to the health care needs of a sizeable section of the rural population (Pieris, 2000).

The relatively weak third pillar of the Sri Lankan welfare state deals with the social services and is examined in a key report, Social Services Commission Report (1947), the Sri Lankan equivalent of the Beveridge Report in Britain. The driving force behind this Report was its Chairman, Sir Ivor Jennings, a leading constitutional theorist and later Vice Chancellor of the University of Ceylon and Cambridge University. Its main focus was on policy questions relating to social security, especially unemployment, financial distress, old age and disability and destitution. However, the Report shows that, while the Commission gave serious consideration to the thinking underlying British social policy,[5] it did not necessarily recommend adopting Beveridge style policies for Sri Lanka.

One of its main recommendations was centred on developing a financially viable plan for social security for wage earners in the public and commercial sectors. One outcome was an Employees' Provident Fund (EPF), established in 1958 and covering all private firms and public bodies as pension provisions existed only for the organized public sector (ILO, 1971). However, the Jennings Report was cast more in the form of an academic exercise in social analysis, planning and reporting, and as a blue print for policy strategies; hence, it did not necessarily get immediately translated into selected programmes and services. Nor did the Report elicit much political interest, mainly because the social security policies it advocated had little relevance for the vast majority of people living in a predominantly agricultural society (Jayasuriya, 2000; Savy, 1974). Both the urban poor and the rural peasantry had access only to social assistance measures and relief programmes such as drought and flood relief, all of which were cast in the style of the early 20th century British Poor Law (Evans, 1978).

Besides the social programmes and services arising from these three major Reports, the other significant aspect of the Sri Lankan welfare state relates to Housing, Public Utilities (e.g., transport, water, posts and telecommunications, and electricity), and the Personal Social Services. The latter were mainly services catering to the needs of disadvantaged and vulnerable groups (e.g., aged, disabled, handicapped children and youth, needy families, sick and injured). Housing, as a distinctive aspect of social policy, was relatively neglected in the early days of the welfare state and limited to the regulation of the rental markets and the promotion of housing investment. One of the main reasons for the low priority accorded to housing policy probably relates to the low rates of urbanization in Sri Lanka (e.g., an increase of only 1 per cent of the urban population over a 25-year period between the Census of 1946 and 1971). The absence of any pattern of rural to urban migration—contrary to other developing countries—is evident in the rural–urban structure of the country which has remained relatively unchanged throughout most of the 20th century (Marga Institute, 1986).

The welfare aspects of housing policies were geared primarily towards alleviating hardships of the middle and low income groups in the urban sector. Thus, much of the housing legislation of this period was based on the Rent Restriction Ordinance, 1942 introduced as a temporary wartime measure to clamp down on the excesses of landlordism. The early housing legislation, mainly focused on tenant and landlord relationships, especially the welfare of tenants, shows that there was little interest in the provision of shelter as a welfare entitlement or a social right.

Although housing did not rate highly as an element of welfare politics, the establishment of a separate Ministry of Housing in 1953, and the passing of the National Housing Act, 1954 marked a major breakthrough in moves towards the development of a national housing policy at a later date. One of the main policy initiatives of the new ministry was to promote housing investment and increase the housing stock through government subsidies to consumers and suppliers of housing (Marga Institute, 1986). Despite these initiatives, 'the expansion of the country's housing stock did not keep pace with the increase of population' (Pieris, 1993: 214). However, the housing sector was drawn more directly into the orbit of social welfare only under the neoliberal regimes of the 1970s. The 'Million Houses Development Programme' (1977–82) sought to provide low cost housing in the urban and urbanized rural sector and for the first time initiated a national housing policy (*Economic Review*, 1975).

The Public Utilities (water, transport, electricity, sewerage, etc.) unlike housing were by nature universal and not limited by economic status. Public utility services such as water and sewerage associated with health and sanitation formed part of the welfare package. Likewise, transport services—which had been previously regarded as an important element of economic policy and geared to economic modernization— were now identified as a component of the social infrastructure. Thus, road services and the impressive network of state managed rail transport services (started in 1867), all of which were critical for the development of the lucrative colonial plantation economy, were reconstituted as a part of the welfare package.

In the heyday of the welfare state in the late 1950s and 1960s, the nationalization of road passenger services and the subsidy for transport was seen as having distinct social welfare benefits. There is no doubt that 'the cheap and extensive transport network … made education, health and other services more easily accessible and spread their benefits to the rural population' (Alailima, 1984: 62). For these reasons, transport constituted a significant item of social expenditure and formed part of the demand politics of welfarism. Given that public utility services in developing countries have had a strong equity element and a redistributive impact, contrary to conventional theorizing about social expenditure (OECD, 1985), transport subsidies should rightly be regarded as belonging to a package of universalistic welfare services and taken account of under social expenditures.

The Personal Social Services, however, remained neglected as an aspect of public policy. Unlike the welfare system in advanced industrial countries, the personal social services failed to elicit much demand for intervention by the state mainly because they dealt with needs customarily provided for by the informal system of family and kin networks. Consequently, there were very few instances of 'free standing services' for special groups—such as the disabled, children, youth, or the aged—in need of rehabilitation, care and probation. In general, the role of the state in relation to the personal social services was that of a reluctant caretaker exercising regulation and control over others providing care and services. The total cost of public welfare and social security schemes constituted less than 1 per cent of public expenditure (Alailima, 1995). While the state could assist with emergency care and assistance, the main social responsibility for these services continued to be with family and kin networks (*Economic Review*, 1978).

In sum, from the beginning of fully responsible self-government and electoral democracy in 1948, there were two dominant themes of competitive politics which have continued to plague Sri Lanka, viz., ethnic and welfare politics. During the first and second decades, from 1948 to 1970, the electoral politics of all governments were plagued by welfarism and the growing tensions of nationalistic and ethnic politics. Cultural nationalist politics were linked to welfare politics since the constituency of the nationalists was drawn mainly from the powerless, socially disfranchised segment of society, i.e., those who did not belong to the Western educated middle class. But during the first two decades after-independence, it was also a matter of political convenience that the culturalist nationalist forces were allied with the organized working class. The politics of this era, not surprisingly, combined welfare issues with linguistic nationalism on the grounds of ensuring a greater measure of distributional equity.

As a result, the welfare politics of this period, structured around a loose political alliance of nationalists and the radical Left, led to the consolidation of the Sri Lanka welfare state in the 1960s (Government of Ceylon, 1963). Continuing the legacy of welfarism of the late colonial state, a distinctive feature of the welfare policy strategy of independent elected governments, especially of the post-1956 era, has been to develop a package of rural policies. The rural component of these policies is evident in liberal credit facilities, land reform and rural amenities, including housing, all of which were beneficial to sections of the rural peasantry. In addition to their economic rationale and consequences, these rural policies helped to consolidate the Sri Lankan welfare state within an institutional framework of a package of economic and social policies targeted regionally and sectorally. These policies, introduced in the 1960s and 1970s, were intended in part to offset the urban bias of welfare policies. But, they also helped to consolidate the alliance politics of this period, representing the combined interests of the peasant rural sector and the urban working class.

It is often overlooked that this package of welfare state policies played a significant role in containing the ethnic politics of this period, and was markedly different from the politics of ethnic accommodation of the pre-independence period which continued into the first decade of independence. The electoral politics associated with welfarism became linked to ethnic politics mainly because rural policies had special significance for the Tamil people. The Tamil people who were mostly concentrated in the north of Sri Lanka were greatly dependent on agriculture for their livelihood, especially the production of 'minor food crops, including bananas, tobacco, vegetables, potatoes, onions, chillies and fruit' (Moore, 1985: 108). Because of this, the predominantly rural Tamil people received considerable economic benefits from the rural policies of the state, which in turn helped to offset the economic loss they suffered when they were deprived of the their main source of livelihood which had been in public sector employment. This disadvantage was a direct consequence of educational reforms introduced in the post-1956 era, making Sinhalese the official language, and leading to what was termed the 'Sinhalisaion of the State' (ibid.).

The regional sectoral social impact of these controversial policies was reflected in changes to the pattern of university admissions as a result of the introduction of district quota admissions to universities, and the standardization of marks[6] according to language medium—Sinhalese or Tamil—in 1974-75. These educational policies, all of which disadvantaged Tamil people in the labour market as a form of affirmative action, were intended to 'neutralize the superior performance of Tamil medium students' (de Silva, 1979), and their privileged position in the labour market. The latter, it was argued, was due to the regional disparities in educational opportunities which favoured Tamil students, especially in science subjects, largely because of their access to better educational facilities.

Against this background, the rural social policies of the welfare state offered the Tamil people some degree of monetary compensation for the economic losses suffered by their becoming less competitive in the labour market, and losing their previously privileged position in the professions and the public sector. It is well documented that until the late 1960s, public sector employment had 'always been proportionately higher than their demographic size' (Tambiah, 1986). Therefore, the policy trade-off evident in the package of welfare state policies was particularly significant because the rural policies provided a highly lucrative alternative source of livelihood for their loss of employment opportunities in the public sector.

The economic benefits derived by the Tamil people from the rural social policies introduced in the 1960s, were dramatically withdrawn when all import controls were removed as a result of the economic liberalization policies introduced in 1977, which included the removal of agricultural subsidies. Thus, with the fall in the price of minor food crops, agricultural production in the Tamil areas (the Jaffna district) fell sharply and caused severe economic hardship (Moore, 1985). This in turn exacerbated latent ethnic tensions and conflicts and destroyed the ethnic accommodation of the immediate post-independence period, which was to a large extent held together by the Sri Lankan welfare state (Gunasinghe, 1984).

In summary, the welfare politics that evolved during the first two decades of independence endeavoured to combine the interests of the peasant rural sector and the urban working class. It was this powerful alliance of interest groups—the political alliance of nationalists and the radical Left—which led to the consolidation of the Sri Lanka welfare state in the 1960s (Government of Ceylon, 1963). The distinctive features of the Sri Lankan welfare state which emerged following the consolidation of numerous social measures in the 1960s may be summarized as follows:

- universalistic social policies in the fields of health, education, subsidised food as an income supplement, and the public utilities, including transport;
- an income redistributive rationale for a high percentage of social expenditure relative to GNP (approximately 10-12 per cent of GNP);
- a social assistance model of social security income maintenance;
- a poorly developed system of 'personal social services' heavily reliant on private charity, benevolence and non-professional human services; and,
- a pronounced urban bias in the delivery of most welfare services and benefits, mitigated by a package of compensatory rural policies.

We may also note in passing that the 'crisis of the welfare state', experienced in the 1970s and 1980s (Dunham and Jayasuriya, 2000; Jayasuriya, L., 2001; Kelegama, 1998; Sandaratne, 2000) was fuelled by the fiscal crisis of the 1970s and also linked with the decline of welfare politics. Indeed, while this may have signalled a shift from *welfare* to *warfare*, they serve 'identical and complementary ends ... (in that they both) derive from the same roots, dynamics, values and ideology' (Gil, 1977: 653).

THE HOW AND WHY OF THE SRI LANKAN WELFARE STATE

The Sri Lankan welfare state of the 1960s was, by any reckoning, in conformity with the understanding of the welfare state as public provision for the protection of its citizens from the consequences of want, ignorance or sickness (Laybourn, 1998). The welfare state, as it evolved in Sri Lanka, was the product of several decades of British colonial rule, and was closely associated with the process of modernization and democratization, extending from the early to the late colonial state.

The democratization process itself was based on the assumption that the colonial state represented 'an absent ruling class' (Mamdani, 1976: 42), whose functions were exercised by the local indigenous bourgeoisie, a Western educated élite. The success of British colonial policy in Sri Lanka rested largely in creating and managing this local élite. Accordingly, one of the objectives of education policy development in the late 19th century was to equip this local élite with knowledge, skill and competence to represent the ruling class as administrators. This was achieved by transplanting British cultural values and liberal political ideas and creating a local ruling class of 'brown sahibs' who helped to sustain British colonial interests.

The ideology of British liberalism transplanted and imposed on Sri Lanka in the early phase of colonial rule helped to shape the Sri Lankan political economy on the basis of three elements, also evident in British colonial policy in India (Stokes, 1959), viz., free trade, evangelicalism, and philosophical radicalism. Free trade, based on the notion of laissez faire policies was critical to the colonial economy, and helped to foster an alliance with a local capitalist class. Evangelicalism, on the other hand, through the work of Christian missionaries, mitigated the adverse effects of unbridled growth by legitimizing the 'civilising mission' of colonial rule. The main function of missionary organizations was to provide social support for colonial rule, enabling a greater degree of acceptance by the ruled. Christianization through education in Sri Lanka was not only an important avenue for social betterment and social mobility, but also directed towards cultural assimilation and co-optation of the educated class.

The third element—philosophical radicalism—gave British liberalism a solid intellectual basis for its social and political commitments. Thus, the utilitarian thinking which guided the political reforms of 1833 had a lasting influence on all aspects of political and social development. As a result, democratic ideas, values and institutions took firm root in the Sri Lankan polity.

In short, the social and political institutions of Sri Lanka, including the welfare state of the 1960s lie firmly anchored to the social and political ideology of British colonialism (Jupp, 1978). Consequently, the evolution of the Sri Lankan welfare state of the 1960s, being rooted firmly in British colonial policy, draws heavily on the intellectual ideas and belief systems derived from Bentham through to Keynes, Beveridge and the Fabian socialist style collectivism. These ideas and belief systems were clearly in the forefront among the western educated élite who were largely responsible for social policy initiatives from the days of the late colonial state to the consolidation of the welfare state in the 1960s.

However, the liberal progressive ideas and political agendas of the political élite were not solely a question of being ideologically driven, but also one of pragmatic convenience to promote measures for greater equity and justice. Indeed, as some analysts have rightly argued, the leading politicians of the post-independence era of welfarism 'were not philosophically committed to redistribution of wealth' but were cast more in the role of 'paternalistic public benefactors' (Manor, 1989: 195). It is somewhat ironical that the conservative politicians who gained political power from the colonial rulers happened to be strong advocates of social liberalism manifest as welfarism, largely to 'ward off attacks from the Marxist Left' (ibid.: 177) or as 'a populist strategy to retain or win political power' (Marga Institute, 1974: 17).

In other words, the 'alliance politics' of the nationalists and the Left (1956–65), strategically used the package of welfare policies—urban and rural welfare measures— to gain political ascendancy in the heyday of 'welfare politics'. At the same time, as some social analysts (e.g., Lakshman, 1989) have pointed out, the very sustenance of the bourgeoisie state required 'social welfarism' in order to keep the masses quiet to avoid revolutionary struggles. Or stated differently, there was a clear legitimizing function for the welfare state, namely, the need to mitigate the adverse consequences of capitalist expansion in a dependent economy (Jayasuriya, 2000). This interpretation exemplifies a combination of the 'élitist' and the pluralist models of social policy, and sees political outcomes as a matter of competition between powerful interest groups (Crowther, 1988; Goldthorpe, 1964).

However, with the crisis of the welfare state and also the collapse of the Westminster style political institutions in the 1970s, there has been a fracturing of the social justice rationale of the earlier welfare state policies (e.g., the greater degree of social mobility, distributive justice and equity evident in the lowering of income inequalities). The deepening crisis of the welfare state and liberal democracy, coupled with the sense of cultural alienation felt by the disempowered indigenous élite (e.g., the failed youth insurrection of the 1970s), has brought to the fore the contradictions and tensions of post-colonialism.

In the new post-colonial state, the nation has been enmeshed in 'two cultures', and 'two societies'. The 'two cultures'—that of the westernized versus the traditional or indigenous—with cross cutting linkages to all other social divisions, ethnic, cultural and regional, is probably one of the lasting legacies of British colonial rule. These 'two cultures' are now confounded with the 'two societies'—the haves and have nots. This is a legacy partly of neoliberalism and a declining welfare state, which has led to a sharp differentiation between the haves and the have nots, the affluent rich and mendicant poor, capital and labour.

These dramatic social changes, alongside a new political ethos, have witnessed the transformation of the Sri Lankan polity from *welfare* to *warfare* in the post-colonial era. The militant post-colonial discourse which emerged from the 1970s has been framed within a culture of an illiberal politics (1977–94), economic liberalism and the dominance of ethnic identity politics over the welfare politics of the earlier era. Although this new ethos was partly reversed in 1994 with a return to the earlier liberal political culture and a moderate form of collectivism, much uncertainty surrounds the Sri Lankan polity in the context of globalization and the 'new politics' after 11 September 2001.

CONCLUSION

In summary, in charting the evolution of the Sri Lankan welfare state, the chapter identifies three distinctive features of its British colonial legacy—the influence of a liberal ideology, processes of democratization and the relative autonomy of the late colonial state. First and foremost, was the impact of the ideological milieu of British colonial policies, as well as the worldview of colonial administrators and local political élites. The late colonial state of the 20th century witnessed the dominance of the ideas of social liberalism and early Fabianism, particularly as they related to notions of modernity and development. This 'welfarist' understanding of the purposes of colonial rule continued to influence governments of all political hues in the first two decades. Clearly, a key feature of the late colonial state was that the Sri Lankan polity was regarded largely as an agency of social development.

Second, one of the central features of the late colonial state was its partial democratization, through the granting of universal franchise and limited indirect rule. Welfarism, which dominated the electoral politics of the late colonial state, was the product of the complex interplay of partial democratization and the search for some degree of political legitimacy. Aspects of this unfolding political dynamic of welfare expansion, stoked by the weakening embers of the late colonial state, continued to reverberate even louder during the first two decades of independence (1948–70).

Third, the relative autonomy of the late colonial state was reflected in the growth of a vibrant civil society in the last decades of colonial rule, the period of partial self-rule. This was manifest in the growth of a working class movement, trade unions, and a range of nationalist/religious/voluntary organizations. This 'civil society' was 'a public sphere constituted through patriarchal discourses' (Srivastava, 1998: 2), and served to exercise considerable pressure on the state to expand its social commitments dramatically in the first two decades of independence. It was these influences that helped to move Sri Lanka from a piecemeal 'welfarism' to an integrated 'welfare state', an exceptional institutional structure for a 'developing society' in the 1960s and 1970s.

Despite the foregoing analysis, there still remain many challenging, unanswered questions in understanding the evolution of social policy in Sri Lanka. From a comparative perspective, perhaps the most problematic of these is the difficult question as to why this form of British colonial rule—a classic instance of a benevolent paternalism—took firm root in Sri Lanka. In other words, how does one explain the success of this novel experiment of British colonial policy in using Sri Lanka as a social laboratory and effecting rapid social changes? Part of the answer probably lies in deep rooted cultural influences emanating from Sri Lanka's rich socio-political history, one endowed with a highly developed literate civilization extending over 2,000 years (Siriweera, 2002).

But more importantly, it needs to be borne in mind that prior to British colonial rule, Sri Lanka had been greatly influenced in a variety of ways by two centuries of European colonization—first by the Portuguese followed by the Dutch (Goonewardene, 1958). Thus, for example, the Dutch who preceded the British as a colonial power 'bridged the gap between medievalism and 19th century colonial rule in Ceylon with a pioneer structure which the British modernized' (Ludowyke, 1967: 134). Sri Lanka, therefore, had been already subject to a modicum of 'westernization' before British colonial rule. This still fails, of course, to answer why the modernization process, when compared with other British colonial settlements, was so easily accomplished in Sri Lanka. The answers to this, however, may have to be located within the broad domain of theorizing about the processes of social and cultural change, in particular contested notions of traditionalism and modernism (Eisenstadt, 1967–68; Horowitz, 1972). These complex questions, along with the more specific issue of the fate of social development and welfarism in the post-colonial era of the last three decades presents a challenging research agenda for the future.

NOTES

1. See listing of constitutional reports and other relevant policy documents in Reports.
2. 'The spirit of utilitarianism sought to justify actions on the basis of contributions towards increasing human satisfactions and decreasing satisfactions' (Sleeman, 1973: 14). Utilitarians encouraged purposive social institutions, e.g., anti-slavery, factory legislation, improving public health, etc., where the greatest good of the greatest number would be provided.
3. Sen (1981) identifies the food subsidy as an example of the concept of 'entitlements', in particular, as a method of universal support, of non-exclusion, guaranteeing the 'right to food' and being effective in famine prevention.
4. J.H.L. Cumpston, the architect of the Report, was a distinguished Australian public servant who as Director-General of Health Services in Australia (1921–45) was responsible for the creation of the Commonwealth Department of Health, Australia (Thome, 1974).
5. Midgley cites the impact of the Beveridge Report on a number of colonial governments as a classic instance of the way in which 'developments in social policy in the metropolitan countries exerted an influence on the colonies' (1984a: 177).
6. Standardization of marks was designed to correct examiner variability between the language media. The intention was 'to arrive at a uniform scale so that in the end the number qualifying from each medium would be proportionate to the number sitting the examination in each medium' (de Silva, 1978).

REFERENCES

Alailima, P. (1984), 'Basic Needs and Employment', *Working Papers, World Employment Programme Research*, Geneva: ILO.

_____ (1995), *Post-Independence Evolution of Social Policy and Expenditure in Sri Lanka*, Colombo: Centre for Women's Research.

Bandarage, A. (1983), *Colonialism in Sri Lanka*, Amsterdam: Mouton.

Bruce, M. (1961), *The Coming of the Welfare State*, London: Batsford.

Crowther, A. (1988), *British Social Policy 1914–1918*, Studies in Economic and Social Policy, London: Macmillan.

Coomaraswamy, R. (1993), 'The Constitution and Constitutional Reform', in K.M. de Silva (ed.), *Sri Lanka: Problems of Governance*, Kandy, Sri Lanka: International Centre for Ethnic Studies.

de Silva, C.R. (1978), 'The Politics of University Admissions: A Review of Some Aspects of the Admissions Policy in Sri Lanka 1971–78', *Sri Lanka Journal of Social Sciences*, 1(2).

_____ (1979), 'The Impact of Nationalism on Education: The Schools Take over (1961) and the University Admissions Crisis 1970–75', in M. Roberts (ed.), *Collective Identities, Nationalisms and Protest in Modern Sri Lanka*, Colombo: Marga Institute.

de Silva, K.M. (1965), *Social Policy and Missionary Organisation in Ceylon 1840–55*, London: Royal Commonwealth Society.

_____ (1981), *A History of Sri Lanka*, London: Oxford University Press.

Dicey, A.V. (1996), *Lectures on the Relation between Law and Public Opinion in England during the Nineteenth Century*, Homes Beach: Gaunt.

Dunham, D. and S. Jayasuriya (2000), 'Equity, growth and the insurrection: Liberalization and the welfare debate in contemporary Sri Lanka', *Oxford Development Studies*, 28(1): 97–110.

Economic Review (1975), *Special Report on Housing and Development*, 21(3 and 4).

_____ (1978), *Social Service, Welfare and Development*, 23(12).

Eisenstadt, S.N. (1967–68), 'Some New Looks of the Problem of Relations between Traditional Societies and Modernization', Review Article, *Economic Development and Cultural Change*, Vol. 16.

Evans, E.J. (1978), *Social policy 1830–1914*, London: Routledge.

Farmer, B.H. (1957), *Pioneer Peasant Colonisation in Ceylon*, London, Oxford: Oxford University Press.

Fernando, L. (1999), 'Three phases of political development after independence', in W.D. Lakshman and C.A. Tisdell (eds), *Facets of Development of Sri Lanka Since Independence*, St. Lucia: University of Queensland Press.

Gil, D. (1977), 'Common roots and functions of the warfare and welfare state', *Journal of Sociology and Social Welfare*, 4(3 and 4): 639–655.

Goldthorpe, J.H. (1964), 'The Development of Social Policy in England 1800–1914', *Transactions of the Fifth World Congress of Sociology*, 4(4): 41–56.

Goonewardene, K.W. (1958), *Foundations of Dutch Power in Ceylon 1636–87*, Amsterdam: Netherlands Institute for International Relations.

Government of Ceylon, Ministry of Finance (1963), *Economic and Social Progress 1956–62*, Supplement to Budget Speech, Colombo: Government Press.

Gunasinghe, N. (1984), 'The open economy and its impact on ethnic relations in Sri Lanka', in Committee for Rational Development (CRD), *Sri Lanka: The Ethnic Conflict*, New Delhi: Navarang.

Gunatilleke, G. (1985), 'Health and development in Sri Lanka: An overview', in S.B. Halstead et al. (eds), *Good Health at Low Cost*, New York: Rockerfeller.

_____ (1993), *Development and Liberalization in Sri Lanka*, Colombo: Marga Institute.

_____ (1999), 'Development policy regimes', in W.D. Lakshman and C.A. Tisdell (eds), *Facets of Development of Sri Lanka Since Independence: Socio-Political, Economic, Scientific, Cultural*, St. Lucia, Brisbane: University of Queensland Press.

Hall, P. (1986), *Governing the Economy: The Politics of State Intervention in Britain and France*, Oxford: Oxford University Press.

Horowitz, I.L. (1972), *Three Worlds of Development: The Theory and Practice of International Stratification*, New York: Oxford University Press.

Houtart, F. (1974), *Religion and Ideology in Sri Lanka*, Colombo: Hansa.

ILO (International Labour Organization) (1971), *Matching Employment Opportunities and Expectations: A Program of Action for Ceylon*, Seers Report Technical Papers, Geneva: ILO.

Jayasuriya, K. (2001), Review essay: 'The making of the Sri Lankan bourgeoisie', Review of K. Jayawardena (2000), *Nobodies to Somebodies: The Rise of the Colonial Bourgeoisie Sri Lanka*, Social Scientists' Association, and Sanjiva Press, Colombo, *Sri Lanka Economic Journal*, 2(1): 168–75.

Jayasuriya, L. (2000), *Welfarism and Politics in Sri Lanka*, Perth: School of Social Work and Social Policy, University of Western Australia.

———— (2001), 'Rethinking social development: Towards an equitable future for Sri Lanka', *South Asian Economic Journal*, 2(1): 105–21.

Jayasuriya, L., G. Fernando and M. Allbrook (1985), 'Sri Lankan social welfare', in J. Dixon and H.S. Kim (eds), *Social Welfare*, London: Croom Helm.

Jayawardena, K. (1972), *The Rise of the Labour Movement in Ceylon*, Durham, North Carolina: Duke University Press.

Jayaweera, S. (1969), 'Development of Secondary Education', in *Education in Ceylon*, Part II, Colombo: Ministry of Education.

Jeffries, C. (1962), *The Path to Independence*, London: Pall Mall Press.

Jones, M. (2000), 'The Ceylon Malaria Epidemic of 1934–35: A Case Study in Colonial Medicine', *Social History of Medicine*, 13(1).

Jupp, J. (1978), *Sri Lanka: Third World Democracy*, London: Frank Cass.

Kannangara, P.D. (1988), 'The Caste Problem and the Study of the Modern Period of Sri Lankan History', *Social Science Review*, 4.

Kearney, R.N. (1971), *Trade Unions and Politics in Ceylon*, New Delhi: University of California Press.

Kelegama, S. (1987), 'Growth and equity—A review of the Sri Lankan experience', *Sri Lanka Economic Journal*, 2(1).

———— (1998), 'Economic Development in Sri Lanka during the 50 Years of Independence: What Went Wrong?', in People's Bank (ed.), *Sri Lanka—The 50 Years of Independence*, Colombo: People's Bank.

Lakshman, W.D. (1989), 'Lineages of Dependent Development: From State Control to the Open Economy', in P. Wignaraja and A. Hussein (eds), *The Challenge in South Asia*, New Delhi: Sage.

Laybourn, K. (1998), The Evolution of British Social Policy and the Welfare State, London: Keele University Press.

Ludowyke, E.F.C. (1967), *A Short History of Ceylon*, New York: Praeger.

Mamdani, M. (1976), *Politics and Class Formation in Uganda*, London: Heinemann.

Manor, J. (1989), *The Expedient Utopian: Bandaranaike and Ceylon*, Cambridge: Cambridge University Press.

Marga Institute (1974), *Welfare and Growth in Sri Lanka*, Colombo: Marga.

———— (1986), *Housing*, Colombo: Marga.

Marshall, T.H. (1973), 'Citizenship and Social Class', in T.H. Marshall (ed.), *Class, Citizenship and Social Development*, Connecticut: Greenwood.

Mendis, G.C. (ed.) (1956), *The Colebrooke–Cameron Papers* (2 Vols), Cambridge: Cambridge University Press.

———— (1957), *Ceylon Today and Yesterday*, Colombo: ANCL.

Midgley, J. (1984a), 'Poor Principles and Social Assistance in the Third World: A Study of the Perpetuation of Colonial Welfare', *International Social Work*, 27(1): 19–29.

———— (1984b), 'Diffusion and the Development of Social Policy: Evidence from the Third World', *Journal of Social Policy*, 13: 167–84.

———— (1998), 'Colonialism and Welfare: A Post-Colonial Commentary', *Journal of Progressive Human Services*, 9(2).

Moore, M. (1985), *The State and Peasant Politics in Sri Lanka*, Cambridge: Cambridge University Press.

OECD (1985), *Social Expenditure 1960–90*, Paris: OECD.

Osmani, S.R. (1993), 'Is There a Conflict between Growth and Welfarism? The Tale of Sri Lanka', *Working Paper No. 109*, Helsinki University, Finland: Wider.

Peiris, G.L. (1993), 'Government and Social Welfare', in K.M. de Silva (ed.), *Sri Lanka: Problems of Governance*, Kandy, Sri Lanka: International Centre for Ethnic Studies.

Perera, N.M. (1944), *The Case for Free Education*, Colombo: Ola Book Company.

Pieris, I. (2000), *Disease, Treatment and Health Behaviour in Sri Lanka*, Sydney: Oxford University Press.

Pieris, R. (1967), 'The Role of the Government in Labour Relations in Ceylon', in *Labour Relations in the Asian Countries*, Tokyo: Japan Institute of Labour.

Ponnambalam, S. (1980), *Dependent Capitalism in Crisis: The Sri Lankan Economy 1948–80*, London: Zed Books.

Russell, J. (1982), *Communal Politics under the Donoughmore Constitution (1931–47)*, Colombo: Tisara Prakasakayo.

Samaraweera, V. (1973), 'The Colebrooke–Cameron Reforms', in K.M. de Silva (ed.), *History of Ceylon*, (Vol. 3), Colombo: University of Ceylon.

Sandaratne, N. (2000), *Economic Growth and Social Transformations*, Colombo: Tamarind.

Savy, R. (1972), *Social Security in Agriculture*, Geneva: ILO.

Sen, A. (1981), *Poverty and Famines: An Essay on Entitlements and Deprivations*, Clarendon: Oxford University Press.

Siriweera, W.I. (2002), *History of Sri Lanka: From Earliest Times up to the Sixteenth Century*, Colombo: Dayawansa Jayakody.

Sleeman, J.F. (1973), *The Welfare State: Its Aims, Benefits and Costs*, London: Allen & Unwin.

Snodgrass, Donald R. (1966), *Ceylon: An Export Economy in Transition*, Homewood: Illinois University Press.

Stokes, E. (1959), *English Utilitarians and India*, Oxford: Oxford University Press.

Tambiah, S.J. (1986), *Sri Lanka: Ethnic Fratricide and the Dismantling of Democracy*, London: Tauris.

Thorne, C. (1974), 'Health and the state', Ph.D dissertation, Canberra: Australian National University.

UNDP (1990–96), *Human Development Reports*, New York: Oxford University Press.

Warnapala, W.A. (1974), *Civil Service Administration in Ceylon*, Colombo: Department of Cultural Affairs, Government of Sri Lanka.

Wilson, A.J. (1973), 'The development of the constitution 1910-1947', in K.M. de Silva (ed.), *The History of Ceylon* (Vol. 3), Colombo: University of Ceylon.

Wright, M. (1950), *The Development of the Legislative Council*, London.

Select Readings

Alailima, P. and N. Sandaratne (1997), 'Sri Lanka's Social Development: A Retrospective Analysis', in Mehotra Santosh and R. Jolly (eds), *Development with a Human Face*, Oxford: Oxford University Press.

Jayawardena, K. (1973), 'Education Policy in the Early 20th Century', in K.M. de Silva (ed.), *History of Ceylon* (Vol. 3), Colombo: University of Ceylon.

Warnapala, W.A. (1973), 'The Emergence of a Welfare Policy', in K.M. de Silva (ed.), *History of Ceylon* (Vol. 3), Colombo: University of Ceylon.

REPORTS

Colebrooke–Cameron Commission Report (1833).

Perry Report (1905), *Report on the Improvement of the Nursing Service of Hospitals,* Sessional Paper No. XXXVI, Colombo: Ceylon Government Press.

Donoughmore Commission Report (1929), *Report of the Special Commission on the (Ceylon) Constitution,* CMD 3131, London: HMSO.

Kannangara Report (1943), *Report of the Special Committee on Education,* Sessional Paper No. XXIV, Colombo: Ceylon Government Press.

Gill Report (1935), *Report on the Malaria Epidemic in Ceylon 1934–35,* Sessional Paper No. XXIII, Ceylon Government Press.

Newnham Report (1936), *Relief of Distress due to Sickness and Shortage of Food,* Sessional Paper No. V, Colombo: Ceylon Government Press.

Wedderburn Report (1934), *Report on Statutory Provision for Poor Relief,* Sessional Paper No. XX, Colombo: Ceylon Government Press.

Corea Report (1937), *Report on Unemployment,* Sessional Paper No. VII, Ceylon Government Press.

Jennings Report (1947), *Report of the Commission on Social Services,* Sessional Paper No. VII, Colombo: Ceylon Government Press.

Soulbury Report (1945), *Report of the Commission on Constitutional Reform,* CMD 7667, HMSO.

Cumpston Report (1950), *Report on the Medical and Public Health Organizations of Ceylon,* Sessional Paper No. III, Colombo: Ceylon Government Press.

Hamlin Report (1957), *Report on Children's Services,* Sessional Paper No. VII, Colombo: Ceylon Government Press.

20

OVERVIEW OF THE HEALTH SECTOR

Amala de Silva

INTRODUCTION

Sri Lanka is often cited internationally as a success story: with an infant mortality rate of 12.2 per 1,000 live births in 2001 and a maternal mortality rate of 2.3 per 10,000 live births in 1996, and male and female life expectancies of 70.7 and 75.4 years respectively (*Annual Health Bulletin*, 2001), it is an outlier among developing countries and the World Health Organization (WHO) classifies it as a low child and adult mortality country in the World Health Report of 2000. Much of this success is attributed to two national policies relating to health: free health care in the public sector and the provision of services close to the client from the 1930s onwards, a concept now advocated strongly by the World Health Organization's Macroeconomics and Health Commission Report of 2001.

Yet, the appropriateness of these very two policies is being questioned in the context of transition. Sri Lanka is facing health transition: the combined effect of demographic and epidemiological transition. The population is ageing rapidly. Currently, over 10 per cent of the population is aged over 60 and this percentage will rise to 13 per cent in 2011 (Indralal de Silva, 1997). The burden of ill health has switched from communicable to non-communicable diseases, with ischaemic heart disease, cerebrovascular disease, pulmonary heart disease and neoplasms among the five leading causes of hospital deaths in 2001. Since the liberalization of the economy in 1977, Sri Lanka has been facing economic transition, from a centrally controlled public sector led economy to one that sees the private sector as its engine of growth. Most significantly, Sri Lanka is also facing rapid social transition as a result of its exposure to factors such as global communication, mass media and information technology, elements that impact on health care, health risks and expectations.

Universal franchise resulted in the widespread development of health facilities (Central Bank, 1998) as politicians strove to satisfy the demands of the electorate. At this time, given the rapidly rising population and the high level of infant and maternal deaths in the country, the emphasis was on providing primary care treatment units that could address the maternal and child care needs of the community and the communicable disease burden. This is the type of close-to-client care that is being recommended for developing countries by the WHO today. In providing this care free and in a widely dispersed network, the state chose to subsidize the supply of health care (WHO, 2002b) rather than demand. No explicit national health policy as regards provision was formulated in this period but the policy of free health care was widely accepted.

As noted in the report of the Presidential Task Force (PTF) in 1992, 'Hitherto, the Ministry of Health formulated policy guidelines on issues as they arose. Whilst some areas of activity were well covered, a number of other areas did not receive attention. As a result, Shri Lanka never had a comprehensive National Health Policy to mould the destinies of health development' (PTF Report, 1992: 1).

Yet, when Task Forces were employed to determine a national health policy as in 1992 and 1996, their policies were not adopted in their entirety due to political upheavals and misgivings. However, attempts have been made to adopt a few elements of these reports in an ad hoc manner, as in the upgrading of one hospital in each district to the level of a District General Hospital as advocated by the 1996 Task Force report.

The needs imposed by health transition are complex: the impacts of such transitions pervade not only the decisions regarding the type of services to be provided but the financing mechanisms needed to provide and access such services as well. The growth of the private health care sector, which occurred within a policy vacuum, apart from the decision in 1977 to permit private practice by state medical officers in their off duty hours, has had its own repercussions on the efficiency and equity of the health system, as a whole. The very nature of the Sri Lankan private health care system that is strongly dependent on the state health care system for its personnel, creates market imperfections and tensions that impact on patient welfare. Subsidizing demand (through public provision, safety net payments for private sector interactions and tax concessions and subsidies) rather than supply could be a means of addressing the equity concerns of the dual health care system emerging in the Sri Lankan context.

The lack of a coherent national health policy, particularly with regard to health financing, has left the country unprepared for the challenges of transition. The Japan International Cooperation Agency (JICA) Master Plan is currently under preparation and it is to be hoped that policy makers will give the challenges of transition and the complexities of coordinating public and private sector activities their due importance.[1]

This chapter seeks to trace the evolution of allopathic[2] health care provision and financing from the 1930s onwards, focusing on the policies that determined such outcomes in the sections that folow immediately. The next two sections highlight the current debates in the fields of provision and financing. The central question the chapter seeks to answer is whether existing policies with regard to health care are outmoded given the complexities of the health challenges posed by transition.

EVOLUTION OF THE HEALTH SYSTEM

Provision

This section focuses on identifying the factors that determined the form and level of health care provision in the country. The evolution of the health system is attributable not only to resource availability and demographic and epidemiological needs but also to political will.

Universal adult franchise in 1931 created the essential link between community needs and government expenditure within a colonized nation, which had long been deprived of a voice. 'Schools, rural hospitals, roads and sub-post offices were among the most common items in the list of demands' (Marga Institute, 1984). It is said that enfranchisement of women in Ceylon resulted from the view that 'women's services would be of special value in coping with the high infant mortality rate in the island and with the need for better housing and improved midwifery and prenatal services' (Myrdal, 1968).

Health policy was focused in this period on the control of major communicable diseases, the provision of mother and child care and ensuring access to the rural poor. Primary health care provision which was the accepted health development strategy in Sri Lanka since the 1930s, with the expansion of field midwife services, the network of rural hospitals, maternity homes and central dispensaries and the emphasis on the control of communicable diseases such as malaria, is considered to have been a forerunner to the WHO's Alma Ata Declaration on Primary Health Care in 1978. Subsequently in 1980, Sri Lanka became a signatory to 'Health for All (HFA) by the year 2000 Convention' of the WHO and health sector documents relate achievements in health indicators to the HFA targets. Sri Lanka's health indicators continued to improve and there were no major health policy debates in Sri Lanka, though by the 1960s resource constraints began to limit state expenditure on health.

Subsidization of supply continued, however, in line with political demands, and the number of health care institutions in the country increased rapidly; from 112 in 1930, to 263 in 1950, 326 in 1970, 397 in 1985 and 510 in 1995 (cited in Sanderatne, 2000). Sanderatne (ibid.) attributes the expansion in the health services in the pre-independence days to strong political commitment of elected representatives after 1931 who were able to pressurize the executive for larger allocations of resources for their constituencies, the impact of the Marxist opposition, the economic capacity that prevailed in the country in this period and subsequently on the need for developing services in the dry zone as a prerequisite to land settlement.

The growth in the number of hospitals between 1940 and 1950 is striking, as is the eightfold increase in maternity homes. The widespread network of health institutions had the advantage of ensuring that any household had some sort of health facility within 2 kilometres from their house (Samarasinghe, 1998). The number of maternity homes and CDs diminishing does not necessarily mean closure of existing facilities. In many cases political will resulted in the upgrading of facilities by name, even if resource levels remained relatively unchanged. Population growth in the 1960s and 1970s provided the rationale for increasing the number of hospitals and hospital beds, and this measure resulted in the number of persons per hospital bed being 554 in 1930 but declining to 385 in 1950, 332 in 1970 and 331 in 1990 (Sanderatne, 2000). The number of health workers kept pace with the population as well but the number of physicians and nurses per 1,00,000 people remains low at 44.8 and 84.4 respectively in 2001. Population per physician has declined in the last decade and was 2,233 in 2001.

The growth in staff levels was uneven. Noteworthy is the fact that while the number of doctors rose by 226 per cent in the period 1990–2000, the growth in the number of nurses lagged significantly behind, though in other time periods the growth in nursing staff was greater than that of medical consultants, as the case should be. The shortage of nurses is currently posing one of the most significant problems with regard to the quality of care in public hospitals and this problem is likely to intensify with the rise in the non-communicable and geriatric disease burden. This also creates a constraint to the development of outreach nursing facilities within the community and domiciliary care, both aspects that are important with the progress of health transition.

Sri Lanka had a policy of free state medical care since 1950. Specialists in government service had, however, been allowed to see private patients up to the early 1970s, when this system was banned. In the period prior to banning private practice, consultants had often seen their patients in a room in their own homes or in small medical facilities involving a few doctors. In addition, there had been a small number of private practitioners functioning in urban settings.

With economic liberalization in 1977, medical consultants in the public sector were again allowed to that private patients in their off hours, either at home, a private outpatient facility, private hospital or nursing home. The word 'channelling'[3] was coined in this period to refer to the situation where the patient is able to consult a public sector specialist in a private sector setting.

The major thrust of the health policy in the 1990s as listed in the PTF Report of 1992 are health promotion, prevention and control of communicable and non-communicable diseases; fostering healthy life styles; human resource development taking into account the changing roles of the public and private sector in the future economic milieu; strengthening the quality and range of services and bridging the gaps, and decentralization of health administration.

The PTF Report of 1992 has in its terms of reference with regard to the determination of a National Health Policy for the country 'maximise the utilization of the available health manpower and facilities by rationalizing their deployment and management in the public and private sector'. In practice, however, the Ministry of Health has made no attempt to coordinate the two segments of the health sector. The regulatory bill, known as the Private Health Institutions Act, has been under discussion on and off for over the past decade. The Board of Investment is currently empowered to deal with foreign hospitals set up within the country which are then beyond the ambit of the Ministry of Health in practice. The Task Force recommendations were never implemented due to a change in government.

Decentralization came with the 13th Amendment of the Constitution in 1987, and resulted in the devolution of a set of functions including health to elected Provincial Councils. This change in policy did not occur in a planned manner and resulted in imbalances and disruptions of services such as in preventive care. Attanayake (2001) notes that a second round of decentralization occurred in 1992 with the transferring of administrative functions from district to sub-district (divisional) level, terming this move deconcentration (see Attanayake, 2001 for details on the impacts of decentralization). However, with larger health institutions such as Teaching Hospitals remaining with the centre and others being taken back to the centre, there has been a trend of concentration as well as insufficient coordination between the centre and the periphery.

The subsequent People's Alliance (PA) government appointed another Task Force, and the report of this Task Force was issued in 1996. The broad aims of the Health Policy of the government were the further increase of life expectancy by the reduction of both communicable and non-communicable preventable deaths and the improvement of the quality of life by reducing preventable diseases, health problems and disability and focusing on health promotion. The report listed 18 strategies. Those that relate to policy on provision were the improvement of existing preventive health programmes, improvement of medical facilities and the development of services including rehabilitation and continuing care based at institutional and community level, increasing accessibility of health care and the improvement of the quality of health care. Non-medical issues were also stressed in these strategies such as respecting and preserving the dignity of the individual, the right to health and community participation.

The Poverty Reduction Strategy Paper (PRSP) prepared by the Ministry of Finance and Planning in 2001 states that the government encouraged the expansion of the private sector, as the public sector was unable to keep pace with the increasing demand for hospital based care and higher quality services. It notes that while the private sector provides nearly half of outpatient care, it still provides only 5 per cent of hospitalization services. This document lists the main goals of the health sector as being the improvement of nutrition, keeping the burden of non-communicable diseases low, eradicating malaria and communicable diseases, ensuring that patients receive medical care of an international standard and providing maximum care to disadvantaged groups. In a bid to achieve these goals, the PRSP identifies five areas of priority health sector reform including three relating to health care provision: the expansion of curative care services at the district level; the expansion of health care services for specific groups such as the elderly, victims of war and conflict and the promotion of special areas of health care such as occupational health problems, mental health and the estate health services; and the development of health promotional programmes, with particular emphasis on outreach through the schools.

Population growth had been a major challenge to health care provision since independence. A national family planning programme was launched in 1965 and was extremely effective. The state promoted family planning as an activity that would benefit acceptors and their families. The stress was on keeping families small and well cared for and the maintenance of proper birth intervals rather than on population control as a national project. The high degree of literacy and female empowerment in Sri Lanka supported this campaign. In 1977, with the liberalization of the economy, an incentive payment scheme for male sterilization was introduced where an allowance was provided to compensate acceptors for their loss of wages and transport costs. Medical consultants too were encouraged to provide this service and non-governmental organizations (NGOs) geared to family planning were strengthened (Samarasinghe, 1998). The total fertility rate (TFR) indicates that the population growth rates are now at replacement level.

The challenge of increasing the quantity of maternal and child care services is now abating but is being replaced by the demands imposed by the epidemiological and demographic challenge: the need for more geriatric care and for services to address specially vulnerable groups and conditions such as the reproductive and mental health needs of youth. The challenge also remains of improving the quality of services both medical and non-medical (as in the concept of responsiveness introduced in the World Health Report of 2000 relating to the treatment of patients as individuals in health care interactions).

Financing

This section examines the financing systems adopted over time in the public and private health sectors of Sri Lanka, relating this information to the needs of the health system in the context of health transition and in line with international financing trends.

From as early as 1903 a system of user fees was in existence in the Ministry of Health. According to the Administrative Report of the Director of Medical and Sanitary Services for 1948:

> The institution of medical care is a responsibility of the Central Government. A national medical service offers free outdoor medical treatment to the people. With regard to indoor treatment it is free to the poorer classes but a small charge is made in the case of certain income groups. A charge of 30 cents per diem is made from those patients with incomes between Rs. 50 and Rs. 83 per mensem for accommodation in a non-paying ward. Where the income exceeds Rs. 83 per mensem a charge of 50 cents is made. (Wickramasinghe, 1949: C7)

These user charges did not impose a burden on the population on the whole for as Rannan-Eliya and de Mel (1996) argue based on the Consumer Finance Survey data of 1953, 90 per cent of the population was at a consumption level of less than Rs 600 per year. Adjusting these figures for the 1940s when this fee structure was in existence, they conclude that over 97 per cent of the rural population would have been exempt. Administrative reports in the 1950s show that revenue collected through these user charges represented less than 1 per cent of total health expenditure, confirming that user charges were a very rare occurrence (Pathmanathan, 2003). Samarasinghe (1998) attributes the fact that user charges were rarely recovered due to self-reporting being used as a means of determining patient income. Health expenditure in this period was borne almost in its entirety by the state. These user charges were scrapped in 1950.

In the post-1931 period, the existence of economic capacity facilitated the expansion of health services and this trend continued until the 1960s, as favourable economic conditions in the plantation sector provided a source of tax revenue to support welfare services including health sector expenditure (Sanderatne, 2000). Low economic growth resulted in resource constraints that led to reductions in the share of health expenditure out of GDP in the 1970s and 1980s (see Table 20.1). Health services had to expand from the 1960s onwards in line with population growth, and continued to do so even in the 1970s (see Table 20.2), but the impact of the resource constraints were felt in the quality of services, the shortage of drugs and the exodus of medical officers to foreign countries.

Table 20.1

Maternal Bed Utilization at Different Levels of Hospital in 1999

By Category of Health Facility	All Births per Day by Category of Hospital	Births per Maternal Bed per Year
Teaching hospital	200.4	59.7
Maternity hospital	76.9	55.8
Provincial hospital	115.2	60.0
Base hospital	234.6	57.6
District hospital	144.7	20.9
Peripheral unit	37.6	13.9
Rural hospital	19.6	7.7
Maternity homes and CDs	7.2	4.9

Source: WHO (2002b).

Table 20.2

Growth of Population, Facilities and Manpower in the Health Sector

							(% change)
	1930–40	1940–50	1950–60	1960–70	1970–80	1980–90	1990–2000
Hospitals	12.5	108.7	9.9	12.8	16.6	11.1	16.8
Maternity homes (some with CDs)		791.7	0.9	–24.1	26.8	–18.3	–23.5
CDs only	6.2	–62.0	17.9	17.3	2.1	–18.0	45.3
Beds	26.5	66.4	49.4	26.6	12.0	–2.0	37.7
Doctors	18.5	66.8	74.0	64.7	6.4	18.7	226.4
Nurses	23.0	86.4	133.0	71.5	23.3	31.3	64.3
Population			31.2	26.5	17.8	15.2	102.0

Sources: Calculations based on Sanderatne (2000), *Annual Health Bulletin*, 2000 and Central Bank, 1998.

In 1977 with the liberalization of the economy the private health sector too blossomed, particularly as a result of re-allowing government medical officers the opportunity for private practice in their off-duty hours. Sanderatne (2000) suggests that this was done to discourage migration of medical officers since it provided a complementary source of income to government salaries. These government salaries have remained relatively low in real terms, and the relatively low cost of government health expenditure is attributed to this in Pathmanathan (2003).

The late 1970s and 1980s were characterized by the structural adjustment programme (see Fernando [2001] for details on health impacts) that sought to create a market oriented, export led economy through the development of market mechanisms in all sectors, the removal of subsidies and price controls and blurring the welfare state image that had prevailed since 1931. Internationally too, this coincided with a period when the World Bank was advocating user charges in the health sector. Policy makers in Sri Lanka were adamant in their refusal to consider user charges (Hsiao, 2000). Instead, they considered the private sector to provide an alternative treatment source that would help reduce government health care costs.

The Health Task Force report of 1992 has the promotion of private sector development in health service delivery as one of its major strategies. Among the proposed policy measures are low interest loans and tax holidays for doctors setting up private practice or nursing homes, use of public health sector facilities in off-duty hours by private sector practitioners, incentives for encouraging foreign clients and the developing of private health insurance. Rannan-Eliya (1997) highlights the fact that the Task Force encourages the expansion of private health insurance for three reasons: first, to support the expansion of the private sector; second, as a mechanism of bringing in extra finances to the health sector; and third, to use such extra finances partly for the support of cost recovery by Ministry of Health (MOH) facilities such as paying wards and the Sri Jayawardenapura General Hospital.

The National Health Policy of 1996 has among its strategies the following: the facilitation of development and regulation of the private health care sector by the government sector and the promotion of better coordination with this sector; more efficient and cost effective health care; and the government commiting additonal funds to health care in meeting priority health needs, especially for health promotion and prevention. Since the Task Force recommendations were not adopted in their entirety, however, many of these issues still remain of importance.

By international standards Sri Lanka's level of health expenditure (both government and private) is low at 3.53 per cent of GDP in 1999 (IPS-MOH, 2002). This phenomenon of low health expenditure and high achievements in health status are considered noteworthy. Rannan-Eliya and de Mel (1996) point out that Sri Lanka completed its demographic transition from high mortality and fertility rates to low mortality and fertility rates in 50 years while maintaining national health expenditure at less than US $8 per capita per annum as measured in constant 1990 US dollars. In 1999 per capita government health expenditure was Rs 1,013 while total health expenditure was Rs 2,068 in current prices (IPS-MOH, 2002). The nominal total per capita health expenditure for 1999 was US $29. In contrast, the Report of the Commission on

Macroeconomics and Health (2001) argues that the provision of essential services, referring to services to attend to major communicable diseases and maternal and prenatal conditions that account for a significant proportion of avoidable deaths in low income countries, would cost US $30 to 45. Sri Lanka being subject to a double burden currently of dealing with the unfinished communicable disease burden such as malaria and diarrhoeal disease morbidity and the challenges posed by non-communicable diseases such as diabetes and ischaemic heart disease, is likely to need an even higher level of health expenditure than this to ensure effective and equitable services for its population.

The distribution of health financing is split in half between public and private sources (IPS-MOH, 2002). It should, however, be noted that this does not suggest that utilization is split equally between the two sectors. The state sector continues to serve large numbers of the public, with inpatient care in particular being predominantly in the public sector. Where financing is concerned, however, 81 per cent of hospital services are financed by the public sector while for ambulatory care 61 per cent of financing is in the private sector. Medical goods are predominantly spent for by the private sector that accounts for 85 per cent of such expenditure. The most striking factor reflected in the National Health Accounts, however, is that only 1 per cent of capital expenditure was borne by the private sector in 1997. The expansion of buildings in the private health sector is recent and the BOI enterprises are likely to have increased this percentage but that private sector investment in the health sector remains low is likely given its emphasis on outpatient care and pharmaceuticals that involve little capital.

The National Health Accounts (IPS-MOH, 2002) shows that of the 50 per cent of health expenditure borne by the private sector, 45 per cent is borne by households in the form of out-of-pocket expenditure, with only 3 per cent coming from employers, 2 per cent from non-profit organizations and 1 per cent from private health insurance. These figures remain almost unchanged over the decade with 44 per cent having accrued from the households and 4 per cent from the employers in 1990.

The PRSP (2001) stresses the introduction of a hospital-based management system. The argument is that such a system would enhance the access of the poor to essential health care services, through the provision of rationalized curative services. Hospital-based management, resulting in institutional autonomy is also supported as a means of enhancing revenue within the hospital, through schemes such as paying wards which currently do not function effectively since the funds accrue to the Consolidated Fund rather than the hospital.

The section on health financing in this document is criticized for its lack of attention to the poor. Its emphasis on health insurance is only of importance if health insurance is seen as a means of diverting the non-poor away from the government health sector, thereby ensuring that the poor are provided with more and better services in the state sector. However, private health insurance, which is most effective in the form of group insurance, is not a valid option in a country where 60.3 per cent of the population is economically inactive (Central Bank, 1999), 7.9 per cent of the population was unemployed in 2001, where only a minority are in wage employment and the highest decile earns only Rs 6,986 per person (Central Bank, 1999: 97). Griffin (1992) discusses the case of farmer organizations in China but for such organizations at the grassroot level to create insurance groups are subject to administrative difficulties and are vulnerable to natural forces.

DEBATES IN THE 21ST CENTURY

Provision: Referral or Voting with the Feet?

With regard to provision, a much-debated issue is that of referral. The over crowding of some secondary and tertiary institutions due to bypassing is as much a source of inefficiency as the under-utilization of maternal and peripheral care institutions. Mass media, the widespread dissemination of information and the rise in social aspirations has contributed to the demand side of this problem. Maldistribution of manpower, equipment and drugs have resulted in the lower level health care facilities being unable to supply efficient services thus creating the push factor towards larger health care institutions.

The referral problem has its roots in the historical evolution of health care provision. Samarasinghe (1998) discusses the fact that maternity homes were originally designed for difficult terrains such as the hill country and remote villages. However, political will resulted in maternity homes not being limited to the planned outposts but being dispersed throughout the country. Another related issue was that originally maternity homes, central dispensaries and rural hospitals were all planned as a part of a cluster provision of services. Political demands resulted in these facilities being provided, in some cases, within short distances of each other, providing competing sources of care using separate health care staff and thereby no longer gaining from their complementarity. Table 20.1 clearly indicates that maternity homes are severely under-utilized. This outcome seems inevitable given that individuals have the option of entering larger hospitals with better facilities not too far from their homes. Maternity homes and CDs have only basic facilities for delivery and post-natal care.

Even in 1948, to quote the Commission on the Organization, Staffing and Operative Methods of Government Departments as cited in Samarasinghe (1998), 'We cannot but regard the building of curative institutions in the absence of staff to man them as creating mere illusion of services to the people. We consider it better to have a properly staffed and thoroughly efficient institution 12 miles away from one's home than an understaffed and inefficient institution nearby.'

This problem of understaffing was a problem in the earlier period but currently the staffing of even smaller health care institutions with medical officers is not a problem. However, poor supervision to ensure that medical officers services are available on a regular basis, shortages of drugs and the expectations of the population geared to demand a higher quality of services particularly with regard to trained staff, equipment and laboratory facilities continues to cause the bypassing of smaller institutions.

In a system that allows for self-referral, bypassing smaller institutions is not costly for the individual: his costs are limited to time and travel costs. Time costs are minimal in economic terms in a labour market system where a large part of the population is self-employed, family worker or unemployed. Transport costs likewise are subsidized by the state if public transport is used. Enforced referral systems, improving lower end facilities, closing down lower end facilities, introducing market forces in the rationing of health care or merely continuing to allow individuals to vote with their feet all remain future policy options.

Enforced referral systems would involve innumerable administrative problems. The implementing of such a scheme would necessitate rigorous education of the public. Back referral is also an important issue, particularly in the context of non-communicable diseases. Measures should be taken to implement back referral policies after ensuring that staff in the lower end hospitals have the necessary drugs and training to monitor patients afflicted by diseases such as hypertension, diabetes and mental illness.

Improving the resources available to health facilities at the lower end of the scale would necessitate more funding for equipment, drugs and laboratory facilities. While this would be a major financial challenge given the current budgetary constraints faced by the country, the even greater challenge would come in the form of ensuring that better qualified staff take up posts in such hospitals and provide efficient service. The latter objective would necessitate economic incentives as well as better supervision.

Rationalizing the hospital structure would necessitate the closing down of under-utilized health care institutions while providing ambulance services for the transport of emergency cases to the larger hospitals. Such a scheme would then be in line with subsidizing demand rather than supply (WHO, 2002b). However, such measures are likely to be politically unacceptable. An alternative strategy would be to change the nature of these institutions from providing maternity care services to providing family health care services including health promotion, health education on non-communicable diseases, monitoring of non-communicable diseases and geriatric day care as proposed in the Family Health Delivery Model proposed by Lavadenz and de Silva in WHO (2002b). The Presidential Task Force of 1992 had put forward a similar proposal: 'The existing Central Dispensaries (CD), Maternity Homes (MH) and CDMHs will be modified/adjusted/strengthened appropriately for providing out-patient care. They will serve as polyclinics to provide first level care. They will be given one common name as Sub-Divisional Health Centre (SDHC).' (Presidential Task Force Report of 1992: 67). Such Sub-Divisional Health Centres were expected to cater to the health needs of a population of about 20,000 and staffed by an MO/AMP/RMP. A Senior Public Health Midwife would be available and would supervise the Gramodaya Health Centres staffed by Public Health Midwives.

An alternative to rigid referral through administrative means is to introduce rationing through market devices. An imposition of a small charge on individuals who bypass health institutions, on the basis of self-referral rather than referral from the lower level of hospitals by medical staff, would generate funds for the secondary and tertiary care systems. This charge is not intended to cover the cost of service, for this would then be a user charge, with its corresponding adverse impacts, nor should it be imposed in the case of emergency services or on those living in the catchment area who could be issued cards to validate residence. The challenge will lie in determining the appropriate charge. In doing so, the administrative costs incurred in collecting this charge will also have to be taken into account. This scheme would have to be supported by complementary activities to develop the lower end health facilities as well.

Financing

Government Financing: Is Sri Lanka Spending Enough?

With regard to financing, current international thinking in the form of the Millennium Development Goals and the Macroeconomic and Health Commission both stress the need for higher government expenditure on the social sector. Whether an optimal level of government expenditure exists and how far Sri Lanka is from this optimal level is an important policy issue. The above question is posed in the context of the historical data presented in Table 20.3.

Table 20.3

GHE/GDP RATIO AND HEALTH INDICATORS

Decade	Government Health Expenditure/GDP (percentage)	Year	Maternal Mortality Rate (per 10,000 live births)	Infant Mortality (per 1,000 live births)
1950s	1.95	1950	55.3	82.3
1960s	2.12	1960	30.2	57.0
1970s	1.81	1970	14.5	47.5
1980s	1.47	1980	6.4	34.4
1990s	1.53	1991	4.2	17.7
		1996	2.3	17.3
		2001	n.a.	12.2

Source: WHO (2002a).

Sri Lanka has achieved significant progress with regard to maternal and infant mortality. The rapid improvement in these health indicators in the 1950s and 1960s is attributed to many factors, including high literacy, female empowerment and the widespread network of health care facilities. The ratio of government health expenditure to GDP in Sri Lanka has always been low by international standards. This is one reason why Sri Lanka is cited as a success: a country with low per capita health expenditure achieving good health indicators as a result of supportive social policy.

Yet, the achievement of further reductions in the mortality rate and the lowering of the morbidity burden in both communicable and non-communicable diseases is likely to be more resource intensive. For example, the reduction in infant mortality is mainly attributable to better antenatal care including nutrition and delivery by trained staff. Currently, the major causes of infant mortality are infant prenatal disorders (especially slow foetal growth, foetal malnutrition and immaturity), diseases of the respiratory system and infections and parasitic diseases (Samarasinghe, 1998). In 1997, the neo-natal mortality rate was 12.8 deaths per 1,000 live births as compared to 17.3 infant deaths per 1,000 live births in 1996. In contrast in 1945 and 1975, there were 140.0 and 45.1 infant deaths per 1,000 live births respectively with neonatal death rates of 75.5 and 27.1. This trend suggests that to achieve further reductions in the infant mortality rate, one would have to target reducing neonatal mortality. Prevention of neonatal deaths necessitates more sophisticated equipment and training, for delivery and man-agement of low birth weight babies. This issue is now in the limelight given the Millen-nium Development Goal (MDG) that sets the target of reducing under five (child) deaths by two-thirds at the 1990 level.

The National Health Policy of 1996 stressed the importance of increasing govern-ment funding for the health sector, with its 18th strategy reading. 'The government is committed to allocate additional funds from government sources and through alterna-tive mechanisms of funding, towards meeting priority health needs especially in the areas of health promotion and prevention' (MOH, Task Force Report, 1996).

Given the need for improving national health performance and facing the chal-lenges of demographic and epidemiological transition and the advocacy of the inter-national organizations such as the UN, WHO and the World Bank, it is clear that the Sri Lankan state is not spending sufficiently on health care provision. While siphoning off demand to the private sector remains a feasible option, this occurs at the cost of efficiency and equity under the present situation where there is a lack of coordination between the state and private sectors and with the market imperfections that charac-terize the Sri Lankan private health system.

The question this raises is the feasibility of expanding government health expendi-ture. Vision 2010 and the PRSP envisage an increase in government spending on health resulting from high economic growth in the economy. Growth rates rising to 8 per cent are predicted in Vision 2010 while 'Regaining Sri Lanka' is based on a 10 per cent growth rate forecast. The likelihood of realizing such high growth rates depend on a number of factors, primarily the achievement of peace in the country, with favourable international trends to increase trade, services and tourism and the im-provement of national efficiency being major concerns as well.

Economic growth per se, however, will not ensure that government allocations to the health sector will rise. This in turn will depend on the buoyancy of government revenue, particularly tax revenue and the competing demands on government rev-enue. The reduction of defence expenditure will only occur gradually and will in turn be absorbed by rehabilitation and reconstruction expenditure in the first few years after peace. It is crucial at this stage that the Ministry of Health ensures that reconstruction of health facilities and the installation of effective health distribution mechanisms in the North and East are priority budgetary issues. The challenges of the transition need to be addressed in the long run and budgetary mechanisms put in place to ensure that the funding needs of the transition are reflected in future allocation decisions. Infla-tion control and exchange rate stability will also be of paramount importance in ensur-ing that health sector allocations remain high in real terms.

The feasibility of alternative sources of government health financing needs to be examined. The PTF Report of 1992 proposes a health earmarked tax on all products that are injurious to health such as alcohol and tobacco at 10 per cent of their retail price and on all outgoing international travellers at the rate of Rs 100 per person. In 2001, tax revenue was Rs 2,05,840 million of which excise tax was Rs 44,978 million (21.9 per cent). Of this tax, Rs 9,795 million was from liquor and Rs 19,268 million from tobacco and cigarettes (Central Bank, 2002). In contrast, health expenditure in 2001 was Rs 22,899 million. Such an ear marked tax would link the adverse effects of liquor, tobacco and cigarettes with the burden it imposes on the health system. It would further have the virtue of ensuring a fixed share of revenue for the health sector. In addition to excise taxes, tax on vehicle insurance is also proposed, as motor traffic accidents currently are a major health burden.

An alternative source of funding would be generating funds from within the health system. User charges have not been considered an appropriate mechanism for Sri Lanka, both due to its political volatility and the worry of its adverse impacts on the health status of the population. The Task Force Report of 1992 proposed the use of paying wards within government hospitals and the permitting of private outpatient care in government hospitals after duty hours as means of generating funding at hospital level. Currently, though the former scheme is in operation on a minor scale, it is not an important source of funding due to inappropriate pricing practices that lead to the subsidization of paying ward care and the lack of incentives to health staff and the hospital due to all earnings being directly channelled to the Consolidated Fund (de Silva et al., 1997). The PRSP stresses the importance of hospital-based management. Such a move would only be meaningful if it ensured a degree of financial autonomy for the health care institution with incentives to its staff to generate funds and act in a cost effective manner.

Private Health Care Market: Imperfect Competition

This section focuses on some of the unusual features of the private health care market in Sri Lanka and discusses the impact of imperfect competition.

First, it questions whether the private health care market in Sri Lanka can in fact be termed a conglomeration of private entities without attributing a major role in its production and distribution decision making to the state. Much discussion has been focused in the Health Economics literature on public–private mix in the health sector: as in the case of public financing and private provision (for example, outsourcing) and private financing and public provision (for example, paying wards in government hospitals). Yet, the situation in Sri Lanka is more complex. Channelling, the phrase used to denote consulting a government sector specialist in the private sector in his off hours, involves government expenditure, not on financing the service provided but on the production of this service. Free medical education, combined with the fact that doctors have an alternative source of wages, act as a subsidy in the provision of private medical care. Likewise, the existence of private practice allows the government to pay lower salaries than would be the demand if government practice were the only source of income. Hence, the two complementary activities act to reduce the cost of each sector.

In the case of the private sector, this subsidization of doctor's charges combined with the rapid expansion of private sector treatment locations, should lead to an over-production of services. This overproduction is not evident as yet, however, for many reasons. First, limitations of the government sector result in pull factors that operate to increase demand. Second, the ageing population and the rise in non-communicable diseases necessitating regular treatment and care have expanded demand. Third, social transition in the form of rising expectations drives consumers to seek private care in order to gain access to specialists and better equipment and technologies. Fourth, the providers of private practice, during their work in the government sector may manipulate the demand for private sector services, through being more accessible and more helpful in the private sector setting, or using the private channelling opportunity as a conduit to the utilization of government sector inpatient care.

Could the government benefit from this situation? Currently, it attempts to tax the salaries of specialists and the profits of the private sector. A more direct measure would be to levy a small service charge on each private sector patient, a user charge for the satisfaction provided in gaining care from a Medical Officer or Specialist trained at government expense, similar to the charge imposed by the private sector institution as hospital charges for a channelled consultation.

The demand side argument for allowing for channelling services emerges from the fact that Sri Lanka had only 683 Specialists in government service in 2001. Individuals seek private health care for three main reasons: first, it allows them choice of medical care provider, and ensures the services of a Specialist, and the Specialist of their choice, rather than being served in the state sector by any medical officer. This is of particular importance given the maldistribution of Specialists in favour of Colombo, and the Western Province. Second, the provision of services outside office hours; finally, the non-medical facilities for inpatient and outpatient care are generally better in the private sector.

Lindbeck (1993) adopts the concept of a wage setting equation in addition to labour demand and labour supply to explain unemployment in New Keynesian macro-economic models. The wage setting equation represents the imperfections of the labour market, whether it is due to the existence of trade unions or efficiency wages. In Lindbeck's model, wages are determined at a point above where the labour demand equals labour supply thus resulting in unemployment. This model can be adapted conversely to represent the case of public sector specialists in the private sector. Here too, fees are set rather than market determined, but with the fees being set below the market clearing fee, resulting, in this context, in an excess demand as reflected by the hardships undergone by patients in getting appointments and the long periods spent in waiting halls.

Four possible reasons exist for this phenomenon of under-pricing. First, there is the equity argument: some consultants argue that they keep their fees low to be accessible even to poorer patients. Second, there is the market share argument, where in an oligopolistic market players are not keen on increasing their fees first, for fear of losing their market share. Third, there is the argument of collusive oligopoly where consultants already in this market guide newcomers on their charges. Finally, there is the signalling argument, whereby long queues and waiting lists are seen as signals of ability and hence are important for stimulating future demand.

Figure 20.1

IMPERFECT MARKET: FEE SETTING

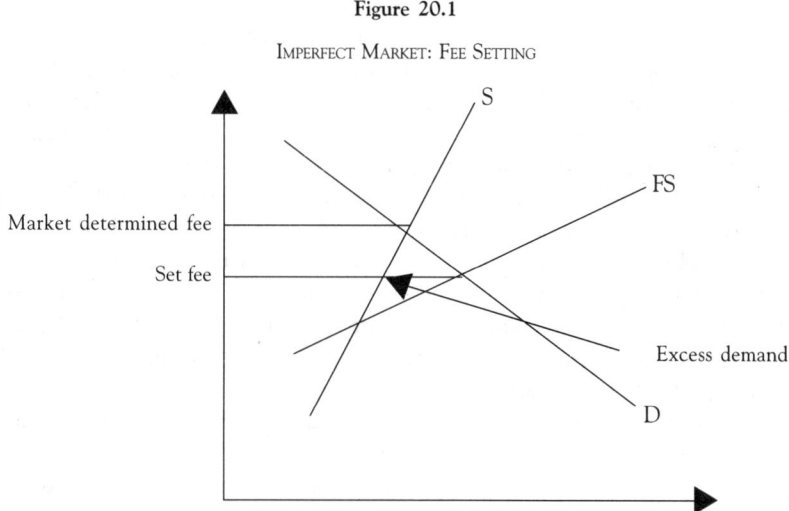

Three alternative measures could be used to deal with the imbalance (Figure 20.1). First, the supply curve could be shifted through increasing the number of consultants but there are likely to be constraints such as the high cost of training, long training periods and the demand for consultants from other countries. Second, steps could be taken to shift the fee setting function. This would lead to an increase in the fees charged and less being supplied under this option. The third alternative would be to reduce the demand for consultant services. This could occur through a referral system being adopted in the private sector. The expansion of full time General Practitioner services could achieve such an outcome.

The channelling market is clearly imperfect. This dual affiliation of Specialists and Medical Officers is adverse to welfare and affects efficiency in both sectors. Currently, there is much debate as to the desirability and feasibility of stopping private practice. The economic constraints currently binding the state sector make it impossible for the government to match the private sector earnings of Specialists or even of medical officers with large private practices. The two cases, however, are different in that while the country still faces a shortage of Specialists, the decision by the government to absorb all medical officers to the state until 2009 is likely to result in an excess of staff beyond the currently envisageable positions in the health system. The state may now have the opportunity of experimenting in the provision of Medical Officers as General Practitioners, either as state employees or encouraging them into full time private practice.

CONCLUSIONS

Currently, the vision of the Ministry of Health is 'To contribute to the social and economic development of Sri Lanka by achieving the highest attainable health status through promotive, preventive, curative and rehabilitative services of high quality made available and accessible to the people of Sri Lanka.' Its mission seeks to achieve this vision through formulating and implementing policies to achieve such ends. However, the vision and mission of the ministry remain rhetoric in the face of the lacuna in the area of national health policy relating to health care provision and financing.

Demographic transition is resulting in the proportion of the elderly rising steadily while the number of children is projected to rise until 2010. The double epidemiological burden imposed by communicable disease morbidity and the rise in the non-communicable disease burden is a further imposition on the health system. Social transition, particularly the rise in expectations, responding to international trends in health care adds to the challenge of providing sufficient, sophisticated and high quality health care to satisfy the demands of the population.

The time is then right to rethink the health care provision and financing models in the country. In 1931, with the introduction of universal franchise politicians determined the supply of health care in line with the electorate's demand for services. These services were then primarily the demands of communicable diseases and maternal and child care necessitating widespread health care networks and an emphasis on primary care. However, many factors have now changed: first, the disease burden is no longer primarily due to communicable diseases; second, people's aspirations have moved beyond mere access to health care to access to modern, sophisticated and, high quality health care; third, transport networks have developed over time and, most importantly, Sri Lanka has been facing economic constraints in the provision of free health care.

Subsidizing supply no longer seems the appropriate strategy. The current demands of the population and the health system make a demand subsidization approach more appropriate. Innovative policies are now needed to grapple with the challenges of transition, the complexities of coordinating public and private sector activity and the enhancement of health financing in the public and private sectors. Health sector planning and policy making must incorporate financing as a central element. This chapter focused on some of the challenges and policy options facing health sector decision makers today. Its primary aim, however, was to highlight the urgent need for a comprehensive national health policy, incorporating health financing explicitly in the policy process in Sri Lanka today.

NOTES

1. Documents being prepared as part of the JICA Master Plan are not reviewed in this chapter as they are still in draft form.
2. The Sri Lankan health system incorporates many forms of health care such as ayurveda, homeopathy, siddha, unani and Chinese medicine in addition to allopathic care but this chapter limits itself to the evolution of allopathic medicine.
3. 'Channelling' is probably a Sri Lankan English term. It is used to express the idea that the patient has the choice (channel = conduit) regarding the care giver.

REFERENCES

Attanayake, Nimal (2001), 'An Assessment of the Effectiveness of Decentralisation of Health Services in Sri Lanka', in Imrana Qadeer, Kasturi Sen and K.R. Nayar (eds), *Public Health and the Poverty of Reforms: The South Asian Predicament*, New Delhi: Sage Publications.

Central Bank of Sri Lanka (1998), 'Economic Progress of Independent Sri Lanka', Central Bank of Sri Lanka, Colombo.

————— (1999), *Report on Consumer Finance and Socio-Economic Survey, 1996/97, Sri Lanka–Part 1*.

————— (2002), *Annual Report*.

Department of Health Services, *Annual Health Bulletin 2000*, Colombo.

—————, *Annual Health Bulletin 2001*, Colombo.

de Silva, Amala, K.C.S. Dalpatadu, S.M. Samarage and A.M. Das (1997), 'Assessment of the Prospects of Paying Wards in Government Hospitals as Complementary Financing for Hospitals', Colombo.

de Silva, W. Indralal (1997), *Population Projections for Sri Lanka: 1991–2041*, Research Studies: Human Resources Development Series No. 2, Colombo: Institute of Policy Studies.

Fernando, Dulitha N. (2001), 'Structural Adjustment Programs and Health Care Services in Sri Lanka—An Overview', in Imrana Qadeer, Kasturi Sen and K.R. Nayar (eds), *Public Health and the Poverty of Reforms: The South Asian Predicament*, New Delhi: Sage Publications.

Griffin, Charles C. (1992), 'Health Care in Asia: A Comparative Study of Cost and Financing', Washington D.C.: World Bank.

Lindbeck, Assar (1993), *Unemployment and Macroeconomics*, Massachusetts: MIT Press.

Marga Institute (1984), *Intersectoral Action for Health: Sri Lanka Study*, Colombo.

Ministry of Health (1996), *National Health Policy*, mimeo.

————— (2002), *Sri Lanka National Health Accounts: Sri Lanka National Health Expenditures, 1990–1999*, Colombo: Nutrition and Welfare and Institute of Policy Studies.

Myrdal, G. (1968), *Asian Drama Vol. 1*, New York: Pantheon Books.

Pathmanathan, Indra (2003), 'Investing in Maternal Health: Learning from Malaysia and Sri Lanka', *Human Development Network* (HNP Series), Washington D.C.: World Bank.

Rannan-Eliya, Ravi P. (1997), 'Analysis of Private Health Insurance in Sri Lanka: Findings and Policy Implications', Institute of Policy Studies Health Policy Programme Occasional Paper No. 3.

Rannan-Eliya, Ravi P. and Nishan de Mel (1996), 'Results of Private Health Insurance Study', Institute of Policy Studies Health Policy Programme Occasional Paper No. 1.

Samarasinghe, Daya (1998), 'Health', in A.D.V. de S Indraratna (ed.), *Fifty Years of Sri Lanka's Independence: A Socio-economic Review*, Colombo: Sri Lanka Institute of Social and Economic Studies.

Sanderatne, Nimal (2000), *Economic Growth and Social Transformations: Five Lectures on Sri Lanka*, Colombo: Tamarind Publications (Pvt) Ltd.

World Health Organization (2001), *Report of the Commission on Macroeconomics and Health*, Geneva: WHO.

_____ (2002a), *Macroeconomics and Health Initiatives—Sri Lanka*, Colombo.

_____ (2002b), *Poverty, Transition and Health: A Rapid Health System Analysis*, Colombo.

SELECT READINGS

de Silva, Amala (1997), 'Health Transition: the Economic Issues', *The Ceylon Medical Journal*, 42(1).

Fernando, George (undated), 'Private Sector Development in the Provision of Health Care Services', *Joint IDA/GOSL Private Sector Assessment (PSA) Study Report*, 1990s.

Fonseka, Carlo, 'Health and Economics 2', *Ceylon Medical Journal*, 36: 133–36.

Jayasuriya, Lucien (1995), 'The Health Services of Sri Lanka Present and Future', *Ceylon Medical Journal*, 4: 107–15.

Ministry of Finance and Planning (2001), *Sri Lanka Poverty Recution Paper*.

_____ *Vision 2010: Sri Lanka*.

Presidential Task Force (1993), *Report of the Presidential Task Force on Formulation of a National Health Policy for Shri Lanka*, Sessional Paper No. II.

Simenov, L.A. (1975), *Better Health for Sri Lanka: Report on a Health Manpower Study*, WHO, New Delhi.

World Health Organization (2000), *The World Health Report 2000*, 'Health Systems: Improving Performance', WHO, Geneva.

Wanasinghe, Shelton and Harshitha Gunaratna (1997), 'Organisation and Financing of Public Sector Health Care Delivery in Sri Lanka: The Need for Radical Changes', Research Studies—Health Economics Series No. 1, Institute of Policy Studies, Colombo.

21

Public Investment in Education: Conceptual Foundations

Harsha Aturupane

Investment in Education: Conceptual Foundations

The economic and social benefits of efficient and equitable investment in education are widely appreciated in modern development policy circles. High quality education enhances reasoning ability, increases cognitive skills, improves problem solving and develops language and mathematical capabilities. Sound education also imparts personal habits of industry and discipline. In addition, good education develops capacity in individuals to be trained for particular occupations and to acquire specific job-related skills. These multiple effects of education enable individuals to accumulate human capital, increase labour productivity and enhance life cycle earnings and economic welfare. Education also produces a variety of social benefits. Well-educated individuals, especially women, are better able to control their fertility and family health, leading to lower child and infant mortality, reduced morbidity and disease burden and higher life expectancy. Education also facilitates social mobility by creating opportunities for poor and disadvantaged groups to raise their economic and social status. A well-designed education system can strengthen social cohesion among different ethnic, religious and cultural groups by contributing to the creation of a multiethnic, multicultural national identity. A wide range of further externality benefits of education have been discussed in the literature, covering aspects of social well-being such as improved political decision making, lower incidence of crime and the higher quality of public services delivered by well-educated government civil servants. Education also produces intergenerational social benefits: increased education in one generation improves schooling, human development and economic progress in the next.

RATIONALE FOR PUBLIC SECTOR INVESTMENT IN EDUCATION

The justification for public investment in education is also now well known in the economic literature. The social benefits of education provide a powerful set of arguments in favour of public investment to achieve the social optimum. Further, there are a set of educational activities, such as curriculum development, accreditation and quality assurance, which contain strong public goods aspects. A second set of arguments arise from characteristics of economic systems such as imperfect capital markets, incomplete future labour markets, and high set-up and transactions costs of education production, which tend to depress private education investment below socially optimal levels. A third group of arguments are based on the notion that education is a merit good and a basic human right, enabling people to access the world of knowledge and information, and empowering individuals to fulfil their innate potential. A fourth set of arguments are based on notions of distributive justice, where education is seen as playing a vital role in equalizing economic opportunities within hierarchically ordered social systems.

These arguments in favour of public investment in education, especially those based on externality benefits and distributive equity, are generally viewed as stronger justifications for state intervention in the lower and middle levels of education, such as primary, basic education and secondary schooling, than in the higher levels of education, such as university bachelor's degrees, which are typically accessed by upper income groups and where individuals are thought to be more likely to capture a larger share of the incremental returns. However, investments in fundamental and basic research, including activities at the highest levels of the tertiary education system such as Ph.D degrees, are considered to generate considerable dynamic externality benefits, so that public investments can be justified on economic grounds.

The arguments in favour of public investment in education do not preclude, at a conceptual level, private investment. An optimal education system is normally considered to contain both private and government institutions, with the state sector concentrating on activities where market failures are most widely prevalent. However, state failures also need to be borne in mind. The range and quality of services delivered by public education institutions depend critically on the objectives, incentives and constraints faced by public officials, such as policy makers, administrators, principals and teachers. An important distinction also needs to be drawn between public financing, such as subsidies to the private sector, and public provision, where the state itself owns and operates education institutions. The optimal mix between public subsidies and public provision depends on the quality and efficiency of each type of education institution, which in turn is critically a function of the opportunity sets, incentive frameworks and constraint functions faced by key agents in the private and public sectors.

THE STRUCTURE OF THE EDUCATION SYSTEM

The formal education system is dominated by the public sector, which accounts for 98 per cent of schools and 97 per cent of student enrolment. Overall, about 4.1 million school children are enrolled in 10,000 public schools and around 93,000 students are enrolled in about 80 private educational institutions. These students follow the national school curriculum and appear for national examinations. In addition, there about 60,000 students enrolled in around 95 international schools, which offer foreign curricula and where students sit for overseas examinations. The formal tertiary education sector is also dominated by the government, with all 13 universities and several institutes of advanced technical education owned by the state. Over 85 per cent of tertiary level enrolment is in public institutions. The establishment of private and international schools and universities is strictly controlled by the government through legislation (Central Bank of Sri Lanka, 1999; Ministry of Education, 1999).

The Sri Lankan public education system, as in most countries, is divided into three main cycles:

1. Primary schooling (grades 1 to 5), containing about 1.8 million students, of whom approximately 50 per cent are female.
2. Secondary schooling (grades 6 to 13), with about 2.3 million students, of whom approximately 50 per cent are female.
3. Tertiary education, consisting of undergraduate or bachelors degree courses, and containing about 42,000 students in internal programmes and around 1,05,000 students in external programmes; postgraduate courses, consisting of diplomas, masters degrees and doctorates, and containing about 20,000 students; and advanced professional and technical courses offered in advanced technical institutions, and containing about 33,000 students.

THE GENERAL EDUCATION SYSTEM

The central characteristic of the education policy framework is the commitment of the state to provide access to primary and secondary education in government schools to all children of school going age. This policy, which has been in force for over 50 years, is implemented through a nation-wide network of about 10,000 schools [see Table 21.1]. The schools are extensively distributed and special provision is made to build and maintain schools in remote areas. In consequence, access to basic education has become nearly universal.[1] There is a school, on average, every 6 square kilometres.

Table 21.1

THE GENERAL EDUCATION SYSTEM, 1999

Province	Square Land Area (km)	Number of Schools	Number of Students	Number of Teachers	Schools per Square (km)	Average School Size	Student Teacher Ratio
Western	3,593	1,454	8,87,445	37,209	2	610	24
Central	5,575	1,519	5,65,436	26,013	4	372	22
Southern	5,383	1,193	5,59,774	27,159	5	469	21
North-Eastern	17,651	1,818	6,29,873	23,010	10	346	27
North-Western	7,506	1,330	4,98,721	23,902	6	375	21
North-Central	9,741	775	2,77,326	12,461	13	358	22
Uva	8,335	836	3,06,581	13,572	10	367	23
Sabaragamuwa	4,921	1,182	4,08,870	19,385	4	346	21
Sri Lanka	62,705	10,057	41,34,026	1,82,711	6	411	23

Sources: Calculated from Ministry of Education and Provincial Council Statistics, and Reports of the Surveyor General's Department.

Even in the large, comparatively lightly populated areas such as the North-Central, North-Eastern and Uva Provinces, there is a school every 10–13 square kilometres. School admission and tuition are free for students.[2] The average school size is moderate, with about 400 students per school. Regional variations in mean school size are low, with the exception of the densely populated, urbanized Western Province, where the school size is nearly 50 per cent higher than the national average. The distribution of teachers across provinces, largely based on a systematic allocation formula, is also fairly even.[3] The average student–teacher ratio is 23:1, and only the war-affected Northern-Eastern Provinces, where teacher retention is difficult, deviates noticeably from this figure with a student–teacher ratio of 27:1.

GOVERNMENT EDUCATION EXPENDITURES

Level and International Comparisons

Public education investment in Sri Lanka has accounted for around 2.5–3 per cent of national income and 9–11 per cent of government spending in recent years (see Appendix Table A-1). This represents a comparatively modest level of education investment by international standards. South Asian countries and low income nations devote, on average, about 3.2 per cent of national income and 11 per cent of government expenditures to education (see Table 21.2). Only Bangladesh within South Asia allocates a lower share of national income to education. The group of lower middle income countries, to which Sri Lanka is expected to belong in the near future, spend over 4 per cent of gross domestic product (GDP) on education. Countries such as

Table 21.2

EDUCATION EXPENDITURE AS A SHARE OF NATIONAL INCOME AND GOVERNMENT
EXPENDITURES, SRI LANKA AND OTHER SELECTED COUNTRIES

Country	Education Expenditure as a Proportion of National Income (%)	Education Expenditure as a Proportion of Government Expenditure (%)	Education Recurrent Expenditure per Student as a Proportion of National Income per Capita (%)	Average Teacher Salaries as a Proportion of National Income per Capita (%)
Sri Lanka	2.7	10.5	9.9	1.5
India	3.2	11.6	16.3	3.0
Bangladesh	2.2	—	—	3.3
Pakistan	2.7	8.1	—	—
Nepal	3.2	13.5	14.5	—
Malaysia	4.9	—	20.7	2.9
Thailand	4.8	20.1	25.3	3.1
South Korea	3.7	17.5	—	4.1
Hong Kong	2.9	—	—	—
Singapore	3.0	23.4	—	—
Costa Rica	5.4	22.8	—	—
South Asia	3.2	11.2	14.5	2.8
Low income countries	3.2	—	16.3	—
Lower middle income countries	4.1	—	18.5	—
Upper middle income countries	5.0	—	23.0	—

Sources: Sri Lanka, calculations from Central Bank of Sri Lanka *Annual Reports*, various issues.
Other Countries, World Development Indicators and UNESCO *Statistical Yearbooks*,
various issues.

Note: The information above for Sri Lanka is computed from 1999 data. Other countries and
regions are from the closest available year in the late 1990s.

Malaysia and Thailand, which act as role models for Sri Lankan policy makers, devote
almost 5 per cent of national income to education. Similarly, recurrent education
spending per capita as a proportion of national income per capita is lower in Sri Lanka,
at about 10 per cent, than the average in South Asia 14.5 per cent, and low and lower
middle income countries, 16.3 per cent and 18.5 per cent respectively. This proportion
is also lower than in countries such as South Korea, Malaysia, Thailand, India and
Nepal.

There are three main reasons for the moderate level of education investments in Sri
Lanka: (*a*) the high level of defence expenditure, which absorbs over 5 per cent of
GDP and crowds out other investments; (*b*) comparatively low teacher salaries; and
(*c*) the small size of the tertiary education sector. Military expenditure in Sri Lanka,
which consumes 5–6 per cent of national income, is at least twice the level in the other
countries cited earlier. Teacher salaries, at 1.5 per cent of per capita income, are
considerably below the proportions in South Asia and countries such as Malaysia,
Thailand, South Korea, India and Pakistan. The Sri Lankan tertiary education sector,
with only about 2–3 per cent of the relevant age group enrolled in internal University

degree programmes, and around 9 per cent of the age cohort enrolled in public tertiary education institutions when external students are counted, is substantially smaller than in nearly all other countries in South Asia, South East Asia and East Asia.

THE HISTORICAL TREND OF GOVERNMENT INVESTMENTS IN EDUCATION

Sri Lanka, at the time of political independence in 1948, had already achieved basic literacy and education levels that many low income countries are still aspiring to reach over 50 years later. According to the population census of 1946, male literacy was 70 per cent and female literacy 44 per cent. During the 1950s and 1960s, the government's priority education policy was to expand the state school system to provide all children in a rapidly rising population access to primary and secondary education. Education resources during this period were chiefly allocated to constructing school buildings and increasing the supply of teachers to keep pace with steeply expanding enrolments. In 1950, there were around 3,200 government schools enrolling about 1.3 million students, and staffed by around 38,000 teachers, with an overall student–teacher ratio of 35:1 (see Table 21.3). There were also about 2,000 university undergraduates and just below 160 University academics, yielding a student–lecturer ratio of 13:1. Education recurrent expenditures through the 1950s grew at about 10 per cent per year in real terms (Snodgrass, 1966). Annual average enrolment growth during 1950–60 was 6 per cent, while the growth rate of teacher numbers was 8 per cent per year. The swift expansion of access to education enabled the country to reach a gross primary enrolment ratio of 100 per cent for males and 90 per cent for females by 1960. However, an important policy measure hampering quality was introduced in the late 1950s with the prohibition of English as a medium of instruction, except for children of foreign or mixed parentage.

Table 21.3

TRENDS IN EDUCATION PROVISION AND ATTAINMENT, 1950–91

	1950	1960	1971	1981	1991
Education expenditure as a % of GDP	2.5	4.4	4.1	2.4	2.5
Government schools	3,188	4,394	8,585	9,521	9,998
Students in government schools	13,49,345	21,92,379	28,28,070	34,51,358	42,58,698
Teachers in government schools	38,086	69,658	94,858	1,35,869	1,77,231
University students	2,036	3,684	12,239	17,656	28,260
University staff	157	269	1,109	1,609	1,811
Adult literacy rate	65	72	79	87	87

Sources: Department of Census and Statistics; Ministry of Education; Central Bank of Sri Lanka; University Grants Commission.

Note: Literacy rates are for 1953 and 1963 respectively.

Through the 1960s the number of schools, students and staff increased sharply in the education system, with public education investment absorbing over 4 per cent of national income. Education recurrent expenditure grew at about 5 per cent per year during the 1960s (see Alailima, 1997). By 1971, there were over 8,500 schools, about 2.8 million students and nearly 95,000 teachers, with a student–teacher ratio of 29:1. The quantity of undergraduates in universities expanded to over 12,000 in 1971, while university staff increased to number about 1,100, producing a student–lecturer ratio of 11:1. As an outcome of the rapid increase in education levels, the male adult literacy rate rose to 79 per cent by 1971. However, some policy measures were introduced during the 1960s that weakened the flow of resources into education. In particular, almost all private schools were taken over and the establishment of new private schools was prohibited in the early 1960s.

The sharp increase in education levels in the population during the 1950s and 1960s was not matched by correspondingly high economic growth, so that the demand for educated labour was lagging behind its supply. This was perceived as a looming social problem even as early as the late 1950s (see Rodrigo et al., 1987). In 1971 an insurrection by the Janatha Vimukthi Peramuna (JVP), led and largely staffed by educated unemployed or under-employed youth, sought to overthrow the government. This insurrection was defeated, but caused policy makers to seriously consider the quality aspects of education in addition to its quantitative expansion.

Government policy through the 1970s and 1980s continued to award priority to the quantitative expansion of the education system. But with the new focus on quality, education reforms were introduced in 1972 emphasizing job-oriented curricula and technical skills from an early age, rather than general learning and a broad basic education. These reforms reflected the conventional wisdom of the time, but were soon perceived as a failure as the graduates of the system were too narrow, inflexible and lacked capacity for training. The proportion of education investment also declined to about 2.5–3 per cent of national income, as economic policies that stifled markets and constrained private sector activity caused the economy to falter, compelling government to contain expenditure. The United National Party (UNP) government which assumed office in 1977 dismissed the education reforms and re-introduced the broad, British style general education system that had existed prior to the 1972 reforms.

The proportion of national income devoted to education remained at about 2.5–3 per cent of national income through the 1980s and 1990s. However, the government in the late 1970s, 1980s and early 1990s introduced several quality enhancing measures. The single, multicampus University of Ceylon was broken up into six autonomous universities in 1979 to facilitate managerial efficiency and promote competition. An Open university to provide distance learning courses was established in 1980. Colleges of Education were set up, in the mid-1980s, to ensure pre-service teacher education for school teachers before they were placed in schools. International schools, operating under the Companies Act and using English as the medium of instruction, were allowed to set up in the early 1990s.

Despite these investments in education quality, the main focus of public policy and government investment in education was on the quantitative expansion of the system. The number of schools increased to about 10,000 in 1991, with around 4.3 million students and 1,77,000 teachers. As an outcome of the continued expansion of the education system, the proportion of students enrolled in secondary education increased from 27 per cent in 1960 to about 70 per cent by the early 1990s. Under-graduate enrolments rose to above 28,000, while university academics exceeded 1,800 by 1991.

However, in the early 1990s, with the aim of providing universal access to general education virtually completed, the focus of public policy shifted to quality enhance-ment. The National Education Commission took a lead role in developing new educa-tion reforms aimed at introducing a new curriculum and promoting student-centred learning and activity based pedagogical methods in schools (see National Education Commission, 1997). Country-wide implementation of these reforms commenced in 1998. Reforms in higher education were also developed to enhance autonomy of universities, especially in resource mobilization and utilization, and to facilitate private sector participation in tertiary education (see Government of Sri Lanka-ADB, 2000; Government of Sri Lanka, 1998).

During the 1990s the trend of education expenditures has been fairly even. Between 1992 and 1999 education expenditure in real per capita terms varied only by a few 100 rupees (see Figure 21.1). There were significant increases in education expenditure in 1992, when the government recruited a large number of teachers, in 1994 when the new People's Alliance Government which assumed office awarded a generous salary increase to teachers, and again in 1998 when the new education reforms were

Figure 21.1

Time Trend of Real Education Expenditure per Student, 1991–99

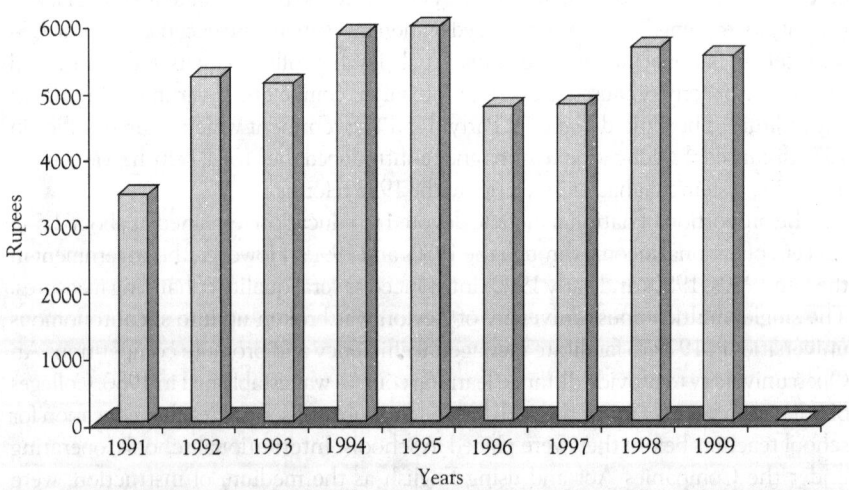

Sources: Calculated from (a) Government of Sri Lanka, Revenue and Expenditure Statements; (b) Statistics of the Ministry of Education; (c) Ministry of Higher Education, Provincial Councils, and University Grants Commission.

implemented nation wide. However, in the intervening years education investment failed to keep pace with inflation, so that the real value of public education spending per student was appreciably lower in 1999 than in 1994–95.

COMPOSITION OF PUBLIC EDUCATION EXPENDITURE

Total education expenditures currently amount to about Sri Lankan Rs 29,000 million annually, of which around Rs 9,500 million (32 per cent) are devoted to primary education, approximately Rs 15,000 million (53 per cent) to secondary education and about Rs 4,500 million (15 per cent) to tertiary education (see Table 21.4). Average recurrent costs per student are highest at tertiary education, followed by secondary and primary schooling. These expenditure levels, unit costs and proportions reflect enrolment numbers and shares, and variations in production costs across education cycles. Tertiary education is typically the most expensive level of education, requiring highly qualified staff, sophisticated technology and advanced equipment and material, resulting in higher human capital and physical resource costs. Secondary education is also normally more expensive than primary education, as secondary teachers tend to be better qualified and paid, and more expensive capital equipment is needed, especially at the senior secondary level. Sri Lanka also has the largest number of students, about 2.3 million or 53 per cent of total enrolment, contained within the secondary cycle.

Unit recurrent education expenditures as a proportion of per capita national income are modest by international standards (see Table 21.4). At the primary and secondary levels, the unit recurrent expenditure proportions in Sri Lanka, 7 per cent and 9 per cent respectively, are well below countries such as Malaysia, Thailand, South Korea, India and Nepal. In relation to India and Nepal, this can partly be attributed to higher internal efficiency and lower teacher salary costs as a proportion of national income. However, in relation to Malaysia, Thailand and South Korea, this is also likely to reflect under-investment in instructional materials, learning resources and quality processes.

Table 21.4

EDUCATION INVESTMENT BY EDUCATION LEVEL, 1999

(rupees million)

Education Level	Recurrent Expenditure	Capital Expenditure	Total Expenditure	Share of Education Expenditure by Level	Unit Recurrent Costs
Primary	7,422	2,066	9,488	32	4,128
Secondary	12,638	2,739	15,377	53	5,410
Tertiary	3,258	1,245	4,503	15	16,290
Total	23,318	6,050	29,368	100	5,380

Sources: Calculated from (*a*) Government of Sri Lanka, Revenues and Expenditure Statements, (*b*) Statistics of the Ministry of Education, (*c*) Ministry of Higher Education, Provincial Councils and University Grants Commission.

Unit recurrent expenditure on tertiary education in Sri Lanka is about 29 per cent of per capita income, again well below the ratios in countries such as India (100 per cent), Thailand (60 per cent) and Malaysia (57 per cent) (see Table 21.5). The comparatively low level of unit expenditures at tertiary level may partly reflect relatively weak academic salaries. However, they are also likely to reflect, at least partially, under-investment in quality inputs and quality processes, and a shortage of research resources.

Table 21.5

UNIT RECURRENT EXPENDITURE ON MAJOR EDUCATION CYCLES: SRI LANKA AND SELECTED COUNTRIES

Country	Recurrent Primary Education Expenditure per Student as a Proportion of National Income per Capita (%)	Recurrent Secondary Education Expenditure per Student as a Proportion of National Income per Capita (%)	Recurrent Tertiary Education Expenditure per Student as a Proportion of National Income per Capita (%)
Sri Lanka	7	9	29
India	9	18	100
Nepal	10	13	115
Malaysia	10	18	57
Thailand	12	11	60
South Korea	18	13	6
Singapore	—	—	28
Costa Rica	—	23	—
South Asia			85

Sources: Sri Lanka, calculations from Central Bank of Sri Lanka *Annual Reports*, various issues. Other Countries, World Development Indicators and UNESCO *Statistial Yearbooks*, various issues.

Note: The information above for Sri Lanka is computed from 1999 data. Other countries and regions are from the closest available year in the late 1990s.

COMPOSITION OF RECURRENT AND CAPITAL EDUCATION BUDGETS

In recent years, about 75–80 per cent of education expenditure has been devoted to recurrent or operating expenses and 20–25 per cent to development or capital expenses (see Figure 21.2). Investments have shifted towards capital expenditures lately, especially 1999–2000, as teacher recruitment has been contained and the emphasis placed on school rationalization, supply of basic facilities and services, and the distribution of quality inputs. The government's tertiary education development programme is also likely to have influenced this process, as new universities were established.

Figure 21.2

Shares of Capital and Recurrent Education Expenditure, 1995–2000

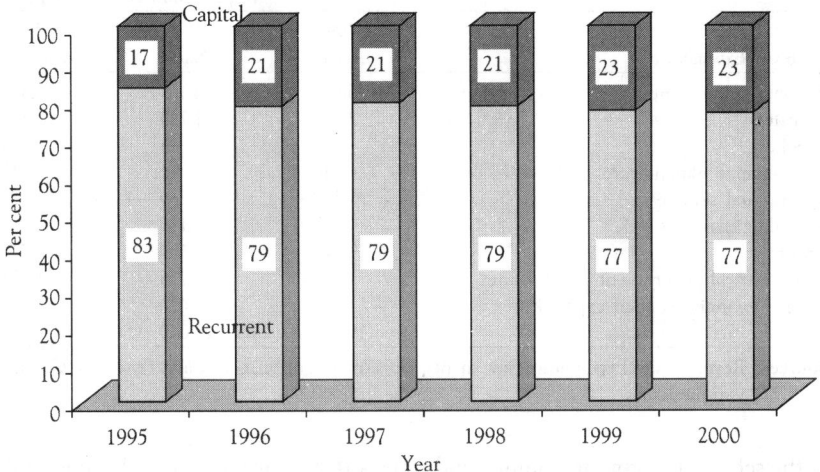

Sources: Calculated from Ministry of Education, Ministry of Higher Education, Provincial Council and University Grants Commission Statistics.

Note: Percentages for 1995–99 are based on actual expenditures. Percentages for 2000 are based on estimates.

Composition of Recurrent Education Expenditure

The largest share of recurrent expenditure, about 80 per cent in recent years, has been allocated to staff emoluments, mainly teacher salaries (see Table 21.6). This is somewhat high by international standards, with the average for low income countries at 68 per cent and the mean for lower middle income countries at 64 per cent. The remuneration of teachers, however, is modest. Teacher salaries as a ratio of per capita income is only 150 per cent for primary teachers and 190 per cent for secondary teachers. This is well below the Asian average for these ratios, about 300 per cent for primary teachers and 400 per cent for secondary teachers. The main reason for the low salaries of Sri Lankan teachers is the relatively high proportion of educated people which has increased the supply of teachers and decreased wage rates.

The second largest element of the recurrent education budget, next to personal emoluments, is transfers. This budget category, which accounts for about 9 per cent of recurrent expenditures, mainly consists of three important incentive programmes to attract children to enrol and attend school: (a) the school uniform programme, by which all students are entitled to one set of free uniforms per year; (b) the textbook programme, by which all students in grades 1–11 are entitled to a set of free textbooks; and (c) the season ticket programme, by which students are entitled to subsidized public transport. These are three universal programmes, in the normal style of Sri Lankan transfer programmes. The coverage, targeting efficiency and cost effectiveness

Table 21.6

COMPOSITION OF GOVERNMENT RECURRENT EXPENDITURE ON GENERAL EDUCATION

(rupees million, current prices)

Recurrent Expenditure	1998 Actual	1999 Actual	2000 Estimated
Personal emoluments	15,900	16,367	18,350
Transfers	2,324	1,723	2,552
Supplies	57	75	138
Maintenance expenditure	14	12	17
Contractual services	358	389	472
Travelling expenses	26	118	37
Grants	522	500	528
Other central government expenditures	322	255	1,085
Other provincial council expenditures	380	620	1,035
Total	19,903	20,060	24,214

Sources: Revenue and Expenditure Statements, Government of Sri Lanka and Provincial Councils, various issues.

of the school uniform programme, and transport subsidy have never been formally assessed. The school textbook programme, however, has been carefully studied (see Lamsco, 1996), and is in the process of undergoing substantial revisions to attract private sector participation in publishing and improve cost effectiveness through higher book re-use and competition.

Composition of Capital Education Expenditure

The main component of capital or investment expenditure on general education, accounting for over 80 per cent of total capital expenditures, is the acquisition of fixed assets (see Table 21.7). This item covers activities such as the procurement of equipment, technology, furniture and tools, and the purchase or construction of buildings, physical facilities and basic services. The other main item of the capital budget is the rehabilitation and improvement of capital assets. This covers activities such as the renovation and refurbishment of buildings and physical facilities, addition of basic services and the replacement of equipment and material.

Table 21.7

COMPOSITION OF GOVERNMENT CAPITAL EXPENDITURE ON GENERAL EDUCATION

(rupees million, current prices)

Capital Expenditure	1998 Actual	1999 Actual	2000 Estimated
Rehabilitation and improvement of capital assets	541	858	614
Acquisition of fixed assets	3,828	3,947	5,870
Total	4,369	4,805	6,484

Sources: Revenue and Expenditure Statements, Government of Sri Lanka and Provincial Councils, various issues.

Public expenditures on tertiary education are dominated by grants to the 13 universities. In 1999, Rs 3,200 million (92 per cent) of all recurrent expenditures was allocated to universities (see Table 21. 8). Similarly, from the capital education budget, Rs 1,200 million (over 99 per cent) was allocated to universities (see Table 21.9). These expenditures reflect the dominance of the university system at the tertiary education level. Non-university institutes and advanced technical education institutions receive only a small fraction of public resources.

Table 21.8

GOVERNMENT RECURRENT EXPENDITURE ON TERTIARY EDUCATION

(rupees million, current prices)

	1998	1999	2000
Recurrent Expenditure	*Actual*	*Actual*	*Estimated*
Transfers to universities	3,177	3,239	3,502
Personal emoluments	9	9	6
Travelling expenses	1	1	1
Supplies	2	3	1
Maintenance expenditure	2	2	1
Contractual services	2	3	2
Other	21	1	3
Total	3,216	3,258	3,517

Sources: Government of Sri Lanka, Revenue and Expenditure Statements.
Notes: Figures may not add up exactly due to rounding.

Table 21.9

GOVERNMENT CAPITAL EXPENDITURE ON TERTIARY EDUCATION

(rupees million, current prices)

	1998	1999	2000
Recurrent Expenditure	*Actual*	*Actual*	*Estimated*
Capital grants to universities	1,199	1,240	1,909
Rehabilitation and improvement of capital assets	1	3	2
Acquisition of fixed assets	0.4	2	0.1
Total	1,201	1,245	1,912

Sources: Government of Sri Lanka, Revenue and Expenditure Statements.
Note: Figures may not add up perfectly due to rounding.

SOURCES OF FINANCING OF GOVERNMENT EDUCATION EXPENDITURE

Education expenditure is mainly financed through domestic revenue, with about 90 per cent of investment met from local sources (see Figure 21.3). Foreign aid loans account for about 8 per cent of expenditures. The World Bank and the Asian Development Bank are the financing sources of these education loans. Foreign grant aid

Figure 21.3

DOMESTIC AND FOREIGN SHARES OF EDUCATION FINANCING, 2000

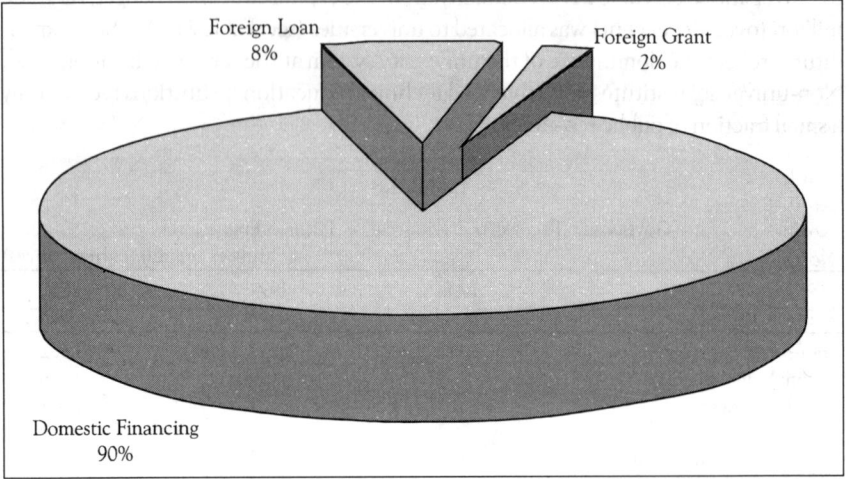

Foreign Loan
8%

Foreign Grant
2%

Domestic Financing
90%

Sources: Calculated from (*a*) Government of Sri Lanka, Revenue and Expenditure Statements; (*b*) Statistics of the Ministry of Education; (*c*) Ministry of Higher Education, Provincial Councils and University Grants Commission.

accounts for the remaining 2 per cent of expenditures. JICA is the chief source of grant aid, followed by DFID, GTZ and SIDA.

EDUCATION ATTAINMENTS

Public investment in education has enabled Sri Lanka to reach high levels of education attainment. The basic quantitative attainments of the Sri Lankan general education system, such as high primary and secondary enrolment, and gender parity in school participation and completion, are now well-known in the development literature (see Kakwani, 1993; UNDP,1990). These attainments can chiefly be attributed to the extensive, country-wide school system providing universal access to primary and secondary education. Gross primary enrolment exceeds 100 per cent in all provinces for which data is available among both male and female children (see Table 21.10). Gross secondary enrolment, too, ranges between 85–98 per cent in all areas. Enrolment in grade 1 is about 93 per cent (see Ministry of Education, 2000). Net school enrolment in basic education, grades 1–9, is over 80 per cent in all regions. Female enrolment in secondary schools exceeds male enrolment in most areas of the country. This can mainly be attributed to greater labour market opportunities for teenage boys, resulting in higher opportunity costs of time spent in school.

Table 21.10

SCHOOL ENROLMENT RATES, BY GENDER AND PROVINCE, 1994

Province	Gross Male Primary Enrolment (%)	Gross Female Primary Enrolment (%)	Gross Secondary Male (%)	Gross Secondary Female (%)	Net School Enrolment Grade 1–9 (%)
Western	104	100	91	89	81
Central	113	108	85	87	84
Southern	105	104	91	97	85
North-Eastern	—	—	—	—	—
North-Western	120	112	90	95	89
North-Central	125	113	91	98	88
Uva	119	114	87	89	89
Sabaragamuwa	115	112	92	94	87
Sri Lanka	112	107	90	92	87

Sources: Calculated from (*i*) Ministry of Education Statistics, and (*ii*) Sri Lanka, Human *Development Report*, UNDP, 1998.

Note: Recent data on the North-Eastern Provinces is not available, as the demographic sample survey from which the information presented above was drawn could not cover the North-East due to the military situation. Parts of this area of the country, especially Jaffna, traditionally had good education attainment indicators, above the national average. However, the war is likely to have adversely affected school attendance, learning and literacy.

Internal efficiency in the primary and junior secondary education cycles are high, with low drop-out and repetition rates (see Table 21.11). The nation-wide drop-out rate averages about 3 per cent at the end of the primary cycle (grade 5), and around 8 per cent at the end of the junior secondary cycle (grade 8). Similarly, repetition rates too are low, averaging 5 per cent at grade 5 and 4 per cent at grade 8. Nearly all children who enter grade 1 are retained in the system through the primary cycle. The coefficient of internal efficiency in Sri Lanka at the primary level is above 90 per cent, as against 67 per cent for India, 68 per cent in Pakistan and 76 per cent

Table 21.11

INDICATORS OF INTERNAL EFFICIENCY, DROP-OUT AND REPETITION RATES, BY PROVINCE, 1998

Province	Grade 5		Grade 8	
	Drop-Out Rates (%)	Repetition Rates (%)	Drop-Out Rates (%)	Repetition Rates (%)
Western	1.1	2.1	6.0	3.1
Central	2.1	4.0	7.2	3.9
Southern	4.7	6.6	8.2	5.8
North-Eastern	5.3	6.1	9.2	4.6
North-Western	2.9	3.9	10.3	2.9
North-Central	3.5	5.3	10.6	6.2
Uva	3.6	5.7	11.9	7.0
Sabaragamuwa	2.9	4.3	8.0	3.5
Sri Lanka	3.3	4.8	8.1	4.1

Sources: Calculated from Provincial Council and Ministry of Education Statistics.

in Bangladesh. It is also only slightly below the level of Malaysia, 98 per cent, and Thailand, 97 per cent.

However, internal efficiency declines sharply at the end of the GCE O/L cycle, grade 11. Only about 35–40 per cent of students sitting the GCE O/L examination meet the qualification criteria to follow GCE A/L classes, and drop-out and repetition rates are thought to be high, although no recent estimates exist. Similarly, at the GCE A/L stage, only about 40–45 per cent pass the examination, and again repetition rates are known to be high.[4] The low proportions passing the GCE O/L and GCE A/L examinations imply that the quality of education is unsatisfactory, as considerably less than half the children are able to reach the minimum standards set by the quality assurance authorities.

Adult literacy rates in the country are well above literacy rates in neighbouring South Asian countries, and close to rates in countries at considerably higher economic levels (see Table 21.12). For instance, Sri Lanka's overall adult literacy rate, 91 per cent, is more than double the literacy rates of Bangladesh, Pakistan and Nepal. It is close to the rates in countries such as Hong Kong and Singapore, which have per capita incomes of about US $25,000 and US $33,000 respectively, in contrast to Sri Lanka's per capita income of US $800. In addition, there is a high level of gender parity in adult literacy. The adult female literacy rate is 88 per cent, more than treble the female literacy rates in Pakistan and Bangladesh, and on par with Hong Kong and Singapore. The female literacy rate as a proportion of the male adult literacy rate, too, is comparable to some of the high performing East and South East Asian countries.

Table 21.12

PATTERNS OF ADULT LITERACY RATES IN SRI LANKA AND SELECTED COUNTRIES, 1997

	Adult Literacy Rate (%)	Female Adult Literacy Rate (%)	Female Adult Literacy as a Proportion of Male Adult Literacy (%)	Per Capita (US$)
Sri Lanka	91	88	93	800
India	54	39	59	370
Bangladesh	39	27	55	360
Pakistan	41	25	46	500
Nepal	38	21	37	220
Malaysia	86	81	90	4,530
Thailand	95	93	96	2,740
South Korea	97	96	97	10,550
Hong Kong	92	88	92	25,200
Singapore	91	87	91	32,810
Costa Rica	95	95	100	2,680
South Asia	—	39	59	452

Source: UNDP (1999), *Human Development Report*.

Education, Poverty Reduction and Economic Welfare

Education investment appears to have had a strong impact on economic welfare and poverty reduction in Sri Lanka. Poverty declines steeply as education levels rise (see Figure 21.4). In 1985–86, poverty incidence was 45 per cent among households whose head was uneducated and 44 per cent among households with a primary educated head. Among households with junior secondary educated heads, poverty incidence was 33 per cent. Poverty rates declined continually across school levels to just 1 per cent among households with heads who were university graduates or higher. A similar pattern was observable in 1995–96, with the poverty distribution having generally shifted downwards, as the economy grew over the decade. Poverty incidence was 40 per cent among households with uneducated heads and 38 per cent among families with primary educated heads. However, poverty fell continually over education levels to 5 per cent among GCE A/L qualified household heads and 1 per cent among graduate household heads.

Economic welfare is also closely related to education. A study of household expenditures among families in poor regions showed that consumption increases sharply as the education level of the household head rises, among both female and male headed

Figure 21.4

Poverty Incidence by Education Level of Household Head

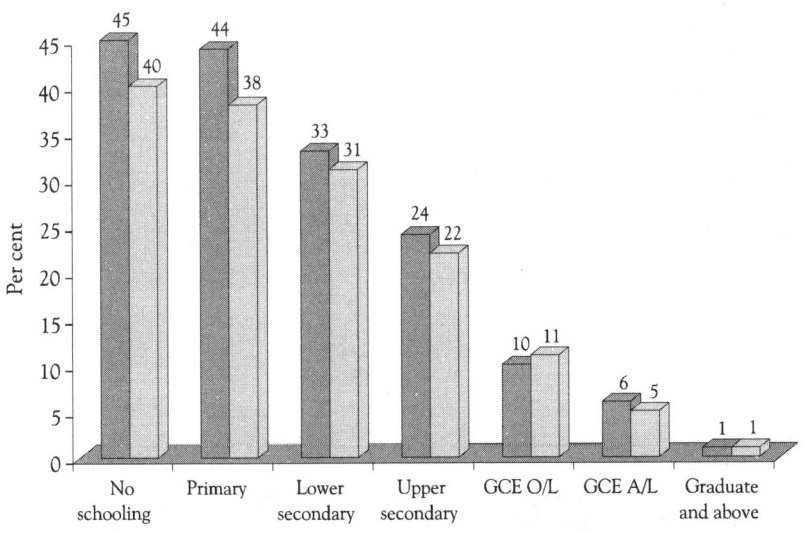

Sources: Gunewardena, 2000.

households (see Aturupane, 1998). All education regression coefficients from lower secondary education upwards are positively signed and statistically significant at conventional levels of confidence (see Table 21.13). Further, the coefficients generally increase as the education level rises. The coefficients suggest that, among male headed households in poor regions, families with junior secondary educated heads consume 20 per cent more than households with uneducated heads. Among households with heads educated up to GCE A/L or above, this consumption differential is 80 per cent

Table 21.13

Multiple Regression Analysis of Economic Welfare, Generalized Least Squares Estimates

Dependant Variable is the Logarithm of Per Capita Consumption Expenditures

Variable	Female Headed Households		Male Headed Households	
	Coefficient	T Ratio	Coefficient	T Ratio
Constant variables related				
to the head of household	6.38	134.95	6.54	85.56
Age 41–50 years	0.03	0.89	0.04	1.04
Age 51–60 years	0.06	1.61	0.08	1.72
Age 61–70 years	0.11	2.71	0.20	2.82
Age 71–80 years	0.09	1.78	0.11	1.46
Primary education	0.08	2.63	0.18	3.18
Junior secondary education	0.24	7.12	0.20	3.50
Upper secondary education	0.28	6.51	0.37	5.88
GCE O/L	0.54	12.45	0.59	8.91
GCE A/L or higher	0.45	7.18	0.88	11.34
Unemployed	0.19	3.49	−0.12	−1.66
Homemaker	0.10	3.36	0.13	1.01
Unable to work	0.10	2.97	−0.04	−0.80
Widow/Widower	0.09	3.96	0.09	−0.36
Separated/Divorced	−0.09	−2.18	−0.08	0.44
Unmarried	0.10	1.72	0.04	2.20
Household variables				
Household size	−0.09	−8.23	−0.11	−6.40
Number of primary earners	0.10	5.39	0.08	2.20
Number of secondary earners	0.09	4.41	0.11	3.96
Number of dependants	−0.01	−0.57	−0.09	−1.08
Urban sector	0.29	11.86	0.38	10.97
Estate sector	−0.06	−1.36	−0.05	−1.19
Test statistics				
Adjusted R^2		0.22		0.32
F		38.22		30.88
		(2,12,801)		(2,11,337)
X^2		158.41		89.64
		(21)		(21)
Sample Size		2,823		1,359

Sources: Aturupane, 1998.

Note: F is a Wald test for joint significance of regression coefficients.

X^2 is the Breusch-Pagan Test for heteroscedasticity.

All 't' values have been estimated using heteroscedasticity consistent standard errors.

higher. Among female headed households, families with junior secondary educated heads consume 8 per cent more than households with uneducated heads. Among households with heads educated up to GCE A/L or higher, this difference in consumption is 72 per cent greater. These findings imply that households enjoy good returns to education, as the estimates of consumption premia over education levels are based on a sample drawn from poor areas, where the earnings and consumption distributions are likely to be considerably lower than the country average.[5]

Households enjoy high welfare gains from education. The impact of education on the economic welfare of households, measured in terms of compensating variations derived from microeconometric estimates of the demand for schooling (see Aturupane, 1999a), is strong and positive among both urban and rural households, and for families where children are attending completely state funded government schools as well as schools that receive private resources (see Table 21.14). The price elasticity of demand for education, too, is low (see Table 21.15), implying that small per pupil increases in non-state revenues will not adversely affect enrolments. These findings suggest that there may be considerable scope for raising private investment in education through the creation of a favourable environment for private sector investment.

Table 21.14

WILLINGNESS TO PAY FOR GENERAL EDUCATION: COMPENSATING VARIATION
ESTIMATES OF REVENUE RAISING MEASURES IN GOVERNMENT SCHOOLS

	Urban Households	Rural Households
De facto free government schools		
Rs 5	5.79	6.00
Rs 10	11.47	11.95
Rs 15	16.21	16.77
De facto resource raising government schools		
Rs 5	6.14	6.21
Rs 10	11.90	12.01
Rs 15	16.75	17.37
Rs 20	21.78	22.02

Source: Aturupane, 1999a.

Table 21.15

ARC PRICES ELASTICITIES OF DEMAND FOR EDUCATION UNDER ALTERNATIVE
REVENUE RAISING MEASURES IN GOVERNMENT SCHOOLS

	Urban Households	Rural Households
De facto free government schools		
Rs 5	−0.0198	−0.0205
Rs 10	−0.0984	−0.1147
Rs 15	−0.1954	−0.2146
De facto resource raising government schools		
Rs 5	−0.0093	−0.0100
Rs 10	−0.0475	−0.0579
Rs 15	−0.0928	−0.1002
Rs 20	−0.1368	−0.1465

Source: Aturupane, 1999a.

CONCLUSION

Overall, Sri Lanka has attained remarkably high levels of primary and secondary education for a poor developing country. Further, these levels of primary and secondary enrolment and completion occur at lower costs than nearly all other countries at comparable or even higher levels of economic development. The long history of public investment in education, aimed chiefly at providing universal access to primary and secondary education, has been mainly responsible for these education attainment levels. The social and economic impact of public investment in education, too, has been highly beneficial. Education contributes strongly to household consumption levels and poverty reduction. In addition, education has a strong impact on the economic welfare of households.

NOTES

1. The only exception is the war-affected areas of the Northern-Eastern provinces, where about 165 schools are not operational. Non-functioning schools are not included in Table 21.1.
2. But schools are allowed to charge for activities such as sports, extra-curricular clubs and societies and school boardings.
3. Although there are problems of intra-provincial teacher deployment between urban and remote rural regions.
4. Data in the early 1990s showed that repetition rates at the GCE O/L were over 40 per cent and at the GCE A/L about 50 per cent. While these rates are likely to have improved more recently, as schools expanded, internal efficiency at these higher schooling levels are still likely to be considerably greater than at the lower grades.
5. Further, the returns to education when calculated on earnings data are likely to be higher than implied above from consumption premia since the earnings distribution is typically less compressed than the consumption distribution.

REFERENCES

Alailima, Patricia (1997), 'Social Policy in Sri Lanka', in W.D. Lakshman (ed.), *Dilemmas of Development, Fifty Years of Economic Change in Sri Lanka*, Sri Lanka: Sri Lanka Association of Economists, Colombo.

Aturupane, Harsha (1998), 'Dimensions of Poverty: The Magnitude of Poverty in the Poorer Areas of Sri Lanka, with Special Emphasis on Female Headed Households', *Upanathi*, 9: 1–20.

——— (1999a), 'Econometric Analysis and Planning in the Social Sectors: an Application to Education in Sri Lanka', in Antonio. L. Fernandez and N.S. Cooray (eds), *Quantitative Tools in Economic Planning: Applications and Issues in Asia*, pp. 163–90, United Nations Center for Regional Development, Nagoya, Japan.

Central Bank of Sri Lanka **(1999)**, *Report of the Socio-Economic Survey, 1996/97.*

_____ , *Annual Reports* (various issues).

Government of Sri Lanka, Presidential Task Force on University Education (1998), Processed.

Government of Sri Lanka-Asian Development Bank (ADB) **(2000)**, Improving Education Planning, Processed.

Gunewardena, Dileni **(2000)**, Consumption Poverty in Sri Lanka, 1985–1996: A Profile of Poverty Based on Household Survey Data, Processed.

Kakwani, N. **(1993)**, 'Performance in Living Standards: an International Comparison', *Journal of Development Economics.*

Lamsco **(1996)**, A Rational Plan for the Development of the Book and Information Sector.

Ministry of Education **(1999)**, *Report of the School Census, 1998.*

_____ **(2000)**, *Preliminary Report of the School Census, 1999.*

National Education Commission **(1997)**, Reforms in General Education, Processed.

Provincial Councils, *Education Statistics* (various issues).

_____ , *Revenue and Expenditure Statements* (various issues).

Rodrigo, Chandra, R.B.M. Korale and D.H.C. Aturupane **(1987)**, 'Employment and Manpower Planning in Sri Lanka', in Rashid Amjad, ed., *Human Resource Planning: The Asian Experience,* New Delhi: ILO, pp. 257–84.

Snodgrass, Donald **(1966)**, *Ceylon: An Export Economy in Transition*, Homewood: Richard and Irwin.

Surveyor General's Department, *Reports* (various issues).

UNDP **(1990)**, *Human Development Report*, New York, U.S.A.

_____ **(1998)**, *Sri Lanka: National Human Development Report*, Colombo: UNDP.

_____ **(1999)**, *Human Development Report*, New York, U.S.A.

UNESCO, *Statistical Yearbooks* (various issues).

University Grants Commission **(1999/2000)**, Sri Lanka Universities Yearbook.

World Bank **(2001)**, *World Development Indicators*, Washington D.C.

SELECT READINGS

Aturupane, Harsha **(1997)**, *Unemployment Among Educated Women*, Colombo: Ministry of Finance and Planning.

_____ **(1999b)**, *Poverty in Sri Lanka: Achievements, Issues and Challenges*, Processed.

Ministry of Finance and Planning, Revenue and Expenditure Statements (various issues).

World Bank **(2000)**, *Higher Education in Developing Countries, Peril and Promise*, Washington D.C.

Appendix

Table 21.1A

EDUCATION EXPENDITURES AS A PROPORTION OF NATIONAL INCOME AND
GOVERNMENT EXPENDITURE, 1996–2000

	1996	1997	1998	1999	2000
Education expenditure as a percentage of GNP	2.7	2.5	2.9	2.7	2.9
Education expenditure as a percentage of government expenditure	9.2	9.5	10.7	10.5	11.0
Education recurrent expenditure as a percentage of government recurrent expenditure	9.1	9.6	11.6	11.3	12.2
Education capital expenditure as a percentage of government capital expenditure	9.5	9.0	8.2	8.5	8.2

Sources: Calculated from *Revenue and Expenditure Statements*, Government of Sri Lanka and Provincial Councils, and *Annual Reports*, Central Bank of Sri Lanka.

Table 21.2A

EDUCATION EXPENDITURES, CAPITAL AND RECURRENT, 1996–2000

	1996 Actual	1997 Actual	1998 Actual	1999 Actual	2000 Estimated
Nominal prices					
Recurrent	16,018	17,757	23,120	23,318	27,731
Capital	4,384	4,592	5,570	6,050	8,410
Total	20,402	22,349	28,690	29,368	36,141
Constant prices (1996=100)					
Recurrent	16,018	16,330	19,622	18,960	21,140
Capital	4,384	4,223	4,727	4,919	6,411
Total	20,402	20,553	24,349	23,879	27,551

Sources: Calculated from *Revenue and Expenditure Statements*, Government of Sri Lanka, and *Annual Reports*, Central Bank of Sri Lanka.

22

POVERTY ALLEVIATION

Buddhadasa Hewavitharana

INTRODUCTION

With its focus on the economics involved, this chapter through its five sections attempts to encompass the past as well as current policy debates on poverty alleviation issues in relation to impediments and obstacles, welfare and income transfers, reformulation and reorientation of programmes and the dynamics of growth, equity and poverty.[1] The fifth section covers the culmination of this series of debates in its 'moment of truth' of poverty eradication through structural change, an issue of fundamental importance which nevertheless had been evaded by all the debates in the past. The concept of techno-socio-economic structural dualism is kept as a backdrop to the topics debated upon so as to keep the roots of poverty and the development economics aspects of poverty alleviation in constant perspective.

There is a rare liveliness that gets imparted to these debates from the fact that they cut through the dividing line between two critical phases in Sri Lanka's economic policy making. The market forces activated by the first round of structural adjustment in 1977 onwards which produced negative effects on the poor signalled the need for evolving policies and measures of poverty alleviation to protect them. In the second round from 1989 onwards, however, the private sector was activated as an engine of growth, signalling the need for linking the poor with the growth process and enabling them to join and work with the market forces in order to grow out of poverty. Policies and strategies suited for the first round came to be critically examined for their relevance for the second, and new ones relevant for market forces-driven poverty eradication had to be evolved. The debates pivot around these issues.

DEBATE ON IMPEDIMENTS AND OBSTACLES TO ALLEVIATING POVERTY

Figure 22.1 depicts the complex of linkages between the poor who are in the Innermost Area (In Ar), and their environment that controls their economic and social well-being. In Ar can be designated as the Micro sphere as its constituents are the households or communities of the poor. It is surrounded by the Local Level sphere (between 1 and 2) containing the Division, the Divisional Secretariat (DSt) and the Pradeshiya Sabha (PS); the Meso sphere (between 2 and 3), constituted by the Province/Region and the Provincial Council (PC); the Macro or the National sphere (between 3 and 4); and the outermost sphere of External Economic Environment (between 4 and 5). A complex of linkages connect In Ar with the outer spheres through planning, decision making, financial

Figure 22.1

THE POOR IN THEIR MICRO-MESO-MACRO SETTING.
THE COMPLEX OF LINKAGES BETWEEN THE TARGET GROUP AND ITS ENVIRONMENT

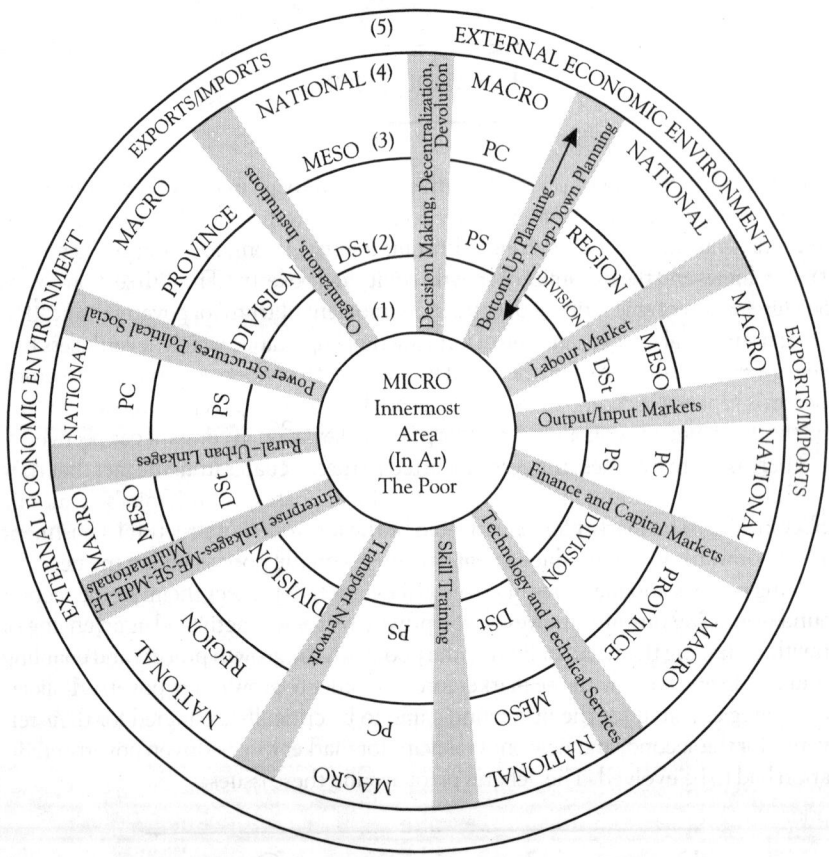

Source: *From Rural Development to Regional Development—A Concept Paper.*
Regional Development Division, Ministry of Finance and Planning, 1994.
Notes: (1)   MICRO, Innermost Area (In Ar), The Poor, Target Group
    (1)–(2)   Division, Divisional Secretariat = DSt, Pradeshiya Sabha = PS
    (2)–(3)   MESO, Sub-National, Province, Provincial Council = PC, Region
    (4)   MACRO, National
    (5)   External, Exports/Imports

and technical services, infrastructure facilities, factor and product markets, industrial and enterprise networks, organizations and social structures. In the flow chart, these linkages are depicted in 12 channels. Five of them penetrate In Ar, while three of them plus another three penetrate the external sphere symbolizing the depths and extents of Micro-Meso-Macro-External linkages.

The poor in In Ar are the casualties of four forms of marginalization. Economic marginalization resulting from an ever increasing population pressure on the limited arable land has ushered in a class comprising of the landless and the near-landless, cultivators of uneconomic holdings and encroachers on infertile state lands. Political marginalization resulting from politicized distribution of safety-net income transfers has ushered in a new breed of poor 'politically marginalized poor' who would, at any given time, constitute a considerable section of the poor, whichever party is in power. Social marginalization is associated with class or caste positions. Spatial marginalization afflicts the communities located in remote areas without access to adequate transport and communication facilities demonstrating thereby the strong linkage between spatial isolation and poverty.

The aim of all targeted and specific poverty alleviation programmes has been to reach out to the poor in In Ar through microlevel interventions to help them to get out of poverty. Politically neutral social mobilization (SM) movement has been able to achieve much in organizing these marginalized groups and giving them a voice. However, a number of impediments, obstacles and barriers of various sorts originating at different levels and from different quarters have plagued these attempts. A lively debate has revolved around these issues.

Macro/National Policies/Programmes Contrary to or at Cross Purposes with Microlevel Interventions

Programme Sustainability

When the government changes, poverty alleviation programmes that had been evolved through dedication and cost get replaced by new ones designed to accommodate political supporters. It leads to a collapse of previous SM-induced structures, an undermining of faith among the poor in SM and to a setting in of SM fatigue.

Saving and Lending

While SM-based voluntary saving and credit discipline were being promoted for the poor, the general policy of all governments of loan forgiveness in government funded credit, for reasons of political expediency, bred a default prone credit culture. Samurdhi's competition for savings assisted by an obligatory element affected the spirit and institutions of voluntary saving.

SM Contradicted by Samurdhi

SM, encouraged by the government and even adopted as its policy, practiced a 'hard' bottom-up approach to social engineering by promoting voluntarism, self-reliance and autonomous development aiming to build up the collective strength of the poor so as to empower them. On a divergent tract, Samurdhi practiced a 'soft' top-down approach through income transfers and dulled the initiative of the poor resulting in ingrained patterns of economic and psychological dependency. The debilitating rivalry and mutual exclusivity of effort unnecessarily restricted the development and innovative potential of all forms of SM while hampering the development of social capital.

Farm Productivity

Stabilization policy measure of freezing agricultural extension cadres defeated the objective of developing productivity levels in farms and raising incomes of small farmers.

Labour Markets

Provision of state sector employment as a means of disbursing political patronage skewed expectations of youth by encouraging them to queue up for government jobs and dampening their enthusiasm for self-employment in income generating activities (IGAs)/microenterprises (MEs).

What emerged from this debate is that for sustainable poverty alleviation there needs to be consistency between macro policy frameworks, institutional change and action at the microlevel. Programmes should have inbuilt checks which prevent them from being manipulated and eroded during political and government changes (GOSL, 2002; GOSL/UNDP, 1998; Gunatilaka and Williams, 1999; NPC, 2001; Nayar and Gunatilaka, 2000; Silva, 1998; UNDP/UNOPS, January 1998).

Blocked Macro-Micro Resource Filters Impede Pro-Poor Allocation of Public Resources

In the sphere of the Division, the DSt comprised of the local line ministry agencies, is the vital filter through which macrolevel public resources can flow into In Ar for poverty alleviation. Another filter at the Division level is the PS and upstream at the meso level are the District Committees and the PC. Facilitating the flows are primarily the planning and decision making/decentralization/devolution channels. Several factors have caused a blocking of these filters leading to inefficiency of pro-poor allocation of public resources.

Failure to Coordinate at DSt

The primary concern of line agencies is to execute programmes that have been decided centrally by using the funds earmarked by the respective funding agency for each project. Evidently, there are no planning systems and coordinating mechanisms that establish a rationale for divisional level resource allocation other than that based on predetermined budgets and multiple sources of predetermined funds. An initiative was taken in some divisions to build an Integrated Poverty Reduction Strategy through a Coordinating Committee. It received only a lukewarm reception from the government stakeholders. It is not a shortage of funds that affects the filter but it is the lack of coordination among government stakeholders and the consequent misallocation of the available resources that blocks the filter. In the consensus that emerged, emphasis was laid on the need for a firm commitment at macro/national level to a strong pro-poor policy, without which no coordination of functions and an integrated use of resources is possible for poverty alleviation at the local level. A corollary to this is the need to decentralize any national level pro-poor plan down to Divisional level action programmes with time bound targets.

Failure to Pool Funds for Pro-Poor Allocation

An unwillingness to pool the resources of the line agencies is a part of the prevailing bureaucratic culture. Decentralized capital budget funds cannot enter into any pool as such a move is impeded by the prevailing political culture. Since the allocation is at the discretion of the MPs, it is subject to narrow political considerations that leave little room for a coordinated and rationalized pro-poor allocation. This problem has worsened with the devolution-related multiplication in the number of politicians at different levels and the complementary proliferation of funds allocated to them. Such expansion of the political power structures blocks the macro-micro filter.

Failure of Demand-Driven, Bottom-Up (B-U) Planned Allocation

Socially mobilized village groups use the mechanisms of B-U planning to have their village plans entered into the Divisional planning process, expecting pro-poor demand-oriented resource allocation. In the absence of pooling and a coordinated allocation of the Division's resources, only such funds as have been provided by the sponsoring project can get allocated for the pro-poor investments demanded. When all the village plans coming through the B-U process cannot be met by project funds, frustration will result. Ironically, it is this very same success in getting village groups to formulate their development plans that 'hits back', by leading to disappointment and demoralization of the poor, if these proposals cannot be financed or do not get considered under the prevailing resource allocation system.

The debate on the latter two topics led to two conclusions. First, the provision of public resources to the neediest poor will remain limited until a genuine decentralized planning process is put in place at the village and Division levels. Second, there is a need to build up the collective strength of the poor on the basis of SM to bargain successfully in the political economic market place for claims on public resources.

Pradeshiya Sabha—Non-Player in Pro-Poor Allocation

The PS is potentially a vital link at the Division level in macro-micro resource flows for two reasons. First, it is main channel to finance local infrastructure that involve irrecoverable costs. Second, it is the local elected body that is duty bound to articulate the concerns of the poor and to see to it that service providers will serve the poor without transaction costs. Far from performing any of these functions, the PS exists on the margin with no capacity for internal resource mobilization or for planning and allocates whatever resources it gets on political considerations.

The Provincial Council—Preoccupied with Power Games

Allocations by the PC are politically determined and come under the pervasive political culture of patronage and revenge. Development according to objective criteria worked out in a plan does not get prioritized by PCs.

A key idea that emerges from the debates on the last two points is the need for a coordinated multilevel strategy for eradication of poverty based on techno-economic considerations and immunized against political manipulation. To support this, macro-meso-micro linkages need to be forged to facilitate resource flows downstream to microlevel where the grassroots level drama of poverty eradication is to be enacted. The same linkages working upstream—micro-meso-macro should facilitate flows of lessons from micro and mesolevel experiences for influencing policy at macrolevel (Amarasinghe and Dale, 1994; GOSL/UNDP, 1998; Gunatilaka and Williams, 1999; Hewavitharana, 2002a; HIRDEP, 1998; Jerve et al., 2003; UNDP, 2001a; Vimaladharma et al., 2000).

Empowerment of the Poor Impeded by Politicization and Bad Governance

To empower the poor is to enable them to gain a command over the resources needed for them to work their way out of poverty. Analysts have argued that the empowerment process has been impeded by the forces of politicization and bad governance. The thrust of the argument is that politicization is the mother of bad governance and disempowerment and that it is from disempowerment that poverty derives. A political culture of patronage and revenge has been reinforced at different levels by the massive increase in the number of politicians and the increase at an exponential rate in the interventions by politicians in every sphere of activity.

Also noted with alarm was a gradual increase in the utilization of the state apparatus as a vehicle for distribution of favours for the supporters of the ruling party and, along with it, a downward trend in good governance involving a rapid decline of transparency and accountability. The lack of transparency at all levels of government, it is argued, has enabled an evolution of particularistic patronage relations while creating opportunities for waste and corruption. The malaise has worsened so much that it is thought that the government apparatus cannot anymore respond impartially to the poor. Contributing to local bad governance is the malfunctioning of the local elective body, the PS. Evaluators are obliged to argue that the SM movement should restructure the rural political economy by seeing to it that the poor are represented by village organizations empowered not by elections but by groups of social mobilizers or catalysts who would bond them together to deal with the PSs' and the PCs.

In contesting the claims on the state for fungible resources, it is the politico-socio-economic elite who will capture these resources for their own private/sectional gains. As earlier noted, an interface between the poor and the public service providers is difficult to be arranged. In this situation, the poor as individuals are incapable of accessing public resources without paying unacceptable transactions costs of a socio-political financial nature. For these reasons, the local politicians and the elite in league with local officials will become the intermediaries for such resource flows and in the process, reinforce the existing power structures and patterns of social relations.

It is necessary to build up countervailing power of the poor that could catalyze a process of building up a new political culture incorporating non-party political processes for poverty eradication. Social mobilization methodology should be practiced to build up the capacity of the poor to resist all types of social, economic and political sources which disempower them, particularly the safety-net income transfer programmes which are often used as instruments of disempowering them (GOSL, 2002; Gunatilaka and Salih, 1999; Hewavitharana, 1997b, 2002a; NPC, 2001; Silva, 1998; UNDP, 1997, 2001a; Vimaladharma et al., 2000).

Welfarism and Income Transfers in Relation to Poverty Alleviation

Welfarism has been the dominant ethos of all government programmes dating back to the pre-independence period. This income transfer element survives up to the present day through metamorphosis. Its incarnation from the early 1990s has been a large direct income transfer component combined with a relatively small development component distributed among half of the population. The reason for this unique phenomenon of income transfers having a life of their own is that they have become intertwined with the political economy of the country.

Techno-Socio-Economic Structural Dualism and Barriers of Dualism

The economy and society of Sri Lanka may be seen to be split and running on two tracks on the lines of 'techno-socio-economic-dualism'. This dualism in the structure arising from technological, sociological and economic factors gets reflected in the following dichotomies between the two sectors:

Sector I—Formal /Organized /Modern /Market oriented / Industrial / Urban
Sector II—Informal /Unorganized /Traditional /Subsistence/Semi-subsistence oriented/
    Small scale farming / Rural Non-farm activities

The dichotomy between the two sectors arises from differences in forms and procedures, the levels of technology, attitudes and behaviour patterns, modes of production,

production sectoral structure, culture and lifestyles. Indeed, Sri Lanka used to be and, despite changes, still is a classic case of dualism due to her colonial legacy of a Sector I comprised of export-oriented plantation agriculture with related service sectors, some industries and the public services and a Sector II comprised of small scale farming and rural non-farm activities with MEs. Given this structure, there are only few backward or forward production linkages between the two sectors. Because of the structural imbalance the factor markets get fractured and fragmented. These manifestations of market imperfections reflect the fact that intersectoral factor flows are obstructed by the 'barriers of dualism', or in other words, market failures, associated with the basic structural imbalance. This causes a perpetuation of dualism because, according to the dynamics of the above model, it is primarily a flow of investment from capital surplus Sector I to create employment in labour surplus Sector II that will erase dualism and reunite the two sectors, the parallel factor markets, the wage rates and other factor prices. The fundamental structural parameters that condition the economic processes and the dynamics therein provide the necessary insights for understanding the structural impoverishment process and possible approaches to eradicating poverty.

The Political Economy of Redistribution

Surplus generation and accumulation occur in Sector I while Sector II holds 90 per cent of the poor. The easy collection of government revenue from direct and indirect tax payers in Sector I furnishes a convenient method of siphoning off a part of the surplus of that sector for distribution in Sector II, where the great majority are non-income tax payers and therefore generally regarded as poor. The focus here is on relative poverty and that fosters the concept of the welfare state and redistributive justice. This concept fashioned the political thinking of all political parties and the welfare transfer policy bias increased over time with competitive populism dominating electoral politics at an increasing rate with each successive election.

In the debate around this issue, the pro-redistribution side put forward the following arguments.

- The State had enough resources (in the initial stages) due to favourable economic conditions and a comprehensive food subsidy was not an unbearable fiscal burden.
- Subsidy levels and nutritional status are correlated as demonstrated by the rise in acute malnutrition (wasting) when the real value of subsidies declined in the early 1980s.[2]

The pro-redistribution side met this with counter arguments.

- The Marxist argument was that what prevails in Sector I is comprador capitalism which does not reinvest surpluses in Sector II because of barriers of dualism, and not much even in Sector I itself, but prefer to remit home the surpluses. Hence, it is social justice to have a part of the surplus redistributed in Sector II to improve its living conditions.

- The development economics argument was that given dualism and lack of linkages between the two sectors, there is little hope for trickle-down from any investment expansion in Sector I to benefit Sector II.
- The political argument was about political, social and economic instability that would block any pruning down of social welfarism in favour of investment and growth.
- The pro-growth argument that income transfers bred 'idlers' and indolence, could not be taken very far because the beneficiaries started taking to the streets whenever welfare expenditure cuts were proposed.
- However, it was their argument that welfare expenditures have not regenerated enough resources to sustain the level of such expenditures, that won the day as the truth of it manifested itself in acute financial difficulties (Hewavitharana, 1993; Ratnayake, 1998; Silva, 1998).

From Universal Subsidies to Targeted Poor and to Safety Net Consumption Transfers

The food subsidy income transfer scheme was faulted for having become a misfit with the new adjustment and stabilization policies, as it was creating pressure on the budget which could not be tolerated under the policy of switching resources to investment. Even with a narrowing down of its coverage from a universal simplistic to a targeted needy, the subsidy bill had kept on rising with the depreciation of the rupee, itself an adjustment policy measure. Hence, the advocacy was to shift to the non-indexed food stamps scheme. The scheme came to be eventually faulted for its incapability to provide food security and to protect the nutritional status. In the meantime, a case was made for the need for safety-nets to protect the vulnerable from fallouts from structural adjustment (SA) measures while bringing those marginalized from the growth process back into the mainstream of development. These arguments promoted a policy shift to targeted income transfers for consumption built into the formal national poverty alleviation programme, Janasaviya (JSP), later succeeded by Samurdhi. The focus in this shift was on targeting the absolutely poor. Thus, it was a shift from relative poverty issues to absolute poverty issues and by implication from the political economy aspects of relative poverty to techno-economic issues in absolute poverty.

The advocacy of this policy shift was derived from two major economic reasonings:

- The growth-oriented policies of de-subsidization, devaluation, increasing of interest rates and import trade liberalization had caused social costs in the forms of employment and income losses. These resulted in a worsening of poverty conditions, an increase of relative poverty and a marginalization of the poor. Thus, a safety net to protect them from such fallouts needed to be devised as a necessary adjunct to the market forces driven growth policy.

- Such a safety net should be regarded only as a temporary device to mitigate those negative short-term effects and to cover the time lag until those marginalized are enabled through a saving and investment component (included in the two programmes) to participate in the mainstream growth process and reap its benefits. This, it was argued could well be the method to ultimately wean the poor from the subsidy-dependency syndrome (Hewavitharana, 1993; Nayar and Gunatilaka, 2000; Ratnayake, 1998).

Politicization of Samurdhi and Its Design Weaknesses Resulting in a Negation of Safety Net Economics

Samurdhi suffered from design and implementation weaknesses, of which have affected its effectiveness in terms of poverty alleviation. Against the background of its design weakness of not having a clearly defined entry mechanism to the programme, it employed the defective implementation modality of political discrimination in beneficiary targeting. It used an extensive network of politically appointed 30,000 'poverty administrators', (Samurdhi Development Officers) who worked at grassroots level identifying and nominating beneficiaries on political grounds. Critics have pointed out how counter-productive such curtailing of people's freedom of political choice can be for alleviating poverty by referring to cross-country evidence to the effect that for poverty programmes to be most effective in reaching the poor, the poor themselves must be able to participate actively and freely in the political process with greater prominence and ease.

Critics brought out supporting data on the targeting inefficiency of Samurdhi. The coverage of Samurdhi transfers at 55 per cent of the population is twice the estimated percentage of the poor. Given such coverage, all poor households in Samurdhi's catchment area should have received benefits, but it was not so in practice. Recent survey research reveals that only 60 per cent in the lowest expenditure quintile receive Samurdhi benefits and that it does not assist 40 per cent in that poorest quintile at all. On the other hand, 44 per cent of its benefits go to top three income quintiles containing the better-off people. Such causative errors of misallocation of resources negate the working of economic dynamics of safety net programmes which require that the positive impact on poverty should be maximized with the least cost and in the shortest possible time.

Given the fact that its coverage was excessive, the Samurdhi budget amounted to as much as 1 per cent of GDP compared to the share of the entire budget for education at 2.5 per cent. Aggravating the situation is its design weakness in the lack of a clear exit mechanism with incentives for the beneficiaries to graduate out of the programme in a sustainable manner within a definable time frame. Such weaknesses negate the economic dynamics of safety net income transfers. Various measures to reduce the number of beneficiaries were proposed, but vested political interests being strong, they had to be abandoned (Aturupane, 1999; GOSL, 2000, 2002; Hewavitharana, 1999; World Bank, 1998, 2000b, 2001).

The concept of social capital and its role in economic development in general and in poverty alleviation in particular, has now gained in recognition. The SM movement for poverty alleviation tries to build up social capital in the individuals at the grassroots level by inculcating qualities of motivation, commitment, devotion for social action and leadership and at the community level by fostering collaborative social relations, collective group action, mutual-aid, self-help groups and participatory planning. As critics have argued, Samurdhi, in letting loose its army of politically motivated public officials holding authority, has hampered what SM movement has been trying to build up. In causing such damage, Samurdhi has defeated its own purpose, which is to alleviate poverty.

Negative Labour Market Effects of Direct Income Transfers

Imperfections in Sri Lanka's labour market are characterized by labour immobility, labour allocation rigidities and labour supply inelasticities. The distortionary effect on the labour market produced by direct income transfers has been put forward as an additional factor that has aggravated the problem of labour market imperfections. As has been cogently argued, JSP with its injections of generous consumption transfers and Samurdhi with its excessive coverage have had negative labour market effects by raising the reservation supply price (reservation wage) of labour.[3] All this is evidence of dynamic economic inefficiency which instead of integrating the poor into the labour market can indirectly lead to a withdrawal from it. In this way, direct income transfers reduce the prospects for factor flows between Sectors I and II which hold the solution for the problem of Structural Dualism (Aturupane, 1999; Hewavitharana, 1993; Sahn and Halderman 1996).

Undermining of Development of Human Resources for Poverty Alleviation by Direct Subsidy Transfers

The newly introduced variable 'W' in the aggregate production function, which stands for behaviour patterns, motivations attitudes, perceptions, mentalities and mind sets, has gained wide recognition as the potentially most dynamic variable, if properly handled, for developing human resources, human capital and social capital required for alleviating poverty. As to what impact the massive subsidy-income transfers have had on these elements of variable 'W' and the implications thereof have led to a productive debate.

- A culture of dependence has been fostered in which low income households have come to possess a handout mentality and depend on income and welfare transfers. It inhibits the culture of self-reliance which SM movement promotes. Given the absence of clear-cut exit procedures in Samurdhi, the effect of its dole system is to generate a reluctance among the beneficiaries to work their way out of poverty. This hinders the promotion of self-employment projects, the main instrument of poverty alleviation.

- The dependency culture has been bolstered by the changes caused in public conception of poverty ever since the introduction of targeted transfer programmes, requiring means tests and identification of who the poor are through public meetings. This decreased the element of shame that was earlier associated with poverty and instead, there occurred a glorification of poverty with an 'official poverty status' as an entitlement. Perceptions crystallized around the poor being 'helpless' and 'innocent' and having a 'right' to government assistance. These perceptions got firmly embedded in the minds of policy makers, politicians and administrators responsible for allocating public funds at national and provincial levels.
- The paternalistic attitude to poverty is a reflection of the outdated traditional welfare thinking that treats the poor as a charge on society, who have to be provided for through handouts of public resources. In contrast, the new positive thinking is that the poor are the untapped resources for bringing about poverty reducing growth.

Several ideas emerged as means of resolving the debate. Implementation of strategies is needed to enable the poor to successfully negotiate with the market, so as to reduce their levels of dependency on political power structures and also rid them of the subservient survival mentality. There is need to emulate the unique Change Agent Programme (CAP) which specialized in promoting behavioural and attitudinal changes with emphasis on self-reliance and self-awareness. Most likely, it is in this arena of the debate on their impact on the variable 'W', that the safety net income transfer programmes met their Waterloo (Aturupane 1999; GOSL, 2000, 2002; GOSL/UNDP, 1998; Silva, 1998; Silva and Gunatilaka, 2000).

Shift From Safety Net Income Transfers to Social Protection Relying on Social Insurance

The advocacy of this policy change draws its inspiration from the Framework for Poverty Reduction (GOSL, 2000), which sets a new role for the government in creating an environment for pro-poor growth through which poverty will be reduced. It is argued that a need for social protection will be increasingly felt as the poor get increasingly dependent on private sector growth for improving their incomes and welfare, and thereby become vulnerable to greater insecurity by having to face greater market failures. When the vulnerability of the poor increases in this manner, 'reactive endeavours' like direct transfers can only be counter productive for they breed the cultures of dependence and indolence. Accordingly, a shift must be effected from transfers to 'work-fare' programmes. To support this, what is needed is a completely new social protection system which helps the poor to develop their entrepreneurial behaviour by facilitating them to manage their risk through a provision of access to social insurance. The Samurdhi Social Security Trust Fund and other private or NGO insurance agencies are to be supported by the government to provide affordable social insurance services to the poor on a commercial and competitive basis. Along with this,

Samurdhi itself is to be revamped by tightening its targeting with new eligibility criteria for income transfers, which will be depoliticized and made to operate subject to exit criteria and procedures. All these measures will be focused on the hard core poor. Over the next decade, as visualized by the Poverty Reduction Strategy (GOSL, 2002), the role of direct transfers will be increasingly reduced and replaced by support for broadening the coverage of social insurance, which will be largely financed on a commercial basis.

POLICY SHIFTS, REFORMULATIONS AND REORIENTATIONS OF PROGRAMMES FOR POVERTY ALLEVIATION

Integrated Rural Development Programmes (IRDPs) in Poverty Alleviation

IRDPs, which started as multisectoral programmes to address regional disparities with the overarching objective of improving the living standards of the poor, came to be enlisted for poverty alleviation as a means of resolving the controversy over macro and micro-policy divergence. SA measures worsened the economic conditions of poor households while the long-standing micro-level policy, on the other hand, was meant to improve the welfare of these households. Safety nets being temporary arrangements, the policy decision taken to resolve this controversy was by getting the IRDPs to place the improvement of incomes of the poor on a more permanent footing.

Evaluations and reviews of the performance of IRDPs in poverty alleviation, however, presented a picture of mixed results in general. Although they had effected much improvement to the living conditions by expanding the physical and social infrastructure in In Ar, their achievements in alleviating income poverty were much less impressive, helping only to prevent further deterioration of the economy of the poor under the impact of SA policies. Their impact on the broader issues on poverty alleviation, viz., inequitable access to productive assets, unemployment and low productivity was only marginal. Basically, these failures can partly be attributed to the very design of these programmes that set too broad a range of objectives leading to a thin spread of investment and activities over too many different sectors in too large an area lacking in any depth of impact. It left little chances for maximizing impact through strategic arrangements for synergy among the activities (Gooneratne et al., 2000; Gunatilaka and Williams, 1999; Jerve et al., 1992, 2003).

By the late 1980s, policy making had reached a crossroad. In response to the first round of SA from 1977 onwards, the task was to counter the negative effects it had produced. In its second round from 1989 onwards, when it activated a private sector-led economic growth process, the task that arose was to help the poor find escape routes by linking them with that process. Logically, what now emerged as the moot point was how the IRDPs which could not help the poor much to overcome the ill effects of market forces under the first round, could now help the poor fit in with market forces to exploit the potentialities of the growth process. The ensuing debate revolved around two types of revisions deemed necessary to enable the programmes to face the challenge. Inward looking revisions sought to reorient corporate capability by redesigning the programmes. Outward looking revisions sought to integrate the development of the In Ar (micro) with that of the region (meso) via newly designed programmes.

Inward Looking Revisions—Reformulation of Hambantota IRDP (HIRDEP)

The increasing of employment for the disadvantaged and the poorest by facilitating full-time work opportunities was introduced as a priority objective in HIRDEP's Perspective Plan for 1994–99. For the first time, it was emphasized that the policy should be one to create wage employment for many and self-employment for some. To ensure the sustainability of MEs/SEs, strategies of private sector leadership, entrepreneurship development and market orientation of enterprises were enlisted.

Although HIRDEP was able to come to terms with the problem of employment and income creation in this manner, its objectives as they were reformulated begged two pertinent questions. How realistic and pragmatic was it to concentrate on the poorest (faithful to the original objectives of HIRDEP) in searching for mechanisms aimed at generating sustainable employment opportunities and incomes over the short term? Of equal importance was the second question—was it possible to implement the new policy and achieve the employment objective without much more dynamism than was found in a 'routine' or 'conventional' poverty alleviation programme? The crux of the problem here was that while introducing the new objectives of employment creation and enlisting the new market-oriented strategies, the conventional objective of enabling people's participation (PP) in decision making too was retained. Designing of strategies to enfold all such 'strange bed fellows' was a stupendous task. Through an exploration of possibilities it was found that after creating hopes among people through SM-led PP, it was difficult and problematic to scale down, adjust or deviate from conventional thinking and routine poverty alleviation procedures and then turn to more dynamic fields, confront and tackle new problems, while remaining within the same IRDP institutional system and procedures. There was no alternative but to completely reorient the institution and the procedures that catalyzed far-reaching changes (Hewavitharana, 2002b; HIRDEP, 1998).

Seeking ways for a complete reorientation, the debate shifted to the interlinked issues of rural economic dynamism, structural change and poverty alleviation. Advancement of the socio-economic conditions of the poor, it was argued, cannot be done in isolation as these are integral to the dynamics of rural economy, which in turn can get activated only by structural changes that involve diversification and surplus accumulation. Within the framework of the new national policy on IRDPs, the Regional

Development Division (RDD) in 1996 virtually 'enforced' a major shift to economic growth by issuing directives to IRDPs which clearly directed them to:

- shed sharp focus on employment creation, especially for educated youth, and on income growth;
- secure active and positive participation of private sector in development planning;
- facilitate and service investment promotion and entrepreneurship;
- encourage market-driven economic activity;
- set up institutional systems and procedures to achieve these ends.

HIRDEP strove to put into practice this neo-liberal development ideology. To activate the private sector, it facilitated the Hambantota District Chamber of Commerce and its Enterprise Service Centre to promote medium (MdEs) and large-scale (LEs) enterprises. MEs were left out. The other institution facilitated by HIRDEP to activate private enterprise was the Social Mobilizer Foundation (SMF), an NGO formed by transforming the former SM network into a network for economic mobilization to promote business development by encouraging members to move on the continuum from ME to SE and to MdE. The ideology of SM-based saving and credit is characterized inter alia by flexibility regarding use of savings, emphasis on gradual improvement, solidarity and mutual trust. Under the new ideology of enterprise-oriented strategies, however, the use of savings for consumption may come under attack as being 'unproductive', causing much damage to the establishment of a saving-credit culture so beneficial to the poor. Another debating point is that under the new ideology, potentially successful members who want to go 'fast and risky' would get targeted for promotion on the 'picking of winners' or 'betting on the strong' strategy. This will leave out the poor members who want to go 'gradual and safe' on the SM-based strategy. The two groups can become complementary to each other if the SMF succeeds in its attempt to ride both horses. If not, the socio-economic dualism that would get recreated will cause damage to unity, solidarity and mutual help fostered by conventional SM (Gunatilaka and Williams, 1999; Jerve et al., 2003).

Looking Outward—Linkages for In Ar with Regional Economy

The neglect of essential structural linkages prevented the bringing of In Ar into the mainstream of socio-economic development. The logical conclusion was that instead of trying to develop In Ar in isolation, efforts must be made to integrate it with the regional (meso level) economy through a network of horizontal and vertical linkages (Gooneratne et al., 2000; Gunatilaka, 1997; Gunatilaka and Salih, 1999; Jerve et al., 2003; UNDP, 1998). The RDD of the Ministry of Planning mooted the idea of moving into regional development planning. In this very first attempt to develop a concept of regional planning, it tried to harness the dynamic economics of linkages—viz., promotion of backward and forward linkages via value addition; strengthening of direct supply linkages between the regional economies and the metropolitan and export markets now weakened by peripherals bypassing them to directly supply the latter; promotion of an inter-linked urban system to strengthen inter-regional linkages in production and trade; facilitation of a Level I for promotion of MEs/IGAs for poverty alleviation and a Level II for promotion of SEs and MdEs, with mutually reinforcing linkages between the two levels.

Without linkages with markets in Sector I, MEs in In Ar (Sector II) will not be stimulated to change over to advanced technologies which hold the key to upgrading of quality and penetration of superior markets. When these do not occur, there will be no mutually supportive increases in the demand for wage goods produced in each sector, no expansion in wage employment and consequently no income multiplier effects, no market expansion and no technology change to complete the vicious circle. With the institution of micro (In Ar)-meso (region) dynamic economic linkages, the interactions between Sectors I and II will increase with respect to technology, markets and wage goods and the resultant income and employment multiplier will relax the circular constraints and narrow down the gap of structural dualism (Hewavitharana, 1995; RDD, 1994). Regional planning that was expected to be carried out within a provincial spatial framework was never able to get off the ground. The seminal ideas that surfaced from the RDD's conceptualization, however, continued to feature in subsequent debates on planning.

The RDD considered the need to replace the IRD concept with a new concept of regional development and the Regional Economic Advancement Programme (REAP) was the result. The REAP was conceived as a transformer which would work to achieve sustainable economic advancement in rural areas, rural economic growth, generation of income and employment through development of enterprises, enhanced participation of the private sector and the commercialization of the stagnating or slow growing rural economy. REAP formulations have been prepared for five districts using the general framework as the guideline.

Based on an analysis of these formulations, a debate is now on regarding how effective REAP can be in addressing poverty alleviation issues. The following are among the arguments focusing on the negative side which are supported by several evaluators and analysts. The potentially pro-poor integrated village development and regional development planning which featured in REAP's original conceptualization have later been dropped. Hambantota REAP will promote only SEs and MdEs and not MEs, ignoring altogether their potential to supplement the growth strategy by reducing the vulnerability of the poor and their role in a possible vertical expansion of enterprises on the ME-SE-MdE continuum. The widely supported two-level/prong approach, which combines poverty alleviation with growth by forging linkages between Prong II promoting SEs, MdEs and LEs and Prong I developing MEs at grassroots level, has not been included in REAP's strategy, totally ignoring the dynamic economics of such vertical linkages that could lead to a mutual reinforcement of the two levels. The formulations do not visualize any partnership arrangements with Community-Based Organizations (CBOs) which are trying to promote self-employment for the poor. Housing development for the poor, which links economic development with social development and which creates wage employment and facilitates ME, SE, MdE development through its pronounced backward and forward linkages, does not feature in the REAP formulations (Gooneratne et al., 2000; HIRDEP, 1998; Jerve et al., 1992, 2003; Lakshman et al., 1994; RDD, 1997; UNDP, 1997).

The Area Based Growth and Equity Programme (ABGEP) was conceptualized to achieve regional economic growth by exploiting new opportunities in competition with national and global market challenges, and distribute the benefits of growth among the poor. In a holistic approach, it will harness the regional resource potential and capitalize on regional opportunities as means of overall development and poverty reduction worked into one coherent strategy. ABGEP was implemented as a pilot project in the poorest province of Uva, on the underlying idea that the promotion of sustainable growth in the poorest region is, by itself, sufficient to address poverty reduction and equity concerns. It deviated from the neo-liberal ideology against protectionism by offering moderate to high subsidies on interest rates for the promotion of enterprises. ABGEP's subsidy policy could prove to be a turning point in the country's on-going debate on subsidies for industrial development.

The verdict of evaluators is that ABGEP is a success with innovative technologies adopted, new products introduced and distant markets penetrated, resulting in the emergence of a new class of small and self-employed entrepreneurs. It has demonstrated that it is possible to encourage private sector-led growth in a marginal region based on private sector initiatives and that they can serve as the basis for economic diversification, higher incomes and reduction of poverty (Tabor et al., 2000; UNDP, 1998; UNOPS/UNDP, 2001).

Policies and Strategies Relating to Growth-Equity-Poverty (G-E-P) Dynamics

---

Structural Adjustment (SA) and G-E-P Dynamics

Researchers on Sri Lanka provide empirical evidence on the negative effects of SA on the economic activities of the poor. Small-scale farming including paddy and particularly the typical poor man's crops, namely, other food crops and subsidiary food crops suffered severely from the stabilization and trade liberalization measures. Many of the poor man's micro/cottage/craft/small industries could not withstand competition from imports of mass produced low-cost consumer goods embodying modern technology. These effects deepened poverty and exacerbated inequity by marginalizing the poor. The World Bank and others oriented towards the neoliberal ideology which inspired SA, however, argued that the growth-favouring SA has led to a notable reduction in consumption poverty and added that it is only in a continued persistence with the reforms to complete their unfinished agenda in liberalizing and strengthening the market economy, that their full beneficial effects could be realized (Glewwe, 1988; Hewavitharana, 1990; World Bank, 1995).

The impact that SA can produce on G-E-P dynamics when it is applied in the setting of structural dualism, however, does not depend on just pressing on with an agenda for maximizing growth. Under SA, it is in Sector I that growth would take place, but its positive effects fail to get fully transmitted to Sector II and thereby the latter is left unassisted in counter balancing the negative effects of SA it has to face. As long as inter-sectoral linkages remain too weak to serve as conduits, the trickle-down from Sector I to II will also remain too weak to play any active role in G-E-P dynamics.

During 1978-86, which experienced the first round of SA and was a period that recorded a high growth rate, the rural sector's poverty (incidence) and inequity (Gini) increased and that too at rates faster than those of their respective national values. During the sub-period, 1985-91, a period of weak growth or stagnation, however, the rural sector's poverty and inequity both declined, the former even faster than the decline in national poverty. Along with these developments, the depth of rural poverty (poverty gap) and the severity of poverty (squared poverty gap) which had earlier increased were also reduced. All these improvements in (E) and (P) took place despite a weak (G) and therefore independently of (G). Probing into these perplexities via a decomposition of the dynamics of poverty change, it is found that a growth in consumption and a better distribution of income contributed almost equally to the reduction of depth and severity of poverty (Datt and Gunawardena, 1994). Providing an insight into these perplexities is the thesis that decreases in poverty (P) and inequity (E minus) with growth (G) are not inevitable, and that such decreases are not possible without explicit and well structured meso policies and micro-interventions to develop economic infrastructure (Adelman and Robinson, 1989) and social infrastructure (Cornea et al., 1987).

In the 1990s, despite a GDP growth at 5 per cent per annum, a halving of the unemployment rate and the enormous efforts put in for poverty reduction via various targeted programmes, poverty incidence (P) showed little or no change, with an esti-mated long-term chronic poverty at 25 per cent. The arguments are that the growth rate (G) has not been high enough; a stronger growth performance would be needed to reduce province-wise disparities, which are in fact widening to increase inequity; and, in the long run nutritional poverty can be eradicated only through a growth rate sustained at a high level. Others, while agreeing fully that a high real rate of growth is a necessary condition—in fact the most powerful engine for poverty reduction—argue that, nevertheless, it is not a sufficient condition. Poverty reduction did not occur because the growth strategies were not sufficiently broad-based and thereby failed to provide opportunities for the poor to participate in the growth process. Thus, G-E-P dynamics depend on both whether or not the growth rate is high enough and the growth strategies are broad-based enough. Sri Lanka has had modest growth accompa-nied by little or no income redistribution, as evident by only a marginal fall in Gini during the 1990s. Hence, macro policy should lay equal emphasis on accelerating the rate of growth and equitable distribution of the benefits of such growth. Realizing that the trickle-down effects do not work, the World Bank and the IMF too are laying emphasis on promoting broad-based growth strategies, like employment intensive pro-duction and participatory processes, for triggering off G-E-P dynamics (GOSL, 2002; Kelegama, 2003).

Income Transfers in G-E-P Dynamics: Role Failures

According to analysts, income transfers have failed either to reduce the incidence of poverty (P) appreciably or make qualitative changes in the economy because they address symptomatic poverty and not structural poverty. Transfers have helped in reducing inequality in income distribution and promoting equity (E) in respect of nutrition but in a mechanical and not in a dynamic way. Such transfers are expensive, temporary solutions and not sustainable. It has been argued that if the poor are just passive recipients of welfare measures such as JSP and Samurdhi benefits, it will be in the nature of a charge on the proceeds of growth that will affect sustained growth (G) by diverting resources away from growth, and that in turn will affect sustained poverty alleviation (P) as well. What emerges is that the old prescription of growth, accompanied by some state-sponsored redistributive efforts in the form of targeted transfer programmes, cannot work because it lacks the requisite dynamics (UNDP, 1998, 2001a; World Bank, 1990).

Both JSP and Samurdhi present development visions and development assistance components which are of a populist nature. Their failure in G-E-P dynamics can be summed up in terms of the dichotomies—Make Believe versus Reality and On Paper versus Actual Practice.

- **Make Believe:** The consumption grant by providing food security will relieve the poor of the anxieties and the struggle to satisfy their basic needs for two years as with JSP. That will enable them to build their capabilities and capacities for improving their quality of life on the basis of self-reliance.
  Reality: As noted earlier, the impact on variable 'W' has tended to be quite the opposite—it has generated cultures of dependence and indolence, reduced work effort, glorified poverty and encouraged laying claim to transfers as a right.
- **On Paper:** Develop a culture of thrift, saving and credit discipline for the development of micro-finance for IGAs/MEs.
  Actual Practice: Samurdhi's forced saving scheme undermined the SM-based voluntary saving and lending culture. Expectations of loan forgiveness associated with state-sponsored credit, that can include Samurdhi credit in public perception, undermined the credit discipline that was being built up. No support services were provided for IGAs/MEs which were left to be self-designed and self-supported resulting in non-sustainability.
- **On Paper:** The capital accumulation based on JSP's saving component was designated to be used as collateral to raise loans from banks under special credit schemes (that would correct credit market failures) to invest in increasing the productivity of their resources and land assets.
  Actual Practice: Beneficiaries were not given the capital accumulated but only the interest from it which was invariably consumed. Typically, the poor do not have many assets of their own to be developed in productivity with the use of bank loans.

- **Make Believe:** Nurture capacities and capabilities through appropriate training to enhance human capital.
  Reality: Under JSP, as seen earlier training was mostly token or a pretence to collect the transfer, an inducement to stay unemployed. No service package arrangements to facilitate the application of skills learned for developing MEs.
- **Make Believe:** The beneficiaries get out of poverty through self-reliance.
  Reality: Both JSP and Samurdhi had no exit mechanisms or procedures. As seen earlier, eligibility conditions in Samurdhi were conducive to a perpetuation of the dependency syndrome.
- **Make Believe:** Reconcile growth (G) and equity (E) objectives within Samurdhi programme.
  Reality: Only 6 per cent of Samurdhi's budget was allocated to capital development, 85 per cent for welfare transfers. As seen earlier, politicized Samurdhi impeded the formation of social capital, a component of variable 'W', which has a potential for triggering off development at the grassroots level.
- **Make Believe:** Complementarity between JSP and Janasaviya Trust Fund (JTF) for balancing of equity (E) with growth (G). JSP provides equity promoting safety net income transfers in Plan I, while in Plan II, JTF will be engaged in growth promoting credit provision for MEs/IGAs, creation of wage employment and productive assets via rural public works.
  Reality: There were no functional linkages directly between the two or indirectly through partner organizations of JTF for any complementarities in field level operations (Hewavitharana, 1993; Ratnayake, 1998).

Irrelevancy of Conventional SM and PP Processes for G-E-P Dynamics

In appreciation of the role played by SM and PP processes in activating the primary factors in the economic and social advancement of the poorer classes, they earned the recognition of analysts as a new development paradigm named as 'alternative development' or 'development from below'. Through their societal transformation strategy, they activated a culture of self-reliance for self-development among the people in In Ar, promoted a saving and lending culture and inculcated credit discipline together with the introduction of lending at market rates to backward communities. They mobilized group activity for collective marketing of produce and purchasing of production inputs with enhanced bargaining power and for gaining access to public resources. IGAs/MEs were promoted mainly on individual basis. Under the PP process, the technique of participatory rural appraisal (PRA) was used to identify and prioritize the economic infrastructure facilities most needed locally by the poor and have the assets constructed with beneficiary participation.

From the perspective of G-E-P dynamics, however, it has been argued that the economic gains from such promotional activities are in the nature of one-off level increases in productivity, incomes and employment and, although they may succeed in reducing poverty (P) and promoting (E), they fail in helping to generate a take off growth dynamic (G) that could set the poor on an autonomous income growth path and pull them out of their poverty in its stride. As pointed out by critics, the SM and PP processes display many weaknesses with respect to G-E-P dynamics. Group-based participatory credit system is not flexible enough in disbursements to cater to the requirements of the enterprising poor and may hold back the more successful individuals under the pressure of the inter se guarantee system. The group system came to be criticized for its weakness in financial intermediation between savers and borrowers, its inability to raise funds for investment on its usual saving and lending basis and the limiting of its lending to consumption purposes. Self-reliance came to be criticized for being an impediment for group dynamics as it could lead to the belief that all problems of the poor could be solved by the poor them-selves and thereby to a neglect of forging external linkages to obtain development inputs to increase the resource capacities of the groups. ·

Once it became clear that the SM process was unable to offset the adverse effects of SA and that even the level effects it produced could not be sustained in the face of inflation, it came to be argued that there was no alternative but to reinstate growth (G), as the vehicle for eradicating poverty (P). Many argued that there has to be a shift from just mobilizing and empowering the poor to the higher plane of getting them into the mainstream of market forces-driven growth process. As a logical sequence to this, it was argued that the mobilization exercise should be remodelled as a holistic commu-nity mobilization (CM) so as to foster a community-driven strategy of investment and enterprise promotion effectively linked with the private sector-led growth (G) effort.

These criticisms notwithstanding, the supporters of SM swung back to defend it pointing to the tasks devolved on it by the prevailing conditions. Propelled by its desires to build up a countervailing power for the poor against politicized interventions, build up their capabilities for successfully negotiating with the market and end their depen-dence on doles and handouts, the National Poverty Conference reaffirmed its faith in SM and self-reliance with EM added. These are valid points, but the point missed here is whether SM/CM + EM can adequately alter the structural parameters of poverty to pull In Ar/Sector II out of its subsistence, low-level equilibrium trap and make it take off on a growth path (Aturupane, 1999; Gunatilaka and Salih 1999; Hewavitharana, 1994, 1997a; HIRDEP, 1996, 1998; Jerve et al., 1992, 2003; Nayar and Gunatilaka, 2000; NPC, 2001; Silva and Gunatilaka, 2000).

Irrelevance of Self-Employment (IGAs and MEs) to G-E-P Dynamics

Rural Non-Farm (R N-F) Activities Born Out of Rural Structural Impoverishment Process Reflect Reverse G-E-P Dynamics

Under the fundamental parameters of the rural structural impoverishment process in Sri Lanka, there was neither a shift of labour from agriculture to industry nor a rural–urban migration. As more labour got 'squeezed out' of agriculture, the R N-F sector had to accommodate a proliferation of last resort activities of a residual nature, otherwise described as distress adaptations characterized by low productivity and low earnings. It is in this manner that the process of structural impoverishment and its deepening has taken place. Hence, it is reverse G-E-P dynamics that work for the continued existence of the subsistence low-level equilibrium trap in which In Ar/ Sector II are caught. Many of the IGAs/MEs promoted by poverty alleviation programmes are more or less replications of the above types of activities.

IGAs and MEs in Poverty Market Trap Cannot Play Any Role in G-E-P Dynamics

Researchers have observed that micro/craft/cottage/small industries, including those promoted by poverty alleviation programmes, depend mostly on local sales and that their growth is hampered by the constraints arising from their being confined to small sized local markets with low purchasing power. MEs that get pushed into poverty market niches face stagnant demand and produce a limited range of low quality goods for which the demand is inelastic. If upgrading of the product is attempted using better technology with a view to catering to superior markets, they would run the risk of falling in between two dilemmas. On the one hand, the concomitant rise in cost of production will get the product priced out of its usual poverty market which can no longer afford it. On the other hand, a shift to upper segments of the market would be risky to attempt because they cannot be sure whether they can compete with the larger firms already catering to such markets, using advanced technology to produce quality products and that too at costs reduced through scale economies. Capital and technology are caught in a vicious circle. When the product is priced cheap, the accumulation of the capital required for technology upgrading is difficult, but without the use of advanced technology higher level markets cannot be penetrated. Rendered unable in this manner to adopt any improved technology, accumulate any capital or enter new markets, a vertical rise on the continuum of ME-SE-MdE is not a possibility. What is possible in the case of rural crafts, as has been argued by a field researcher, is a continuation of the survival modality of reproduction of crafts, which by implication means that the continuation of artisan craft production depends on the continued existence of the poor. On these grounds it is held that IGAs and MEs embodying the self-employment mode are irrelevant for G-E-P dynamics (Gunatilaka, 1997; Hesselberg, 1980; Hewavitharana, 1986, 1990, 1992).

Relevance of Wage Employment to G-E-P Dynamics in Contrast with Self-Employment (IGAs/MEs)

Field researchers argue that a lack of motivation (an element of variable 'W') among operators is a key reason for the weakness of MEs. The poor simply do not perceive self-employment as a secure means of crossing the threshold of poverty. They prefer the security of wage employment. For the youth, self-employment only helps to mark time while they search for wage employment in Sector I. This lack of motivation in turn can be traced to several causes. An aspirations mismatch is in operation as consumers' aspirations for incomes and jobs, stimulated by the consumerism of an open economy, soar above what self-employment can offer. The non-entrepreneurial housewife bias commonly found in self-employment means that the operators do not have the time or inclination to raise IGAs beyond the level of a secondary earning activity supportive of their subsistence. Hoping to get the poorest on to a growth path via MEs is like betting on the weak as they are the least able in terms of skills, aptitudes and attitudes towards risk to adopt or experiment with new technology in undertaking investments.

Generation of wage employment is crucial for reducing poverty and that it is the only way out of poverty for the majority of the poor. Hence, from the perspective of G-E-P dynamics, the policy should be to promote enterprises among rural higher income groups who have greater capacity to face risks in making the investments to generate and provide employment for others (Gunatilaka, 1997; Gunatilaka and Salih, 1999; Hewavitharana, 1994; Lakshman et al., 1994; Silva, 1998).

Paradigm Shift from Conventional SM to a Redesigned SM of Real Relevance to G-E-P Dynamics

Conceptual Framework

The poverty problems aggravated by the ongoing growth process cannot be allowed to linger on until the invisible hand will correct them through the normal economic process. Growth is absolutely essential, but it should be defined in a manner that its touchstone is what it does to the poor. Hence, one must adopt the policy of 'poverty reducing growth at the micro level'. The poor should be regarded as untapped resources; if these were to be mobilized in such a way that the poor act as active agents of socio-economic development and work themselves out of poverty through productive activities, then poverty will get reduced while making a contribution to growth (G).

A Paradigm Shift to a Redesigned SM

The instrumental roles the redesigned SM was expected to play in promoting G-E-P dynamics can be highlighted as follows. (a) Shift away from organizing for self-help to economically empowering the poor on a market oriented production based strategy; assist them by carrying out feasibility studies, making cost estimates, facilitating flow of the needed resources, providing technical assistance and bringing them in to credit lines. (b) Shift the poor away from income transfers and handouts to an autonomous development path of self-reliant working with market forces, induced by commercial profits and gains in incomes and employment. (c) Shift from planning for demands (what one wants) as done under conventional SM to planning a portfolio of opportunities (what one can do) to better themselves on the basis of identifications at household, group and community levels. (d) Shift from seeing the poor as passive recipients of benefits to seeing them as active agents of development, and unleashing their untapped potential for economic activities by providing them with a level playing field for production via removal of micro-level obstacles in the forms of unequal access to capital, markets and development services.

While acknowledging these objectives, evaluators were obliged to raise the question whether micro-level achievements can be sustained without G-E-P dynamics being promoted at national/macro level. The debate on this point remains unresolved (Hewavitharana, 2002a; ISACPA, 1992; SAPAP/UNDP, 1996; UNDP, 2001a, 2001b; UNDP/UNOPS, 1998; Vimaladharma et al., 2000).

CULMINATION OF THE ECONOMIC DEBATES ON POVERTY ALLEVIATION POLICY: PRO-POOR STRUCTURAL CHANGE FOR PRO-POOR GROWTH

Issues Raised by Evaluators/Analysts

It is the lack of high growth rates that emerges as the fundamental problem, not the lack of any specialized and specifically targeted ME support projects. These can facilitate micro finance (MF) and ME growth on any scale only if the fundamental economic conditions are in place. Inconsistency between macro policies and poverty reduction measures is a policy paradox that involves implementing of measures to develop MEs at the micro level, but allowing an unfavourable macroeconomic environment that is not conducive to a high rate of growth. Also, the anti-poor biases of too many policies have rendered poverty alleviation efforts futile. As has been observed, a change over to pro-poor macro policy or 'change from above' has been slow while micro-level-induced policy change or 'change from below' has been taking place, albeit in a piecemeal way. Clearly, the upshot of these arguments is to bring the growth rate to the centre and to make the macroeconomic dynamism associated with it the crucially necessary framework for the G-E-P dynamics.

Given the sluggish growth at the macro level and economic stagnation at the meso level, Sector II continues to be caught in the subsistence low-level equilibrium trap. In this trap situation with its vicious circle that allows no progress, any small gains from IGAs/MEs are swallowed up by inflation and changing terms of trade between Sectors I and II. Growth in the past has failed to generate enough momentum to pull out the less responsive rural sector (Sector II) in its wake. Until enough dynamism can be generated to loosen this trap, both policy makers and the poor will have to reconcile themselves to holding operations that concentrate on micro-level interventions to promote MEs that cannot make any progress. What is required are investments so strategically planned as to achieve the twin objectives of breaking into the vicious circle of the trap while integrating the rural economy (Sector II), with the more dynamic urban sector (Sector I), and so launch it on to a dynamic growth path.

These arguments which deal with the fundamentals of structural dualism carry certain far-reaching implications. Poverty alleviation depends not on intermediated resource flows but on the dynamism of national and local economy and, most importantly, on the capacity of the poor to share in that dynamism. Given the conditions of structural dualism, it is imperative to incorporate a process of realizing structural change in the rural economy (Sector II) into models of poverty alleviation. The effecting of structural change in Sector II to integrate it with Sector I by means of strategically planned investments to break the barriers of dualism to accessing skills development facilities, infrastructure facilities, capital and technology, that prevent the participation of the poor in the growth process, should constitute the core of a new model for poverty alleviation (Aturupane, 1999; Gunatilaka and Williams, 1999; HIRDEP, 1998; ISACPA, 1992; Nayar and Gunatilaka, 2000; Silva and Gunatilaka, 2000; UNDP, 1998, 2001a, 2001b; UNDP/UNOPS, 1998).

The Innovative Concept of Pro-Poor Growth

It addresses G-E-P dynamics from three perspectives. First, a high rate of growth, with the poor adequately connected with the growth process, will create ample opportunities for them to improve their incomes and living conditions. Second, growth integrated with poverty reduction is not only possible but also essential if persistent poverty is to be overcome. Third, while raising the rate of growth (G), the institutions that reinforce equity should be strengthened (E), via broad-based participation in economic activities. This means that Institutional Economics has to take over the task of stimulating the role of 'E' in G-E-P dynamics by encouraging community mobilization and community-based action and delivery in order to ensure that the poor participate fully in working out appropriate solutions to eradicate poverty.

How to Manage G-E-P Dynamics in a Private Sector-Led Process of Economic Growth

The government will maintain a stable macroeconomic environment, a prerequisite for growth in investment, output, income and employment. It will encourage the private sector to participate in the provision and management of infrastructure facilities, social services and in the operation of commercial enterprises hitherto controlled by the government. It will act as facilitator and catalyst to help the poor to get organized for community-based action to gain access to competitive markets and to augment their productivity levels. Thus, the erstwhile social engineering efforts devoted to social mobilization will now get reoriented to enable commercial gains. The government will avoid poverty alleviating measures that increase dependence on state and thus act as a drag on growth. If this policy were to be adhered to, it will end the debate on income transfers and begin a weaning of the poor from doles and handouts. It could at last cure the economy of the earlier noted unfavourable effects of these measures on work effort, labour force participation, factor mobilization and the efficiency of the labour market and the behavioural variable 'W' and, as a bonus, release the resources required to finance the badly needed big investment push effort.

The Innovative Concept of Pro-Poor Structural Change

The effecting of a gradual shift from the economy of Sector II, based on low productivity subsistence oriented agriculture, to the higher productivity services and industrialization of Sector I is the primary means by which economic development contributes to poverty reduction. The specific objective of such engineering with structures is to enable a process in which the poor are 'pulled' out of the low productivity trap by its positive forces or at least prevented from being prematurely 'pushed' into the trap by the earlier noted negative forces of structural impoverishment. Structural change has to be so strategized as to create opportunities for the poor to participate in the growth process. A revitalization of rural development, it is argued, is necessary to prepare a foundation for accelerated income growth, the employment multiplier and economic diversification in Sector II. This is to be achieved by commercialization of farming and raising of investment and returns in agriculture by means of a more stable market-based trade and price policy, focusing of research and extension on competitiveness and productivity improvement, liberalization of the land market, fostering of R N-F activities, electrification and promotion of SEs and MdEs.

Departing from earlier notions on the subject, the encouragement of rural to urban migration has been put forward as a new poverty reduction initiative. It is argued that the poor who have been thus trapped into low productivity farming in marginal and uneconomic farms in Sector II, would do better by migrating to urban areas with high growth potential in Sector I. Their migration needs to be facilitated by equipping them with the necessary skills and ability and by helping them with low-cost housing.[4] Industry-based secondary town development with industrial parks will make industrial employment opportunities accessible to the poor while spreading widely the benefits of industrialization. Pro-poor transport and communication initiatives, including ports, highways and integrated road networks to connect poor communities with rapidly growing domestic and international markets and lower order towns with higher order ones, will give effect to pro-poor structural change and play a vital role in G-E-P dynamics. These connectives will widen the opportunities for the poor, especially those in spatially marginalized In Ar, to participate in the growth process, reduce regional disparities in poverty levels, reduce the segmentation of urban (Sector I) and rural (Sector II) markets and work towards integrating the two sectors.

Epilogue

Is the pro-poor growth debate the one that will end all debates on poverty alleviation? As far as theory and concepts are concerned it could be so, for it goes into the fundamentals, the structural roots of poverty issues. The preceding debates were of the kind that focused mostly on symptomatic poverty and pivoted around the changes in particular policies, programmes or innovations, in terms of their consequences or impacts and their operational efficiency or otherwise. Structural dualism, which is at the root of structural poverty, a running theme in this chapter, was ignored by all these debates until this last culminating one. So the G-E-P dynamics were ignored. The debates may not have come to an end but may well continue around issues in implementation of the concept of pro-poor growth. The summoning of sufficient political will required for the adoption of the purely economic logic-based pro-poor growth concept for implementation may prove to be difficult, given the attractiveness to those who seek power of other programmes that can be politicized. If the government was to commit itself to this policy, the blocked macro-micro filters will get cleared and public resources will be enabled to flow into In Ar in a coordinated manner for its integrated development. For that to become a reality, however, the agenda of the National Poverty Reduction Strategy, which is the implementation plan for the pro-poor growth concept, has to be decentralized down to the divisional level with time-bound targets. This has not happened as yet. Debates can go on and on in these two arenas.

NOTES

1. Among the great many contributors to these debates were the World Bank, UNDP, ESCAP, GOSL, Independent South Asian Commission for Poverty Alleviation, South Asian Poverty Alleviation Programme, NORAD, HIRDEP, Regional Development Division of the Ministry of Policy Implementation, researchers of the IPS, Ministry officers and numerous local and foreign programme evaluators and reviewers. It was not possible to acknowledge each one separately against each point made. Hence the relevant important contributors are listed collectively at the ends of the sub-sections.
2. The pro-growth side argued back that there was a pre-empting of resources for consumption, resulting in a deprivation of investment of resources.
3. Under JSP, beneficiaries, if unemployed, could collect their transfer incomes by putting in even nominal or token 'work' as community service for 20 days. This can be an inducement to stay unemployed, work less or pretend to work. Under Samurdhi, beneficiaries cease to receive transfers when income exceeds Rs 2,000 per month, which can lead to a decrease in work effort, or, when one member of the family finds employment, can act as a disincentive to find employment.
4. This initiative can be expected to end the long drawn out debate in the country on the pros and cons of rural to urban migration. The 1972–76 Five-Year Plan, prepared during a centrally commanded economic regime, disapproved rural to urban migration on grounds that it would impoverish the rural sector more due to the brawn and brain drain it causes. Hence, rural development efforts were oriented to retaining them in the rural sector even by helping them with survival strategies. Now it is the opposite, with rural–urban migration being seen as a vital role player in G-E-P dynamics, fitting in well with a market forces driven economy.

REFERENCES

Adelman, Irma and Sherman Robinson (1989), 'Income Distribution and Development', in Hollis Chenery and T.N. Srinivasan, (eds.), *Handbook of Development Economics*, Vol. 2, Amsterdam: North-Holland.

Amarasinghe, Patrick and Reidar Dale (1994), *Review of Divisional and Local Level Planning in HIRDEP*, Sri Lanka, mimeo.

Aturupane, Harsha (1999), *Poverty in Sri Lanka: Achievements, Issues and Challenges*. Paper prepared for the Workshop on Poverty Alleviation, Ministry of Planning, mimeo.

Cornea, G., R. Jolly and Frances Stewart (eds) (1987), *Adjustment with a Human Face*, Vol. 2. Oxford: Oxford University Press.

Datt, Gaurav and Dileni Gunawardena (1994), *Some Aspects of Poverty in Sri Lanka: 1985–90*. Washington D.C: World Bank Policy Research Department, mimeo.

Glewwe, P. (1988), 'Economic Liberalization and Income Inequity: Further Evidence from Sri Lankan Experience', *Journal of Development Economics*, 28(2).

Gooneratne, Wilbert, M.M. Karunanayake and S.M. Senanayake (2000), *Comparative Study of REAP Formulation Documents*. Report prepared for Royal Netherlands Embassy, mimeo.

Government of Sri Lanka (GOSL) (November 2000), *Sri Lanka: A Framework for Poverty Reduction*, Colombo.

————— (June 2002), *Connecting to Growth: Sri Lanka's Poverty Reduction Strategy*, Colombo.

GOSL/United Nations Development Programme (UNDP) (1998), *Cluster Evaluation Report*. Joint Evaluation Mission, mimeo.

Gunatilaka, R. (1997), *Credit-Based Participatory Poverty Alleviation Strategies in Sri Lanka—What Have We Learned?* Colombo: Institute of Policy Studies.

Gunatilaka, R. and R. Salih (May 1999), How Successful is Samurdhi's Savings and Credit Programme in Reaching the Poor? Colombo: Institute of Policy Studies, mimeo.

Gunatilaka, R. and T.W. Williams (December 1999), *The Integrated Rural Development Programme in Sri Lanka: Lessons of Experience for Poverty Reduction*. Colombo: Institute of Policy Studies.

Hesselberg, J. (1980), *Artisan Production: The Case of Puwakdandawa*. Oslo University, Oslo, mimeo.

Hewavitharana, Buddhadasa (1986), *Industrialization, Employment and Basic Needs: Sri Lanka*. International Labour Organization, Working Paper No.60, Geneva.

————— (1990), *Rural Non-Farm Employment: Problems, Issues and Strategies*, Colombo: Institute of Policy Studies.

————— (1992), *Industrial Development and Location: Spatial Patterns and Policies—Sri Lanka*. Nagoya: UNCRD.

————— (1993), 'The Sri Lankan Approach to Poverty Alleviation in the Context of Sustainability and Pragmatism', in *Economic Growth and Human Development with Equity, Security and Sustainability, National and Regional Perspectives.* Colombo: Society for International Development, Sri Lanka Chapter.

————— (1994), *Build Up A Bank And Grow With It: The Janashakthi Bangku Sangam*. Colombo: Women's Development Federation/Janasaviya Trust Fund.

————— (1995), *Policy Guidelines for Regional and Rural Development Planning*. Prepared for the RDD and Swedish Embassy, mimeo.

————— (1997a), *Social Mobilization Approach to Integrated Rural Development in Badulla District*. Prepared for RDD and UNDP, mimeo.

————— (1997b), *Economic Consequences of the Devolution Package, and an Evaluation of Decentralization*, Colombo: Sinhala Weera Vidahana.

————— (1999), 'The Two Leading Meso Policy Interventions for Rural Poverty Alleviation— Sri Lanka—A Case Study', in *Rural Poverty Alleviation in Asia and the Pacific*, Tokyo: A.P.O.

————— (2002a), UNDP Supported Initiatives in Poverty Alleviation in Sri Lanka, mimeo.

————— (2002b), Key Lessons From Pioneering New Development Approaches of Integrated Rural Development Programme, Hambantota (HIRDEP), mimeo.

HIRDEP (1996), *Annual Programme—1997*. Hambantota: IRDP Office.

————— (1998), *Annual Work Programme—1999*. Hambantota: IRDP Office.

ISACPA (1992), *Meeting the Challenge*, New Delhi.

Jerve, A.M. et al. (1992), *Evaluation Report 4.91, HIRDEP, Sri Lanka*. Norway: Chr. Michelsen Institute.

————— (1996), 'Potentialities of Meso Policy Options in the context of Adjustment, Poverty and Equity: Relevance of Sri Lankan Experience', *Journal of Asian Productivity Organization*, Summer.

————— (2003), *Sustaining Local Level Development: What Worked and What Did Not*, Norway: Chr. Michelsen Institute.

Kelegama, Saman (2003), 'Poverty Situation and Policy in Sri Lanka', in C.M. Edmonds (ed.), *Reducing Poverty in Asia: Emerging Issues in Growth, Targeting, and Measurement*, UK: Edward Elgar.

Lakshman, W.D., S.S. Vidanagama and S.H.P. Senanayake (1994), *Self Employment Within a Framework of Structural Adjustment*, SL EA-SIDA, Colombo, mimeo.

NPC (2001), *Report on National Poverty Conference.*

Nayar, N. and R. Gunatilaka (2000), *Sri Lanka's Microfinance Sector: Environment, Policies and Practices.* Report prepared for Ministry of Samurdhi, Sri Lanka.

Ratnayake, R.M.K. (1998), Poverty in Sri Lanka: Incidence and Poverty Reduction Strategies. Ministry of Samurdhi, Youth Affairs and Sports, Colombo, mimeo.

Regional Development Division (RDD) (1994), *From Rural Development to Regional Development, A Concept Paper*, mimeo.

_____ (1997), *Regional Development Programme Framework*, Draft.

Sahn, D.E. and Harold Alderman (1996), 'The Effect of Food Subsidies on Labour Supply in Sri Lanka', *Economic Development and Cultural Change*, 4(1).

South Asia Poverty Alleviation Programme (SAPAP)/UNDP (1996), *Annual Progress Report, Sri Lanka.*

Silva, K.T. (1998), *Sociological Perspectives Relating to Selected Aspects of Poverty in Sri Lanka.* Paper presented to Ministry of Planning, mimeo.

Silva, K.T. and R. Gunatilaka (May 2000), *Final Evaluation of the Change Agent Programme*, mimeo.

Tabor, S.R., H.P. Wijewardana and S.S. Mudalige (2000), *Area Based Growth With Equity Programme.* Report of the Evaluation Mission, mimeo.

UNDP (June 1997), *First Country Cooperation Framework, Sri Lanka 1997–2002*, mimeo.

_____ (August 1998), *Area Based Growth With Equity Programme*, Programme Support Document, mimeo.

_____ (2001a), *Evaluation of the South Asia Poverty Alleviation Programme—An Overview*, mimeo.

_____ (2001b), *UN Development Assistance Framework for Sri Lanka*, 2002–2006.

UNDP/UNOPS (January 1998), *South Asia Poverty Alleviation Programme: Mid-Term Evaluation Report.*

UNOPS/UNDP (2001), *Area Based Growth With Equity, Sri Lanka*, Programme Findings and Recommendations, Kuala Lumpur, mimeo.

Vimaladharma, K.P., S. de Mel and S. Ranasinghe (2000), *Impact Assessment Study, Sri Lanka*, South Asia Poverty Alleviation Programme, mimeo.

World Bank (1990), *Report on Employment and Poverty Alleviation Project*, Washington D.C.

_____ (1995), *Sri Lanka Poverty Assessment*, Washington D.C.

_____ (1998), *World Bank Implementation Completion Report*, Poverty Alleviation Project, Washington D.C.

_____ (2000b), *An Empirical Evaluation of the Samurdhi Programme*, Background Paper for World Bank's Work on Poverty, Sri Lanka, World Bank, Washington D.C.

_____ (2001), *Poverty Assessment in Sri Lanka.*

SELECT READINGS

Guru-Gharana and Kishor Kumar (1997), Macroeconomic Policies and Poverty Alleviation in South Asia. Kathmandu: Nepal Foundation for Advanced Studies.

Hewavitharana, Buddhadasa (1996), 'Potentialities of Meso Policy Options in the Context of Adjustment, Poverty and Equity: Relevance of Sri Lankan Experience', *Journal of Asian Productivity Organization*, Summer.

HIRDEP (1993), *Perspectice Plan for 1994–1995*, Hambantota, IRDP Office.

Stewart, Frances (1995), *Adjustment and Poverty.* London: Routledge.

Todaro, Michael P. (1985), *Economic Development in the Third World.* New York: Longman Inc.

World Bank (2000a), *World Bank Country Report. Sri Lanka, Recapturing Missed Opportunities*, Washington D.C.

Biographical Sketch of Gamani Corea

Gamani Corea was born on 4 November 1925 in Sri Lanka. After attending Royal College, Colombo, and the University of Ceylon in 1944, he continued his studies, from 1945 to 1952, in the United Kingdom, first at Corpus Christi College, Cambridge and then at Nuffield College, Oxford.

Gamani Corea was first appointed to the post of Secretary General of the United Nations Conference on Trade and Development (UNCTAD) in 1973 and continued until 31 December 1984. After the initial term of three years, he was re-appointed thrice, his fourth term covering the period December 1982 until the end of 1984. While Secretary General of UNCTAD, Corea also held the position of Under Secretary General of the United Nations.

Corea holds the following degrees: BA, MA (Cantab); BA, MA (Oxon); D.Phil (Oxon); Doctor (Honoris Causa) University of Nice, France; D.Litt (Hon) University of Colombo, Sri Lanka; D.Sc (Hon) University of Kelaniya, Sri Lanka.

Career

National

Before assuming duties as Secretary General of UNCTAD, Corea served Sri Lanka as:

- Ambassador to the European Economic Community, Belgium, Luxembourg and the Netherlands (1973).
- Deputy Governor and Senior Deputy Governor of the Central Bank of Ceylon (1970–73).
- Permanent Secretary, Ministry of Planning and Economic Affairs, Government of Ceylon (1965–70).
- Secretary, Cabinet Planning Committee, Government of Ceylon (1965–70).
- Director of Economic Research, and Assistant to the Governor, Central Bank of Ceylon (1960–64).
- Secretary, National Planning Council and Director, Planning Secretariat, Government of Ceylon (1956–60).
- Economist and later Director, Planning Secretariat, Government of Ceylon (1952–56) and Research Officer, Central Bank of Ceylon (1959).

After relinquishing his duties at UNCTAD, Corea served in Sri Lanka as:

- Chairman, Board of Governors, Institute of Policy Studies, Sri Lanka (1989 to date).
- Chancellor, Open University of Sri Lanka (1981 to date).
- Chairman Emeritus, Board of Governors, Marga Institute of Development Studies, Sri Lanka (1973–96).
- Chairman, Foreign Affairs Study Group, Government of Sri Lanka.
- Special Adviser to the Ministry of Foreign Affairs, Colombo.
- Chairman, Committee on 'SAPTA and Sri Lanka' (appointed by the President of Sri Lanka, 1997/98).
- Chairman, Industrial Task Force, Ministry of Industrial Development (1995–98).

International

- Chief, United Nations Planning Mission to British Honduras (1962).
- Member (1965–72) and Chairman (1972–74), United Nations Committee on Development Planning.
- Chairman of First and Second UNCTAD Expert Groups on International Monetary Issues (1965 and 1969).
- Chairman of the UN Cocoa Conference 1972, which resulted in the International Cocoa Agreement.
- Chairman, Expert Group on Development and Environment, Founex (1971).
- Chairman, ECAFE Expert Group on Regional Performance Evaluation during the Second UN Development decade (1972–73).
- Chairman, Conference on the 'Crisis in Planning' Institute of Development Studies, University of Sussex (1970).
- Chairman, Inaugural Meeting, Third World Forum, Karachi (1975).
- Chairman, ILO Meeting on Evaluation of Comprehensive Employment Missions to Colombia, Kenya, Iran and Sri Lanka (1973).
- Special Representative of the Secretary General of the UN Conference on Human Environment (1971–72).
- Secretary General of the United Nations Conference on the Least Developed Countries, Paris (1981).
- Member, UN Panel of Eminent Persons on South Africa and Transnational Corporations (September 1985).
- Member, UN Panel of Eminent Persons on the 'Relationship between Disarmament and Development' (April 1986).
- Team Leader, UNDP High Level Multi-Disciplinary Mission to Qatar (April 1987).
- Chairman, United Nations General Assembly; Ad Hoc Committee of the Whole on an International Development Strategy for the 4th Development Decade, 1989–90).

- Member, South Commission (1987–90).
- Member of the Board, South Centre (1995–98).
- Chairman, Expert Group on Third World Debt, Non-Aligned Movement (NAM) (1996).
- Chairman, Ad Hoc Panel of Economists, NAM (1997–98).
- Chairman of the Research and Policy Committee, South Centre (1998–2002).
- Chairman, South Commission (2002–03).

Memberships in Societies and Other Academic Activities

- Member of Governing Body International Foundation for Development Alternatives.
- Member, Board of Management, Bandaranaike Centre for International Studies.
- Chairman, Association of Former International Civil Servants, Colombo.
- Member, National Science and Technology Commission, Sri Lanka.
- Visiting Fellow, Institute of Development Studies, University of Sussex (1973).
- Research Fellow, International Development Research Centre of Canada (1973).
- Visiting Fellow, Nuffield College, Oxford University (1974–79).
- Fellow Commoner, Corpus Christi College, Cambridge University (1985–86).
- Vice President for Asia, Inter Presa Service, Rome (1985–89).
- President, Sri Lanka Economic Association (1985–91).
- Member of Governing Council, University of Ceylon (1965–69).
- Member, National Science Council of Ceylon (1967–70).
- President, Section F, Ceylon Association for the Advancement of Science (1961–62).
- General President, Ceylon Association for the Advancement of Science (1971).
- President, National Academy of Science of Sri Lanka (1994–97).
- Board Member, Seylan Bank, Sri Lanka (1988–to date).
- Life Member, Organization of Professional Associations, Sri Lanka.
- Patron, Symphony Orchestra of Sri Lanka.

Publications

Books

- *The Insatiability of an Export Economy*, Marga Publication, Colombo, 1975.
- *Need for Change: Toward the New International Economic Order*, Pergamon Press, Oxford, 1980.
- *Taming Commodity Markets: The Integrated Programme and the Common Fund in UNCTAD*, Manchester University Press, Manchester, 1992.

Articles

- 'Ceylon', in *Asian Economic Development*, Cranley Onslow-Wiedenfeld and Nicolson (eds), 1965.
- 'The Debt Problems of Developing Countries', *UN Journal of Development Planning*, 1970.
- 'Aid and the Economy', *Marga Quarterly Journal*, Vol. 1, No. 1, 1971.
- 'Ceylon in the 60s', *Marga Quarterly Journal*, Vol. 1, No. 2, 1971.
- 'Human Environment Stockholm Conference', *Marga Quarterly Journal*, Vol. 2, No. 1, 1972.
- 'International Monetary System and Developing Countries', *Central Bank of Ceylon Staff Studies*, Vol. 1, No. 2, 1972.
- 'The Food Drive in Ceylon', *Finance and Development: Essays in Honour of Lady Hicks*, Macmillan, 1973.
- 'Redistribution on a Global Scale', *Economic Review*, People's Bank, Vol. 1, No. 10, 1976.
- 'UNCTAD and the New International Economic Order', 1976 Stevenson Memorial Lecture; *International Affairs*, 1977.
- 'The Quest for an International Commodity Policy', Boyd Orr Memorial Lecture, University of Glasgow, 1977.
- 'The Integrated Programme for Commodities: An Appraisal', *Central Bank of Ceylon: Occasional Paper*, No. 1, August 1981.
- 'Indira Gandhi and the North-South Dialogues', in *Indira Gandhi—Statesmen, Scientists, Scholars and Friends Remember*, Vikas Publishing House, New Delhi, 1985.
- 'Will this warning be heeded?', Book Review in *Trade and Development—An UNCTAD Review*, No. 6, 1985.
- 'UNCTAD—The Changing Scene', in *UNCTAD and the South-North Dialogue*, M. Zammit Cutajar (ed.), Pergamon Press, 1985.
- 'Creating a Framework to Strengthen and Stabilize International Commodity Markets', in *Negotiating World Order*, Alan K. Hendrickson (ed.), Tufts University, US, 1986.

- 'The Crisis: Some Reflections', *The World Economy in Transition*, Pergamon Press, 1986.
- Inaugural Address, *Sri Lanka Economic Journal*, Vol. 1, No. 1, 1986.
- 'Obstacles to South-South Cooperation', in *Facets of Development in Independent Sri Lanka: Ronnie De Mel Felicitation Volume*, Government Press, Sri Lanka, 1986.
- 'Adjustment and Growth', in *Structural Adjustment & Growth*, Sri Lanka Association of Economists, 1986.
- 'The Future of Commodities', *Central Bank of Sri Lanka: Occasional Papers*, No. 15, 1987.
- 'Regional Cooperation in South Asia: Perspective and Prospects', *South Asia Journal*, Vol. 1, No. 1, 1987.
- 'The Prospects for Our Poor' (Fourth N.M. Perera Memorial Lecture, 21 August 1986), *Sri Lanka Economic Journal*, Vol. 2, No. 1, 1987.
- 'UNCTAD as a Negotiating Forum', in *Peace through Economic Justice— Essays in memory of Manual Pérez Guerrero*, Mikio Tajima (ed.), Victor Chevalier, Switzerland, 1988.
- 'Third World Cooperation & Development Crisis' (Inaugural Senaka Bibile Lecture, 21 December 1987), *Sri Lanka Economic Journal*, Vol. 3, No. 2, 1988.
- 'Disarmament & Development', *Sri Lanka Economic Journal*, Vol. 3, No. 2, 1988.
- 'Privatisation of Public Enterprises', A Seminar Keynote Address, *Economic Review*, People's Bank, Vol. 13, Nos 11 and 12, 1988.
- 'Sri Lanka's Economy and the External Environment', *Economic Review*, People's Bank, Vol. 14, Nos 1 and 2, 1988.
- 'The Negotiating Platform of the Group of 77', *RIS Digest*, New Delhi, March–June, 1989.
- 'New Development Strategy for the 1990s', *Economic Review*, People's Bank, Vol. 15, No. 10, 1990.
- 'Prospects for South-South Cooperation', *Economic Review*, People's Bank, Vol. 15, No. 11, 1990.
- 'Our Foreign Economic Policy', *Economic Review*, People's Bank, Vol. 16, No. 10, 1991.
- 'International Development Perspectives for the 90s', Distinguished Lecture, Pakistan Society of Development Economists, 7th AGM, Islamabad, 10 January 1991; *Pakistan Development Review*, Vol. 30, No. 4, 1991.
- 'Development in Asia: Perspectives & Issues for the Nineties', *Sri Lanka Economic Journal*, Vol. 8, No. 1, 1993.
- 'Development Perspectives and Fiscal Policy', *Sri Lanka Tax Review*, Vol. 2, No. 1, 1994.
- 'World and Asian Development Perspectives in the 1990s', in *Essays in Honour of A.D.V. de S. Indraratna*, A.D.V. de S. Indraratna Felicitation Committee, 1994.

- 'Democratization should be an end itself, not just the means to achieving high growth rates', *Economic Review*, People's Bank, Vol. 21, No. 9, 1995.
- 'Third Wave of Asian Development will, to a great extent, depend on the success of the international policies of SAARC countries in their progress towards industrialization', *Economic Review*, People's Bank, Vol. 22, No. 2, 1996.
- 'Reflections on Rahul Prebisch', *South Asia Economic Journal*, Vol. 4, No. 1, 2003.

Corea has written 'Forewords' for a number of books. Among them are: (*a*) Syed Nawab Haider Naqvi, *Development Economics: A New Paradigm*, Sage Publications, New Delhi, 1993; (*b*) Laksiri Jayasuriya, *Welfare & Politics in Sri Lanka: Experience of a Third World Welfare State*, School of Social Work and Social Policy, University of Western Australia, 2000; and (*c*) Ric Shand, *Irrigation & Agriculture in Sri Lanka*, Institute of Policy Studies, Sri Lanka, 2002.

HONOURS, DISTINCTIONS AND AWARDS

- 'Order of the Yugoslav Flag with a Ribbon', for the Promotion of International Understanding, Government of Yugoslavia, 1985.
- Award of 'Deshamanya', Sri Lanka, First Honours List, Independence Day, 4 February 1986.
- Sahabdeen Foundation Award for International Understanding.
- Viswa Prasadeni, 1996.
- Lanka Abhimanaya, 2003.
- Honorary Fellow, Corpus Christi College, Cambridge.
- Honorary Fellow, Institute of Development Studies, University of Sussex.
- Fellow and Member of the Council, National Academy of Science of Sri Lanka.
- Honorary Fellow, Bandaranaike Centre for International Studies.
- Senior Fellow, Institute of Fundamental Studies, Sri Lanka.

FESTSCHRIFT

Policies for Development, Essays in Honour of Gamani Corea, Sydney Dell (ed.), Macmillan, 1988.

About the Editor and Contributors

The Editor

Saman Kelegama is the Executive Director of the Institute of Policy Studies of Sri Lanka. Prior to assuming duties as the Director, he was a Fellow of the Institute from 1990 to 1994. He also serves on many official committees of the Government of Sri Lanka as an independent member. Dr Kelegama has served in a number of government bodies as a Board Member, including the Board of Investment (1994–95), the Public Enterprise Reform Commission (1995), the Human Resources Development Council (1995–97), the Industrial Task Force (1995–99), the Industrialization Commission (1997–99), the Small and Medium Industry Task Force (2001–2002), Fair Trading Commission (1995–2002), and Regaining Sri Lanka Policy Development Committee on Infrastructure (2002–03). He has also served as a Board Member in a number of private sector institutions.

Outside Sri Lanka, Saman Kelegama serves as a Governing Board Member of the South Asia Centre for Policy Studies, Dhaka, Bangladesh and the Centre for Regulation and Competition, University of Manchester, UK. He has been a Visiting Fellow at the Institute of Social Studies, The Hague (1993), the Australia–South Asia Research Centre of the Australian National University, Canberra (1998), and has been conferred many academic awards, including the Government of India Distinguished Visiting Scholar (1997).

The Contributors

Prema-chandra Athukorala is Professor of Economics in the Research School of Pacific and Asian Studies at the Australian National University and Fellow of the Academy of Social Science in Australia. His publications include eight books; two edited volumes and over 100 papers in the areas of development macroeconomics, trade and development and international labour migration.

Harsha Aturupane is a Senior Economist at the World Bank. He graduated from the University of Colombo and obtained his doctorate at Cambridge. He has written extensively in education economics, labour economics, poverty and human development. His recent work has included economic analyses, project preparation, supervision, evaluation and completion for the World Bank in several South Asian countries.

Sarath Dasanayaka is currently Head of the Department of Management of Technology, and Research Coordinator for MBA programmes in the Faculty of Engineering, University of Moratuwa, Sri Lanka. He is engaged as a lead researcher for many international research projects, as an Associate in various research networks, a Visiting Professor for some Asian universities and as a consultant for international and local organizations.

A.D.V. de S. Indrartna is Emeritus Professor of Economics, University of Colombo, a Fellow of the National Academy of Science, a former General President of the Sri Lanka Association for the Advancement of Science (1998) and is the current President of the Sri Lanka Economic Association. He was the Chairman of the Fair Trading Commission from 2002–03. He has more than 30 years of teaching and research experience at the university level and has been honoured with DLitt from the University of Colombo.

Amala de Silva is currently Senior Lecturer at the University of Colombo. She graduated from the University of Colombo and holds a doctorate in Economics from the University of Sussex. She was a Rockerfeller Global Health Leadership Fellow at WHO, Geneva (1999/2000). Her areas of research include healthcare costing, responsiveness of health systems, maternal mortality, poverty and health, and migration.

David Dunham is the Deputy Rector of the Institute of Social Studies (ISS), the Hague, the Netherlands. He has served as Professor of Geography and Regional Planning and as Dean at the ISS and was the Resident Coordinator of the Institute of Policy Studies in Sri Lanka (1991–99). He has edited a book and authored a number of articles on the Sri Lankan economy.

Godfrey Gunatilleke is the founder Executive Director of the Marga Institute in Sri Lanka (Centre for Development Studies) where he directed a programme of multidisciplinary research and development during 1972–95. He served in the Sri Lanka Administrative Service and the National Planning Council. He has written extensively on development issues in Sri Lanka and was honoured by the University of Colombo with DLitt and by the Government of Sri Lanka with the title Deshamanya (1994).

Buddhadasa Hewavitharana is Emeritus Professor of Economics at the University of Peradeniya. He obtained his doctorate from the London School of Economics and has specialized in Development Economics and Economic Planning and was the Head/ Department of Economics, Commerce and Statistics at University of Peradeniya. He was also Economic Advisor to the Ministry of Finance (1970–75) and is a Founder Member of the National Development Trust Fund for Poverty Alleviation and of the Institute of Policy Studies of Sri Lanka.

Laksiri Jayasuriya is currently Hon. Senior Research Fellow, University of Western Australia, Perth, and is a Fellow of the Australian Academy of Social Science. Until his retirement, he held the Foundation Chair of Social Work and Social Administration at the University of Western Australia. He was formerly the Dean/Social Science and Professor of Sociology and Social Welfare, University of Colombo.

Sisira Jayasuriya is the Director of the Asian Economics Centre, Department of Economics, University of Melbourne and Visiting Professor at the Institute of Policy Studies, Colombo. His research and publications cover topics on trade, environment and macroeconomic issues in developing countries, with special emphasis on South and Southeast Asia.

Lal Jayawardena is an Honorary Fellow of King's College, Cambridge, where he graduated with 'a double first' in the Economics Tripos of Cambridge University. He was also awarded the Ellen McArthur Prize of Cambridge University for his doctoral thesis. He has served in the Government of Sri Lanka as Secretary to the Treasury, Economic Advisor to the President, as Ambassador to the Benelux countries and High Commissioner in the UK. He was the first Director of the World Institute for Development Economics Research of the United Nations University. (He passed away on 8 April 2004.)

Nihal Kappagoda is a consultant on Sovereign Debt Management, residing in Canada. In Sri Lanka, he worked at the Central Bank and headed the External Resources Department. Subsequently, he held senior positions in the International Development Research Centre, the Asian Development Bank and the Commonwealth Secretariat. He has been a consultant to international financial institutions for the past 15 years.

H.N.S. Karunatilake was the Governor of the Central Bank of Sri Lanka from 1988 to 1992. He has degrees in Economics from the University of Ceylon, London School of Economics and Harvard University. He received a Ph.D in Economics from the University of London and was appointed Research Fellow in Economics at Harvard University. He has written 20 books and has published over 200 articles in local and international journals.

J.B. Kelegama has served in the Government of Sri Lanka as the Secretary to the Ministry of Commerce, Director of Commerce, Director of Economic Affairs to the Treasury, and Chairman of the Tea Commission. He obtained his doctorate from Oxford and was the Professor of Economics at the University of Kelaniya and served as the Chancellor of the Rajarata University. He was also a UN consultant. He has written extensively on economic issues and is a recipient of the honours Deshamanya (1994) and Artha Shasthra Shiromani (2002).

Malathy Knight-John is a Research Fellow at the Institute of Policy Studies specializing in privatization, competition policy and regulation. She has written a number of articles on these subjects. Currently she is pursuing doctoral studies at the University of Manchester, UK.

Raja B.M. Korale is the former Head of the Department of Census and Statistics and Director of Employment, Ministry of Planning. He was the first Sri Lankan to be elected as a member of the International Statistical Institute. During 1999–2003 he worked as a consultant to the ILO, UNFPA, the World Bank and the Asian Development Bank. He has authored serveral papers on employment and unemployment, migration, poverty, cost of living, survey design and sampling and statistical management.

W.D. Lakshman is Professor of Economics at the University of Colombo. He obtained his doctorate from Oxford and served as the Head of the Department of Economics, University of Colombo, and as Vice Chancellor of the University. He was also the President of the Sri Lanka Association of Economists and the editor of the Association's journal, Visiting Professor at Ryukoku University, Japan, and other universities. He has edited several volumes and authored many articles on the Sri Lankan economy.

Chandana Perera is presently a Senior Lecturer in the Department of Management of Technology, University of Moratuwa, Sri Lanka and also serves as the coordinator for the MBA programme in Management of Technology. He has served as a resource person for APO and JICA. His main teaching and research areas include operations management, technology management and innovation management.

Sarath Rajapatirana is a Visiting Scholar at the American Enterprise Institute. Previously, he was Division Chief and Economic Advisor at the World Bank. He graduated from the University of Sri Lanka and the University of Minnesota and was a Fulbright Scholar. He has authored six books and numerous articles.

Nimal Sanderatne is Visiting Senior Fellow at the Postgraduate Institute of Agriculture of the University of Peradeniya and Chairman of the Centre for Poverty Analysis (CEPA). He was formerly Director of Economic Research, and Director of Statistics of the Central Bank of Sri Lanka; Chairman of the Bank of Ceylon; Chairman of the National Development Bank and Senior Fellow and Senior Visiting Fellow of the Institute of Policy Studies.

D.D.M. Waidyasekera is a former Commissioner of Inland Revenue and Secretary to the 1990 Taxation Commission. He is a Fellow of the Institute of Taxation (Sri Lanka) and a member of the Royal Economic Society. He has written extensively on taxation and fiscal policy matters and presented papers at various forums.

Dushni Weerakoon is a Research Fellow of the Institute of Policy Studies of Sri Lanka. She holds a doctorate in Economics from the University of Manchester, UK. Her research and publications cover issues related to regional trade integration, macroeconomic policy and international economics.

Ravindra A. Yatawara is Assistant Professor of Economics at the University of Delaware, USA, and is a Visiting Research Fellow at the Institute of Policy Studies of Sri Lanka. He received his Ph.D in Economics from Columbia University and was recently in the core team that drafted the Private Sector Productivity Policy for Sri Lanka.

INDEX